DISTRIBUTED SYSTEMS

Vol. I:

Distributed Processing Systems

The Artech House Computer Library

Techniques in Data Communications by Ralph Glasgal
Advances in Computer Communications and Networking, Wesley Chu, ed.
Advances in Computer System Security, Rein Turn, ed.
Advances in Computer System Security, Vol. II, Rein Turn, ed.
Advances in Microprogramming, Efrem Mallach and Norman Sondak, eds.
Proceedings, Conference on Advanced Research in VLSI, 1982, MIT
Graphical and Binary Image Processing and Applications, J.C. Stoffel, ed.
Error-Control Coding and Applications by Djimitri Wiggert

RELATED TITLES

Communications

Microcomputer Tools for Communication Engineering by S.T. Li, J.C. Logan, J.W. Rockway, and D.W.S. Tam
Error-Control Coding and Applications by Djimitri Wiggert
Antenna Design Using Personal Computers by David M. Pozar
Radar Calculations Using Personal Computers by William A. Skillman

Business

Electronic Information Processing by W.V. Smith
Micrographics Handbook by Charles Smith

Technology in Medicine

Computers in Nutrition by C. Maloff and R.W. Zears
Management and Clinical Engineering, C.A. Caceres, ed.
The Management of Technology in Health and Medical Care, C.A. Caceres, ed.
Computers in Medical Administration, Norman Sondak and Florence Kavaler, eds.
Computers and Medicine, Vernon Sondak, Howard Schwartz, and Norman Sondak, eds.
Evaluating Telecommunication Technology in Medicine by David Conrath, Earl Dunn, and Christopher Higgins

DISTRIBUTED SYSTEMS

Vol. I:

Distributed Processing Systems

Wesley W. Chu, Editor

ARTECH HOUSE, INC.
610 Washington Street
Dedham, MA 02026

International Standard Book Number (Vol. I): 0-89006-212-9
International Standard Book Number (2 vols.): 0-89006-214-5
Library of Congress Catalog Card Number: 86-70445

86 87 10 9 8 7 6 5 4 3 2 1

PREFACE

During the past decades, both VLSI and computer communications have provided the foundation to accelerate the development of distributed systems in the 80's. With the advent of VLSI, low cost microprocessor and memory chips become available. Thus, distributed processing systems become economically feasible. Further, with the advent of computer communication and networking during the past decade, remote terminals and computers are commonly connected together to allow resource sharing of hardware, software, and data bases.

Since a distributed processing system consists of many processors, it has several advantages over single processor systems, such as providing higher availability, flexibility, and improved response time. However, it also creates many new and complex design issues such as how to partition an application task into modules and allocate to the set of processors, and methods for providing efficient interprocess communication, and efficient task scheduling. Other issues that need to be considered are how to provide user transparency and how to provide fault tolerance to processors and data bases in a distributed environment and methods for debugging and maintaining software systems in distributed systems.

The sharing of data bases among a set of computers also adds new dimensions to the data base design problem. Technical issues that need solutions are techniques to partition, distribute, and allocate files and data bases; methods to organize an efficient integrated directory system; integrating views from different data bases; solutions for efficient data translation among heterogeneous data bases; techniques to provide data consistency among the set of replicated data bases; and optimal query processing that requires accessing data from different sites.

A large body of knowledge and techniques concerning distributed systems has been developed during the past decades. This information is scattered in various conference proceedings, transactions, and journals. A textbook to summarize these results is very desirable, since there is a critical need in the technical community for textbooks as well as reference materials. However, due to the time required to prepare such a text, the time usually required for publication, and the rapid technological changes and growth in this field, publishing a book containing up-to-date information as well as technical depth in computer communications at this time is very difficult, if not impossible. Therefore, we have taken a different approach. We have selected a set of reprints representing significant advances in distributed systems during the past decades. We have organized them into this book with the objective of answering some of the questions which have arisen about the planning and designing of distributed processing systems and distributed data base systems.

Since distributed processing systems and distributed data base systems are closely related, they are considered together in this volume. This book consists of two major integral volumes: distributed processing systems and distributed data base systems. For the distributed processing systems (Volume I), it covers such topics as task allocation, distributed operating systems, interconnection networks, distributed system design methodology, fault tolerant design, cache memory for distributed systems, and case studies of commercial distributed systems. For the distributed data base systems (Volume II), it covers such issues as distributed data base design methodology, concurrency control, query optimization, fault tolerant design, interconnection of heterogeneous data base systems, and case studies of operational distributed data base systems.

This collection of reprints can be used as texts or reference books for a graduate course in distributed systems. It is an outgrowth of a short course entitled "Distributed Data Base Systems," which has been offered at UCLA for a period of five years. Most of the papers in these volumes have also been used in a first year graduate course entitled "Distributed Processing and Distributed Data Base Systems." These books are also a valuable reference source for engineers or scientists who are engaged in the design and development of distributed processing and distributed data base systems.

Considering the large number of fine papers available, and the limited number that we can collect into this set of books, the selection of the set of papers for these volumes has been a difficult task. Many excellent papers that could not be included here are mentioned in the list of references.

Several authors have added comments on and corrections to their papers. This material is appended to their papers.

We wish to express our appreciation to all of the authors and publishers for permission to reprint the papers in this book. The majority of the papers are publications of the IEEE, ACM, VLDB, and AFIPS. We have also received helpful comments from J.F. Bartlett, J. Gray, T. Lang, B. Lindsay, and G. Wiederhold in selecting the materials for this book.

WESLEY W. CHU
Los Angeles, California

TABLE OF CONTENTS

Vol. I: DISTRIBUTED PROCESSING SYSTEMS

Chapter 1

TASK ALLOCATION IN DISTRIBUTED SYSTEMS

Task allocation is one of the important problems in distributed processing system design. The factors that influence task allocation are task execution time, interprocessor communications, precedence relation among tasks, and data allocation.

Load balancing is a commonly used criterion for allocation. However, the processor load should not only consider accumulative execution time but also the loading requirements for handling the interprocessor communications which consist of overhead in processor communication as well as file or data access. Thus, the frequency of usage of files as well as tasks also plays an important role in allocation. The problem is further complicated by the precedence relationship among tasks; that is, a task cannot be executed until its preceding task has been executed, which affects the task response time. Therefore, for a thread that consists of a long sequence of tasks, precedence relation plays an important role in task allocation. For more discussion of this subject, see [CHU 86].

Because load balancing depends on allocation, finding the optimal task allocation is a complex task. An approximation for the objective function for load balancing is to minimize the heaviest loaded processor (bottleneck processor). Such optimization usually yields balanced loads because, if the bottleneck processor is not minimized, the loading among the processors will not be balanced. Further, if the task allocation yields high interprocessor communications, then the process loading will be high and the bottleneck processor will not be minimized. Therefore, the allocation generated from minimizing the bottleneck processor yields fairly balanced loads among processors [CHU 86].

In this chapter, the first paper by Chu, *et al.*, provides an overview of task allocation in distributed processing systems. The second paper provides a model to estimate the interprocessor communication among program modules and file access. The third paper by Shen and Tsai proposes a graph matching approach for solving the task assignment problem. The optimization criterion used is to minimize the interprocessor communication and balancing processor loading. There are many task allocation models available. For further information, the interested reader should refer to [GYLY 76, JENN 77, CHU 78, EFE 82, MA 82].

There are many aspects of task allocation that still need further research. For example, how to determine the optimal number of multiple copies of a module and data that achieve desired system performance (e.g., response time, availability) and how to allocate them optimally.

Load balancing increases throughput but creates interprocessor overhead. This research suggests that a programming approach is the task allocation strategy most likely to balance these conflicting factors.

Task Allocation in Distributed Data Processing

Wesley W. Chu, Leslie J. Holloway, Min-Tsung Lan, and Kemal Efe
University of California at Los Angeles

The advent of LSI technology and low-cost microprocessors has made distributed computing an economic reality in today's computing environment. The modularity, flexibility, and reliability of distributed processing makes it attractive to many types of users, and several distributed processing systems have been designed and implemented in recent years. Distributed processing applications range from large data base installations where processing load is distributed for organizational efficiency to high-speed signal processing systems where extremely fast processing must be performed in a real-time environment. But, like any new concept, distributed processing has problems which must be solved before it can become part of the accepted processing repertoire of system designers.

A serious problem is the degradation in throughput caused by the saturation effect. In an ideal multiple processor environment, we would expect throughput to increase linearly as the number of processors increases. That is, we expect to double throughput by doubling the number of processors available to perform a task, if the modules being processed are independent of each other (excluding the effects of control overhead, which we would expect to decrease performance). This expected performance is shown by the "ideal" curve in Figure 1. Early experience in multiple processor systems, however, has demonstrated behavior in operational systems is more like the "actual" curve. In practice, the throughput in a multiple processor system increases significantly only for the first few additional processors. At some point the throughput actually begins to decrease with each additional processor—this can be as few as three or four if the system is improperly designed. Examples of this phenomenon are documented by Chu[1] and Jenny.[2] This decrease in throughput is due to excessive interprocessor communication. Like the thrashing behavior observed in early memory paging systems, the decrease in performance due to interprocessor communication—IPC—is caused by processing overhead. This overhead is incurred when software modules resident on different processors must communicate with each other. Software overhead is incurred for communication protocols and for the management of the distributed storage and external resources. There are also delays in processing due to waiting time in queues at both the sending and the receiving ends of the communication path. The extra processing and waiting time due to IPC grows rapidly and system

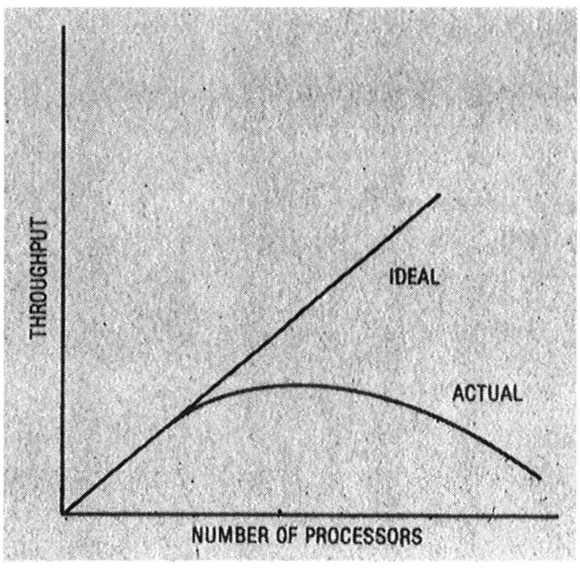

Figure 1. The saturation effect.

performance quickly begins to degrade. This degradation in throughput for incremental increase in computing resources is the saturation effect.

In order to avoid the saturation effect, we must investigate the nature of IPC. IPC cost is incurred when data is transferred from one module to a module residing in a different processor. IPC is, therefore, a function of intermodule communication—IMC—and the module allocation. IMC is the amount of data to be transferred between each pair of modules. This is independent of the allocation. Clearly, IPC = IMC if the two modules are not coresident. When modules are coresident on a processor, no IPC cost is incurred. (We have assumed here that overhead due to communiction between coresident modules is negligible.)

Task partitioning and task allocation are the two steps necessary to minimize IPC. Task partitioning refers to the breakdown of a processing task into several individual modules with minimum IMC. This can be considered a software design issue.[3,2] Task allocation is the process of allocating modules to processors with minimum overhead due to IPC.

We will assume that the task partitioning process has been performed by the software designer and that each task arrives in the distributed processing system already partitioned into a set of modules along its own natural boundaries, a concept discussed in some detail by Jenny.[2] In this article, we emphasize how to optimally allocate modules to processors. Since the number of modules is usually much larger than the number of processors, several modules may be assigned to the same processor. This assignment of clusters of modules to processors is often referred to as task partitioning. We find this terminology confusing, and differentiate between task partitioning and task allocation as defined above.

In the next section we define a generic distributed processing system and discuss the basic issues involved in developing a task allocation strategy. The subsequent section discusses model formulation and solution strategies for the task allocation problem by introducing two major approaches researchers are currently pursuing: a graph theoretic approach and a programming approach.

Because of the computational complexity of optimum solution strategies, a need has arisen for a simplified, suboptimum approach to the task allocation problem. Results from some current research efforts are presented in the section on heuristic approaches. A fundamental need in task allocation is the development of a strategy for assigning costs to intermodule communication. This issue is addressed in the subsequent section. We conclude with a brief summary of the state of the task allocation problem, and suggestions for future research.

Task allocation strategy

The task allocation environment. Distributed processing enhances system performance by employing several processors to handle the processing load. A representation of a generic distributed processing system is shown in Figure 2. The key elements in this system are a set of modules to be processed, $\{M_1, M_2, \ldots M_m\}$, and a module allocation mechanism, S, which assigns each of the m modules to one of the n processors, $\{P_1, P_2, \ldots P_n\}$. It is convenient to consider a module an indivisible entity, the smallest viable computational unit. In

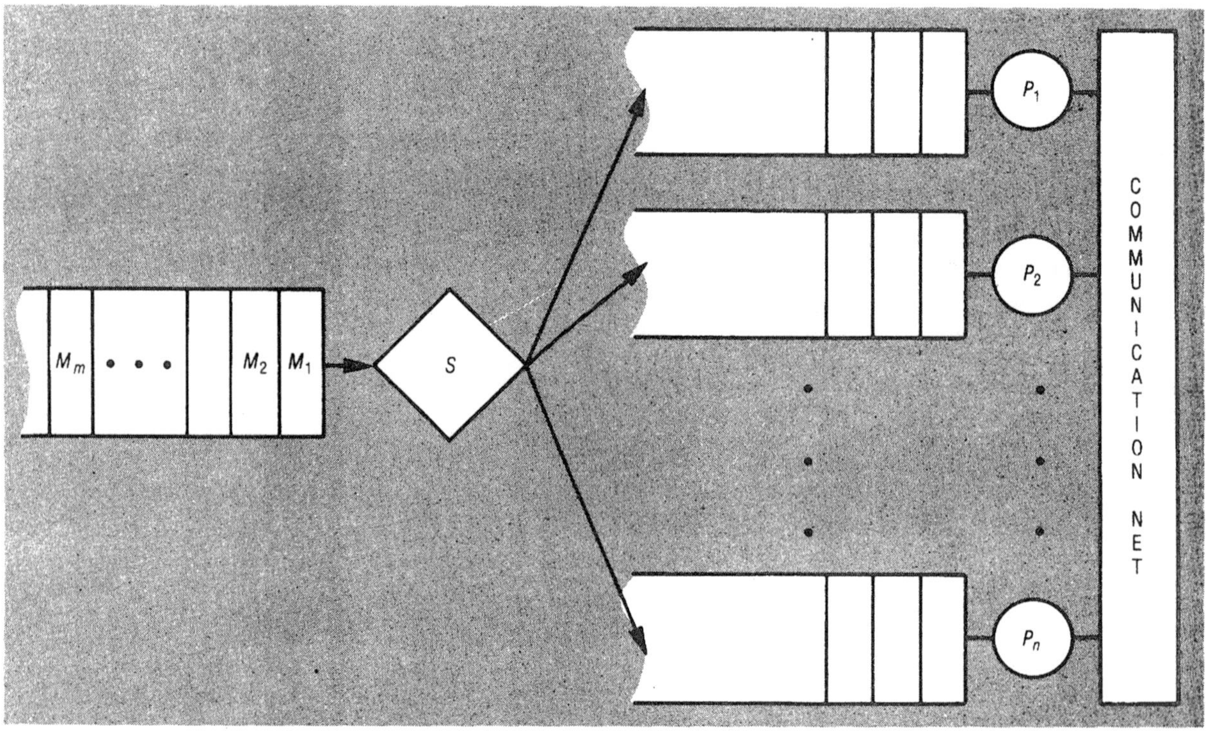

Figure 2. A distributed processing system.

general, the number of modules is much larger than the number of processors. The set of *m* modules makes up a task; a task is a single processing entity. The processors in this environment communicate among themselves via an interconnection mechanism. Modules may be assigned to different processors. When modules have data to communicate to one another, the processors to which they are assigned must then communicate with each other. Therefore, processors share resources, and communication among processors is essential.

The IMC between any pair of modules is determined by the software design and is a fixed attribute of the modules at the time of module allocation. Since the amount of IMC may vary considerably from one pair of modules to another, the way in which modules are allocated to processors can change the overall processing cost dramatically. For example, if two modules, M_i and M_j, have high mutual IMC and they are assigned to different processors, the IPC load will be high. Total processing costs could be decreased by assigning M_i and M_j to the same processor. On the other hand, if two modules have little IMC and no precedence relations, assigning them to different processors may well speed up overall processing time.

Factors affecting system performance. Assuming independent processing modules, intuition suggests the maximum throughput allocation strategy is one which assigns modules to processors so that all processors in the system are approximately evenly loaded. This balanced-load allocation strategy is shown in Figure 3 for an example system. The incoming task has been partitioned into a set of six noncommunicating modules, $\{M_1, M_2, \ldots, M_6\}$, which are to be allocated among the three available processors, $\{P_1, P_2, P_3\}$. We assume each module has identical processing requirements and each processor has identical processing abilities. For simplicity, let us also assume the processing speed of each processor is one module per unit of time. For the illustrated case, the system is able to process the task in two time units.

Let us study the behavior of IPC for the same set of modules and processors. We now assume the incoming task consists of six modules with a known IMC profile. If we attempt to maximize system performance by minimizing IPC without considering load balancing, all modules will be assigned to the same processor as shown in Figure 4. This allocation strategy produces a minimum IPC allocation, but processing time for the task increases by a factor of three.

It is clear that two conflicting factors, load balancing and IPC, influence the allocation strategy for optimal system performance. Maximum throughput is achieved by load balancing (in the absence of IPC), which tries to distribute modules as much as possible, but overhead due to IPC drives the allocation strategy to cluster modules to as few processors as possible. The task allocation problem is to assign modules to processors for maximum system performance (as measured by throughput) by balancing these two competing factors.

Applications of task allocation. The task allocation problem is important in the initial design phase of a distributed processing system, in the normal operational mode, and in the reconfiguration phase of a dynamic reallocation environment.

During the design phase, it is necessary to evaluate competing design configurations including network topology, channel bandwidth, number of processors, etc. Task allocation allows determination of the value of these parameters to achieve a desired level of performance.

In the normal operational mode of certain real-time distributed systems, such as on-board signal processing, it is important to assign incoming modules to processors to meet critical timing constraints. An additional complication arises in this mode due to the presence of unfinished modules still resident in processor queues, and in the processors themselves, at the time of a new task allocation. It cannot be assumed that all processors are ready and available at task allocation time. An additional feature must be introduced into the strategy to allow for the effect

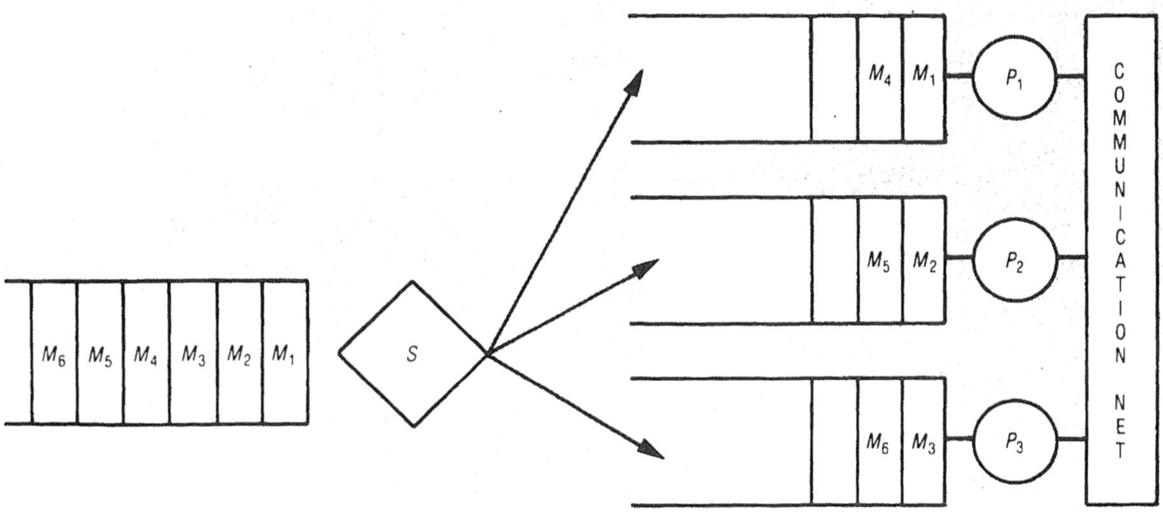

Figure 3. Balanced load allocation strategy.

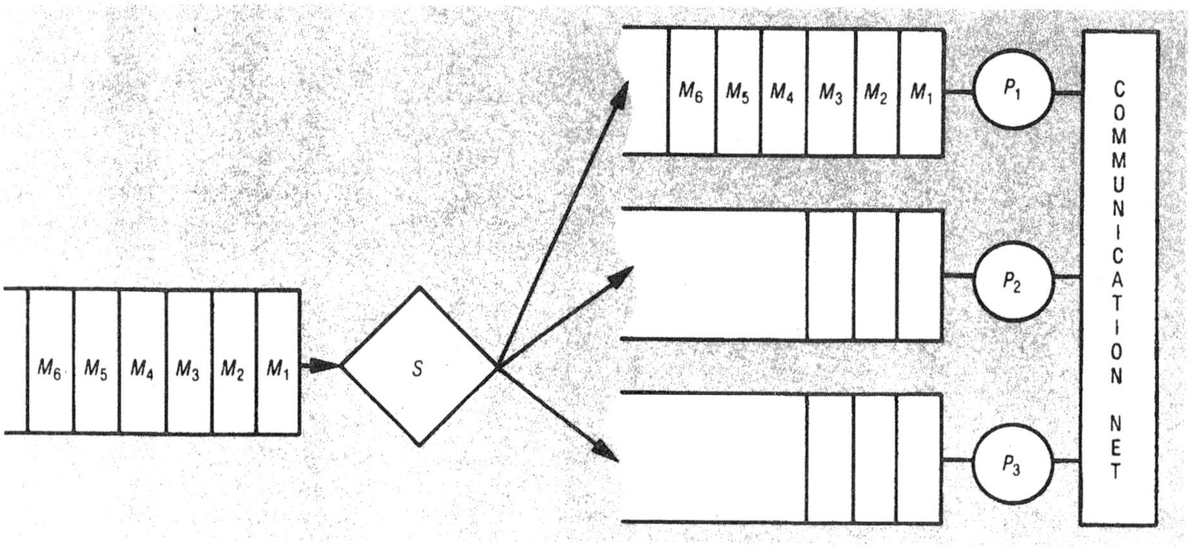

Figure 4. Minimum IPC allocation strategy.

of current system state on the task allocation.

Task allocation is also important during reconfiguration due to changing operating environment. These changes may be a result of changes in task input rate, in processing, channel capacity, etc. Task allocation should provide a strategy to reallocate modules dynamically, and the process should be transparant to the user.

Further, we must assume that system resources are limited. That is, the number of available processors, processor speed, memory capacity, and number and types of peripheral devices are fixed and limited by available system resources. In real-time applications, allowed elapsed time is also a limited resource. In this case, the module allocation methodology should be simple and fast enough to meet system performance requirements.

Model formulation and solution strategy

The task allocation problem is related to other distributed processing problems, such as the file allocation problem in distributed data base systems[4] and the task scheduling problem in queueing networks.[5,6,7] Queueing models, however, do not consider IPC and are therefore inappropriate. We will introduce two of the task allocation strategies that *do* consider IPC: a graph theoretic approach and an integer programming approach.

Graph theoretic approach. Several task allocation researchers have chosen a graph theoretic approach.[2,8,9,10] This method represents the modules to be allocated as a set of nodes in a graph. We assume the IMC cost between each pair of modules is known, represented by the weight of a nondirected arc connecting the two nodes. An IMC cost of zero means no communication takes place between the two modules, and therefore they are not connected in the graph. An IMC cost of infinity means these two nodes *must* be assigned to the same processor. The arc weights then represent the cost of communication between a pair of modules not coresident on a processor. Any pair of coresident modules is assumed to have zero IPC cost.

The task allocation strategy in this model is to minimize total cost, defined as the sum of processing cost and IPC cost. These costs are functions of the module-to-processor allocation. In order to represent the allocation of modules to processors we define an assignment matrix X such that

$$x_{i,k} = \begin{cases} 1 \text{ if module } M_i \text{ is assigned to processor } P_k \\ 0 \text{ otherwise} \end{cases}$$

Processing cost is given by the Q matrix,

$$Q = \{q_{i,k}\}, i=1, \ldots m, k=1, \ldots n$$

where $q_{i,k}$ represents the processing cost for module M_i on processor P_k. We assume this cost is available. It is a

Table 1.
Intermodule communication costs.

MODULE	A	B	C	D	E	F
A		6	4	0	0	12
B			8	12	3	0
C				0	11	0
D					5	0
E						0
F						

Table 2.
Processing costs.

MODULE	P_1 COST	P_2 COST
A	5	10
B	2	∞
C	4	4
D	6	3
E	5	2
F	∞	4

measure of the processing requirements of the module. A value of infinity, $q_{i,k} = \infty$, implies that module M_i cannot be executed at processor P_k.

Let $c_{i,j}$ represent the IMC cost between modules M_i and M_j. The total cost for processing a given task can then be expressed as a function of the allocation, X.

$$\text{Cost}(X) = \sum_{k} \sum_{i} \{ q_{i,k} x_{i,k} + \sum_{l<k} \sum_{j<i} c_{i,j} x_{i,k} x_{j,l} \} \quad (1)$$

The first summation term of (1) represents the processing cost for each module on its assigned processor. The second term represents the IPC cost between non-coresident modules. The minimum cost allocation is obtained by performing a min-cut algorithm on the graph.[11]

To illustrate, consider an example from Stone.[9] The task consists of six modules, {A,B,C,D,E,F}, which have IMC costs as given in Table 1 and processing costs as given in Table 2, on two processors, P_1 and P_2. The graph in Figure 5 can then be constructed with nodes for each of the modules and IMC costs on the arcs joining the nodes. In order to represent processing costs, as desired in the cost equation, two additional nodes are added to the graph to represent the two available processors, P_1 and P_2. The cost of running each module on processor P_1 is denoted on the arc joining that module node to node P_2. Similarly, the cost of running each module on processor P_2 is denoted on the arc joining that module node to node P_1. If we perform a min-cut algorithm on the graph in Figure 6, we obtain the cut shown by the heavy dark line. This provides the minimum cost allocation of the given modules between two processors. As we can see from the unbalanced allocation in this example, this strategy provides no mechanism for load balancing.

While this method is attractive in its simplicity, it has several serious limitations. First, the basic min-cut solution provides for a minimum cost allocation between two to three processors. In general, an extension of this method to an arbitrary number of processors requires an n-dimensional min-cut algorithm which quickly becomes computationally intractable.[11] This limits the usefulness of the method in many applications. An extension of this method to allow allocation among four or more processors has been proposed for cases where the IMC pattern can be constrained to be a tree.[10]

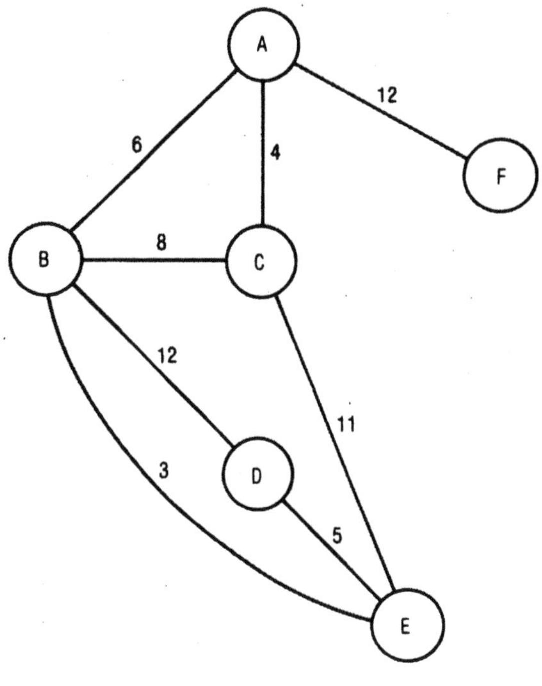

Figure 5. Communication graph.

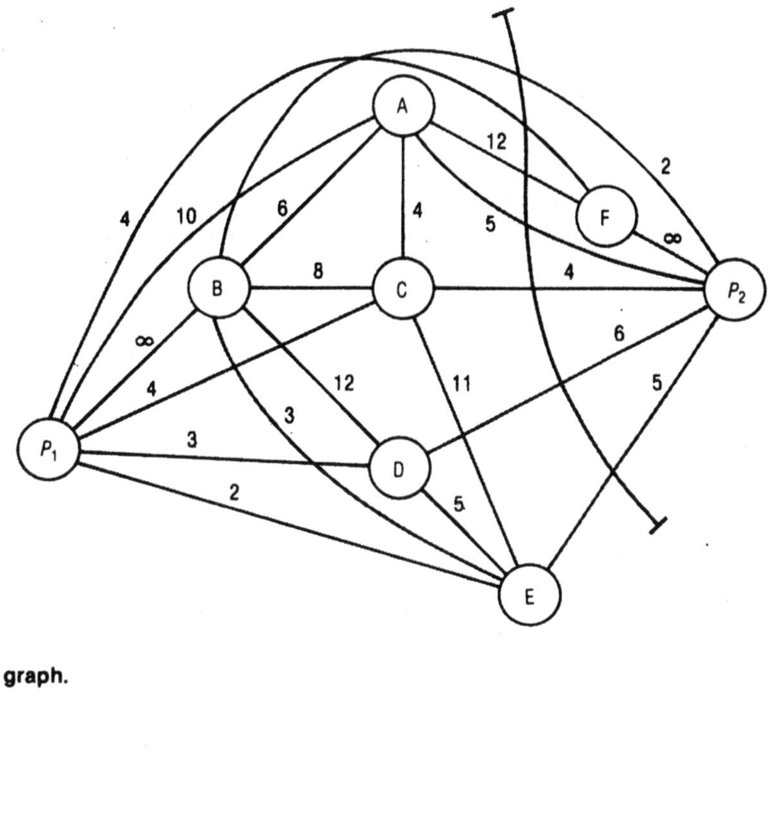

Figure 6. Complete graph.

This method provides neither a mechanism for representing limited resources in memory size or processing time, nor a mechanism for load balancing. An extension to include a restricted memory constraint is complex, and the solution is NP-complete.[8] Another drawback of this method is its inability to measure the impact of queueing delays on throughput. These delays are introduced into the system when more than one module is assigned to a single processor. Also, no mechanism is available for preservation of data flow precedence. These shortcomings suggest that the graph theoretic approach is not the best solution to the module allocation problem.

Integer 0-1 programming approach. A method applied with some success to the file problem and task allocation problem formulates the model as an optimization problem, and then solves it via a mathematical programming technique.[4,12]

As in the previous model, we wish to maximize system performance by minimizing total system cost, as defined in Equation (1). The minimization again takes place over the module allocation, X. Processing cost can be represented by the Q matrix defined above. In order to represent the IPC costs in this model we will replace the single cost matrix C with the product of a volume matrix and a distance matrix. We define IMC by a volume matrix,

$$V = \{v_{i,j}\}, i=1, \ldots m, j=1, \ldots m$$

where $v_{i,j}$ represents the volume of data sent from module M_i to module M_j. If $v_{i,j} = 0$, then module M_i does not communicate with module M_j.

Consider the distributed processing environment portrayed in Figure 2. We define a distance matrix on the set of processors

$$D = \{d_{k,l}\}, k=1, \ldots n, l=1, \ldots n$$

where n is the number of processors. The distance, $d_{k,l}$, is a measure of the communication cost between P_k and P_l. If two processors are not connected, then $d_{k,l} = \infty$. This distance measure allows the model to represent the processor interconnection in the network. By allowing $d_{k,k}$ to be nonzero, we can represent a cost of communication between coresident modules. This can be a useful feature in some distributed processing environments. The properties of the distance matrix are discussed in some detail in Lee.[13] We assume the distances are known and fixed for all pairs of processors.

We can now formulate the objective function for the model.

$$\text{Cost}(X) = \sum_k \sum_i \{q_{i,k}x_{i,k} + \sum_{l<k} \sum_{j<i} wv_{i,j}d_{k,l}x_{i,k}x_{j,l}\} \quad (2)$$

The first summation term of (2) represents the processing cost for each module on its assigned processor. The second term sums the volume-distance products that represent IPC cost. For a given assignment X, each pair of modules has a volume of data given by V, to be communicated between two processors given by the assignment at a distance given by D. The normalization constant w is used to scale processing cost and IPC cost to account for any differences in measuring units.

Load balancing will be achieved through imposition of constraints. The constraints we have identified as significant in our environment are memory size, processor speed, and real-time constraints on processing time. Processor speed is reflected in the processing cost matrix Q, so we need only discuss the memory size constraint and the real-time constraint.

A limited memory environment is represented by the constraint

$$\sum s_i x_{i,k} \leq R_k, k=1, \ldots n \quad (3)$$

where s_i represents the amount of memory storage required by module M_i and R_k represents the memory capacity at processor P_k. Equation (3) states that the amount of memory consumed by all modules assigned to a processor must not exceed its memory capacity.

The real-time constraint is given by

$$\sum u_i x_{i,k} \leq T_k, k=1, \ldots n \quad (4)$$

where u_i represents processing time required by module M_i, and T_k represents the required time limit for processing the modules that reside in processor P_k for a given task. Equation (4) states that the length of time required to process all the modules assigned to a single processor must not exceed the required real-time limit.

We may now perform the task allocation for any given system by minimizing Equation (2) subject to the constraints of Equations (3) and (4). This can be solved as a nonlinear 0-1 integer programming problem. Further, the nonlinear 0-1 equation can be linearized by adding further constraints, which greatly simplifies the solution process. A problem consisting of 8000 constraints and 2500 unknowns can be solved on a CDC 6000 series computer in a few minutes.[14] This represents a problem of approximately 15 processors and 25 modules.

Time-critical applications demand other approaches. One is to use approximate solution strategies for the above model. Such solution strategies include goal programming[15,16] and quadratic assignment algorithms.[17] Another approach to the complexity problem is to generate optimum allocations, off-line, over some range of possible processing environments and to store tables of these allocations for use in real time by table look-up. Such techniques can be useful in a dynamic assignment environment.

The above formulation of the task allocation problem provides a good representation of the task allocation environment. It is a flexible technique because it allows constraints to be introduced into the model as appropriate to the application. This is difficult or impossible with the graph theoretic approach.

The integer 0-1 programming model falls short in two important areas: the representation of the effects of current system state in the real-time constraint, and representation of the effects of precedence relations in the data flow among the modules. Further study is required here because both factors introduce queueing delays into the system in a complex manner. Under these considerations, the real-time constraint becomes

$$\sum_i f_i(u_i x_{i,k}, p_{i,j}) \leq T_k, k=1, \ldots n, \; i, j=1, \ldots m \quad (5)$$

where $p_{i,j}$ represents the precedence relation between modules M_i and M_j. The function f_i then represents the processing time, including queueing delay, for processing module M_i at processor P_k.

Heuristic methods

Some simplifying assumptions reduce the amount of computing time for module allocation: processors in the network are homogeneous; they are fully connected; and the effect of precedence relationships among modules can be ignored. Under these assumptions, a heuristic module clustering algorithm (grouping modules with high intermodule communication cost) can be used for module allocation subject to the real-time and memory constraints. Such an algorithm has been proposed by Gylys.[12]

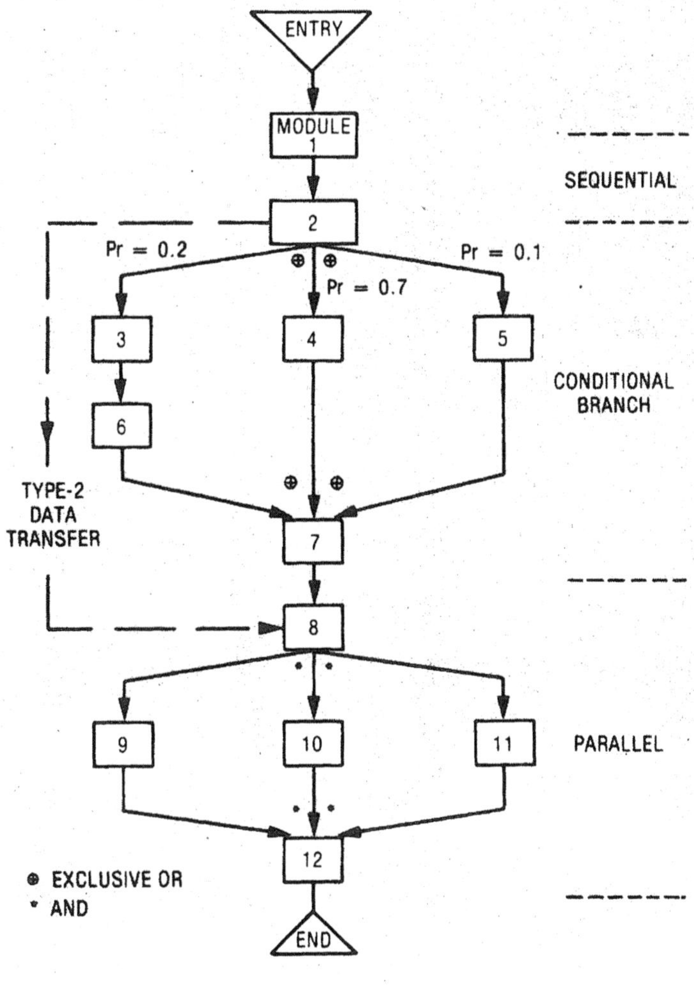

Figure 7. A control flow graph.

The process of assigning two modules to the same processor is called fusion. In this algorithm, after finding a pair of modules—fusion of which will eliminate the greatest amount of IPC cost—we check to see whether this fusion satisfies the real-time and memory constraints. If it does, that module pair is fused. Otherwise, the eligible pair with the next highest IMC cost is chosen as a possible candidate. We repeat this process until a fusion is made. That module pair is then represented by a module cluster for the next iteration. This fusing process continues until all eligible pairs are allocated.

In the above algorithm, the real-time constraint does not consider the queueing delays and precedence relationships among modules, since both are difficult to estimate or model. Since we know balancing the load among the set of processors yields high throughput and faster response time, we propose replacing the real-time constraint with a load-balancing constraint. This should yield a faster computational solution, since it is a simpler constraint.

We propose that the module allocation for minimizing IPC costs and satisfying the load-balancing and memory constraints be treated in two stages. The modules are first fused among a set of processors with a clustering algorithm. We then check to see whether or not the system satisfies the load-balancing requirements and memory constraints. Since it is difficult—if not impossible—to achieve perfect load balancing, we consider the system balanced if the loading of the processors is within a certain tolerance of the ideal level; we reassign some modules from processors exceeding the tolerance level to processors that are below this level.

Although heuristic algorithms achieve only a suboptimum solution, they are useful in applications where an optimum solution is not required, not obtainable, or cannot be obtained within the critical time limit.

Estimation of intermodule communication

The task allocation strategies discussed above depend on the availability of IMC measurements. In this section, we develop a methodology to estimate IMC. This methodology will be particularly useful in the early design phase of a distributed processing system, before the programs are actually coded. It will also enhance the performance of a partitioning compiler to compile and then partition the compiled code.[18] The concept of this methodology is based on the program specifications and the module interreference patterns.

In this section, we represent the task and the intermodule data transfers by a flow graph, then develop equations to estimate the intermodule communication using branching probabilities and loop frequencies. To facilitate discussion, we classify the IMC into three categories for (1) shared or intermediate data transfer, (2) distributed database management, and (3) system control. IMC due to system control refers to scheduling of distributed system resources and their management, including task scheduling, synchronization, processor status and/or peripheral device status broadcasting, maintenance of data base consistency, system reconfiguration information, etc. Since these are fixed overhead costs, we will consider only the first two categories of IMC.

IMC for shared or intermediate data transfer. The module partitioning of a task in a control and data flow graph is represented in Figure 7. A control and data flow graph has an entry point and a termination point. A distributed task can have multiple entry points and multiple termination points, as shown within the dotted square boundary in Figure 8. These multiple entry points and termination points can be combined into a single entry point and a single termination point, as shown. Therefore, we need only consider single-entry single-termination control flow graphs.

The rectangular block in Figure 7 represents a computational module, and the directed arc represents the precedence relationship between the two connected modules. When there is an arc from M_i to M_j, it implies data transfer from M_i to M_j. If M_i and M_j are not allocated to the same processor, there is a transfer of data from one processor to another, referred to as the type-1 data transfer.

Data may have to be transferred from one module to another even when there is no direct connecting arc between the two modules. Consider the example in Figure 7. M_2 may generate data to be used by M_8 but not by M_3 through M_7. In this case, it is desirable to have M_2 transfer these data directly to M_8 instead of routing them through M_3, M_6, and M_7 (assuming that M_2, M_3, M_6, M_7, and M_8 are not coresident in the same processor). This type of data transfer, the type-2 data transfer, is represented by dotted lines in the figure.

There are three basic types of control flow: sequential, conditional branching (Exclusive OR), and parallel (AND). As will become clear, all control flow can be represented as a combination of these three basic types.

The loop control flow as shown in Figure 9 is a variant of conditional branching because the control is conditionally branched back to some previous point in the program. There are two categories of loops in a sequential program. For example, let us consider the DO loops in the following Fortran program.

```
      DO 10 I  =  1, 15
      SUMA  =  SUMA + A(I)
   10 SUMB  =  SUMB + B(I)
      DO 12 I  =  1, 15
      C(I)  =  A(I) + B(I)
   12 D(I)  =  C(I) ** 2
```

There are two loops in this program. The first one must be executed in a sequential manner; that is, the loop for index $I = k+1$ should not be executed before the loop for $I = k$ is completed. If we examine the second loop, we find it is actually a set of 15 parallel-executable sequences, with two statements in each sequence. Therefore, it should be represented with the AND-type control flow in the graph.

The control flow at the conditional branching points and the number of times a loop will be repeated may be constant (given in the system or program design specifications) or data dependent. When these parameters are data dependent, their values must be obtained through experience or simulations. In the following discussion, let us assume: (1) the probability that each arc will be chosen is known at each conditional branching point; (2) the average number of times each loop is executed is known.

With these assumptions, we can proceed to calculate the number of times an arc *i-j* is traversed, $N^a_{i,j}$, and the number of times a module M_i is executed, N^m_i. If we can obtain these values, we are able to calculate the IMC for common data, $v_{i,j}$, as follows:

$$v_{i,j} = \begin{cases} v'_{i,j} * N^a_{i,j} & \text{for type-1 data transfer} \\ v''_{i,j} * N^m_i & \text{for type-2 data transfer} \\ 0 & \text{otherwise;} \end{cases} \tag{6}$$

where $v'_{i,j}$ = the volume of data transfer required each time the connecting arc *i-j* is traversed, and $v''_{i,j}$ = the volume of data transfer required along the dotted line *i-j* each time M_i is executed.

The $N^a_{i,j}$ is easily obtained from N^m_i as follows: (1) if there is a sequential control flow from M_i to M_j and there is no other arc leaving M_i, then

$$N^a_{i,j} = N^m_i \tag{7}$$

(2) If more than one Exclusive-OR arcs leaves M_i, then the $N^a_{i,j}$ for each such arc *i-j* is

$$N^a_{i,j} = N^m_i \times \Pr(i,j) \tag{8}$$

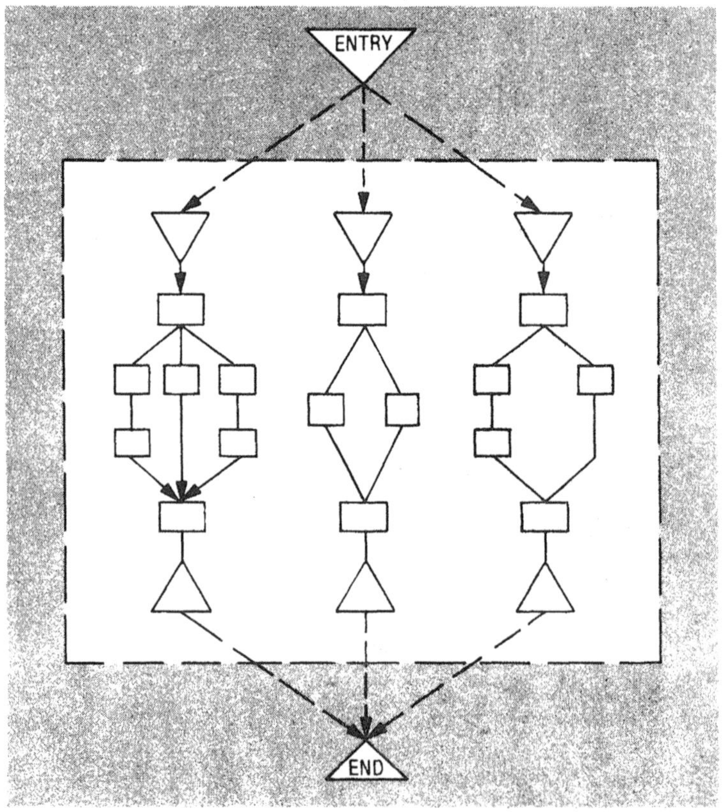

Figure 8. Combining several control flow graphs into one.

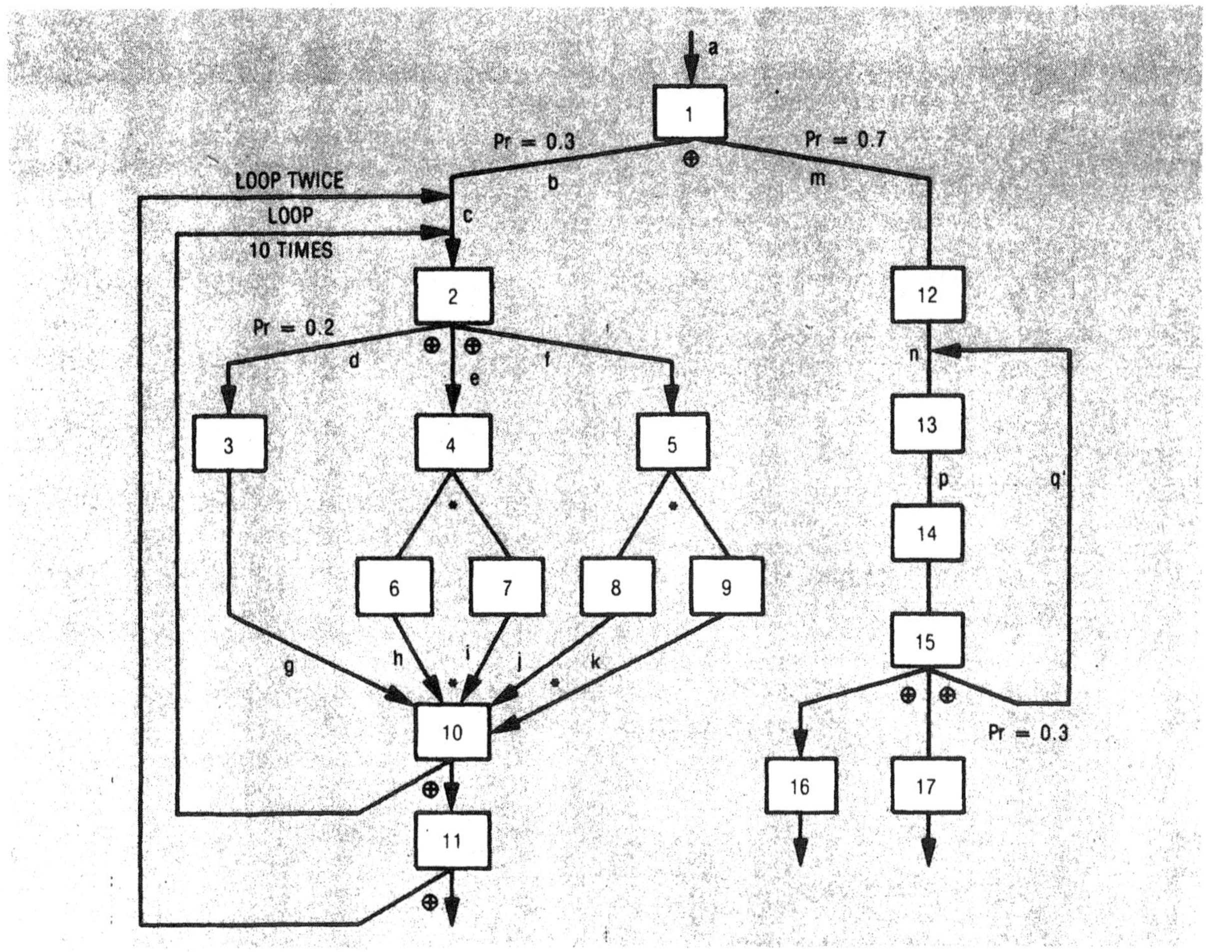

Figure 9. Graph for N^a and N^m calculation.

where $\Pr(i,j)$ is the probability that arc i-j is chosen. For example, if M_2 in Figure 7 is executed 10 times within a certain period (e.g., a job cycle or a certain mission) and $\Pr(2,3) = 0.2$, then $N^a_{2,3} = 10 \times 0.2 = 2$ times. (3) If there are more than one AND arcs leaving M_i, then every such arc i-j has an $N^a_{i,j}$ as

$$N^a_{i,j} = N^m_i \tag{9}$$

Having shown the calculation of the $N^a_{i,j}$'s in terms of the N^m_i's, we can now show the calculation of the N^m_j's in terms of the $N^a_{i,j}$'s. That is, we want to show that the number of times a module M_j is executed can be obtained from the number of times all its incoming arcs are traversed. The following is a set of three rules corresponding to the three basic types of control flow: (1) If the control passes through a sequential flow arc, from M_i into M_j, then

$$N^m_j = N^a_{i,j} \tag{10}$$

This is illustrated at M_2 in Figure 7 where $N^m_2 = N^a_{1,2}$. (2) If there are more than one Exclusive-OR arcs meeting at a single module M_j, then

$$N^m_j = \sum_i N^a_{i,j} \tag{11}$$

where the summation takes place over all the modules M_i which have an outgoing arc connected to module M_j, since only one of these arcs may be traversed at a time. This is illustrated at module M_7 where

$$N^m_7 = N^a_{6,7} + N^a_{4,7} + N^a_{5,7}$$

(3) If more than one AND arcs (i-j)'s merge into a single module M_j, then

$$N^m_j = \text{any}(N^a_{i,j}) \tag{12}$$

since all these arcs are invoked at the same time. This is illustrated at M_{12} in Figure 7 where

$$N^m_{12} = N^a_{9,12} = N^a_{10,12} = N^a_{11,12}$$

All other cases can be decomposed into one or more of the above three basic cases. For example, the number of times M_{10} in Figure 9 is executed can be obtained as

$$N^m_{10} = N^a_{3,10} + N^a_{6,10} + N^a_{8,10}$$

because arcs 6-10 and 7-10 can be merged into a single arc with the number of traversals equal to $N^a_{6,10}$ $(= N^a_{7,10})$.

Likewise, arcs 8-10 and 9-10 can be merged into a single arc.

If M_j is the first module within a specific loop with loop index range I, and if $N^a_{i,j}$ for the arc i-j which leads into module M_j has been calculated, then

$$N^m_j = N^u_{i,j} \times I \qquad (13)$$

For example, N^m_2 in Figure 9 is equal to $N^u_{1,2} \times 2 \times 10$. If arc a is traversed 10 times, then arc d is traversed $10 \times 0.3 \times 2 \times 10 \times 0.2$ times.

Let us examine another situation. Assume a conditional branching point exists, emanating from a module M_i, and the control might branch back to a previous module with a given probability, Pr. Note that this is not a fixed-index-range loop. Then, the first module M_j encountered after the branching back has

$$N^m_j = \mathrm{N}^a_{i,j} \times \sum_{k=0}^{\infty} \qquad (14)$$

If $N^m_{12} = 100$ in Figure 9 and $\mathrm{Pr} = 0.3$, then

$$N^m_{13.} = 100 \sum_{k=0}^{\infty} (0.3)^k$$
$$= 100 * 1/(1 - 0.3)$$
$$= 143.$$

To compute the N^m's and N^u's, we always start from the top of the control flow graph and deal with the outermost loop first. Once we obtain all N^u's and N^m's, we can use Equation (6) to compute all desired IMC, the $v_{i,j}$'s. Since the estimation of $v'_{i,j}$ and $v''_{i,j}$ are identical, it is sufficient to consider only one of them, the $v'_{i,j}$. It is simply

$$v'_{i,j} = O(i) \cap I(j) \qquad (15)$$

where $O(i)$ = output from M_i, i.e., the set of new data generated by M_i; $I(j)$ = input to M_j, i.e., the set of data generated from other modules and used by M_j for its computation.

IMC for distributed data base management. The data base-related activities of a module can be grouped into three classes: (1) Read (Get) data from the data base, (2) Write (Insert) data into the data base, and (3) Modify (Rewrite) data in the data base (see Figure 10). The files of a distributed data base are placed at various processor locations. Interprocessor communication is involved when a program module at a processor needs to access a file at another processor.

With the aid of a control flow graph, we can estimate the frequency—$f_{i,k}$—with which the kth I/O statement in module M_i accesses file j. Then the communication volume $v_{i,j}$ is

$$v_{i,j} = \sum_k f_{i,k} d_{i,k,j} \qquad (15)$$

where $d_{i,k,j}$ is the volume of communication invoked by executing the kth I/O statement in M_i under the condition that module M_i and file j are not allocated at the same processor. The actual value of $d_{i,k,j}$ depends on such parameters as record length, communication protocol used, and query complexity.

Conclusions and future directions

The object of task allocation is to counterbalance the related but opposite factors of interprocessor communication cost and load balancing, to achieve maximum throughput and to satisfy real-time constraints. Assuming a task is partitioned into modules, models are

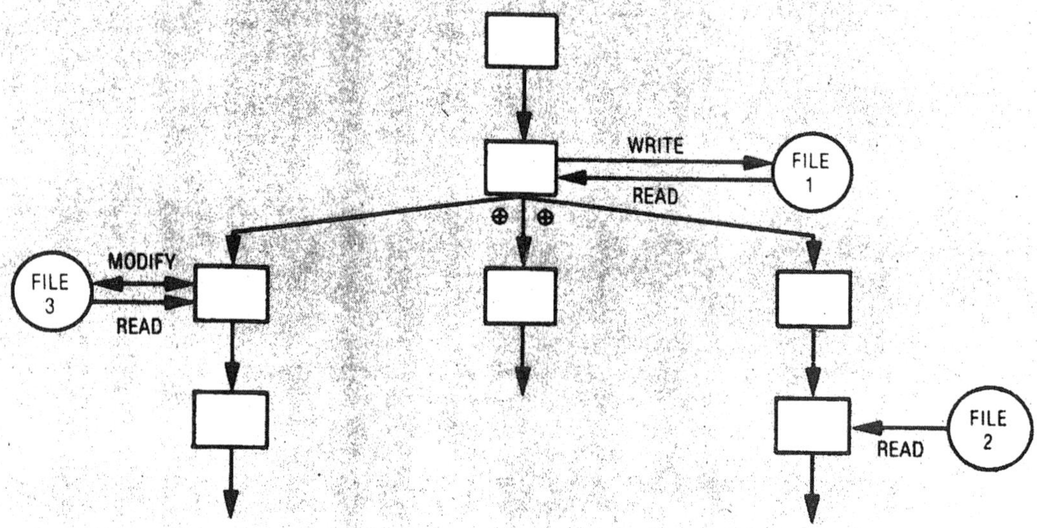

Figure 10. Distributed data base activities.

developed to accomplish task allocation to minimize total processing cost.

A graph model represents modules as nodes in a graph and the intermodule communication cost as weights on the nondirected arcs connecting the nodes of the graph. The task allocation methodology is to allocate modules to processors so that total processing cost is minimized. Total processing cost is the sum of module processing cost and interprocessor communication cost. Standard min-cut algorithms can obtain the optimum task allocation. However, the computation costs become intractable for n-dimensional (n-processor assignment) min-cut algorithms. Moreover, this model does not consider load balancing and resource limitation issues.

The integer 0-1 programming model minimizes total processing cost subject to such resource limitation constraints as memory capacity and real-time requirements. The real-time constraint is rather complex; it must include the queueing delay at various processor queues and the precedence relations between the modules. However, the integer programming model does consider the system resource limitations and real-time requirements, necessary attributes for any methodology to be useful under real system requirements. Although there are problems in accurate representation of real-time constraints and computation problems in solving large-scale problems, there have been some promising results with this methodology.

Heuristic models provide approximate solutions to the task allocation problem. The basic idea of heuristic methods is to find an allocation to balance the costs between IPC and load balancing. This technique requires much less computation time than integer programming methods. As a result, it can solve time-critical cases and also larger dimensional problems.

Control flow graphs can be constructed to represent module interrelationships. The intermodule communication cost can then be estimated from the control and data flow graph, based on the frequency of module references as well as the module I/O characteristics. The module interrelationships are important both for estimating interprocessor communication and for representing queueing delays in interprocessor communication.

Task partitioning is an important problem in distributed processing systems, a problem far from being solved. How will the relationships among response time, precedence relations, and queueing delay be expressed? How will we express the dynamics of IPC, particularly in light of data dependency in system operation time? How will tradeoffs of replicated programs and data files for response time and reconfiguration considerations, etc., be included? Much more work will be required to resolve these and other questions. ■

Acknowledgments

This research is in part supported by the US Office of Naval Research, Contract No. N00014-75-C-0650, and in part by the US Army, Contract No. DASG60-79-C-0087.

References

1. W.W. Chu, D. Lee and B. Iffla, "A Distributed Processing System for Naval Data Communication Networks," *AFIPS Conf. Proc.*, Vol. 47, NCC 1978, pp. 783-793.
2. C.J. Jenny, "Process Partitioning in Distributed Systems," *Digest of Papers NTC '77*, 1977, pp. 31:1-1—10.
3. M.P. Mariani and D.F. Palmer, *Tutorial: Distributed System Design*, IEEE Computer Society, 1979.*
4. W.W. Chu, "Optimal File Allocation in a Multiple Computing System," *IEEE Trans. Computers*, Vol. C-18, No. 10, Oct. 1969, pp. 885-889.
5. V. Balachandran, J.W. McCredie and V.I. Mikhail, "Models of the Job Allocation Problem in Computer Networks," *Digest of Papers COMPCON Fall 76*, Sept. 1976, pp. 211-214.*
6. F. Baskett, K.M. Chandy, R.R. Muntz and F.G. Palacios, "Open, Closed and Mixed Networks of Queues with Different Classes of Customers," *J. ACM*, Vol. 22, No. 2, Apr. 1975, pp. 248-260.
7. Y. Chow and W.H. Kohler, "Models for Dynamic Load Balancing in a Heterogeneous Multiple Processor System," *IEEE Trans. Computers*, Vol. C-28, No. 5, May 1979, pp. 354-361.
8. G.S. Rao, H.S. Stone and T.C. Hu, "Assignment of Tasks in a Distributed Processor System with Limited Memory," *IEEE Trans. Computers*, Vol. C-28, No. 4, Apr. 1979, pp. 291-299.
9. H.S. Stone, "Multiprocessor Scheduling with the Aid of Network Flow Algorithms," *IEEE Trans. Software Eng.*, Vol. SE-3, No. 1, Jan. 1977, pp. 85-93.
10. H.S. Stone and S.H. Bokhari, "Control of Distributed Processes," *Computer*, July 1978, pp. 97-106.
11. F. Harary, *Graph Theory*, Addison-Wesley, New York, N.Y., 1969.
12. V.B. Gylys and J.A. Edwards, "Optimal Partitioning of Workload for Distributed Systems," *Digest of Papers, COMPCON Fall 76*, Sept. 1976, pp. 353-357.*
13. R.P. Lee, *Optimal Task and File Assignment in a Distributed Computing Network*, Doctoral Dissertation, UCLA, 1977.
14. P.L. Price and D.W. Smith, "Analysis and Use of an Integer Programming Model for Optimally Allocating Files in a Multiple Computer System," DTNSRDC-78/102, David W. Taylor Naval Ship and Research and Development Center, Bethesda. Md., Nov. 1978.
15. J.P. Ignizio, *Goal Programming and Extensions*, D. C. Heath and Co., Indianapolis, Ind., 1976.
16. S.M. Lee, *Goal Programming for Decision Analysis*, Auerbach Publishers, Pennsauken, N.J., 1972.
17. G.W. Graves and A.B. Whinston, "An Algorithm for the Quadratic Assignment Problem," *Management Sci.*, Vol. 17, 1970, pp. 453-471.
18. O. El-Dessouk, W. Huen and M. Evans, "Towards a Partitioning Compiler for a Distributed Computing System," *Proc. Int'l Conf. Distributed Computing Systems*, 1979, pp. 296-304.

* These tutorials and digests are available from the IEEE Computer Society Publications Office, 5855 Naples Plaza, Suite 301, Long Beach, CA 90803.

Wesley W. Chu is a computer sciences professor at UCLA and a consultant to government and industry. At UCLA he directs research groups in computer communications and networking and in distributed processing and data bases. He is an editor on several computer publications, has edited two textbooks, and authored more than 50 articles on information processing systems and computer communications.

From 1960 to 1969 he worked in private industry on design of large-scale computers, switching circuits, and computer communications. Between 1970 and 1977 he was an ACM National Lecturer, an IEEE Distinguished Visitor, chairman of ACM SIGCOMM, on the IEEE Computer Communications Technical Committee, chairman of the ACM Interprocess Communication Workshop, technical program chairman of the Fourth Data Communication Symposium, and chairman of the IEEE Lake Arrowhead workshop on networking and distributed data bases.

He is a member of Tau Beta Pi, Eta Kappa Nu, Phi Tau Phi, and Sigma Xi. A fellow of the IEEE, he received his BS and MS degrees from the University of Michigan and PhD in electrical engineering from Stanford.

Leslie J. Holloway is a research assistant in computer science at UCLA, and a PhD candidate in distributed processing. She is a Doctoral Fellow and staff engineer at Hughes Aircraft Company in the Systems Engineering Department of the Software Engineering Lab. She holds BA and MA degrees in mathematics from UCLA and is a member of the IEEE Computer Society, AAAI, and Pi Mu Epsilon.

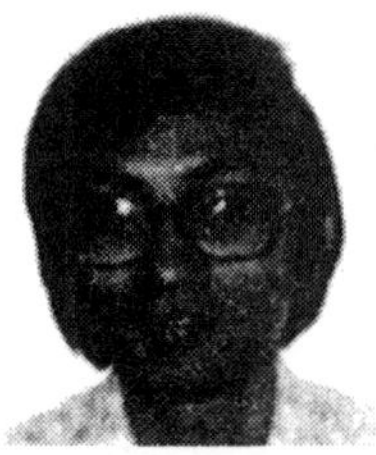

Min-Tsung Lan is a PhD student and research assistant in the Computer Science Department at UCLA, where he is working on the distributed processing problem. From 1974 to 1976 he was a computer system engineer for the China Steel Corporation on Taiwan. In 1978-79 he was on the technical staff of the Technology Service Corporation in Santa Monica, California. He received his BS in electrical engineering from National Taiwan University in 1974 and MS in computer science from the University of Nebraska in 1977.

Kemal Efe is a Research Fellow in computer science at the University of Leeds in England. His research interests are computer arithmetic, job control, and operating system interfaces of job control languages. He has worked as a project engineer for Turkish Electronical Industries and Trade Corporation, and is a member of the Electrical Engineer's Association of Turkey. Mr. Efe received his BS in electrical engineering from the Technical University of Istanbul in 1977 and completed his MS in computer science at UCLA in 1980.

Estimation of Intermodule Communication (IMC) and Its Applications in Distributed Processing Systems

WESLEY W. CHU, FELLOW, IEEE, MIN-TSUNG LAN, STUDENT MEMBER, IEEE, AND JOSEPH HELLERSTEIN

***Abstract*— Communication among program modules plays an important role in the performance of distributed processing systems. In this paper, a model for estimating intermodule communication (IMC) is developed. The model derives communication volume based on module invocation rates and file access probabilities via the control-and-data-flow graph. The IMC model is validated by simulation experiments. Interprocessor communication (IPC) and system resources utilization can be estimated from the IMC. We show that IMC and IPC are useful in finding good module assignments in distributed processing systems.**

***Index Terms*— Control and data flow graph, distributed processing, intermodule communication (IMC), interprocessor communication (IPC), module assignment, multiprocessing, parallel processing, performance measurement, real-time systems, task assignment.**

I. Introduction

With the advent of technology for high-speed computer communication and VLSI, distributed processing has become economically feasible. Distributed processing has the potential for providing lower cost, better response time, and higher availability than centralized processing. However, compared to centralized systems, the design and implementation of distributed systems are much more complex and so have been the subject of intensive research [1]–[7], [10], [11], [13]. A key factor affecting the performance of distributed systems is *interprocessor communication (IPC)* [4] which consists of all messages exchanged among computers (processors) and shared memories. Once the location of program modules (module assignment) and shared files (file assignment) is given and the nature of communication control overhead of the operating system is known, IPC can be derived from *intermodule communication (IMC)* which quantifies the amount of communication among modules. Thus, estimating IPC requires the knowledge of IMC. In this paper, we first characterize IMC and develop a model for estimating both the IMC and module execution time (ET). Next, we present the results of measurements taken from a simulated space defense system and use these measurements to validate the IMC and ET models. The IMC incurred for control functions in distributed processing systems is then discussed. Finally, we present the applications of IMC in the estimation of IPC and system resource utilization, and in module assignment for a real-time distributed processing system.

Manuscript received March 22, 1983; revised January 13, 1984. This work was supported by the Ballistic Missile Defense Advanced Technological Center under Contract DASG60-79-C-0087.

W. W. Chu and M. -T. Lan are with the Department of Computer Science, University of California, Los Angeles, CA 90024.

J. Hellerstein was with the Department of Computer Science, University of California, Los Angeles, CA 90024. He is now with the IBM T. J. Watson Research Center, Yorktown Heights, NY 10598.

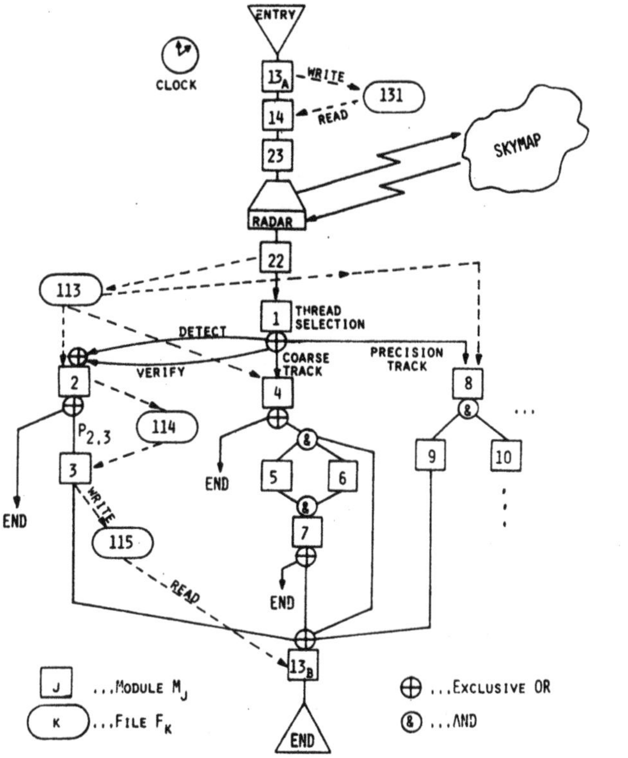

Fig. 1. A control-and-data-flow graph for a space-defense application task.

II. Analytical Model for IMC Estimation

A distributed application consists of J program modules $M_1, M_2, \cdots, M_J$ running on S computers. Fig. 1 shows a *control-and-data-flow graph* of an application task. The granularity of modules is at the subroutine level rather than the instruction level as is being used in data flow machines [12]. A control-and-data-flow graph is a control flow graph superimposed by files and the associated data flow between modules and files. The graph has an entry point and a termination point [5]. Each square box represents a computational module, and each directed *arc* represents the precedence relationship between the two connected modules. The sequence of module execution is referred to as the *control flow*. Module M_j causes M_n to follow it by sending an *enablement* to M_n's computer which is referred to as "M_j enables M_n." Files are represented by ellipses. *Data flow* is represented by broken lines and consists of reads and writes by modules to the set of K shared data files $F_1, F_2, \cdots, F_K$. Modules communicate through shared files and module enablements; such communication is referred to as *intermodule communication (IMC)*.

A. Estimation of Key Parameters

Three types of IMC exist: module-to-module (M–M) for module enablements, module-to-file (M–F) for file updates (writes), and file-to-module (F–M) for file reads (Fig. 1). Here we estimate each for all specified time intervals (t_h, t_{h+1})'s. (Note that h is simply an integer index; we reserve i and j for indexing other items in this paper.) The interval size, $t_{h+1} - t_h$, for the estimation should be properly selected. Too short intervals prevent us from observing the trend of workload changes while too long intervals are not sensitive enough to reveal the dynamic behavior.

For M–M IMC, the number of module M_n enablements by M_j during time interval (t_h, t_{h+1}) is

$$N_j(t_h, t_{h+1})\, p_{jn}(E;\, t_h, t_{h+1})$$

where $N_j(t_h, t_{h+1})$ = *number of times module M_j executes* during (t_h, t_{h+1}), referred to as *execution frequency* of M_j, and $p_{jn}(E;\, t_h, t_{h+1})$ = probability that an execution of M_j enables M_n, referred to as *enablement probability*.

Thus, the M–M IMC volume from M_j to M_n is

$$V_{jn}(E;\, t_h, t_{h+1}) = N_j(t_h, t_{h+1})\, p_{jn}(E;\, t_h, t_{h+1}) L_{jn}(E;\, t_h, t_{h+1}) \quad (1)$$

where $L_{jn}(E;\, t_h, t_{h+1})$ = average number of words (enablement-message length) sent from M_j to M_n when M_j enables M_n.

For M–F IMC, the number of updates to F_k by M_j is

$$N_j(t_h, t_{h+1})\, p_{jk}(W;\, t_h, t_{h+1})$$

where $p_{jk}(W;\, t_h, t_{h+1})$ = probability that an execution of M_j updates file F_k. Therefore, the *IMC message volume* (number of words) sent from M_j to F_k is

$$V_{jk}(W;\, t_h, t_{h+1}) = N_j(t_h, t_{h+1})\, p_{jk}(W;\, t_h, t_{h+1}) L_{jk}(W;\, t_h, t_{h+1}) \quad (2)$$

where $L_{jk}(W;\, t_h, t_{h+1})$ = average number of words (record length) written per update.

Similarly, the F–M message volume for read response sent from file F_k to M_j is

$$V_{jk}(R;\, t_h, t_{h+1}) = N_j(t_h, t_{h+1})\, p_{jk}(R;\, t_h, t_{h+1}) L_{jk}(R;\, t_h, t_{h+1}) \quad (3)$$

where $p_{jk}(R;\, t_h, t_{h+1})$ = probability that an execution of M_j reads file F_k, and $L_{jk}(R;\, t_h, t_{h+1})$ = average number of words M_j reads from F_k.

Finally, the accumulative execution time (AET) for M_j during (t_h, t_{h+1}) is

$$T_j(t_h, t_{h+1}) = N_j(t_h, t_{h+1}) X_j(t_h, t_{h+1}) \quad (4)$$

where $X_j(t_h, t_{h+1})$ = average execution time (ET) of M_j during (t_h, t_{h+1}). This time can be expressed in terms of machine-language instructions (MLI) executed.

Since (1)–(4) require values for $N_j(t_h, t_{h+1})$, we show how it can be estimated in the next section.

B. Estimation of $N_j(t_h, t_{h+1})$

To estimate $N_j(t_h, t_{h+1})$, we use only the control flow portion of the graph. There are three basic types of control flows: sequential, conditional branching (EXCLUSIVE OR), and parallel (AND). Loop control flow is a variant of conditional branching because the control is conditionally branched back to some previous point. Therefore, in this paper, we assume control flow graphs with no loops.

Estimation for the execution frequency of module M_j within (t_h, t_{h+1}), $N_j(t_h, t_{h+1})$, requires knowledge of the enablement probabilities $p_{ij}(E;\, t_h, t_{h+1})$ for all incident arcs $(i{-}j)$'s from M_i's into M_j. Enablement probabilities must satisfy the following two conditions.

1) If more than one EXCLUSIVE OR arc leaves M_i, then every such arc $i{-}m$ has an enablement probability $p_{im}(E;\, t_h, t_{h+1})$ such that $\sum_m p_{im}(E;\, t_h, t_{h+1}) = 1$.

2) If there are more than one AND arcs leaving M_i, each arc $i{-}m$ has $p_{im}(E;\, t_h, t_{h+1}) = 1$. Note that sequential flow is a special case of EXCLUSIVE OR flow (and AND flow) where only one arc leaves M_i and $p_{im}(E;\, t_h, t_{h+1}) = 1$.

A control flow graph with no loops can be viewed as an acyclic directed graph and hence has a *partial ordering* of modules where the relation "partial order" is denoted as $M_i < M_j$ when M_i enables M_j. We can use the *topological sorting algorithm* [9] to embed the partial order of the J modules into a linear order and rename these modules into $M_1, M_2, \cdots, M_J$ such that whenever M_i enables M_j, $i < j$. Let the entry node be M_0 and assume the number of entries into the control flow graph, $N_0(t_h, t_{h+1})$, is given. To estimate $N_j(t_h, t_{h+1})$'s, we consider the modules M_j's *in their ordered sequence* $j = 1, 2, \cdots, J$. Doing so ensures that for each j, $N_i(t_h, t_{h+1})$ is known if M_i enables M_j.

The following estimation rules are used.

1) If M_j has only one incident arc and this arc emits from M_i, then

$$N_j(t_h, t_{h+1}) \approx N_i(t_h - \Delta_{ij}, t_{h+1} - \Delta_{ij}) \cdot p_{ij}(E;\, t_h - \Delta_{ij}, t_{h+1} - \Delta_{ij}) \quad (5)$$

where the notation "≈" indicates an approximate estimation, and Δ_{ij} is the average M_i-to-M_j *enablement delay*. An enablement delay is the duration starting from when M_i completes its execution and enables M_j until when M_j completes its execution. This includes the wait time of M_j in scheduling queue plus its own execution time. Normally the module execution time is much smaller than the time interval $(t_{h+1} - t_h)$. (See the discussion on interval size at the beginning of Section II-A.) If the wait time is also small, then Δ_{ij} is negligible compared to $(t_{h+1} - t_h)$ and (5) reduces to

$$N_j(t_h, t_{h+1}) \approx N_i(t_h, t_{h+1})\, p_{ij}(E;\, t_h, t_{h+1}) . \quad (6)$$

For example, if M_2 in Fig. 1 executes ten times within a time

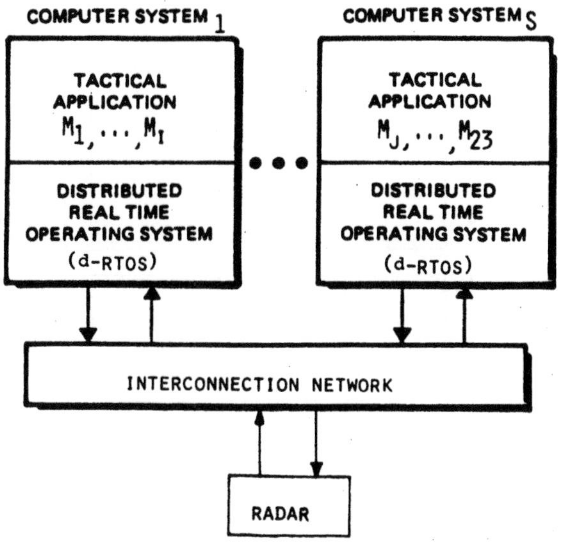

Fig. 2. The Distributed Processing Architecture Design (DPAD) system.

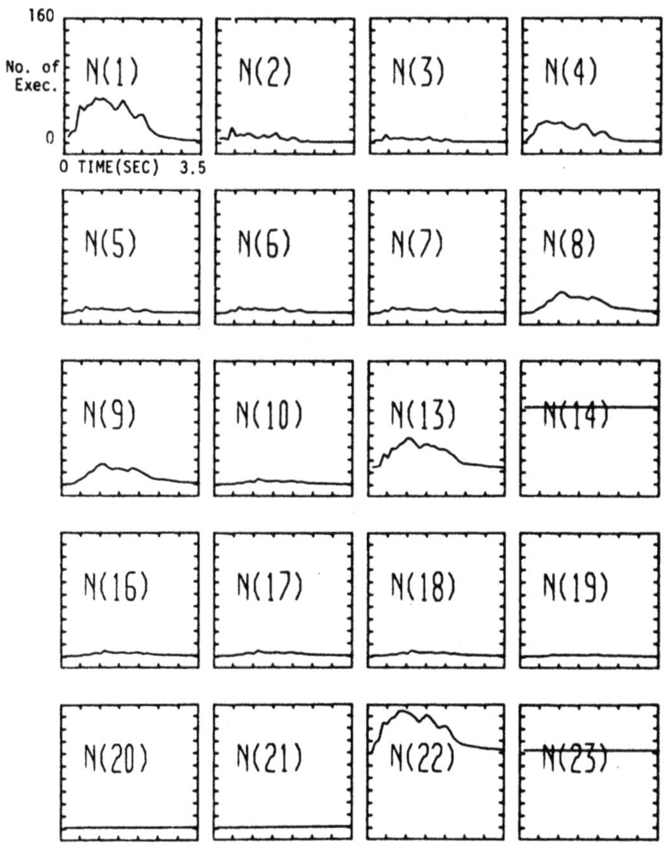

Fig. 3. Number of module executions.

interval, $p_{2,3}(E) = 0.5$, and $\Delta_{2,3}$ is negligible, then M_3 executes $10 \times 0.5 = 5$ times within that same interval.

2) If multiple arcs $(i-j)$'s enter module M_j in the EXCLUSIVE OR manner, then

$$N_j(t_h, t_{h+1}) \approx \sum_i N_i(t_h - \Delta_{ij}, t_{h+1} - \Delta_{ij}) \cdot p_{ij}(E; t_h - \Delta_{ij}, t_{h+1} - \Delta_{ij}). \quad (7)$$

Equation (7) *sums over* all the modules M_i which have an outgoing arc connected to module M_j since any of these M_i's

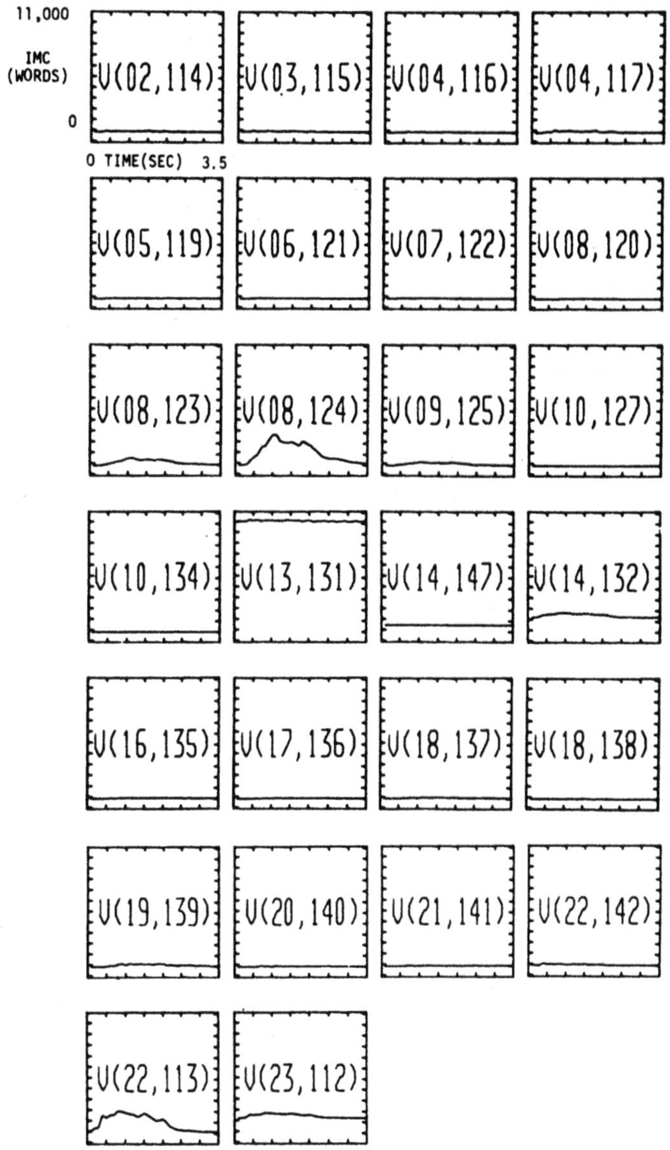

Fig. 4. Module-to-file (M–F) IMC for the example.

might enable M_j. For example, consider M_{13} in Fig. 1 and assume $\Delta_{i,13}$'s are negligible. Then

$$N_{13}(t_h, t_{h+1}) \approx N_3(t_h, t_{h+1}) + N_7(t_h, t_{h+1})\, p_{7,13}(E) + N_4(t_h, t_{h+1})\, p_{4,13}(E) + N_9(t_h, t_{h+1}).$$

3) If multiple arcs $(i-j)$'s join at M_j in the AND manner, M_j cannot enter the scheduling queue until all its predecessor modules M_i's have completed their execution. If such a wait time is negligible, then

$$N_j(t_h, t_{h+1}) \approx \operatorname{any}_i [N_i(t_h, t_{h+1})\, p_{ij}(E; t_h, t_{h+1})] \quad (8)$$

since all these predecessor modules enable M_j the same number of times. For example, for M_7 in Fig. 1 we have $N_7(t_h, t_{h+1}) \approx N_5(t_h, t_{h+1}) \times 1.0 \approx N_6(t_h, t_{h+1}) \times 1.0$. If enablement delays are not small, then from the predecessors M_i's we must determine the module M_b that finishes execution last and (8) becomes

$$N_j(t_h, t_{h+1}) \approx N_b(t_h - \Delta_{bj}, t_{h+1} - \Delta_{bj}). \quad (9)$$

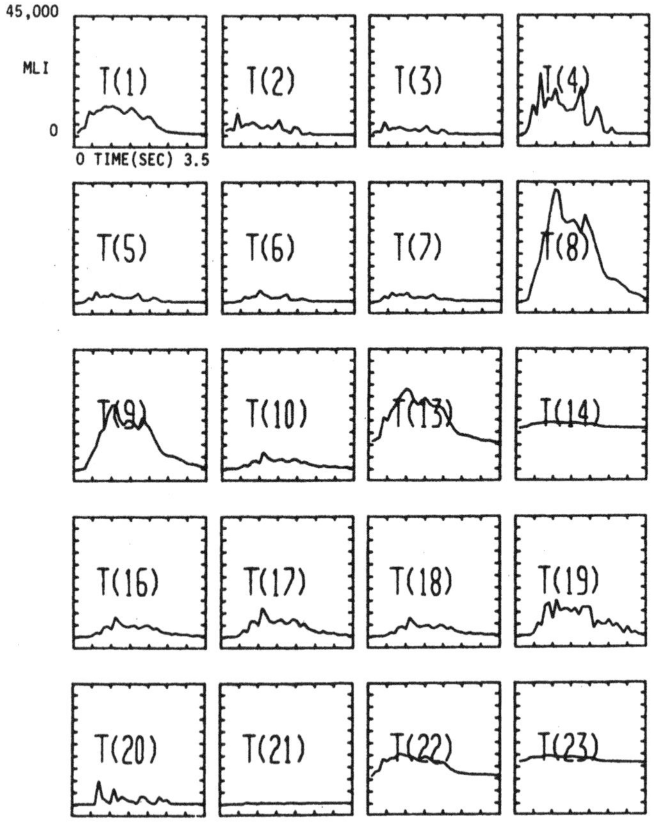

Fig. 5. Accumulative module execution time.

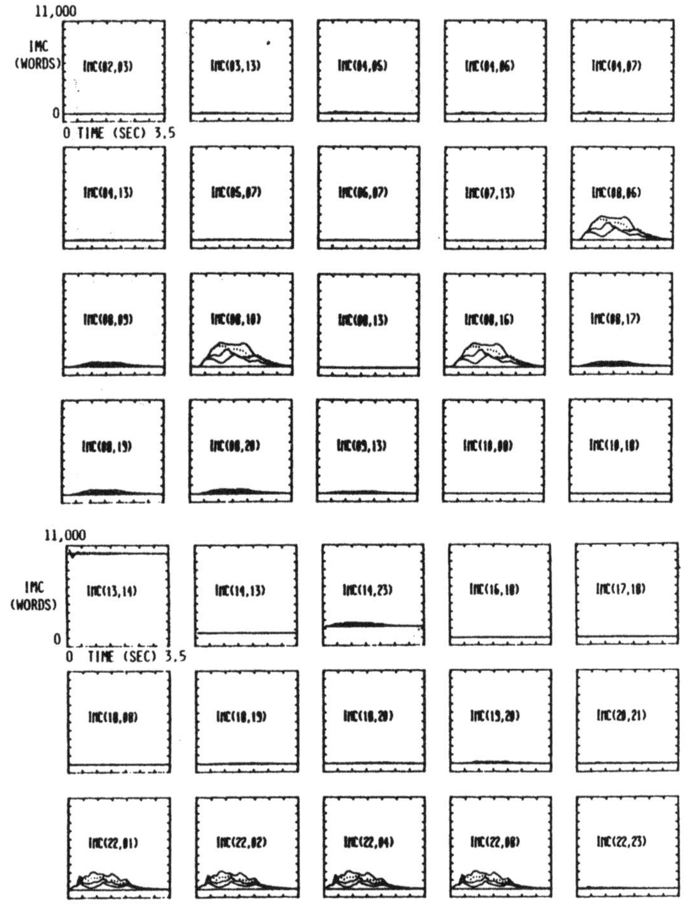

Fig. 6. IMC between module pairs.

To compute all the $N_j(t_h, t_{h+1})$'s, we always start from the top of the control flow graph, obtaining them in the topologically sorted sequence. Once we know how to obtain all $N_j(t_h, t_{h+1})$'s, we can use (1)–(4) to estimate the desired IMC and AET profiles.

In the estimation of IMC and AET, some values may be difficult to obtain, e.g., enablement probabilities $p_{ij}(E; t_h, t_{h+1})$'s and average module execution time X_j in (4) for some modules. In these cases, a simulation can be used to estimate these values. Since such a simulation is applied to a smaller subsystem, it usually is much simpler than simulating the entire system.

III. IMC Measurements

In this section, we present measurements of IMC for the Distributed Processing Architecture Design (DPAD) system which was developed to manage the data processing and radar resources for a space defense application [6], [8]. The DPAD system consists of four components: 1) the radar interface, 2) the interconnection network, 3) the distributed real-time operating system (d-RTOS), and 4) 23 tactical application modules (Fig. 2). Measurements were made on the DPAD simulator at the University of California, Los Angeles (UCLA). This simulator consists of a fully coded d-RTOS, simulators for the other three components, and statistics recording and reporting facilities. In the simulator, the radar interface uses a detailed *sky map* as the driving scenario; the network delay is assumed to be negligible. Below we discuss the d-RTOS and application modules.

Residing on each computer is an identical copy of the d-RTOS, responsible for scheduling application modules, shared data management, and resource management. The d-RTOS assumes that if a module references a shared file, then a copy of that file is present on the computer to which the module is assigned. Thus, we do not consider F–M IMC in this example because every module reads only local file copies and this incurs no IPC. M–F and M–M IMC are accomplished as follows. When a module M_j updates a file F_k, M_j places an entry for F_k in the Task Completion Queue (TCQ) of the d-RTOS. When d-RTOS reads the TCQ, it formats and sends a file-update message to all computers which have a copy of that file. Similarly, when M_j enables M_n, M_j places an entry for M_n in the TCQ. The d-RTOS then sends an enablement message to the computer where M_n is assigned.

The DPAD system is driven by a clock and radar returns. There are 23 tactical application modules; however, modules M_{11}, M_{12}, and M_{15} are not currently implemented in the simulator. A portion of the control-and-data-flow is shown in Fig. 1. M_{13} consists of two separate routines: M_{13A} and M_{13B}. M_{13A} is periodically enabled every 1 ms to schedule radar commands: it enables M_{14} which in turn enables M_{23}. All other modules are enabled by the radar returns, directly or indirectly. Returns of different types (e.g., Detect, Verify, Coarse Track, or Precision Track) are processed by different

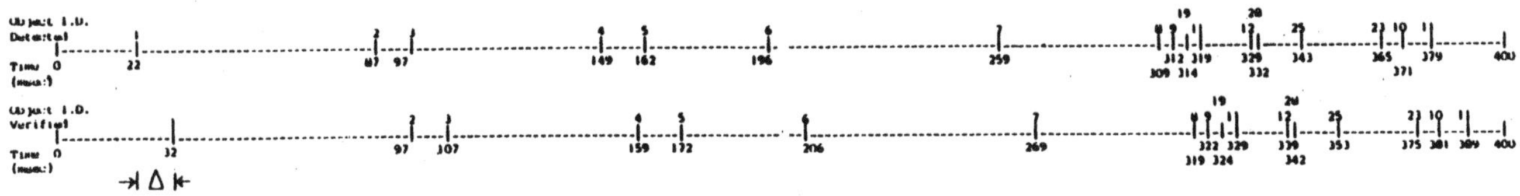

(a)

Time Interval t_h	0	100	200	300	400	500	600	700	800	900					1400					1900					2400					2900
t_{h+1}	100	200	300	400	500	600	700	800	900	1000					1500					2000					2500					3000
$N_{22}(d)$	3	3	1	10	4	5	4	6	5	3	2	5	4	4	5	2	2	2	2	3	0	0	1	0	0	0	0	0	0	0
$N_{22}(v)$	2	3	2	10	3	6	4	6	5	2	3	5	2	5	6	2	2	1	3	3	0	0	1	0	0	0	0	0	0	0
$N_2(t_h, t_{h+1})$	5	6	3	20	7	11	8	12	10	5	5	10	6	9	11	4	4	3	5	6	0	0	2	0	0	0	0	0	0	0

$N_{22}(d)$ = Number of object detections
= Number of M_{22} executions for detection processing
$N_{22}(v)$ = Number of object verifications
= Number of M_{22} executions for verification processing

(b)

Fig. 7. Execution frequency of module M_2 during each interval. (a) Detection time and verification time of objects. (b) Number of objects detected and verified during each interval.

threads of modules; M_1 does the thread selection. All files in the DPAD are named with an integer number greater than 100.

Fig. 3 presents the number of executions for each module during 100 ms intervals. $N_j(t_h, t_{h+1})$ is plotted as a point and the points are connected to show the changing trend of activities. These $N_j(t_h, t_{h+1})$'s are average values obtained from measurements of ten replications (i.e., ten simulation runs using independent random number streams). Since M–M IMC volume (for enablement messages) is much smaller than M–F IMC volume, we only plot the latter. Fig. 4 shows the average M–F IMC obtained from the same ten replications. Note that only 26 $V_{jk}(W)$'s are nonzero and thus shown here. They are all plotted on the same scale to reveal the relative magnitude. The $V_{jk}(W)$ varies with module-file pair and time. For example, $V_{8,124}(W)$ is quite large during 1–2 s, $V_{6,121}(W)$ is always small, and $V_{13,131}(W)$ is always large. The AET, $T_j(t_h, t_{h+1})$, are displayed in Fig. 5 and show the relative processing requirements of the 20 modules.

An alternative way to present the file-access IMC is shown in Fig. 6 where the M–F IMC and F–M IMC are *combined* into one set of figures. Each figure represents the file-update IMC sent from a module M_j to another module M_n, consisting of the file-update messages written by M_j to *one or more* files (F_k's) which are later read by M_n. This combined IMC can be derived from (2).

$$\mathrm{IMC}_{jn}(t_h, t_{h+1}) = N_j(t_h, t_{h+1}) \sum_{k \in K(j,n)} p_{jk}(W; t_h, t_{h+1}) L_{jk}(W; t_h, t_{h+1}) \tag{10}$$

where $K(j, n)$ = the set of files which are both updated by M_j and read by M_n. This IMC presentation provides a way to identify heavily communicating program module pairs. Note that each figure in Fig. 6 contains five curves (instead of one), each representing the IMC for a simulated sky scenario with a different number of detected objects.

IV. An Example of Analytical IMC Estimation

In this section, we apply the estimation model developed in Section II to the DPAD Detect/Verify processing for modules M_{22}, M_1, M_2, and M_3. Detect/Verify processing determines the presence of potentially threatening objects and consists of: 1) a radar-search return with object detection that causes modules M_{22}, M_1, and M_2 to execute in sequence (i.e., in their topologically sorted order), 2) a radar-verify delay of 9–15 ms, and 3) a radar-verify return that causes modules M_{22}, M_1, M_2, and M_3 to execute in sequence. A radar-search return with no detection is simply discarded by M_{22} and so M_1, M_2, and M_3 are not enabled. We shall estimate $N_2(t_h, t_{h+1})$ and the IMC written by M_2 which consists of 13 words to update file F_{114} (i.e., $L_{2,114}(W)$ = 13) whenever M_2 enables M_3.

We let $N_j(d; t_h, t_{h+1})$ be the number of module M_j executions for Detect processing, $N_j(v; t_h, t_{h+1})$ be the M_j executions for Verify processing, and $N_j(t_h, t_{h+1})$ be the total M_j executions for both Detect and Verify processing. Clearly,

$$N_j(t_h, t_{h+1}) = N_j(d; t_h, t_{h+1}) + N_j(v; t_h, t_{h+1}) .$$

Because each module's execution time is short (less than 1 ms) compared to the measurement interval ($t_{h+1} - t_h$ = 100 ms),

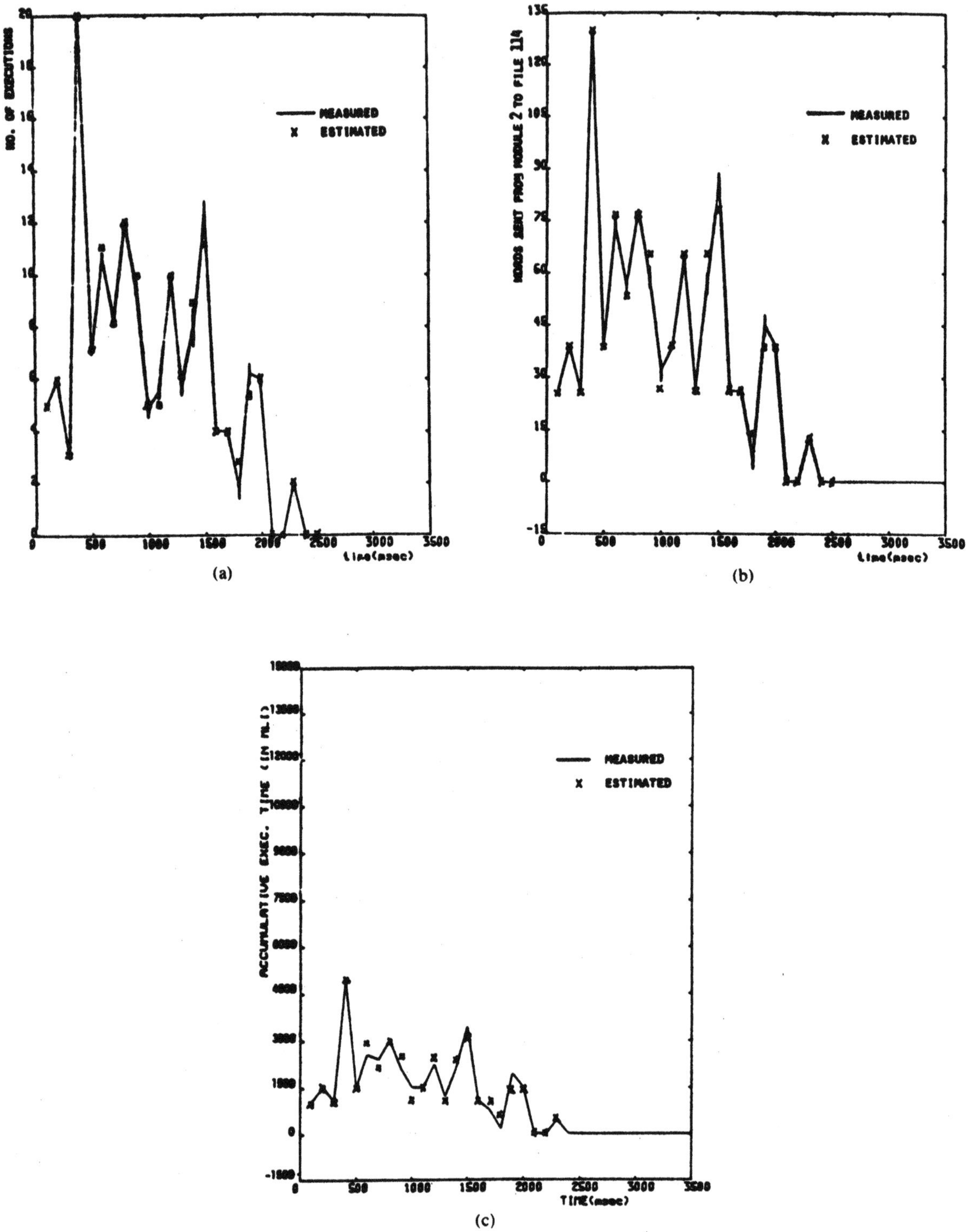

Fig. 8. Comparison between measured and estimated values. (a) Number of module M_2 executions, $N_2(t_h, t_{h+1})$. (b) M–F IMC from M_2 to F_{114}, $V_{2,114}(W; t_h, t_{h+1})$. (c) Module M_3 accumulative execution time $T_3(t_h, t_{h+1})$.

$$N_j(d;\ t_h, t_{h+1}) \approx N_{22}(d;\ t_h, t_{h+1}) \quad \text{for } j = 1, 2$$

and

$$N_j(v;\ t_h, t_{h+1}) \approx N_{22}(v;\ t_h, t_{h+1}) \quad \text{for } j = 1, 2, 3\,.$$

The radar detection time for each object and, thus, the number of radar detections in 100 ms intervals [i.e., $N_{22}(d;\ t_h, t_{h+1})$] are computed from the input scenario (the sky map). For simplicity, only the first 400 ms of radar-detect and radar-verify operations are shown in Fig. 7(a). The time-shift due to radar-verify delay ($\Delta \approx 10$ ms) is shown in the figure, i.e.,

$$N_{22}(v;\ t_h, t_{h+1}) \approx N_{22}(d;\ t_h - 10, t_{h+1} - 10)\,.$$

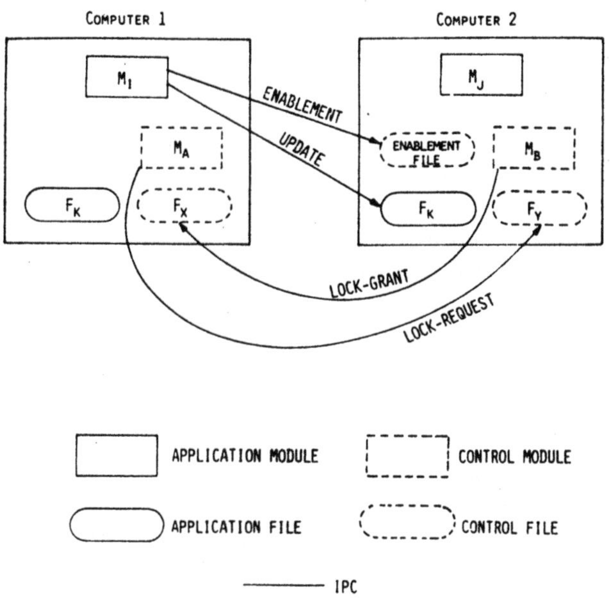

Fig. 9. IPC in a distributed processing system.

ASSIGNMENT	A			B		
COMPUTERS	1	2	3	1	2	3
MODULE #	2	3	1	1	13	3
	5	4	7	2	14	5
	8	6	14	4	23	7
	9	10	16	6		9
	19	13	18	8		17
	20	17	21	10		18
		22	23	16		19
						20
						21
						22
AVERAGE MODULE LOAD	0.218	0.365	0.417	0.205	0.517	0.288

ASSIGNMENT A: BASED ONLY ON BALANCING MODULE LOAD
ASSIGNMENT B: BASED ON BOTH MODULE LOAD AND IMC

Fig. 10. Two module assignments for the DPAD system.

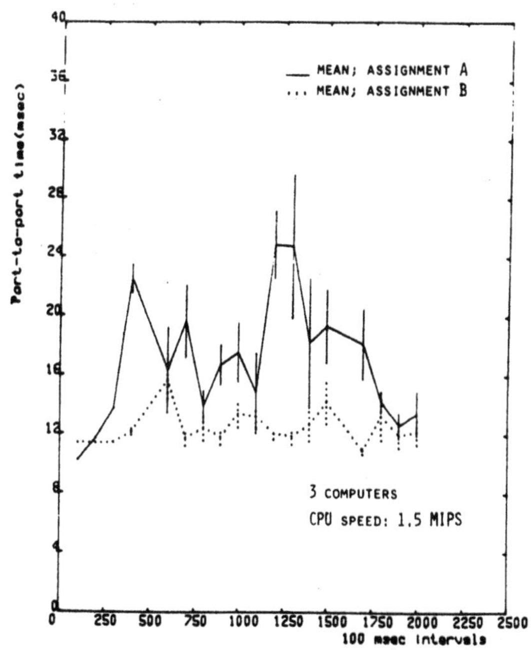

Fig. 11. Port-to-port time for Detect/Verify thread.

Fig. 7(b) shows how $N_2(t_h, t_{h+1})$ was estimated. From (2) we can obtain $V_{2,114}(W; t_h, t_{h+1})$ as follows:

$$V_{2,114}(W; t_h, t_{h+1}) \approx N_2(v; t_h, t_{h+1}) \times 13(\text{words}).$$

Fig. 8(a) and (b) plots the estimates for $N_2(t_h, t_{h+1})$ and $V_{2,114}(W; t_h, t_{h+1})$ along with their measured values. Since the average execution time for M_3 [i.e., $X_3(t_h, t_{h+1})$] is 500 MLI and $N_3(t_h, t_{h+1}) = N_3(v; t_h, t_{h+1})$, the AET for M_3 [i.e., $T_3(t_h, t_{h+1})$] is estimated from (4). Both the estimated and measured AET are shown in Fig. 8(c). All three charts in Fig. 8 exhibit close correspondence between the estimated and measured values.

V. CONTROL IMC

In Sections II–IV, only *application IMC* was studied. However, distributed processing systems require a significant number of control functions to support application file access (e.g., read-requests, lock-requests, and lock-releases) and to maintain the distributed processing system (e.g., status monitoring). These functions are carried out by *control modules*, resulting in *control IMC*.

Control IMC consists of reads and updates (writes) by control modules (e.g., lock managers) to *control files* (e.g., lock status files). Once the file access and distributed system maintenance functions are known, control IMC can be derived from application IMC. For example, in Fig. 9, assume that module M_i at computer 1 updates application file F_k at computer 2 for $N_i(t_h, t_{h+1})$ times during (t_h, t_{h+1}). Since every F_k update requires a lock-request and a lock-grant, control module M_A at computer 1 writes $N_i(t_h, t_{h+1})$ lock-request messages to control file F_Y at computer 2 while M_B at computer 2 writes $N_i(t_h, t_{h+1})$ lock-grant messages to F_X at computer 1.

VI. APPLICATIONS

A. *Derivation of Interprocessor Communication (IPC)*

Interprocessor communication (IPC) consists of all messages exchanged among computers and all interactions with shared memories. IPC is created by IMC that crosses a computer boundary, i.e., the sender and receiver are not located on the same computer. This happens when a module writes to a remote file copy (M–F) or reads a remote file copy (F–M), or when a module enables a remote module (M–M). We note that an enablement is actually a special case of a file write (to the enablement-queue file) and a file read (from the enablement-queue file).

IPC depends on aspects of system configuration and operation such as: 1) the assignment of modules to computers determines where updates to files originate and the destination for read-responses; 2) the assignment of files to computers and shared memories determines the destination for file updates; and 3) selecting which copy of a file to read (referred to as *read-copy selection*) determines the origin of read-responses. In a system with each file fully replicated at all computers, a file update must be sent to all computers. If the system has a broadcast bus, the update IMC is sent out only once; for a point-to-point connection network, however, *multiple* update IMC messages need to be sent, one to each computer, thus incurring a heavy communication overhead on the sending computer. As to file reads, if a file copy exists at the local computer where a reading module resides, no IPC is incurred. Otherwise, the reading computer incurs IPC to read a remote copy. From IMC and the above design considerations, IPC is calculated by summing across all instances of M–F, F–M, and M–M IMC which cross a computer boundary.

B. Calculation of System Resource Utilization

The utilization of a system resource (i.e., computer, shared memory, or bus channel) is defined as the fraction of time the resource is busy. Resource utilization is an important measure in distributed processing systems since it is directly related to queueing delays and throughput. Each IPC message incurs a processing cost at the sending computer *and* a processing cost at the receiving computer. It also increases network traffic. Therefore, IPC degrades the performance of distributed processing systems.

The utilization of a computer can be estimated from AET, the processing cost for sending and receiving IPC messages at this computer site, and operating system overhead. The utilization of a channel can be derived from the channel bandwidth (in words/s) and the IPC volume to be sent on this channel.

C. Module Assignment in a Real-Time Distributed System

Module assignment to computers has a great impact on response time. In general, this requires such considerations as file assignment and read-copy selection. We shall use the DPAD system as an example. In the DPAD, a file is replicated on those computers where a module reads the file, so only module assignment need be considered.

Fig. 10 shows two module assignments for the DPAD System. Module assignment *A* only considers balancing the module processing load (due to AET) among computers. For example, both modules M_{13} and M_{14} have large accumulative execution time (see Fig. 5), so they are assigned to different computers.

Module assignment *B* considers both module processing load and IMC. This assignment uses the following two principles.

1) M_i and M_j are colocated (i.e., assigned to the same computer) if there exists a large IMC volume between them. This eliminates the large IPC which would otherwise be incurred.

2) All the other modules are assigned so as to balance load. Since there is a large IMC between modules M_{13} and M_{14} (Fig. 6), they were colocated. Similarly, M_6, M_8, M_{10}, and M_{16} were colocated.

Using the UCLA DPAD Simulator, response times (referred to as port-to-port times) were measured for both module assignments. Fig. 11 portrays these measurement results (with 90-percent confidence intervals) for the DPAD Detect/Verify processing thread. The overall superiority of assignment *B* demonstrates that IMC data play an important role in module assignment.

VII. Conclusions

In this paper, a model is developed based on control-and-data-flow graphs for estimating intermodule communication (IMC) and module's accumulative execution time (AET). The input parameters used in the model either are readily available to system designers or can be obtained through simulation. And there are two ways to present the IMC data: IMC between modules and files *and* IMC between module pairs. The IMC and AET of a space defense application were measured and presented. These measurements compare very closely to the values obtained from the proposed estimation model. For a given file assignment and module assignment, the interprocessor communication (IPC) and system resources utilization can be calculated from the IMC data. IMC and IPC information are useful in finding good module assignments. Our studies revealed that IMC plays an important role in the performance of distributed processing systems.

Acknowledgment

The authors wish to thank Dr. M. Green for his assistance in installing the DPAD Simulator at UCLA.

References

[1] R. G. Arnold, R. P. Ramseyer, L. B. Wing, and E. A. Householder, "MMBC architecture," in *Proc. 1st Int. Conf. Distrib. Comput. Syst.*, Oct. 1979, pp. 707–724.

[2] C. T. Baker, "Logical distribution of applications and data," *IBM Syst. J.*, vol. 19, no. 2, pp. 171–192, 1980.

[3] W. W. Chu, "Optimal file allocation in a multiple computer system," *IEEE Trans. Comput.*, vol. C-18, pp. 885–889, Oct. 1969.

[4] W. W. Chu, D. Lee, and B. Iffla, "A distributed processing system for naval data communication networks," in *Proc. AFIPS Conf. (NCC)*, vol. 47, 1978, pp. 783–793.

[5] W. W. Chu, L. J. Holloway, M. T. Lan, and K. Efe, "Task allocation in distributed data processing," *Computer*, vol. 13, pp. 57–69, Nov. 1980.

[6] M. Green, E. Y. S. Lee, S. Majumdar, and D. C. Shannon, "A distributed real-time operating system," in *Proc. Symp. Distrib. Data Acquisition, Computing and Control*, Dec. 1980, pp. 175–184.

[7] K. Haessig and C. J. Jenny, "Partitioning and allocating computational objects in distributed computing systems," in *Proc. IFIP Cong. '80*, Melbourne, Australia, Oct. 1980, pp. 593–598.

[8] R. H. Hoffman, R. W. Smith, and J. T. Ellis, "Simulation software development for the BMDATC DDP Underlay experiment," in *Proc. 4th Int. Comput. Software and Applications Conf. (COMPSAC)*, Oct. 1980, pp. 569–577.

[9] D. E. Knuth, *The Art of Computer Programming, Vol. 1: Fundamental Algorithms*. Reading, MA: Addison-Wesley, 1973.

[10] P. Y. R. Ma, E. Y. S. Lee, and M. Tsuchiya, "A task allocation model for distributed computing systems," *IEEE Trans. Comput.*, vol. C-31, pp. 41–47, Jan. 1982.

[11] H. S. Stone and S. H. Bokhari, "Control of distributed processes," *Computer*, vol. 11, pp. 97–106, July 1978.

[12] P. C. Treleaven, D. R. Brownbridge, and R. P. Hopkins, "Data-driven and demand-driven computer architecture," *Ass. Comput. Mach. Comput. Surveys*, vol. 14, no. 1, pp. 93–143, Mar. 1982.
[13] C. R. Vick, "A dynamically reconfigurable distributed computing system," Ph.D. dissertation, Dep. Electrical Engineering, Auburn Univ., Auburn, AL, Dec. 1979.

Wesley W. Chu (S'62–M'67–SM'74–F'78) received the B.S. and M.S. degrees from the University of Michigan, Ann Arbor, in 1960 and 1961, and the Ph.D. degree in electrical engineering from Stanford University, Stanford, CA, in 1966.

From 1961 to 1962 he worked on switching circuit design at the General Electric Computer Department (now Honeywell), Phoenix, AZ; from 1964 to 1966 he worked on the design of large-scale computers at IBM, Menlo Park and San Jose, CA; and from 1966 to 1969 he researched on computer communications at Bell Laboratories, Holmdel, NJ. He joined the University of California, Los Angeles (UCLA) in 1969, and is currently a Professor in the Department of Computer Science. He directs a research group at UCLA in the areas of computer communications and networking, distributed processing, and distributed databases. He is also a Consultant to government agencies and private industries. He is a Member of Technical Review Committee for the Western Union Telegraph Co., NJ, where he reviews various technical programs related to computer networking and distributed processing systems. He has authored or coauthored more than 60 articles on information processing systems and computer communications and has edited two textbooks: *Advances in Computer Communications* (Dedham, MA: Artech House, 1st ed., 1974 and 2nd revised ed., 1977), and *Centralized and Distributed Database Systems* (coedited with P. P. Chen) (IEEE Computer Society, 1979).

Dr. Chu is a member of Tau Beta Pi, Eta Kappa Nu, Phi Tau Phi, and Sigma Xi. He was an ACM National Lecturer from 1972 to 1973, IEEE Distinguished Visitor from 1973 to 1974, Chairman of the ACM SIGCOMM from 1973 to 1977, a member of the IEEE Technical Committee on Computer Communications, Chairman of the 1975 ACM Interprocess Communication Workshop, Technical Program Chairman of the Fourth Data Communication Symposium in 1975, and Chairman of the IEEE Lake Arrowhead Workshop on Computer Networking and Distributed Databases in 1977. He was an Associate Editor for the IEEE TRANSACTIONS ON COMPUTERS for the field of computer networking and distributed processing systems (1978–1982) and received a meritorious award for his service to the IEEE in 1983. He is currently a member of the Editorial Board of *Computer Networks* and the *International Journal on Computers and Electrical Engineering* and an Associate Editor for the *Journal of Computer Networks*.

Min-Tsung Lan (S'79) received the B.S. degree in electrical engineering from National Taiwan University in 1974, the M.S. degree in computer science from the University of Nebraska, Lincoln, in 1977, and is currently a Ph.D. degree candidate and Research Assistant in the Department of Computer Science at the University of California, Los Angeles (UCLA).

His research interests include distributed system simulation, performance modeling, and task assignment for distributed processing systems. From 1974 to 1976 he was a computer system engineer for the China Steel Corporation, Taiwan. In 1978 he was with the Nebraska State Department of Labor and in 1979 he was on the Technical Staff of the Technology Service Corporation, Santa Monica, CA. He was also a part-time employee with the OAO Corporation, Los Angeles.

Joseph Hellerstein was born in Indianapolis, IN, in 1952. He received the B.A. degree in mathematics, with honors, from the University of Michigan, Ann Arbor, in 1974, and the M.S. and Ph.D. degrees in computer science from the University of California, Los Angeles (UCLA) in 1979 and 1984, respectively.

From 1974 to 1978 he worked as a Software System Designer for Honeywell, developing communications, operating systems, and network software. From 1978 to 1984 he was a Research Assistant working on the ARPA Packet Radio contract and the Ballistic Missile Defense Distributed Processing contract. His research interests include computer systems performance modeling, distributed processing systems, and distributed database systems.

A Graph Matching Approach to Optimal Task Assignment in Distributed Computing Systems Using a Minimax Criterion

CHIEN-CHUNG SHEN AND WEN-HSIANG TSAI, MEMBER, IEEE

***Abstract*—A graph matching approach is proposed in this paper for solving the task assignment problem encountered in distributed computing systems. A cost function defined in terms of a single unit, time, is proposed for evaluating the effectiveness of task assignment. This cost function represents the maximum time for a task to complete module execution and communication in all the processors. A new optimization criterion, called the minimax criterion, is also proposed, based on which both minimization of interprocessor communication and balance of processor loading can be achieved. The proposed approach allows various system constraints to be included for consideration. With the proposed cost function and the minimax criterion, optimal task assignment is defined. Graphs are then used to represent the module relationship of a given task and the processor structure of a distributed computing system. Module assignment to system processors is transformed into a type of graph matching, called weak homomorphism. The search of optimal weak homomorphism corresponding to optimal task assignment is next formulated as a state-space search problem. It is then solved by the well-known *A** algorithm in artificial intelligence after proper heuristic information for speeding up the search is suggested. An illustrative example and some experimental results are also included to show the effectiveness of the heuristic search.**

***Index Terms*—*A** algorithm, distributed computing systems, graph matching, interprocessor communication, load balancing, minimax criterion, state-space search, weak homomorphism.**

I. Introduction

DISTRIBUTED computing systems have become more and more attractive and important in recent years due to the advancement of VLSI and computer networking technologies. Distributed computing systems not only provide the facility for utilizing remote computer resources or data not existing in local computer systems but also increase the throughput by providing facilities for parallel processing [1]. Furthermore, the modularity, flexibility, and reliability of distributed computing systems make them attractive to many types of applications. But there are some major problems that prevent widespread use of the distributed computing system [1], [2], [16]. One of the problems is the degradation in throughput caused by the "saturation effect" due to excessive interprocessor communication by data and control messages transferred from one program module to another residing in different processors [2].

Thus, the purpose of task assignment in distributed computing systems is to reduce the job turnaround time and increase the throughput. This can be done by maximizing and balancing the utilization of resources while minimizing the communication between processors [1]. While minimizing interprocessor communication tends to assign the whole task to a single processor, load balancing tries to distribute the program modules of the task evenly among the processors. Therefore, there exists conflict between these two criteria and a compromise must be made to obtain an optimal policy for task assignment.

Several approaches to task assignment in distributed computing systems have been suggested [1]–[12], [16]. They can be roughly classified into three categories, namely, graph-theoretic [3]–[6], mathematical programming [2], [16], and heuristic methods [1]. The graph-theoretic method uses a graph to represent a task, and applies the minimal-cut algorithm to the graph to get the task assignment with minimum interprocessor communication. The mathematical programming approach formulates task assignment as an optimization problem, and solves it with mathematical programming techniques. And the heuristic method provides fast but suboptimal algorithms for task assignment, which are useful for applications where an optimal solution can not be obtained in real time.

Most of the above methods adopt some types of cost function to evaluate the effectiveness of task assignment algorithms [1]–[12], [16]. The most commonly used cost function is defined as the sum of the interprocessor communication cost and the processing cost. But these two types of cost are measured in different units, and it is difficult to give a reasonable meaning to the resulting cost summation.

In this paper, we propose a new task assignment model for distributed computing systems, based on a graph matching approach and a more meaningful cost function for task assignment optimization. Each graph match corresponds to a specific task assignment. Cost values are defined in terms of a single unit, time. Minimization of cost functions is based on a so-called minimax criterion. The proposed model allows easy incorporation of most system constraints encountered in

Manuscript received November 9, 1983; revised May 7, 1984.

The authors are with the Institute of Computer Engineering, National Chiao Tung University, Hsinchu, Taiwan 300, Republic of China.

applications. A state-space search method [15] is employed for finding optimal task assignment corresponding to minimum-cost graph matching. Useful heuristic information to speed up the search is also suggested. Optimal solutions guaranteed by the proposed approach are important for non-real-time applications where the resulting assignment will be repeatedly executed on a distributed computing system. And speedup in solution search is useful for real-time applications.

In the remainder of this paper, we describe system assumptions, the cost function, and the minimax criterion in Section II. In Section III, we formulate the graph matching model, and in Section IV, we review the state-space search algorithm and apply it to the search of optimal solutions. An illustrative example and some experimental results are given in Section V, followed by conclusive remarks in the last section.

II. Assumptions, Costs, and Optimization Criterion

Various assumptions made about the distributed computing system considered in this paper are first described in the following.

1) The processors in the system are heterogeneous. That is, a single program module, if executed on different processors, will require different amounts of running time, which specify different degrees of preference of the module on the processors.

2) Nonidentical communication links are used by the processors for message transmission. That is, an identical amount of message, if transmitted through different communication links, will require different amounts of transmission time, which specify different degrees of preference of the message on the links.

3) The processors in the system need not be fully connected. But the link between any two processors is symmetric, i.e., the time to transmit a certain amount of message from one processor to another is identical to that to transmit the same message in the reverse direction.

4) There exists little or no precedence relationship or synchronization requirement among the program modules so that processor idleness is negligible during task execution, provided that module partition has been resolved satisfactorily.

Based on the above assumptions, the cost function and the minimax criterion proposed for task assignment optimization are described in the following.

After a task is partitioned into suitable modules, let $t_p^e(A)$ denote the total time spent for module execution, and $t_p^c(A)$ be the total time for interprocessor communication delay, both in some processor p according to a certain task assignment A. Let

$$t_p(A) = t_p^e(A) + t_p^c(A)$$

which is the total time spent in processor p for task assignment A. We call $t_p(A)$ the *processor turnaround time of p*. This turnaround time is different for each distinct processor. Let

$$t(A) = \max_p t_p(A)$$

which we call the *task turnaround time of A*. It is easy to see that $t(A)$ is the total time required to complete the whole task according to assignment A under the assumption of negligible processor idleness. Therefore, $t(A)$ may be, from the point of reducing total processing time, used as a cost measure for the effectiveness of task assignment A. The smaller $t(A)$ is, the better A is. An optimal task assignment thus may be defined as the one A_o which minimizes the task turnaround time $t(A)$, i.e.,

$$t(A_o) = \min_A t(A) = \min_A \max_p t_p(A).$$

This means that we want to minimize the maximum processor turnaround time, resulting in the so-called *minimax criterion*. $t(A_o)$ will be called the *minimum task turnaround time*.

III. Graph Matching Model

Graphs are of a type of very general data structure for system representation. The graph matching problem is that of finding an efficient algorithm to compare two given graphs to see how well they match in a certain sense. A survey of such problems and the algorithms for solving them can be found in [13], [14]. Based on the purpose or the criterion of matching, there are various types of graph matching. The type we consider in this paper is weak homomorphism which is defined as follows.

Definition 1: Let $G_1 = (V_1, E_1)$ and $G_2 = (V_2, E_2)$ be two graphs where V_i $(i = 1, 2)$ are the vertex sets and E_i $(i = 1, 2)$ are the edge sets of G_1 and G_2, respectively. G_1 is weakly homomorphic to G_2 if there exists a mapping (possibly many-to-one) M: $V_1 \rightarrow V_2$ such that if edge $(a, b) \in E_1$, then edge $(M(a), M(b)) \in E_2$, and we say that there is a weak homomorphism from G_1 to G_2.

As mentioned before, a task submitted into a distributed computing system is partitioned into suitable modules and then assigned to processors. Each task thus can be represented by an undirected graph $T = (V_T, E_T)$, which we call the *task graph* where 1) V_T is a set of vertices each of which represents a module of the task; 2) $E_T \subseteq V_T \times V_T$ is a set of edges each of which represents the intermodule communication between the two modules at the ends of the edge.

Similarly, the processors in a distributed computing system can also be represented by an undirected graph $P = (V_P, E_P)$, which we call the *processor graph* where 1) V_P is a set of vertices representing the processors in a distributed computing system; 2) $E_P \subseteq V_P \times V_P$ is a set of edges representing the communication links between processors.

Because two related modules may be assigned to a single processor, we add a self-looping edge to each vertex in the processor graph to follow the weak homomorphism definition, as will be clear in the following discussion.

Fig. 1 shows a typical task graph and Fig. 2 shows a typical processor graph.

For a task assignment A to be acceptable, any two modules a and b which communicate with each other *must* be assigned either to a single processor X or to two processors X and Y with a communication link between them. In terms of graph-theoretic terminologies just defined and considering the task assignment A as defining a mapping M from the task graph T to the processor graph P, we see this requirement means that if edge $(a,b) \in E_T$, then it must be true that edge $(X,X) \in E_P$, or that edge $(X,Y) \in E_P$. Edge (X,X) is always included in the processor graph P as mentioned previously. By Definition 1, this in turn means that there must exist a weak homomorphism from T to P. Therefore, the task assignment problem can be transformed into the problem of finding a weak homomorphism from the task graph T to the processor graph P with minimum task turnaround time. We call such a weak homomorphism the *optimal weak homomorphism from T to P*. Now, we have to discuss how task turnaround time (i.e., the cost value) can be computed for each mapping or weak homomorphism.

Definition 2: Vertex Transformation—Let T and P be the task graph and the processor graph defined previously. If M is a mapping from T to P defined by a task assignment A, then we use $a \rightarrow M(a)$ to denote the assignment of module $a \in V_T$ to processor $M(a) \in V_P$, and call it a vertex transformation.

Let C_p be a nonnegative real-valued cost function defined on all vertex transformations such that $C_p\ (a \rightarrow M(a))$ denotes the execution time of module a on processor $M(a)$.

Definition 3: Edge Transformation—Similarly, we use $(a,b) \rightarrow (M(a), M(b))$ to denote the assignment of module communication between modules a and b to the communication link between processors $M(a)$ and $M(b)$, and call it an edge transformation.

Let C_c be another nonnegative real-valued cost function defined on all edge transformations such that $C_c\ ((a,b) \rightarrow (M(a), M(b)))$ denotes the communication time between modules a and b using the communication link $(M(a), M(b))$. If $M(a)$ is equal to $M(b)$, i.e., if modules a and b are assigned to the same processor, then the cost is defined to be zero. For those edges (a,b) nonexistent in E_T, the costs for assigning them to any communication links are also set zero.

If there are n modules $m_1, m_2, \cdots, m_n$ in a task and m processors $p_1, p_2, \cdots, p_m$ in a distributed computing system, we can use an n by m matrix X to represent the mapping M: $V_P \rightarrow V_T$ where

$$X_{ij} = \begin{cases} 1, & \text{if module } i \text{ is assigned to processor } j; \\ 0, & \text{otherwise.} \end{cases}$$

Thus, the total execution time of all the modules assigned to processor j is

$$PT_j = \sum_{i=1}^{n} [C_p(m_i \rightarrow p_j) \cdot X_{ij}]. \tag{1}$$

Let L be an m by m matrix representing the configuration

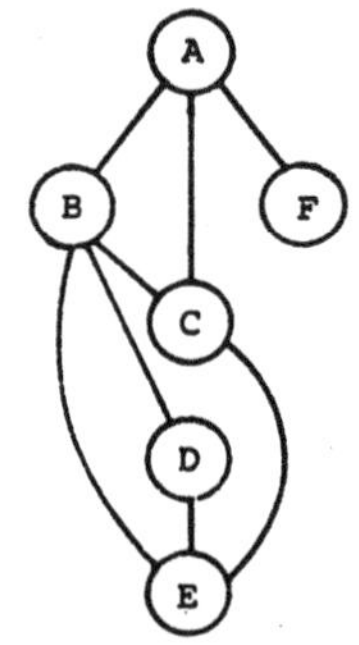

T = (V_T, E_T) where

V_T = {A, B, C, D, E, F},

E_T = {(A,B),(A,C),(A,F),(B,C),(B,D),(B,E),(D,E),(C,E)}.

Fig. 1. Task graph.

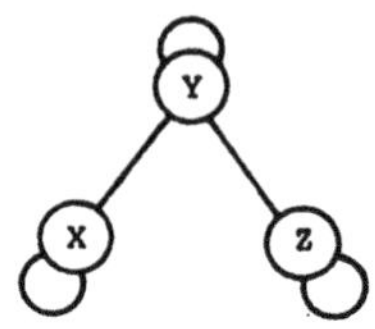

P = (V_P,E_P) where

V_P = {X, Y, Z},

E_P = {(X,Y),(Y,Z),(X,X),(Y,Y),(Z,Z)}.

Fig. 2. Processor graph.

structure of the processors in a distributed computing system where

$$L_{ij} = \begin{cases} 1, & \text{if processors } i \text{ and } j \text{ are connected to each other;} \\ 0, & \text{otherwise.} \end{cases}$$

Let R be an n by n matrix representing the intermodule communication relationship of a task where

$$R_{ij} = \begin{cases} 1, & \text{if modules } i \text{ and } j \text{ communicate with each other;} \\ 0, & \text{otherwise.} \end{cases}$$

Thus, the total communication time spent in processor j is

$$CT_j = \sum_{k=1}^{m} \sum_{s=1}^{n} \sum_{t=1}^{n} [C_c((m_s, m_t) \rightarrow (p_j, p_k)) \cdot X_{sj} \cdot X_{tk} \cdot R_{st} \cdot L_{jk}]. \tag{2}$$

In the above equation, X_{sj} and X_{tk} are included to indicate whether m_s is assigned to p_j and whether m_t is assigned to p_k.

According to (1) and (2) the processor turnaround time of processor j is equal to

$$TA_j = PT_j + CT_j. \tag{3}$$

Recalling that the task turnaround time is just the maximum of all the processor turnaround times, we can define the cost of a mapping M defined by a task assignment to be

$$\text{COST}(M) = \max_{1 \le j \le m}(TA_j). \tag{4}$$

According to the minimax criterion, our goal in this paper now is to find an optimal mapping M^* which is a weak homomorphism such that

$$\text{COST}(M^*) = \min_{M} \text{COST}(M).$$

This optimal weak homomorphism M^* not only minimizes the interprocessor communication time but also achieves load balancing and will be found by the state-space search method described in the next section.

IV. State-Space Search Method

In this section, the problem of finding the optimal weak homomorphism between two graphs will be formulated as a state-space search problem, and the well-known A^* algorithm in artificial intelligence will be used for solving this problem [15]. With the A^* algorithm, not only the optimal weak homomorphism is guaranteed to be found, but the search will also speed up. Note that this approach so far has not been considered in any other investigation on task assignment in distributed computing systems.

In a state-space search problem, each state description is denoted by a *node*. *Operators* applicable to nodes are defined for generating successors of nodes, called *node expansion*. A *solution path* of a search problem is a path in the state space defined by a sequence of operators which leads a *start node* to one of the *goal nodes* [15]. In our case here, a solution path defines the optimal weak homomorphism which is a weak homomorphic mapping M with minimum COST(M). We now formulate the state-space search method as follows.

1) State Description: Let ordered pair set $K = \{(i,x) \mid i \in V_T, \text{ and } x \in V_P\}$ denote the partially developed mapping M corresponding to a tree node n in the search tree. Each ordered pair (i,x) means that module i is assigned to processor x, i.e., $M: i \rightarrow x$ or $x = M(i)$. Let $K_G = \{i \mid (i,x) \in K\}$ and $i_{\max} = \max_{i \in K_G} i$.

2) Initial State: The initial state is $K \neq \emptyset$, the empty set.

3) Operators: An operator adds new *valid* pairs (j,y) to K. The procedure is as follows. First, form a set of candidate ordered pairs

$$D = \{(j,y) \mid j = i_{\max} + 1, y \in V_P\}.$$

Next, check all candidate pairs one by one for validity, using vertex adjacency information in the task graph T and the processor graph P. A candidate pair $(j,y) \in D$ is said to be *valid* if for each $(i,x) \in K$ it is true that if edge $(i,j) \in E_T$, then either edge $(x,y) \in E_P$ or $x = y$. This validity check is necessary to preserve the property of weak homomorphism (see Definition 1). Each candidate pair (j,y) represents a possible additional assignment of module j to processor y, but if j communicates with any other module i already assigned to a processor x (i.e., $i \in K_G$), then j should also be assigned either to processor x or to another distinct processor y which has a communication link to x. Let D' be the set of all valid pairs in D. Then the operator finally updates set K as the union of old K and D'.

Note that the operator is defined in such a way that it always expands the partially developed mapping M (as represented by K) by assigning the module *with next larger index number* $j = i_{\max} + 1$ (see the definition of D above) to each of all the processors y in V_P. It is in this way that developing of partial mapping can be kept in order until all possible module assignments are exhaustively considered (see Fig. 5 for an illustration).

4) Goal State: Any state K with $V_T = K_G$ is a goal state; that is, the search stops when all modules are assigned completely.

The above formulation just offers a search scheme for finding a homomorphic mapping corresponding to a task assignment; it does not include computation of cost values. Next, we use the A^* algorithm described in Nilsson [15] to find optimal weak homomorphisms.

In an A^* algorithm, an evaluation function is used to order nodes for expansion, and is guaranteed to find a solution path optimal in the sense that the path cost is minimized, if the evaluation function is properly defined. More specifically, according to Nilsson [15], if we define an evaluation function as

$$f(n) = g(n) + h(n)$$

where $g(n)$ is the minimum path cost from the start node to node n in the state space, and $h(n)$ is a lower-bound estimate, using any heuristic information available, of the minimum path cost $h^*(n)$ from node n to a goal node, then as long as $h(n) \leq h^*(n)$ for all n (i.e., $h(n)$ is *consistent*), the A^* algorithm using such an evaluation function will be guaranteed to find an optimal solution path in the state space after expanding fewer nodes during the search than any uninformed algorithms. In other words, such a heuristic search algorithm can speed up the search of an optimal weak homomorphism, which is usually time consuming for graphs with large numbers of vertices and edges.

According to the previous formulation of task assignment as the graph matching problem, a node n in the state space denotes a partially developed homomorphic mapping which assigns part of the modules of a task to processors. Thus, we can let the evaluation function at node n in the state space be

$$f(n) = g(n) + h(n) \tag{5}$$

where the value of $g(n)$ is the total minimum cost of the vertex and edge transformations included in the partially developed mapping M corresponding to n, and the value of the heuristic function $h(n)$ is an estimate of the value $h^*(n)$ which is the minimum cost of the vertex and edge transformations required to complete the partial mapping M.

To calculate $g(n)$, we first set up the X and R matrices as mentioned in the previous section for the partial mapping M corresponding to node n, and then use (1), (2), (3), and (4) to calculate the cost of a partial mapping M which defines $g(n)$.

As to the heuristic function $h(n)$ in (5), it can be defined by several different approaches. The simplest way is to set $h(n) \equiv 0$ for all n, and the resulting search is a uniform-cost search [15] which nevertheless is still guaranteed to find an optimal weak homomorphism. To be more efficient in the search, nonzero $h(n)$ values, of course, should be used, and this has been found possible as is discussed in the following.

Let M be the corresponding partial mapping at search tree node n. When using (4) to find the cost of M, try to find the k such that

$$\begin{aligned} \text{COST}(M) &= \text{COST}(TA_k) \\ &= \max_{1 \leq j \leq m} (TA_j). \end{aligned}$$

That is, processor k is currently with the maximum processor turnaround time in the partial task assignment. Let MK be the set of modules assigned to processor k by the partial mapping M, and MK' be the set of all the remaining modules not assigned by M. Then, define $LK = \{(a,b) \mid a \in MK', b \in MK, \text{ and } (a,b) \in E_T$ (edge set of task graph)$\}$ which denotes a set of the edges representing all the communications between the modules in MK and MK', and define $B = \{a \mid (a,b) \in LK\}$ which denotes the set of those unassigned modules in MK' communicating with the modules in processor k. The heuristic information useful for defining $h(n)$ is observed as follows. When the state-space search process goes forward, each module a in B will *have to* be assigned either to processor k or to a processor l connected through a communication link to processor k so that communication between module a and those modules in k can be accomplished. But these two different types of assignments will result in different amounts of partial processor turnaround time being increased at processor k. To keep $h(n)$ as a lower bound of $h^*(n)$, we must find out the smallest amount for each module a in B and then sum up these amounts for all the modules in B as the value $h(n)$, as is calculated in the following algorithm.

Algorithm 1: Computation of $h(n)$. M is the corresponding partial mapping at search tree node n.

Step 1): Find the k such that

$$\mathrm{COST}(M) = \mathrm{COST}(TA_k) = \max_{1 \le j \le m}(TA_j).$$

Step 2): Find the sets MK, MK', LK, and B as defined previously.

Step 3): For each $a \in B$, find $L_a = \{b \mid (a,b) \in LK\}$ which is the set of the modules in processor k communicating with module $a \in B$.

Step 4): Define $AC_a = \min_{1 \le l \le m}[\sum_{b \in L_a} C_c((b,a) \rightarrow (p_k, p_l))]$ where l denotes any processor connected to processor k, and define $AP_a = C_p(a \rightarrow p_k)$. If there exists no processor l connected to processor k, then AC_a is set infinite.

Step 5): Let $I_a = \min(AC_a, AP_a)$. Then compute the heuristic function $h(n)$ as

$$h(n) = \sum_{a \in B} I_a.$$

It is not difficult to see that $h(n)$ is a consistent lower bound of $h^*(n)$ for all n, so the state-space search will be guaranteed to find an optimal weak homomorphism using the algorithm described in the following.

Algorithm 2: Find an optimal weak homomorphism between two graphs.

Step 1): Put the initial node $K = \emptyset$ on a list called OPEN, and set $f(K) = 0$ where f is an evaluation function defined by (5).

Step 2): Remove from OPEN the node n with a smallest f value and put it on a list called CLOSED.

Step 3): If n satisfies the goal state defined in the previous section, then find out the corresponding graph mapping M as the desired homomorphism and exit. Otherwise, continue.

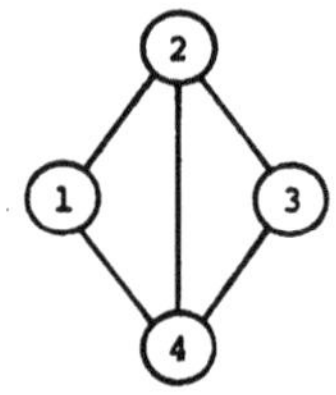

T = (V_T, E_T) where

V_T = {1,2,3,4},

E_T = {(1,2),(2,3),(3,4),(4,1),(2,4)}.

Fig. 3. Task graph.

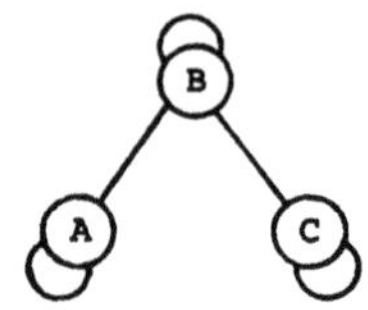

P = (V_P, E_P) where

V_P ={ A,B,C},

E_P = {(A,B),(B,C),(A,A),(B,B),(C,C)}.

Fig. 4. Processor graph.

Step 4): Expand node n, using operators applicable to n, and compute the value $f(n') = g(n') + h(n')$ for each successor n' of n where $g(n')$ is computed according to (1), (2), (3), and (4), and $h(n')$ is computed according to Algorithm 1. Put all the successors of n on OPEN.

Step 5): Go to Step 2).

In Step 4), if $h(n')$ is always set 0, then Algorithm 2 is a uniform-cost search. Otherwise, it is an A^* algorithm.

V. Illustrative Example

Here, we give an example to illustrate the mapping between the task graph and the processor graph by the proposed state-space search method. Task graph T and processor graph P are shown in Figs. 3 and 4.

The intermodule communication time and the module processing time are listed in Tables I and II.

Using the vertex and edge transformation notations defined previously, we have

$$C_p(1 \rightarrow A) = 10, \quad C_p(3 \rightarrow A) = 70,$$
$$C_p(1 \rightarrow B) = 20, \quad C_p(3 \rightarrow B) = 50,$$
$$C_p(1 \rightarrow C) = 30, \quad C_p(3 \rightarrow C) = 80,$$
$$C_p(2 \rightarrow A) = 40, \quad C_p(4 \rightarrow A) = 50,$$
$$C_p(2 \rightarrow B) = 5, \quad C_p(4 \rightarrow B) = 80,$$
$$C_p(2 \rightarrow C) = 10, \quad C_p(4 \rightarrow C) = 20,$$

and

$$C_c((1,2) \rightarrow (A,B)) = C_c((1,2) \rightarrow (B,C)) = 20,$$
$$C_c((2,3) \rightarrow (A,B)) = C_c((2,3) \rightarrow (B,C)) = 5,$$
$$C_c((3,4) \rightarrow (A,B)) = C_c((3,4) \rightarrow (B,C)) = 35,$$
$$C_c((4,1) \rightarrow (A,B)) = C_c((4,1) \rightarrow (B,C)) = 40,$$
$$C_c((2,4) \rightarrow (A,B)) = C_c((2,4) \rightarrow (B,C)) = 70.$$

Then, using Algorithm 2 as an ordered-search algorithm, we can find an optimal weak homomorphism $M^*: V_T \rightarrow V_P$ and compute the minimum task turnaround time. Fig. 5

TABLE I
INTERMODULE COMMUNICATION TIME

	module 1	2	3	4
module 1	0	20	0	40
2	20	0	5	70
3	0	5	0	35
4	40	70	35	0

TABLE II
MODULE PROCESSING TIME

	processor A	B	C
module 1	10	20	30
2	40	5	10
3	70	50	80
4	50	80	20

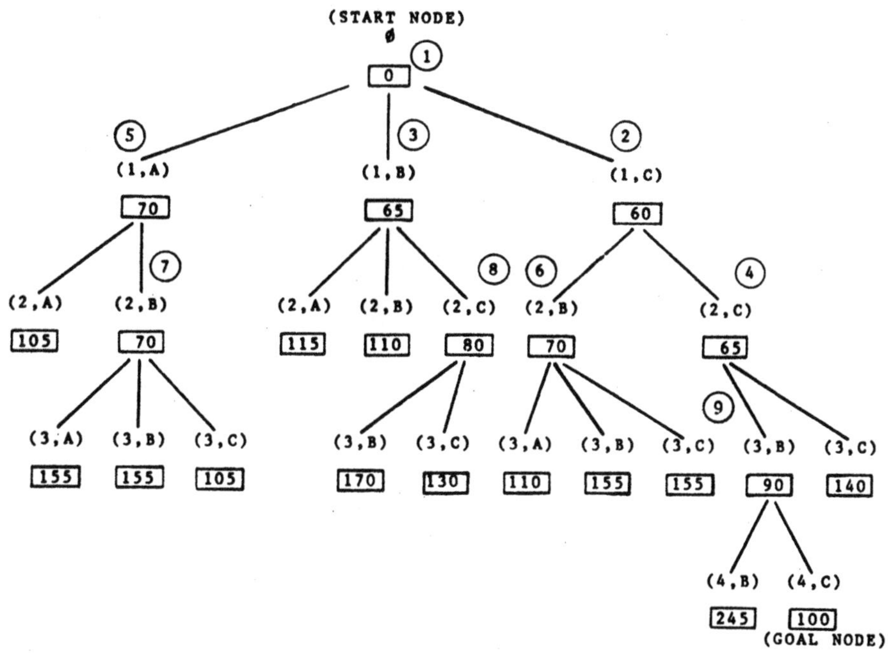

Fig. 5. State-space search tree of the illustrative example (circled numbers indicate node expansion order, and squared numbers indicate node costs).

shows the resulting search tree. The optimal weak homomorphism M^*, as shown, is

$$M^*: \begin{cases} 1 \rightarrow C \\ 2 \rightarrow C \\ 3 \rightarrow B \\ 4 \rightarrow C \end{cases}$$

which defines the optimal assignment of task T to distributed computing system P, and the minimum task turnaround time of this assignment is 100.

As shown in Fig. 5, totally only 9 state-space nodes are expanded and 23 nodes generated before the goal node is found. The search concentrates rather well on the right path to the goal node with only a few branches elsewhere. To prove that such concentration is a result from utilizing the heuristics proposed previously, we further reuse Algorithm 2 as a uniform-cost algorithm (by setting $h(n)$ zero for all nodes) to find the optimal weak homomorphism again. The resulting state-space search tree is too large to be included here as a figure. We only mention that totally 22 state-space nodes are expanded in the tree with 49 nodes generated.

More experiments have been performed on a CDC CYBER 170/720 computer for some other cases to test the effectiveness of the heuristic function $h(n)$ used in Algorithm 2. The results [18] show that in most cases with module numbers and processor numbers less than 10, the number of generated nodes by Algorithm 2 is about a half of that generated by the uniform-cost algorithm. It is also found in these cases that the complexity of Algorithm 2 as defined by the number of generated nodes is approximately to the order of N^2, although optimal task assignment, like many other graph matching problems, needs exponential time in the worst case [17].

VI. Conclusions

In this paper, we describe a graph matching approach to task assignment optimization. Optimal task assignment is transformed into the search problem of optimal weak graph homomorphism, which is then solved by heuristic state-space search using the A^* algorithm. The approach uses the task turnaround time as the cost measure and the minimax criterion as the criterion for assignment optimization. This approach allows various system constraints to be easily included for consideration. It minimizes interprocessor communication and optimizes load balancing by minimizing the task turnaround time.

There are M^N possible assignments to be considered in an assignment problem with M processors and N modules, and actual computation using an enumerative algorithm requires time to the order of M^N [10]. The state-space heuristic search algorithm proposed in this paper is shown effective by an illustrative example and some case studies for speeding up solution search. Further research can be directed to the improvement of the proposed lower-bound estimate $h(n)$ of $h^*(n)$ in Algorithm 1 and the inclusion of precedence consideration into the proposed algorithms.

References

[1] K. Efe, "Heuristic models of task assignment scheduling in distributed systems," *Computer*, vol. 15, pp. 50–56, June 1982.

[2] W. W. Chu, L. J. Holloway, M. T. Lan, and K. Efe, "Task allocation in distributed data processing," *Computer*, vol. 13, pp. 57–69, Nov. 1980.

[3] H. S. Stone and S. H. Bokhari, "Control of distributed processes," *Computer*, vol. 11, pp. 97–106, July 1978.

[4] H. S. Stone, "Multiprocessor scheduling with the aid of network flow algorithms," *IEEE Trans. Software Eng.*, vol. SE-3, pp. 85–93, Jan. 1977.

[5] T. C. K. Chow and J. A. Abraham, "Load balancing in distributed systems," *IEEE Trans. Software Eng.*, vol. SE-8, July 1982.

[6] S. H. Bokhari, "Dual processor scheduling with dynamic reassignment," *IEEE Trans. Software Eng.*, vol. SE-5, July 1979.

[7] ——, "On the mapping problem," *IEEE Trans. Comput.*, vol. C-30, pp. 207–214, Mar. 1981.

[8] H. S. Stone, "Critical load factors in two-processor distributed systems," *IEEE Trans. Software Eng.*, vol. SE-4, pp. 254–258, May 1978.

[9] G. S. Rao, H. S. Stone, and T. C. Hu, "Assignment of tasks in a distributed processor system with limited memory," *IEEE Trans. Comput.*, vol. C-28, pp. 291–299, Apr. 1979.

[10] C. C. Price, "The assignment of computational tasks among processors in a distributed system," in *Proc. Nat. Comput. Conf.*, May 1981, pp. 291–296.

[11] L. Kleinrock and A. Nilsson, "On optimal scheduling algorithms for time-shared systems," *J. ACM*, vol. 28, no. 3, pp. 477–486, July 1981.

[12] Y. C. Chow and W. Kohler, "Models for dynamic load balancing in a heterogeneous multiple processor system," *IEEE Trans. Comput.*, vol. C-28, pp. 354–361, May 1979.

[13] W. H. Tsai, "Graph matching problems: A survey and a tutorial," in *Proc. 1st Conf. Comput. Algorith.*, Hsinchu, Taiwan, China, July 1982.

[14] W. H. Tsai and K. S. Fu, "Subgraph error-correcting isomorphisms for syntactic pattern recognition," *IEEE Trans. Syst. Man, Cybern.*, vol. SMC-13, pp. 48–62, Jan./Feb. 1983.

[15] N. J. Nilsson, *Problem Solving Methods in Artificial Intelligence*. New York: McGraw-Hill, 1971.

[16] P. R. Ma, E. Y. S. Lee, and M. Tsuchiya, "A task allocation model for distributed computing systems," *IEEE Trans. Comput.*, vol. C-31, pp. 41–47, Jan. 1982.

[17] R. C. Read and D. G. Corneil, "The graph isomorphism disease," *J. Graph Theory*, pp. 339–363, 1977.

[18] C. C. Shen and W. H. Tsai, "A graph matching approach to optimal task assignment in distributed computing systems using a minimax criterion," Inst. Comput. Eng., Nat. Chiao Tung Univ., Hsinchu, Taiwan, Republic of China, Tech. Rep., July 1983.

Chien-Chung Shen was born in Taiwan, Republic of China, on July 15, 1960. He received the B.S. and M.S. degrees in computer engineering from National Chiao Tung University, Hsinchu, Taiwan, in 1982 and 1984, respectively.

From 1982 to 1984, he served as a Teaching and Research Assistant in the Institute of Computer Engineering, National Chiao Tung University. His research interests include artificial intelligence, pattern recognition, graph theory, database design, and computer-aided design of VLSI.

Wen-Hsiang Tsai (S'79–M'80) was born in Tainan, Taiwan, Republic of China, on May 10, 1951. He received the B.S. degree from National Taiwan University, Taipei, Taiwan, in 1973, the M.S. degree from Brown University, Providence, RI, in 1977, and the Ph.D. degree from Purdue University, West Lafayette, IN, in 1979, all in electrical engineering.

From 1973 to 1975, he served in the Chinese Navy as an Electronics Officer. From 1977 to 1979, he worked as a Research Assistant in the Advanced Automation Research Laboratory, School of Electrical Engineering, Purdue University. Since November 1979, he has been on the faculty of the Institute of Computer Engineering at National Chiao Tung University, Hsinchu, Taiwan. His current research interests are image processing and pattern recognition, computer vision applications in robotics and automation, and parallel processing and multiprocessor systems.

Chapter 2

DISTRIBUTED OPERATING SYSTEMS

An operating system in a distributed system needs to coordinate the operations of the set of processes that reside on the set of computers. The basic operations are the following: interprocess communications, transparent access to data files, replication of files and process for fault tolerance, process scheduling and migration to achieve response time requirements or to maximize system throughput. Due to the cost-performance trade-offs, not all of the above mentioned operations have actually been implemented in the available distributed operating systems. In fact, certain aspects, such as process scheduling and migration for efficiency, are still under research investigation.

In this chapter, we shall examine the disciplines as well as some of the distributed operating systems. The first paper by Per Brinch Hansen describes the structure of a multiprogram system which can be extended to create and control communications of a hierarchy of processes. In the second paper, Spector presents a communication model for efficient remote communication on a local network and also implementation considerations for a communication system. In the third paper, Rashid and Robertson describe a communication oriented operating system with emphasis on transparency, network access, and fault tolerant behavior. The fourth paper by Cheriton and Zwaenepoel describes the performance of diskless workstations that use a message oriented kernel to provide local and network interprocess communication. The fifth paper by Walker, *et al.*, presents the distributed Unix based operating system which supports transparent access to data access through a network-wide file system, allows automatic replication of storage, and supports transparent distributed process execution. The last paper by Green, *et al.*, presents a distributed real time operating system which supported a distributed computer simulation with set specific services. The operating system is tailored to a specific space defense application for achieving maximum performance and minimum overhead.

For further information on distributed operating systems, the interested reader should refer to [THOM 73, BRYA 81, POPE 81, VANT 84].

The Nucleus of a Multiprogramming System

PER BRINCH HANSEN
A/S Regnecentralen, Copenhagen, Denmark

This paper describes the philosophy and structure of a multiprogramming system that can be extended with a hierarchy of operating systems to suit diverse requirements of program scheduling and resource allocation. The system nucleus simulates an environment in which program execution and input/output are handled uniformly as parallel, cooperating processes. A fundamental set of primitives allows the dynamic creation and control of a hierarchy of processes as well as the communication among them.

KEY WORDS AND PHRASES: multiprogramming, operating systems, parallel processes, process concept, process communication, message buffering, process hierarchy, process creation, process removal
CR CATEGORIES: 4.30, 4.31, 4.32, 4.41

1. Introduction

The multiprogramming system developed by Regnecentralen for the RC 4000 computer is a general tool for the design of operating systems. It allows the dynamic creation of a hierarchy of processes in which diverse strategies of program scheduling and resource allocation can be implemented.

For the designer of advanced information systems, a vital requirement of any operating system is that it allow him to change the mode of operation it controls; otherwise his freedom of design can be seriously limited. Unfortunately, this is precisely what present operating systems do not allow. Most of them are based exclusively on a single mode of operation, such as batch processing, priority scheduling, real-time scheduling, or conversational access.

When the need arises, the user often finds it hopeless to modify an operating system that has made rigid assumptions in its basic design about a specific mode of operation. The alternative—to replace the original operating system with a new one—is in most computers a serious, if not impossible, matter because the rest of the software is intimately bound to the conventions required by the original system.

This unfortunate situation indicates that the main problem in the design of a multiprogramming system is not to define functions that satisfy specific operating needs, but rather to supply a system nucleus that can be extended with new operating systems in an orderly manner. This is the primary objective of the RC 4000 system.

In the following, the philosophy and structure of the RC 4000 multiprogramming system is explained. The discussion does not include details of implementation; size and performance are presented, however, to give an idea of the feasibility of this approach. The functional specifications of the multiprogramming system are described in detail in a report [1] available from Regnecentralen.

2. System Nucleus

Our basic attitude during the designing was to make no assumptions about the particular strategy needed to optimize a given type of installation, but to concentrate on the fundamental aspects of the control of an environment consisting of parallel, cooperating processes.

Our first task was to assign a precise meaning to the process concept, i.e. to introduce an unambiguous terminology defining what a process is and how it is implemented on the actual computer.

The next step was to select primitives for the synchronization and transfer of information among parallel processes.

Our final decisions concerned the rules for the dynamic creation, control, and removal of processes.

The purpose of the system nucleus is to implement these fundamental concepts: simulation of processes; communication among processes; creation, control, and removal of processes.

3. Processes

We distinguish between internal and external processes, roughly corresponding to program execution and input/output.

More precisely, an *internal process* is the execution of one or more interruptable programs in a given storage area. An internal process is identified by a unique process name. Thus other processes need not be aware of the actual location of an internal process in the store, but can refer to it by name.

A sharp distinction is made between the concepts program and internal process. A *program* is a collection of instructions describing a computational process, whereas an internal process is the execution of these instructions in a given storage area.

In connection with input/output, the system distinguishes between peripheral devices, documents, and external processes.

A *peripheral device* is an item of hardware connected to the data channel and identified by a device number. A *document* is a collection of data stored on a physical medium, such as a deck of punched cards, a printer form, a reel of magnetic tape, or a file on the backing store.

An *external process* is the input/output of a given document identified by a unique process name. This concept implies that internal processes can refer to documents by name without knowing the actual devices on which they are mounted.

Multiprogramming and communication between internal and external processes are coordinated by the system nucleus—an interrupt response program with complete control of input/output, storage protection, and the interrupt system. We do not regard the system nucleus as an independent process, but rather as a software extension of the hardware structure, which makes the computer more attractive for multiprogramming. Its function is to implement our process concept and primitives that processes can invoke to create and control other processes and communicate with them.

So far we have described the multiprogramming system as a set of independent, parallel processes identified by names. The emphasis has been on a clear understanding of relationships among resources (store and peripherals), data (programs and documents), and processes (internal and external).

4. Process Communication

In a system of parallel, cooperating processes, mechanisms must be provided for the synchronization of two processes during a transfer of information.

Dijkstra has demonstrated that indivisible lock and unlock operations operating on binary semaphores are sufficient primitives from a logical point of view [3]. We have been forced to conclude, however, that the semaphore concept alone does not fulfill our requirements of safety and efficiency in a dynamic environment in which some processes may turn out to be black sheep and break the rules of the game.

Instead we have introduced message buffering within the system nucleus as the basic means of process communication. The system nucleus administers a common pool of *message buffers* and a *message queue* for each process.

The following primitives are available for the communition between internal processes:

send message (receiver, message, buffer),
wait message (sender, message, buffer),
send answer (result, answer, buffer),
wait answer (result, answer, buffer).

Send message copies a message into the first available buffer within the pool and delivers it in the queue of a named receiver. The receiver is activated if it is waiting for a message. The sender continues after being informed of the identity of the message buffer.

Wait message delays the requesting process until a message arrives in its queue. When the process is allowed to proceed, it is supplied with the name of the sender, the contents of the message, and the identity of the message buffer. The buffer is removed from the queue and made ready to transmit an answer.

Send answer copies an answer into a buffer in which a message has been received and delivers it in the queue of the original sender. The sender of the message is activated if it is waiting for the answer. The answering process continues immediately.

Wait answer delays the requesting process until an answer arrives in a given buffer. On arrival, the answer is copied into the process and the buffer is returned to the pool. The result specifies whether the answer is a response from another process or a dummy answer generated by the system nucleus in response to a message addressed to a nonexisting process.

The procedure wait message forces a process to serve its queue on a first-come, first-served basis. The system, however, also includes two primitives that enable a process to wait for the arrival of the next message or answer and serve its queue in any order.

This communication scheme has the following advantages.

The multiprogramming system is dynamic in the sense that processes can appear and disappear at any time. Therefore a process does not in general have a complete knowledge of the existence of other processes. This is reflected in the procedure wait message, which makes it possible for a process to be unaware of the existence of other processes until it receives messages from them.

On the other hand, once a communication has been established between two processes (i.e. by means of a message) they need a common identification of it in order to agree on when it is terminated (i.e. by means of an answer). Thus we can properly regard the selection of a buffer as the creation of an identification of a conversation. A happy consequence of this is that it enables two processes to exchange more than one message at a time.

We must be prepared for the occurrence of erroneous or malicious processes in the system (e.g. undebugged programs). This is tolerable only if the system nucleus ensures that no process can interfere with a conversation between two other processes. This is done by storing the identity of the sender and receiver in each buffer and checking it whenever a process attempts to send or wait for an answer in a given buffer.

Efficiency is obtained by the queueing of buffers, which enables a sending process to continue immediately after delivery of a message or an answer, regardless of whether or not the receiver is ready to process it.

To make the system dynamic, it is vital that a process can be removed at any time, even if it is engaged in one or more conversations. In this case, the system nucleus leaves all messages from the removed process undisturbed in the queues of other processes. When these processes answer them, the system nucleus returns the buffers to the common pool.

The reverse situation is also possible: during the removal of a process, the system nucleus finds unanswered messages sent to the process. These are returned as dummy answers to the senders.

The main drawback of message buffering is that it introduces yet another resource problem, since the common pool contains a finite number of buffers. If a process were allowed to empty the pool by sending messages to ignorant processes, which do not respond with answers, further communication within the system would be blocked. Consequently a limit is set to the number of messages a process can send simultaneously. By doing this, and by allowing a process to transmit an answer in a received buffer, we have placed the entire risk of a conversation on the process that opens it.

5. External Processes

Originally the communication primitives were designed for the exchange of messages between internal processes. Later we also decided to use *send message* and *wait answer* for communication between internal and external processes.

For each kind of external process, the system nucleus contains a piece of code that interprets a message from an internal process and initiates input/output using a storage area specified in the message. When input/output is terminated by an interrupt, the nucleus generates an answer to the internal process with information about actual block size and possible error conditions. This is essentially the implementation of the external process concept.

We consider it to be an important aspect of the system that internal and external processes are handled uniformly as independent, self-contained processes. The difference between them is merely a matter of processing capability. A consequence of this is that any external process can be replaced by an internal process of the same name if more complex criteria of access and response become desirable.

External processes are created on request from internal processes. *Creation* is simply the assignment of a name to a particular peripheral device. To guarantee internal processes exclusive access to sequential documents, primitives are available for the *reservation* and *release* of external processes.

Typewriter consoles are the only external processes that can send messages to internal processes. The operator opens a conversation by pushing an interrupt key and typing the name of the internal receiver followed by a line of text.

A file on the backing store can be used as an external process by copying a description of the file from a catalog on the backing store into the system nucleus; following this, internal processes can initiate input/output by sending messages to the file process.

Real-time synchronization of internal processes is obtained by sending messages to a clock process. After the elapse of a time interval specified in the message, the clock returns an answer to the sending process.

In general, external processes can be used to obtain synchronization between internal processes and any signal from the external world. For example, an internal process may send a message to a watchdog process and receive an answer when a magnetic tape is mounted on a station. In response, the internal process can give the station a temporary name, identify the tape by reading its label, and rename the station accordingly.

6. Internal Processes

A final set of primitives in the system nucleus allows the creation, control, and removal of internal processes.

Internal processes are created on request from other internal processes. *Creation* involves the assignment of a name to a contiguous storage area selected by the parent process. The storage area must be within the parent's own area.

After creation, the parent process can load a program into the child process and *start* it. The child process now shares computing time with other active processes including the parent process.

On request from a parent process, the system nucleus waits for the completion of all input/output initiated by a child process and *stops* it. In the stopped state, the process can still receive messages and answers in its queue. These can be served when the process is restarted.

Finally, a parent process can *remove* a child process in order to assign its storage area to other processes.

According to our philosophy, processes should have complete freedom to choose their own strategy of program scheduling. The system nucleus only supplies the essential primitives for initiation and control of processes. Consequently, the concepts of program loading and swapping are not part of the nucleus. Time-sharing of a common storage area among child processes on a swapping basis is possible, however, because the system does not check whether internal processes overlap each other as long as they remain within the storage areas of their parents. Swapping from process A to process B can be implemented in a parent process as follows: stop(A); output(A); input(B); start(B).

7. Process Hierarchy

The idea of the system nucleus has been described as the simulation of an environment in which program execution and input/output are handled uniformly as parallel, cooperating processes. A fundamental set of primitives allows the dynamic creation and control of processes as well as communication among them.

For a given installation we still need, as part of the system, programs that control strategies of operator communication, program scheduling, and resource allocation; but it is essential for the orderly growth of the system that these *operating systems* be implemented as other programs. Since the difference between operating systems and production programs is one of jurisdiction only, this problem is solved by arranging the internal processes in a *hierarchy* in which parent processes have complete control over child processes.

After initial loading, the internal store contains the system nucleus and a basic operating system, S, which can create parallel processes, A, B, C, etc., on request from consoles. The processes can in turn create other processes, D, E, F, etc. Thus while S acts as a primitive operating system for A, B, and C, these in turn act as operating systems for their children, D, E, and F. This is illustrated by Figure 1, which shows a family tree of processes on the left and the corresponding storage allocation on the right. This family tree of processes can be extended to any level, subject only to a limitation of the total number of processes.

In this multiprogramming system, all privileged functions are implemented in the system nucleus, which has no built-in strategy. Strategies can be introduced at the various higher levels, where each process has the power to control the scheduling and resource allocation of its children. The only rules enforced by the nucleus are the following: a process can only allocate a subset of its own resources (including storage and message buffers) to its children; a process can only start, stop, and remove its own children (including their descendants). After removal of a process, its resources are returned to the parent process.

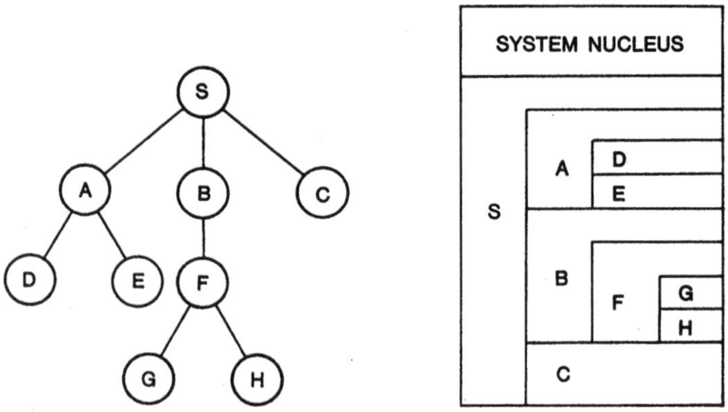

Fig. 1

Initially all system resources are owned by the basic operating system S. For details of process control and resource allocation, the reader should consult the manual of the system [1].

We emphasize that the only function of the family tree is to define the rules of process control and resource allocation. Computing time is shared by round-robin scheduling among active processes regardless of their position in the hierarchy, and each process can communicate with all other processes.

Regarding the future development of operating systems, the most important characteristics of the system can now be seen as the following.

1. New operating systems can be implemented as other programs without modification of the system nucleus. In this connection, we should mention that the ALGOL and FORTRAN languages for the RC 4000 contain facilities for calling the nucleus and initiating parallel processes. Thus it is possible to write operating systems in high-level languages.

2. Operating systems can be replaced dynamically, thus enabling an installation to switch among various modes of operation; several operating systems can, in fact, be active simultaneously.

3. Standard programs and user programs can be executed under different operating systems without modification, provided there is common agreement on the possible communication between parents and children.

8. Implementation

The RC 4000 is a 24-bit, binary computer with typical instruction execution times of 4 microseconds [2]. It permits practically unlimited expansion of the internal store and standardized connection of all kinds of peripherals. Multiprogramming is facilitated by program interruption, storage protection, and privileged instructions.

The present implementation of the system makes multiprogramming feasible with a minimum store of 16K–32K words backed by a fast drum or disk. The system nucleus includes external processes for a real-time clock, typewriters, paper tape input/output, line printer, magnetic tape, and files on the backing store. The size of the nucleus and the basic operating system is as follows:

	words
primitives	2400
code for external processes	1150
process descriptions and buffers	1250
system nucleus	4800
basic operating system	1400
	6200

The communication primitives are executed in the uninterruptable mode within the system nucleus. The execution times of these set a limit to the system's response to real-time events:

	msec
send message	0.6
wait answer	0.4
wait message	0.4
send answer	0.6

An analysis shows that the 2 milliseconds required by a complete conversation (the sum of the four primitives) are used as follows:

	percent
validity checking	25
process activation	45
message buffering	30

This distribution is so even that one cannot hope to increase the speed of the system by introducing additional, ad hoc machine instructions. The only realistic solution is to make the hardware faster.

The primitives for creation, start, stop, and removal of processes are implemented in an anonymous internal process within the system nucleus to avoid intolerably long periods in the uninterruptable mode. Typical execution times for these are:

	msec
create process	3
start process	26
stop process	4
remove process	30

The excessive times for the start and removal of an internal process are due to the peculiar storage protection system of the RC 4000, which requires the setting of a protection key in every storage word of a process.

9. Conclusion

Ideas similar to those described here have been suggested by others [4–6]. We have presented our system because we feel that, taken as a whole, it represents a systematic and practical approach to the design of replaceable operating systems. As an inspiration to other designers, it is perhaps most important that it illustrates a sequence of design steps leading to a general system nucleus, namely, the definition of the process concept, the communication scheme, and the dynamic creation and structuring of processes.

We realize, of course, that a final evaluation of the system can only be made after it has been used to design a number of operating systems.

Acknowledgments. The design philosophy was developed by Jørn Jensen, Søren Lauesen, and the author. Leif Svalgaard participated in the implementation and testing of the final product.

Regarding fundamentals, we have benefited greatly from Dijkstra's analysis of cooperating sequential processes.

RECEIVED JULY, 1969; REVISED JANUARY, 1970

REFERENCES

1. *RC 4000 Software: Multiprogramming System.* P. Brinch Hansen (Ed.). A/S Regnecentralen, Copenhagen, 1969.
2. *RC 4000 Computer: Reference Manual.* P. Brinch Hansen (Ed.). A/S Regnecentralen, Copenhagen, 1969.
3. DIJKSTRA, E. W. Cooperating Sequential Processes. Math. Dep., Technological U., Eindhoven, Sept. 1965.
4. HARRISON, M. C., AND SCHWARTZ, J. T. SHARER, a time sharing system for the CDC 6600. *Comm. ACM 10,* (Oct. 1967), 659.
5. HUXTABLE, D. H. R., AND WARWICK, M. T. Dynamic supervisors—their design and construction. Proc. ACM Symp. on Operating System Principles, Gatlinburg, Tenn., Oct. 1–4, 1967.
6. WICHMANN, B. A. A modular operating system. Proc. IFIP Cong. 1968, North Holland Pub. Co., Amsterdam, p. C48.

Operating Systems

Performing Remote Operations Efficiently on a Local Computer Network

Alfred Z. Spector
Stanford University

A communication model is described that can serve as a basis for a highly efficient communication subsystem for local networks. The model contains a taxonomy of communication instructions that can be implemented efficiently and can be a good basis for interprocessor communication. These communication instructions, called remote references, cause an operation to be performed by a remote process and, optionally, cause a value to be returned. This paper also presents implementation considerations for a communication system based upon the model and describes an experimental communication subsystem that provides one class of remote references. These remote references take about 150 microseconds or 50 average instruction times to perform on Xerox Alto computers connected by a 2.94 megabit Ethernet.

CR Categories and Subject Descriptors: C.2.2 [**Computer Communication Networks**]: Networks Protocol—protocol architecture; C.2.4 [**Computer Communication Networks**]: Distributed Systems—*network operating systems*; C.2.5 [**Computer Communication Networks**]: Local Networks—buses, rings; D.4.4 [**Operating Systems**]: Communication Management—*message sending, network communication*; D.4.5 [**Operating Systems**]: Organization and Design—*distributed systems.*

General Terms: Performance, Reliability

Additional Key Words and Phrases: efficient communication, transactions, communication models

1. Introduction

This paper discusses efficient communication techniques for very high speed local networks. A major question that this paper attempts to answer is how to reduce the traditionally high processing overhead of network communication. This overhead, characterized by the time to send a null message and receive a null answer, was reported by Peterson to be about 20 milliseconds on a variety of systems [21]. If communication processing overhead can be reduced and processors are interconnected with high bandwidth, low latency networks, distributed programs having a relatively fine granularity of parallelism can be executed. Networks operating at up to 100 megabits/second, developed at TRW, Mitsubishi, and Xerox, exemplify the technology that will permit small data transmission times to be achieved [2], [13], [23].

Ultimately, studies of efficient communication must be concerned with the specification and implementation of language-level primitives. For example, Cook, Hoare, Liskov, and Nelson have written about remote procedure calls and message passing primitives [4], [10], [17], [19]. However, we concentrate on a communication subsystem on which to base these language-level primitives. To provide overall efficiency, this intermediate communication subsystem must be a good foundation on which to implement the desired high level primitives. Also, it must be specialized enough to be implemented efficiently using the semi-reliable packet transmission facility that most local networks provide. Efficient implementations may require the use of microcode or specialized hardware.

The particular communication subsystem that we propose differs from typical network communication subsystems in two ways. First, we advocate an integrated implementation approach rather than the layered approach discussed by Zimmerman [31]. Though layered approaches facilitate the use of similar communication subsystems on heterogeneous networks and permit simplified design and maintenance of network software, the crossing of layer boundaries results in decreased efficiency. Second, we place more emphasis on ensuring that the functions provided by the communication subsystem are suitable for implementing high level primitives. Rather than providing, for example, only a transmission function for asynchronous byte streams, we propose that the communication subsystem provide functions that can be used more easily in implementing high level communication primitives. These functions must not be too complex (e.g., guaranteeing reliability when it is not necessary) nor must they be so simple that implementations of high level primitives using them are difficult or inefficient. In some instances, we hope for almost a trivial mapping from language-level functions to those provided by the communication subsystem. In related work, Nelson and Popek have discussed the benefits of streamlined implementations of communication primitives in the context of programming language constructs and operating systems, respectively, [19], [22].

The initial sections of this paper discuss functions that should be provided by a communication subsystem

This work was supported by a Fannie and John Hertz Foundation Graduate Fellowship. Some of this work came about as a result of the author's work at IBM's San Jose Research Laboratory. Firmware and software were developed on equipment given to Stanford University by the Xerox Corporation.

Author's present address: Alfred Z. Spector, Department of Computer Science, Carnegie-Mellon University, Pittsburgh, PA 15213.

and techniques for implementing these functions. More specifically, Sec. 2 presents a communication model called the *remote reference/remote operation* model in which a taxonomy of communication primitives is defined. We argue that a communication subsystem suggested by this model can provide powerful primitives yet be implemented efficiently. Section 3 presents implementation considerations for such a subsystem, and Sec. 4 exemplifies a highly reliable communication primitive that it could provide.

Section 5 adds substance to the discussion of the remote reference/remote operation model by describing an experiment in which a simple type of communication instruction was microcoded on Xerox Alto computers using the 2.94 megabit experimental Ethernet. (Information on the Alto and the Ethernet can be found in [18] and [30].) We show that these instructions execute quickly: they typically take about 150 microseconds or about 50 macroinstruction times on this hardware. This time is about two orders of magnitude faster than could be expected if they were implemented in a conventional way. This improvement in performance is due to three factors: the specialization of the communication interface, the use of simplified protocols, and the direct implementation in microcode.

2. The Remote Reference/Remote Operation Model

In the remote reference/remote operation model, a process executes communication instructions called *remote references*; each remote reference causes a single *remote operation* to be performed by a remotely located process. The remote operation may return a value to the caller. A remote reference is analogous to a subroutine call instruction that specifies certain properties concerning the execution of the subroutine. During the execution of any remote reference, the process that issues the reference is called the *master* and the process that executes the operation is called the *slave*.

Remote operations can vary greatly in complexity, from the simplicity of a memory access to the complexity of an asynchronously executing subroutine. For example, the message passing "send" operation causes a data block to be placed on the receiver's message queue and provides an indication of the success of that operation. In this case, the sender is the master, and the queue manager (at the remote site) is the slave.

There are four reasons why this model includes primitives that not only transmit data but also initiate operations and return their results.

1. *Utility of Primitives.* An implementation of high level primitives based upon remote references can be efficient because remote references are relatively powerful and reduce the need for costly software (and protocol) layering on top of them. Examples of communication primitives that can be naturally implemented using remote references are remote memory references, remote subroutine calls, and message passing operations. Specific examples include the SIGP operation on the IBM 370 [11], "requests" in the Tandem Guardian system [1], and certain Cm* operating system functions [14], [20].

2. *Support for Reliability.* In the case of a transmission medium with high reliability such as a local network, Saltzer [24] suggests that providing "end-to-end" reliability is often more important than providing reliable message transmission. Because references initiate remote operations, such "end-to-end" reliability can be supported by remote references; references can have an attribute that ensures that an operation is performed, not merely that a message is delivered. (As will be discussed in Sec. 3.3, the communication system can only assist in providing high reliability; the remote operation must also be specially implemented.)

3. *Potential for Protocol Simplification.* Many types of remote references can be implemented using simpler protocols than are required for more general and common communication mechanisms such as byte stream primitives.

4. *Potential for Efficient Implementation.* Remote references are specific enough that they can be specially implemented, perhaps in microcode or hardware.

2.1 Definitions and Assumptions

The remote reference/remote operation model provides a basis for communication on a system comprised of *processors* connected by a *local network*, as shown in Fig. 1. To discuss the model fully, we must first specify some aspects of the underlying system architecture.

Data is exchanged between machines by the transmission of *packets* over a local network—a high bandwidth, low latency communication medium having high reliability and low cost. With respect to reliability, the local network provides four transmission properties: First, if a packet is transmitted enough times, it will reach its destination. Second, packets corrupted during transmission are automatically discarded. Third, packets are not duplicated by the network. Finally, packets arrive in the order in which they are sent. Thus, local network failures result only in lost packets. The reader should note that this paper does not discuss internetworks.

Fig. 1. Underlying Architecture.

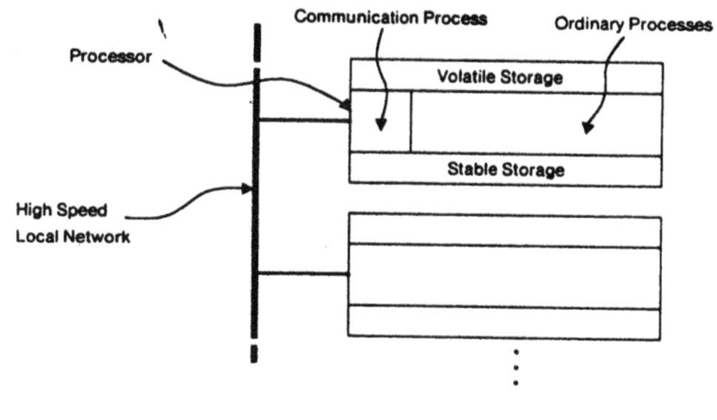

As will become clear in Sec. 2.3, some remote references are intended to provide very fine grain communication. Such remote references are practical only if transmission latencies are very small for short packets. If many (e.g., 100) processors must also be supported, a high capacity (e.g., 100 megabits/second) network may be necessary.

In the model, processors occasionally fail in a detectable fashion and are then restarted. In addition, processors contain *processes* with names unique to that processor. There are two classes of processes: *regular processes* that disappear after a processor failure and *recoverable processes* that are automatically reincarnated after a processor crash and are reset to one of several predetermined states. Recoverable processes require the availability of *stable storage*—storage that survives failures [16]. Processors are sufficiently reliable to allow recoverable processes to make progress.

We assume that the regular and recoverable processes are used to provide one or more *ordinary* processes that are used by applications. We also assume the existence of a distinguished process called the *communication process*. This process is recoverable and is specially implemented—off-loaded or at interrupt level—so that it can be activated rapidly. Though its implementation must permit the execution of simple functions quickly, it must also be able to do more complex operations requiring stable storage. (The need for this is described in Sec. 2.3.) The communication process does not have the full capabilities of other processes, but it can perform the following functions efficiently.

1. The transmission and reception of packets on the local network. Only the communication process accesses the network-specific hardware directly.
2. The manipulation of specialized communication state information. The communication process can quickly access the state tables described in Sec. 3.1. Some table entries need to be saved in stable storage.
3. The execution of communication primitives issued by other processes on the same processor. This process implements the communication interface seen by other processes.
4. The execution of simple operations initiated by a remote communication process; i.e., simple requests can be directed to a remote communication process for efficient processing.

2.2 Model Description

Figure 2 illustrates the remote reference/remote operation model in the absence of communication or processor failures. A reference is initiated by an action labeled **Reference-Commit.** At a later time, a request is received on the slave processor, and the communication process initiates the appropriate remote operation by issuing an action called **Op-Begin-Commit.** The remote operation is complete only when the action labeled **Op-End-Commit** has been executed. If the remote operation produces

Fig. 2. Normal Operation of Remote References.

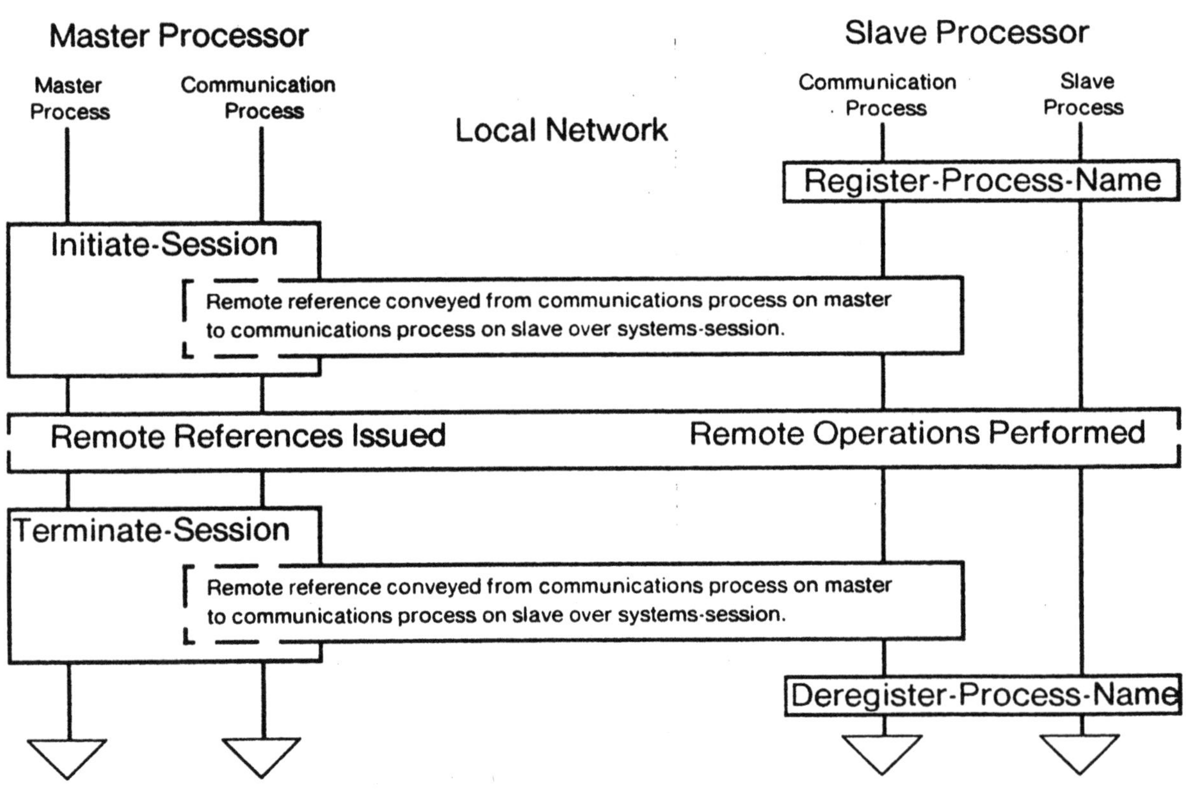

a value, the communication process on the slave issues a *response* to the master, which causes the action labeled **Result-Commit** to be executed. For remote reference types having certain reliability semantics, some of these four actions must be *atomic* (i.e., execute indivisibly) and either correctly write a record on stable storage, or fail completely and do nothing. (See [9] for a discussion of atomic actions.)

There are many possible protocols for implementing remote references. In simple cases, upon executing a remote reference, a master issues a request packet to a slave and possibly awaits a subsequent response packet from that slave. In other cases, the protocol is much more complex. Section 3.4 contains a more detailed discussion of this.

2.3 Reference Taxonomy

Remote references have associated with them five attribute classes. These are based on the following: varying reliability semantics, whether a value is returned, how the remote operation occurs temporally with respect to the reference, the need for flow control, and the kind of process by which the operation will be performed. These attribute classes have been selected to span the space of possible implementation strategies—and costs—as well as to provide a rich set of primitives with which to communicate. Sections 2.3.1 through 2.3.5 describe these five different attributes in more detail.

2.3.1 Reliability

Careful specification of the performance of remote references under different failure conditions is important in distributed systems, because we often desire the system to tolerate failures. The attributes discussed in this section provide for various degrees of robustness under conditions of communication and processor failures. They are summarized in Table I and described below.

The four reliability attributes, listed in increasing order of function complexity and implementation cost, are as follows: **maybe, at-least-once, only-once-type-1,** and **only-once-type-2.** Their names arise from the semantics that these attributes provide under conditions of communication failures.

In the absence of communication or processor failures, all references initiate one **Op-End-Commit** and, if required, one **Result-Commit.** The effect of the four attributes under conditions of communication failure (i.e., lost packets) is summarized below.

The **maybe** attribute: An **Op-End-Commit** to be performed zero or one times. If the **Op-End-Commit** is performed, the **Result-Commit** will occur zero or one times.

The **at-least-once** attribute: An **Op-End-Commit** will be performed one or more times. The **Result-Commit** will also occur one or more times.

The **only-once-type-1** or **only-once-type-2** attribute: Exactly one **Op-End-Commit** and one **Result-Commit** will occur regardless of communication failures.

A slave processor failure may cause **maybe, at-least-once,** and **only-once-type-1** references to fail: that is, in addition to their normal semantics under communication failures, we must add the possibility that no **Op-End-Commit** and **Result-Commit** will occur. A failed master processor causes problems similar to those of a failed slave processor except that the **Result-Commit** is *guaranteed* not to occur. Table I summarizes these points.

The **only-once-type-2** attribute applies to references issued to recoverable slaves from both recoverable and nonrecoverable master processes. **Only-once-type-2** references cause exactly one **Op-End-Commit** to be executed, regardless of failures. The **Result-Commit** always occurs if the master process is recoverable.

Table I. Reliability Semantics Survey.

Protocol Class	Reference Semantics Under Different Failure Conditions				
	No Failures	Lost Packets	Lost Packets & Slave Failure	Lost Packets & Master Failure	Lost Packets, Master & Slave Failure
Maybe	op performed: 1 result-commit: 1	op performed: 0,1 result-commit: 0,1	op performed: 0,1 result-commit: 0,1	op performed: 0,1 result-commit: 0	op performed: 0,1 result-commit: 0
At-Least-Once	op performed: 1 result-commit: 1	op performed: ≧ 1 result-commit: ≧ 1	op performed: ≧ 0 result-commit: ≧ 0	op performed: ≧ 0 result-commit: 0	op performed: ≧ 0 result-commit: 0
Only-Once-Type-1	op performed: 1 result-commit: 1	op performed: 1 result-commit: 1	op performed: 0,1 result-commit: 0,1	op performed: 0,1 result-commit: 0	op performed: 0,1 result-commit: 0
Only-Once-Type-2	op performed: 1 result-commit: 1	op performed: 1 result-commit: 1	op performed: 1 result commit: 1	regular master process op performed: 1 result commit: 0 recoverable master process op performed: 1 result-commit: 1	regular master process op performed: 1 result-commit: 0 recoverable master process op performed: 1 result-commit: 1

These attributes have a major effect on the protocol that is needed to implement remote references. Protocol considerations are discussed in Sec. 3.4.

2.3.2 Value and Novalue References

All references, except those with **maybe** semantics, explicitly return a value to the master process. These are called **value** references. In Fig. 2, **Result-Commit** labels the time at which a value is returned. This value is either provided by the remote operation or by the communication system; in the latter case, it provides an indication that the remote operation has been performed. For **only-once-type-2** references, which guarantee that a remote operation will be performed, this response allows the master process to know *when* the remote operation has occurred.

To permit greater efficiency, we allow **maybe** references to not return a value. These are called **novalue** references. **Maybe** references do not require a response to achieve their reliability semantics; hence, it would be inefficient to require a response for operations that produce no value.

2.3.3 Synchrony

Remote operations that execute synchronously with respect to a calling processor are called **processor-synchronous.** Operations that execute synchronously with respect to the calling process only are called **process-synchronous**: in this case, the processor may execute another process while the remote operation is being performed. Operations that execute asynchronously with respect to only the calling process are called **asynchronous.** The order in which remote operations complete (i.e., execute **Op-End-Commit**) is independent of the order of the **asynchronous** references that initiate them. In summary, a master process can issue **processor-synchronous**, **process-synchronous**, or **asynchronous** references.

References have been divided into these three synchrony classes because of the different implementation efficiency that is possible for each. For example, **processor-synchronous** references can be implemented very efficiently and permit fine grained communication; **process-synchronous** references require task switching on the master; and **asynchronous** references usually require more complex protocols due to the existence of multiple outstanding requests. These considerations are presented in more detail in Sec. 3.2.

2.3.4 Inter-Reference Flow Control

Flow control has many meanings, but we consider flow control as a resource reservation system that guarantees a resource is available on the slave. Usually, this is buffering space for requests. Thus, flow control ensures that a master issues requests to a slave below a predetermined rate. Flow control is not useful for **process-synchronous** or **processor-synchronous** references, because with these a process cannot issue a new reference until the last reference has been acted upon. However, **asynchronous** references can be either **flow-controlled** or **not-flow-controlled.** When required, flow control adds to the cost of executing remote references.

2.3.5 Operation Types: Primary and Secondary

Operations are **primary** if they are performed by a remote communication process and **secondary** if they are performed by an ordinary process. **Primary** operations can be executed rapidly on the remote processor, because the communication process can be activated without substantial overhead. Furthermore, requests do not cause scheduling or require additional queueing, because there is only one communication process per processor, and we assume that it can be run with low overhead. Finally, the caveat that **primary** operations must be simple (to avoid overloading the communication process) is a factor contributing to the high speed at which they run. Examples of **primary** references are causing data to be enqueued in a process' mailbox and initiating remote memory operations.

In comparison, **secondary** operations require request demultiplexing, request queueing, and more costly process switching on the remote side. Remote subroutine calls are typical examples of **secondary** references.

2.4 Discussion

This communication model provides a large number of well-specified communication primitives. Table II summarizes the feasible reference types. Because many types of references are available, and because they differ greatly in implementation costs, distributed systems need only pay for what they use. Because each reference type provides only highly specific functions, implementations can be specialized thereby supporting highly efficient operation.

Though a communication system based upon the model need not provide all of these reference types,

Table II. Reference Type Summary.

Synchrony Class	Op-Type Class	Flow-Control Class	Reliability Class	Value Returning Class
Processor-Synchronous (See 3)	Primary	Flow-Controlled (See 2)	Maybe	Value
			At-Least-Once	
Process-Synchronous	Secondary	Not-Flow-Controlled	Only-Once-Type-1	No-Value (See 1)
Asynchronous			Only-Once-Type-2 (See 4)	

1) Only Maybe references can have No-Value.
2) Only Asynchronous references may be Flow-Controlled.
3) Processor-Synchronous references should be Primary.
4) Only-Once-Type-2 references must be directed to recoverable slaves.

many have direct uses in distributed systems. **Primary, processor-synchronous** references are useful for sharing memory, enqueueing small blocks of data, signalling remote processors, etc. **Primary, process-synchronous** and **primary, asynchronous** references are useful for implementing message passing primitives. **Secondary, process-synchronous** references are useful for implementing remote subroutine calls and cross-network paging. Finally, **secondary, asynchronous** references have their place in the parallel execution of remote subroutine calls. Even the **maybe** reliability attribute is useful; an example is the transmission of packetized speech.

3. Implementation Considerations

The preceding section described a communication model and introduced a taxonomy of primitives. Whereas Sec. 2 concentrated on defining the semantics of remote references, this section presents implementation considerations for a communication subsystem based upon the model. We envision that such a system would predefine some remote references and provide mechanisms for the definition of others. Predefined remote references would include **primary** remote references and remote references that are used in the definition of others. The predefined **primary** references would be highly optimized and provide low overhead fine granularity communication.

First, this section describes *sessions*; these are connections between processes over which references are conveyed. Then, general implementation issues regarding the reliability and synchrony attributes are presented. This section concludes with a discussion of protocols and the circumstances under which they can be used.

3.1 Sessions and Sockets

A session, as defined in this paper, is a logical connection over which a single master process can issue requests and a single slave process can issue responses. Associated with a session are the semantic attributes of the references which are conveyed over it. For some attributes, considerable state information (for such purposes as flow control or duplicate detection) must be maintained. In this work processes are assumed to be located on fixed processor nodes for the life of the session.

When a session is established, one *socket* is created on each of the master and slave processors. These sockets serve three main functions: First, packets associated with that session are addressed using references to these sockets. Second, sockets contain information that permits requests and responses to be mapped to individual processes. Third and most importantly, they contain state information that enables sessions to provide specific semantic attributes for references conveyed during that session. Sockets for active sessions are contained in a per-processor socket table that is accessed by the communication process and implemented using both volatile and stable storage.

There are two types of sockets: *regular* sockets, which do not survive processor crashes and *recoverable* sockets, which use stable storage and do survive crashes. Recoverable sockets can be used by recoverable processes to ensure that their communication capabilities are not lost after processor failures. After a failed processor has been restarted, a recoverable process associated with recoverable sockets can continue executing references if it is a master or receiving requests if it is a slave. No regular sockets survive a processor restart.

A session can be considered to be a distributed abstract data object that is manipulated by two cooperating communication processes via the two sockets. There are four major operations allowed during sessions.

Issue-Reference permits a master process to initiate a remote operation on the slave and causes a **Reference-Commit** to occur locally.

Receive-Response permits a master process to receive a response from a slave and causes a **Result-Commit**. In some instances, a master may have a **Receive-Response** outstanding and receive an interrupt when a response arrives. Sometimes, **Receive-Response** is issued in combination with **Issue-Reference.**

Receive-Request permits a slave to receive a request from its master. In some instances, a slave may have a **Receive-Request** outstanding and may receive an interrupt when a request arrives.

Return-Response allows a slave to return a result to its master and causes an **Op-End-Commit** to be executed locally.

Issue-Reference, **Receive-Response**, **Receive-Request**, and **Return-Response** are generic names for primitives whose implementations are application dependent: in fact, their call syntax will often be modified to reduce overhead. For example, a normal memory reference may result in an **Issue-Reference** if a segmentation table specifies that the memory reference should be issued over a session.

Two sessions are maintained between each pair of communication processes to permit each communication process to act as both a master and a slave to each other's communication process. These sessions, called *systems-sessions*, allow other sessions between noncommunication processes to be created and destroyed. Communiction processes provide the following primitives.

Register-Process-Name is processed locally on the slave processor and registers a slave process name with the local communication process, and it specifies how requests for that process will be conveyed to it; for example, via interrupt or queueing. It also specifies the type of session in which the slave will participate. This permits the communication process to respond to requests asking for sessions with this slave.

Deregister-Process-Name is processed locally on the slave processor and expunges a slave process name from the socket table of the local communication process. It cannot be issued if a session is established. (The session must first be terminated with **Terminate-Session**.)

Initiate-Session is executed by a master and establishes a session with a previously registered slave. It requires as arguments the remote slave process name and address, the desired type of session (see Sec. 2.3), and an indication of the disposition for responses received from the slave. It returns a session number. **Initiate-Session** initiates a remote reference to the communication process on the slave. This predefined remote reference serves the purpose of an initial connection protocol such as PUP's rendezvous protocol [3]. Additionally, it allows the presetting of defaults for that session.

Terminate-Session eliminates a session. This predefined remote reference requires the session number as an argument and initiates a remote reference to the remote communication process. It can be executed by either a master or slave.

Figure 3 illustrates the initiation and termination of a session.

In summary, the communication process performs four main functions: it maintains systems-sessions; it supervises the initiation and closing of the other sessions; it accepts references from a master process, initiates their remote execution and possibly performs certain actions to inform the master of the result; and it accepts remote requests from the network, awakens the slave process, if necessary, and possibly sends responses to the master.

The concepts of sessions and sockets are not unique to this work. For example, sockets are called half-sessions in SNA [5] and TCB's in TCP [12], and sessions are implemented in Level 5 in the OSI protocol hierarchy [8]. However, in this work, there are many types of sessions, each fulfilling particular needs; the diversity of session types, in many instances, permits simpler protocols to be used. Additionally, the sessions in this model subsume the function of a few layers in general network hierarchies; this reduces the need for inefficient protocol layering.

3.2 The Synchrony Attributes

Processor-synchronous references can be performed efficiently if requests and responses are short, and if the specified remote operation can be executed quickly. They are useful when the cost of doing the remote operation is lower than the additional overhead that would be incurred with **process-synchronous** or **asynchronous** references. When errors occur that would unduly slow the operation of **processor-synchronous** references, the reference can time-out and be re-executed in a **process-synchronous** fashion. In this way, the master processor will not be halted for too long.

Process-synchronous references are the next most efficient references, because they do not require a master process to account explicitly for multiple outstanding requests. **Asynchronous, only-once** references of both types require a more complex protocol than **processor-synchronous** or **process-synchronous** references, because a master can issue new references before previous references have completed. Because of this, slaves cannot

Fig. 3. Session Initiation and Termination.

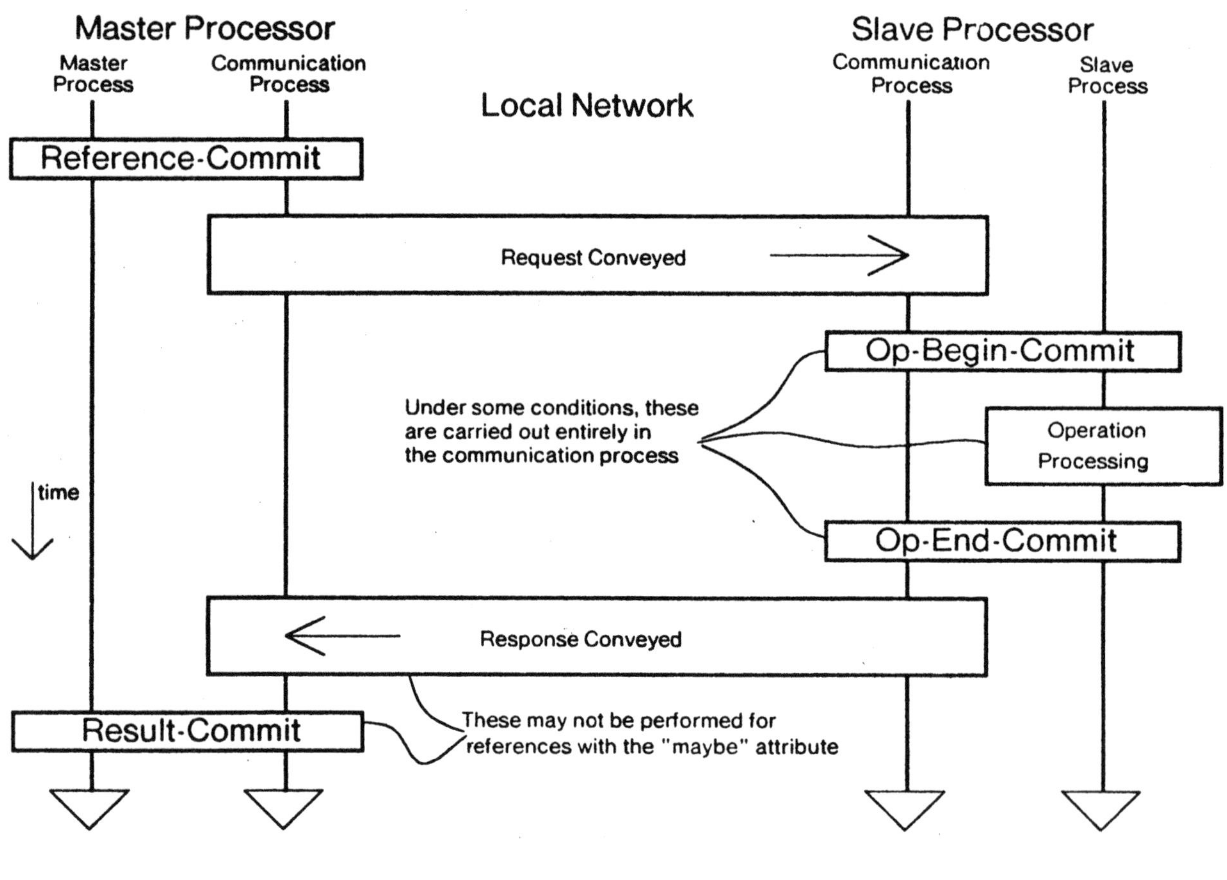

automatically discard saved state information concerning a previous request when a new request arrives.

With **process-synchronous** and **asynchronous** references, each response must be demultiplexed and queued to an individual process, and request–response correlation is more complicated. Additionally, potentially costly process switches often occur.

Asynchronous references may require flow control. When needed, flow control requires that the master save information that reflects the amount of storage space reserved for buffering additional requests on the slave. Maintaining this information requires additional information to be transferred between the slave and the master.

3.3 The Reliability Attributes

Maybe references do not require any retransmission mechanism. However, to achieve **at-least-once** semantics, the master must transmit a request to the slave until either a valid response is returned, or it can be determined that a processor failure has occurred. **Only-once-type-1** semantics additionally require that information must be saved by the communication process on the slave to permit the suppression of duplicate requests and allow response retransmissions.

Implementations of **only-once-type-2** references are similar to those of **only-once-type-1**, except that the session state must be maintained in recoverable sockets on both master and slave. The slave process must be recoverable, and the remote operations that it executes must be transactions; for example, once a remote operation executes **Op-Begin-Commit**, it will either execute **Op-End-Commit** or fail and leave no trace. In addition, both **Reference-Commit** and **Op-End-Commit** must be atomic, and both must commit state to stable storage. **Result-Commit** and **Op-Begin-Commit** may be atomic and may commit state to stable storage in some instances.

We should also note that for all **only-once-type-2** references, **Result-Commit** cannot occur until a valid response is received from the slave. If the duration of **only-once-type-2** references is always to be small, a back-up processor (that can reference stable storage) must be available for the slave to minimize the duration of failures. Also, **only-once-type-2** references require heavy use of stable storage. Traditional implementations such as mirrored disks are probably not suitable for reasons of efficiency.

3.4 Protocol

The reference attributes, the amount of time required for the remote operation to be performed, and the amount of data that must be conveyed between master and slave affect the communication protocols that can be used to implement remote references. The first protocol issue concerns requests and responses that do not fit in a single packet. This issue is important because local networks may enforce small maximum packet sizes to lower the transmission latency for small packets or to decrease the size of the packet buffers that run at the speed of the network.

Requests and responses that do not fit within a single packet can be transmitted as *multipackets*, or sequences of packets. Multipackets are an extension of the basic transmission facilities of the network to permit the efficient transmission of larger amounts of data. Multipackets take advantage of the underlying reliability of the network; hence, packets in a multipacket are neither acknowledged nor retransmitted. Many schemes are possible for multipackets; we describe a scheme based upon the use of a checksum over all packets in the multipacket in [26]. Aside from the checksum, this scheme requires only one byte of overhead per packet and permits single packet requests and responses to be interleaved with the receipt or transmission of multipackets.

Once arbitrarily long requests and responses can be issued, three protocols, the *request* (**R**) protocol, the *request/response* (**RR**) protocol, the *request/response/acknowledge–response* (**RRA**) protocol, are satisfactory for implementing the various types of remote references. (Occasionally, other protocols provide higher performance; these are discussed in [26].) Flow-control can be added to the **RR** and **RRA** protocol by providing *allocation* fields in responses that indicate the amount of space reserved on the slave for additional requests.

The **R** protocol is useful for **maybe, novalue, not-flow-controlled** references. Data is encapsulated into a request and transmitted to the slave.

The **RR** protocol is useful for many types of references. With it, the master initiates a remote operation by issuing a request, and the slave returns a result (either an explicit value or an acknowledgment) by issuing a response. In the **RR** protocol, requests and responses must contain a unique identifier that permits them to be matched to each other. The **RR** protocol is efficient to implement and can be used when the following two conditions are satisfied.

1. The master does not have to buffer too much data while it is awaiting a response from the slave. If the requests are very long and the remote operation requires a long time, buffer space may be wasted.

2. The slave does not have to buffer too much data. For example, consider using this protocol to implement **asynchronous, only-once** references of both types. The **only-once** property requires that the slave retain sufficient information so it can issue duplicates until the master has reliably received a response. Because this protocol does not inform the slave when a response has been received, the slave can never reclaim storage used for storing duplicate responses.

With **processor-synchronous** and **process-synchronous** references, the issuance of a new reference implies the receipt of the previous response. Because of this fact, the **RR** protocol is potentially useful for all **process-synchronous** and **processor-synchronous** references. It is also useful for **asynchronous, maybe, value** references,

asynchronous, maybe, novalue, flow-controlled references, and **asynchronous, at-least-once** references because these do not require any inter-reference state to be maintained on the slave. The **RR** protocol will always be the protocol of choice for **synchronous** references because requests and responses are necessarily short. Whether or not the **RR** protocol is used for **process-synchronous** references depends upon the length of requests and responses.

The **RRA** protocol can be used to lower the amount of storage that must be buffered on the slave. In this protocol, the slave's response is acknowledged, allowing the slave to reclaim space devoted to storing that response. It is similar to the **RR** protocol except that the master additionally issues an acknowledge–response to indicate that it has received certain responses, and the unique identifiers contained in requests and responses must be sequence numbers (i.e., ordered.) The acknowledge–response is interpreted as acknowledging the receipt of all responses that have a sequence number $\leq$ M, for some M. This interpretation ensures that the loss of an acknowledge–response is harmless. When a slave receives an acknowledge–response, M, it is free to delete all saved state asssociated with responses that have sequence numbers $\leq$ M.

With the **RRA** protocol, the master may not be able to acknowledge all responses immediately. This is because the master may receive responses for **asynchronous** references out of order. The master will be able to acknowledge a newly received response immediately only if all responses with lower sequence numbers have arrived. (If this causes an important delay in deleting state on the slave, a separate sequence number for responses can be added by the slave, and acknowledge–responses can acknowledge this sequence number.)

The **RRA** protocol may be useful for **only-once, process-synchronous** references, but more usually would be used for **only-once, asynchronous** references. The acknowledge–response packet is required for **asynchronous** references because a new request does not ensure that the last response has been received.

In all protocols using regular sockets, the slave must be able to eliminate sockets associated with crashed masters. Many techniques are available: for example, upon recovery, the master communication process could issue references—over the systems session—to communication processes on processors with which it may have communicated, requesting that regular sockets be eliminated. Alternatively, regular sockets could timeout.

4. An Example: Only-Once-Type-2, Asynchronous References

This section contains a brief discussion of one rather complex reference type: an **only-once-type-2, asynchronous, value** reference. (In this description, we consciously ignore flow-control and addressing considerations due to space limitations.) The purpose is not to fully specify an implementation but to demonstrate that this model includes rather complex primitives and to exemplify the **only-once-type-2** attribute. An example of such a reference type is a remote reference that reliably causes a slave process to write a page onto remote secondary storage, unlock that page, and return a version number.

In an implementation using the **RRA** protocol, if **Reference-Commit** is successfully executed, a stable entry (containing the request, with sequence number N, that is to be sent to the slave) is made atomically in the master's socket. (Sequence numbers are ordered, and new remote references initiate transmission of requests with higher sequence numbers.) The request is then repeatedly transmitted by the master to the slave until **Result-Commit** occurs.

After the requested operation is performed and **Op-End-Commit** is executed, the slave issues a response, containing the result and the sequence number N, to the master. Normally, the master receives this response, and it executes **Result-Commit. Result-Commit** attempts to commit atomically to stable storage both the reference's result and an indication that the reference has completed.

After **Result-Commit** has occurred, the master sends an acknowledge–response to the slave. The acknowledge–response contains a sequence number M, M $\leq$ N, and indicates that the master has received all responses through sequence number M. The acknowledge–response does not need to be sent reliably to the slave because each future acknowledge–response will acknowledge at least as many responses as did the previous one. After the master has issued the acknowledge–response, the communication process can reclaim all storage except for the indication that the reference has completed. This protocol is illustrated in Fig. 4.

On the slave, **Op-End-Commit** must be an atomic action that first checks the operation that is about to be committed to see that it is not a duplicate. If the operation is not a duplicate, it then commits the reference result, sequence number, and any operation-dependent data to stable storage. The slave then sends a response to the master, containing either the previous or the new result.

Fig. 4. Illustration of RRA Protocol for **only-once-type-2, Asynchronous** References. Illustrated case is where there are no lost packets.

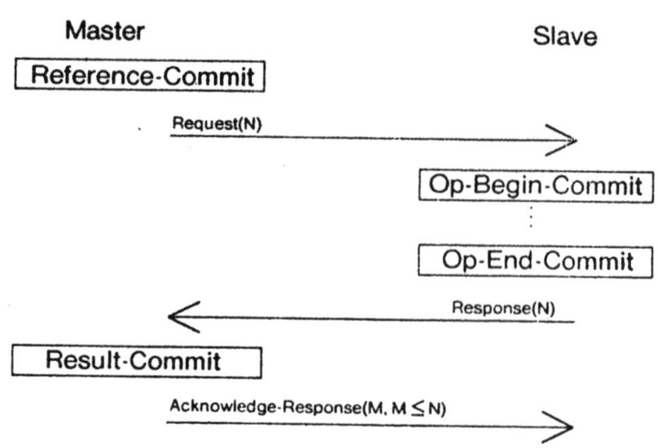

Fig. 5. ESP Packet Format.

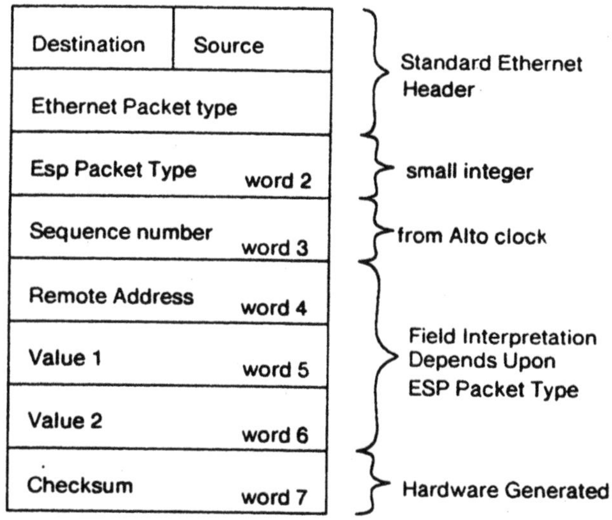

In fact, the code sequence on the slave from **Op-Begin-Commit** to **Op-End-Commit** corresponds to a transaction where the *begin-transaction* takes a unique identifier as an argument and the *commit-transaction* commits the transaction only if the invocation associated with that unique identifier has not already committed.

5. A Case Study: Only-Once-Type-1, Primary, Processor-synchronous References

In the previous sections, many types of remote references were described. The references vary substantially, both in their intended use, and in their implementation. In this section, however, we turn away from the generality of the model in order to study in detail one class of primitives. Our three goals are as follows: to show how the remote reference model terminology applies to a specific example; to illustrate the direct implementation approach that we advocate and show that specialized implementations are feasible; and to show some performance statistics that are indicative of the communication efficiency possible on local networks.

Below, we describe two implementations (one in software, the other in microcode) of **only-once-type-1, value, not-flow-controlled, primary, processor-synchronous** references using a request/response protocol. The software version is a layered implementation with which the performance of the microcoded version can be compared.

The implemented references are called RLDA, RSTA, RENQUEUE, RDEQUEUE, and RCS, and initiate remote load, remote store, remote enqueue, remote dequeue, and remote compare and swap operations, respectively, on a remote machine. The latter operation is similar to the IBM 370 *CS* instruction [11]. The exact semantics of these references are summarized in the appendix. Both implementations use an **RR** protocol which is called "ESP" for *E*fficient *S*ynchronous *P*rotocol. (See Fig. 5 for the packet format.)

The work was done on Xerox Alto computers, a microcoded 16-bit machine with an internal cycle time of 180 nanoseconds, a writeable control store, and a memory bandwidth of 29 megabits/second. The Altos [28], [31] are interconnected with a 2.94 megabit Ethernet. Though the Ethernet is somewhat slower than the networks with which we are primarily concerned and cannot be extended to work at high speeds with the short packets that are used, it is a satisfactory experimental vehicle.

The Alto's macroinstruction set as well as its peripheral device controllers are implemented on the micromachine through the operation of up to 16 microcoded tasks, each executing 32-bit microinstructions. Mechanisms exist to switch between tasks in one microcycle. Because I/O device controllers—including the task that controls the Ethernet—are implemented as microcoded tasks, they can use the full processing capability and temporary storage of the micromachine, and can access main memory easily.

The emulator task microcode that was used provides a macroinstruction set similar to a Data General Nova [7] and executes macroinstructions at about 330 KIPS. No protection or virtual memory facilities are implemented on the Alto.

5.1. Implementation—Software Version

We first implemented a software package that provides five subroutines that implement the RLDA, RSTA, RCS, RENQUEUE, and RDEQUEUE references. These subroutines cause a request packet to be transmitted to a remote Alto and return control when a proper response packet is received or when an error condition is detected. On the remote site, a slave process executes the desired operations and returns an appropriate response.

The software is written entirely in BCPL [6] and uses the raw datagram facilities of PUP Level 0 for packet transport [3]. Sessions are maintained between each pair of communicating processors. Duplicate elimination is handled by the sequence number field of the ESP packet.

5.2. Implementation—Microcode Version

For the purposes of this study, it was sufficient to implement two separate sets of microcode: one allows an Alto to act as a slave that executes and responds to ESP request packets; the other allows an Alto to act as a master and issue RLDA, RSTA, RCS, RENQUEUE and RDEQUEUE instructions, formatting request packets, and awaiting responses. The two sets of microcode could be combined to provide exactly the same function as that provided by the software version, including compatibility with standard PUP communication. However, this would require time-consuming modifications to the Ethernet control task and is not necessary to prove the efficiency that can be achieved for **only-once-type-1, primary, processor-synchronous** references.

Though the microcode is quite similar to the software, it does differ in some respects. First, incoming requests are not queued, because queueing a request would require almost as much work as processing it. Second, the processing time of a request is small in comparison to the amount of time that the Ethernet hardware is busy. Third, microcoded instruction decoding is performed to make the references more efficient. Finally, substantial performance benefits are realized by overlapping memory accesses with processing.

The microcode is simple due to more convenient handling of errors, multitasking, and timeouts in the micromachine. It comprises about 280 instructions though this number could be reduced by more clever microcoding. A total of 7 hardware registers are used in processing. The microcode executing on the slave uses an additional 728 (256 × 3) words of main memory to store the last sequence number and response values for all possible machines connected on the Ethernet. This corresponds to the socket table in Sec. 3.1.

Use of the new instructions is illustrated by the description of RCS in Fig. 6. Instructions take arguments in two general registers as well as in the two words following the operation code. They skip return on success and return results in one or two registers.

On error returns, the sequence number of the request is returned, allowing for additional software retransmission of the request. In our model, this would be done by re-executing the reference as a **process-synchronous** operation and instructing the communication system to use the previous sequence number. To provide the proper error semantics in light of remote processor failure, a flag can be maintained on the slave that is set to 0 when a machine has been restarted after a failure. If a request arrives and finds this flag set to 0, a response can indicate that a machine failure has occurred prior to this request. Requests always set this flag to 1.

Upon receipt of control following a remote instruction, the microcode first collects information from various places and assembles it in a 7-word block of memory. This includes the machine number of both source and destination, the system time (which is used as a sequence number), various data values from the general registers and the words following the instruction, etc. Before the packet is transmitted, one internal register is set with the number of retransmissions and another with a counter that is continuously counted down to allow for

Fig. 6. Instruction Call Sequence for RCS.

```
                <store to-be-checked value in acc. 0>
                <store to-be-stored value in acc. 1>
                <store remote address: >
                <store remote machine number: >
                RCS (opcode 63003)
                1 word for remote machine number <-
                1 word for remote address <-
ERROR-RETURN:   <2 instructions to handle error case>
NORMAL-RETURN:
```

timeouts. A transmission count of 2 and a timeout interval of 3 milliseconds is currently used—a time long enough to permit a long packet on the Ethernet to pass. The small transmission count ensures that the processor does not suspend its operation for too long. With these parameters, the *maximum* time a remote reference can halt processing is 6 milliseconds.

When a response packet is received, its source and sequence number are checked to ensure that it is a response for the last request. If these numbers match, values are placed in one or two general registers and the instruction returns. If they do not match, either the machine waits for another packet, retransmission is attempted, or the instruction returns and indicates an error.

At the remote site, the microcode continually checks the Ethernet to see if a new packet has arrived. If an ESP packet arrives, the source byte is used to index into the socket table.If the sequence number of the received packet is the same as that in the corresponding table entry, the request is a duplicate and a response is generated using the state information saved after the first request. If the sequence number differs, the operation specified by the ESP packet type is performed using the remote address and value fields as arguments. Up to two values resulting from this operation as well as the new sequence number are placed in the table. Finally, a response packet is generated using these values.

5.3. Performance

In the software version, approximately 210 remote references can be executed per second on an unloaded Ethernet; this corresponds to 4.8 milliseconds/reference or about 1500 macro instruction times. Running at maximum speed, two machines communicating using this software package can impose a 1.8 percent load on the Ethernet. Using RSTA instructions, this corresponds to a 3.4 kilobit effective transfer rate. This software implementation is likely to be at least three times faster than any implementation using the PUP byte system protocol—a protocol that provides a full duplex, reliable byte stream protocol from one machine to another. This difference is due to the more complex protocol used by the reliable byte stream protocol and the more general interfaces that it provides.

The microcode version is capable of supporting 6450 references per second corresponding to a time of 155 microseconds/reference. As another characterization, each remote reference takes about 50 macro instruction times. Figure 7 shows a breakdown of the time spent when an RLDA instruction is executed, assuming no contention on the Ethernet. This time is representative of the times of the other instructions as well. Of the 155 microseconds required, transmission time accounts for more than half: 85 microseconds. Local processing leading up to the request requires 28 microseconds, processing at the remote site requires 31 microseconds, and local processing after the response is received requires 11 microseconds.

Fig. 7. Breakdown of Time Spent in RLDA Instruction, Microcoded Version.

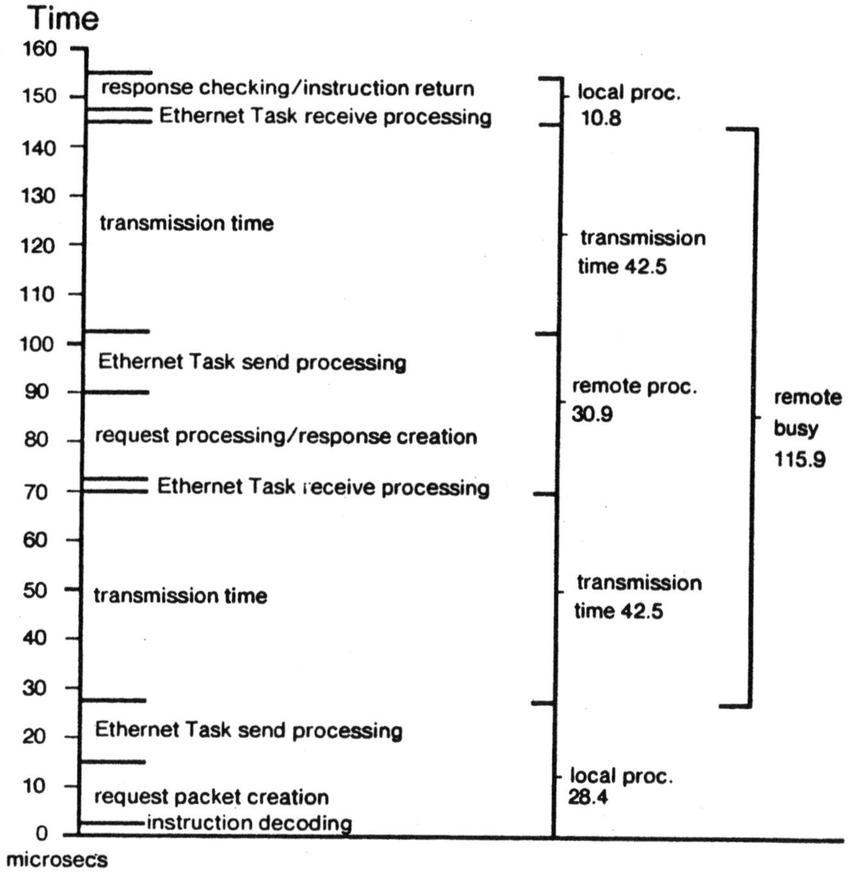

The slave's Ethernet transceiver or processor is busy for 116 microseconds per request. Thus, a shared memory could support a maximum of 8600 references per second. A processor could initiate 6450 remote instructions per second, placing a load on the Ethernet of about 55 percent. In practice, neither the shared memory nor a processor issuing references would operate at their maximum rates.

We have measured a single processor issuing RLDA's to a remote memory at the rate of 5000 per second. The difference between 5000 and the theoretical maximum of 6450 can be accounted for by the time necessary to execute the instruction loop iterating over the RLDA's. The Ethernet load generated by this test was 42 percent or 1.28 megabits. As one would expect, practically no retransmissions or timeouts occurred during this test. Though one would not use RLDA instructions to provide high data throughput, the effective transmission data rate in this test was 80 kilobits. Table III summarizes these yardsticks.

If a processor executed an instruction stream that contained 1 percent remote references, a processor would slow from executing about 330,000 instructions/second to about 220,000 instructions/second, a 33 percent speed degradation. This slowing has implications with respect to the types of distributed programs that could be supported.

In a more complex test, where two machines attempted to generate 5000 requests per second to a slave, severe contention problems on the shared memory occurred. The high load on the memory coupled with the fact that a slave does not listen to the Ethernet while it is processing a request results in many request retransmissions—a type of thrashing. The occurrence of this problem demonstrates that overuse of a resource in this environment is quite harmful.

Finally, in a test to determine if the Ethernet is a limiting factor with two outstanding sessions, two machines made requests to two separate shared memories and collectively put a load on the network of about 64 percent of 1.92 megabits. There were very few collisions or retransmissions but transmission times were longer due to the possibility of having to wait for a packet to pass. The longer transmission times reduced the number of references each machine could generate to about 3750 per second or about 1250 per second less than when only a single session was in use.

Table III. Performance Summary. The parenthesized measurements were achieved in a BCPL program and include iteration overhead.

Description	Software	Microcode
RSTA's/second (achieved)	210	6450 (5000)
microseconds/RSTA	4800	155
Ethernet load (achieved) 1 master => 1 slave	1.8%	55% (43%)
Real Data Rate (achieved)	3.4 Kbits	103 (80) Kbits

5.4 Case Study Results

The case study demonstrated that relatively simple **only-once-type-1, primary, processor-synchronous** references can be implemented efficiently. The performance results show that the microcoded implementation executes about 30 times faster than the software implementation, and probably an additional 3 times faster than a software version built upon a general purpose byte stream protocol. The performance improvement is not surprising given the task switching, queueing, and subroutine calls in the software implementation. What is more surprising and important is the ease with which the direct microcoded implementation could be done.

The timings of the microcoded version show that **processor-synchronous** references are sometimes useful. Some remote references (particularly those that require the transmission of only a few data words) can be performed faster than the time to do a few task switches. Except in rare cases where errors or transmission delays are encountered, the simplification resulting from the **processor-synchronous** attribute can be beneficial.

The good performance of the microcoded version depends heavily upon the rapid decoding of the remote reference and the low process switch time to the communication process. The microtask organization of the Alto hardware facilitated both of these. The performance of the microcoded version would be much improved by the substitution of a 10 megabit Ethernet and slightly different hardware. Certainly, remote reference times could be well under 100 microseconds with these changes.

One point that the case study was *not* trying to make concerns the utility of unprotected shared memory in distributed systems. Where reliability is desired, direct memory reads and writes are potentially dangerous. The enqueue and dequeue instructions are more likely to foster reliability. Additional work on references like those described above must include consideration of protection and virtual memory.

6. Architectural Considerations

Two questions arise from the earlier sections of this work. The first concerns the proper hardware configuration for supporting very efficient implementations of remote references. Particularly, the network controller and underlying type of network are affected. The second involves the class of distributed programs that might be supported on such systems.

With respect to the local network controller, it must be closely integrated with the processor if fine granularity communication is to be supported. The communication process, as defined in the model, can be multiplexed on the processor or implemented on the network controller. However, in either case, process switches to the communication process must be inexpensive and **primary** operations must be executed rapidly. These restrictions require that the communication process must have fast access to main processor memory. In addition, low latency, high bandwidth stable storage is necessary for efficient implementations of **only-once-type-2** references. To lower contention problems on a slave, the network controller should allow reception of back-to-back packets.

The Cm* Kmap [27] is similar in function to a local network controller that can support the communication process. In fact, the Kmap has all the necessary properties (e.g., fast access to processor memory and small process switch times) except the ability to use stable storage. Both Cm* operating systems, StarOS [14] and Medusa [20], use the horizontal microcode executed by the Kmap in much the way that we would have the communication subsystem use the facilities of the local network controller.

With respect to the local network, the reduction in communication processing overhead may lead to increased bandwidth requirements. In addition, if fine granularity communication is important, the network must support the use of small packet lengths to ensure that fine granularity communication does not incur long delays. This combination of small packet sizes and high bandwidth requirements (say, 100 megabits) would probably not allow contention networks like the Ethernet to be used. Ring networks like those of Cambridge [29], TRW [2], or MIT [25] are better suited to high speed, small packet size requirements. We discuss these network-related issues in more detail in [26].

Turning to the implications of more efficient communication, typical applications for local network-based systems such as mail servers and replicated file systems could be more efficiently implemented. It is also possible to consider using such a local network-based architecture for supporting distributed programs of the type that might be executed on shared memory multiprocessors. However, assuming a matched technology (e.g., fifty cached, 1 MIPS, 32-bit processing nodes, two 100 megabit/second ring networks) and about 50 percent network utilization, shared memory access would probably be about two orders of magnitude more costly than local memory accesses. While this is much better than the four orders of magnitude that might be found in traditional communication systems, the few hundred nanoseconds required for a cached reference is difficult to approach with a bit-serial communication link crossing a few hundred meters. Hence, unless multiprocessor algorithms make less than 1 percent of their memory accesses globally, this architecture could not support them.

On the other hand, this architecture would be suitable for multiprocessor algorithms that use somewhat less finely granular communication. If the communication mix were to include some larger block transfers, high data communication rates between processors could be sustained. Thus, an architecture based upon efficient communication on a high speed local network seems to fit somewhere between a shared memory multiprocessor and a conventional network-based system. In some ways, the resulting architecture is similar to the Tandem NonStop System [15].

One other issue affecting distributed programs concerns the utility of **only-once-type-2** references. Though the availability of low latency stable storage could make implementations of **only-once-type-2** references and their corresponding remote operations quite efficient, the fact that the references contain the transaction commit might result in decreased flexibility. A transaction commit that covers the work performed by multiple references is an alternative approach. More work on transaction-based distributed systems will be necessary to resolve this point.

7. Summary

We presented a communication model that includes a taxonomy of communication instructions, called remote references. The specialization of the references permits efficient implementations, and the semantic attributes of the references make them a good basis for the construction of distributed programs. Though relatively complete, the taxonomy could be extended to include more complex types of sessions, such as those with multiple slaves, and to include other semantic attributes such as intra-reference flow control for references having very variable size requests and responses.

Following the discussion of the model, we presented issues that arise when implementing a communication subsystem based upon the model. The experimental communication subsystem for the Altos shows that a streamlined system based upon the model can be implemented with great efficiency.

To demonstrate further the utility of the remote reference/remote operation model, a reasonable subset of communication primitives must be selected and a complete communication subsystem designed. Not all references can be implemented as efficiently as those in the example. But without doubt, they could be implemented much more efficiently than the normal communication mechanisms that are currently used on local networks.

Acknowledgments. I am indebted to Jim Gray and Richard Pattis for their many readings of this document. I would also like to thank Forest Baskett, David Gifford, John Hennessy, Cynthia Hibbard, Bruce Lindsay, Patricia Selinger, and the referees for valuable suggestions and comments.

Appendix

Reference Semantics

```
DEFINE RLDA(MACHINE-NUMBER, ADDRESS) =
  IF NO RESPONSE
    RETURN [ERROR-CONDITION, INTERNAL-SEQ-NUMBER]
    RETURN MACHINE-NUMBER[ADDRESS]
```

```
DEFINE RSTA(MACHINE-NUMBER, ADDRESS, VALUE) =
  IF NO RESPONSE
    RETURN [ERROR-CONDITION, INTERNAL-SEQ-NUMBER]
  MACHINE-NUMBER[ADDRESS] := VALUE
DEFINE RCS(MACHINE-NUMBER, ADDRESS, VALUE-1, VALUE-2) =
  IF NO RESPONSE
    RETURN [ERROR-CONDITION, INTERNAL-SEQ-NUMBER]
  IF MACHINE-NUMBER[ADDRESS] EQ VALUE-1
  THEN BEGIN
    MACHINE-NUMBER[ADDRESS] := VALUE-2
    RETURN IS-EQUAL
  END ELSE BEGIN
    VALUE-1 := MACHINE-NUMBER[ADDRESS]
    RETURN IS-NOT-EQUAL
  END
DEFINE RENQUEUE(MACHINE-NUMBER, ADDRESS, VALUE) =
  IF NO RESPONSE
    RETURN [ERROR-CONDITION, INTERNAL-SEQ-NUMBER]
  IF FULL-QUEUE(MACHINE-NUMBER[ADDRESS])
    THEN RETURN IS-FULL
  ELSE ENQUEUE(MACHINE-NUMBER[ADDRESS], VALUE)
DEFINE RDEQUEUE(MACHINE-NUMBER, ADDRESS) =
  IF NO RESPONSE
    RETURN [ERROR-CONDITION, INTERNAL-SEQ-NUMBER]
  IF EMPTY-QUEUE(MACHINE-NUMBER[ADDRESS])
    THEN RETURN IS-EMPTY
    ELSE RETURN DEQUEUE(MACHINE-NUMBER[ADDRESS])
```

Notes: All remote references are done atomically. The expression referred to as MACHINE-NUMBER[ADDRESS] refers to absolute memory address ADDRESS on the processor referred to by MACHINE-NUMBER.

Received 9/81; revised 11/81; accepted 12/81

References

1. Barlett, Joel F. A nonStop™ kernel. *Proc. 8th Symp. on Operating System Principles*, Dec. 1981, 22–29.
2. Blauman, Sheldon. Labeled slot multiplexing: a technique for a high speed fiber optic based loop network. *Proc. 4th Berkeley Conference on Distributed Data Manipulation and Computer Networks*, (Aug 1979), 309–321.
3. Boggs, David R., Shoch, John F., Taft, Edward A. and Metcalfe, Robert M. *Pup: an internetwork architecture*. Report CSL-79-10, Xerox Palo Alto Research Center, 1979.
4. Cook, R.P. * MOD—a language for distributed programming. *IEEE Trans. on Software Engineering SE6*, 6 (Nov. 1980), 563–571.
5. Cypser, R.J. *Communications Architectures for Distributed Systems*. Addison-Wesley, Reading, MA, 1978.
6. Curry, James E. et al. *BCPL Reference Manual*. Xerox Palo Alto Research Center, 1979.
7. *Introduction to Programming The Nova Computers*. 093-000067, Data General Corp., Southboro, MA, 1972.
8. Folts, Harold C. Coming of age: a long-awaited standard for heterogeneous networks. *Data Communications*, (Jan. 1981).
9. Gray, J., McJones, P., Blasgen M., Lindsay, B., Lorie, R., Price T., Potzulo, F., and Traiger, I. The recovery manager of a database management system. *Computing Surveys 13*, 2 (June 1981), 223–242.
10. Hoare, C.A.R. Communicating sequential processes. *Comm. ACM 12*, 8 (Aug. 1978), 666–677.
11. *IBM System 370 Principles of Operation*. GA22-7000-5, IBM Corporation, Poughkeepsie, 1976.
12. *DOD Standard Transmission Control Protocol*. Report RFC-761, Information Sciences Institute, Marina del Ray, 1980.
13. Ikeda, K., Ebihara, Y., Ishizaka, M., Fujima, T., Nakamura, T., and Kazuhiko, N. Computer network coupled by 100 MBPS optical fiber ring bus—system planning and ring bus subsystem description. *Proc. Compcon*, Nov. 1980, 159–165.
14. Jones, A.K., Chansler, R.J., Durham, I., Schwans, K., and Vegdahl, S.R. Staros, a multiprocessor operating system for the support of task forces. *Proc. 7th Symp. on Operating System Principles*. Dec. 1979, 117–127.
15. Katzman, J.A. A fault tolerant computing system. *11th Hawaii Int. Conf. on System Sciences*. (Jan. 1978); Also appears in Siewiorek, O., Bell, G., and Newell, A.: *Computer Structures: Principles and Examples*. McGraw-Hill, New York, 1981.

16. Lampson, B. and Sturgis, H.K. *Crash Recovery in a Distributed System.* (unpublished), Xerox Palo Alto Research Center, 1979.
17. Liskov, Barbara. *Linguistic support for distributed programs: a status report.* Laboratory for Computer Science Computation Structures Group Memo 201, MIT, Cambridge, 1980.
18. Metcalfe, R.M., and Boggs, D.R. Ethernet: distributed packet switching for local computer networks. *Comm. ACM 19*, 7 (July 1976) 395–404.
19. Nelson, Bruce Jay. *Remote Procedure Call.* Ph.D. Dissertation, Report CMU-CS-81-119, Carnegie-Mellon University, Pittsburgh, PA, 1981.
20. Ousterhout, John K., Scelza, Donald, A., and Sindhu, Pradeep. Medusa: an experiment in distributed operating system structure. *Comm. ACM 23*, 2 (Feb. 1980), 92–105.
21. Peterson, James L. Notes on a workshop on distributed computing. *Operating Systems Review 13*, 3 (July 1979), 18–27.
22. Popek, G., et al. Locus: A network transparent, high reliability distributed system. *Proc. 8th Symp. on Operating System Principles*, Dec. 1981, 169–177.
23. Rawson, E.G., and Metcalfe R.M. Fibernet: multimode optical fibers for local computer networks. *IEEE Trans. on Computer Communication COM-26*, 7 (July 1978), 983–990.
24. Saltzer, J.H. End-to-end arguments in system design. *Proc. 2nd Int. Conf. on Operating Systems.* Paris (April 1981).
25. Saltzer, J.H., Clark, D., and Reed, D. *Version Two Ring Network.* Laboratory for Computer Science Report, MIT, Cambridge, 1981.
26. Spector, Alfred Z. *Multiprocessing Architectures for Local Computer Networks.* Ph.D. Dissertation, Report STAN-CS-81-874, Stanford University, 1981.
27. Swan, R.J., Fuller, S.H., and Siewiorek, D.P. Cm* A modular multi-microprocessor. *Proc. of the National Computer Conference.* June 1977, 636–644.
28. Thacker, C.P., McCreight, E.M., Lampson B.W., Sproull, R.F., and Boggs, D.R. Alto: A personal computer. In Siewiorek, O., Bell, G., and Newell, A. *Computer Structures: Readings and Examples.* Second ed. McGraw Hill, New York, 1981.
29. Wilkes, M.V., and Wheeler, D.J. The Cambridge digital communication ring. *Proc. Local Area Communication Network Symposium.* Boston, May 1979.
30. *ALTO: A Personal Computer System Hardware Manual.* Xerox Palo Alto Research Center, 1979.
31. Zimmerman, H. OSI reference model—the ISO model of architecture for open systems interconnection. *IEEE Trans. on Communication COM-28*, 4 (Apr. 1980), 425–432.

Accent: A communication oriented network operating system kernel

Richard F. Rashid
George G. Robertson
Department of Computer Science
Carnegie-Mellon University
Pittsburgh, PA 15213

Abstract

Accent is a communication oriented operating system kernel being built at Carnegie-Mellon University to support the distributed personal computing project, Spice, and the development of a fault-tolerant distributed sensor network (DSN). Accent is built around a single, powerful abstraction of communication between processes, with all kernel functions, such as device access and virtual memory management accessible through messages and distributable throughout a network. In this paper, specific attention is given to system supplied facilities which support transparent network access and fault-tolerant behavior. Many of these facilities are already being provided under a modified version of VAX/UNIX. The Accent system itself is currently being implemented on the Three Rivers Corp. PERQ.

Keywords: Inter-process communication, networking, virtual memory, paging, UNIX, PERQ, VAX, network operating systems, distributed computation.

This research was sponsored by the Defense Advanced Research Projects Agency (DOD), ARPA Order No. 3597, monitored by the Air Force Avionics Laboratory Under Contract F33615-78-C-1551.

The views and conclusions contained in this document are those of the authors and should not be interpreted as representing official policies, either expressed or implied, of the Defense Advanced Research Projects Agency or the US Government.

1. Introduction

Two independent projects, one for the development of a fault-tolerant distributed sensor network (DSN) and one for a distributed personal computing environment (Spice) are currently underway at CMU. Both projects require as their foundation a network operating system which allows flexible, transparent access to distributed resources. Accent[1] has been developed to satisfy the requirements of these projects.

Specifically, Accent was built to conform to the following design constraints which were viewed as essential to the success of large distributed systems such as Spice and DSN:

- *Modular decomposition.* It must be possible to decompose large problems into smaller modular units which can be run concurrently on a single processor or optionally distributed between several processors on a network.

- *Multiple language support.* The system should support not one but many language environments and provide tools for close interaction between languages.

- *Protection.* Within both the Spice and DSN environments, a single machine may be running a number of processes written by different individuals at different times. In Spice, for example, such programs as mail service daemons, games, editors, compilers and debuggers may all be running simultaneously to satisfy the desires of a particular user. If interactions between these processes were

[1] Accent is a registered trademark of Accent International, Inc. The product it designates is sold as a spice and its only ingredient is monosodium glutamate (MSG).

unpredictable, chaos could result. Blame for errors could not properly be assigned without knowledge of all the programs running at the time of an error.

- *Rapid error detection and tools for transparent fault-recovery, debugging and monitoring.* Multiple process debugging and monitoring, both on a single processor and over a network connection, are essential to building a reliable distributed system. Tools for rapid error detection and fault recovery are also necessary if the system is to be usable and maintainable.

- *Transparent network access.* The location of resources in the distributed system has to be transparent. Without transparent access, processes could not be transported from one machine to another and the decomposition of a task across machine boundaries would be impossible.

- *Uniform access to resources.* It should be possible for any feature provided by the kernel to be provided instead by a process. This includes functions normally thought to be exclusively the preserve of an operating system, such as virtual memory management.

- *Explicit representation of knowledge.* Where possible, information about the functioning of processes is made explicit rather than procedurally embedded. This allows greater latitude for optimization and error detection.

Accent satisfies these constraints by:

- providing the ability to create and control a large number of independent processes on a single processor and supporting a sophisticated form of inter-process communication;

- supporting the notion of multiple, independent virtual address spaces and a virtual machine specification which can accommodate diverse interpretations of process state;

- supplying two kinds of protection: 1) address space protection, to insure that no process can affect another except through the use of the inter-process communication facility, and 2) access protection in the communication facility itself to prevent unauthorized communication between processes;

defining inter-process communication in a way that allows transparent debugging, monitoring and fault recovery;

- taking advantage of these same mechanisms to allow transparent network extension independent of network hardware or protocols;

- allowing all services except the basic communication primitives to be viewed by processes as being provided through a communication interface; and

- structuring message communication to allow intermediary processes such as debuggers, protocol converters or network communication servers to better interpret the contents and purpose of messages.

Accent stands out as a relatively pure example of a *communication oriented* operating system -- i.e. an operating system which uses the abstraction of communication between processes as its basic organizing principle. The integration of virtual memory support, file access and inter-process communication in Accent makes possible performance improvements over previous communication oriented systems (e.g. [1]) as well as a more "transparent" network operating system design.

2. System overview

Physically, the distributed system built around Accent can be viewed as a loosely-connected collection of *host machines*, each with its own primary and secondary storage. The notion of a host machine is flexible in that it can include either uni-processors or tightly coupled multi-processors. In addition, no specific assumptions are made about the technology or topology of the underlying communication network which links together these host machines. The initial host machine chosen for Spice/DSN, the Three Rivers Corporation PERQ, is a uni-processor which currently possesses a 3MHz Ethernet [5] and will eventually possess a 10MHz Ethernet.

Each host machine on the network possesses an *operating system kernel* which in turn supports a collection of *processes* (See Figure 7-1.)

The function of the system kernel is to provide an execution environment for processes running on its host machine. This includes

- *inter-process communication,*

- *virtual memory management, and*

- *process management.*

In addition, the kernel provides

- *the low-level functions of process creation and*

destruction,

- *access to devices through inter-process communication,*

- *support for language and application specific microcode, and*

- *rudimentary support for process monitoring and debugging.*

These kernel functions are similar to those provided by the RIG operating system [1], [2] and satisfy the requirements for a distributed operating system kernel suggested by Watson [4].

The system as a whole can be viewed as having a number of layers, with the system kernel at the bottom and layers of processes providing successively more complex services building upon each other. Inter-process communication (IPC) is the glue which binds processes together. It provides a uniform interface at each level of the system. All objects and services in the system (including those provided by the kernel) are accessible through IPC. Even though the IPC facility of the Accent kernel is defined solely in terms of communication between processes on the same machine, communication can be extended transparently over a network by processes called *network servers*.

3. Inter-process communication

Although processes are the active components of the system, the notion of process is a poor one on which to base a communication facility. Different languages may define multiple concurrent tasks within a single kernel-supported process. Moreover, a given service may be provided over a period of time by a number of different processes.

The basic transport abstraction of the IPC is the notion of a *port*. A port is a protected kernel object into which messages may be placed by processes and from which messages may be removed. All services and facilities provided by a process are made available to other processes through one or more ports.

Ports are intended to be used by processes to represent specific services or data structures. For example, a file system process might associate a separate port with each open file, or a virtual terminal handling process might allocate a port to represent each virtual terminal. However, no restriction is placed on their use. Ports may be used by processes to communicate information in any mutually convenient way.

Logically associated with each port is a queue on which reside messages sent to that port but not yet removed from it by a process. The ability to remove messages from a port is called *receive access*. Only one process may have receive access to a port at a time, although receive access to a port may be transferred to another process in a message.

Ports cannot be directly manipulated or named by a process. Instead, the kernel provides processes with a secure *capability* to send a message to a port and/or extract (receive) a message from it. This capability is a local name for a system object, much in the way a UNIX file descriptor is a local name for a system maintained file, pipe, or device [11]. Port capabilities may be passed in messages, handed down to process children, or destroyed. A given process may have only one local name for a given port at a time. Whenever a port name is passed in a message the system kernel must map that name from the local name space of the sending process into the name space of the receiving process.

The ability to manipulate access to ports allows for the redirection of communication from one process to another and the explicit management of communication between two processes by a third process. It also allows a port to be used to refer to a specific service or process-provided object even in situations in which that service or object is handled by different servers at different times. Neither the address (i.e. the location) or the name of a process can be determined from a capability to send a message to one of its ports. See Figure 7-2.

3.1. Ports

3.1.1. Creating, accessing and destroying ports

A port is created by a process through an *AllocatePort* system call. It is a system object, distinct from the process which created it, but initially *owned* by the creating process. The result of the *AllocatePort* call is a local port name which refers to the created port. This name is logically an index into a correspondence table maintained by the kernel for each process. It has meaning only when used by that process.

Initially the owner of a port also has receive access to it. Ownership of a port and receive access are, however, logically distinct. Ownership of a port may be passed in a message from one process to another, but not shared. Receive access to a port may also be passed in a message but not shared. These restrictions prevent multiple servers from managing the same queue, and are necessary to avoid serious problems which occur when access to a single queue is shared by processes on different machines.

If a single process both owns and has receive access to a port, that process may destroy the port by performing a *DeallocatePort* system call. A process with a capability (local name) to a port may release the capability via the same system call.

A port is automatically destroyed when its owner and the process with receive access to it both die. In either case, all processes with access to that port are notified via emergency messages. If the same process does not both own and have receive access to a port, then the deallocation of the port name by either process results in an emergency error message being sent to the other accompanied by full access rights to that port (i.e., both ownership and receive rights).

The purpose of distinguishing receive access from ownership is to allow a process to take over services or functions provided by other processes in the event those processes should die or malfunction. This is particularly important when writing fail-soft software and can also be used to provide orderly shut-down of services after catastrophic failures.

3.1.2. Software or pseudo interrupts

In the case where a process does not wish to wait for messages explicitly, it is possible to enable a software interrupt which will be triggered upon message reception. The interrupt service routine, executing in the context of that process, can then receive the incoming message and process it or notify the main program of the event in a user defined manner. A mechanism such as this can allow processes which are inherently compute bound to react quickly to incoming messages without using some form of message polling. It can also be used as a way of triggering language defined exceptions across process boundaries.

3.1.3. Flow control

The message queues attached to ports have a finite length. This prevents a sending process from queueing more messages to a receiving process than can be absorbed by the system and provides a means for controlling the flow of data between processes of mismatched processing speed.

Subject to implementation restrictions on maximum port size, the process with receive rights to a port is allowed to specify its *backlog* -- the maximum number of normal messages which may be queued for that port at one time. Should a process attempt to send a message to a full port, one of three things may happen depending on options specified by the sender:

1. The process is suspended until the message can be placed in the queue.

2. The process is notified of an error condition (after perhaps allowing itself to be suspended for up to a specific period of time waiting for the message to be sent).

3. The message is accepted and the kernel sends a message to the sending process when that message can actually be placed in the queue. A maximum of one message per sending process per receiving port may be outstanding in this fashion.

These three options correspond to three different programming situations:

1. The first option is the one most likely to be used by a 'user process' when communicating with a 'server process'. In this situation the user process does not care if it is suspended for some time waiting for a message to be delivered to the server (as in the case of a remote procedure call).

2. The second option is used when a process does not care whether a particular message is sent to a destination, but is using the message only to wake up a dormant partner. The fact that other messages are in the queue for the partner's port indicates that the partner is already scheduled to be activated.

3. The third option is the one most likely to be used by a service process when dealing with a user process. The server probably cannot afford to be suspended waiting on a user to clear its queue. It may also not want to just throw away the message or poll the user explicitly until the message can be sent. The system provides an explicit message event corresponding to the unblocking of the user's port queue.

The flow control scheme described here is not the only reasonable technique for restricting the flow of messages between processes. Other possible mechanisms include limiting the total number of messages which may be outstanding from a given process (as in Brinch Hansen's RC4000 system or CMU's Hydra) or limiting the outstanding messages from a given process to a particular port. Experience with RIG, however, has shown that the exact flow control policy is much less important to overall system performance than the higher level communication protocols devised to solve individual problems. For example, independent of system supplied flow control, processes may choose to communicate is a lock-step fashion via a request/reply or remote procedure call protocol.

3.1.4. Waiting for messages

Although particular protocols may specify synchronous behavior, the receipt of a message is inherently an asynchronous event. In a network environment in particular it becomes possible for error conditions to cause messages to be sent to a process at almost any time. Mechanisms must therefore be provided for a process to check the state of its ports, to wait for activity on one or more of its ports, and to receive messages selectively. It should also be possible for a process to specify a maximum amount of time to wait for a message before reawakening.

Four basic primitives are provided for accomplishing this task. *Receive(SetOfPorts,Message,Timeout)* waits for at most *Timeout* milliseconds and if a message is available during that time from any of the ports designated by *SetOfPorts* then the message is read into *Message* and a boolean value of true is returned. *MessageWait(SetOfPorts,Timeout)* performs a similar function, but does not receive the pending message. It returns the capability of the port from which the next message would be received. *Preview(SetOfPorts,Message,Timeout)* is again similar to *Receive*, but it reads only the header of the next waiting message and does not actually dequeue that message from the port queue. *PortsWithMessagesWaiting(SetOfPorts)* is an informational routine which checks the status of all ports and returns the set of ports with messages waiting.

3.1.5. Sending and receiving kernel messages

Each newly created process has access to two ports whose primary purpose is to allow messages to be sent to and received from the Accent kernel. The first is called the *kernel port* of the process and the kernel logically has the receive rights for this port while the created process has the send rights. The second is called the *data port* and it is normally used by a process to receive messages from the kernel.

The father of a process can, at the time of process creation, ask that other ports to which it has access be given to its child process. The father can also get access to the kernel and data port of the child process. This, taken together with the ability to send port access rights in messages, is the basic mechanism for establishing communication between processes.

3.2. Messages

A message is logically a collection of typed data objects copied from the address space of the sender at the time of a message send call and into the address space of the receiver when a receive call is performed. Physically, a message is divided into two parts: 1) the message header -- which contains information normally associated with all messages and 2) an optional sequence of typed data objects to be sent. The purpose of this division is primarily to optimize the transmission of short control messages and to make it easier for the kernel to find critical information which must always be contained in a message -- such as its destination port.

3.2.1. The message header

The message header contains a small amount of system required message information and is used to form an anchor for the structured part of a message. At minimum it specifies the type of a message and contains a capability for the destination port of a message and a field for a capability (which may be empty) to be used for a reply. The destination and reply ports are more commonly referred to as the *remote* and *local* ports, respectively. The header also contains an ID field to be used for discriminating messages and a pointer to the structured data part of the message.

The header may be checked without actually receiving the data portion of a message by calling *Preview*. The purpose of this facility is to allow a process to check the ID of the message received and select an appropriate message structure for receiving it.

The type of a message contains information which determines the kind of service it requires of the IPC. The following service classes are provided:

- *Flow control*. Normally messages are flow controlled according to the above procedure. The message type can specify, however, that a larger flow control backlog should apply to this message. This allows special high priority messages to be sent to otherwise full ports.

- *Priority*. A range of message priorities is provided. Messages waiting at the same port with different priorities will be received according to the order of their priorities.

- *Sequentiality*. Messages from the same process to a particular port with the same priority are normally guaranteed to arrive in the order they were sent (FIFO). It is possible to relax this constraint by noting in the message type that the order of reception of a particular message is unimportant.

- *Reliability*. A message is guaranteed to arrive at its destination reliably, as long as the destination exists long enough for the message to be received. A message could simply be advisory, however, and it may be unimportant that it arrive at its destination. A message may therefore contain in its message type an indication that it may be delivered unreliably.

- *Maximum age*. A message could become out of date after a certain length of time has passed. A message may therefore be marked as having a maximum age after which it may be destroyed rather than delivered.

- *Security*. A message may be marked as requiring special procedures for ensuring the security of its data. Messages containing password information would fall into this class. Messages marked as 'secure' are encrypted when transmitted on a network or placed on a storage medium which may not be secure.

Two message types have been given special names and play a dominant role in communication:

1. *Normal messages*. A 'normal' message is flow controlled, sequential, reliable, not secure, of lowest priority and has no maximum age. This is the default message type and is assumed to satisfy most communication requirements.

2. *Emergency messages*. Emergency messages are specially flow controlled, sequential, reliable, not secure, of highest priority, and have no maximum age. Emergency messages play an important role in error handling. Because of their high priority, they are guaranteed to be received before any normal messages sent to a port. Their purpose is to allow urgent information to be delivered to a process regardless of that process' current message backlog or message queue. They are used for error notification, special event processing, and debugging.

The notion of message type allows the programmer the ability to specify the exact requirements of his IPC use. This gives the underlying system more information about a message and thus makes possible optimizations in the delivery and management of messages. This use of message types is consistent with the overall goal of making as much of the inner workings of the communication system as possible *visible* to the 'outside world' rather than hidden inside compiled algorithms, thus allowing greater flexibility in optimization, management and monitoring.

Service class information can be considered in some cases as advise. The system may choose, for example, to deliver a message reliably which has been marked as unreliable without affecting the correctness of the programs which use unreliable messages. For the most part service class information has a direct effect only on the management of message traffic by network servers and other intermediary processes.

3.2.2. Message structure

The structured data part of a message is described in detail in [8]. Currently any data structure which contains no self references can be described. A message format which allows an arbitrary graph to be transmitted is now being designed for the DSN project. The purpose of message structure is to provide a standard protocol for communicating typed information. Among the important kinds of typed data which can be passed are capabilities for ports. Only port capabilities are currently checked by the system kernel for correctness. All other data is passed unchecked by the kernel, but may be interpreted, if necessary, by intermediary processes such as network servers or debuggers.

3.3. Exceptional condition handling

Distributed programming imposes a heavy responsibility to handle a multitude of error conditions. Message activity can be pipelined or multiplexed, and the relationships between incoming and outgoing messages can be much richer than in a conventional programming environment (i.e., one in which subroutines are used as the primary structuring mechanism). A faulty process could conceivably crash many processes by sending illegal messages, making it very hard to identify the source of the problem. As a practical matter, it is difficult to ensure complete compatibility between similar programs written by different individuals in different languages. Supposedly interchangeable processes may differ in subtle ways. A failure in a message-based system can quickly lead to finger-pointing.

A variety of facilities for protection, error detection and error handling have been built into the IPC. Illegal process addresses are noted within the send and receive primitives, and the appropriate error returned to the offending process. In addition, processes are protected from accidental or malicious access through the use of port capabilities rather than global port or process identifiers. Whenever a port is destroyed the kernel notifies all processes which still have access to that port via an emergency message. Emergency messages themselves are important because the give processes a a way to reliably communicate errors in situations where normal communication channels are blocked. Software interrupts allow processes to handle error conditions without interfering with normal execution.

3.4. Network inter-process communication

3.4.1. The notion of an intermediary process

The fact that messages are sent to ports rather than processes and that ports are only referred to indirectly by processes allows a single process N to act as an intermediary for communication between two distinct process groups, A and B. Such an intermediary process allocates ports which 'mirror' only those ports used by each of the two process groups for communication with the other. When a message is sent between the two groups it arrives at one of these 'alias' ports and is forwarded to its appropriate final destination. Processes in group A believe that the intermediary ports of N are in fact owned by processes in group B, since all messages sent to those ports have the effect of being delivered to ports which are in fact owned by group B processes. The same is true for processes in group B. Because messages are typed, capabilities for ports can be passed in messages in the same way that they are passed by the kernel, with N substituting the names of its 'alias' ports for those of the corresponding 'real' ports of A and B. Whenever a new, previously unseen, port of A is sent to B in a message, N creates a new local port to correspond to it and passes that onto B in the forwarded message. It is in this way that new communication connections are made between A and B through N. Of course, N must provide some means by which A and B establish an initial connection. This could be done either through string name lookup or through some special function provided by N and known to A and B. See Figure 7-3.

3.4.2. The network server as an intermediary process

A network server which provides a transparent network extension of the IPC can function much like the intermediary process described in the previous section. In the case of inter-machine communication, the process groups A and B are the processes of two host machines X and Y respectively. Two network servers are required, N_1 and N_2 which communicate with each other across a network to provide the correspondence between 'alias' ports. The kernel requires no knowledge of networking or networks for such a mechanism to be provided. See Figure 7-4.

The primary requirement of a network server is that it provide some form of reliable, flow controlled communication between machines which can accommodate the semantics of local IPC communication. A communication path for messages to a port on another machine on the network is identified with a port which belongs to the network server and to which processes may send messages to be forwarded across the network. As in the case of the intermediary process, a process A on machine X can possess a capability for a port to which messages can be sent destined for a process B on machine Y. This capability is in fact a capability for a port owned by a network server N_1 on X, but this is both unknowable and unimportant to A. The exact nature of the connection, the protocols used, the topology of the network, and even the existence of multiple competing networks linking X and Y can be hidden from process A.

For this reason, there is no requirement that there be only a single network server or that all network servers use the same communication protocols or even that 'network servers' actually implement communication on a physical communication link. This allows multiple competing versions of network software to be written and debugged or multiple network links to be provided without affecting the system kernel or existing software.

Where efficiency is critical, the fact that the kernel can act like a process allows the implementation of the network server in the Accent kernel.

3.4.3. Port migration

Just as a network server can fabricate a local port to correspond to a remote port, it is also possible for a port to be 'passed' between processes through a network server. One requirement of this scheme is that there be a way for network servers to know when a message contains a port capability. Along with each such capability sent in a message goes an implicit network connection which would be needed should a message be sent to that port. It is the responsibility of the network server to convert any references to capabilities found in messages forwarded over a network into capabilities local to its host machine.

3.4.4. The use of message types

The concept of message type is important to the efficient functioning of a network server. Message service classes encoded into the message type, such as *unreliable*, *maximum age*, and *security* can be directly translated into actions which can be taken by the network server to speed service or make communication more secure. For example, a distributed sensor net with real time constraints could mark messages containing audio data as having a specific lifetime or as not requiring reliable transmission. If such messages arrive too late they could have no use to the tracking processes. Also, redundancy in the handling of audio data for tracking purposes could make retransmission of error packets unnecessary. At the same time a network server may choose to ignore such advisory class distinctions in the name of simplicity or debugging (where reproducibility is more important than speed).

3.4.5. The use of structured messages

Message structuring is important not only for handling the transmission of port capabilities across networks but also for data conversion in networks with machines which have widely varying data representations for integers, reals, characters, etc. As stated above, it would be appropriate in such networks to reserve certain 'user types' which would have network understood meanings. In this way network servers could provide for data conversion across machine boundaries. Specifically, process A on machine X is communicating with process B on machine Y. A sends B a message containing arbitrary data. The kernel on X packages the data into a host-dependent linearized form and delivers it to the network server, which then delivers the data across the network in a manner which Y can understand. The network server on Y unpacks the data into the host-dependent linearized form for Y and delivers the message to its kernel. If word-size mismatches occur, B can specify in its receive that the data should either be truncated or expanded.

By having this translation performed by the network server rather than the end processes, greater location and implementation independence are obtained and the knowledge of which machines are actually in communication can be hidden by the network. In addition, the translation of data need occur only once rather than twice.

3.4.6. Issues in process migration

The definition of the IPC makes it possible for a process B to migrate from one machine to another on the network without a cooperating process A being aware of the change as long as the network servers involved handle the transfer of the logical communication channel between A and B. Accent provides the tools for migrating processes since all relevant process state (microstate, port queues, and memory) can be extracted from a process and transmitted over a network. When migration occurs due to a hardware problem, however, higher level mechanisms are required for fault-tolerant behavior. In such a case the recreated state of the migrated process probably corresponds to the last 'good' or checkpointed process state and some message communication may have gone on since it was saved. The issue of process migration for fault-tolerance in Accent is therefore not only a kernel problem but also one of properly structuring message communication into atomic transactions.

4. Virtual memory management

In Accent, virtual memory, file storage and IPC are integrated together in a way that preserves the logical structure of inter-process communication while providing performance advantages over previous communication based operating systems. This same melding of virtual memory with IPC makes it possible for Accent to allow one process to manage the virtual address space of another (either by allocating virtual memory from the kernel and sending it to another process or by explicitly managing page faults) and in so doing provides a clean, kernel-transparent mechanism for cross-network paging.

4.1. Virtual memory and files

The virtual address space of an Accent process is flat and linearly addressable. On the PERQ this address space is 2**32 sixteen bit words. An *Accent segment* is the basic unit of virtual memory allocation and secondary storage management. All randomly accessible secondary storage is considered part of the virtual memory of the system and is organized into Accent segments and managed by the kernel.

There are two kinds of Accent segments: *temporary* and *permanent*. Temporary segments are allocated by processes as required for their memory needs and are released when all processes which have access to them are terminated. The storage contained in permanent segments form the basis for the Accent file system. Permanent segments are allocated by sending messages to a special port normally supplied only to special processes. They do not disappear except by explicit request.

Normally, new segments are allocated by the kernel in response to a *CreateSegment* message, with the kernel responding in a message with the newly created segment's identifier. A segment can be explicitly destroyed through the use of a *DestroySegment* message. The data contained in a segment can be read into a processes virtual address space using a *ReadSegment* message. The reply to a ReadSegment message contains the newly allocated pages which are introduced into the requesting process' address space through reception of the message. Similarly, data can be explicitly transferred out of a process' address space through the use of a *WriteSegment* message.

4.2. Optimizing message transfers

Messages are logically copied from a process' address space into a kernel message data structure upon transmission and are logically copied from the kernel to a process' address space upon message reception. Since data is never shared between processes, message communication over a network has precisely the same semantics as local message communication.

Double copy semantics need not, however, imply actually copying the data twice. If a process sends a message pointing to pages in its virtual memory and either releases the memory or simply never changes it, double copy semantics can be preserved by marking the pages referenced in the message as copy-on-write and not actually copying them into the supervisor's address space. Moreover, if the receiver of the message doesn't care about its placement or desires that it be placed in its memory on the same page boundaries no copy of data need be performed at all. Instead, the data pages may be placed directly into the address map of the receiving process.

Thus, when a process sends a message to a port, whole virtual memory pages referenced in the message are not copied but instead marked as copy-on-write in the address space of the sender. Should the sender attempt to change any or all of these pages, new virtual pages will be allocated, filled with the appropriate data, and placed in its address space. On reception into an area of the receiver's virtual memory which is properly aligned, pages referred to in the incoming message are mapped in rather than copied. If the receive desires a different alignment of data than that specified by the sender, a copy operation will be performed.

The utilization of virtual memory by the IPC represents a functionally transparent *optimization* which is not required either for the functioning of the IPC or the virtual memory management facility. Nevertheless, this optimization can be of value in increasing the speed of communication between processes on the same host.

4.3. Optimizing message transfers: an example

The advantage of integrating virtual memory, file storage and IPC is graphically illustrated by the example of file system access provided through messages sent to and from a file system process. The file system process can read secondary storage by sending a message to the kernel. The kernel then sends back a message which contain the virtual pages requested by the file system. This message need look no different than any other message containing data. Moreover the requested pages need never be copied, but are simply placed into the address space of the file system in the normal way that data is placed into the address space of any process when received in a message. If a user requests a block of data, however large, the file system can send it that block in a message, again without ever having the underlying data referenced by either the kernel or the file system. In this way the speed advantages of large PMAPed [3] files can be obtained through the reception of normal IPC messages without resorting to special file mapping primitives.

4.4. Process directed management of virtual memory and network paging

Another advantage of the Accent approach to virtual memory is that it allows virtual memory to be considered a process provided resource. A process can create a *pseudo segment* and "read" it into an unused part of its address space. It is then possible for a process to send another process these 'pseudo pages' in a message. When the message is received, these pages are placed into the address map of the receiving process. When these pages are referenced by the receiving process, messages requesting their contents are sent to a port belonging to the process which created the segment When a changed 'pseudo page' is about to be purged from main memory, its new contents are also sent in a message. This allows a process which is not the kernel to provide kernel-like management of secondary storage. In particular, it makes cross-network paging possible using the standard IPC facility as well as the 'demand transmission' of pages of large messages sent over a network through a network server process.

5. Process Management

The process management system forms the third major part of the operating system kernel. It interacts with the virtual memory management and inter-process communication systems to provide the execution environment for processes running on a host machine.

As mentioned earlier, all communication between a user process and the kernel is through a port, called its *kernel port*, which is created when the process is created. Since ports can be sent in messages to other processes, it is possible for process A to send its kernel port to process B. The process system is designed so that process B can manage process A's behavior, much the same way the virtual memory system allows one process to manage another's virtual memory. This mechanism forms the basis for remote debugging and monitoring systems.

A number of issues were addressed in building the process management component of Accent:

- *Simple user interface.* From the user's point of view, the process system is quite simple. The basic primitives allow process creation and destruction with *Fork* and *Terminate*, process monitoring with *Status*, and process control with *SetPriority*, *SetLimit* (which sets a runtime time limit), *Suspend*, and *Resume*.

- *Multiple language support.* Mechanisms are provided for supporting languages with different notions of process state. In particular, different languages will have different underlying microcode support. In order to support multiple languages at this level, most of the process mechanisms are forced down to the microcode level. A *MicroKernel* has been defined to provide this support. The MicroKernel consists of all the language independent microcode support, including process queue management, process state switch and context swap, low level scheduling, I/O support, interrupt support, and virtual address translation. The MicroKernel is defined so that language microcode interfaces to it in a small number of well-defined ways (e.g., the number of registers to include in context swap is language dependent and is stored in a fixed register).

- *High performance.* The context swap mechanism is language independent, yet quite fast. Since the virtual memory system requires no change of page map on context swap, only language dependent microcode registers need to be swapped. In the current version of the Accent kernel microcode a context switch from one PASCAL virtual machine to another requires 50 microseconds (or about the cost of two PASCAL procedure calls).

- *Scheduling control.* The process scheduling system provides time slice scheduling with sixteen priority levels. Preemption is provided to enable time critical processes to meet their demands. Aging is provided to support some degree of fairness in scheduling.

- *Simple interrupt structure.* The traditional interrupt structure is not being supported in this system. Hardware interrupts are serviced in the MicroKernel, and processes waiting on service are simply awakened. Preemptive scheduling is used if the awakened process is time critical. At the process level, there is no notion of hardware interrupt. However, there is a notion of software interrupt, which is tied closely to the inter-process communication system. Any receipt of a normal or emergency message will flag a software interrupt for the receiving process. Since different languages will represent software interrupts in different ways, it is left to the language microcode support to interpret the interrupt flag (on resumption from a context swap) and reflect it to the user in whatever way is appropriate for that language.

6. Current status of Accent

An implementation of the Accent IPC facility as a communication facility for VAX/UNIX has been in use since March, 1980 [7]. Network servers written in PASCAL have also been implemented and are now in use. The PERQ implementation of the full Accent kernel is now (September 1980) being tested and refined.

7. Final thoughts

One of the first (and suprisingly most controversial) decisions made in the design of Accent was the determination that every kernel supported process should have a logically distinct and independent address space. The reasons for this decision were:

- Not all languages are "safe" in the sense that a properly compiled and loaded program can be expected to respect the integrity of storage which is not its own. Examples of unsafe languages include BCPL, C, and PASCAL. Even languages which are often thought of as safe have embarrassing loopholes which make address space protection important.

- It is usually easier to construct a runtime environment for a language if it does not have to be integrated into the same address space as other language environments. Moreover, decisions about the use of an address space by a language, once made, need not be reviewed every time a new language gets added to the system. This is simply a modularity argument, but it can be important in practice.

- Both DSN and Spice have the requirement that a single processor may need to support a large number of simultaneous processes, many of them written by different individuals with varying levels of programming expertise. It is important for the isolation of problems that errors generated in a given subsystem not be allowed to propagate at random through other subsystems. Address space protection provides an important tool for controlling inter-program error propagation.

- It is very difficult to provide truly transparent

networking if processes can potentially have interactions which the system itself cannot detect.

This decision to support multiple independent address spaces on a single personal computer should be contrasted with the approach being taken by others currently doing similar research. The XEROX Pilot operating system [10], for example, provides a single (currently 24 bit) address space for all concurrent processes it supports. It can do this because it supports only one programming language (MESA) which has been designed to reduce the probability of inter-program contamination.

One significant disadvantage of the Accent approach is that it is often time-consuming for existing computers to switch from one logical address space to another. One reason for Pilot's single address space design is that its target machine has a single large set of virtual address mapping registers which would have to be updated in order to switch contexts. As another example, the VAX 11/780 uses a content addressable address translation buffer to provide both a larger address space and faster context switching. Unfortunately the buffer must be flushed on a context switch and refilling the buffer for the new process results in switching times on the order of hundreds of microseconds.

'Message-based' has often in the past been synonymous with 'slow', largely because of the cost of context-switching and the lack of microcode support for message-passing primitives comparable to the support which exists in most hardware architectures for procedure-calling. Some machines, however, do provide acceptable address space switching times. The PRIME 750, for example, can switch address spaces in less than ten microseconds [6]. The key to the PRIME approach is the use of the process identifier as part of the virtual address. In the PERQ system we have adopted a similar scheme with the result that context switching times are comparable to two PERQ procedure calls. In addition, the Accent message-passing scheme, even though it provides for a the handling of large, complex data structures, also allows simple messages to be constructed and passed between processes using microcode support similar in complexity to that for subroutine argument passing in PASCAL [9].

The decision to build a communications based system on the notion of protected ports and port capabilities was based on considerable past experience with message based operating systems both at CMU and the University of Rochester. Ports simplify the problems of network communication and protection by decoupling networking from intra-machine communication and providing an abstraction of function which does not depend upon a particular implementation of processes. Ports can be used to represent functions independent of how those functions are implemented. They can be used to specify kernel objects (such as files or process management functions) or objects maintained by processes. All access to the outside world is mediated through ports with the notion of system call reduced to the notion of sending and receiving messages.

Protection derives from the fact that ports are protected kernel objects to which processes only have a local reference. The right to send a message to a port cannot be forged or accidentally created. This prevents processes which are either buggy or malevolent from gaining fraudulent access to resources and it allows the writer of a process to make a positive statement about the correctness of his program based on precise knowledge of which other processes are allowed to communicate with it.

The existence of access lists also provides the kernel with complete knowledge of the communication rights of processes. It is not possible for a process to hide a reference to another process' port in its private address space. The system can know who is talking with whom and notify processes which have access to a port when that port is destroyed. Knowledge of inter-process communication paths can also be used as an aid in intelligently scheduling systems with tightly coupled communicating processes.

Finally, the fact that the location of a port can change at will as can the nature of the process serving it, without affecting the processes using the port allows transparent process migration and fail-soft performance.

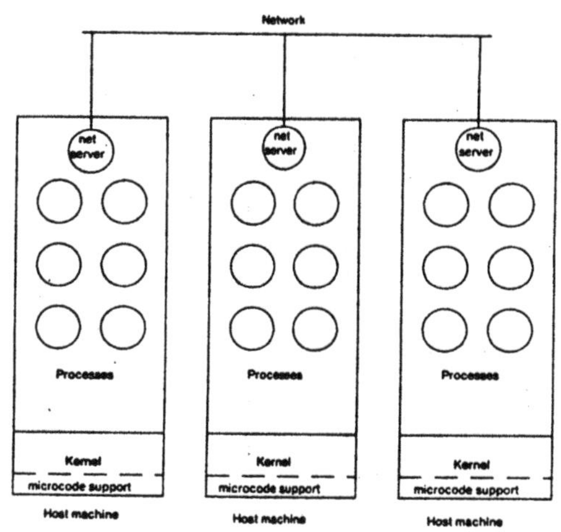

Figure 7-1: Overview of system

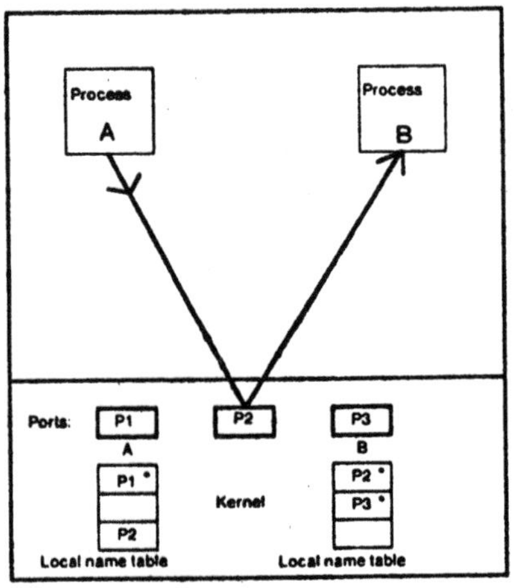

Figure 7-2: Path of message communication

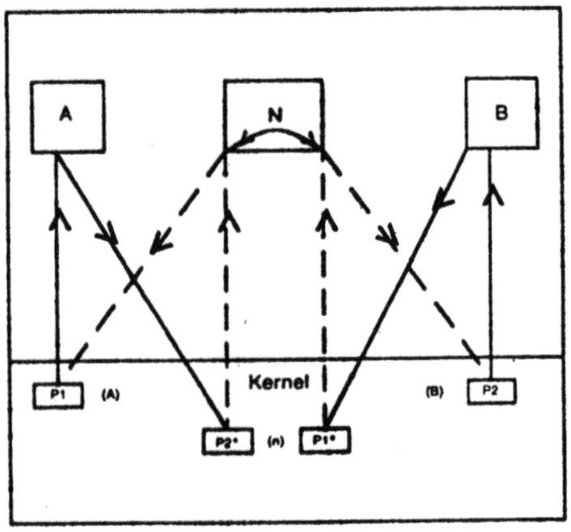

Figure 7-3: Communication via an intermediary process

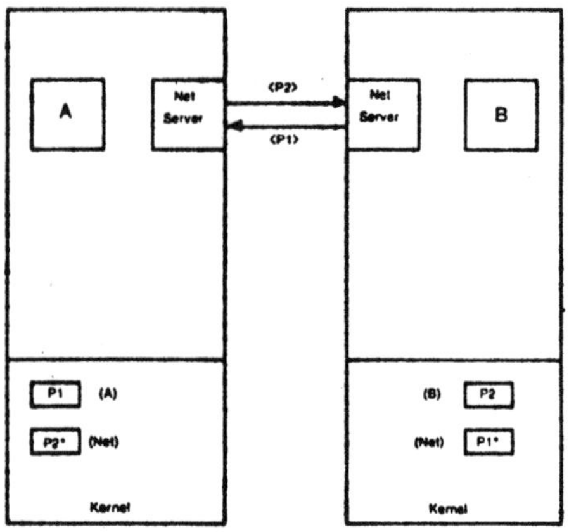

Figure 7-4: Network communication

Bibliography

1. J.E. Ball, J.A. Feldman, J.R. Low, R.F. Rashid, and P.D. Rovner. "RIG, Rochester's Intelligent Gateway: System overview." *IEEE Trans. on Software Eng. 2*, 4 (December 1976), 321-328.

2. J. E. Ball, E. Burke, I. Gertner, K. A. Lantz, and R. F. Rashid. Perspectives on message-based distributed computing. Proceedings 1979 Networking Symposium, IEEE, December, 1979, pp. 46-51.

3. Bobrow, D.G., Burchfiel, J.D., Murphy, D.L. and Tomlinson, R.S. "TENEX, a paged time sharing system for the PDP-10." *Comm. ACM 15*, 3 (March 1972), 135-143.

4. Lampson, Butler, ed.. *Distributed Systems Architecture and Implementation: An Advanced Course*. Springer-Verlag, 1981.

5. Metcalf, Robert and Boggs, David. "Ethernet: Distributed Packet Switching for Local Computer Networks." *Comm. ACM 19*, 7 (July 1976), 395-404.

6. ----. Prime Reference Guide: System architecture and instructions. Tech. Rept. IDR3060, Prime Computer, Inc., July, 1978.

7. R. Rashid. An inter-process communication facility for UNIX. Tech. Rept. CMU-CS-80-124, Computer Science Department, Carnegie-Mellon University, February, 1980.

8. R. Rashid. Accent: A network operating system for SPICE/DSN. Tech. Rept. , Computer Science Department, Carnegie-Mellon University, May, 1981.

9. R. Rashid. The Accent kernel interface manual. Tech. Rept. , Computer Science Department, Carnegie-Mellon University, September, 1981.

10. Redell, D.D., Dalal, Y.K., Horsley, T.R., Lauer, H.C., Lynch, W.C., McJones, P.R., Murray, H.G. and Purcell, S.C. Pilot: An operating system for a personal computer. Proceedings of the 7th Symposium on Operating Systems Principles, December, 1979, pp. 106-107.

11. Ritchie, D.M. and Thompson, K. "The UNIX time-sharing system." *Bell System Technical Journal* (July 1978).

The Distributed V Kernel and its Performance for Diskless Workstations

David R. Cheriton and Willy Zwaenepoel

Computer Systems Laboratory
Departments of Computer Science and Electrical Engineering
Stanford University

Abstract

The distributed V kernel is a message-oriented kernel that provides uniform local and network interprocess communication. It is primarily being used in an environment of diskless workstations connected by a high-speed local network to a set of file servers. We describe a performance evaluation of the kernel, with particular emphasis on the cost of network file access. Our results show that over a local network:

1. Diskless workstations can access remote files with minimal performance penalty.
2. The V message facility can be used to access remote files at comparable cost to any well-tuned specialized file access protocol.

We conclude that it is feasible to build a distributed system with all network communication using the V message facility even when most of the network nodes have no secondary storage.

1. Introduction

The distributed V kernel is a message-oriented kernel that provides uniform local and network interprocess communication. The kernel interface is modeled after the Thoth [3, 5] and Verex [4, 5] kernels with some modifications to facilitate efficient local network operation. It is in active use at Stanford and at other research and commercial establishments. The system is implemented on a collection of MC68000-based SUN workstations [2] interconnected by a 3 Mb Ethernet [9] or 10 Mb Ethernet [7]. Network interprocess communication is predominantly used for remote file access since most SUN workstations at Stanford are configured without a local disk.

This paper reports our experience with the implementation and use of the V kernel. Of particular interest are the controversial aspects of our approach, namely:

1. The use of diskless workstations with all secondary storage provided by backend file servers.
2. The use of a general purpose network interprocess communication facility (as opposed to special-purpose file access protocols) and, in particular, the use of a Thoth-like interprocess communication mechanism.

The more conventional approach is to configure workstations with a small local disk, using network-based file servers for archival storage. Diskless workstations, however, have a number of advantages, including:

1. Lower hardware cost per workstation.
2. Simpler maintenance and economies of scale with shared file servers.
3. Little or no memory or processing overhead on the workstation for file system and disk handling.
4. Fewer problems with replication, consistency and distribution of files.

The major disadvantage is the overhead of performing all file access over the network. One might therefore expect that we use a carefully tuned specialized file-access protocol integrated into the transport protocol layer, as done in LOCUS [11]. Instead, our file access is built on top of a general-purpose interprocess communication (IPC) facility that serves as the transport layer. While this approach has the advantage of supporting a variety of different types of network communication, its generality has the potential of introducing a significant performance penalty over the "problem-oriented" approach used in LOCUS.

Furthermore, because sequential file access is so common, it is conventional to use streaming protocols to minimize the effect of network latency on performance. Instead, we adopted a synchronous "request-response" model of message-passing and data transfer which, while simple and efficient to implement as

This work was sponsored in part by the Defense Advanced Research Projects Agency under contracts MDA903-80-C-0102 and N00039-83-K-0431.

well as relatively easy to use, does not support application-level use of streaming.

These potential problems prompted a performance evaluation of our methods, with particular emphasis on the efficiency of file access. This emphasis on file access distinguishes our work from similar studies [10, 13]. The results of our study strongly support the idea of building a distributed system using diskless workstations connected by a high-speed local network to one or more file servers. Furthermore, we show that remote file access using the V kernel IPC facility is only slightly more expensive than a lower bound imposed by the basic cost of network communication. From this we conclude that relatively little improvement in performance can be achieved using protocols further specialized to file access.

2. V Kernel Interprocess Communication

The basic model provided by the V kernel is that of many small processes communicating by messages. A process is identified by a 32-bit globally unique *process identifier* or *pid*. Communication between processes is provided in the form of short fixed-length messages, each with an associated reply message, plus a data transfer operation for moving larger amounts of data between processes. In particular, all messages are a fixed 32 bytes in length.

The common communication scenario is as follows: A *client* process executes a ***Send*** to a *server* process which then completes execution of a ***Receive*** to receive the message and eventually executes a ***Reply*** to respond with a reply message back to the client. We refer to this sequence as a *message exchange*. The receiver may execute one or more ***MoveTo*** or ***MoveFrom*** data transfer operations between the time the message is received and the time the reply message is sent.

The following sections describe the primitives relevant to this paper. The interested reader is referred to the V kernel manual [6] for a complete description of the kernel facilities.

2.1. Primitives

Send(message, pid)

Send the 32-byte message specified by *message* to the process specified by *pid*. The sender blocks until the receiver has received the message and has sent back a 32-byte reply using ***Reply***. The reply message overwrites the original message area.

Using the kernel message format conventions, a process specifies in the message the *segment* of its address space that the message recipient may access and whether the recipient may read or write that segment. A segment is specified by the last two words of a message, giving its start address and its length respectively. Reserved flag bits at the beginning of the message indicate whether a segment is specified and if so, its access permissions.

pid = Receive(message)

Block the invoking process, if necessary, to receive a 32-byte message in its message vector. Messages are queued in first-come-first-served (FCFS) order until received.

(pid, count) = ReceiveWithSegment(message, segptr, segsize)

Block the invoking process to receive a message as with ***Receive*** except, if a segment is specified in the message with read access, up to the first *segsize* bytes of the segment may be transferred to the array starting at *segptr*, with *count* specifying the actual number of bytes received.

Reply(message, pid)

Send a 32-byte reply contained in the message buffer to the specified process providing it is awaiting a reply from the replier. The sending process is readied upon receiving the reply; the replying process does not block.

ReplyWithSegment(message, pid, destptr, segptr, segsize)

Send a reply message as done by ***Reply*** but also transmit the short segment specified by *segptr* and *segsize* to *destptr* in the destination process' address space.

MoveFrom(srcpid, dest, src, count)

Copy *count* bytes from the segment starting at *src* in the address space of *srcpid* to the segment starting at *dest* in the active process's space. The *srcpid* must be awaiting reply from the active process and must have provided read access to the segment of memory in its address space using the message conventions described under ***Send***.

MoveTo(destpid, dest, src, count)

Copy *count* bytes from the segment starting at *src* in the active process's space to the segment starting at *dest* in the address space of the *destpid* process. The *destpid* must be awaiting reply from the active process and must have provided write access to the segment of memory in its address space using the message conventions described under ***Send***.

SetPid(logicalid, pid, scope)

Associate *pid* with the specified *logicalid* in the specified scope, which is one of local, remote or both. Example *logicalid's* are *fileserver, nameserver*, etc.

pid = GetPid(logicalid, scope)

Return the process identifier associated with *logicalid* in the specified scope if any, else 0.

2.2. Discussion

The V kernel's interprocess communication is modeled after that of the Thoth and Verex kernels, which have been used in multi-user systems and real-time applications for several years. An extensive discussion of this design and its motivations is available [5], although mainly in the scope of a single machine system. We summarize here the highlights of the discussion.

1. Synchronous request-response message communication makes programming easy because of the similarity to procedure calls.
2. The distinction between small messages and a separate data transfer facility ties in well with a frequently observed usage pattern: A vast amount of interprocess communication is transfer of small amounts of control information (e.g. device completion) while occasionally there is bulk data transfer (e.g. program loading).
3. Finally, synchronous communication and small, fixed-size messages reduce queuing and buffering problems in the kernel. In particular, only small, fixed-size message buffers

must be allocated in the kernel and large amounts of data are transferred directly between users' address spaces without extra copies. Moreover, by virtue of the synchrony of the communication, the kernel's message buffers can be statically allocated. As exemplified in Thoth, these factors make for a small, efficient kernel.

The V message primitives appear ill-suited in several ways for a network environment, at least on first observation. The short, fixed-length messages appear to make inefficient use of large packet sizes typically available on local networks. The synchronous nature of the message sending would seem to interfere with the true parallelism possible between separate workstations. And the economies of message buffering afforded by these restrictions in a single machine implementation are less evident in a distributed environment. Finally, the separate data transfer operations ***MoveTo*** and ***MoveFrom*** appear only to increase the number of remote data transfer operations that must be implemented in the distributed case.

However, our experience has been that the V message primitives are easily and efficiently implemented over a local network. Moreover, we have found that the semantics of the primitives facilitated an efficient distributed implementation. The only major departure from Thoth was the explicit specification of segments in messages and the addition of the primitives ***ReceiveWithSegment*** and ***ReplyWithSegment***. This extension was done for efficient page-level file access although it has proven useful under more general circumstances, e.g. in passing character string names to name servers.

3. Implementation Issues

A foremost concern in the implementation of the kernel has been efficiency. Before describing some of the implementation details of the individual primitives, we list several aspects of the implementation that are central to the efficient operation of the kernel.

1. Remote operations are implemented directly in the kernel instead of through a process-level network server. When the kernel recognizes a request directed to a remote process, it immediately writes an appropriate packet on the network. The alternative approach whereby the kernel relays a remote request to a network server who then proceeds to write the packet out on the network incurs a heavy penalty in extra copying and process switching. (We measured a factor of four increase in the remote message exchange time.)

2. Interkernel packets use the "raw" Ethernet data link level. The overhead of layered protocol implementation has been described many times [10]. An alternative implementation using internet (IP) headers showed a 20 percent increase in the basic message exchange time, even without computing the IP header checksum and with only the simplest routing in the kernel. While we recognize the tradeoff between internet functionality and local net performance, we have chosen not to burden the dominant (local net) operation with any more overhead than is strictly necessary.

3. The synchronous request-response nature of a reply associated with each message is exploited to build reliable message transmission directly on an unreliable datagram service, i.e. without using an extra layer (and extra packets) to implement reliable transport. The reply message serves as an acknowledgement as well as carrying the reply message data.

4. The mapping from process id to process location is aided by encoding a host specification in the process identifier. The kernel can thus determine quickly whether a process is either local or remote, and in the latter case on which machine it resides.

5. There are no per-packet acknowledgements for large data transfers (as in ***MoveTo*** and in ***MoveFrom***). There is only a single acknowledgement when the transfer is complete.

6. File page-level transfers require the minimal number of packets (i.e. two) because of the ability to append short segments to messages using ***ReceiveWithSegment*** and ***ReplyWithSegment***.

The following sections look at particular aspects of the implementation in greater detail.

3.1. Process Naming

V uses a global (flat) naming space for specifying processes, in contrast to the local port naming used in DEMOS [1] and Accent [12]. Process identifiers are unique within the context of a local network. On the SUN workstation, it is natural for the V kernel to use 32-bit process identifiers. The high-order 16 bits of the process identifier serve as a *logical host identifier* subfield while the low-order 16 bits are used as a locally unique identifier.

In the current 3 Mb Ethernet implementation, the top 8 bits of the logical host identifier are the physical network address of the workstation, making the process identifier to network address mapping trivial. In the 10 Mb implementation, a table maps logical hosts to network addresses. When there is no table entry for the specified logical host, the message is broadcast. New "logical host-to-network address" correspondences can be discovered from messages received. However, each node must at least know or discover its own logical host identifier during kernel initialization.

The use of an explicit host field in the process identifier allows distributed generation of unique process identifiers between machines and allows an efficient mapping from process id to network address. In particular, it is very efficient to determine whether a process is local or remote. This "locality" test on process identifiers serves as the primary invocation mechanism from the local kernel software into the network IPC portion. In general, most V kernel operations differ from their Thoth implementation by a call to a "non-local" handler when one of the process identifier parameters fails to validate as a local process. With the exception of ***GetPid***, kernel operations with no process identifier parameters are implicitly local to the workstation.

GetPid uses network broadcast to determine the mapping of a logical process identifier to real process identifier if the mapping is not known to the local kernel. Any kernel knowing the mapping can respond to the broadcast request. The addition of local and remote scopes was required to discriminate between server processes that serve only a single workstation and those that serve the network.

3.2. Remote Message Implementation

When a process identifier is specified to ***Send*** with a logical host identifier different from that of the local machine, the local pid validation test fails and ***Send*** calls ***NonLocalSend*** which handles transmission of the message over the network.

The ***NonLocalSend*** routine writes a interkernel packet on the network addressed to the host machine of this process or else broadcasts the packet if the host machine is not known. When the host containing the recipient process receives the packet, it creates an *alien* process descriptor to represent the remote sending process using a standard kernel process descriptor[1] and saves the message in the message buffer field of the alien process descriptor. When the receiving process replies to the message, the reply is transmitted back to the sender as well as being saved for a period of time in the alien descriptor. If the sender does not receive a reply within the timeout period T, the original message is retransmitted by the sender's kernel. The receiving kernel filters out retransmissions of received messages by comparing the message sequence number and source process with those represented by the aliens. The kernel responds to a retransmitted message by discarding the message and either retransmitting the reply message or else sending back a "reply-pending" packet to the sending kernel if the reply has not yet been generated. It also sends back a reply-pending packet if it is forced to discard a new message because no (alien) process descriptors are available. The sending kernel concludes the receiving process does not exist (and thus the ***Send*** has failed) if it receives a negative acknowledgement packet or it retransmits N times without receiving either a reply message or a reply-pending packet.

This description supports the claim made above that reliable message transmission is built immediately on top of an unreliable datagram protocol with the minimal number of network packets in the normal case.

3.3. Remote Data Transfer

MoveTo and ***MoveFrom*** provide a means of transferring a large amount of data between remote processes with a minimal time increase over the time for transferring the same amount of data in raw network datagrams. ***MoveTo*** transmits the data to be moved in a sequence of maximally-sized packets to the destination workstation and awaits a single acknowledgement packet when all the data has been received. Given the observed low error rates of local networks, full retransmission on error introduces only a slight performance degradation. We have, however, implemented retransmission from the last correctly received data packet in order to avoid the pitfall of repeated identical failures arising when back-to-back packets are consistently being dropped by the receiver. The implementation of ***MoveFrom*** is similar except a ***MoveFrom*** request is sent out and acknowledged by the requested data packets, essentially the reverse of ***MoveTo***.

As in the local case, major economies arise with ***MoveTo*** and ***MoveFrom*** because, by their definitions, there is no need for queuing or buffering of the data in the kernel. The V kernel moves the data directly from the source address space into the network interface, and directly from the network interface to the destination address space[2].

3.4. Remote Segment Access

The message and data transfer primitives provide efficient communication of small amounts and large amounts of data, less than 32 bytes or several tens of network packets. However, page-level file access requests involve an intermediate amount of data that is not efficiently handled by the Thoth primitives when implemented over a local network.

V file access is implemented using an I/O protocol developed for Verex [4]. To read a page or block of a file, a client sends a message to the file server process specifying the file, block number, byte count and the address of the buffer into which the data is to be returned. The server reads the data off disk, transfers it into the remote buffer using ***MoveTo***, and then replies, confirming the amount of data read. In the common case of the data fitting into a single network packet, this requires 4 packet transmissions (assuming no retransmissions): one for the ***Send***, 2 for the ***MoveTo*** and one for the ***Reply***. This is double the number of packets required by a specialized page-level file access protocol as used, for instance, in LOCUS [11] or WFS [14].

To remedy this problem, we made some modifications to the original Thoth kernel interface. First, we added the primitives ***ReceiveWithSegment*** and ***ReplyWithSegment***. Second, we required explicit specification of segments in messages (as described in Section 2.1). Using this explicit specification, ***Send*** was then modified to transmit, as part of the network packet containing the message, the first part of a segment to which read access has been granted, if any. Using the ***ReceiveWithSegment*** operation, the recipient process is able to receive the request message and the first portion of the segment in a single operation. By setting the size of the initial portion of the segment sent to be

[1] Use of standard kernel process descriptors for aliens reduces the amount of specialized code for handling remote messages. However, alien processes do not execute and can reasonably be thought of as message buffers.

[2] This is possible with a programmed I/O interface, as used by the SUN 3 Mb Ethernet interface as well as the 3COM 10 Mb Ethernet interface. A conventional DMA interface may require a packet assembly buffer for transmission and reception.

at least as large as a file block, a file write operation is reduced to a single two packet exchange. In this fashion, read access to small segments (such as single block disk write operations) is handled efficiently. The ***ReplyWithSegment*** operation eliminates the extra packets in the case of a file read by combining the reply message packet with the data to be returned.

Advantages of this approach include:

1. The advantages of the Thoth IPC model with the network performance of a WFS-style file access protocol.
2. Compatibility with efficient local operation. For instance, segments may be accessed directly if in the same address space or if the recipient process operates a DMA device.
3. Use of ***ReceiveWithSegment*** and ***ReplyWithSegment*** is optional and transparent to processes simply using ***Send***.

An expected objection to our solution is the apparent asymmetry and awkwardness of the message primitives. We feel the asymmetry may be appropriate given the prevalent asymmetry of communication and sophistication between client and server processes. Also, it is not unexpected that there be some conflict between efficiency and elegance. Given that applications commonly access system services through stub routines that provide a procedural interface to the message primitives, it is not inappropriate to make some compromises at the message level for efficiency.

We now turn to the discussion of the performance evaluation of the kernel. We first define the term *network penalty* as a reasonable lower bound on the cost of network communication. Subsequently we discuss the efficiency of the kernel, both in terms of message passing and file access.

4. Network Penalty

Our measurements of the V kernel are primarily concerned with two comparisons:

1. The cost of remote operations versus the cost of the corresponding local operations.
2. The cost of file access using V kernel remote operations versus the cost for other means of network file access.

An important factor in both comparisons is the cost imposed by network communication. In the first comparison, the cost of a remote operation should ideally be the cost of the local operation plus the cost of moving data across the network (data that is in shared kernel memory in the local case). For instance, a local message ***Send*** passes pointers to shared memory buffers and descriptors in the kernel while a remote message ***Send*** must move the same data across the network. In the second comparison, the basic cost of moving file data across the network is a lower bound on the cost for any network file access method.

To quantify the cost of network communication, we define a measure we call the *network penalty*. The network penalty is defined to be the time to transfer n bytes from one workstation to another in a network datagram on an idle network and assuming no errors. The network penalty is a function of the processor, the network, the network interface and the number of bytes transferred. It is the minimal time penalty for interposing the network between two software modules that could otherwise transmit the data by passing pointers. The network penalty is obtained by measuring the time to transmit n bytes from the main memory of one workstation to the main memory of another and vice versa and dividing the total time for the experiment by 2. The experiment is repeated a large number of times for statistical accuracy. The transfers are implemented at the data link layer and at the interrupt level so that no protocol or process switching overhead appears in the results. The assumptions of error-free transmission and low network utilization are good approximations of most local network environments.

Network penalty provides a more realistic minimum achievable time for data transfer than that suggested by the physical network speed because it includes the processor and network interface times. For instance, a 10 Mb Ethernet can move 1000 bits from one workstation to another in 100 microseconds. However, the time to assemble the packet in the interface at the sending end and the time to transfer the packet out of the interface at the receiving end are comparable to the time for transmission. Thus, the time for the transfer from the point of view of the communicating software modules is at least two or three times as long as that implied by the physical transfer rate.

Measurements of network penalty were made using the experimental 3 Mb Ethernet. In all measurements, the network was essentially idle due to the unsociable times at which measurements were made. Table 4-1 lists our measurements of the 3 Mb network penalty for the SUN workstation using the 8 and 10 MHz processors with times given in milliseconds. The network time column gives the time for the data to be transmitted based on the physical bit rate of the medium, namely 2.94 megabits per second.

Network Penalty

Bytes[3]	Network Time	Network Penalty	
		8 MHz	10 MHz
64	.174	0.80	0.65
128	.348	1.20	0.96
256	.696	2.00	1.62
512	1.392	3.65	3.00
1024	2.784	6.95	5.83

Table 4-1: 3 Mb Ethernet SUN Network Penalty (times in msec.)

The network penalty for the 8 MHz processor is roughly given by $P(n) = .0064 * n + .390$ milliseconds where n is the number of bytes transferred. For the 10 MHz processor, it is $.0054 * n + .251$ milliseconds.

[3]We only consider packet sizes that fit in a single network datagram.

The difference between the network time, computed at the network data rate, and the measured network penalty time is accounted for primarily by the processor time to generate and transmit the packet and then receive the packet at the other end. For instance, with a 1024 byte packet and an 8 MHz processor, the copy time from memory to the Ethernet interface and vice versa is roughly 1.90 milliseconds in each direction. Thus, of the total 6.95 milliseconds, 3.80 is copy time, 2.78 is network transmission time and .3 is (presumably) network and interface latency. If we consider a 10 Mb Ethernet with similar interfaces, the transmission time is less than 1 millisecond while the copy times remain the same, making the processor time 75 percent of the cost in the network penalty. The importance of the processor speed is also illustrated by the difference in network penalty for the two processors measured in Table 4-1.

With our interfaces, the processor is required to copy the packet into the interface for transmission and out of the interface on reception (with the interface providing considerable on-board buffering). From the copy times given above, one might argue that a DMA interface would significantly improve performance. However, we would predict that a DMA interface would not result in better kernel performance for two reasons. First, the kernel interprets a newly arrived packet as it copies the packet from the network interface, allowing it to place much of the packet data immediately in its final location. With a DMA interface, this copy would be required after the packet had been DMA'ed into main memory. Similarly, on transmission the kernel dynamically constructs a network packet from disparate locations as it copies the data into the network interface. Most DMA interfaces require the packet to be assembled in one contiguous area of memory, implying the need for a comparable copy operation. Finally, there is not currently available (to our knowledge) a network DMA interface for the Ethernet that moves data faster than a 10 MHz Motorola 68000 processor as used in the SUN workstation. In general, the main benefit of a smart network interface appears to be in offloading the main processor rather than speeding up operations that make use of network communication.

5. Kernel Performance

Our first set of kernel measurements focuses on the speed of local and network interprocess communication. The kernel IPC performance is presented in terms of the times for message exchanges and the data transfer operations. We first describe how these measurements were made.

5.1. Measurement Methods

Measurements of individual kernel operations were performed by executing the operation N times (typically 1000 times), recording the total time required, subtracting loop overhead and other artifact, and then dividing the total time by N. Measurement of total time relied on the software-maintained V kernel time which is accurate plus or minus 10 milliseconds.

Measurement of processor utilization was done using a low-priority "busywork" process on each workstation that repeatedly updates a counter in an infinite loop. All other processor utilization reduces the processor allocation to this process. Thus, the processor time used per operation on a workstation is the elapsed time minus the processor time allocated to the "busywork" process divided by N, the number of operations executed.

Using 1000 trials per operation and time accurate plus or minus 10 milliseconds, our measurements should be accurate to about .02 milliseconds except for the effect of variation in network load.

5.2. Kernel Measurements

Table 5-1 gives the results of our measurements of message exchanges and data transfer with the kernel running on workstations using an 8 MHz processor and connected by a 3 Mb Ethernet. Note that *GetTime* is a trivial kernel operation, included to give the basic minimal overhead of a kernel operation. The columns labeled Local and Remote give the elapsed times for these operations executed locally and remotely. The Difference column lists the time difference between the local and remote operations. The Penalty column gives the network penalty for the amount of data transmitted as part of the remote operation. The Client and Server columns list the processor time used for the operations on the two machines involved in the remote execution of the operation. Table 5-2 gives the same measurements using a 10 MHz processor. The times for both processors are given to indicate the effect the processor speed has on local and remote operation performance. As expected, the times for local operations, being dependent only on the processor speed, are 25 percent faster on the 25 percent faster processor. However, the almost 15 percent improvement for remote operations indicates the processor is the most significant performance factor in our configuration and is not rendered insignificant by the network delay (at least on a lightly loaded network).

A significant level of concurrent execution takes place between workstations even though the message-passing is fully synchronized. For instance, transmitting the packet, blocking the sender and switching to another process on the sending workstation proceeds in parallel with the reception of the packet and the readying of the receiving process on the receiving workstation. Concurrent execution is indicated by the fact that the total of the server and client processor times is greater than the elapsed time for a remote message exchange. (See the Client and Server columns in the above tables.)

5.3. Interpreting the Measurements

Some care is required in interpreting the implications of these measurements for distributed applications. Superficially, the fact that the remote *Send-Receive-Reply* sequence takes more than 3 times as long as for the local case suggests that distributed applications should be designed to minimize inter-machine communication. In general, one might consider it impractical to

Kernel Performance

Kernel Operation	Elapsed Time			Network Penalty	Processor Time	
	Local	Remote	Difference		Client	Server
GetTime	0.07	-	-	-	0.07	-
Send-Receive-Reply	1.00	3.18	2.18	1.60	1.79	2.30
MoveFrom: 1024 bytes	1.26	9.03	7.77	8.15	3.76	5.69
MoveTo: 1024 bytes	1.26	9.05	7.79	8.15	3.59	5.87

Table 5-1: Kernel Performance: 3 Mb Ethernet and 8 MHz Processor (times in milliseconds)

Kernel Operation	Elapsed Time			Network Penalty	Processor Time	
	Local	Remote	Difference		Client	Server
GetTime	0.06	-	-	-	0.06	-
Send-Receive-Reply	0.77	2.54	1.77	1.30	1.44	1.79
MoveFrom: 1024 bytes	0.95	8.00	7.05	6.77	3.32	4.78
MoveTo: 1024 bytes	0.95	8.00	7.05	6.77	3.17	4.95

Table 5-2: Kernel Performance: 3 Mb Ethernet and 10 MHz Processor (times in milliseconds)

view interprocess communication as transparent across machines when the speed ratio is so large. However, an alternative interpretation is to recognize that the remote operation adds a delay of less than 2 milliseconds, and that in many cases this time is insignificant relative to the time necessary to process a request in the server. Furthermore, the sending or client workstation processor is busy with the remote ***Send*** for only 1.44 milliseconds out of the total 2.54 millisecond time (using the 10 MHz processor). Thus, one can offload the processor on one machine by, for instance, moving a server process to another machine if its request processing generally requires more than 0.67 milliseconds of processor time, i.e. the difference between the local ***Send-Receive-Reply*** time and the local processor time for the remote operation.

5.4. Multi-Process Traffic

The discussion so far has focused on a single pair of processes communicating over the network. In reality, processes on several workstations would be using the network concurrently to communicate with other processes. Some investigation is required to determine how much message traffic the network can support and also the degradation in response as a result of other network traffic.

A pair of workstations communicating via ***Send-Receive-Reply*** at maximum speed generate a load on the network of about 400,000 bits per second, about 13 percent of a 3 Mb Ethernet and 4 percent of a 10 Mb Ethernet. Measurements on the 10 Mb Ethernet indicate that for the packet size in question no significant network delays are to be expected for loads upto 25 percent. Thus, one would expect minimal degradation with say two separate pairs of workstations communicating on the same network in this fashion. Unfortunately, our measurements of this scenario turned up a hardware bug in our 3 Mb Ethernet interface, a bug which causes many collisions to go undetected and show up as corrupted packets. Thus, the response time for the 8 MHz processor workstation in this case is 3.4 milliseconds. The increase in time from 3.18 milliseconds is accounted for almost entirely from the timeouts and retransmissions arising (roughly one per 2000 packets) from the hardware bug. With corrected network interfaces, we estimate that the network can support any reasonable level of message communication without significant performance degradation.

A more critical resource is processor time. This is especially true for machines such as servers that tend to be the focus of a significant amount of message traffic. For instance, just based on server processor time, a workstation is limited to at most about 558 message exchanges per second, independent of the number of clients. The number is substantially lower for file access operations, particularly when a realistic figure for file server processing is included. File access measurements are examined in the next section.

6. File Access Using the V Kernel

Although it is attractive to consider the kernel as simply providing message communication, a predominant use of the message communication is to provide file access, especially in our environment of diskless personal workstations. File access takes place in several different forms, including: random file page access, sequential file reading and program loading. In this section, we assume the file server is essentially dedicated to serving the client process we are measuring and otherwise idle. A later section considers multi-client load on the file server.

We first describe the performance of random page-level file access.

6.1. Page-level File Access

Table 6-1 list the times for reading or writing a 512 byte block between two processes both local and remote using the 10 MHz processor. The times do not include time to fetch the data from disk but do indicate expected performance when data is buffered in memory. A page read involves the sequence of kernel operations: ***Send--Receive--ReplyWithSegment.*** A page write is ***Send--ReceiveWithSegment--Reply.***

difference between the client processor time for remote page access and for local page access, namely 1.3 milliseconds. A processor cost of more than 1.3 milliseconds per request can be expected from the estimation made earlier using LOCUS figures.

These measurements indicate the performance when file reading and writing use explicit segment specification in the message and ***ReceiveWithSegment*** and ***ReplyWithSegment.*** However, a file write can also be performed in a more basic Thoth-like way using the ***Send-Receive-MoveFrom-Reply*** sequence. For a 512 byte write, this costs 8.1 milliseconds; file reading is similar using ***MoveTo.*** Thus, the segment mechanism saves 3.5 milliseconds on every page read and write operation, justifying this extension to the message primitives.

Random Page-Level Access

	Elapsed Time			Network Penalty	Processor Time	
Operation	Local	Remote	Difference		Client	Server
page read	1.31	5.56	4.25	3.89	2.50	3.28
page write	1.31	5.60	4.29	3.89	2.58	3.32

Table 6-1: Page-Level File Access: 512 byte pages (times in milliseconds)

The columns are to be interpreted according to the explanation given for similarly labeled columns of Tables 5-1 and 5-2. Note that the time to read or write a page using these primitives is approximately 1.5 milliseconds more than the network penalty for these operations.

There are several considerations that compensate for the cost of remote operations being higher than local operations. (Some are special cases of those described for simple message exchanges.) First, the extra 4.2 millisecond time for remote operations is relatively small compared to the time cost of the file system operation itself. In particular, disk access time can be estimated at 20 milliseconds (assuming minimal seeking) and file system processor time at 2.5 milliseconds.[4] This gives a local file read time of 23.8 milliseconds and a remote time of 28.1 milliseconds, making the cost of the remote operation 18 percent more than the local operation.

This comparison assumes that a local file system workstation is the same speed as a dedicated file server. In reality, a shared file server is often faster because of the faster disks and more memory for disk caching that come with economy of scale. If the average disk access time for a file server is 4.3 milliseconds less than the average local disk access time (or better), there is no time penalty (and possibly some advantage) for remote file operations.

Second, remote file access offloads the workstation processor if the file system processing overhead per request is greater the

[4] This is based on measurements of LOCUS [11] that give 6.2 and 4.3 milliseconds as processor time costs for 512-byte file read and write operations respectively on a PDP-11/45, which is roughly half the speed of the 10 MHz Motorola 68000 processor used in the SUN workstation.

6.2. Sequential File Access

Sequential file access is the predominant pattern for file activity in most systems. Efficient file systems exploit this behavior to reduce the effect of disk latency by prefetching file pages (read-ahead) and asynchronously storing modified pages (write-behind). File access and file transfer protocols typically implement streaming to reduce the effect of network latency on sequential file access.

Using the V kernel message communication between a workstation and a file server, the file server can implement read-ahead and write-behind to reduce the effect of disk latency. However, there is no streaming in the network IPC to deal with network latency.

Two factors suggest that streaming can be done without in a local network environment. First, local networks have a low latency as a consequence of their high speed and low delay. Second, although V kernel IPC is logically synchronous, significant concurrency arises in the network implementation, further reducing the effects of network latencies. The presence of streaming adds a significant cost to the protocol in terms of buffer space, copying time and complexity of code. Moreover, buffering effectively puts a disk cache on the workstation, thus raising problems of cache consistency between the different workstations and the file server.

To get a realistic measure of sequential file access performance, we modified the test program used for measuring page read times by the addition of a delay in the server process corresponding to the disk latency. Because we assume the file server is doing read-ahead operations, the delay is interposed between the reply to one request and the receipt of the next request. We contend that this program closely approximates the performance of a workstation sequentially reading a file as rapidly as possible from an otherwise idle file server. The results are shown in Table 6-2

Sequential Page-Level Access

Disk Latency	Elapsed Time per Page Read
10	12.02
15	17.13
20	22.22

Table 6-2: Seq. File Access: 512 byte pages (times in msec.)

These results indicate that, for reasonable values of disk latency, the elapsed time for sequential file access is within 10 to 15 percent from the minimum achievable (the disk latency). It follows that a streaming protocol cannot improve on the performance measured for V kernel file access by more than 15 percent.

Moreover, consider the two cases for the application, namely: Reading faster than the disk latency and reading slower than the disk latency. Suppose an application is reading file pages over the network using a streaming protocol. If it is reading faster than the disk can deliver, it will operate much like the V kernel model in attempting to read a page not yet available, possibly requesting this page from the file server, blocking waiting for the page, having the page returned into the local page buffers, copying the page into its application buffer and then continuing. Thus, performance of a streaming file access implementation can be expected to be similar to our results. For instance, comparing our results with the LOCUS figures for remote sequential file access with a disk latency of 15 milliseconds, the average elapsed time per page is essentially equal to the LOCUS figure of 17.18 milliseconds.

If an application is reading pages sequentially slower than the disk latency time, with say 20 milliseconds between every read request, the page should be available locally on each read with a streaming protocol. In this case, the elapsed time for the read should be 1.3 milliseconds compared to 5.6 milliseconds remotely. However, because read operations occur at most every 20 milliseconds, the speedup by replacing non-streamed file access with streamed file access is limited to 20 percent or less.

Moreover, a streaming protocol would introduce extra processing overhead for copying and buffering readahead pages in this circumstance. Assuming the application was reading slowly because it was compute-bound between read operations, the streaming protocol processing overhead would further slow down the application From this analysis, it is clear that streaming has limited potential for speedup over non-streamed file access when pages are accessed from disk with the latencies we have discussed.

In most systems, sequential file access is used extensively for program loading. However, program loading can be performed more efficiently with the V kernel using *MoveTo*. It is therefore not reliant on the performance figures of this section and is discussed below.

6.3. Program Loading

Program loading differs as a file access activity from page-level access in that the entire file containing the program (or most of it) is to be transferred as quickly as possible into a waiting program execution space. For instance, a simple command interpreter we have written to run with the V kernel loads programs in two read operations: the first read accesses the program header information; the second read copies the program code and data into the newly created program space. The time for the first read is just the single block remote read time given earlier. The second read, generally consisting of several tens of disk pages, uses *MoveTo* to transfer the data. Because *MoveTo* requires that the data be stored contiguously in memory, it is often convenient to implement a large read as multiple *MoveTo* operations. For instance, our current VAX file server breaks large read and write operations into *MoveTo* and *MoveFrom* operations of at most 4 kilobytes at a time. Table 6-3 gives the time for a 64 kilobyte Read. (The elapsed time for file writing is basically the same as for reading and has been omitted for the sake of brevity. Note also that network penalty is not defined for multi-packet transfers.) The transfer unit is the amount of data transferred per *MoveTo* operation in satisfying the read request.

The times given for program loading using a 16 or 64 kilobyte transfer unit corresponds to a data rate of about 192 kilobytes per second, which is within 12 percent of the data rate we can achieve on a SUN workstation by simply writing packets to the network interface as rapidly as possible. Moreover, if the file server retained copies of frequently used programs in memory, much as

Program Loading

	Elapsed Time			Network Penalty	Processor Time	
Transfer unit	Local	Remote	Difference		Client	Server
1 Kb	71.7	518.3	446.5	434.5	207.1	297.9
4 Kb	62.5	368.4	305.8	*	176.1	225.2
16 Kb	60.2	344.6	284.3	*	170.0	216.9
64 Kb	59.7	335.4	275.1	*	168.1	212.7

Table 6-3: 64 kilobyte Read (times in milliseconds)

many current timesharing systems do, such program loading could achieve the same performance given in the table, independent of disk speed. Thus, we argue that ***MoveTo*** and ***MoveFrom*** with large transfer units provide an efficient program loading mechanism that is as fast as can be achieved with the given hardware.

7. File Server Issues

File server performance is a critical issue for diskless workstations. Unfortunately, we do not yet have experience with a V kernel-based file server. Thus, this section describes what we believe are the key issues and estimates performance without providing conclusive data. In general, we view the processor as the key resource to consider in file server performance because, as argued earlier, the network bandwidth is plentiful and disk scheduling and buffering issues are identical to those encountered in conventional multi-user systems.

The number of workstations a file server can support can be estimated from processor requirements. If we estimate page read or write processing overhead as roughly 3.5 milliseconds for file system processing (from LOCUS) plus 3.3 milliseconds for kernel operation (from Table 6-1]), a page request costs about 7 milliseconds of processor time. Program loading appears to cost about 300 milliseconds for an average 64 kilobyte program. Estimating that 90 percent of the file requests are page requests, the average request costs 36 milliseconds. Thus, a file server based on the SUN workstation processor could support about 28 file requests a second. From this we estimate that one file server can serve about 10 workstations satisfactorily, but 30 or more active workstations would lead to excessive delays. However, a diskless workstation system can easily be extended to handle more workstations by adding more file server machines since the network would not seem to be a bottleneck for less than 100 workstations.

For some programs, it is advantageous in terms of file server processor requirements to execute the program on the file server, rather than to load the program into a workstation and subsequently field remote page requests from it. Large programs, executing for a short time and doing a lot of file access while executing are in this class, especially if they require only limited interaction with the user.

On this basis, a file server should have a general program execution facility and the ability to selectively execute certain programs. The need for this execution facility is a further argument for using a general interprocess communication mechanism in place of a specialized page-level file access protocol. With the V kernel, all inter-program communication and interaction takes place through the IPC facility, including: file access, argument passing, debugger control and termination notification. Thus, execution of a program in the file server rather than the client's workstation does not change the program's execution environment nor the client's interaction with the program, i.e. it is transparent except for performance.

8. Measurements with the 10 Mb Ethernet

Our limited access to a 10 Mb Ethernet has precluded basing our measurements on this standard local network. However, some preliminary figures using the 10 Mb Ethernet indicate the effect of using a faster network and slightly faster network interfaces. First, the remote message exchange time is 2.71 milliseconds using an 8 MHz processor, roughly the time for the 10 MHz processor on the 3 Mb network and .5 milliseconds better than the 8 MHz processor on the 3 Mb network. Second, the page read time is 5.72 milliseconds. Finally, the program loading time is much improved, achieving 255 milliseconds for a 64 kilobyte load using 16 Kb transfer units. We have not identified to what degree the improvement is due to the faster network speed versus the differences in the network interface.

9. Related Work

There are a number of previous and concurrent efforts in providing communication mechanisms for distributed systems. For brevity, we compare our work with only a representative sample that characterizes the search for, and evaluation of, suitable models and implementations.

Spector's remote reference study [13] considered the feasibility of implementing remote load and store operations over a local network. Nelson's work on remote procedure calls [10] investigates network communication for procedure-based systems analogous to what the V kernel provides for message-based systems. Rashid and Robertson's Accent kernel [12] implements a message system with a number of features such as non-blocking message sending that are not provided by the V kernel. Finally, LOCUS [11] integrates network communication into a UNIX-like system in the form of transparent remote file access.

Our work has followed the pattern of Spector's and Nelson's work in using a *request-response* form of communication (in place of streaming) and stripping away protocol layers for adequate performance. However, we share Spector's concern about the utility of an unprotected globally shared memory in a distributed system, which is essentially the functionality provided by his primitives. The V kernel provides a strong degree of separation between processes and supports protected provision of services in a multi-user, multi-workstation environment by limiting interprocess communication to the kernel IPC primitives.

Our approach differs from Nelson's primarily in our use of a separate interconnection mechanism from procedure calls, namely messages, and some of the ensuing differences in semantics. Fundamentally, the V kernel provides a base on which to build a remote procedure call mechanism by the addition of suitable compiler and run-time support. Under more detailed examination, many slight differences appear that reflect long-established differences in the construction of procedure-based versus message-based systems, although it is not clear these differences result in any significant difference in overall performance.

The V kernel performance is roughly comparable to that of the software implementations developed by Spector and Nelson, allowing for the non-trivial differences in operation semantics and host processors. We would hypothesize that V kernel performance could be improved by a factor of 30 using microcode, similar to the improvement observed by Spector and Nelson for their primitives. Unfortunately, neither Spector nor Nelson provides results that afford a comparison with our file access results. In general, their work has concentrated on the speed of the basic mechanism and has not been extended to measure performance in a particular application setting.

In comparison to Accent, the V kernel provides a primitive form of message communication, and benefits accordingly in terms of speed, small code size and ability to run well on an inexpensive machine[5] without disk or microcode support. For instance, Accent messages require an underlying transport protocol for reliable delivery because there is no client-level reply message associated with every ***Send*** as in the V kernel. We do not at this time have performance figures for Accent.

LOCUS does not attempt to provide applications with general network interprocess communication but exploits carefully honed problem-oriented protocols for efficient remote file access. It is difficult to compare the two systems from measurements available given the differences in network speeds, processor speeds and measurement techniques. However, from the specific comparisons with LOCUS presented earlier, we would expect overall file access performance for the V kernel to be comparable to LOCUS running on the same machines and network.

However, the memory requirements for the V kernel are about half that of LOCUS compiled for the PDP-11 and probably more like one fourth when LOCUS is compiled for a 32-bit processor like the 68000. Thus, for graphics workstations or process control applications, for instance, the V kernel would be more attractive because of its smaller size, real-time orientation and its provision of general interprocess communication. However, the V kernel does not provide all the functionality of the LOCUS kernel which includes that of the UNIX kernel and more. When required with V, these additional facilities must be provided by server processes executing either on client workstations or network server machines.

10. Conclusions

We conclude that it is feasible to build a distributed system using diskless workstations connected by a high-speed local network to one or more file servers using the V kernel IPC. In particular, the performance study shows that V kernel IPC provides satisfactory performance despite its generality. Because the performance is so close to the lower bound given by the network penalty, there is relatively little room for improvement on the V IPC for the given hardware regardless of protocol and implementation used.

The efficiency of file access using the V IPC suggests that it can not only replace page-level file access protocols but also file transfer and remote terminal protocols, thereby reducing the number of protocols needed. We claim that V kernel IPC is adequate as a transport level for all our local network communication providing each machine runs the V kernel or at least handles the interkernel protocol. We do, however, see a place for these specific protocols in internetworking situations.

In addition to quantifying the elapsed time for various operations, our study points out the importance of considering processor requirements in the design of distributed systems. More experience and measurement of file server load and workstation file access behavior is required to decide whether file server processing is a significant problem in using diskless workstations.

The V kernel has been in use with the diskless SUN workstations, providing local and remote interprocess communication, since September 1982. It is currently 38 kilobytes including code, data and stack. The major use of the network interprocess communication is for accessing remote files. Our file servers are currently 6 VAX/UNIX systems running a kernel simulator and file server program which provides access to UNIX system services over the Ethernet using interkernel packets. A simple command interpreter program allows programs to be loaded and run on the workstations using these UNIX servers. Our experience with this software to date supports the conclusions of the performance study that we can indeed build our next generation of computing facilities [8] using diskless workstations and the V kernel.

Acknowledgements

We are indebted to all the members of the V research group at Stanford, which at this point includes two faculty members and roughly ten graduate students. In particular, we wish to thank Keith Lantz for his patient comments on a seemingly endless sequence of drafts and Tim Mann for his many contributions to the design and the implementation of the kernel. We would also like to thank the referees whose comments and suggestions helped to enhance the clarity of the paper.

References

1. F. Baskett, J.H. Howard and J.T. Montague. Task Communication in DEMOS. Proceedings of the 6th Symposium on Operating System Principles, ACM, November, 1977, pp. 23-31. Published as *Operating Systems Review* 11(5).

2. A. Bechtolsheim, F. Baskett, V. Pratt. The SUN Workstation Architecture. Tech. Rept. 229, Computer Systems Laboratory, Stanford University, March, 1982.

[5] A diskless SUN workstation is much less than the cost of a PERQ.

The LOCUS Distributed Operating System[1]

Bruce Walker, Gerald Popek, Robert English, Charles Kline and Greg Thiel[2]

University of California at Los Angeles

Abstract

LOCUS is a distributed operating system which supports transparent access to data through a network wide filesystem, permits automatic replication of storage, supports transparent distributed process execution, supplies a number of high reliability functions such as nested transactions, and is upward compatible with Unix. Partitioned operation of subnets and their dynamic merge is also supported.

The system has been operational for about two years at UCLA and extensive experience in its use has been obtained. The complete system architecture is outlined in this paper, and that experience is summarized.

1 Introduction

LOCUS is a Unix compatible, distributed operating system in operational use at UCLA on a set of 17 Vax/750's connected by a standard Ethernet[3]. The system supports a very high degree of *network transparency,* i.e. it makes the network of machines appear to users and programs as a single computer; machine boundaries are completely hidden during normal operation. Both files and programs can be moved dynamically with no effect on naming or correct operation. Remote resources are accessed in the same manner as local ones. Processes can be created locally and remotely in the same manner, and process interaction is the same, independent of location. Many of these functions operate transparently even across heterogeneous cpus.

LOCUS also provides a number of high reliability facilities, including flexible and automatic replication of storage at a file level, a full implementation of nested transactions[MEUL 83], and a substantially more robust data storage facility than conventional Unix systems. All of the functions reported here have been implemented, and most are in routine use.

This paper provides an overview of the basic LOCUS system architecture. The file system, especially its distributed naming catalog, plays a central role in the system structure, both because file system activity typically predominates in most operating systems and so high performance is critical, and because the generalized name service provided is used by so many other parts of the system. Therefore, the file system is described first. Remote processes are discussed next, including discussions of process creation, inter-process functions and error handling.

An important part of the LOCUS research concerns recovery from failures of parts of the system, including partition of a LOCUS system into separated but functioning subnetworks. The next sections of this paper discuss the several LOCUS facilities dedicated to recovery. First is the merging of the naming catalog; the hierarchical directory system. The handling of other object types in the file system is also briefly considered. These recovery algorithms

---

[1] This research was supported by the Advanced Research Projects Agency under research contract DSS-MDA-903-82-C-0189.

[2] Current address of Bruce Walker, Charles Kline and Greg Thiel: LOCUS Computing Corporation, 3330 Ocean Park Blvd., Santa Monica, Ca. 90405.

[3] Initial work was done on DEC PDP-11/45's and VAX 750's using both 1 and 10 megabit ring networks.

are designed to permit normal operation while resources are arriving and departing. Last, the protocols which LOCUS sites execute in order to maintain and define the accessible members of a network, i.e. the network topology, are discussed. These protocols are designed to assure that all sites converge on the same answer in a rapid manner.

The paper concludes with a set of observations regarding the use of LOCUS in production settings, especially the value of its network transparent interface.

2 Distributed Filesystem

2.1 Filesystem overview

The LOCUS filesystem presents a single tree structured naming hierarchy to users and applications. It is functionally a superset of the Unix tree structured naming system. There are three major areas of extension. First, the single tree structure in LOCUS covers all objects in the filesystem on all machines. LOCUS names are fully transparent; it is not possible from the name of a resource to discern its location in the network. Such location transparency is critical for allowing data and programs in general to move or even be executed from different sites. The second direction of extension concerns replication. Files in LOCUS can be replicated to varying degrees, and it is the LOCUS system's responsibility to keep all copies up to date, assure that access requests are served by the most recent available version, and support partitioned operation.

To a first approximation, the pathname tree is made up of a collection of filegroups, as in a conventional Unix environment[1]. Each group is a wholly self contained subtree of the naming hierarchy, including storage for all files and directories contained in the subtree. Gluing together a collection of filegroups to construct the uniform naming tree is done via the *mount* mechanism. Logically mounting a filegroup attaches one tree (the filegroup being mounted) as a subtree within an already mounted tree. The glue which allows smooth path traversals up and down the expanded naming tree is kept as operating system state information. Currently this state information is replicated at all sites. To scale a LOCUS network to hundreds or thousands of sites, this "mount" information would be cached.

[1] The term filegroup in this paper corresponds directly to the Unix term filesystem.

A substantial amount of the LOCUS filesystem design, as well as implementation, has been devoted to appropriate forms of error and failure management. These issues will be discussed throughout this paper. Further, high performance has always been a critical goal. In our view, solutions to all the other problems being addressed are really not solutions at all unless their performance is suitable. In LOCUS, when resources are local, access is no more expensive than on a conventional Unix system. When resources are remote, access cost is higher, but dramatically better than traditional layered file transfer and remote terminal protocols permit. Measured performance results are presented in [GOLD 83].

2.2 File Replication

2.2.1 Motivation for Replication

Replication of storage in a distributed filesystem serves multiple purposes. First, from the users' point of view, multiple copies of data resources provide the opportunity for substantially increased availability. This improvement is clearly the case for read access, although the situation is more complex when update is desired, since if some of the copies are not accessible at a given instant, potential inconsistency problems may preclude update, thereby decreasing availability as the level of replication is increased.

The second advantage, from the user viewpoint, concerns performance. If users of the file exist on different machines, and copies are available near those machines, then read access can be substantially faster compared to the necessity to have one of the users always make remote accesses. This difference can be substantial; in a slow network, it is overwhelming, but in a high speed local network it is still significant[1].

In a general purpose distributed computing environment, such as LOCUS, some degree of replication is essential in order for the user to be able to work at all. Certain files used to set up the user's environment must be available even when various machines have failed or are inaccessible. The startup files in Multics, or the various Unix shells, are ob-

[1] In the LOCUS system, which is highly optimized for remote access, the cpu overhead of accessing a remote page is twice local access, and the cost of a remote open is significantly more than the case when the entire open can be done locally.

vious examples. Mail aliases and routing information are others. Of course, these cases can generally be handled by read-only replication, which in general imposes fewer problems[1].

From the system point of view, some form of replication is more than convenient; it is absolutely essential for system data structures, both for availability and performance. Consider a file directory. A hierarchical name space in a distributed environment implies that some directories will have entries which refer to files on different machines. There is strong motivation for storing a copy of all the directory entries in the backward path from a file at the site where the file is stored, or at least "nearby". The principal reason is availability. If a directory entry in the naming path to a file is not accessible because of network partition or site failure, then that file *cannot be accessed,* even though it may be stored locally. LOCUS supports replication at the granularity of the entire directory (as opposed to the entry granularity) to address this issue.

Second, directories in general experience a high level of read access compared to update. As noted earlier, this characteristic is precisely the one for which a high degree of replicated storage will improve system performance. In the case of the file directory hierarchy, this improvement is critical. In fact, the access characteristics in a hierarchical directory system are, fortunately, even better behaved than just indicated. Typically, the top of the hierarchy exhibits a very high level of lookup, and a correspondingly low rate of update. This pattern occurs because the root of the tree is heavily used by most programs and users as the starting point for name resolution. Changes disrupt programs with embedded names, and so are discouraged. The pattern permits (and requires) the root directories to be highly replicated, thus improving availability and performance simultaneously. By contrast, as one moves down the tree toward the leaves, the degree of shared use of any given directory tends to diminish, since directories are used to organize the name space into more autonomous subspaces. The desired level of replication for availability purposes tends to decrease as well. Further, the update traffic to directories near the leaves of the naming tree tends to be greater, so one would have less directory replication to improve performance.

The performance tradeoffs between update/read rates and degree of replication are well known, and we have already discussed them. However, there are other costs as well. For example, concurrency control becomes more expensive. Without replication the storage site can provide concurrency control for the object since it will know about all activity. With replication some more complex algorithm must be supported. In a similar way, with replication, a choice must be made as to which copy of an object will supply service when there is activity on the object. This degree of freedom is not available without replication. If objects move, then, in the no replication case, the mapping mechanism must be more general. With replication a move of an object is equivalent to an add followed by a delete of an object copy.

2.2.2 Mechanism Supporting Replication

File replication is made possible in LOCUS by having multiple physical containers for a logical filegroup. A given file belonging to logical filegroup X may be stored at any subset of the sites where there exist physical containers corresponding to X. Thus the entire logical filegroup is not replicated by each physical container as in a "hot shadow" type environment. Instead, to permit substantially increased flexibility, any physical container is incomplete; it stores only a subset of the files in the subtree to which it corresponds.

To simplify access and provide a basis for low level communication about files, the various copies of a file are assigned the same file descriptor or inode number within the logical filegroup. Thus a file's globally unique low-level name is:
<logical filegroup number, file descriptor (inode) number>
and it is this name which most of the operating system uses.

In the case where not all sites are communicating and even for a short time while they are communicating right after a file update, not all the copies of the file are necessarily up to date. To record this and to ensure that the latest copies will be used for any accesses, each copy has a version vector associated with it that maintains necessary history information. See [PARK83].

[1] The problems which remain are present because few files are strictly read-only; it is just that their update rate is low. When an update is done, some way to make sure that all copies are consistent is needed. If the rate is low enough, manual methods may suffice.

2.3 Accessing the Filesystem

There were several goals directing the design of the network-wide file access mechanism. The first was that the system call interface should be uniform, independent of file location. In other words, the same system call with the same parameters should be able to access a file whether the file is stored locally or not. Achieving this goal of transparency would allow programs to move from machine to machine and allow data to be relocated.

The primary system calls dealing with the filesystem are *open, create, read, write, commit, close* and *unlink*. After introducing the three logical sites involved in file access and the file access synchronization aspect of LOCUS, these system calls are considered in the context of the logical tasks of file reading, modifying, creating and deleting.

2.3.1 LOCUS Logical Sites for Filesystem Activities

LOCUS is designed so that every site can be a full function node. As we saw above, however, filesystem operations can involve more than one host. In fact there are three logical functions in a file access and thus three logical sites. These are:

a. *using site*, (US), which issues the request to open a file and to which pages of the file are to be supplied,
b. *storage site*, (SS), which is the site at which a copy of the requested file is stored, and which has been selected to supply pages of that file to the using site,
c. *current synchronization site*, (CSS), which enforces a global access synchronization policy for the file's filegroup and selects SSs for each open request. A given physical site can be the CSS for any number of filegroups but there is only one CSS for any given filegroup in any set of communicating sites (i.e. a partition). The CSS need not store any particular file in the filegroup but in order for it to make appropriate access decisions it must have knowledge of which sites store the file and what the most current version of the file is.

Since there are three possible independent roles a given site can play (US, CSS, SS), it can therefore operate in one of eight modes. LOCUS handles each combination, optimizing some for performance.

Since all open requests for a file go through the CSS function, it is possible to implement a large variety of synchronization policies. In LOCUS, so long as there is a copy of the desired resource available, it can be used. If there are multiple copies present, the most efficient one to access is selected. Other copies are updated in background, but the system remains responsible for supplying a mutually consistent view to the user. Within a set of communicating sites, synchronization facilities and update propagation mechanisms assure consistency of copies, as well as guaranteeing that the latest version of a file is the only one that is visible.

Since it is important to allow modification of a file even when all copies are not currently accessible, LOCUS contains a file reconciliation mechanism as part of the recovery system (described in section 4).

2.3.2 Strategy for Distributed Operation

LOCUS is a procedure based operating system - processes request system service by executing system calls, which trap to the kernel. The kernel runs as an extension to the process and can sleep on behalf of the process. In general, application programs and users cannot determine if any given system call will require foreign service. In fact, most of the high level parts of the system service routines are unaware of the network. At the point within the execution of the system call that foreign service is needed, the operating system packages up a message and sends it to the relevant foreign site. Typically the kernel then sleeps, waiting for a response, much as it would after requesting a disk i/o to be performed on behalf of a specific process.

This flow of control structure is a special case of remote procedure calls. Operating system procedures are executed at a remote site as part of the service of a local system call. Figure 1 traces, over time, the processing done at the requesting and serving site when one executes a system call requiring foreign service.

2.3.3 Reading Files

To read a file, an application or system supplied program issues the *open* system call with a filename parameter and flags indicating that the open is for read. As in standard Unix, pathname searching (or directory interrogation) is done within the operating

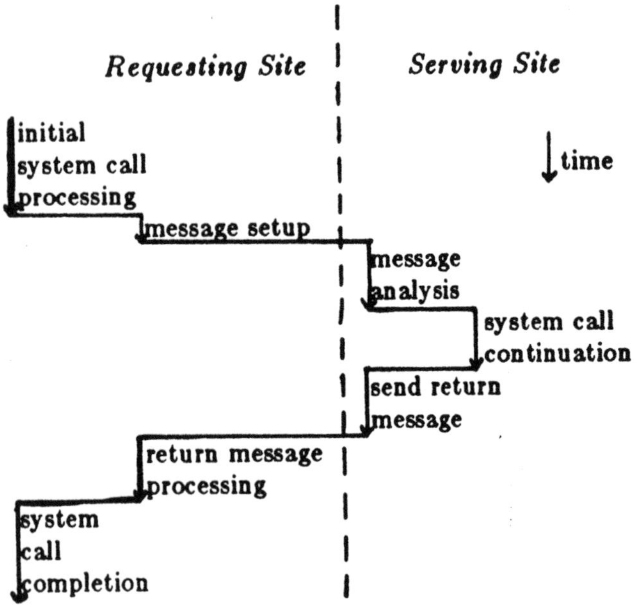

Figure 1: Processing a System Call Requiring Foreign Service

system open call.[1] After the last directory has been interrogated, the operating system on the requesting site has a <logical filegroup number, inode number> pair for the target file that is about to be opened. If the inode information is not already in an incore inode structure, a structure is allocated. If the file is stored locally, the local disk inode information is filled in. Otherwise very little information is initially entered.

Next, the CSS is interrogated. If the local site is the CSS, only a procedure call is needed. If not, the CSS is determined by examining the logical mount table, a message is sent to the CSS, the CSS sets up an incore inode for itself, calls the same procedure that would have been called if the US is the CSS, packages the response, and sends it back to the US. The CSS is involved for several reasons. One is to enforce synchronization controls. Enough state information is kept incore at the CSS to support those synchronization decisions. For example, if the policy allows only a single open for modification, the site where that modification is ongoing would be kept incore at the CSS. Another reason for contacting the CSS is to determine a storage site. The CSS stores a copy of the disk inode information whether or not it actually stores the file. Consequently it has a list of packs which store the file. Using that information and mount table information the CSS can select potential storage sites. The potential sites are polled to see if they will act as storage sites.

Besides knowing the packs where the file is stored, the CSS is also responsible for knowing the latest version vector. This information is passed to potential storage sites so they can check it against the version they store. If they do not yet store the latest version, they refuse to act as a storage site.

Two obvious optimizations are done. First, in it's message to the CSS, the US includes the version vector of the copy of the file it stores, if it stores the file. If that is the latest version, the CSS selects the US as the SS and just responds appropriately to the US. Another simplying case is when the CSS stores the latest version and the US doesn't. In this case the CSS picks itself as SS (without any message overhead) and returns this information to the US.

The response from the CSS is used to complete the incore inode information at the US. For example, if the US is not the SS then all the disk inode information (eg. file size, ownership, permissions) is obtained from the CSS response. The CSS in turn had obtained that information from the SS. The most general open protocol (all logical functions on different physical sites) is:

US --> CSS	OPEN request
CSS --> SS	request for storage site
SS --> CSS	response to previous message
CSS --> US	response to first message.

Figure 2 displays this generally message sequence.

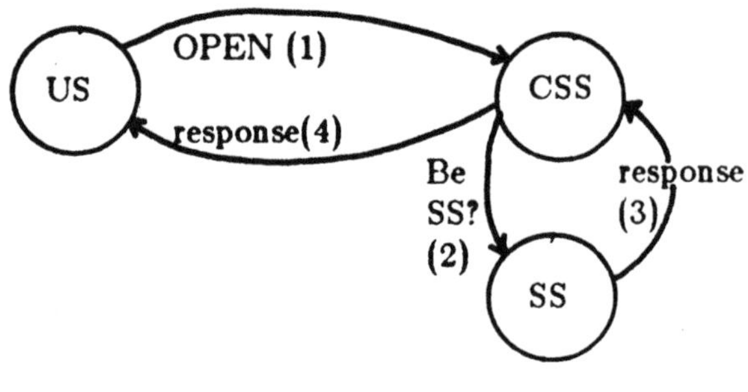

Figure 2: Open Protocol

[1] Pathname searching is described in the next section.

After the file is open, the user level process issues read calls. All such requests are serviced via kernel buffers, both in standard Unix and in LOCUS. In the local case, data is paged from external storage devices into operating system buffers and then copied from there into the address space of the process. Access to locally stored files is the same in LOCUS as in Unix, including the one page readahead done for files being read sequentially.

Requests for data from remote sites operates similarly. Instead of allocating a buffer and queueing a request for a page from a local disk, however, the operating system at the US allocates a buffer and queues a request to be sent over the network to the SS. The request is simple. It contains the <logical filegroup, inode number> pair, the logical page number within the file and a guess as to where the incore inode information is stored at the SS. The CSS is out of the i/o communication.

At the SS, the request is treated, within the operating system, as follows:

a. The incore inode is found using the guess provided;
b. The logical page number is translated into a physical disk block number;
c. A standard low level operating system routine is called to allocate a buffer and get the appropriate page from disk (if it is not already in a buffer);
d. The buffer is queued on the network i/o queue for transmission back to the US as a response to a read request.

The protocol for a network read is thus:[1]

US --> SS	request for page *x* of file *y*
SS --> US	response to the above request

As in the case of local disk reads, readahead is useful in the case of sequential behavior, both at the SS, as well as across the network.

One of several actions can take place when the *close* system call is invoked on a remotely stored file, depending on how many times the file is concurrently open at this US.

[1] There are *no* other messages involved; no acknowledgements, flow control or any other underlying mechanism. This specialized protocol is an important contributor to LOCUS performance, but it implies the need for careful higher level error handling.

If this is not the last close of the file at this US, only local state information need be updated in most cases. However, if this is the last close of the file, the SS and CSS must be informed so they can deallocate incore inode structures and so the CSS can alter state data which might affect it's next synchronization policy decision. The protocol is[1]:

US --> SS	US close
SS --> CSS	SS close
CSS --> SS	response to above
SS --> US	response to first message

Closes of course can happen as a result of error conditions like hosts crashing or network partitions. To properly effect closes at various logical sites, certain state information must be kept in the incore inode. The US of course must know where the SS is (but then it needed that knowledge just to read pages). The CSS must know all the sites currently serving as storage sites so if a certain site crashes, the CSS can determine if a given incore inode slot is thus no longer in use. Analogously, the SS must keep track, for each file, of all the USs that it is currently serving.

The protocols discussed here are the lowest level protocols in the system, except for some retransmission support. Because multilayered support and error handling, such as suggested by the ISO standard, is not present, much higher performance has been achieved.

2.3.4 Pathname Searching

In the previous section we outlined the protocol for opening a file given the <logical filegroup number, inode number> pair. In this section we describe how that pair is found, given a character string name.

All pathnames presented to the operating system start from one of two places, either the root (/) or the current working directory of the process presenting the pathname. In both cases an inode is incore at the US for the directory. To commence the pathname searching, the <logical filegroup, inode number> of the starting directory is extracted from

[1] The original protocol for close was simply:

US --> SS	US close of file *y*
SS --> US	SS close of file *y*

However, we encountered a race condition under this scheme. The US could attempt to reopen the file before the CSS knew that the file was closed. Thus the responses were added.

the appropriate inode and an internal open is done on it. This is the same internal open that was described at the start of the previous section, but with one difference. A directory opened for pathname searching is not open for normal READ but instead for an internal unsynchronized read. The distinction is that no global locking is done. If the directory is stored locally and there are no propagations pending to come in, the local directory is searched without informing the CSS. If the directory is not local, the protocol involving the CSS must be used but the locking is such that updates to the directory can occur while interrogation is ongoing. Since no system call does more than just enter, delete, or change an entry within a directory and since each of these actions are atomic, directory interrogation never sees an inconsistent picture.

Having opened the initial directory, protection checks are made and the directory is searched for the first pathname component. Searching of course will require reading pages of the directory, and if the directory is not stored locally these pages are read across the net in the same manner as other file data pages. If a match is found, the inode number of that component is read from the the directory to continue the pathname search. The initial directory is closed (again internally), and the next component is opened. This strategy is continued up to the last component, which is opened in the manner requested by the original system call. Another strategy for pathname searching is to ship partial pathnames to foreign sites so they can do the expansion locally, avoiding remote directory opens and network transmission of directory pages. Such a solution is being investigated but is more complex in the general case because the SS for each intermediate directory could be different.

Some special care is necessary for crossing filegroup boundaries, as discussed earlier, and for creating and deleting files, as discussed later.

2.3.5 File Modification

Opening an existing file for modification is much the same as opening for read. The synchronization check at the CSS is different and the state information kept at all three logical sites is slightly different.

The act of modifying data takes on two forms. If the modification does not include the entire page, the old page is read from the SS using the read protocol. If the change involves an entire page, a buffer is set up at the US without any reads. In either case, after changes are made, the page is sent to the SS via the write protocol, which is simply[1]:

US –> SS Write logical page x in file y

The action to be taken at the SS is described in the next section in the context of the commit mechanism.

The close protocol for modification is similar to the read case. However, at the US all modified pages must be flushed to the SS before the close message is sent. Also, the mechanism at the SS interacts with the commit mechanism, so we turn to it now.

2.3.6 File Commit

The important concept of atomically committing changes has been imported from the database world and integrated into LOCUS. All changes to a given file are handled atomically. Such a commit mechanism is useful both for database work and, in general, and can be integrated without performance degradation. No changes to a file are permanent until a commit operation is performed. *Commit* and *abort* (undo any changes back to the previous commit point) system calls are provided, and closing a file commits it.

To allow file modifications to act like a transaction, it is necessary to keep both the original and changed data available. There are two well known mechanisms to do so: a) logging and b) shadow pages or intentions lists [LAMP 81a]. LOCUS uses a shadow page mechanism, partly because Unix file modifications tend to overwrite entire files, and partly because high performance shadowing is easier to implement.

The US function never deals with actual disk blocks but rather with logical pages. Thus the entire shadow page mechanism is implemented at the SS and is transparent to the US. At the SS, then, a new physical page is allocated if a change is made to an existing page of a file. This is done without any extra i/o in one of two ways: if an entire page is being changed, the new page is filled in with the new data and written to the storage medium; if the change is not of the entire page, the old page is read, the name of the buffer is changed to the new page, the changed data is entered and this new page is written to the storage medium. Both these cases leave the

[1] There are low level acknowledgements on this message to ensure that it is received. No higher level response is necessary.

old information intact. Of course it is necessary to keep track of where the old and new pages are. The disk inode contains the old page numbers. The incore copy of the disk inode starts with the old pages but is updated with new page numbers as shadow pages are allocated. If a given logical page is modified multiple times it is not necessary to allocate different pages. After the first time the page is modified, it is marked as being a shadow page and reused in place for subsequent changes.

The atomic commit operation consists merely of moving the incore inode information to the disk inode. After that point, the file permanently contains the new information. To abort a set of changes rather than commit them, one merely discards the incore information since the old inode and pages are still on disk, and free up page frames on disk containing modified pages. Additional mechanism is also present to support large files that are structured through indirect pages that contain page pointers.

As is evident by the mechanism above, we have chosen to deal with file modification by first committing the change to one copy of a file. Via the centralized synchronization mechanism, changes to two different copies at the same time is blocked, and reading an old copy while another copy is being modified is prevented.[1] As part of the commit operation, the SS sends messages to all the other SS's of that file as well as the CSS. At a minimum, these messages identify the file and contain the new version vector. Additionally, for performance reasons, the message can indicate: a) whether it was just inode information that changed and no data (eg. ownership or permissions) or b) which explicit logical pages were modified. At this point it is the responsibility of these additional SS's to bring their version of the file up to date by propagating in the entire file or just the changes. A queue of propagation requests is kept by the kernel at each site and a kernel process services the queue.

Propagation is done by "pulling" the data rather than "pushing" it. The propagation process which wants to page over changes to a file first internally opens the file at a site which has the latest version. It then issues standard read messages either for all the pages or just the modified ones. When each page arrives, the buffer that contains it is renamed and sent out to secondary storage, thus avoiding copying data into and out of an application data space, as would be necessary if this propagation mechanism were to run as an application level process. Note also that this propagation-in procedure uses the standard commit mechanism, so if contact is lost with the site containing the newer version, the local site is still left with a coherent, complete copy of the file, albeit still out of date.

Given this commit mechanism, one is always left with either the original file or a completely changed file but never with a partially made change, even in the face of local or foreign site failures. Such was not the case in the standard Unix environment.

2.3.7 File Creation and Deletion

The system and user interface for file creation and deletion is just the standard Unix interface, to retain upward compatibility and to maintain transparency. However, due to the potential for replicated storage of a new file, the create call needs two additional pieces of information - how many copies to store and where to store them. Adding such information to the create call would change the system interface so instead defaults and per process state information is used, with system calls to modify them.

For each process, an inherited variable has been added to LOCUS to store the default number of copies of files created by that process. A new system call has been added to modify and interrogate this number. Currently the initial replication factor of a file is the minimum of the user settable number-of-copies variable and the replication factor of the parent directory.

Initial storage sites for a file are currently determined by the following algorithm:

a. All such storage sites must be a storage site for the parent directory;
b. The local site is used first if possible;
c. Then follow the site selection for the parent directory, except that sites which are currently inaccessible are chosen last.

This algorithm is localized in the code and may change as experience with replicated files grows.

As with all file modification, the create is done at one storage site and propagated to the other storage sites. If the storage site of the created file is not local, the protocol for the create is very similar

[1] Simultaneous read and modification requests, even when initiated at different sites is allowed. Page-valid tokens are managed by the kernels for this purpose. Only one storage site can be involved, unlike the case when there are only multiple readers.

to the remote open protocol, the difference being that a placeholder is sent instead of an inode number. The storage site allocates an inode number from a pool which is local to that physical container of the filegroup. That is, to facilitate inode allocation and allow operation when not all sites are accessible, the entire inode space of a filegroup is partitioned so that each physical container for the filegroup has a collection of inode numbers that it can allocate.

File delete uses much of the same mechanism as normal file update. After the file is open for modification, the US marks the inode and does a commit, which ships the inode back to the SS and increments the version vector. As part of the commit mechanism, pages are released and other sites are informed that a new version of the file exists. As those sites discover that the new version is a delete, they also release their pages. When all the storage sites have seen the delete, the inode can be reallocated by the site which has control of that inode (i.e. the storage site of the original create).

2.4 Other Issues

The LOCUS name service implemented by the directory system is also used to support interprocess communication and remote device access, as well as to aid in handling heterogeneous machine types in a transparent manner. We turn to these issues now.

2.4.1 Site and Machine Dependent Files

There are several aspects to the hardware heterogeneity problem, such as number representation, byte ordering, instruction set differences and special hardware constraints (eg. floating point availability). Strong file typing and conversions during transmission can help some of these problems[1]. Here we address only the file naming problem.

While globally unique user visible file naming is very important most of the time, there can be situations where an uttered filename wants to be interpreted specially, based on the context under which it was issued. The machine-type context is a good example. In a LOCUS net containing both DEC PDP-11/45s and DEC VAX 750s, a user would want to type the same command name on either type of machine and get a similar service. However, the load modules of the programs providing that service could not be identical and would thus have to have different globally unique names. To get the proper load modules executed when the user types a command, then, requires using the context of which machine the user is executing on. A discussion of transparency and the context issue is given in [POPE 83a]. Here we outline a mechanism implemented in LOCUS which allows context sensitive files to be named and accessed transparently.

[1] Solutions to the number representation and byte ordering problems have not yet been implemented.

Basically the scheme consists of four parts:

a. Make the globally unique name of the object in question refer to a special kind of directory (hereafter referred to as a *hidden directory)* instead of the object itself.
b. Inside this directory put the different versions of the file, naming them based on the context with which they are associated. For example, have the command */bin/who* be a hidden directory with the file entries *45* and *vax* that are the respective load modules.
c. Keep a per-process inherited context for these hidden directories. If a hidden directory is found during pathname searching (see section 4.4 for pathname searching), it is examined for a match with the process's context rather than the next component of the pathnames passed to the system.
d. Give users and programs an escape mechanism to make hidden directories visible so they can be examined and specific entries manipulated.

As we shall see in section 3, not only does this naming scheme allow us to store and name load modules for different sites, but allows us to transparently run a requested command on the site for which a load module exists.

2.4.2 Other Filesystem Objects

In LOCUS, as in Unix, the name catalog also includes objects other than files; devices and interprocess communication (ipc) channels are the best known.

LOCUS provides for transparent use of remote devices in most cases[1]. This functionality is exceedingly valuable, but involves considerable care. The

[1] The only exception is remote access to raw, non-character devices and these can be accessed by executing processes remotely.

implementation architecture is beyond the scope of this paper.

Interprocess communication (ipc) is often a controversial subject in a single machine operating system, with many differing opinions. In a distributed environment, the requirements of error handling impose a number of additional requirements that help make design decisions, potentially easing disagreements.

In LOCUS, the initial ipc effort was further simplified by the desire to provide a network-wide ipc facility which is fully compatible with the single machine functions that were already present in Unix. Therefore, in the current LOCUS system release, Unix *named pipes* and *signals* are supported across the network. Their semantics in LOCUS are identical to those seen on a single machine Unix system, even when processes are resident on different machines in LOCUS. Just providing these seemingly simple ipc facilities was non-trivial, however. Details of the implementation are given in [WALK83].

3 Remote Processes

Transparent support for remote processes requires a facility to create a process on a remote machine, initialize it appropriately, support cross machine, inter-process functions with the same semantics as were available on a single machine, and reflect error conditions across machine boundaries. Each of these is discussed below.

3.1 Remote Process Creation

LOCUS permits one to execute programs at any site in the network, subject to permission control, in a manner just as easy as executing the program locally. In fact, one can dynamically, even just before process invocation, select the execution site. No rebinding or any other action is needed. The mechanism is entirely transparent, so that existing software can be executed either locally or remotely, with no change to that software.

The decision about where the new process is to execute is specified by information associated with the calling process. That information, currently a structured advice list, can be set dynamically. Shell commands to control execution site are also available.

Processes are typically created by the standard Unix *fork* call. Both fork and *exec*, the Unix call which installs a load module into a process and starts execution, are controlled by site information in the process environment. If exec is to occur remotely, then the process is effectively moved at that time. By doing so it is feasible to support remote execution of programs intended for dissimilar cpu types.

In both cases, a process body is allocated at the destination site following a message exchange between the calling site and the new process site. More significant, it is necessary to initialize the new process' environment correctly. This requires, for Unix compatibility, that the parent and child process share open file descriptors (which contain current file position pointers[1]), a copy of other process state information.

In the case of a fork, the process address space, both code and data, must be made a copy of the parents'. If the code is reentrant, and a copy already exists on the destination machine, it should be used. In any case, the relevant set of process pages are sent to the new process site.

For optimization purposes, a *run* call has been added that is similar to the effect of a fork followed by a exec. If the run is to execute remotely, the effect is a local fork and a remote exec. However, run is transparent as to where is executes. Run avoids the copy of the parent process image which occurs with fork, and includes parameterization that permits the caller to set up the environment of the new process, be local or remote.

3.2 Inter-process Functions

The semantics of the available functions by which processes interact determines, to a large extent, the difficulty involved in supporting a transparent process facility. In Unix, there are explicit functions such as signals and pipes (named or not), but there are also implicit mechanisms; shared open files are the most significant. The most difficult part of these functions' semantics is their expectation of shared memory. For example, if one process sharing an open file reads or writes a character, and then another does so, the second process receives or alters

[1] To implement this functionality across the network we keep a file descriptor at each site, with only one valid at any time, using a token scheme to determine which file descriptor is currently valid.

the character following the one touched by the first process. Pipes have similar characteristics under certain circumstances.

All of these mechanisms are supported in LOCUS, in part through a token mechanism which marks which copy of a resource is valid; access to a resource requires the token. This concept is used at various levels within the system. While in the worst case, performance is limited by the speed at which the tokens and their associated resources can be flipped back and forth among processes on different machines, such extreme behavior is exceedingly rare. Virtually all processes read and write substantial amounts of data per system call. As a result, most collections of Unix processes designed to execute on a single machine run very well when distributed on LOCUS.

3.3 Error Handling

In LOCUS, process errors are folded into the existing Unix interface to the degree possible. The new error types primarily concern cases where either the calling or called machine fails while the parent and child are still alive. When the child's machine fails, the parent receives an error signal. Additional information about the nature of the error is deposited in the parent's process structure, which can be interrogated via a new system call. When the parent's machine fails, the child is notified in a similar manner. Otherwise, the process interface in LOCUS is the same as in Unix.

4 LOCUS Recovery Philosophy

The basic approach in LOCUS is to maintain, within a single partition, strict synchronization among copies of a file so that all uses of that file see the most recent version, even if concurrent activity is taking place on different machines. Each partition operates independently, however. Upon merge, conflicts are reliably detected. For those data types which the system understands, automatic reconciliation is done. Otherwise, the problem is reported to a higher level; a database manager for example, who may itself be able to reconcile the inconsistencies. Eventually, if necessary, the user is notified and tools are provided by which he can interactively merge the copies.

An important example where replicated operation is needed, in a distributed system, is the *name service,* the mechanism by which the user sensible names are translated into internal system names and locations for the associated resource. Those mapping tables must themselves be replicated, as already pointed out. A significant part of the basic replication mechanism in LOCUS is used by its name service, or directory system, and so we will concentrate on that part of recovery in the remainder of our discussion.

4.1 Partitions

Partitions clearly are the primary source of difficulty in a replicated environment. Some authors have proposed that the problem can be avoided by having high enough connectivity that failures will not result in partitions. In practice, however, there are numerous ways that effective partitioning occurs. In single local area networks, a single loose cable terminator can place all machines in individual partitions of a single node. Gateways between local nets fail. Long haul connections suffer many error modes. Even when the hardware level is functioning, there are miriad ways that software levels cause messages not to be communicated; buffer lockups, synchronization errors, etc. Any distributed system architectural strategy which depends for its correct and convenient operation on the collection of these failure modes being exceedingly infrequent is a fragile model, in our judgment. In addition, there are maintenance and hardware failure scenarios that can result in file modification conflict even when two sites have never executed independently at the same time. For example, while site B is down, work is done on site A. Site A goes down before B comes up. When site A comes back up, an effective partition merge must be done.

Given partitioning will occur, and assuming replication of data is desired for availability, reliability, and performance, an immediate question is whether a data object, appearing in more than one partition, can be updated during partition. In our judgment, the answer must be yes. There are numerous reasons. First, if it is not possible, then availability goes down, rather than up, as the degree of replication increases. Secondly, the system itself must maintain replicated data, and permit update during partitioned mode. Directories are the obvious example. Solutions to that problem may well be made available to users at large. Third, in many environments, the probability of conflicting updates is low. Actual intimate sharing is often not the rule. Thus, unless the user involved needed to get at an alternate copy because of system failures, a policy of allowing update in all partitions will not lead to conflicting updates. To forbid update in all partitions, or all except one, can be a severe constraint, and in most cases will have been unnecessary.

Given the ability to update a replicated object during partition, one must face the problem of mutual consistency of the copies of each data object. Further, the merge procedure must assure that no updates are lost when different copies are merged. Solutions proposed elsewhere, such as primary copy [ALSB76], majority consensus [THOM78], and weighted voting [MENA77] are excluded. They all impose the requirement that update can be done in at most one partition. Even methods such as that used in Grapevine [BIRR82] are not suitable. While Grapevine assures that copies will eventually reach a consistent state, updates can be lost.

It is useful to decompose the replication/merge problem into two cases. In the first, one can assume that multiple copies of a given object may be reconciled independently of any other object. That is, the updates done to the object during partition are viewed as being unrelated and independent of updates (or references) to other objects.

The second case is the one that gives rise to transactions. Here it is recognized that changes to sets of objects are related. Reconciliation of differing versions of an object must be coordinated with other objects and the operations on those objects which occurred during partition.

LOCUS takes both points of view. The basic distributed operating system assumes, as the default, that non-directory file updates and references are unrelated to other non-directory files. The steps which are taken to manage replication under those assumptions are discussed in the next section. In addition, LOCUS provides a full nested transaction facility for those cases where the user wishes to bind a set of events together. Case specific merge strategies have been developed. The recovery and merge implications of these transactions are discussed later.

4.2 Detection of Conflicting Updates to Files

Suppose file f was replicated at sites S_1 and S_2. Initially assume each copy was identical but after some period sites S_1 and S_2 partitioned. If f is modified at S_1 producing f_1 then when S_1 and S_2 merge the two copies of f will be inconsistent. Are they then in conflict? No. The copy at S_1 (f_1) should propagate to S_2 and that will produce a consistent state. The copies of the object would be in conflict if during the partition not only was S_1's copy modified to produce f_1 but S_2's copy was modified to produce f_2. At merge a conflict should be detected. As already pointed out the system may be able to resolve the conflict. This is just a simple example. There could be several copies of the object and the history of the modifications and partitions can be complex. Detecting consistency under the general circumstances is non-trivial, but a elegant solution is presented in [PARK83], and is implemented in LOCUS.

For some types of system supported single file structures the system can mechanically resolve those conflicts which are detected. Directories and mailboxes have relatively simple semantics (add and delete are the major operations) and can be done in this manner. These cases are critical to LOCUS, and will be discussed below.

4.3 File System Merge

A distributed file system is an important and basic case of replicated storage. The LOCUS file system is a network wide, tree structured directory system, with leaves being data files whose internal structure is unknown to the LOCUS system nucleus. All files, including directories, have a *type* associated with them. The type information is used by recovery software to take appropriate action. Current types are:

- directories
- mailboxes (several kinds)
- database files
- untyped files

The LOCUS recovery and merge philosophy is hierarchically organized. The basic system is responsible for detecting all conflicts. For those data types that it manages, including internal system data as well as file system directories, automatic merge is done by the system. If the system is not responsible for a given file type, it reflects the problem up to a higher level; to a recovery/merge manager if one exists for the given file type. If there is none, the system notifies the owner(s) of the file that a conflict exists, and permits interactive reconciliation of the differences. Transaction recovery and merge can also be supported across partitions in LOCUS. See [FAIS81, THIE83 and MEULL83].

4.4 Reconciliation of a Distributed, Hierarchical Directory Structure

In this section, we consider how to merge two copies of a directory that has been independently updated in different partitions. Logically, the directory structure is a tree[1] but any directory can be replicated. A directory can be viewed as a set of records, each one containing the character string comprising one element in the path name of a file. Associated with that string is an index that points at a descriptor (inode) for a file or directory. In that inode is a collection of information about the file. LOCUS generally treats inode as part of the file from the recovery point of view. The significance of this view will become apparent as the reconciliation procedure is outlined.

To develop a merge procedure for any data type, including directories, it is necessary to evaluate the operations which can be applied to that data type. For directories, there are two operations:

insert (character string path element) and
remove (character string path element).

Although these operations have rather simple semantics, the merge rules are not so simple, primarily because:

a) operations (remove, rename and link) may be done to a file in a partition which does not store the file;

b) a file which was deleted in one partition while it was modified in another, wants to be saved;

c) a directory may have to be resolved without either partition storing particular files.

With these situations in mind, we note that no recovery is needed if the version vector for both copies of the directory are identical. Otherwise the basic rules are:

1. Check for name conflicts. For each name in the union of the directories, check that the inode numbers are the same. If they aren't, both file names are slightly altered to be distinguished. The owners of the two files are notified by electronic mail that this action has been taken.
2. The remaining resolution is done on an inode by inode basis, with the rules in general being:
   a) if the entry appears in one directory and not in the other, propagate the entry;
   b) if a deleted entry exists in one directory and not in the other, propagate the delete, unless there has been a modification of the data since the delete;
   c) if both directories have an entry and neither is deleted, no action is necessary;
   d) if both directories have an entry and one is a delete and other is not, the inode is interrogated in each partition; if the data has been modified since the delete, either a conflict is reported or the delete is undone; otherwise the delete is propagated.

Further augmentation to the directory merge algorithm must be done because of *links*. The complete algorithm is given in [POPE83b].

Since recovery may have to be run while users are active, it is necessary that regular traffic be allowed. To accommodate this, we support demand recovery, which is to say that a particular directory can be reconciled out of order to allow access to it with only a small delay.

4.5 Reconciliation of Mailboxes

Automatic reconciliation of user mailboxes is important in the LOCUS replication system, since notification of name conflicts in files is done by sending the user electronic mail. It is desirable that, after merge, the user's mailbox is in suitable condition for general use.

Fortunately, mailboxes are even easier to merge than directories. The reason is that the operations which can be done during partitioned operation are the same: insert and delete, but it is easy to arrange for no name conflicts, and there are no link problems. Further, since mailboxes are not a system data structure, and generally are seen only by the small number of mail programs, support for deletion information can be easily installed.

[1] With the exception of links.

Thus, for each different mail storage format[1] there is a mail merge program that is invoked after the basic file system has been made consistent again. These programs deal with conflicted files detected by the version vector algorithm which the typing system indicates are mail files.

4.6 Conflicts Among Untyped Data Objects

When the system has no mechanisms to deal with conflicts, it reports the matter to the user. In LOCUS, mail is sent to the owner(s) of a given file that is in conflict, describing the problem. It may merely be that certain descriptive information has been changed. Alternately, the file content may be in conflict. In any case, files with unresolved conflicts are marked so normal attempts to access them fail, although that control may be overridden. A trivial tool is provided by which the user may rename each version of the conflicted file and make each one a normal file again. Then the standard set of application programs can be used to compare and merge the files.

5 Dynamic Reconfiguration

5.1 Introduction

Transparency in LOCUS applies not only to the static topology of the network, but to the configuration changes themselves. The system strives to insulate the users from reconfigurations, providing continuing operation with only negligible delay. Requiring user programs to deal with reconfiguration would shift the network costs from the operating system to the applications programs.

This section discusses the concept of transparency as it relates to a dynamic network environment, gives several principles that the operating system should follow to provide it, and presents the reconfiguration protocols used in LOCUS. The protocols make use of a high-level synchronization strategy to avoid the message overhead of two-phased commits or high-level ACKs, and are largely independent of the specific architecture of LOCUS.

[1] There are two storage formats in LOCUS; one in which multiple messages are stored in a single file, the default, and another where each message is a different file, and messages are grouped by parent directory. This second storage discipline is used by the mail program *mh*.

The high-level protocols of LOCUS assume that the underlying network is fully connected. By this we mean that if site A can communicate with site B, and site B with site C, then site A can communicate with site C. In practice, this may be done by routing messages from A to C through B, although the present implementation of LOCUS runs on a broadcast network where this is unnecessary. The assumption of transitivity of communication significantly simplifies the high-level protocols used in LOCUS.

The low-level protocols enforce that network transitivity. Network information is kept internally in both a high-level status table and a collection of virtual circuits.[1] The two structures are, to some extent, independent. Membership in the partition does not guarantee the existence of a virtual circuit, nor does an open virtual circuit guarantee membership in the partition. Failure of a virtual circuit, either on or after open, does, however, remove a node from a partition. Likewise removal from a partition closes all relevant virtual circuits. All changes in partitions invoke the protocols discussed later in this paper.

The system attempts to maintain file access across partition changes. If it is possible, without loss of information, to substitute a different copy of a file for one lost because of partition, the system will do so. If, in particular, a process loses contact with a file it was reading remotely, the system will attempt to reopen a different copy of the same version of the file.

The ability to mount filegroups independently gives great flexibility to the name space. Since radical changes to the name space can confuse users, however, this facility is rarely used for that purpose, and that use is not supported in LOCUS. The reconfiguration protocols require that the mount hierarchy be the same at all sites.

[1] The virtual circuits deliver messages from *site* A to *site* B (the virtual circuits connect sites, not processes) in the order they are sent. If a message is lost, the circuit is closed. The mechanism defends the local site from the slow operation of a foreign site.

5.2 Requirements for the Reconfiguration Protocols

The first constraint on the reconfiguration protocol is that it maintain consistency with respect to the internal system protocols. All solutions satisfying this constraint could be termed correct. Correctness, however, is not enough. In addition to maintaining system integrity, the solution must insulate the user from the underlying system changes. The solution should not affect program development, and it should be efficient enough that any delays it imposes are negligible.

As an example of a "correct" but poor solution to the problem, the system could handle only the boot case, where all machines in the network come up together. Any failures would be handled by a complete network reboot. Such a solution would easily satisfy the consistency constraint; however, one might expect murmurs of complaint from the user community.

Similarly, a solution that brings the system to a grinding halt for an unpredictable length of time at unforseeable intervals to reconstruct internal tables might meet the requirement of correctness, but would clearly be undesirable.

Optimally, the reconfiguration algorithms should not affect the user in any matter whatsoever. A user accessing resources on machine A from machine B should not be affected by any activity involving machine C. This intuitive idea can be expressed in several principles:

1. User activity should be allowed to continue without adverse affect, provided no resources are lost.
2. Any delay imposed by the system on user activity during reconfiguration should be negligible.
3. The user should be shielded from any transient effects of the network configuration.
4. Any activity initiated after the reconfiguration should reflect the state of the system after the reconfiguration.
5. Specialized users should be able to detect reconfigurations if necessary.
6. No user should be penalized for increased availability of resources.[1]

All these principles are fairly intuitive. They merely extend the concept of network transparency to a dynamic network and express a desire for efficiency. They do, however, give tight constraints on the eventual algorithms. For example, those operations with high delay potentials must be partitioned in such a way that the tasks relevant to a specific user request can be run quickly, efficiently, and immediately.

The principles have far-reaching implications in areas such as file access and synchronization. Suppose, for example, a process were reading from a file replicated twice in its partition. If it were to lose contact with the copy it was reading, the system should substitute the other copy (assuming, of course, that it is still available). If a more recent version became available, the process should continue accessing the old version, but this must not prevent other processes from accessing the newer version.

These considerations apply equally to all partitions, and no process should loose access to files simply because a merge occurred. While the LOCUS protocols insure synchronization within a partition, they cannot do so between partitions. Thus, it is easy to contrive a scenario where the system must support conflicting locks within a single partition, and invoke any routines necessary to deal with inconsistencies that result.

5.3 Protocol Structure

As noted before, the underlying LOCUS protocols assume a fully-connected network. To insure correct operation, the reconfiguration strategy must guarantee this property. If, for instance, a momentary break occurs between two sites, all other sites in the partition must be notified of the break. A simple scan of available nodes is insufficient.

The present strategy splits the reconfiguration into two stages: first, a *partition* protocol runs to find fully-connected sub-networks; then a *merge* protocol runs to merge several such sub-networks into a full partition. The partition protocol affects only those sites previously thought to be up. It divides a partition into sub-partitions, each of which is guaranteed to be fully-connected and disjoint from all other

[1] This last point may cause violations of synchronization policies, as discussed below.

sub-partitions. It detects all site and communications failures and cleans up all affected multi-site data structures, so that the merge protocol can ignore such matters. The merge protocol polls the set of available sites, and merges several disjoint sub-partitions into one.

After the new partition is established, the recovery procedure corrects any inconsistencies brought about either by the reconfiguration code itself, or by activity while the network was not connected. Recovery is concerned mainly with file consistency. It schedules update propagation, detects conflicts, and resolves conflicts on classes of files it recognizes.

All reconfiguration protocols are controlled by a high-priority kernel process. The partition and merge protocols are run directly by that process, while the recovery procedure runs as a privileged application program.

5.4 The Partition Protocol

Communication in a fully-connected network is an equivalence relation. Thus the partitions we speak about are partitions, in the strict mathematical sense of the set of nodes of the network. In normal operation, the site tables reflect the equivalence classes: all members of a partition agree on the status of the general network. When a communication break occurs, for whatever reason, these tables become unsynchronized. The partition code must re-establish the logical partitioning that the operating system assumes, and synchronize the site tables of its member sites to reflect the new environment.

In general, a communication failure between any two sites does not imply a failure of either site. Failures caused by transmission noise or unforeseen delays cannot be detected directly by foreign sites, and will often be detected in only one of the sites involved. In such situations, the partition algorithm should find maximum partitions: a single communications failure should not result in the network breaking into three or more parts.[1] LOCUS implements a solution based on iterative intersection.

[1] Breaking a virtual circuit between two sites aborts any ongoing activity between those two sites. Partition fragmentation must be minimized to minimize the loss of work.

A few terms are helpful for the following discussion. The *partition set*, P_α, is the set of sites believed up by site α. The *new partition set*, P_α', is the set of sites known by α to have joined the new partition.

Consider a partition P after some set of failures has occurred. To form a new partition, the sites must reach a consensus on the state of the network. The criterion for consensus may be stated in set notation as: for every $\alpha,\beta \in P$, $P_\alpha = P_\beta$. This state can be reached from any initial condition by taking successive intersections of the partition sets of a group of sites.

When a site α runs the partition algorithm, it polls the sites in P_α. Each site polled responds with its own partition set $P_{pollsite}$. When a site is polled successfully, it is added to the new partition set P_α', and P_α is changed to $P_\alpha \cap P_{pollsite}$. α continues to poll those sites in P_α but not in P_α' until the two sets are equal, at which point a consensus is assured, and α announces it to the other sites.

Translating this algorithm into a working protocol requires provisions for synchronization and failure recovery. These two requirements are antagonistic—while the algorithm requires that only one active site poll for a new partition, and that other sites join only one new partition, reliability considerations require that sites be able to change active sites when one fails—and make the protocol intrinsically complex. Space precludes including the details of the algorithm.

5.5 The Merge Protocol

The *merge* procedure joins several partitions into one. It establishes new site and mount tables, and re-establishes CSS's for all the file groups. To form the largest possible partition, the protocol must check all possible sites, including, of course, those thought to be down[1]. In a large network, sequential polling results in a large additive delay because of the timeouts and retransmissions necessary to determine the status of the various sites. To minimize this effect, the merge strategy polls the sites asynchronously.

[1] In a large network with gateways one can optimize by polling the gateways.

The algorithm itself is simple. The site initiating the protocol sends a request for information to all sites in the network. Those sites which are able respond with the information necessary for the initiating site to build the global tables. After a suitable time, the initiating site gives up on the other sites, declares a new partition, and broadcasts its composition to the world.

The algorithm is centralized and can only be run at one site, and a site can only participate in one protocol at a time, so the other sites must be able to halt execution of the protocol. To accomplish this, the polled site sends back an error message instead of a normal reply:

```
IF ready to merge THEN
        IF merging AND actsite == locsite THEN
                IF fsite < locsite THEN
                        actsite := fsite;
                        halt active merge;
                ELSE decline to merge
                FI
        ELSE actsite := fsite;
        FI
ELSE decline to merge
FI
```

If a site is not ready to merge, then either it or some other site will eventually run the merge protocol.

The major source of delay in the merge procedure is in the timeout routines that decide when the full partition has answered. A fixed length timeout long enough to handle a sizeable network would add unreasonable delay to a smaller network or a small partition of a large network. The strategy used must be flexible enough to handle the large partition case and the small partition case at the same time.

The merge protocol waits longer when there is a reasonable expectation that further replies will arrive. When a site answers the poll, it sends its partition information in the reply. Until all sites believed up by some site in the new partition have replied, the timeout is long. Once all such sites have replied, the timeout is short.

5.6 The Cleanup Procedure

Even before the partition has been reestablished, there is considerable work that each node can do to clean up its internal data structures. Essentially, each machine, once it has decided that a particular site is unavailable, must invoke failure handling for all resources which it's processes were using at that site, or for all local resources which processes at that site were using. The action to be taken depends on the nature of the resource and the actions that were under way when failure occurred. The cases are outlined in the table below.

Local Resource in Use Remotely

Resource	Failure Action
File (open for update)	Discard pages, close file and abort updates
File (open for read)	Close file

Remote Resource in Use Locally

Resource	Failure Action
File (open for update)	Discard pages, set error in local file descriptor
File (open for read)	Internal close, attempt to reopen at other site

Interacting Processes

Failure Type	Action
Remote Fork/Exec, remote site fails	return error to caller
Fork/Exec, calling site fails	notify process
Distributed Transaction	abort all related subtransactions in partition

Once the machines in a partition have mutually agreed upon the membership of the partition, the system must select, for each filegroup it supports, a new synchronization site. This is the site to which the LOCUS file system protocols direct all file open requests. Once the synchronization site has been selected, that site must reconstruct the lock table for all open files from the information remaining in the partition. If there are operations in progress which would not be permitted during normal behavior, some action must be taken. For example, file X is open for update in two partitions, the system policy permits only one such use at a time, and a merge occurs. The desired action is to permit these operations to continue to completion, and only then perform file system conflict analysis on those resources.[1] Finally, the recovery procedure described in section 4 is run for each filegroup to which it is necessary.

After all these functions have been completed, the effect of topology change has been completely processed. For most of these steps, normal processing at all of the operating nodes continues unaffected. If a request is made for a resource which has not been merged yet, the normal order of processing is set aside to handle that request. Therefore, higher level reconfiguration steps, such as file and directory merge, do not significantly delay user requests.

5.7 Protocol Synchronization

The reconfiguration procedure breaks down into three distinct components, each of which has already been discussed. What remains is a discussion of how the individual parts are tied together into a robust whole. At various points in the procedure, the participating sites must be synchronized, and control of the protocol must be handed to a centralized site. Those sites not directly involved in the activity must be able to ascertain the status of the active sites to insure that no failures have stalled the entire network.

One approach to synchronization would be to add ACKs to the end of each section of the protocol, and get the participants in lock-step before proceeding to the next section. This approach increases both the message traffic and the delay, both critical performance quantities. It also requires careful analysis of the critical sections in the protocols to determine where a commit is required, and the implementation of a commit for each of those sections. If a site fails during a synchronization stage, the system must still detect and recover from that failure.

LOCUS reconfiguration uses an extension of a "failure detection" mechanism for synchronization control. Whenever a site takes on a passive role in a protocol, it checks periodically on the active site. If the active site fails, the passive site can restart the protocol.

As the various protocols execute, the states of both the active and the passive sites change. An active site at one instant may well become a passive site the next, and a passive site could easily end up waiting for another passive site. Without adequate control, this could lead to circular waits and deadlocks.

One solution would be to have passive sites respond to the checks by returning the site that they themselves are waiting for. The checking site would then follow that chain and make sure that it terminated. This approach could require several messages per check, however, and communications delays could make the information collected obsolete or misleading.

Another alternative, the one used in LOCUS, is to order all the stages of the protocol. When a site checks another site, that site returns its own status information. A site can wait only for those sites who are executing a portion of the protocol that precedes its own. If the two sites are in the same state, the ordering is by site number. This ordering of the sites is complete. The lowest ordered site has no site to legally wait for; if it is not active, its check will fail, and the protocol can be re-started at a reasonable point.

While no synchronization "failures" can cause the protocols to fail, they can slow execution. Without ACKs, the active site cannot effectively push its dependents ahead of itself through the stages of the protocol. Nor can it insure that two passive sites always agree on the present status of the reconfiguration. On the other hand, careful design of the message sequences can keep the windows where difficulties can occur small, and the normal case executes rapidly.

6 Experience

Locus has now been operating for about two years at UCLA, and has been installed at a few other sites. Most of the experience with a large network configuration has occurred at UCLA. A 17 Vax-11/750 Ethernet network is the host facility, with additional machines, including a Vax-11/780, to be added shortly. The network is typically operated as three separate Locus networks; one for production use, one as a beta test net, and a few machines for developing new system software. On the beta net, for example, it has recently been typical to have 5 machines operational with about 30-40 users. The production net configuration is correspondingly larger. These systems are used for virtually all the interactive computing in the UCLA Computer Science Department, except for those classes using the Vax-11/780 that has not yet been converted. We estimate that over 100,000 connect hours have been

[1] LOCUS currently does not support this behavior.

delivered by the Vax Locus networks by early 1983. Most of the user experience with Locus has been acquired on a version of the system that did not support replication of files, the nested transaction facility or general remote process forking. The following observations largely reflect the experience at UCLA.

First, it is clearly feasible to provide high performance, transparent distributed system behavior for file and device access, as well as remote, interprocess interaction. Measurements consistently indicate that Locus performance equals Unix in the local case, and that remote access in general, while somewhat slower than when resources are local, is close enough that no one typically thinks much about resource location because of performance reasons. This ability to provide a substantial degree of *performance transparency* surprised us. There is still no indication that Ethernet bandwidth is any significant limitation. It is, however, difficult to swap load images across the network with high performance because of the software cost of packet disassembly and reassembly for the current hardware and low level protocols. Much larger configurations clearly cannot share the same broadcast cable of that bandwidth, of course.

Most of the problems which were encountered by users resulted from those situations where transparency was not completely supported, either because the implementation was not finished, or because explicit decisions to make exceptions were made. Overwhelming however, experience with transparency has been very positive; giving it up, once having had it, would be nearly unthinkable.

LOCUS executes programs locally as the default. We found that the primary motivation for remote execution was load balancing. Remote process execution is also used to access those few peripheral devices which are not remotely transparent. We expect that the remote processing facility will also be heavily used when a LOCUS network is composed of heterogeneous cpus. The non-Vax machines at UCLA (PDP-11's) were decommissioned before the remote processing facilities were generally available, so this activity is not heavily represented in operational experience.

Experience with replicated storage was limited at the time this paper was written, so few firm conclusions can be drawn, except that we certainly cursed its absence.

As usual, the tasks involved in providing a reasonably production quality environment were far more extensive and much more painful than anyone had anticipated, even though we held university standards for 'production quality', and we all knew to expect this phenomenon.

We estimate that, from the project inception in 1979 till early 1983, about 50 man years were spent on Locus. This effort included almost a year in a conceptual phase (transparency was only a vague idea at that time, for example), an extensive design phase that lasted almost a year, initial construction on PDP-11s, multiple ports to the Vax and Ethernet, development of the general-use, development and testing configuration at UCLA, extensive debugging, some redesign and reimplementation to more fully maintain Unix compatibility, and a significant number of masters and PhD theses. Nevertheless, a great deal remains at the time this paper was written. Fortunately, most of that work is now being done in a commercial environment rather than by a university research project.

7 Conclusions

The most obvious conclusion to be drawn from the LOCUS work is that a high performance, network transparent, distributed file system which contains all of the various functions indicated throughout this paper, is feasible to design and implement, even in a small machine environment.

Replication of storage is valuable, both from the user and the system's point of view. However, much of the work is in recovery and in dealing with the various races and failures that can exist.

Nothing is free. In order to avoid performance degradation when resources are local, the cost has been converted into additional code and substantial care in implementation architecture. LOCUS is approximately a third bigger than Unix and certainly more complex.

The difficulties involved in dynamically reconfiguring an operating system are both intrinsic to the problem, and dependent on the particular system. Rebuilding lock tables and synchronizing processes running in separate environments are problems of inherent difficulty. Most of the system-dependent problems can be avoided, however, with careful design.

The fact that LOCUS uses specialized protocols for operating system to operating system communication made it possible to control message traffic quite selectively. The ability to alter specific protocols to simplify the reconfiguration solution was particularly appreciated.

The task of developing a protocol by which sites would agree about the membership of a partition proved to be surprisingly difficult. Balancing the needs of protocol synchronization and failure detection while maintaining good performance presented a considerable challenge. Since reconfiguration software is run precisely when the network is flaky, those problems are real, and not events that are unlikely.

Nevertheless, it has been possible to design and implement a solution that exhibits reasonably high performance. Further work is still needed to assure that scaling to a large network will successfully maintain that performance characteristic, but our experience with the present solution makes us quite optimistic.

In summary, however, use of LOCUS indicates the enormous value of a highly transparent, distributed operating system. Since file activity often is the dominant part of the operating system load, it seems clear that the LOCUS architecture, constructed on a distributed file system base, is rather attractive.

8 Acknowledgements

The authors would like to thank all those members of the research contract who have helped, over the years, in the design, implementation and support of LOCUS. In addition, special recognition should be given to Terry Gray, who is responsible for keeping the LOCUS facility running at UCLA.

9 Bibliography

ALSB 76 Alsberg, P. A., Day, J. D., *A Principle for Resilient Sharing of Distributed Resources,* Proceedings of Second International Conference on Software Engineering, October 1976.

BARL 81 Bartlett J.F., *A NonStop Kernel,* Proceedings of the Eighth Symposium on Operating Systems Principles, Pacific Grove, California, December 1981.

BIRR 82 Birrell, A. D., Levin, R., Needham, R. M., Schroeder, M. D., *Grapevine: An Exercise in Distributed Computing,* CACM, Vol. 25, No. 4, April 1982, pp. 260-274.

DION 80 Dion, J., *The Cambridge File Server,* Op. Sys. Rev, 14(4), pp. 26-35, Oct. 1980.

FAIS 81 Faissol, S., *Availability and Reliability Issues in Distributed Databases,* Ph. D. Dissertation, Computer Science Department, University of California, Los Angeles, 1981.

GOLD 83 Goldberg, A., and G. Popek, *Measurement of the Distributed Operating System LOCUS,* UCLA Technical Report, 1983.

GRAY 78 Gray, J. N., *Notes on Data Base Operating Systems,* Operating Systems, Lecture Notes in Computer Science 60, Springer-Verlag, 1978, 393-481.

HOLL 81a Holler E., *Multiple Copy Update,* Distributed Systems - Architecture and Implementation, Lecture Notes in Computer Science 105, Springer-Verlag, 1981, 284-303.

HOLL 81b Holler E., *The National Software Works (NSW),* Distributed Systems - Architecture and Implementation, Lecture Notes in Computer Science 105, Springer-Verlag, 1981, 421-442.

JONE 82 Jones, M.B., R. F. Rashid and M. Thompson, *Sesame: The Spice File System,* Draft from CMU, Sept. 82.

LAMP 81a Lampson B.W., *Atomic Transactions,* Distributed Systems - Architecture and Implementation, Lecture Notes in Computer Science 105, Springer-Verlag, 1981, 246-264.

LAMP 81b Lampson B.W., *Ethernet, Pub and Violet,* Distributed Systems - Architecture and Implementation, Lecture Notes in Computer Science 105, Springer-Verlag, 1981, 446-484.

LAMP 82 Lampson, B.W. and H.E. Sturgis, *Crash Recovery in a Distributed Data Storage System,* CACM (to appear)

LELA 81 LeLann G., *Synchronization,* Distributed Systems - Architecture and Implementation, Lecture Notes in Computer Science 105, Springer-Verlag, 1981, 266-282.

LIND 79 Lindsay, B. G. et. al., *Notes on Distributed Databases,* IBM Research Report RJ2571(33471), IBM Research Laboratory, San Jose, CA, July 14, 1979, 44-50.

MENA 77 Menasce, D. A., Popek, G. J., Muntz, R. R., *A Locking Protocol for Resource Coordination in Distributed Systems,* Technical Report UCLA-ENG-7808, Dept. of Computer Science, UCLA, October 1977.

MEUL 83 Meuller E., J. Moore and G. Popek, *A Nested Transaction System for LOCUS,* SOSP '83.

MITC 82 Mitchell J.G. and J. Dion, *A Comparison of Two Network-Based File Servers,* CACM, Vol. 25, No. 4, April 1982.

NELS 81 Nelson, B.J., *Remote Procedure Call,* Ph.D. Dissertation, Report CMU-CS-81-119, Carnegie-Mellon University, Pittsburgh, 1981.

PARK 83 Parker, D. Stott, Popek, Gerald J., Rudisin, G., Stoughton, A., Walker, B., Walton, E., Chow, J., Edwards, D., Kiser, S., and Kline, C., *Detection of Mutual Inconsistency in Distributed Systems,* IEEE Transactions of Software Engineering, May 1983.

POPE 81 Popek, G., Walker, B., Chow, J., Edwards, D., Kline, C., Rudisin, G., and Thiel, G., *LOCUS: A Network Transparent, High Reliability Distributed System,* Proceedings of the Eighth Symposium on Operating Systems Principles, Pacific Grove, California, December 1981.

POPE 83a Popek, Gerald J., and Walker, Bruce J., *Network Transparency and its Limits in a Distributed Operating System,* Submitted for Publication.

POPE 83b Popek G.J., et.al., *LOCUS System Architecture,* LOCUS Computing Corporation Technical Report, 1983.

RASH 81 Rashid, R.F., and Robertson, G.G., *Accent: A Communication Oriented Network Operating System Kernel,* Proceedings of the Eighth Symposium on Operating Systems Principles, Pacific Grove, California, December 1981.

REED 78 Reed, D. P., *Naming and Synchronization in a Decentralized Computer System,* Technical Report MIT/LCS/TR-205, Laboratory for Computer Science, M.I.T., 1978.

REED 80 Reed, D.P, and Svobodova L, *SWALLOW: A Distributed Data Storage System for a Local Network,* Proc. of the International Workshop on Local Networks, Zurich, Switzerland, August 1980.

RITC 78 Ritchie, D. and Thompson, K., *The UNIX Timesharing System,* Bell System Technical Journal, vol. 57, no. 6, part 2 (July - August 1978), 1905-1930.

SALT 78 Saltzer J.H., *Naming and Binding of Objects,* Operating Systems, Lecture Notes in Computer Science 60, Springer-Verlag, 1978, 99-208.

SPEC 81 Spector, A. Z., *Performing Remote Operations Efficiently on a Local Computer Network,* CACM, Vol. 25, No. 4, April 1982.

STON 76 Stonebraker, M., Wong, E., Kreps, P., *The Design and Implementation of Ingres,* ACM Transactions on Database Systems, Vol. 1, No. 3, Sept. 1976, pp. 189-222.

STUR 80 Sturgis, H.E. J.G, Mitchell and J. Israel, *Issues in the Design and Use of a Distributed File System,* Op. Sys. Rev, 14(3), pp. 55-69, July 1980.

SVOB 81 Svobodova, L., *A Reliable Object-Oriented Data Repository For a Distributed Computer,* Proceedings of the Eighth Symposium on Operating Systems Principles, Pacific Grove, California, December 1981.

THIE 83 Thiel, G., *Partitioned Operation and Distributed Data Base Management System Catalogues*, Ph.d. Dissertation, Computer Science Department, University of California, Los Angeles, June 1983.

THOM 78 Thomas, R.F., *A Solution to the Concurrency Control Problem for Multiple Copy Data Bases*, Proc. Spring COMPCON, Feb 28-Mar 3, 1978.

WALK 83 Walker, B.J., *Issues of Network Transparency and File Replication in Distributed Systems: LOCUS*, Ph.D. Dissertation, Computer Science Department, University of California, Los Angeles, 1983.

WATS 81 Watson R.W., *Identifiers (Naming) in Distributed Systems*, Distributed Systems - Architecture and Implementation, Lecture Notes in Computer Science 105, Springer-Verlag, 1981, 191-210.

A DISTRIBUTED REAL TIME OPERATING SYSTEM

Michael L. Green, Edward Y.S. Lee, Samprakash Majumdar, Douglas C. Shannon

TRW Defense and Space Systems Group
Redondo Beach, Ca. 90278

Abstract

A distributed-Real Time Operating System (d-RTOS) is described which supported a distributed computer simulation with the following services: A Data Input Handler, Clock Manager, Conditional Enablement Handler, Reconfiguration Prescheduler, Scheduler, Task Completion Handler and Resource Manager. These services were tailored to a ballistic missile defense (BMD) application to achieve maximum performance at minimum overhead. The experiment proved that d-RTOS is efficient for BMD applications. The d-RTOS may be extended to other classes of distributed computer applications.

Introduction

A distributed computer simulation was conducted at the Advanced Research Center in Huntsville, Alabama, using a network of eight VAX 11/780 computers [1]. The simulation included a distributed-Real Time Operating System (d-RTOS) which employed a functioning distributed data base manager, distributed resource manager and process executive, and models of the target application software. This paper describes an overview of the d-RTOS. Companion papers describe the data base manager and resource manager [2, 3].

The d-RTOS was developed to both explicitly perform and functionally simulate the execution of several key d-RTOS tasks including the following:

(1) Dispatcher - cycles through six d-RTOS tasks.
(2) Initialization Routine - initializes variables and arrays.
(3) Data Input Handler - processes incoming task enablements and replicated file updates from other simulated computers.
(4) Clock Manager - monitors the real time clock for time enablements.
(5) Conditional Enablement Handler - checks for a matching pair of conditional enablements.
(6) Reconfiguration Prescheduler - generates a reconfiguration enablement when all requested resource management status reports have been received.
(7) Scheduler - selects, on a priority First-In First-Out (FIFO) basis, a task in the local task enablement queue and executes the selected task.
(8) Task Completion Handler - processes task enablements and outgoing replicated file updates generated by a local task completion.
(9) Resource Manager - detects one or more overloaded computers and redistributes their load.

Each computer in the simulated BMD defense unit contains a distributed-Real Time Operating System (d-RTOS), that is an operating system which acts independently but cooperatively with the other computers in the defense unit. A block diagram for the d-RTOS for a single computer is shown in Figure 1. This figure shows the control and data flow within a computer and the data flow to and from the other computers in the defense unit. The d-RTOS and application task models are presented as if they were in a true tactical environment.

Data is shared in a single computer (without overhead) between all d-RTOS and application tasks using FORTRAN named commons. Between computers, updates to replicated files and task enablements are formatted into a variable length message using a three-word tactical header and transmitted over a simulated shared bus or direct link.

The objectives of the d-RTOS are to simplify the design and to speed the execution of the application tasks for use in a distributed environment. The d-RTOS is not a general purpose operating system but is highly specialized to take advantage of every peculiarity of the BMD construct.

The d-RTOS model is transparent to the application tasks. Each application task is unaware that it is being executed on a distributed architecture. It need not know where the other application tasks are resident or where updates to its replicated files are sent. In addition, when an application task is enabled, all its files have already been updated by the d-RTOS data base manager and are waiting for it locally for immediate processing.

The d-RTOS uses a write-oriented design philosophy. When an application task updates a replicated file, these updates are transferred by the data base manager as soon as possible to all relevant computers. Thus an application task need never request data files since all data files are transferred as soon as they are updated. This design philosophy encourages parallelism between data flow and task execution, trading off message traffic for computation and reconfiguration speed.

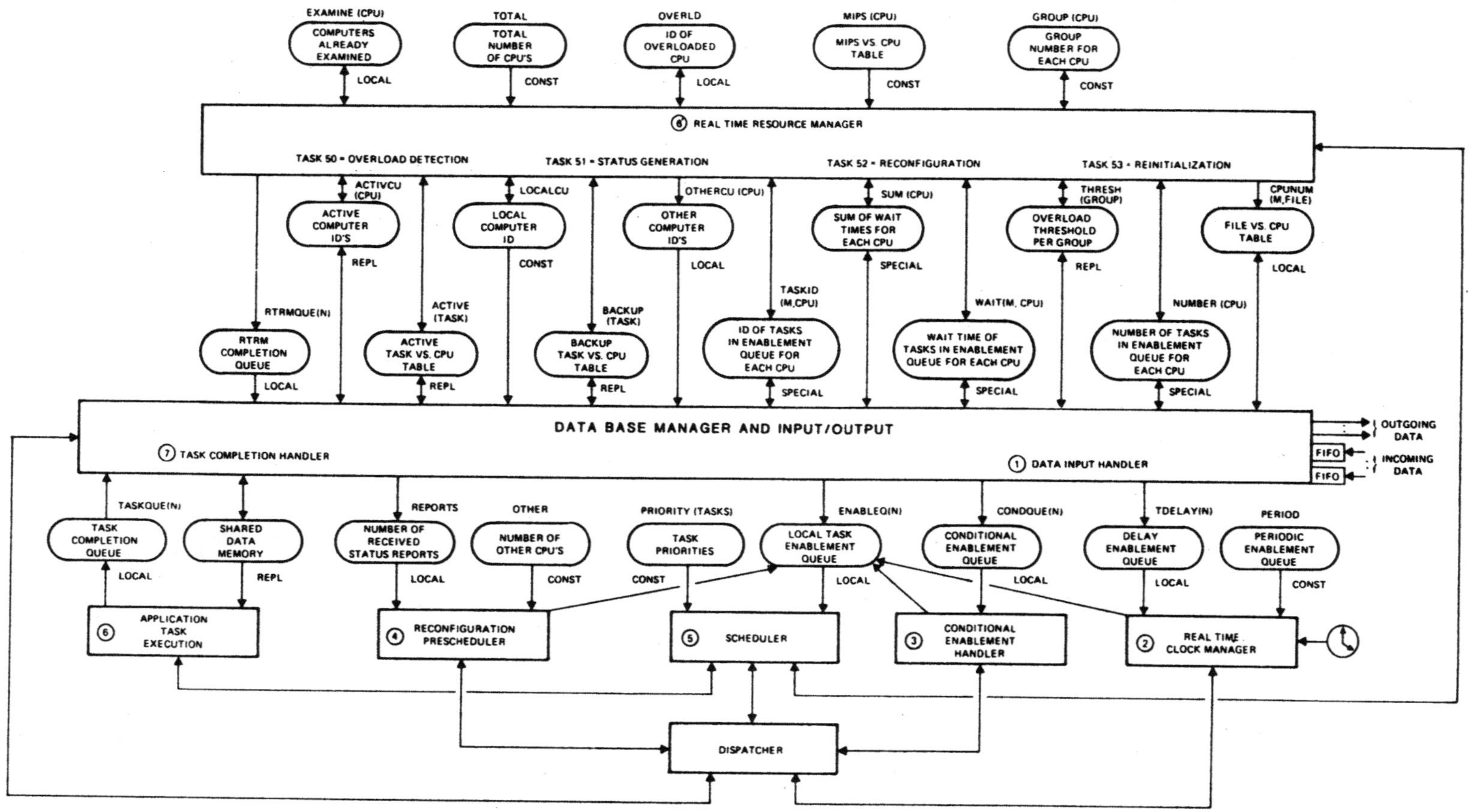

Figure 1. Distributed-Real Time Operating System (r-RTOS) for each Computer

The Real Time Resource Manager is used to balance the task load across all the computers in the defense unit. Load balancing is accomplished by locally detecting an overloaded condition, querying all other computers for their loading status and then dynamically changing the allocation of tasks to computers. The Resource Manager is fully distributed and consists of five tasks which reside on each computer in the defense unit.

Fundamental Assumptions

Several fundamental assumptions have been made in order to improve performance and to simplify the design of a tactical distributed RTOS for the Distributed Data Processing (DDP) Simulation Experiment [4, 5].

Assumption 1 - Files read by two or more computers in the DDP architecture will be replicated. These replicated files will be updated whenever a completing task updates its local files.

Assumption 2 - Updates for a file are only written into that part of the file corresponding to a unique ID.

Assumption 3 - A file may be written into by only one task in the DDP architecture. Several tasks may read a file.

Assumption 4 - Each computer has infinite main storage. Therefore, there is no limit as to the number of tasks and data files that can be stored within each computer. For this experiment, this memory will be assumed to be of a single high speed level. Thus a task can be enabled without dispatch and initialization overhead.

Assumption 5 - Computers are so closely spaced that communications between computers are error free. Thus error checking, acknowledgements, retransmissions, etc., will not be required nor modeled.

Assumption 6 - Computers are interconnected using point-to-point direct connections or shared buses, and FIFO buffers. FIFO buffers are assumed to be of infinite length, therefore overflow protection will not be required.

Assumption 7 - Within each computer all d-RTOS and application tasks can communicate with each other through FORTRAN common memory, i.e., local reads and writes are not required (zero overhead).

Detail of the Distributed Real Time Operating System

The Dispatcher

The simulated defense unit is dormant until the defense command authority transmits an initialization call to each computer. The dispatcher is the main program within each computer (see Figures 1 and 2). It initializes variables and arrays through a call to the Initialization Routine and then requests permission to start. When permission is received it begins cycling through six d-RTOS tasks: The Data Input Handler, Clock Manager, Conditional Enablement Handler, Reconfiguration Prescheduler, Scheduler, and Task Completion Handler. Through these six d-RTOS tasks, the Dispatcher executes either directly or indirectly all relevant d-RTOS and application tasks. If a d-RTOS task is called that has no entries in its input queue(s), it simply returns control to the Dispatcher. Otherwise, it performs its required function and, if necessary, calls other d-RTOS tasks and then returns to the Dispatcher.

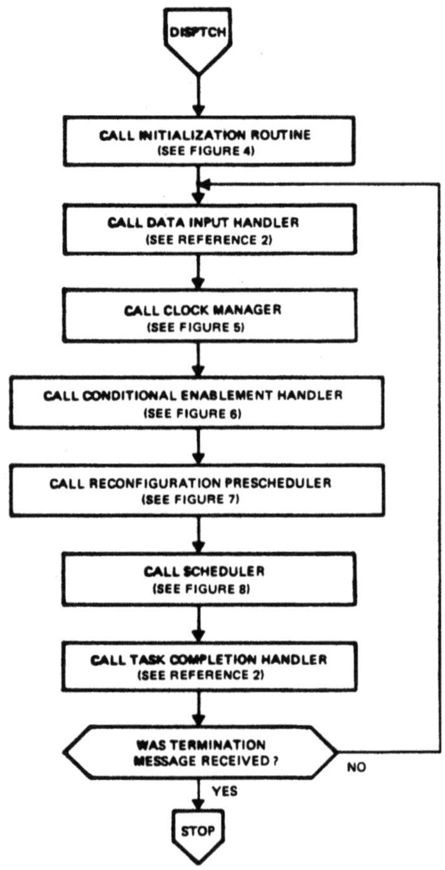

Figure 2. The Dispatcher

The cyclic nature of the execution sequence within each computer is graphically displayed in Figure 3. The execution time required by any d-RTOS task can range from negligible when its input queue(s) are empty, to the largest part of a cycle. The execution time of a cycle, being merely the sum of its composite parts, may also vary over a wide range.

The Initialization Routine

The initialization routine is used to initialize the variables and arrays used by d-RTOS and the application model within a computer (see Figures 2 and 4). It is called only once as the defense unit is readied for engagement. Since initialization occurs only during the preengagement period, its execution time is ignored.

The Clock Manager

An application task may write a task delay enablement into its task completion queue (see Figure 1). The Task Completion Handler (part of the data base manager) reads this task delay enablement and routes it to the computer which will eventually execute this task at the appropriate time. When the task delay enablement arrives at the destination computer, the Data Input Handler stores it in the local task delay enablement queue.

The Real Time Clock Manager is called once per cycle (see Figures 1, 3, and 5). It examines the real time clock and at the proper time places a task enablement in the local task enablement queue for task delay enablements (at a time specified by an application task) and for periodic enablements (every N milliseconds).

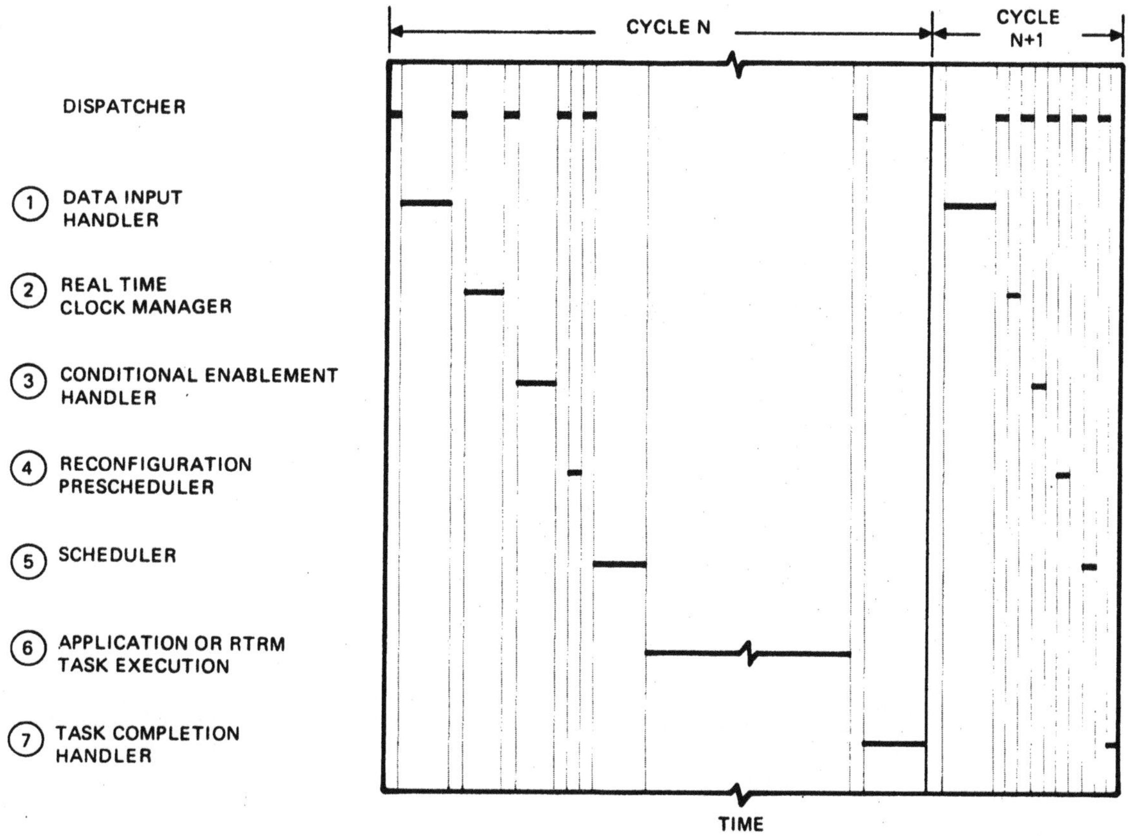

Figure 3. Execution Sequence Within Each Computer

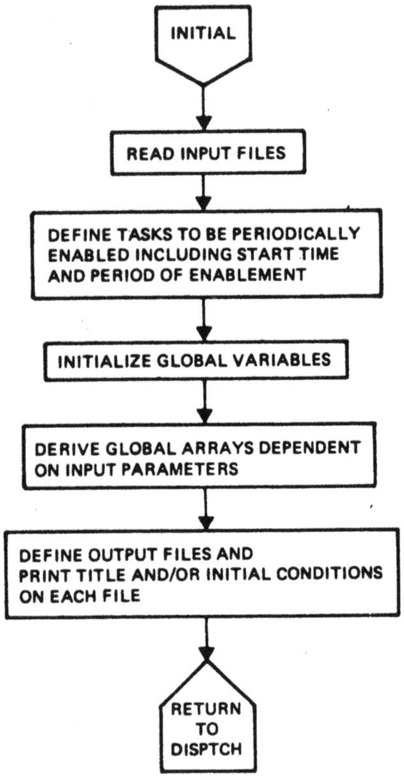

Figure 4. The Initialization Routine

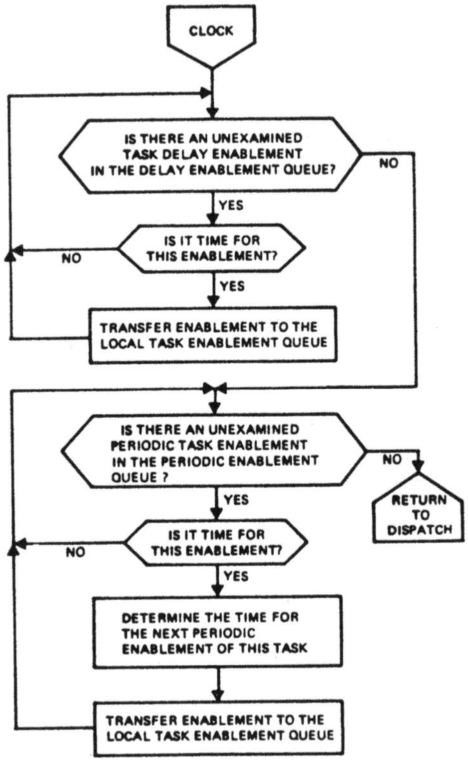

Figure 5. The Clock Manager

The Conditional Enablement Handler

A conditional enablement scheme is available in which two different application tasks operating on the same instance must both request the enablement of a third task before that task can be enabled. Each of the three tasks involved can be resident on different computers or can be reallocated to other computers by the resource manager without affecting the conditional enablement.

The scheme works as follows: Two application tasks independently write a conditional enablement into their respective task completion queues (see Figure 1). The Task Completion Handler of the local computer (part of the data base manager) reads each of these conditional enablements and routes them to the computer that will eventually execute this task. When each conditional enablement arrives at the destination computer, the Data Input Handler stores it in the conditional enablement queue.

The Conditional Enablement Handler is called once per cycle (see Figures 1, 3, and 6). It checks the conditional enablement queue for a matching pair of conditional enablements containing the same task number and the same instance ID but which are requested by different tasks. If such a pair of conditional enablements is found, it places an enablement in the local task enablement queue which will be processed by the Scheduler during a later part of the cycle.

The Reconfiguration Prescheduler

The Real Time Resource Manager (RTRM) consists of four d-RTOS tasks: Overload Detection, Status Report Generation, Reconfiguration and Reinitialization. The Overload Detection task (DETECT) is periodically enabled every 20 milliseconds via the Clock Manager. DETECT checks for an overloaded condition within the local task enablement queue. If an overload is detected, DETECT requests a status report from the other computers in the defense unit by writing an enablement for the Status Report Generation task in the RTRM Completion Queue. When all the status reports have been returned, the Reconfiguration Prescheduler places an enablement for the Reconfiguration task in the local task enablement queue. The Reconfiguration task attempts to redistribute the task load from one or more overloaded computers to one or more lightly loaded computers (see Figures 1, 3, and 7, and the companion paper entitled "A Distributed Real Time Resource Manager" [3].

The Scheduler

Each computer has its own local task enablement queue (array ENABLEQ). A task enablement can be placed in this queue from several different d-RTOS Tasks (see Figure 1):

- When an enablement is received from another computer, the Data Input Handler stores it in ENABLEQ.
- The Clock Manager monitors the real time clock and at the specified time places a delay enablement or periodic enablement in ENABLEQ.
- The Conditional Enablement Handler checks for a matching pair of conditional enablements and if found, places an enablement in ENABLEQ.
- When all the requested status reports have been returned, the Reconfiguration Prescheduler places an enablement for the Reconfiguration task in ENABLEQ.
- An application task can write an enablement for another application task into the task completion queue. A resource management task can write an enablement for another resource management task into the RTRM completion queue. The Task Completion Handler transfers these enablements either to ENABLEQ or to another computer after referring to the "Task vs. CPU" table.

The Scheduler examines the task enablement(s) placed in ENABLEQ by one or more of the above d-RTOS tasks. It selects on a priority first-in first-out basis one of these task enablements, it executes the selected task, and then returns control to the Dispatcher (see Figures1, 3, and 8).

Data Base Management

The Data Base Manager (DBM) of the distributed Real Time Operating System (d-RTOS) serves several very important functions in the overall d-RTOS design. It controls the flow of data and enablements among application tasks both within the local CPU and between the local CPU and other CPU's. It maintains all the replicated files and tables needed by the application tasks and the Real Time Resource Manager (RTRM), making sure all updates are performed correctly. It also services the four important queues related to task execution under the d-RTOS design. For more details, see the companion paper entitled "A Distributed Data Base Manager" [2].

Simulation Analysis Tools

This section presents a sample of the output listings available to analyze the performance of the simulation.

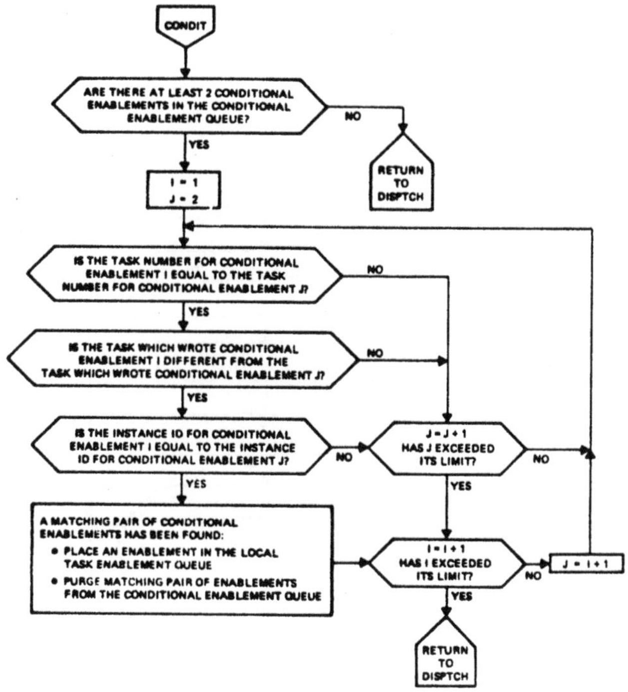

Figure 6. The Conditional Enablement Handler

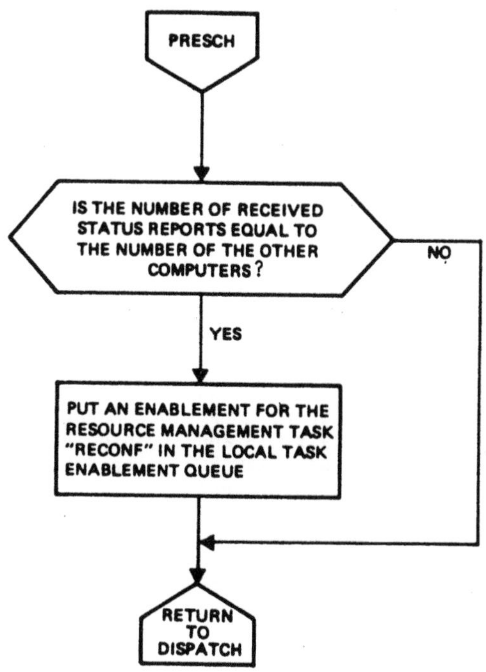

Figure 7. The Reconfiguration Prescheduler

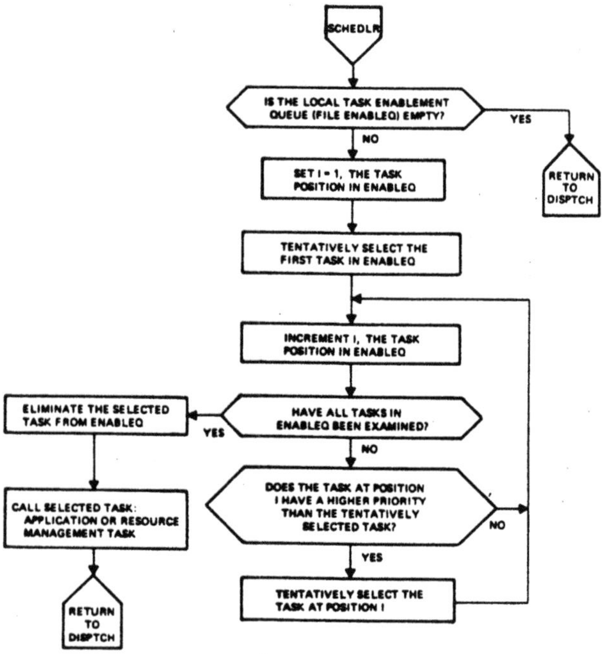

Figure 8. The Scheduler

Full Trace of the Run

A d-RTOS cycle may contain 6 d-RTOS tasks and 1 application or resource management task (see Figures 1 and 3). Application or resource management tasks are only selected and executed by the Scheduler if the relevant enablement is written into the local task enablement queue by another d-RTOS task. If a d-RTOS task executes in less than 15 machine language instructions (indicating that its input queue(s) are empty), it is defined as "idle" and it is not displayed in the full trace of the run.

As an example of the trace output, Figure 9 shows several d-RTOS cycles of tactical computer 2 in a six-computer architecture testcase. In cycle 1, 1 microsecond after BMD processing was initiated, the first non-idle d-RTOS task was executed, the Real Time Clock Manager. The Clock Manager placed an enablement for tasks 13 and 14 into the local task enablement queue (ENABLEQ). The Scheduler then examined these enablements and selected the highest priority task, task 13. Task 13 ran and wrote into the task completion queue that it updated files 129, 128 and 131 (see Figure 1). The Task Completion Handler examined the task completion queue and with the aid of the File versus CPU table concluded that all 3 updated files were non-replicated.

In the second cycle, the scheduler selected the task enablement remaining in the local task enablement queue, task 14. Task 14 ran and wrote into the task completion queue that it updated files 147, 146 and 132 and that it requests the enablement of task 23. The Task Completion Handler examined this queue and concluded that only file 132 was replicated on another computer. The updated part of file 132 (6 actual words and 4 fictitious words making up a 10-word simulated tactical file update) were appended to a 3-word tactical header and transmitted to tactical computer 1. The Task Completion Handler next processed the task 23 enablement and with the aid of the Task versus CPU table concluded that this enablement should be placed in the local task enablement queue.

Note that no cycles are printed between cycles 3 and 74. These cycles are defined as "empty". An empty cycle does not contain an application task and all six d-RTOS tasks which are executed are "idle"; an idle task executes in less than 15 machine language instructions (see Figure 3).

Utilization Factors

The utilization factor is defined as the percentage of the time that a computer is utilized executing a specific type of code. Figure 10 shows the utilization factors for the following types of code:

- TASKS - all the application tasks
- SCHED - the d-RTOS Scheduler
- RTOS - the d-RTOS Clock Manager, Conditional Enablement Handler and Reconfiguration Prescheduler
- RTRM - the d-RTOS Resource Management tasks
- DATAIN - the d-RTOS Data Input Handler
- INPUT - the d-RTOS FIFO buffer to memory task
- COMPL - the d-RTOS Task Completion Handler
- OUT - the d-RTOS memory to output port task
- TOTAL - all of the above
- IDLE - 100% - TOTAL = utilization factor of all d-RTOS tasks executing in less than 15 machine language instructions

The column labeled INSTRUCTIONS shows the accumulated machine language instructions per approximately 10 millisecond interval. The four columns labeled CYCLES show the number and percentage of active and empty cycles. An empty cycle does not contain an application task and all six d-RTOS tasks which are executed are "idle". (An idle task executes in less than 15 machine language instructions.) An active cycle contains at least one non-idle d-RTOS or application task.

Other Tools

Several other output listings are also available to aid in the analysis of the simulation:

- Port-to-Port Times
- Incoming Messages from SETS (the threat)
- Maximum Number of Words in each FIFO
- Maximum Number of Words sent out per Cycle

```
*****************************************************************************************************

BMD DATA PROCESSING WAS INITIATIATED BY THE DU COMMAND AUTHORITY  2982.000 SECONDS AFTER THE ENEMY MISSILES WERE LAUNCHED

*****************************************************************************************************

2 * * * * *     CYCLE       1               ENABTOT  2                  1 MICROSECONDS   * * * * * *
D-RTOS TASK 62, CLOCK:  TIME ENABLEMENT(S) ARE WRITTEN IN ENABLEQ FOR TASK(S):  13  14
D-RTOS TASK 65, SCHEDLR:  EXAMINED ENABLEQ AND SELECTED TASK 13
        N     ENABLEQ(N,1)  ENABLEQ(N,2)  ENABLEQ(N,3)
        1         13            62            0
        2         14            62            0
TASK 13, TRPS RAN.  IT WAS ENABLED BY: 62 FOR IMAGE ID:        0
D-RTOS TASK 66, COMPLET:   TASK 13 UPDATED NON-REPLICATED FILE 129
D-RTOS TASK 66, COMPLET:   TASK 13 UPDATED NON-REPLICATED FILE 128
D-RTOS TASK 66, COMPLET:   TASK 13 UPDATED NON-REPLICATED FILE 131

5 * * * * *     CYCLE       2               ENABTOT  1                184 MICROSECONDS   * * * * * *
D-RTOS TASK 65, SCHEDLR:  EXAMINED ENABLEQ AND SELECTED TASK 14
        N     ENABLEQ(N,1)  ENABLEQ(N,2)  ENABLEQ(N,3)
        1         14            62            0
TASK 14, TRMS, SCHEDULED    1  RADAR COMMANDS FOR SETS
IT UPDATED FILES 132,146,147 AND PLACED AN ENABLEMENT FOR TASK 23 INTO TASKQUE
D-RTOS TASK 66, COMPLET:   TASK 14 UPDATED NON-REPLICATED FILE 147
D-RTOS TASK 66, COMPLET:   TASK 14 UPDATED NON-REPLICATED FILE 146
D-RTOS TASK 66, COMPLET:   6 +  4 WORD(S) OF REPLICATED FILE 132 SENT TO COMPUTER(S):   1
D-RTOS TASK 66, COMPLET:   PLACED AN ENABLEMENT FOR TASK 23 IN ENABLEQ

5 * * * * *     CYCLE       3               ENABTOT  1                277 MICROSECONDS   * * * * * *
D-RTOS TASK 65, SCHEDLR:  EXAMINED ENABLEQ AND SELECTED TASK 23
        N     ENABLEQ(N,1)  ENABLEQ(N,2)  ENABLEQ(N,3)
        1         23            14            1
TASK 23, THE RADAR COMPUTERS OUTPUT TASK, SENT  1 RADAR COMMANDS TO SETS.   IT UPDATED FILE 112 (&153) AND 145.   RDRSETS:
             1        SRCH        3689         1         0          0
D-RTOS TASK 66, COMPLET:   1 +  0 WORD(S) OF REPLICATED FILE 145 SENT TO COMPUTER(S):   1
D-RTOS TASK 66, COMPLET:   6 +  4 WORD(S) OF REPLICATED FILE 112 SENT TO COMPUTER(S):  10

2 * * * * *     CYCLE      74               ENABTOT  1               1000 MICROSECONDS   * * * * * *
D-RTOS TASK 62, CLOCK:  TIME ENABLEMENT(S) ARE WRITTEN IN ENABLEQ FOR TASK(S):  14
D-RTOS TASK 65, SCHEDLR:  EXAMINED ENABLEQ AND SELECTED TASK 14
        N     ENABLEQ(N,1)  ENABLEQ(N,2)  ENABLEQ(N,3)
        1         14            62            0
TASK 14, TRMS, SCHEDULED    1  RADAR COMMANDS FOR SETS
IT UPDATED FILES 132,146,147 AND PLACED AN ENABLEMENT FOR TASK 23 INTO TASKQUE
D-RTOS TASK 66, COMPLET:   TASK 14 UPDATED NON-REPLICATED FILE 147
D-RTOS TASK 66, COMPLET:   TASK 14 UPDATED NON-REPLICATED FILE 146
D-RTOS TASK 66, COMPLET:   6 +  4 WORD(S) OF REPLICATED FILE 132 SENT TO COMPUTER(S):   1
D-RTOS TASK 66, COMPLET:   PLACED AN ENABLEMENT FOR TASK 23 IN ENABLEQ

1 * * * * *     CYCLE      75               ENABTOT  1               1097 MICROSECONDS   * * * * * *
D-RTOS TASK 61, DATAIN:   PLACED AN ENABLEMENT FOR TASK 22 IN ENABLEQ
D-RTOS TASK 61, DATAIN:   8 + 24 WORD(S) OF REPLICATED FILE 111 TRANSFERRED FROM FIFO 10 TO SHARED MEMORY
D-RTOS TASK 65, SCHEDLR:  EXAMINED ENABLEQ AND SELECTED TASK 23
        N     ENABLEQ(N,1)  ENABLEQ(N,2)  ENABLEQ(N,3)
        1         23            14            1
        2         22            62            1
TASK 23, THE RADAR COMPUTERS OUTPUT TASK, SENT  1 RADAR COMMANDS TO SETS.   IT UPDATED FILE 112 (&153) AND 145.   RDRSETS:
             2        SRCH        4514        16         0          0
D-RTOS TASK 66, COMPLET:   1 +  0 WORD(S) OF REPLICATED FILE 145 SENT TO COMPUTER(S):   1
D-RTOS TASK 66, COMPLET:   6 +  4 WORD(S) OF REPLICATED FILE 112 SENT TO COMPUTER(S):  10
```

Figure 9. Example of Full Trace of the Run

	UTILIZATION FACTORS	(PERCENT)									INSTRUCTIONS	CYCLES			
TIME	TASKS	SCHED	RTOS	RTRM	DATAIN	INPUT	COMPL	OUT	TOTAL	IDLE	TOTAL	ACTIVE	%	EMPTY	%
10003	22.5	3.3	0.3	0.0	0.2	3.2	4.0	2.5	36.0	64.0	7597	25	5.9	396	94.1
20001	18.6	2.9	0.3	0.0	0.0	0.0	3.4	1.9	27.0	73.0	5674	22	4.6	452	95.4
30013	33.1	4.5	0.3	0.0	0.0	2.0	5.5	5.1	50.4	49.6	10762	33	9.8	303	90.2
40008	20.5	3.3	0.3	0.0	0.0	0.7	4.1	2.8	31.7	68.3	6674	25	5.6	422	94.4
50003	20.5	3.3	0.3	0.0	0.0	0.7	4.1	2.8	31.7	68.3	6674	25	5.6	422	94.4
60014	20.5	3.3	0.3	0.0	0.0	0.7	4.0	2.8	31.6	68.4	6674	25	5.6	423	94.4
70176	38.3	3.8	0.5	0.0	0.0	0.6	4.7	2.8	50.7	49.3	10982	29	8.6	308	91.4
80004	23.6	3.4	0.3	0.0	0.0	0.7	4.1	3.0	35.2	64.9	7294	26	6.2	393	93.8
90007	20.2	3.2	0.3	0.0	0.0	0.7	3.8	2.4	30.5	69.5	6421	24	5.3	430	94.7
100010	20.2	3.2	0.3	0.0	0.0	0.7	3.8	2.4	30.5	69.5	6421	24	5.3	430	94.7
AVERAGE	UTILIZATION:		TASKS = 23.8%			D-RTOS = 11.7%			D-RTOS/TOTAL RATIO =		0.33				
110002	24.1	3.6	0.3	0.0	0.2	3.8	4.4	3.0	39.4	60.6	8344	28	7.0	372	93.0
120004	25.2	3.5	0.3	0.0	0.4	5.7	4.1	2.7	41.9	58.1	8878	26	6.8	359	93.2
130008	37.3	4.9	0.3	0.0	0.2	7.2	6.1	5.8	61.8	38.2	13280	37	14.0	228	86.0
140014	26.7	3.9	0.3	0.0	0.4	4.1	4.8	3.7	43.8	56.2	9305	30	8.0	345	92.0
150347	74.3	1.5	0.4	0.0	0.2	0.1	1.6	0.7	78.7	21.3	17651	11	7.3	139	92.7
160012	43.5	6.7	0.3	0.0	0.2	5.2	8.0	6.9	70.8	29.2	14800	47	22.8	159	77.2
170249	44.5	4.3	0.5	0.0	0.4	6.1	5.3	3.6	64.6	35.4	14236	33	13.1	218	86.9
180000	28.2	3.9	0.3	0.0	0.2	3.9	4.7	3.9	45.1	54.9	9351	30	8.4	327	91.6
190008	21.8	3.5	0.3	0.0	0.0	1.3	4.2	2.8	34.0	66.0	7168	26	6.0	408	94.0
202068	39.2	3.1	0.2	0.0	0.3	3.2	3.6	2.5	52.2	47.8	13434	28	7.3	357	92.7
AVERAGE	UTILIZATION:		TASKS = 36.5%			D-RTOS = 16.7%			D-RTOS/TOTAL RATIO =		0.31				
210001	30.2	4.7	0.4	0.0	0.2	4.8	5.5	3.8	49.5	50.5	8375	28	10.4	242	89.6
220004	25.0	3.6	0.3	0.0	0.2	3.8	4.4	3.0	40.3	59.7	8545	28	7.1	367	92.9
230390	39.9	5.2	0.4	0.0	0.2	7.6	6.2	6.2	65.7	34.3	14686	40	16.0	210	84.0
240013	29.6	4.3	0.1	0.0	0.6	7.5	5.5	4.5	52.2	47.8	10718	32	10.3	280	89.7
250430	31.3	4.3	0.4	0.0	0.5	11.1	5.1	4.2	56.8	43.2	12673	35	11.4	271	88.6
264139	64.8	2.3	0.3	0.0	0.5	4.8	2.7	1.9	77.3	22.7	22968	23	10.6	193	89.4
270081	71.9	4.5	0.5	0.0	0.9	11.0	3.1	4.3	96.2	3.8	12572	13	100.0	0	0.0
280228	62.2	7.6	0.3	0.0	0.3	6.9	10.2	7.7	95.2	4.8	21240	62	100.0	0	0.0
290007	41.2	4.8	0.5	0.0	0.7	11.9	5.8	4.7	69.6	30.4	14709	38	18.3	170	81.7
302133	62.8	3.8	0.2	0.0	0.7	8.3	4.4	3.5	83.8	16.2	22132	34	23.6	110	76.4
AVERAGE	UTILIZATION:		TASKS = 45.9%			D-RTOS = 22.8%			D-RTOS/TOTAL RATIO =		0.33				
310008	37.2	5.1	0.4	0.0	0.7	10.6	6.1	4.2	64.3	35.7	10896	32	16.4	163	83.6
320234	31.1	3.9	0.3	0.0	0.7	11.0	4.7	3.5	55.2	44.8	12070	31	10.0	279	90.0
330011	40.7	5.4	0.3	0.0	0.2	5.8	6.6	6.6	65.6	34.4	13806	39	16.5	198	83.5
340012	28.7	4.2	0.3	0.0	0.4	6.9	5.2	4.3	50.0	50.0	10651	31	9.2	306	90.8
350097	78.1	1.7	0.4	0.0	0.4	5.3	1.8	1.2	88.8	11.2	19574	12	15.0	68	85.0
360015	67.4	6.9	0.3	0.0	0.5	5.8	7.9	6.5	95.4	4.6	20788	49	100.0	0	0.0
370085	42.5	4.8	0.3	0.0	0.2	10.6	6.0	4.9	69.2	30.8	15051	41	18.9	176	81.1
380423	44.8	4.9	0.6	0.0	0.9	9.3	5.7	4.9	71.0	29.0	15857	38	17.9	174	82.1
390057	49.4	4.0	0.1	0.0	0.6	5.0	4.8	3.7	67.6	32.4	14033	29	13.4	187	86.6
400006	56.1	4.9	0.3	0.0	0.7	9.7	5.7	4.5	81.9	18.1	17738	36	27.3	96	72.7
AVERAGE	UTILIZATION:		TASKS = 47.6%			D-RTOS = 23.3%			D-RTOS/TOTAL RATIO =		0.33				
410004	28.6	3.8	0.3	0.0	0.5	10.6	4.7	3.4	51.9	48.1	11083	35	10.9	287	89.1
423821	66.7	2.4	0.4	0.0	0.4	4.7	2.7	1.9	79.1	20.9	23717	24	11.9	177	88.1
430029	57.2	8.3	0.4	0.0	0.6	8.7	9.6	9.9	94.7	5.3	12920	35	100.0	0	0.0
440004	43.1	5.0	0.3	0.0	0.4	9.0	6.8	6.0	70.6	29.4	15232	45	21.4	165	78.6
451314	71.8	2.0	0.4	0.0	0.5	3.1	2.1	1.2	81.1	18.9	19924	15	10.1	133	89.9
460027	68.1	6.5	0.3	0.0	0.4	6.2	7.2	6.8	95.6	4.4	18314	39	100.0	0	0.0
470269	47.5	5.3	0.4	0.0	0.2	4.9	6.8	5.1	70.1	29.9	15511	43	19.7	175	80.3
480308	44.6	4.9	0.5	0.0	0.7	12.9	5.8	5.0	74.4	25.6	16185	37	20.2	146	79.8
490006	27.1	4.0	0.1	0.0	0.4	7.2	5.1	3.9	47.9	52.1	9884	31	9.1	308	90.9
500131	70.7	4.0	0.3	0.0	0.9	7.2	4.1	3.4	90.5	9.5	20042	29	38.2	47	61.8
AVERAGE	UTILIZATION:		TASKS = 52.5%			D-RTOS = 23.1%			D-RTOS/TOTAL RATIO =		0.31				

Figure 10. Utilization Factors

- Number of Words sent out per 10 Milliseconds
- Radar Command Offset
- Resource Manager
  - Maximum Length and Wait Times of ENABLEQ
  - Resource Management Thread
  - Trace of the Reconfiguration Task

Summary and Conclusions

A distributed-Real Time Operating System (d-RTOS) was developed to support research in distributed computer system design. It is a highly specialized operating system designed to take full advantage of the peculiarities of a ballistic missile defense (BMD) application. It provides many special services to support the application software: Data Input Handler, Clock Manager, Conditional Enablement Handler, Reconfiguration Prescheduler, Scheduler, Task Completion Handler and Resource Manager. Since BMD applications are both demanding and time critical, the d-RTOS was designed to provide maximum performance at minimum overhead. It is believed those objectives were met. Analysis, refinement, and extension of the d-RTOS design are planned in the coming year.

Acknowledgement

The work described in this paper was performed as part of the research in Phase III of the Distributed Processing Architecture Design (DPAD) program sponsored by the U.S. Army Ballistic Missile Defense Advanced Technology Center (BMDATC) Data Processing Directorate under Contract DASG60-79-C-0039. The simulation experiment was performed with cooperation from personnel from TRW, General Research Corp. (GRC) and System Development Corp. (SDC). The authors wish to thank them for all the assistance provided.

References

[1] W. C. McDonald, J. R. Reynolds and H. D. Welch, "Distributed Simulation Host: A Distributed Testbed", 4th International Computer Software and Applications Conference (COMPSAC), Oct. 1980, Chicago.

[2] E.Y.S. Lee, M. L. Green and D. C. Shannon, "A Distributed Data Base Manager", a companion paper for this symposium.

[3] S. Majumdar and M. L. Green, "A Distributed Real Time Resource Manager", a companion paper for this symposium.

[4] R. H. Hoffman, R. W. Smith and J. T. Ellis, "Simulation Software Development", 4th International Computer Software and Applications Conference (COMPSAC), Oct. 1980, Chicago.

[5] M. L. Green, E.Y.S. Lee, S. Majumdar and D. C. Shannon, "Special Report Phase III of Distributed Processing Architecture Design (DPAD) Program - The DDP Underlay Simulation Experiment: Tactical Applications and d-RTOS Models", TRW Defense and Space Systems Group, 15 May 1980.

Chapter 3

INTERCONNECTION NETWORKS

Concurrent processing in a distributed system depends on the interconnection network among processors and memory modules. Various network interconnection architecture and switching strategies are available and have been proposed. Selecting the appropriate interconnection network and control strategy to satisfy a certain cost-performance is an important architecture design issue. The interconnection network solution depends on the processor and memory architecture, operating systems, and the application program characteristics.

In this chapter, the first paper by Feng provides an overview of various interconnection networks and their design considerations. The second paper by Chen, Lawrie, Yew, and Padua summarizes many of the results dealing with the shuffle-exchange type of network for synchronic and asynchronic processing. The last paper by Ajmone Marsan, *et al.*, presents the performance analysis of interconnection networks for multiprocessor systems.

There are many aspects of interconnection networks that have been reported in the literature. For further information, the interested reader should refer to [BARN 81, DIAS 81, SIEG 81a, KRUS 83, PADM 83].

Concurrent processing depends on interconnection networks for communication among processors and memory modules. Various network topologies and switching strategies are covered here.

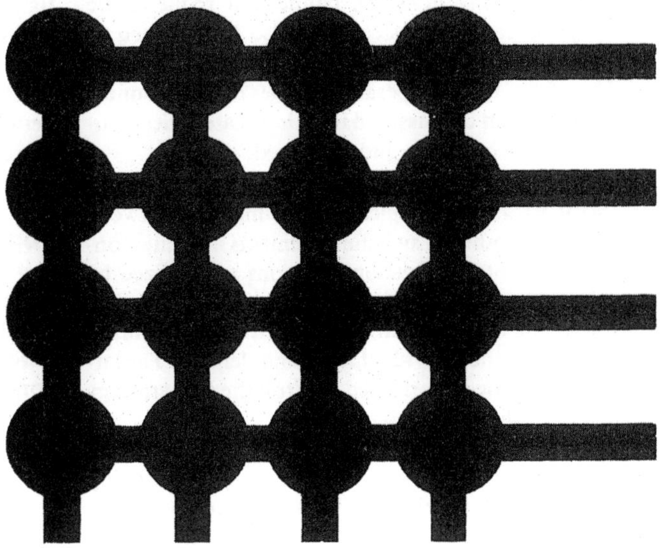

A Survey of Interconnection Networks

Tse-yun Feng
The Ohio State University

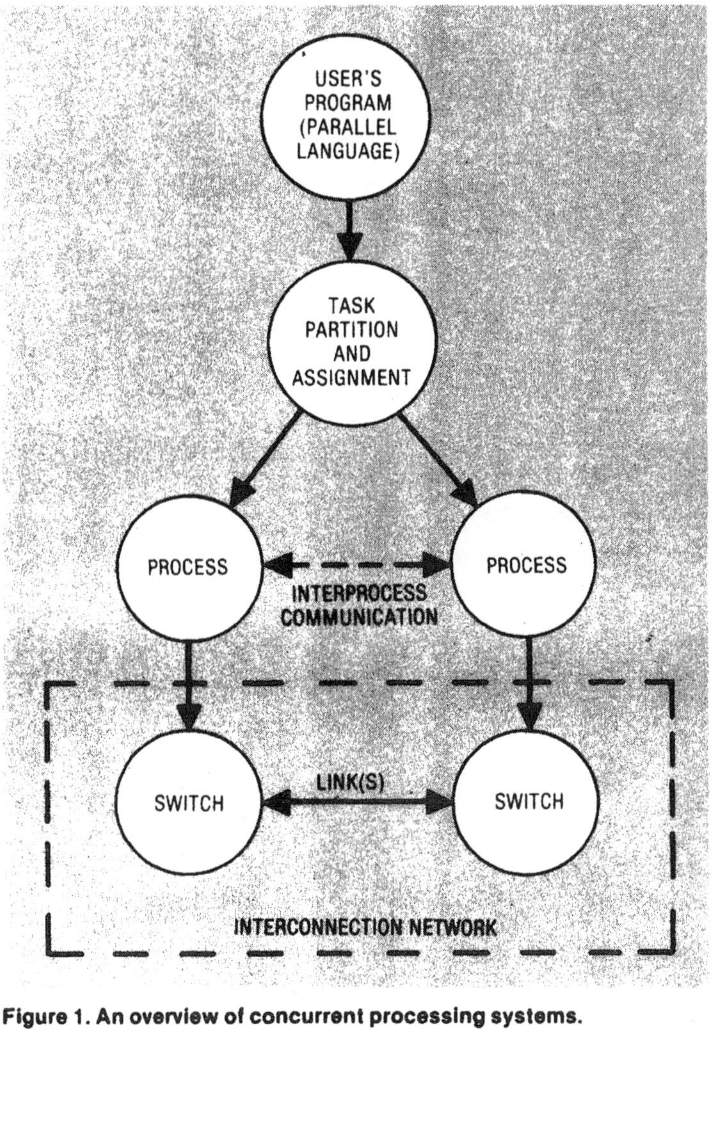

Figure 1. An overview of concurrent processing systems.

Concurrent processing of data items is considered a proper approach for significantly increasing processing speed.[1] In many real-time applications—such as image processing and weather computation, which need an instruction execution rate of more than one billion floating-point instructions per second—concurrent processing is unavoidable. And now, with the advent of LSI technology, it is economically feasible to construct a concurrent processing system by interconnecting hundreds—even thousands—of off-the-shelf processors and memory modules.

A basic concurrent processing system is shown in Figure 1. Processes, generated by compiling and partitioning a user's program, are assigned to individual processors, and an interconnection network implements interprocess communication. A general model of the hardware system is shown in Figure 2. The interconnection network facilitates communication not only among the n processors and the m memory modules but also between the processors and memory modules.

Many interconnection networks have been reviewed in other surveys.[2-9] In this article we consider interconnection networks from a practical design viewpoint. We examine design decisions that are essential in choosing a cost-effective communication network, survey the various topologies and communication protocols, and discuss connection issues related to concurrent processing.

Design decisions

In selecting the architecture of an interconnection network, four design decisions can be identified.[10] They concern operation mode, control strategy, switching method, and network topology.

Operation mode. Two types of communication can be identified: synchronous and asynchronous. Synchronous communication is needed for processing in which communication paths are established synchronously for either a data manipulating function[11] or a data/instruction broadcast. Asynchronous communication is needed for multiprocessing in which connection requests are issued dynamically. A system may also be designed to facilitate both synchronous and asynchronous processing. Therefore, typical operation modes of interconnection networks can be classified into three categories: synchronous, asnychronous, and combined.

Control strategy. A typical interconnection network consists of a number of switching elements and interconnecting links. Interconnection functions are realized by properly setting control of the switching elements. The control-setting function can be managed by a centralized controller or by the individual switching element. The latter strategy is called distributed control; the first strategy is called centralized control.

Switching methodology. The two major switching methodologies are circuit switching and packet switching. In circuit switching, a physical path is actually established between a source and a destination. In packet switching, data is put in a packet and routed through the interconnection network without establishing a physical connection path. In general, circuit switching is much more suitable for bulk data transmission, and packet switching is more efficient for short data messages. Another option, integrated switching, includes capabilities of both circuit switching and packet switching. Therefore, three switching methodologies can be identified: circuit switching, packet switching, and integrated switching.

Network topology. A network can be depicted by a graph in which nodes represent switching points and edges represent communication links. The topologies tend to be regular and can be grouped into two categories: static and dynamic. In a static topology, links between two processors are passive and dedicated buses cannot be reconfigured for direct connections to other processors. On the other hand, links in the dynamic category can be reconfigured by setting the network's active switching elements.

The cross product of the set of categories in each design decision—{operation mode} × {control strategy} × {switching methodology} × {network topology}—represents a space of interconnection networks. Obviously, the cross product contains some uninteresting cases, but a network designer can obtain a meaningful subspace by exercising a practical view of engineering technology.

Topologies

Network topology is a key factor in determining a suitable architectural structure, and many topologies have been considered for telephone switching connections.[12] Here, we review those proposed or used for connections in tightly coupled multiple-processor systems (see Figure 3).

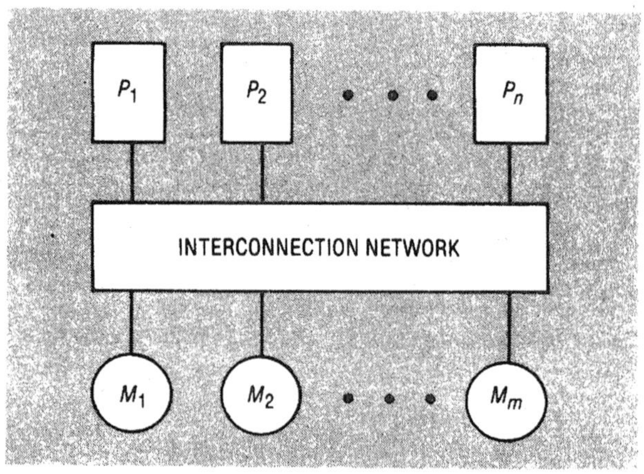

Figure 2. Hardware model of concurrent processing systems.

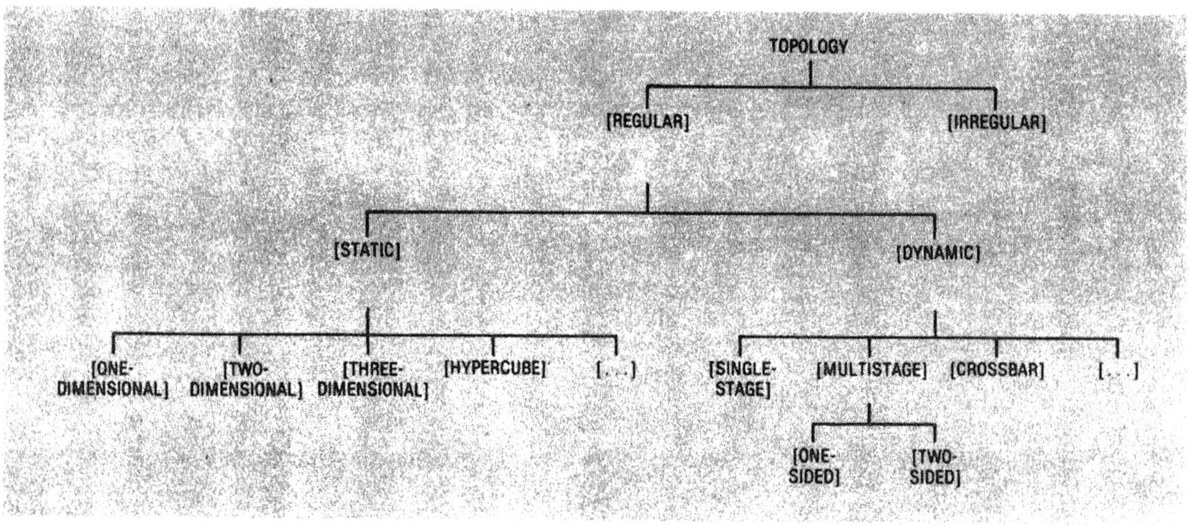

Figure 3. Topologies of interconnection networks.

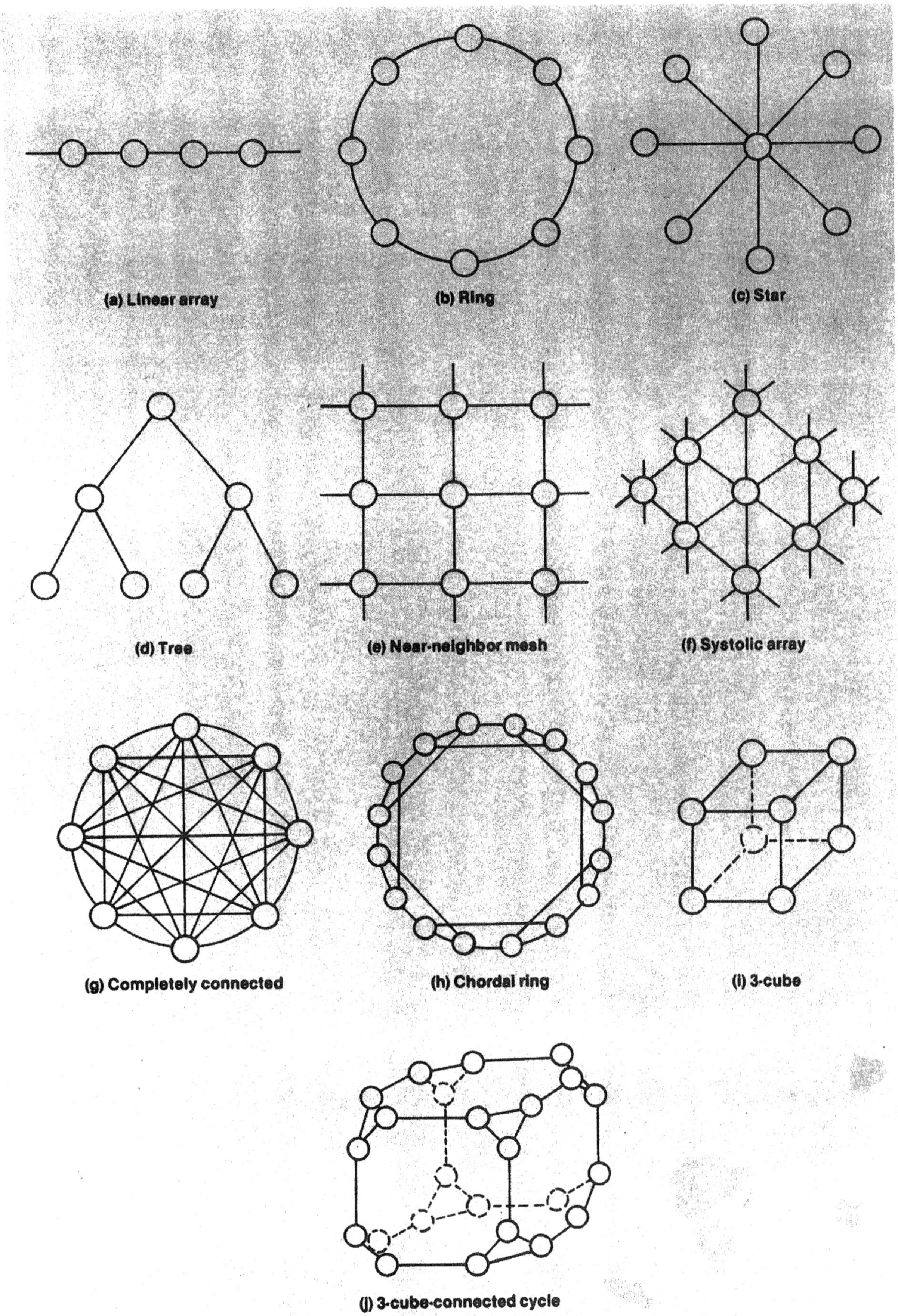

Figure 4. Examples of static network toplogies: (a) one dimensional; (b-f) two dimensional; and (g-j) three dimensional.

Static. Topologies in the static category can be classified according to dimensions required for layout—specifically, one-dimensional, two-dimensional, three-dimensional, and hypercube as shown in Figure 3. Examples of one-dimensional topologies include the linear array used for some pipeline architectures (Figure 4a).[13] Two-dimensional topologies include the ring,[14,15] star,[16] tree,[17] near-neighbor mesh,[18] and systolic array.[13] Examples are shown in Figure 4b-f. Three-dimensional topologies include the completely connected,[19] chordal ring,[20] 3-cube,[21] and 3-cube-connected-cycle[22] networks depicted in Figure 4g-j. A *D*-dimensional, *W*-wide hypercube contains *W* nodes in each dimension, and there is a connection to a node in each dimension. The near-neighbor mesh and the 3-cube are actually two- and three-dimensional hypercubes, respectively. The cube-connected-cycle is a deviation of the hypercube. For example, the 3-cube-connected-cycle shown in Figure 4j is obtained by replacing each node of the 3-cube by a 3-node cycle. Each node in the cycle is connected to the corresponding node in another cycle.

Dynamic. There are three topological classes in the dynamic category: single-stage, multistage, and crossbar (see Figure 5).

Single-stage. A single-stage network is composed of a stage of switching elements cascaded to a link connection pattern. The shuffle-exchange network[23] is a single-stage network based on a perfect-shuffle connection cascaded to a stage of switching elements as shown in Figure 5a. The single-stage network is also called a recirculating network because data items may have to recirculate through the single stage several times before reaching their final destination.

Multistage. A multistage network consists of more than one stage of switching elements and is usually capa-

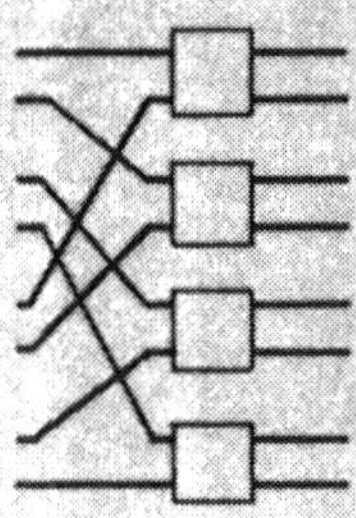

(a) 8 x 8 shuffle-exchange

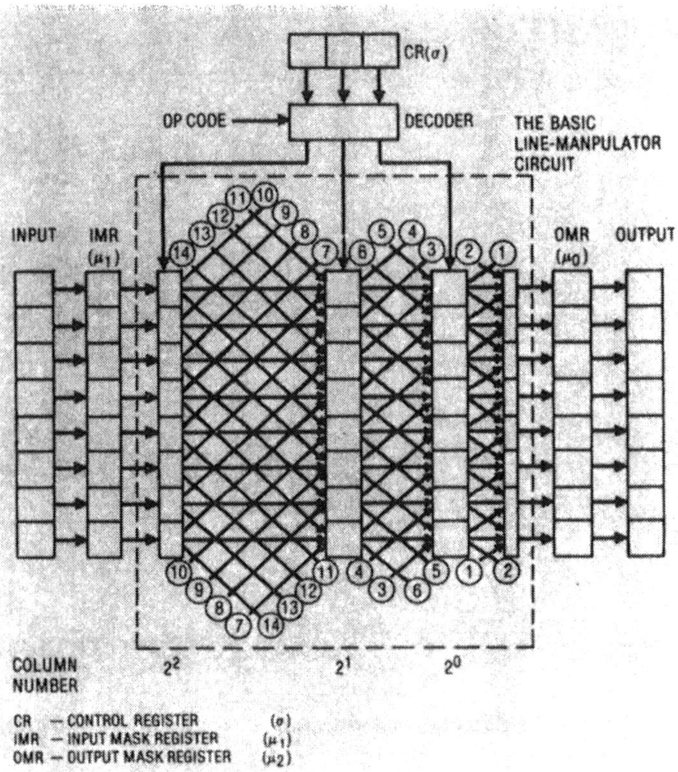

(b) 8 x 8 data manipulator[11]

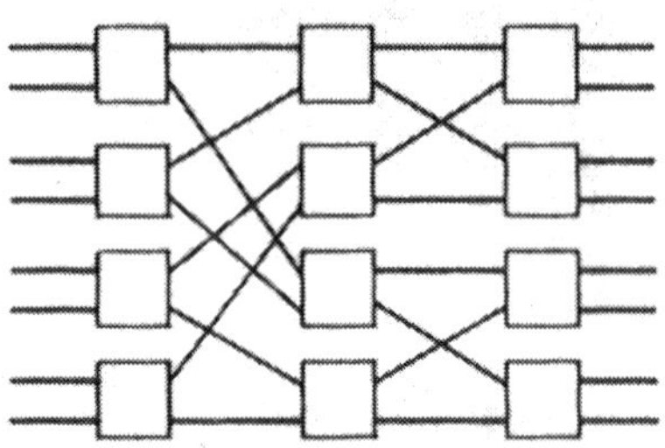

(c) 8 x 8 baseline

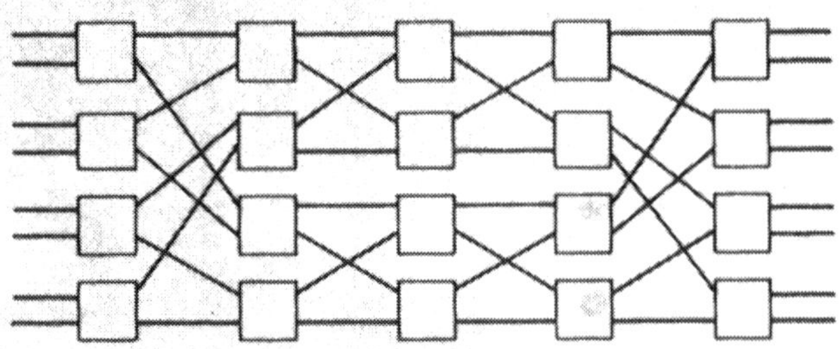

(d) 8 x 8 Benes

Figure 5. Examples of dynamic network topologies: (a) single stage; (b-i) multistage; and (j) crossbar. (Cont'd on p. 16.)

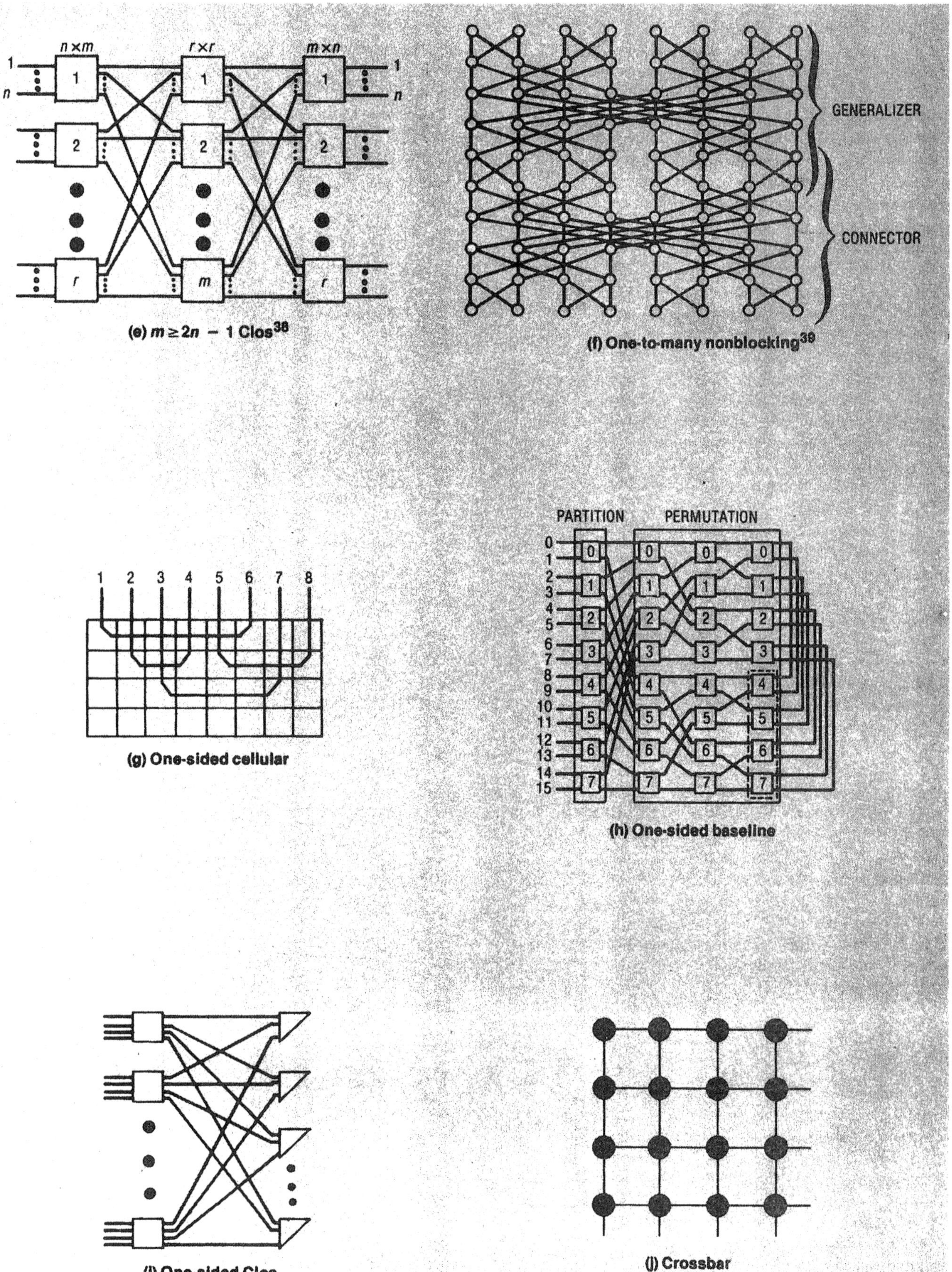

(e) $m \geq 2n - 1$ Clos[38]

(f) One-to-many nonblocking[39]

(g) One-sided cellular

(h) One-sided baseline

(i) One-sided Clos

(j) Crossbar

Figure 5 (cont'd from p.15). Examples of multistage and crossbar (j) dynamic network topologies.

ble of connecting an arbitrary input terminal to an arbitrary output terminal. Multistage networks can be one-sided or two-sided. The one-sided networks, sometimes called full switches, have input-output ports on the same side. The two-sided multistage networks, which usually have an input side and an output side, can be divided into three classes: blocking, rearrangeable, and nonblocking.

In blocking networks, simultaneous connections of more than one terminal pair may result in conflicts in the use of network communication links. Examples of this type of network, which has been extensively investigated, include data manipulator,[24] baseline,[25,26] SW banyan,[27] omega,[28] flip,[29] indirect binary n-cube,[30] and delta.[31] A topological equivalence relationship has been established for this class of networks in terms of the baseline network.[25,26] A data manipulator and a baseline network are shown in Figure 5b and 5c.

A network is called a rearrangeable nonblocking network if it can perform all possible connections between inputs and outputs by rearranging its existing connections so that a connection path for a new input-output pair can always be established. A well-defined network, the Benes network[12] shown in Figure 5d, belongs to this class. The Benes rearrangeable network topology has been extensively studied for use in synchronous data permutation[32-35] and asynchronous interprocessor communication.[36,37]

A network which can handle all possible connections without blocking is called a nonblocking network. Two cases have been considered in the literature. In the first case, the Clos network[38] shown in Figure 5e, a one-to-one connection is made between an input and an output. The other case considers one-to-many connections.[39] Here, a generalized-connection network topology is generated to pass any of the N^N mapping of inputs onto outputs where N is the number of inputs or outputs (see Figure 5f). In a one-sided network (or full switch), one-to-one connection is possible between all pairs of terminals.[40,41] A cellular implementation, a base-line topology construction, and a Clos construction are shown in Figure 5g-i.

Crossbar. In a crossbar switch every input port can be connected to a free output port without blocking. Figure 5j shows a schematic which is similar to one used in C.mmp.[42] A crossbar switch called a versatile line manipulator has also been designed and implemented.[43,44]

Communication protocols

The switching methodology and the control strategy are implemented in switching elements (or switching points) according to required communication protocols. The communication protocols can be viewed on two levels. The first level concerns switching control algorithms which generate necessary control settings on switching elements to ensure reliable data routings from source to destination. The first-level protocols are referred to as routing techniques here. The second level is concerned with the link control procedure that provides the handshaking process among switching points. The handshaking process is a basic function implemented by switching elements.

Routing techniques. The routing techniques depend on the network topology and the operation mode used. More or less, each multiple-processor system needs a routing algorithm. Here, we use several well-defined routing algorithms for examples.

Near-neighbor mesh. Bitonic sort has been adapted by several authors[45-47] for the routing of an $n \times n$ mesh-connected, single instruction-multiple data stream system. The procedure developed by Nassimi[47] is as follows:

```
Procedure SORT (n,n)
  1) K ← S ← 1
  2) While K < n do
       a) consider the n × n processor array as com-
          posed of many adjacent K × 2K subarrays
       b) do in parallel for each K × 2K array
          HORIZONTAL_MERGE(K, 2K)
       c) S ← S + 1
       d) Consider the n × n processor array as
          composed of many adjacent 2K × 2K
          subarrays
       e) do in parallel for each 2K × 2K subarray
          VERTICAL_MERGE(2K, 2K)
       f) S ← S + 1; K ← 2 * K
  end
end SORT
```

The HORIZONTAL_MERGE sorts a bitonic sequence arranged in two arrays with the increasing sequence on the

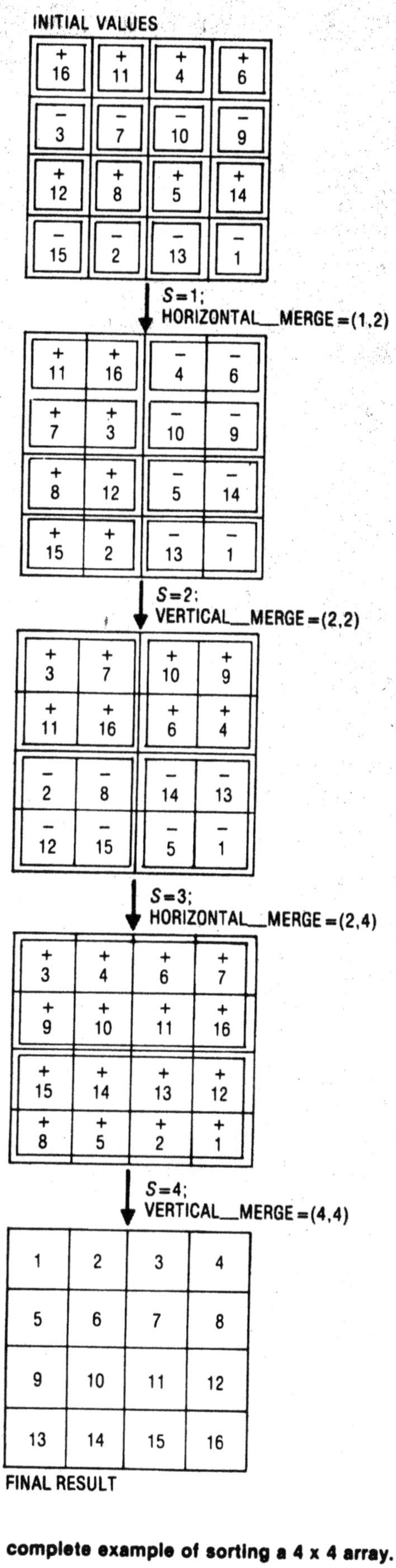

Figure 6. A complete example of sorting a 4 x 4 array.

left array and the decreasing sequence on the right array, or vice versa. Similarly, the VERTICAL_MERGE sorts a bitonic sequence arranged in two arrays with the increasing sequence on the upper array and the decreasing sequence on the lower array, or vice versa. A complete example of sorting a 4×4 array is shown in Figure 6. The order into which a subarray gets sorted is determined by the SIGN function, "+" and "−", used during a comparison-interchange where "+" is for nondecreasing order and "−" is for nonincreasing order. In Figure 6, the initial values given go through an HM sort on two 1×1 arrays, a VM sort on two 1×2 arrays, an HM sort on two 2×2 arrays, and finally a VM sort on two 2×4 arrays.

Shuffle-exchange network. Both centralized and distributed routings have been worked out for the shuffle-exchange network. It has been shown that the shuffle-exchange network can realize an arbitrary permutation in $3(\log_2 N) - 1$ passes where N is the network size.[48] An example is shown in Figure 7 for the following permutation:

$$p = \begin{pmatrix} 0 & 1 & 2 & 3 & 4 & 5 & 6 & 7 & 8 & 9 & 10 & 11 & 12 & 13 & 14 & 15 \\ 14 & 12 & 5 & 7 & 15 & 8 & 9 & 13 & 4 & 3 & 10 & 6 & 1 & 0 & 2 & 11 \end{pmatrix}$$

The control setting developed consists of three matrices, $\overline{F}$, $\overline{S}$, and $\overline{T}$. Among these three control matrices, $\overline{S}$ is independent of the permutation and $\overline{F}$ and $\overline{T}$ are modified matrices obtained by performing some prescribed operations on the control matrix for the Benes binary network. The detailed transformation is shown in Wu and Feng.[48] The shuffle-exchange network can also be constructed to adapt to a distributed control scheme. The construction can be considered as a sorting network, and the binary codes of the destination names are used as the values to be sorted.[23,49] Figure 8 illustrates an example for 2^n elements where $n = 4$. Each of the n^2 steps in this scheme consists of a perfect-shuffle followed by simultaneous operations performed on 2^{n-1} pairs of adjacent elements. Each of the latter operations is either "0" (no operation, straight connection), "+" (comparator module which sends the larger value to the lower link), or "−" (a reverse comparator module). The sorting proceeds in n stages of n steps each: during stage s, for $s \leq n$, we do $n - s$ steps in which all operations are "0", followed by s steps in which the operations consist alternately of 2^t "+" followed by 2^t "−" for $t = 1, 2, \ldots, s$. During the last stage, all operations are "+".

Data manipulator. A centralized control scheme is designed for implementing data manipulating functions such as permuting, replicating, spacing, masking, and complementing.[11] To implement a data manipulating function, proper control lines of the six groups ($U_1^{2^i}$, $U_2^{2^i}$, $H_1^{2^i}$, $H_2^{2^i}$, $D_1^{2^i}$, $D_2^{2^i}$) in each column must be properly set through the use of the control register and the associated decoder. A "duplicate spaced substrings down" operation is illustrated in Figure 9. The two substrings to be duplicated are AB and EF. For this operation the control line groups $D_1^{2^i}$ and $H_1^{2^i}$ or $H_1^{2^i}$ and $H_2^{2^i}$ are activated, depending on whether the control bit is 1 or 0 as determined by substring length. In this example, the substring is 2; thus, only the control bit for column 2^1 has a value of 1, all others are 0's. Thus, in columns 2^2 and 2^0, $H_1^{2^i}$ and $H_2^{2^i}$ are activated, and in column 2^1, $D_1^{2^i}$ and $H_1^{2^i}$ are activated. With this control pattern, the substrings can be generated at the output register.

A distributed control scheme has also been developed by McMillen and Siegel.[50] It uses a routing tag which contains $2n$ bits and is of the form $F = (f_{2n-1} \cdot\cdot f_{n+1} f_n f_{n-1} \cdot\cdot f_1\ f_0)$. The n low-order bits represent the magnitudes of the route, and the n high-order bits represent the sign corresponding to the magnitudes. In stage i, a given switching element examines bits i and $n+i$ of the routing tag. If $f_i = 0$, the straight link is used, regardless of the value of f_{n+i}. If $f_i = 1$, bit $n+i$ is examined. If $f_{n+i} = 0$, the $+2^i$ link is used; if $f_{n+i} = 1$, the -2^i link is used. The source processor generates its own routing tag. For example, in a data manipulator of $N = 2^4$, if the source is 13 and the destination is 6, one possible value for F is 00000111. The path traversed is straight, $+2^2$, $+2^1$, $+2^0$. Multiple paths exist between a source-destination pair. For example, an alternative routing tag from source 13 to destination 6 is (0001 1001). The example is shown in Figure 10. A general rule to calculate the routing tag is shown as

$$D = S + (-1)^{f_{2n-1}}(f_n 2^{n-1}) + (-1)^{f_{2n-2}}(f_{n-1} 2^{n-2}) + \ldots (-1)^{f_n}(f_0 2^0)$$

where S and D are the addresses of the source and the destination, respectively.

Baseline network. Routing techniques for baseline networks described here are also useful for other topological-

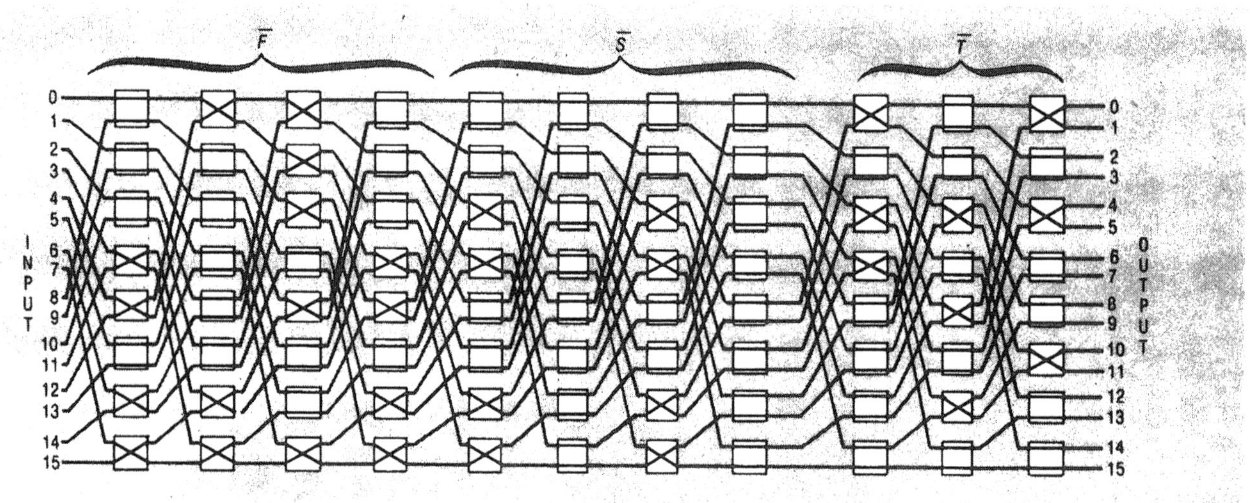

Figure 7. An example for universal realization of permutations.[48]

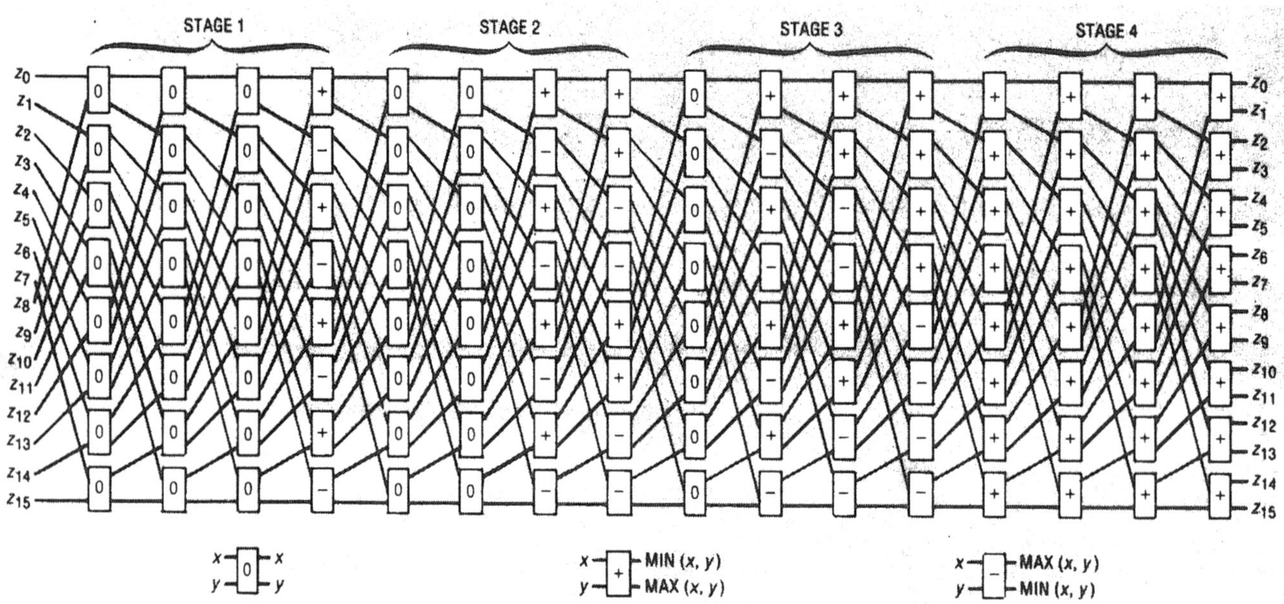

Figure 8. Sorting with shuffle-exchange. (Adapted from *The Art of Computer Programming, Vol. 3: Sorting and Searching* by D. E. Knuth; Addison-Wesley, Reading, Mass., © 1973.)

ly equivalent blocking multistage networks.[25] Basically, two types of routing are available: recursive routing and destination tag routing.[25,28,51] The recursive routing algorithm determines the control pattern according to permutation names. For some permutation, useful in parallel processing, the control pattern can be calculated recursively on the fly as the data pass through the network. Six categories of such permutations have been identified. For our purpose, we describe one here and show the recursive routing algorithm. The flip permutation function[29] is described as follows:

$$F_k^{(n)}\ (0 \le k < 2^n):\ p(X^r \oplus k) = X \text{ and } p(X \oplus k) = X^r$$

where X^r is the number whose binary representation is the reverse of X. Let $k = 2k^1 + k_0$ and $[L;R]$ denote the cascaded matrix whose left part and right part are L and R, respectively. Also let $V^{(n-1)}(b)$ be the 2^{n-1} bit vector whose components are all equal to b. The control pattern $K^{(n)}$ of the flip function can then be expressed in terms of the following recursive formula:

$$K^{(n)}(F_k^{(n)}) = [V^{(n-1)}(k_0);\ K^{(n-1)}(F_k^{(n)})],$$

where

$$K^{(1)}(F_k^{(n)}) = [V^{(n-1)}(k)].$$

For example, assuming

$$p = \begin{pmatrix} 0 & 1 & 2 & 3 & 4 & 5 & 6 & 7 \\ 1 & 5 & 3 & 7 & 0 & 4 & 2 & 6 \end{pmatrix}$$

p can be described by

$$F_4^{(3)}: p(X^r \oplus 4) = X.$$

Accordingly, we have

$$K^{(3)}(F_4^{(3)}) = [V^2(0);\ V^{(2)}(0);\ V^{(2)}(1)].$$

Hence

$$K^{(3)}(p) = \begin{bmatrix} 0 & 0 & 1 \\ 0 & 0 & 1 \\ 0 & 0 & 1 \\ 0 & 0 & 1 \end{bmatrix}.$$

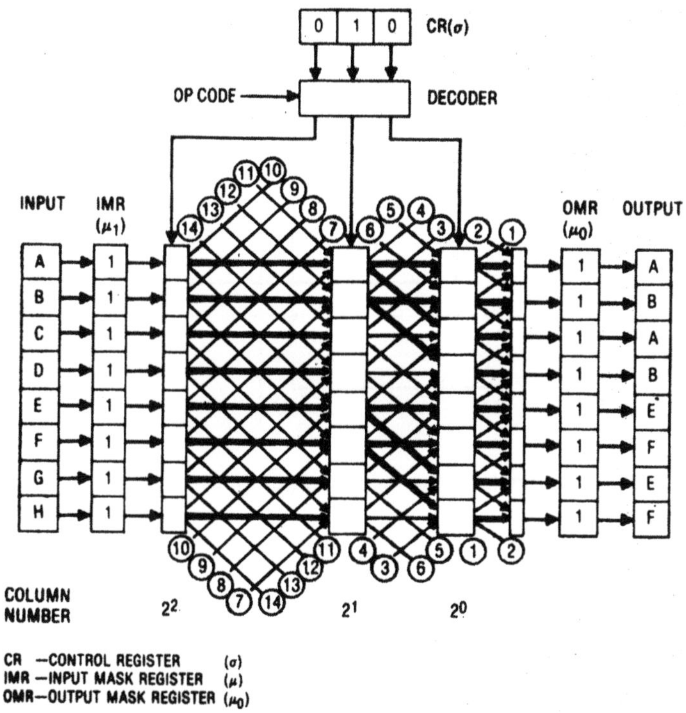

Figure 9. Duplicate spaced substring down on data manipulator.[11]

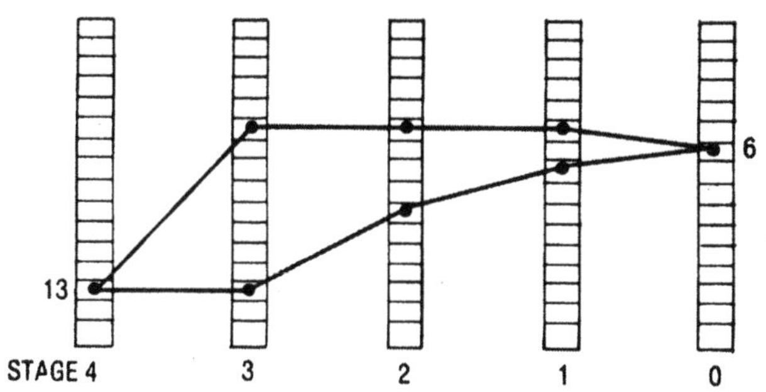

Figure 10. Distributed routing on the data manipulator.

The destination tag routing uses the binary representation of the destination as a routing tag. Let the source terminal link and destination terminal link be A and Z, respectively. Also, let the binary representation of Z be $z_{n-1}z_{n-2}\ldots z_0$. Starting at A, the first node to which A is connected is set to switch A to the upper link if $z_{n-1}=0$ or the lower link if $z_{n-1}=1$. The second node in the path is again set to switch A to the upper link if $z_{n-2}=0$ or the lower link if $z_{n-2}=1$. This scheme is continued until we get the proper destination. For example, in Figure 11, $A=2$ and $Z=11$ (i.e., $z_3z_2z_1z_0=1011$). Switching element 1 of the left-most stage switches A to the lower link because $z_3=1$. At the next stage, switching element 4 switches A to the upper link because $z_2=0$. Again, switching element 4 in the third stage and switching element 5 in the right-most stage both switch A to the lower links because $z_1=z_0=1$. If we consider Z as the source and A as the destination, using the binary representation of A as the routing tag and repeating the same routing procedure will lead us to choose the same path. This routing tag algorithm will connect the only path available between a source and a destination and is extremely suitable for a distributed control scheme. A conflict resolution scheme[25] has also been developed for implementing destination tag routing in terms of centralized control.

Benes network. Sequential routing algorithms[34,52] need $O(N \log N)$ steps where N is the network size. Many researchers have worked toward improving this time complexity in terms of parallel processing technique,[53] heuristic method,[37] or recursive formula.[35] Here, we demonstrate the very basic routing algorithm, called the looping algorithm. The basic principle, in terms of the permutation to be realized by the Benes binary network shown in Figure 5d, is

$$p = \begin{pmatrix} 0 & 1 & 2 & 3 & 4 & 5 & 6 & 7 \\ 3 & 7 & 4 & 0 & 2 & 6 & 1 & 5 \end{pmatrix}$$

The loop algorithm starts recording the permutation, *p*, as shown in Figure 12. The two output numbers of a switching element in the output stage are shown in the same column, and the two input numbers of a switching element in the input stage are shown in the same row. We then choose an arbitrary entry in the chart as a starting point. For example, electing to start at row 23 and column 01, we then look for a same-row or column entry to form a loop and, in Figure 12, choose row 23 and column 45. The process continues until we obtain a loop by re-entering row 23 and column 01. The loop's member entries are then assigned "*a*" and "*b*" alternately. The second loop can be formed in the same way. Then, we assign input and output lines named "*a*" to subnetwork *a* and those named "*b*" to subnetwork *b*. The control of the input and output switching elements must be set as depicted in Figure 13. This looping algorithm can be applied recursively to the two subnetworks.

Construction of interconnection networks. Interconnection networks are usually designed so they can be constructed of a single type of modular building block called a switching element. The switching element realizes communication protocols which specify the control strategy and the switching methodology.

The logic design of switching elements has been explored in many projects,[54-56] including recent LSI implementations.[10,57] Here, we describe in more detail three designs that have been implemented and are operational.

Flip network 2 × 2 switching element. The flip network uses centralized control and circuit switching.[29] The 2 × 2 switching element can be set by a control line into a direct-connection or crossed-connection state. Assume that I_0, I_1, O_0, O_1, and C represent the two inputs, the two outputs, and the switching element control. The switching element's output function can be expressed as follows:

$$O_0 = \overline{C} I_0 + C \cdot I_1, \text{and}$$

$$O_1 = \overline{C} I_1 + C \cdot I_0$$

where $C=0$ means straight connection and $C=1$ crossed connection (see Figure 14).

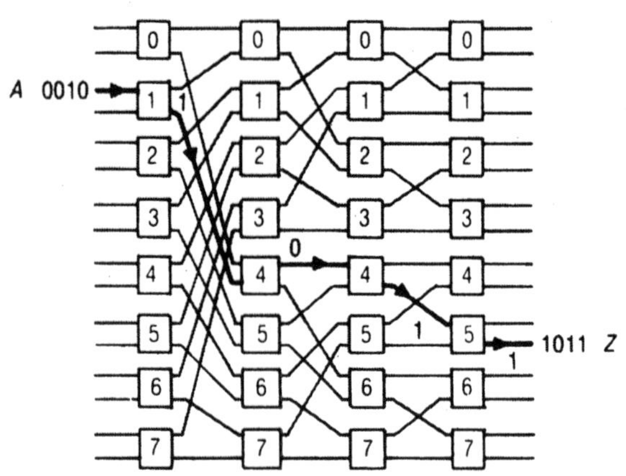

Figure 11. Distributed routing on a baseline network.

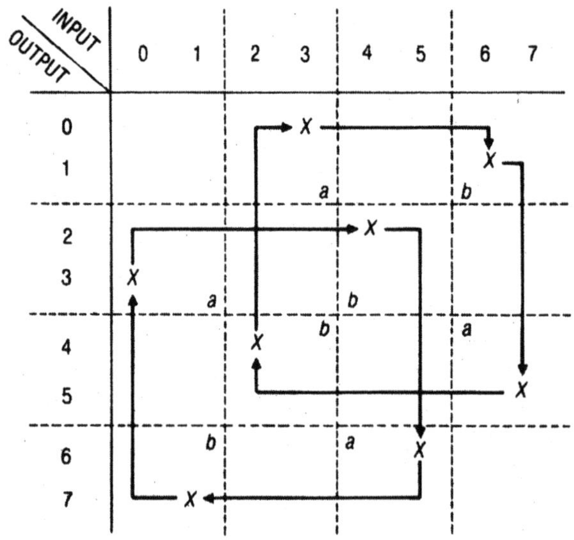

Figure 12. An example of the looping algorithm.

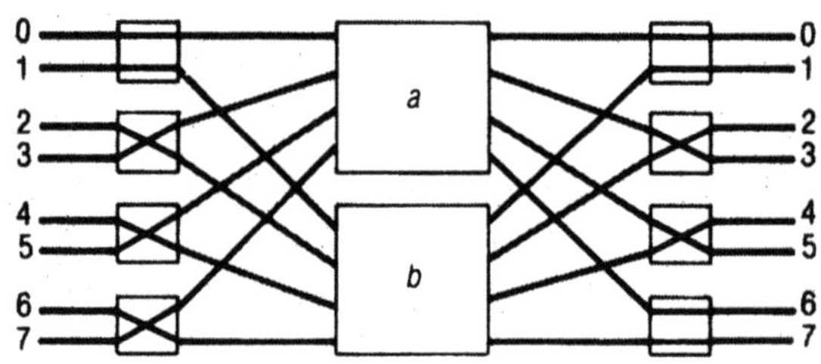

Figure 13. Control setting result from the first iteration of the looping algorithm.

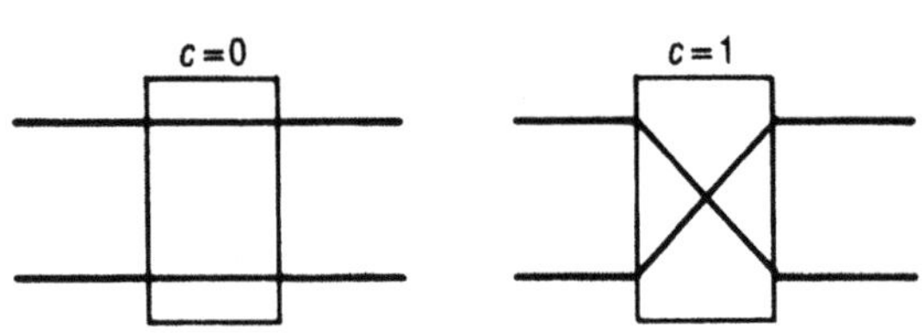

Figure 14. A 2 x 2 switching element.

Dimond 2 × 2 switching element. A switching element with two input and output ports, called Dimond for dual interconnection modular network device,[58] allows modular construction of interconnection networks. A packet of messages (containing routing information) arriving at a Dimond is switched to a designated output port, where it is stored in a register. Figure 15 shows an implementation of Dimond which requires one control clock for all interconnected switching elements. The central clock has two phases. In the first clock phase, it is determined which inputs have to be copied into which registers. The copy allowances so determined are stored in four flip-flops: C_{00}, C_{01}, C_{10}, and C_{11} (C_{01} is the allowance for copying in_0 into reg_1). In addition, output signals of copy acknowledgments ($cack_0$ and $cack_1$), internal control signals ($cross_0$, $fill_0$, and $fill_1$) are generated. More precisely, we have the following:

$$C_{00} = creq_0 \cdot \overline{des_0} \cdot \overline{stat_0} \cdot (\overline{creq_1} + des_1 + \overline{prio}) \;;$$

$$C_{01} = creq_0 \cdot des_0 \cdot \overline{stat_1} \cdot (\overline{creq_1} + \overline{des_1} + \overline{prio}) \;;$$

$$C_{10} = creq_1 \cdot \overline{des_1} \cdot \overline{stat_0} \cdot (\overline{creq_0} + des_0 + prio) \;;$$

$$C_{11} = creq_1 \cdot des_1 \cdot \overline{stat_1} \cdot (\overline{creq_0} + \overline{des_0} + prio) \;;$$

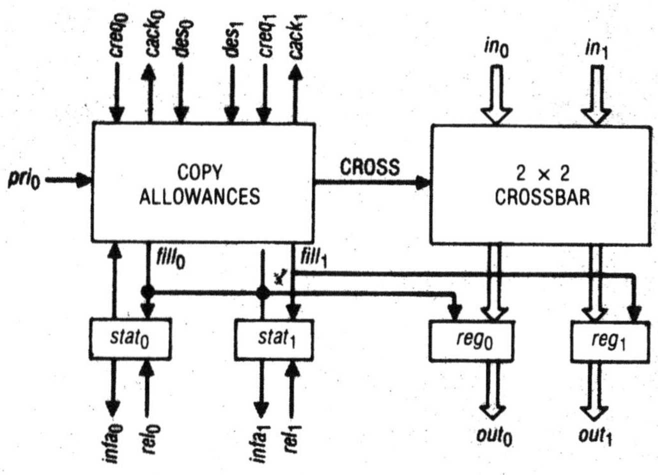

Figure 15. A 2 x 2 dual interconnecting modular network device—Dimond[58]—for packet switching.

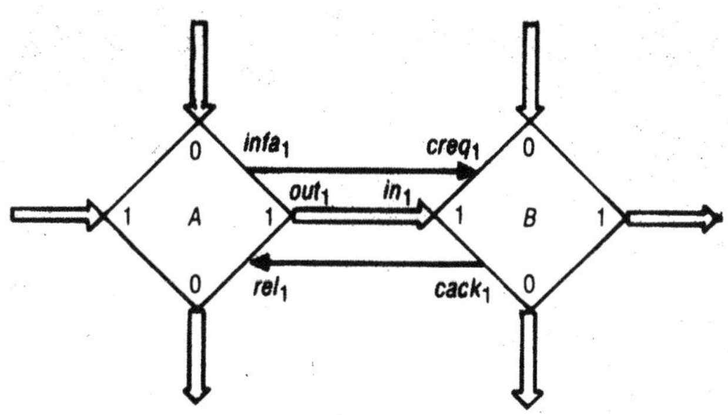

Figure 16. Connecting two Dimonds.[58]

$$Cack_0 = C_{00} + C_{01} \;;$$

$$Cack_1 = C_{10} + C_{11} \;;$$

$$Cross = C_{00} + C_{11} \;;$$

$$Fill_0 = C_{00} + C_{10} \;;$$

$$Fill_1 = C_{01} + C_{11} \;;$$

where *prio* is the priority line indicating the index (0,1) of the input served first in the event of conflict, and des_0 and des_1 are destination lines for in_0 and in_1. In the second clock phase, two actions are performed concurrently. Inputs are copied into the output register, if required, and the status flip-flops, $stat_0$ and $stat_1$ (status of reg_0 and reg_1, respectively) are adapted. Precisely, we have the following:

$$Fill_0 \rightarrow reg_0 = cross \cdot in_0 + \overline{cross} \cdot in_1 \;;$$

$$Fill_1 \rightarrow reg_1 = \overline{cross} \cdot in_0 + cross \cdot in_1 \;;$$

$$Fill_0 \cdot \overline{rel_0} \rightarrow stat_0 = 1 \;;$$
$$rel_0 \rightarrow stat_0 = 0 \;;$$

$$Fill_1 \cdot \overline{rel_1} \rightarrow stat_1 = 1 \;;$$
$$rel_1 \rightarrow stat_1 = 0 \;.$$

The information-available lines are connected to the status flip-flops:

$$infa_0 = stat_0 \;;$$
$$infa_1 = stat_1 \;.$$

The interconnection of two Dimonds is shown in Figure 16, which depicts the relation of handshaking lines.

64 × 64 switching element. A centralized-control and circuit-switching 64 × 64 versatile data manipulator[11] (see Figure 17) is operating in conjunction with the Staran computer at the Rome Air Development Center.[44] The data manipulator operates under the control of the Staran computer's parallel input-output unit. The contents of the input and output masks, of the address control register, and of the input and output control registers, as well as the data to be manipulated, are entered via the 256-bit wide PIO buffer interface. The manipulated data leave the data manipulator via the same interface. The data manipulator's instruction repertoire allows one to load the various address registers and masks and to start and stop data manipulation. Self-test is performed by loading address and input-data registers, allowing verification of correct operation without assistance from the Staran computer. There are 64 × 64 cells in the basic crossbar circuit. The output gate of cell (*i,j*) is controlled by the *i*th address control register through a decoder. The decoder has 64 outputs to control the 64 output gates in a basic-crossbar-circuit row.

Connection issues for concurrent processing

Two approaches—array processing and multiprocessing—have been tried to provide processing concurrency.

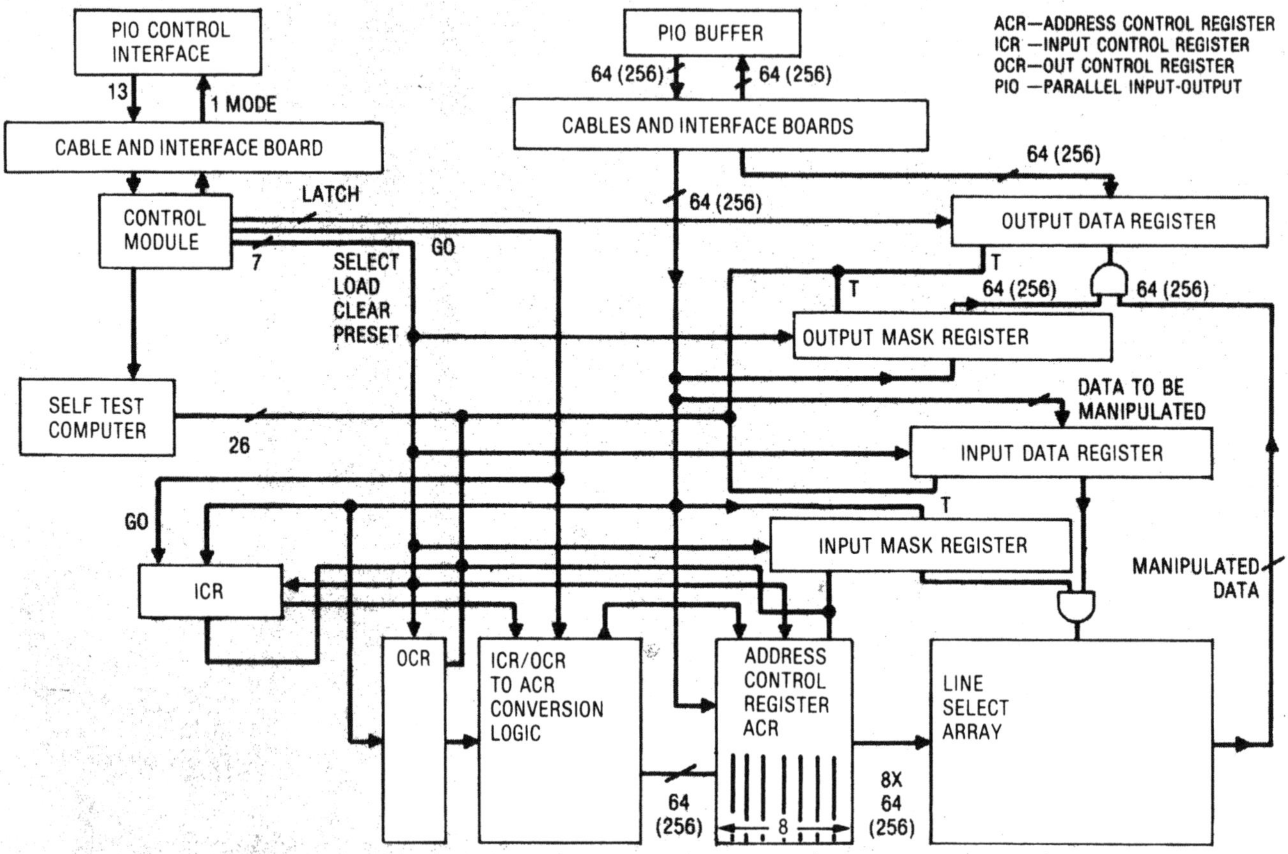

Figure 17. Block diagram of a versatile data manipulator.

Since array processors, which consist of multiple processing elements and parallel memory modules under one control unit, can handle single instructions and multiple data streams, they are also known as SIMD computers. Existing examples include Illiac IV and Staran. An overall SIMD machine organization[59] is shown in Figure 18. The N processing elements, or PEs, are connected by two interconnection networks to the M parallel memory modules. The control unit in the center provides control over PEs and memory modules.

Array processors allow explicit expression of parallelism in user programs. The compiler detects the parallelism and generates object code suitable for execution in the multiple processing elements and the control unit. Program segments which cannot be converted into parallel executable forms are executed in the control unit; program segments which can be converted into parallel executable forms are sent to the PEs and executed synchronously on data fetched from parallel memory modules under the control of the control unit. To enable synchronous manipulation in the PEs, the data are permuted and arranged in vector form. Thus, to run a program more efficiently on an array processor, one must develop a technique for vectorizing the program (or algorithm). The interconnection network plays a major role in vectorization.

The second approach for concurrent processing uses multiprocessing. The multiprocessor can handle multiple

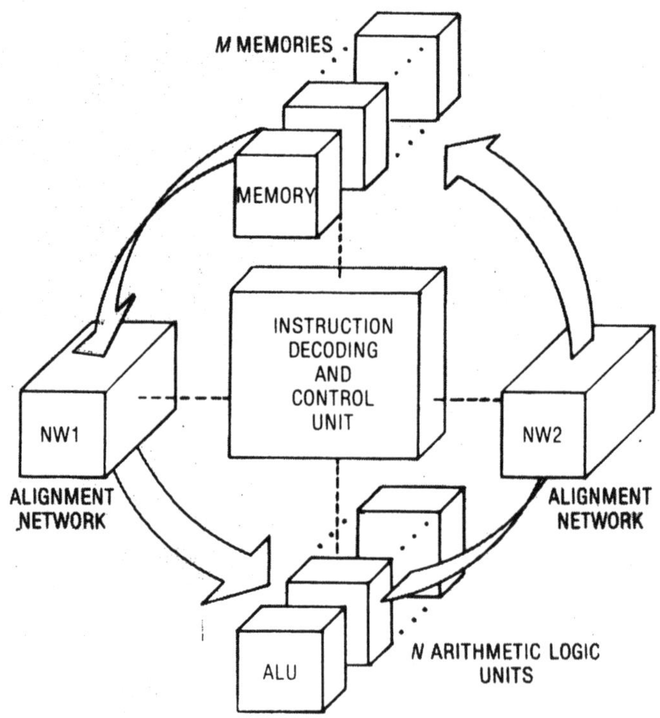

Figure 18. SIMD model.[59]

instructions and multiple data streams and hence is called an MIMD processor. Examples of the MIMD architecture include HEP,[60] data flow processor,[61] and flow model processor.[62] A configuration of MIMD architecture[62] is shown in Figure 19. The *N* processing elements are connected to the *M* memory modules by an interconnection network. The activities are coordinated by the coordinator. Unlike the control unit in an array processor, the coordinator does not execute object code; it only implements the synchronization of processes and smooths out the execution sequence. Again, the compiler must be designed to partition a computation task and assign each piece to individual processing elements. Effective partitioning and assignment are essential for efficient multiprocessing. The criterion is to match memory bandwidth with the processor processing load, and the interconnection network is a critical factor in this matching.

Below, we address some problems and results regarding the role of the interconnection network in concurrent processing.

Combinatorial capability. In array processing, data are often stored in parallel memory modules in skewed forms that allow a vector of data to be fetched without conflict.[63-65] However, the fetched data must be realigned in prescribed order before they can be sent to individual PEs for processing. This alignment is implemented by permutation functions of the interconnection network, which also realigns data generated by individual PEs into skewed form for storage in the memory modules.

In the computer architecture project, one should question whether the interconnection network chosen can efficiently perform the alignment. The rearrangeable network and the nonblocking network can realize every permutation function, but using these networks for alignment requires considerable effort to calculate control settings. A recursive routing mechanism has been provided for a few families of permutations needed for parallel processing[35]; however, the problem remains for the realization of general permutations. Many articles[45,51,66,67] concentrating on the permutation capabilities of single-stage net-

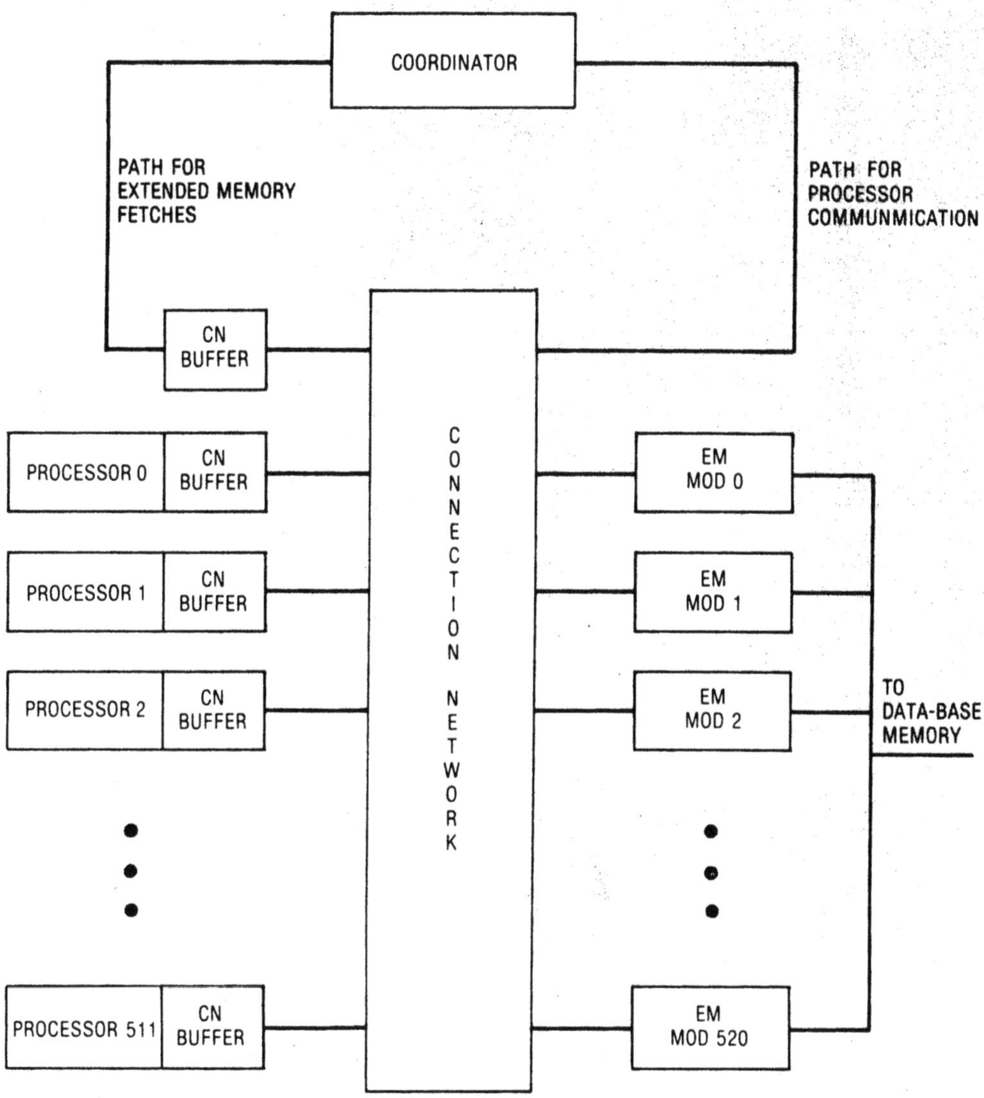

Figure 19. MIMD model.

works and blocking multistage networks have shown that these networks cannot realize arbitrary permutations in a single pass. Recent results show that the baseline network can realize arbitrary permutations in just two passes[51] while other blocking multistage networks, such as the omega network, need at least three passes.[66] As mentioned previously, the shuffle-exchange network can realize arbitrary permutations in $3(\log_2 N) - 1$ passes where N is the network size.[48]

Task assignments and reconfiguration. Consider a parallel program segment using M memory modules and N processing elements. During execution, data is usually transferred from memory modules to processing elements or vice versa. It is also necessary to transfer data among processing elements for data sharing and synchronization. Simultaneous data transfers through the interconnection network, which implements the transfers, may result in contention for communication links and switching elements. In case of conflict, some of the data transfers must be deferred; consequently, throughput decreases because the processing elements which need the deferred data cannot proceed as originally expected. To minimize delays caused by communication conflicts, program codes must be assigned to proper processing elements and data assigned to proper memory modules. The assignment of data to memory modules, called mapping,[68] has recently been extended to include assignment of program modules to processing elements.[69]

A configuration concept has been proposed to better use the interconnection network.[51] Under this concept, a network is just a configuration of another one in the same, topologically equivalent class.[25] To configure a permutation function as an interconnection network, we can assign input/output link names in a way that realizes the permutation function in one conflict-free pass. The problem of assigning logical names that realize various permutation functions without conflicts is called a reconfiguration problem. It has been shown that, through the reconfiguration process, the baseline network can realize every permutation in one pass without conflicts.[69] This implies that concurrent processing throughput could be enhanced by proper assignment of tasks to processing elements and data to memory modules.

Partitioning. In partitioning—that is, dividing the network into independent subnetworks of different sizes—each subnetwork must have all the interconnection capabilities of a complete network of the same type and size. Hence, with a partitionable network, a system can support multiple SIMD machines. By dynamically reconfiguring the system into independent SIMD machines and properly assigning tasks to each partition, we can use resources more efficiently.

Several authors have noted the importance of partitioning.[30] One recent study[70] shows that single-stage networks, such as the shuffle-exchange and Illiac networks, cannot be partitioned into independent subnetworks, but blocking multistage networks, such as the baseline and data manipulator, can be partitioned.

Bandwidth of interconnection networks. The bandwidth can be defined as the expected number of requests accepted per unit time. Since the bus system cannot provide sufficient bandwidth for a large-scale multiprocessor system and the crossbar switch is too expensive, it is particularly interesting to know what kind of bandwidth various interconnection networks can provide.

The analytic method has been used to estimate bandwidth.[31,71,72] However, one cannot obtain a closed-form solution, and the analytic model is sometimes too simplified. Just for example, one result showed that for a blocking multistage interconnection network of size 256 × 256, the bandwidth is 77 requests (per memory cycle) and for a crossbar switch of the same size, the bandwidth is 162. However, the crossbar costs about 20 times as much as the multistage network, and with buffering (packet switching), the performance of the multistage network is quite comparable to the crossbar switch.[71]

Numerical simulation, also used to estimate the bandwidth,[71] can simulate actual PE connection requests by analyzing the program to be executed. The access conflicts in the network and memory modules can be detected as shown by Wu and Feng.[25] Using the simulation method, Barnes[73] concluded that the baseline network is more than adequate to support connection needs of a proposed MIMD system which can execute one billion floating-point instructions per second.

Reliability. Reliable operation of interconnection networks is important to overall system performance. The reliability issue can be thought of as two problems: fault diagnosis and fault tolerance. The fault-diagnosis problem has been studied for a class of multistage interconnection networks constructed of switching elements with two valid states.[74] The problem is approached by generating suitable fault-detection and fault-location test sets for every fault in the assumed fault model. The test sets are then trimmed to a mimimal or nearly minimal set. Detecting a single fault (link fault or switching-element fault) requires only four tests, which are independent of network size. The number of tests for locating single faults and detecting multiple faults are also workable.

The second reliability problem mainly concerns the degree of fault tolerance.[75] It is important to design a network that combines full connection capability with graceful degradation—in spite of the existence of faults. ■

Acknowledgment

The author wishes to acknowledge the original contribution of Dr. C. Wu in preparing this article.

References

1. T. Feng, editor's introduction, special issue on parallel processors and processing, *Computing Surveys*, Vol. 9, No. 1, Mar. 1977, pp. 1-2.

2. C. V. Ramamoorthy, T. Krishnarao, and P. Jahanian, "Hardware Software Issues in Multi-Microprocessor Computer Architecture," *Proc. First Annual Rocky Mountain Symp. Microcomputers,* 1977, pp. 235-261.

3. K. J. Thurber, "Interconnection Networks—A Survey and Assessment," *AFIPS Conf. Proc.*, Vol. 43, 1974 NCC, pp. 909-919.

4. K. J. Thurber, "Circuit Switching Technology: A State-of-the-Art Survey," *Proc. Compcon Fall 1978,* Sept. 1978, pp. 116-124.

5. K. J. Thurber and G. M. Masson, *Distributed-Processor Communication Architecture,* Lexington Books, Lexington, Mass., 1979, 252 pp.

6. H. J. Siegel, "Interconnection Networks for SIMD Machines," *Computer,* Vol. 12, No. 6, June 1979, pp. 57-66.

7. H. J. Siegel, R. J. McMillen, and P. T. Mueller, Jr., "A Survey of Interconnection Methods for Reconfigurable Parallel Processing Systems," *AFIPS Conf. Proc.*, Vol. 48, 1979 NCC, pp. 387-400.

8. G. M. Masson, G. C. Gingher, and Shinji Nakamura, "A Sampler of Circuit Switching Networks," *Computer,* Vol. 12, No. 6, June 1979, pp. 32-48.

9. T. Feng and C. Wu, *Interconnection Networks in Multiple-Processor Systems,* Rome Air Development Center report, RADC-TR-79-304, Dec. 1979, 244 pp.

10. C. Wu and T. Feng, "A VLSI Interconnection Network for Multiprocessor Systems," *Digest Compcon Spring 1981,* pp. 294-298.

11. T. Feng, "Data Manipulating Functions in Parallel Processors and Their Implementations," *IEEE Trans. Computers,* Vol. C-23, No. 3, Mar. 1974, pp. 309-318.

12. V. Benes, *Mathematical Theory of Connecting Networks,* Academic Press, N.Y., 1965.

13. H. T. Kung, "The Structure of Parallel Algorithms," in *Advances in Computers,* Vol. 19, M. C. Yovits, ed., Academic Press, N.Y., 1980.

14. D. J. Farber and K. C. Larson, "The System Architecture of the Distributed Computer System—the Communications System," *Proc. Symp. Computer Comm. Networks and Teletraffic,* Brooklyn Polytechnic Press, Apr. 1972, pp. 21-27.

15. C. C. Reames and M. T. Liu, "A Loop Network for Simultaneous Transmission of Variable Length Messages," *Proc. Second Symp. Computer Architecture,* Jan. 1975, pp. 7-12.

16. S. I. Saffer et al., "NODAS—The Net Oriented Data Acquisition System for the Medical Environment," *AFIPS Conf. Proc.*, Vol. 46, 1977 NCC, pp. 295-300.

17. J. A. Harris and D. R. Smith, "Hierarchical Multiprocessor Organization," *Proc. Fourth Symp. Computer Architecture,* Mar. 1977, pp. 41-48.

18. G. H. Barnes et al., "The Illiac IV Computer," *IEEE Trans. Computers,* Vol. C-17, No. 8, Aug. 1968, pp. 746-757.

19. E. M. Aupperle, "MERIT Computer Network: Hardware Considerations," in *Computer Networks,* R. Rustin, ed., Prentice-Hall, Englewood Cliffs, N.J., 1972, pp. 49-63.

20. B. W. Arden and H. Lee, "Analysis of Chordal Ring Network," *IEEE Trans. Computers,* Vol. C-30, No. 4, April 1981, pp. 291-295.

21. H. Sullivan, T. R. Bashkow, and K. Klappholz, "A Large Scale Homogeneous, Fully Distributed Parallel Machine," *Proc. Fourth Symp. Computer Architecture,* Nov. 1977, pp. 105-125.

22. F. P. Preparata and J. Vuillemin, "The Cube-Connected Cycles: A Versatile Network for Parallel Computation," *Comm. ACM,* Vol. 24, No. 5, May 1981, pp. 300-309.

23. H. S. Stone, "Parallel Processing with the Perfect Shuffle," *IEEE Trans. Computers,* Vol. C-20, No. 2, Feb. 1971, pp. 153-161.

24. T. Feng, *Parallel Processing Characteristics and Implementation of Data Manipulating Functions,* Rome Air Development Center report, RADC-TR-73-189, July 1973.

25. C. Wu and T. Feng, "On a Class of Multistage Interconnection Networks," *IEEE Trans. Computers,* Vol. C-29, No. 8, Aug. 1980, pp. 694-702.

26. C. Wu and T. Feng, "On a Distributed-Processor Communication Architecture," *Proc. Compcon Fall 1980,* pp. 599-605.

27. L. R. Goke and G. J. Lipovski, "Banyan Networks for Partitioning Multiprocessing Systems," *Proc. First Annual Computer Architecture Conf.*, Dec. 1973, pp. 21-28.

28. D. H. Lawrie, "Access and Alignment of Data in an Array Processor," *IEEE Trans. Computers,* Vol. C-24, No. 12, Dec. 1975, pp. 1145-1155.

29. K. E. Batcher, "The Flip Network in STARAN," *Proc. 1976 Int'l Conf. Parallel Processing,* Aug. 1976, pp. 65-71.

30. M. C. Pease, "The Indirect Binary n-Cube Microprocessor Array," *IEEE Trans. Computers,* Vol. C-26, No. 5, May 1977, pp. 548-573.

31. J. H. Patel, "Processor-Memory Interconnections for Multiprocessors," *Proc. Sixth Annual Symp. Computer Architecture,* Apr. 1979, pp. 168-177.

32. A. Waksman, "A Permutation Network," *J. ACM,* Vol. 9, No. 1, Jan. 1968, pp. 159-163.

33. A. E. Joel, Jr., "On Permutation Switching Networks," *B.S.T.J.*, Vol. 67, 1968, pp. 813-822.

34. D. C. Opferman and N. T. Tsao-Wu, "On a Class of Rearrangeable Switching Networks—Part I: Control Algorithm; Part II: Enumeration Studies of Fault Diagnosis," *B.S.T.J.*, 1971, pp. 1579-1618.

35. J. Lenfant, "Parallel Permutations of Data: A Benes Network Control Algorithm for Frequently Used Permutations," *IEEE Trans. Computers,* Vol. C-27, No. 7, July 1978, pp. 637-647.

36. T. Feng, C. Wu, and D. P. Agrawal, "A Microprocessor-Controlled Asynchronous Circuit Switching Network," *Proc. Sixth Annual Symp. Computer Architecture,* 1979, pp. 202-215.

37. Y-C. Chow, R. D. Dixon, T. Feng, and C. Wu, "Routing Techniques for Rearrangeable Interconnection Networks," *Proc. Workshop on Interconnection Networks,* Apr. 1980, pp. 64-69.

38. C. Clos, "A Study of Nonblocking Switching Networks," *Bell System Tech. J.*, Vol. 32, 1953, pp. 406-424.

39. C. D. Thompson, "Generalized Connection Networks for Parallel Processor Intercommunication," *IEEE Trans. Computers,* C-27, No. 12, Dec. 1978, pp. 1119-1125.

40. J. Gecsei, "Interconnection Networks from Three-State Cells," *IEEE Trans. Computers,* Vol. C-26, No. 8, Aug. 1977, pp. 705-711.

41. Y-C. Chow, R. D. Dixon, and T. Feng, "An Interconnection Network for Processor Communication with Optimized Local Connections," *Proc. 1980 Int'l Conf. Parallel Processing,* Aug. 1980, pp. 65-74.

42. W. A. Wulf and C. G. Bell, "C.mmp—A Multimicroprocessor," *AFIPS Conf. Proc.*, Vol. 41, 1972 FJCC, pp. 765-777.

43. T. Feng, *The Design of a Versatile Line Manipulator,* Rome Air Development Center report, RADC-TR-73-292, Sept. 1973.

44. W. W. Gaertner, *Design, Construction, and Installation of Data Manipulator,* Rome Air Development Center report, RADC-TR-77-166, May 1977, 80 pp.

45. S. E. Orcutt, "Implementation of Permutations Functions in an Illiac IV-Type Computer," *IEEE Trans. Computers,* Vol. C-25, No. 9, Sept. 1976, pp. 929-936.

46. C. D. Thompson and H. T. Kung, "Sorting on a Mesh-Connected Parallel Computer," *Comm. ACM,* Vol.20, No. 4, Apr. 1977, pp. 263-271.

47. D. Nassimi and S. Sahni, "Bitonic Sort on a Mesh-Connected Parallel Computer," *IEEE Trans. Computers,* Vol. C-28, No. 1, Jan. 1979, pp. 2-7.

48. C. Wu and T. Feng, "Universality of the Shuffle-Exchange Network," *IEEE Trans. Computers,* Vol. C-30, No. 5, May 1981.

49. D. E. Knuth, *The Art of Computer Programming, Vol. 3: Sorting and Searching,* Addison-Wesley, Reading, Mass., 1973.

50. R. J. McMillen and H. J. Siegel, "MIMD Machine Communication Using the Augmented Data Manipulator Network," *Proc. Seventh Symp. Computer Architecture,* June 1980, pp. 51-58.

51. C. Wu and T. Feng, "The Reverse-Exchange Interconnection Network," *IEEE Trans. Computers,* Vol. C-29, No. 9, Sept. 1980, pp. 801-811; also *Proc. 1979 Int'l Conf. Parallel Processing,* pp. 160-174.

52. S. Anderson, "The Looping Algorithm Extended to Base 2^t Rearrangeable Switching Networks," *IEEE Trans. Comm.,* Vol. COM-25, No. 10, Oct. 1977, pp. 1057-1063.

53. G. Lev, N. Pippenger, and L. G. Valiant, "A Fast Parallel Algorithm for Routing in Permutation Networks," *IEEE Trans. Computers,* Vol. C-30, No. 2, Feb. 1981, pp. 93-100.

54. D. H. Lawrie, *Memory-Processor Conneciton Networks,* UIUCDCS-R-73-557, University of Ilinois, Urbana, Feb. 1973.

55. *Numerical Aerodynamic Simulation Facility Feasibility Study,* Burroughs Corporation, Mar. 1979.

56. U. V. Premkuma, R. Kapur, M. Malek, G. J. Lipovski, and P. Horne, "Design and Implementation of the Banyan Interconnection Network in TRAC," *AFIPS Conf. Proc.,* Vol. 49, 1980 NCC, pp. 643-653.

57. M. A. Franklin, "VLSI Performance Comparison of Banyan and Crossbar Communication Networks," *IEEE Trans. Computers,* Vol. C-30, No. 4, Apr. 1981, pp. 283-290.

58. P. G. Jansen and J. L. W. Kessels, "The DIMOND: A Component for the Modular Construction of Switching Networks," *IEEE Trans. Computers,* Vol. C-29, No. 10, Oct. 1980, pp. 884-889.

59. D. J. Kuck, "A Survey of Parallel Machine Organization and Programming," *Computing Surveys,* Vol. 9, No. 1, Mar. 1977, pp. 29-59. Also in *Proc. 1975 Sagamore Computer Conf. Parallel Processing,* pp. 15-39.

60. B. J. Smith, "A Pipelined, Shared Resource MIMD Computer," *Proc. 1978 Int'l Conf. Parallel Processing,* pp. 6-8.

61. J. B. Dennis, "Data Flow Supercomputers," *Computer,* Vol. 13, No. 11, Nov. 1980, pp. 48-56.

62. S. F. Lundstrom and G. Barnes, "A Controllable MIMD Architecture," *Proc. 1980 Int'l Conf. Parallel Processing,* pp. 19-27.

63. D. J. Kuck, "ILLIAC IV Software and Application Programming," *IEEE Trans. on Computers,* Vol. C-17, No. 8, Aug. 1968, pp. 758-770.

64. K. E. Batcher, "The Multi-Dimensional Access Memory in STARAN," *IEEE Trans. Computers,* Vol. C-26, No. 2, Feb. 1977, pp. 174-177.

65. D. H. Lawrie and C. Vora, "The Prime Memory System for Array Access," *Proc. 1980 Int'l Conf. Parallel Processing,* pp. 81-87.

66. A. Shimer and S. Ruhman, "Toward a Generalization of Two- and Three-Pass Multistage, Blocking Interconnection Networks," *Proc. 1980 Int'l Conf. Parallel Processing,* pp. 337-346.

67. T. Lang and H. S. Stone, "A Shuffle-Exchange Network with Simplified Control," *IEEE Trans. Computers,* Vol. C-25, No. 6, Jan. 1976, pp. 55-65.

68. H. T. Kung and D. Stevenson, "A Software Technique for Reducing the Routing Time on a Parallel Computer with a Fixed Interconnection Network," in *High Speed Computer and Algorithm Organization,* Academic Press, N.Y., 1977, pp. 423-433.

69. C. Wu and T. Feng, "A Software Technique for Enhancing Performance of a Distributed Computer System," *Proc. Compsac 80,* Oct. 1980, pp. 274-280.

70. H. J. Siegel, "The Theory Underlying the Partitioning of Permutation Networks," *IEEE Trans. Computers,* Vol. C-29, No. 9, Sept. 1980, pp. 791-801.

71. D. M. Dias and J. R. Jump, "Analysis and Simulation of Buffered Delta Networks," *IEEE Trans. Computers,* Vol. C-30, No. 4, Apr. 1981, pp. 273-282.

72. D. A. Padua, D. J. Kuck, and D. H. Lawrie, "High-Speed Multiprocessors and Compilation Techniques," *IEEE Trans. Computers,* Vol. C-29, No. 9, Sept. 1980, pp. 763-776.

73. G. H. Barnes, "Design and Validation of a Connection Network for Many-Processor Multiprocessing Systems," *Proc. 1980 Int'l Conf. Parallel Processing,* pp. 79-80.

74. C. Wu and T. Feng, "Fault Diagnosis for a Class of Multistage Interconnection Networks," *Proc. 1979 Int'l Conf. Parallel Processing,* pp. 269-278.

75. J. P. Shen and J. P. Hayes, "Fault Tolerance of a Class of Connecting Networks," *Proc. Seventh Symp. Computer Architecture,* 1980, pp. 61-71.

Tse-yun Feng is a professor in the Department of Computer and Information Science, Ohio State University, Columbus. Previously, he was on the faculty at Wayne State University, Detroit, and Syracuse University, New York. He has extensive technical publications in the areas of associative processing, parallel and concurrent processors, computer architecture, switching theory, and logic design, and has received a number of awards for his technical contributions and scholarship.

A past president of the IEEE Computer Society (1979-80), Feng was a distinguished visitor (1973-78), and has served as a reviewer, panelist, or session chairman for various technical magazines and conferences. He also initiated the Sagamore Computer Conference on Parallel Processing and the International Conference on Parallel Processing.

He received the BS degree from the National Taiwan University, Taipei, the MS degree from Oklahoma State University, Stillwater, and the PhD degree from the University of Michigan, Ann Arbor, all in electrical engineering.

Networking techniques allow several processors within a multiprocessing system to cooperate efficiently on a single large problem.

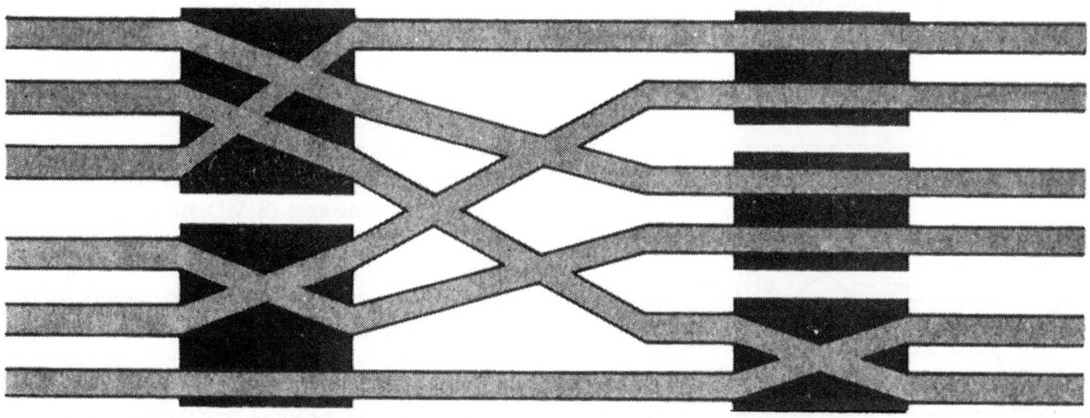

Interconnection Networks Using Shuffles

P-Y. Chen, D. H. Lawrie, and P-C. Yew, University of Illinois at Urbana-Champaign
D. A. Padua, Universidad Simón Bolívar, Venezuela

In recent years, research interest in the design of multiprocessor computer systems in which a large number of processors can be applied to a single problem has grown. This increased interest has been motivated by applications such as weather prediction, airframe design, radar tracking, and image processing, where performance requirements far exceed the capabilities of single-processor architectures. Any multiprocessor system that employs more than one processor per job must be designed to allow efficient communication between processors, and between memories and processors, lest the advantages of multiprocessing be negated by inefficient communication. As the number of processors grows, the interconnection design becomes more critical as crossbar or centralized bus schemes become impractical.

These systems can be viewed as networks having N inputs and N outputs, which can be connected to memories, or processors, or both. We can divide networks of this type into two categories: single-stage interconnection networks, or SSINs, and multistage interconnection networks, or MSINs. A single-stage network consists of a single, fixed interconnection together with a set of switches capable of permuting the inputs of the connected processors. In this article, we restrict our discussion of single-stage networks to those using a fixed "shuffle" interconnection of the kind shown in Figure 1.[1] Multistage networks, which have been studied extensively in recent years,[2-16] usually consist of at least log N stages of switching elements interconnected by a fixed interconnection. We restrict our discussion of multistage networks to those with log N or 2 log N stages interconnected by shuffles.

We can also divide networks into those that use circuit switching and those that use packet switching to communicate information (although SSINs, by definition, are used only in the packet switching mode). A circuit switching network is one that forms a connection (circuit) between any input port i and any output port j and can maintain this connection for an arbitrary length of time. In a packet switching network, fixed-length packets of information, consisting of anywhere from one bit to thousands of words, depending on the design of the network, are addressed to their destinations and may be stored and forwarded at several intermediate points along the way. In the context of multiprocessor interconnection, packet

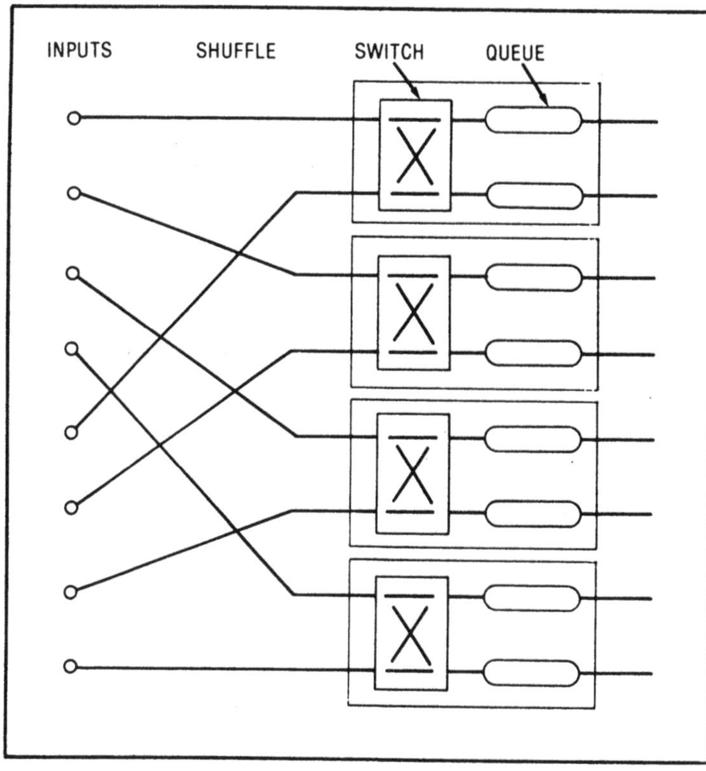

Figure 1. Shuffle connection and a queued, single-stage, shuffle-exchange network.

switching networks typcially transmit packets of, at most, several words over distances of tens of meters.

Finally, we can divide these networks into single-instruction-stream/multiple-data-stream, or SIMD, and multiple-instruction-stream/multiple-data-stream, or MIMD, systems.[17] In SIMD systems, we are interested in establishing a set of N or fewer circuits, or in sending a set of N or fewer messages, in the shortest possible time: for example, if we wanted to perform an operation on a vector of data. In MIMD applications, we are interested in minimizing the average delay for each circuit or message or in maximizing throughput (messages completed per unit of time).

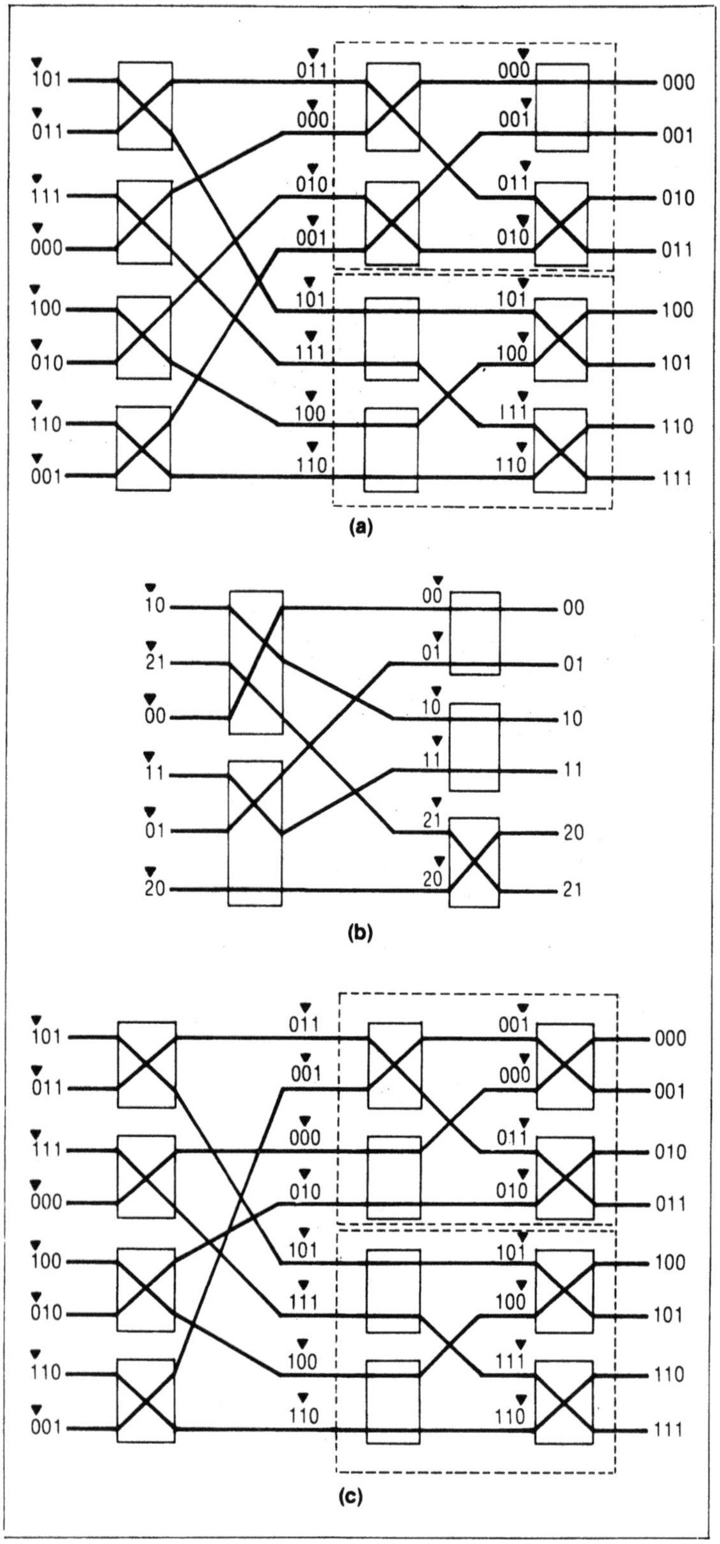

Figure 2. Local sorting: (a) radix-sort with radix system (2,2,2); (b) radix-sort with radix system (3,2); (c) possible alternative to (a).

We are basically concerned with two measures of system performance. First, the delay (turnaround) for a set of circuits or messages (SIMD applications) or for each message (MIMD applications); and second, the bandwidth (throughput) of each type of network in terms of the number of messages completed per unit of time.*

We also discuss the hardware complexity of these networks, although the rules for quantifying this complexity have become difficult since the advent of VLSI technology. For example, we know that the gate count in a log-N-stage network is proportional to $N \log N$. But the area required for the shuffle interconnection is proportional to $(N/\log N)^2$;[18,19] thus, for the log-N-stage shuffle exchange network, the VLSI area would be at least $N^2/\log N$. (A recent result establishes a lower bound of N^2.) Research into the VLSI complexity of these networks is still in its infancy. Furthermore, pin limitations make it unlikely that entire networks would be implemented on a single substrate. So, to simplify the discussion, we define hardware complexity in terms of the number of switches (2×2 or larger) employed in each network. (This has some intuitive appeal simply because the number of gates and the number of interconnections are proportional to the number of switches.) We emphasize, though, that the detailed design of these networks may favor the selection of one network over another independently of our complexity measures.

SIMD applications

Single-stage networks (those that are mesh connected and shuffle connected) were among the first to be used for SIMD machines,[1,20-22] and they are still popular because of their low cost. However, they are more difficult to use, since to operate them efficiently may require significant changes to application algorithms.[23,24] More recently, a number of multistage networks have been proposed for SIMD applications. One important use of a multistage network in a SIMD system is basically as a permutation network. Multistage networks can also be designed to allow various "broadcast" capabilities (i.e., one-to-many mappings of inputs to outputs), in addition to permutations,[10,25] but these capabilities are less than perfectly understood. Multistage networks are usually discussed from the point of view of circuit-switching applications, but they can also be used for packet switching, and they can be pipelined to enhance throughput.[26]

*For certain networks used in SIMD applications, such as the omega network, these measures are not meaningful, since they can produce certain connections in a fixed amount of time while they cannot produce certain other connections at all, at least in a single pass. In these cases, we define a third quality, or characteristic: the types of connections that a network can or cannot produce.

Many of these multistage networks are designed to produce all permutations of their inputs. However, because of the complexity of their control algorithms, they tend to be inappropriate for use in SIMD applications, where many different permutations have to be performed in a short time. This has led to a search for multistage networks with faster control algorithms. In order to get these faster control algorithms, designers have had to sacrifice the ability to perform all permutations, and have had to concentrate on subsets consisting of "useful" permutations. Many networks of this type have been proposed. Surprisingly, most depend on what might be called a universal topology: exchange elements interconnected by a "shuffle" connection. The multistage shuffle networks actually belong to a more general class of networks, which are constructed from a limited version of radix-sort algorithms.[27] This class of networks and its variations include the banyan network,[28] the omega network,[10] the baseline network,[12,16] the delta network,[29] the indirect binary n-cube network,[13] and others. The simplicity of the network-control algorithm, and the moderate hardware complexity, together with the short network delay, make these networks suitable for SIMD systems.

Radix-sort and network construction

The radix-sort algorithm, as described by Gear,[27] takes account of the representation of keys in order to do the sorting. The keys are usually expressed in some radix system. For example, the number 14 (base 10) is represented in the binary radix system (2,2,2,2) as 1110, in radix system (3,2,3) as 202, in radix system (3,3,3) as 112. According to Gear, the sorting algorithm "can be likened to the method of alphabetizing a list of names by first sorting them into 26 piles based on the first letter, and then, treating each pile separately, alphabetizing them on the second letter, and so on . . ." Eventually, we will have a sorted name list in alphabetical order.

If we try to implement this algorithm in hardware, we need a completely connected network (e.g., a crossbar switch) between steps. However, if we are willing to sacrifice some sorting capabilities, the hardware complexity can be greatly reduced. The idea is to perform sorting *locally*. Figure 2 shows just such a scheme. At each stage, the keys are partitioned into groups based on the radix used for the corresponding digit positions. In Figures 2a and 2c, the radices used are all 2s, so keys are partitioned into pairs at each stage. In Figure 2b, the radix system is (3,2), so the keys are partitioned into three keys per group at the first stage, and two keys per group at the second stage.

Using Figure 2a as an example, at the first stage, the keys are sorted into two piles based on the first digit (which is of radix 2). The upper pile includes all the keys with the first digit equal to 0; the lower pile includes all the keys with the first digit equal to 1. Within each pile, the keys are sorted locally on the second digit at the second stage, and so on. The same algorithm is also applied in Figure 2b. (For simplicity, we consider only binary networks—those constructed with keys represented in the binary system).

Obviously, these networks cannot handle all of the permutations, because if either of the two keys in a group belong to the same pile, the "wires" between stages will have to reject one of them. (That is, each wire allows only one key to go through at any time.) For example, the networks in Figure 2a cannot realize the identity mapping ($i \rightarrow i$, $1 \leq i \leq N$). However, if we put a fixed "bit-reversal" connection in front of the network, the identity mapping can be realized. Furthermore, if we rearrange the switching elements in each stage, it is easy to verify that this network is topologically equivalent to a class of very regular networks called the omega networks.[10,12,30] In these networks, each stage consists of a shuffle connection followed by switching elements. Similarly, if the bit-reversal connection is at the end of the network, the network will be topologically equivalent to the indirect binary n-cube networks.[13] Also, with some other fixed connection in front of the network or at its end, we will have networks like the baseline network and the banyan network (S = 2, F = 2).[16]

Many more networks can be constructed using this limited version of the radix-sort algorithm. For example, the order of the keys within each pile is unimportant. Figure 2c shows a network, topologically different from the previous networks, that still uses the same limited version of radix-sort. This network belongs to the class of delta networks proposed by Patel.[29]

Control algorithms and network capabilities

The control algorithms on these networks are straightforward. At stage i, the ith bit of the keys is used for sorting. Assume that the keys with the ith bit equal to 0 are sorted to the upper pile and the keys with the ith bit equal to 1 are sorted to the lower pile, as in Figure 2a. Then switching elements will be set as shown in Figure 3. The bits used to sort the keys are used to set switching elements; they are the control bits of the switching elements. If both control bits of a switching element are zeroes or ones, as in Figures 3c and 3d, then "conflicts" will occur and the permutation will not be realized.

If the number of network inputs is N, the network will contain $(N/2) \log N$ switching elements. Since each switching element has two nonconflict states—(a) and (b) in Figure 3—and each key has only one unique path from its original position to its final destination (because it must belong to the correct "pile" at each stage), the total number of permutations that the network can handle is $2^{(N/2)(\log N)}$, which is $\sqrt{N^N}$. For $N = 8$, this is only about 10 percent of the total number of permutations. Fortunately, for networks like the omega network, the base-

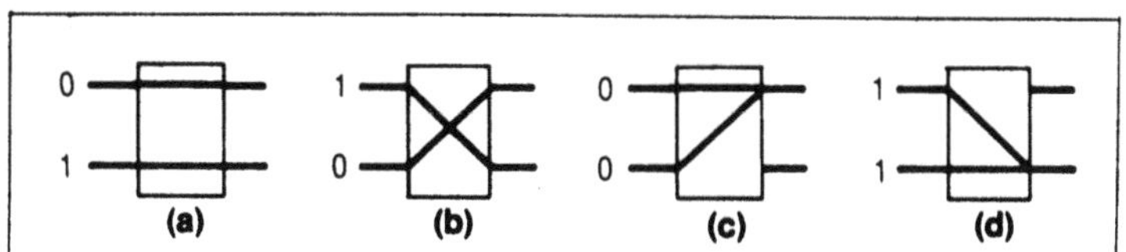

Figure 3. Switch settings for the control algorithm in Figure 2a: (a) and (b), nonconflict states; (c) and (d), conflict states.

line network, and the indirect binary n-cube network, most of the frequently used permutations that are required to access multidimensional array elements are included in that small portion.[10] However, a class of permutations called bit-permute-complement permutations[23] cannot be realized. A shuffle permutation and a bit-reversal permutation belong to this class. Later, we will see that we can enhance network capabilities to include these permutations as well as some others.

Capability enhancement schemes. The capabilities of this class of networks are limited by the number of states ($\sqrt{N}^N$, as described before) the network can represent. Since each message has only one unique path from its original position to its final positions, the only way to enhance the network capability is to break this constraint. Several schemes have been proposed, including queues, decomposition methods, mapping, and conflict-state elimination.

Queues. Queues are the most straightforward way to enhance the network capability. The basic idea is that when a conflict occurs in a switching element, one of the messages will be stored in a queue. Lang was the first to propose queues in these networks;[31] his proposal used a single shuffle-exchange stage that is discussed below. Chen[26] studied the case of a multistage network with queues for SIMD applications. By using a Markov analysis (verified by simulation), he showed that permutations can be performed in an average of $1.5 \log N$ ($N \geq 32$) with an average queue length less than 0.3. Note that, since it is not known a priori how long a given permutation will take, this technique is useful only in cases where deterministic times are not required.

Decomposition methods. These methods accomplish arbitrary permutations by decomposing the permutation into one or more intermediate permutations, each of which is within the capabilities of the network even though the original permutation is not. The set of messages will be moved to some intermediate locations after each pass through the network; several passes later (typically, two or three), the keys will be sorted. These methods were first proposed by Pease[13] and by Lenfant and Tahe.[32] Pease used a typical LU decomposition algorithm with pivoting for those permutations whose mapping can be represented in a matrix form. After the decomposition, the keys for those intermediate permutations can be obtained. The overhead required for these decomposition algorithms, however, is frequently too great to permit their use in SIMD applications.

Mapping from looping algorithms for Benes networks. Using various looping algorithms,[33] Benes networks can realize any permutation. However, these looping algorithms take $O((\log N)^4)$ time.[34]

Two passes through the baseline network[16] and three passes through the omega network[35] have the same capability as a Benes network. The control algorithms for the Benes network, therefore, can be mapped to these networks and can be used for any permutation. However, the mapped control algorithm will have, at best, the same order of complexity as the original control algorithm—$O((\log N)^4)$. Once again, the overhead required to control these networks makes these methods impractical in many SIMD applications.

Conflict-state elimination. Conflict states will arise in a switching element. There is, however, a natural way to eliminate them. If a permutation can be realized by a network, the two control bits at the inputs of a switching element must be different. This must be true for all of the switching elements in the network as well. The implication of this is that one of the control bits is enough to control a switching element. Figure 4 shows two such schemes. In Figure 4a, the control bit at the upper input is used; in Figure 4b, the control bit at the lower input is used. No conflict states will arise in these two schemes. Moreover, if a permutation can be realized by the network using the original control scheme (that is, if both control bits are used at a switching element), there will be no difference between the switch settings for the original control scheme and for the conflict-eliminated control scheme. Since the conflict states are eliminated, we can go through the network using the original keys as many times as necessary without computing the keys for the intermediate locations, as the decomposition methods required. It can be shown that in two passes through the omega network, many frequently used permutations, including bit-permute-complement permutations, can be realized.[36] We can also concatenate several omega networks, rather than going through the same omega network several times, to make the network usable as a circuit switching network. This scheme can also be applied to the Benes network.[37]

Figure 4. Switch settings for conflict-state-elimination scheme when (a) upper control bit and (b) lower control bit is used.

Single-stage networks

For networks like the omega network and the indirect binary n-cube network, the network configuration is actually very uniform. Each stage of the network contains a fixed connection (for example, a shuffle connection in the omega network) and $N/2$ switching elements. It is possible to use just one stage of the network (see Figure 1) to emulate the functions of the original network (which has multiple stages). This has been suggested by a number of people.[21,22,38] However, the single-stage network does not necessarily work in the same way the original multistage network does. Two possible differences are

(1) The multistage network can be used in both the circuit switching mode and the packet switching mode. The single-stage network can only be used in the packet switching mode.

(2) In the multistage network, messages must go through all stages before reaching their destination. In a single-stage network, messages can arrive

at the destination faster because some will arrive at their destination after each iteration.

Lang[31] studied a single-stage network that included queues and found that, in the worst case, queue length could approach $O(\sqrt{N})$ and the worst-case permutations (such as bit reversal) require $O(\sqrt{N})$ time. Chen[26] also studied queued single-stage networks and has shown that the average time to finish a permutation is $O(\log N)$. If deterministic performance is not required, therefore, single-stage networks can be cost-effective choices over multistage networks, since both take $O(\log N)$ time.

MIMD interconnection networks

In a MIMD machine, each processing element has its own control unit. Consequently, the measures used to evaluate MIMD interconnection networks are different from those used for SIMD networks; the measures of a MIMD network are the average time it takes a message to traverse the network (called average delay) and the bandwidth of the network.

The results reported here are all analytical. This allows us to present the above measure for large values of N (as we said above, our networks have N inputs with $N = 2^n$). The model we use for MIMD interconnection networks is the equiprobable independent reference model, whose assumptions are that:

(1) each message has probability $1/N$ of having a particular network output as its destination, and
(2) the destination of a message is independent of the destination of any other message.

Single-stage interconnection networks. An N-input SSIN contains N tokens. These are packet holders; a token may contain a packet or it may be empty. The network operates in steps called cycles. At the beginning of a cycle, the N tokens are at the input of the exchange elements, one token at each input. During the cycle, the tokens go first through the shuffle connection and then through the exchange element. At the end of the cycle, the tokens are again at the input of the exchange elements, ready for the next cycle. In each exchange element, there are two ports—an input port through which packets are placed into empty tokens, and an output port through which the tokens are emptied. A packet consists of two components, a message and a destination tag. The destination tag is simply a $\log_2 N$-bit number $b_0 b_1 . . . b_{n-1}$ used to route the packet. Two routing algorithms might be considered. The first, the log N routing algorithm, requires a counter in each packet. At the beginning of any cycle, this counter has a value between 0 and $\log N - 1$. This value is the number of the destination-tag bit to be used to route the packet through the exchange element. When a packet is introduced into the network, its counter is zero, and, under ideal circumstances, the counter will increase by one every time the packet goes through an exchange element. When the counter reaches log N, the packet is at its destination. The second algorithm, the fast finishing algorithm, uses the whole destination tag to route the packet. Combinational logic, or a table in the exchange element, is searched to determine the output port to which the packet is to be routed.[36] This output, if taken, will allow the packet to reach its destination in the minimum possible number of cycles. With this algorithm, the number of cycles a packet will take to traverse the network from origin to destination could be less than log N.

In general, however, because of conflicts at the exchange elements, the time it takes a packet to reach its destination could be longer than log N under either routing algorithm. Conflicts arise when, according to the routing algorithm, two packets at the input of an exchange element are to be routed to the same output. These conflicts are dealt with in the following way.

First, consider a single-stage network that uses the simple routing algorithm. At each output, the exchange elements will have a register and, possibly, a FIFO queue (see Figure 1). If there is no conflict, during the first part of a cycle the packet at the exchange element input will be moved to the output determined by the routing algorithm, and its counter is incremented by one. When there is a conflict, one of the packets will be selected and moved to the output 0_1 determined by the destination-tag, and its counter will be incremented. This leaves two possibilities: if there are no queues or if the queue at 0_1 is full, the other packet will be routed toward the other output, and its counter will be set to zero; on the other hand, if there is a queue at 0_1 with at least one empty slot, the other packet will be routed to this queue, and its counter will be incremented.

During the second part of a cycle, the packets at the output registers will be routed through the shuffle interconnection. A network using the fast-finishing algorithm will behave in the same way, except that there is no need to deal with the counter.

When there is a conflict, the selection of one of the packets can be accomplished either through random priority or CTF priority techniques. Random priority, as its name indicates, selects a packet at random, while CTF priority selects the packet closer to finishing, and, in the case of a tie, then selects a packet at random. For the log N routing algorithm, selecting the packet closer to its destination is equivalent to selecting the packet with the larger counter. Other priority algorithms are possible—for example, giving priority to the message that has been in the network the longest.

Another technique used to deal with conflicts is the use of several single-stage networks in combination, which can not only increase the bandwidth of the network but also decrease the average delay if the networks are interconnected appropriately. Specifically, we could interconnect the corresponding exchange elements of the networks and in some way move packets from one to another to avoid conflicts. Such an arrangement is called a cooperating multiple-layer single-stage network.

Clearly, there are many possibilities for the design of single-stage interconnection networks. Basically, we could classify them according to four orthogonal criteria:

(1) queue length,
(2) routing algorithm,
(3) priority algorithm, and
(4) number of cooperating layers.

As we have said, the measures of performance are average delay and bandwidth. The average delay is measured by the number of cycles it takes a packet to reach its destination after it is introduced into the network. The bandwidth is measured in the number of packets reaching their destination per cycle. The use of a cycle as the basic measure makes it possible to compare the different techniques. However, this simple measure is a compromise, since, depending on the technology and the implementation, the cycle time of one technique could differ from that of the others.

Average delay and bandwidth are measured as a function of N and of the fraction of the tokens carrying packets, called the load. The way these parameters influence the performance depends on the type of network. The influence of the load on the average delay for two types of SSIN is shown in Figure 5 for $N = 2^{10}$. The influence of N on the average delay and bandwidth for the same networks is shown in Figures 6 and 7 for loads of 0.25 and 0.50. As should be expected, the average delay grows with N and with the load. Note, however, that we measure delay only in the network, and do not include the time a message must wait to enter the network. (See Padua et al.[39] for our analysis of this effect on performance.) As we can see from Figure 5, the priority algorithm has a profound effect on packet delay as the load increases. One would expect bandwidth to increase as the load increases. However, for the random-priority case, it can be shown that to increase the load beyond a critical point actually decreases bandwidth (see Figure 8). For the CTF priority case, bandwidth increases monotonically with the load, but delays can get unacceptably large unless the load is kept small. However, as we shall see, if we use queues or several cooperating layers, then delays can be held to an acceptable (though less than optimum) level even if the load is large.

For a given SSIN and a given load, we define the optimum average delay and bandwidth as the values obtained for those measures if conflicts never arise. The most interesting result of the SSIN analysis is that the average delay and the bandwidth can get very close to the optimum, given a reasonable load. In Figures 6, 7, 9, and 10, the average delay and bandwidth of SSINs with one layer and queue length of 0 are compared to the optimum; the results are shown for loads of 0.25 and 0.50.

Significant improvements of these results have been obtained in two ways. First, we use more than one layer and allow messages to be switched between layers to avoid

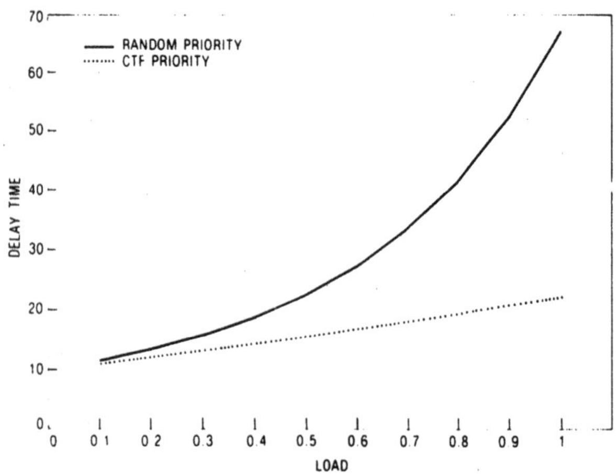

Figure 5. Packet delay vs. network load with queue = 0, layers = 1, full log N routing, $N = 2^{10}$.

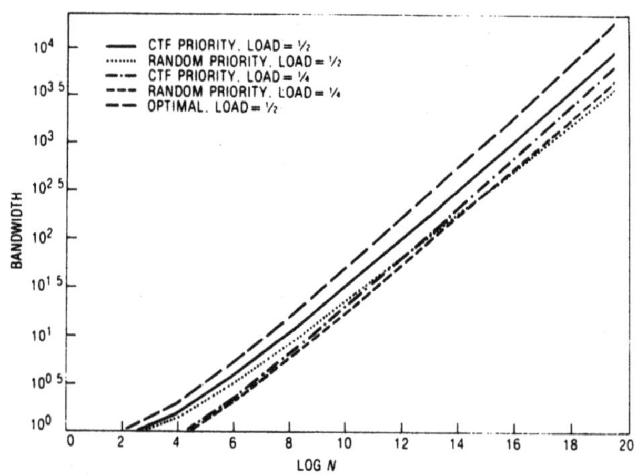

Figure 7. Bandwidth vs. N with queue = 0, layers = 1, full log N routing.

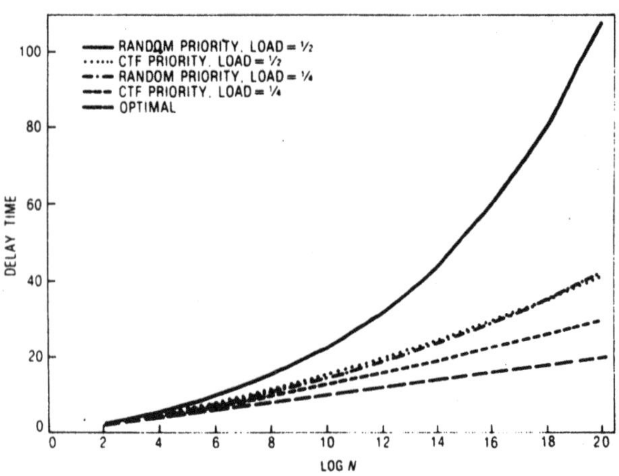

Figure 6. Packet delay vs. N with queue = 0, layers = 1, full log N routing.

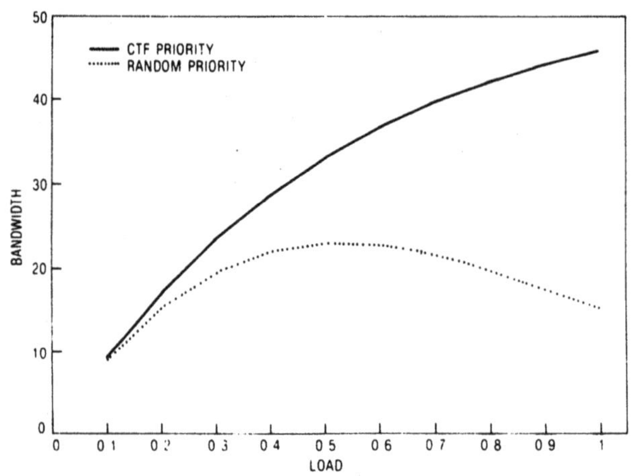

Figure 8. Bandwidth vs. load for random and CTF priority.

conflicts wherever possible (layer-switching). Using this technique, we can achieve delays very close to log N even with loads approaching 1.0. For loads of 0.25, using fast-finish routing, we can produce delays that are less than log N. However, by using queues, we can get results almost as good, and queues are much easier to implement than layer-switching.

As we said earlier, packets can be queued at the outputs of each switch instead of being routed the wrong way. One advantage of queueing is that packet delay is less sensitive to network load; this is illustrated in Figure 11. Also, note that it does not take a very long queue to achieve the same benefits as an infinite queue.

In Figures 12 and 13, we show the average packet delay assuming loads of 0.5 and 1.0, respectively. As can be seen, even with a load of 1.0 and a queue length of only 2, delay is very close to the optimal value of log N. Figures 14 and 15 show the bandwidth for loads of 0.5 and 1.0, respectively. Again, results very close to optimal can be achieved with a queue length of only 1 or 2. Even further improvements could be made by using fast-finish routing. CTF priority, however, would not have much effect, since it would be used only when a queue is full—a rare occurrence.

Multistage interconnection networks. Since Dias and Jump (see this issue, pp. 43-53) cover multistage interconnection networks in MIMD applications, we discuss this issue only briefly. Either packet switching or circuit switching techniques could be used here. Circuit switch-

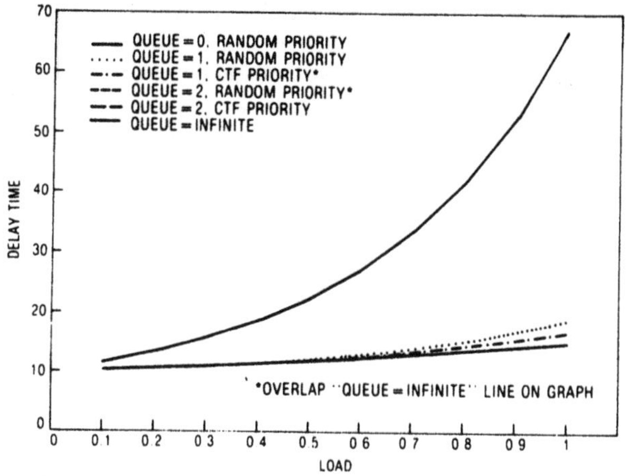

Figure 11. Delay vs. load with various queue lengths, N = 1024, layers = 1, log N routing.

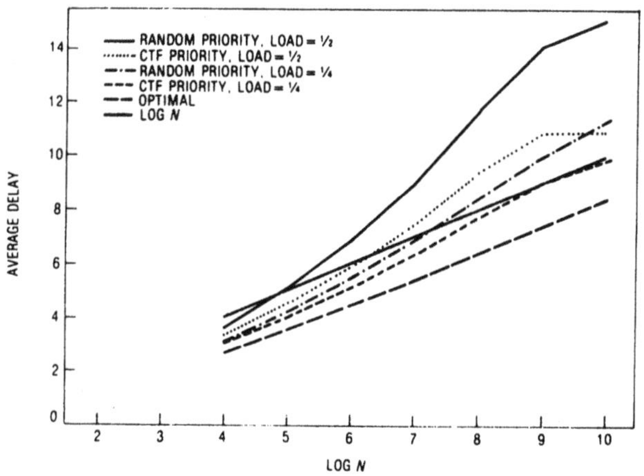

Figure 9. Packet delay vs. N with fast-finishing routing, queue = 0, layers = 1.

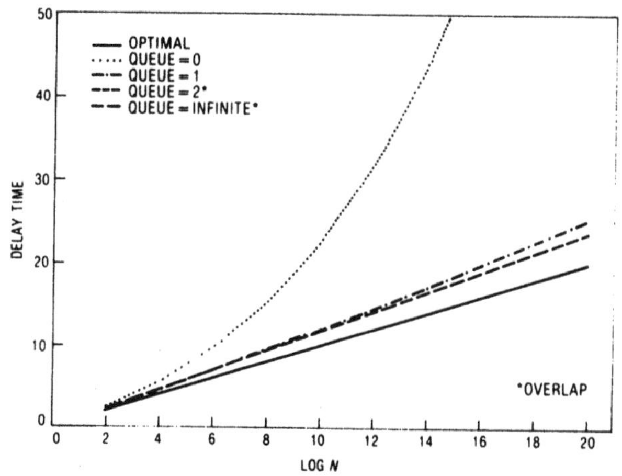

Figure 12. Packet delay vs. N with various queue lengths, load = 0.5, log N routing, random priority.

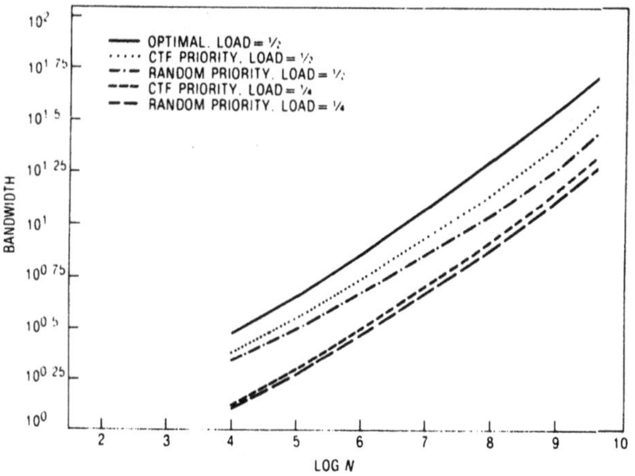

Figure 10. Bandwidth vs. N with fast-finishing routing, queue = 0, layers = 1.

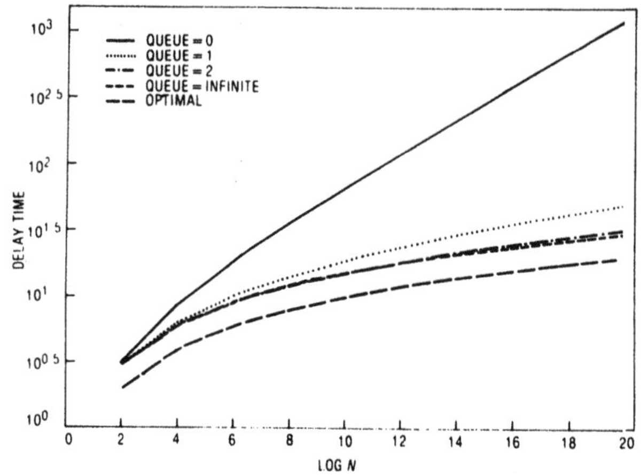

Figure 13. Packet delay vs. N with various queue lengths, load = 1.0, log N routing, random priority.

ing techniques for MIMD applications have been proposed for the Burroughs FMP, a MIMD machine,[2] and have been studied by others.[26,40] Circuit switching is especially appropriate when a large amount of data is to be transmitted between any given pair of ports, or when the amount of data varies greatly. For example, a single data path can be established between the ports, and data can then be transmitted bit serially. However, it is also possible to use a multistage network to transmit fixed-sized packets. In this case, we can add queues to the networks to improve delay time, and we can use pipelining techniques to improve throughput and hardware utilization.[26,29,41,42]

Conclusion

We have summarized many of the results dealing with interconnection networks for SIMD and MIMD computers. SIMD computers ideally require a network capable of performing permutations of data—for example, between memories and processors—in a deterministic and short amount of time. Networks capable of performing all permutations dynamically, where the permutations change constantly, are difficult to design. Crossbar networks are generally too costly when N grows large. Other networks that are capable of performing all permutations but that are cheaper, with $O(N \log N)$ complexity like that of the Benes network, have control algorithms that take too long to allow frequent changes of the permutation. By restricting the set of permutations the network will perform to a "basic" set, we can achieve $O(\log N)$ time with $O(\log N)$ complexity.

There are various ways of augmenting the basic network to perform permutations not in the basic set. They include multiple passes through the basic network using a modified control algorithm, the use of the more general looping control algorithm, and the use of queues. Clearly, however, any time we step outside the basic set of permutations, we give up time, complexity, or determinism.* Much research is being done to develop algorithms and compilation techniques that stay within the basic sets of permutations.

For MIMD computers, other techniques seem more appropriate. Although it is more difficult to restrict permutations to the basic set, deterministic times for permutations are not as important. Probabilistic networks are therefore popular. Here, we can use single or multistage, queued, shuffle-connected networks to perform packet switching with delays close to log N and bandwidth/hardware ratios approaching their theoretical limit. ■

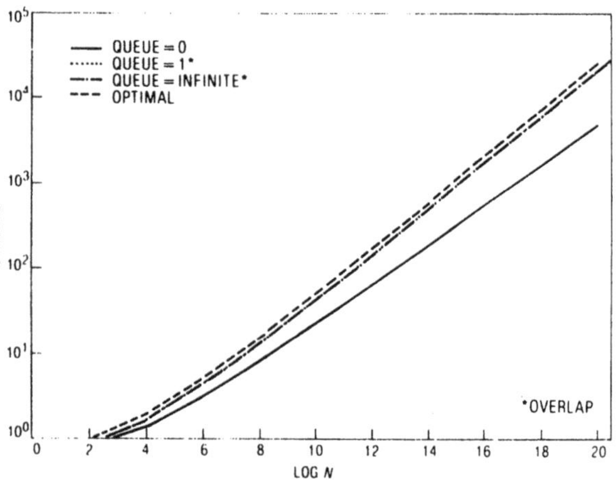

Figure 14. Bandwidth as a function of *N* for various queue sizes, load = 0.5, log *N* routing, random priority.

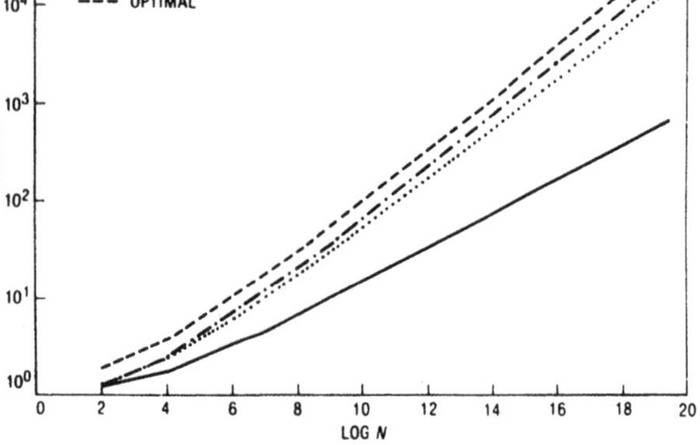

Figure 15. Bandwidth as a function of *N* for various queue sizes, load = 1.0, log *N* routing, random priority.

Acknowledgment

This work was supported in part by the National Science Foundation under Grant No. US NSF MCS80-01561 and by the US Department of Energy under Grant No. US DOE DE-AC02-81ER10822.

References

1. H. S. Stone, "Parallel Processing with the Perfect Shuffle," *IEEE Trans. Computers,* Vol. C-20, No. 2, Feb. 1971, pp. 153-161.
2. G. H. Barnes, "Design and Validation of a Connection Network for Many—Processor Multiprocessor Systems," *Proc. 1980 Int'l Conf. Parallel Processing,* Aug. 1980, pp. 79-80.
3. K. E. Batcher, "Sorting Networks and Their Applications," *AFIPS Conf. Proc.,* Vol. 32, 1968 SJCC, pp. 307-314.
4. K. E. Batcher, "The Flip Network in STARAN," *Proc. Int'l Conf. Parallel Processing,* Aug. 1976, pp. 65-71.
5. V. E. Benes, *Mathematical Theory of Connecting Networks and Telephone Traffic,* Academic Press, NY, 1965.
6. T-y. Feng and C. L. Wu, "Interconnection Networks in Multiple Processor Systems," Rome Air Development Center Technical Report No. RADC-TE-79-304, Rome, NY, Dec. 1979.

*If determinism is not required, then queued single-stage networks can perform any permutation in an average time of $O(\log N)$. This can be quite effective, since it requires only $O(N)$ complexity.

7. L. R. Goke and G. J. Lipovski, "Banyan Networks for Partitioning Multiprocessor Systems," *First Ann. Symp. Computer Architecture,* Dec. 1973, pp. 21-28.

8. A. E. Joel, Jr., "On Permutation Switching Networks," *Bell System Technical J.,* Vol. 27, 1968, pp. 813-822.

9. T. Lang and H. Stone, "A Shuffle-Exchange Network with Simplified Control," *IEEE Trans. Computers,* Vol. C-25, No. 1, Jan. 1976, pp. 55-65.

10. D. H. Lawrie, "Access and Alignment of Data in an Array Processor," *IEEE Trans. Computers,* Vol. C-24, No. 12, Dec. 1975, pp. 1145-1155.

11. G. M. Masson, "Binomial Switching Networks for Concentration and Distribution," *Computer,* Vol. 25, No. 9, Sept. 1977, pp. 873-883.

12. D. S. Parker, "Topics in Conjugation, Huffman Tree Construction, Non-linear Recurrences, and Permutation Networks," University of Illinois at Urbana-Champaign Department of Computer Science Report No. 78-930, Oct. 1978.

13. M. C. Pease, "The Indirect Binary n-Cube Microprocessor Array," *IEEE Trans. Computers,* Vol. C-26, No. 5, May 1977, pp. 458-473.

14. N. Pippenger, "On the Complexity of Strictly Non-Blocking Networks," *IEEE Trans. Communications,* Vol. COM-22, 1974, pp. 1890-1892.

15. H. J. Siegel and S. D. Smith, "Study of Multistage SIMD Interconnection Networks," *Proc. 5th Ann. Symp. Computer Architecture,* Apr. 1978, pp. 223-229.

16. C. Wu and T. Feng, "On a Class of Multistage Interconnection Networks," *IEEE Trans. Computers,* Vol. C-29, No. 9, Sept. 1980, pp. 694-702.

17. M. J. Flynn, "Some Computer Organizations and Their Effectiveness," *IEEE Trans. Computers,* Vol. C-21, No. 9, Sept. 1972, pp. 948-960.

18. C. D. Thompson, "A Complexity Theory for VLSI," PhD thesis, Carnegie Mellon University, Pittsburgh, PA, 1980.

19. D. Kleitman, F. T. Leighton, M. Lepley, and G. L. Miller, "New Layouts for the Shuffle-Exchange Graph," *Proc. ACM Ann. Symp. Theory of Computation,* May 1981.

20. J. Gregory and R. McReynolds, "The SOLOMON Computer," *IEEE Trans. Computers,* Vol. EC-12, No. 6, Dec. 1963, pp. 774-781.

21. J. T. Schwartz, "Ultracomputers," *ACM Trans. Programming Languages and Systems,* Vol. 2, No. 4, Oct. 1980, pp. 484-521.

22. M. C. Pease, "Organization of Large Scale Fourier Processors," *J. ACM,* Vol. 16, No. 3, July 1969, pp. 474-482.

23. D. Nassimi and S. Sahni, "An Optimal Routing Algorithm for Mesh-Connected Parallel Computers," *J. ACM,* Vol. 27, No. 1, Jan. 1980, pp. 6-29.

24. D. Nassimi and S. Sahni, "Bitonic Sort on a Mesh-Connected Parallel Computer," *IEEE Trans. Computers,* Vol. C-28, No. 1, Jan. 1979, pp. 2-7.

25. D. Nassimi and S. Sahni, "Data Broadcasting in SIMD Computers," *IEEE Trans. Computers,* Vol. C-30, No. 2, Feb. 1981, pp. 101-107.

26. P. Y. Chen, "Multiprocessor Systems: Interconnection Networks, Memory Hierarchy, Modeling and Simulations," PhD thesis, University of Illinois at Urbana-Champaign, in preparation.

27. G. W. Gear, *Computer Organization and Programming,* (2nd. ed.), McGraw-Hill, Hightstown, N.J., 1974, pp. 388-392.

28. G. J. Lipovski, "The Architecture of a Large Associative Processor," *AFIPS Conf. Proc.,* Vol. 36, 1970 SJCC, pp. 385-396.

29. J. H. Patel, "Processor-Memory Interconnections for Multiprocessors," *Proc. 6th Ann. Symp. Computer Architecture,* Apr. 1979, pp. 168-177.

30. C. Wu and T. Feng, "The Universality of Shuffle-Exchange Networks," *IEEE Trans. Computers,* Vol. C-30, No. 5, May 1981, pp. 324-331.

31. T. Lang, "Interconnections between Processors and Memory Modules Using the Shuffle-Exchange Network," *IEEE Trans. Computers,* Vol. C-25, No. 5, May 1976, pp. 496-503.

32. J. Lenfant and S. Tahe, "Permuting Data with the Omega Network," Rome Air Development Center Technical Report, Rome, NY, Nov. 1978.

33. D. C. Opferman and N. T. Tsao-Wu, "On a Class of Rearrangeable Switching Networks," *Bell System Technical J.,* Vol. 50, No. 5, June 1971, pp. 1579-1618.

34. D. Nassimi and S. Sahni, "Parallel Algorithms to Set Up the Benes Permutation Network," Tech. Rpt. No. 79-19, University of Minnesota, Minneapolis, 1979.

35. D. S. Parker, "New Points of View on 3-Stage Rearrangeable Switching Networks," *Proc. Workshop in Interconnection Networks,* (H. J. Siegel, ed.), Lafayette, IN, Apr. 21-22, 1980, pp. 56-63.

36. P-C. Yew, "On the Design of Interconnection Networks for Parallel and Multiprocessor Systems," PhD thesis, University of Illinois at Urbana-Champaign Department of Computer Science Report No. 81-1059, Mar. 1981.

37. P-C. Yew and D. H. Lawrie, "An Easily Controlled Network for Frequently Used Permutations," *Proc. Workshop on Interconnection Networks* (H. J. Siegel, ed.), Lafayette, IN, Apr. 21-22, 1980, pp. 72-73; also *IEEE Trans. Computers,* Vol. C-30, No. 4, Apr. 1981, pp. 296-298.

38. D. H. Lawrie and D. A. Padua, "Analysis of Message Switching with Shuffle-Exchanges in Multiprocessors," *Proc. Workshop on Interconnection Networks* (H. J. Siegel, ed.), Lafayette, IN, Apr. 21-22, 1980, pp. 116-123.

39. D. A. Padua, D. J. Kuck, and D. H. Lawrie, "High-Speed Multiprocessors and Compilation Techniques," *IEEE Trans. Computers,* Vol. C-29, No. 9, Sept. 1980, pp. 763-776.

40. J. E. Wirsching and T. Kishi, "CONET—A Connection Network Model," *Proc. Workshop on Interconnection Networks* (H. J. Siegel, ed.), Lafayette, IN, Apr. 21-22, 1980, pp. 105-106.

41. D. M. Dias and J. R. Jump, "Packet Communication in Multistage Shuffle-Exchange Networks," *Proc. 1980 Int'l Conf. Parallel Processing,* Aug. 1980, pp. 327-328.

42. D. M. Dias and J. R. Jump, "Analysis and Simulation of Buffered Delta Networks," *IEEE Trans. Computers,* Vol. C-30, No. 4, April 1981, pp. 273-282.

Pin-Yee Chen is currently completing the PhD degree in computer science at the University of Illinois at Urbana-Champaign. He received the BSEE degree from the National Taiwan University, Taipei, and the MS degree from Yale University. His major area of study is the design and analysis of multiprocessor systems. His current interests include parallel and distributed processing, computer architecture, computer systems peformance evaluation, computer communication, and local networks.

Chen is a member of the IEEE Computer Society and the ACM.

Duncan H. Lawrie has worked with parallel computation and other very large computation systems since 1966, when he worked on the ILLIAC IV computer. He has contributed to the design of several other machines, including, most recently, the Burroughs Scientific Processor. He is an associate professor of computer science at the University of Illinois at Urbana-Champaign. He is a member of Tau Beta Pi, Eta Kappa Nu, Sigma Xi, ACM, IEEE, and the AAUP.

Lawrie has served as a referee for the *IEEE Transactions on Computers* and for several national conferences. He was program co-chairman for the Symposium on High Speed Computer and Algorithm Organization, program co-chairman for the 9th International Conference on Parallel Processing, a member of the program committee for the Workshop on Interconnection Networks, and program co-chairman for the 1980 International Conference on Parallel Processing.

David Padua is currently professor agregado at the Universidad Simon Bolivar in Venezuela. Before that he was a visiting assistant professor of computer science at the University of Illinois at Urbana-Champaign, where he received the PhD degree in computer science in 1980. Born in Caracas, Venezuela, he was granted a licentiate in computer science by the Universidad Central de Venezuela in 1973, and taught mathematics and computer science at that university and at Universidad Simon Bolivar.

Pen-Chung Yew is a visiting assistant professor of computer science at the University of Illinois at Urbana-Champaign. He received his BSEE degree from National Taiwan University in 1972 and the MS and PhD degrees in computer science from the University of Massachusetts at Amherst and the University of Illinois at Urbana-Champaign, respectively, in 1977 and 1981. His current research interests include interconnection networks and multiprocessor organization. He is a member of Sigma Xi, Phi Kappa Phi, ACM, and IEEE.

Modeling Bus Contention and Memory Interference in a Multiprocessor System

MARCO AJMONE MARSAN, MEMBER, IEEE, GIANFRANCO BALBO, GIANNI CONTE, MEMBER, IEEE, AND FRANCESCO GREGORETTI

***Abstract*—Stochastic models of contention for shared resources in an experimental multiprocessor prototype are presented and are validated with simulation and measurement results. Three modeling techniques are used (stochastic Petri nets, Markov chains, and queueing networks) that represent the system operations as Markovian stochastic processes. Each technique is best suited to a specific stage of the analysis. An integrated use of these techniques represents a very powerful tool for the performance analysis of multiprocessor systems and provides ways of investigating several extensions of the prototype architecture. Simulation results and measurements performed on the hardware prototype validate the analysis and show that the accuracy of the analytical results is excellent.**

***Index Terms*—Bus contention, Markov chains, memory interference, message passing, multiprocessors, performance evaluation, Petri nets, queueing networks.**

I. Introduction

DECREASING costs of CPU and memory modules have recently spurred new research efforts in the field of multiprocessor systems. Multiprocessor systems are also becoming increasingly interesting because of the growth of computer applications that can profit from the use of these structures. Examples of applications are found in the fields of artificial intelligence [9], control of industrial processes [38], packet switching systems [29], and telephone switches [14]. Many other experimental multiprocessor systems are presently being built in research laboratories and universities.

A prototype architecture (TOMP, TOrino MultiProcessor) is currently under development at Politecnico of Torino, Torino, Italy [15]. The present version of this system comprises three Zilog Z8001 processors tightly coupled via a global bus and with shared memories. A distributed operating system kernel allows the exchange of information among processes on a message-passing basis. Main goals of the research project that have led to this experimental setup are the development of efficient modular multiprocessor structures, the study of efficient interprocessor communication schemes, and the implementation of hardware aids for multiprocessor software.

The efficiency of a multiprocessor system depends upon many factors related to different hardware and/or software components (contention for shared resources, synchronization of tasks, operating system, etc.). The architecture designer must thus be concerned with the reduction of the overhead introduced by the interconnection structure in order to insure that contention for shared resources (buses, common memories, I/O devices, etc.) is kept minimal. In fact, tight bottlenecks at this level can be detrimental to the global system performance and cannot be recovered at higher levels.

A qualitative ranking of architecture alternatives can often be made by skilled designers. However, a quantitative comparison for cost/performance tradeoffs requires the availability of suitable system modeling tools. The architecture of TOMP has been selected as a good compromise between performance and implementation cost after a comparative analysis of several alternatives [2]. To further study the characteristics of the selected structure, other models have been developed that take into account additional details of the system behavior and that explore possible extentions. To assist the design of the system control programs, higher level models of software behavior are now being studied.

The operations of a tightly coupled multiprocessor system can be very complex even in the case of a small system such as the present version of TOMP. A broad spectrum of models can thus be derived depending upon the level of detail used for the representation of the system behavior. A very detailed description of the system leads to extremely complex models (the limiting case being the construction of a system emulator) whose analysis is often very costly and whose verification becomes intractable. More abstract views of the system can be used where the compound effect of several factors is represented in a probabilistic manner. The models obtained in this way are usually simpler and can in general be solved with a limited effort. The models we have developed for the performance evaluation of TOMP fall in this latter class and rely on a set of assumptions that makes them Markovian.

Several authors have already developed stochastic models of interference among processors in multiprocessor systems. The earlier works were concerned with the performance loss due to memory interference in crossbar systems [4], [5], [21], [35], [39]. Rapidly decreasing costs of CPU's and memories suggest the use of simpler interconnection structures such as shared buses or shuffle exchange networks. A few perfor-

Manuscript received February 5, 1982; revised July 14, 1982. This work was supported in part by the Italian National Research Council (CNR) as part of the Computer Science Program, MUMICRO Project, under Contract 81.01527.97, and in part by the North Atlantic Treaty Organization (NATO) under Research Grant 012.81.

M. Ajmone Marsan, G. Conte, and F. Gregoretti are with the Istituto di Elettronica e Telecomunicazioni, Politecnico di Torino, Corso Duca degli Abruzzi 24, Torino, Italy.

G. Balbo is with the Istituto di Scienze dell'Informazione, Universita' di Torino, Corso M. D'Azeglio 42, Torino, Italy.

mance studies of bus-oriented multiprocessor architectures have recently been published [1], [2], [17], [20], [39].

This paper reports on further developments of the work presented in [2] where four different bus-oriented multiprocessor architectures were examined using a single modeling technique for their performance comparison. In this paper, the selected architecture is investigated in more detail using different modeling approaches (Markov chains, stochastic Petri nets, queueing networks), each one being best suited for a specific field of analysis, but having similar underlying stochastic properties. The accuracy of the obtained performance predictions and the effectiveness of the probabilistic description of the system behavior have been successfully tested with measurements performed on the real system.

II. The Multiprocessor System Model

The architecture considered in this study is shown in Fig. 1. Each processor is associated with a local memory composed of two sections, one of which is private, the other being common. Private memory areas can be accessed only by local processors, whereas common memory areas are accessible to all processors in the system. Throughout this paper we assume that the multiprocessor system is made up of N identical processor-memory modules.

A processor reaches its private memory (private access) using a private bus (PB). Accesses to the local module of the common memory (local access) are accomplished using the private bus and the local bus (LB). To reach a nonlocal portion of the common memory (external access), a processor uses its private bus, the global bus (GB), and the bus local to the destination memory module. Contention arises in the use of the global bus and of the common memory modules and a processor is delayed when the resources it is trying to access are busy. Arbitration units, needed to manage multiple requests for GB and LB, can implement different strategies. In the case of the TOMP prototype, a fixed priority policy has been chosen for GB and a FIFO discipline is used to manage LB. Fig. 2 shows the prototype setup based on six boards: three for the CPU's and three for the common parts of the local memories and for the distributed arbiter of the global bus.

Processors are assumed to execute a continuous flow of instructions stored in their own private memories. These instructions are logically grouped into tasks that cooperate by passing messages through memory areas. Modeling this system at the message passing level corresponds to the identification of processing periods (CPU bursts) that require access to private memories and transfer periods that require access to common memory areas to pass messages. CPU bursts and transfer periods actually correspond to the execution of many elementary instructions.

Communication between tasks allocated to the same processor takes place through private memory only. Communication between tasks allocated to different processors must use common memory. Shared buses are used only to access common memory areas; thus the exchange of information is relevant to our models only when the communicating tasks reside on different processors.

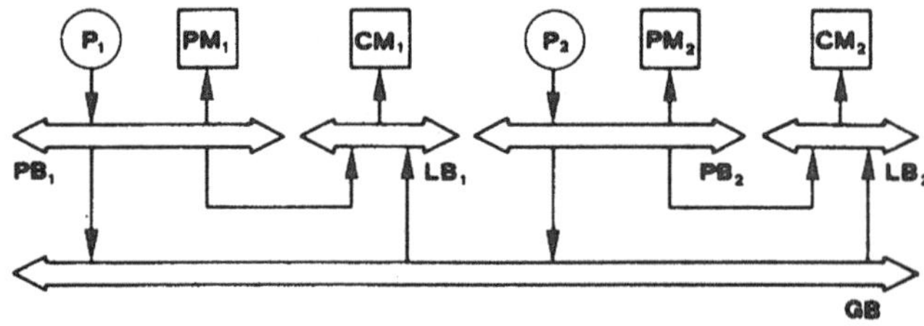

Fig. 1. Architecture of TOMP in the case of two processors.

Fig. 2. View of the present version of the TOMP prototype.

The execution of tasks cooperating in a message passing fashion therefore amounts to repeatedly executing a "CPU burst-transfer period" cycle. Contention for the use of shared resources, such as buses and common memory modules, can add a queueing period component to the execution cycle.

We can classify the state of a processor as follows.

1) Active—The processor executes in its private memory.

2) Accessing—The processor exchanges messages with other cooperating processors by writing into (or reading from) common memory areas.

3) Queued—The processor queues waiting to access common memory areas.

4) Blocked—The processor working on its local common memory module, is blocked when preempted by some other processor accessing the same common memory area.

Parameters of our models are the average CPU burst length $(1/\lambda)$ and the average transfer period duration $(1/\mu)$. The system load factor ρ is defined as the ratio λ/μ. The performance index used in this paper is the average number of active processors, called processing power and denoted by P.

External accesses are made to send messages to other processors; messages are received by the destination processes by means of local accesses. Assuming that each message is eventually read, the numbers of external and local accesses made by each processor are asymptotically equal. We can thus assume that a CPU burst is followed half of the time by an external access request and half of the time by a local access request.

Besides being analytically tractable, Markovian models often yield reasonably good estimates of the performance of real systems [10]. In order to make our models Markovian, the following additional assumptions are introduced.

1) The lengths of CPU bursts and access periods are assumed to be independent exponentially distributed random variables.

2) When a processor requires access to a common memory module, a path is immediately established (with no delay) between the processor and the referenced memory module, provided that the memory is accessible (the global bus is available and the memory is free).

3) If a path cannot be established, the processor idles, waiting for the necessary resource(s).

4) Upon memory access completion, the memory and the global bus are immediately released (with no delay) and the processor returns to its active state.

5) External access requests from each processor are directed to any nonlocal common memory module with probability $1/(N-1)$.

Assumptions 2 and 4 imply that we neglect the times needed for bus arbitration and release. This is a consequence of our rather abstract view of the system behavior. Nothing, however, prevents from adding both arbitration and release times to the access time in the period of average duration $1/\mu$m used in the model.

The goal of this paper is the development of stochastic models for studying the performance loss due to contention for physical resources. Our main concern not being an accurate model of the system workload, we have chosen to keep it as simple as possible to facilitate the analysis of the system; the choices of exponential distributions and of symmetric workload, while not strictly necessary to preserve the Markovian properties of the models, are thus introduced to simplify the analysis.

III. Modeling Techniques

As we said in the introduction, this paper reports on the study of the performance of TOMP using different analytical modeling techniques, all based on the theory of Markovian stochastic processes. Each technique is best suited to a specific field or stage of the performance analysis.

Stochastic Petri nets (*SPN*'s) are introduced first as a useful graphical tool for the precise description of the system operations, and as a modeling technique that allows an easy evaluation of the performance of small systems.

SPN's are extremely versatile and are an excellent analysis tool in the initial stage of a study. They can be used by system designers with hardly any modeling experience and with no knowledge of the theory of Markovian processes since the model solution can be automatically obtained from the graphical description [27]. Several design options can thus be tested for performance improvements with very little effort.

A weak point of *SPN*'s is that the graphical representation rapidly becomes very cumbersome when the size of the multiprocessor system to be modeled increases. Moreover, the number of states of the Markovian process underlying the *SPN* representation of the system shows an exponential growth as a function of the number of system components.

Subsequent steps in the performance evaluation of a system can be done by the direct use of Markov chains (*MC*'s). The probabilistic analysis of these models is identical to that used for *SPN*'s, but the *SPN* descriptive power is lost. Much more insight is now required in the development of the model and some modeling steps, such as the *MC* state definition and the evaluation of the state transition rates, are left to the analyst. On the other hand, a careful analysis of the system structure may reveal symmetries that can be exploited to reduce the number of states using such techniques as "lumping" [24]. An *MC* model is less versatile than the one, since a change in the assumptions requires the study of a different *MC*. Larger, but still moderate size systems can be analyzed in this way. The use of approximations may further expand the applicability of *MC* models [1], [2].

Another analytical approach is that of using queueing network (*QN*) models, for which a wide gamut of exact and approximate solution methods has been published in the literature [8], [18]. Computationally efficient approximate solution methods exist that allow the analysis of fairly large systems, possibly with multiple bus interconnection structures. Models derived in this way have little versatility and modifications in the assumptions often lead to intractable queueing networks.

Simulation and measurements were employed to validate analytical results. Different from the previous approaches, simulation models can be very general and do not need the introduction of Markovian or independence assumptions. They can thus be used to investigate the impact that these assumptions have on the performance estimates provided by the other methods. A simulation study of the effect of Markovian and symmetry assumptions on the performance of multiprocessor systems similar to those discussed in this paper can be found in [1].

IV. Stochastic Petri Net Models

Graph models of computer systems have been developed by many authors. Much of the work in this field refers to the original ideas of C. A. Petri and the derived models are generally known as Petri nets [32], [33]. These models have recently become very popular for the representation of distributed computing systems because of their capability of clearly describing concurrency, conflicts, and synchronization of tasks.

Original Petri nets were used to represent the logic behavior of computer systems with no timing and performance considerations. Some work has recently been done to include the notion of time into Petri net models. In some cases, fixed times were used leading to deterministic models [26], [40]. Several authors have, on the other hand, suggested the introduction of random firing times in Petri nets [27], [28], [36], so that the resulting models are stochastic in nature.

In this paper, we refer to the work of M. K. Molloy [27] and use the models he proposed, named stochastic Petri nets (*SPN*'s), to analyze the performance behavior of the multiprocessor system described in Section II.

An *SPN* has a set of places P, a set of transitions T, a set of directed arcs A, and an initial marking M. A firing rate in the set G is associated to each transition. A formal definition of an *SPN* is the following:

$$SPN = (P, T, A, M, G) \tag{1}$$

where

$$\begin{aligned} P &= [p_1, p_2, \cdots, p_n] \\ T &= [t_1, t_2, \cdots, t_m] \\ A &\subset (P \times T)\, U\, (T \times P) \\ M &= [m_1, m_2, \cdots, m_n] \\ G &= [g_1, g_2, \cdots, g_m]. \end{aligned} \tag{2}$$

In the graphical representation of *SPN*'s, places are drawn as circles and transitions as bars. Arcs connect places to transitions and transitions to places. A marking is defined by assigning a given number of tokens (drawn as black dots) to each place. A place is an input to a transition whenever an arc exists from that place to that transition. A place is an output of a transition whenever an arc exists from that transition to that place. A transition is enabled when all of its input places contain at least one token. Enabled transitions fire after an exponentially distributed random time. The rate associated to the transition determines the parameter of the exponential distribution. The firing of a transition removes one token from each of its input places and puts one token in each of its output places. The firing of a transition may thus disable conflicting transitions.

Molloy has shown that *SPN*'s are isomorphic to continuous time *MC*; *SPN* markings correspond to *MC* states. It is thus possible to obtain the steady-state probability of each marking and from it, to derive performance indexes.

Consider, for instance, the multiprocessor system described in Section II. Its behavior is described by the *SPN* of Fig. 3 in the case of two processors and one global bus.

The assumptions on the multiple processor workload determine the firing rate of each transition, giving

$$\begin{aligned} g_1 = g_5 = g_8 = g_{12} &= \lambda/2 \\ g_4 = g_7 = g_{11} = g_{14} &= \mu. \end{aligned} \tag{3}$$

The other transitions correspond to operations (bus arbitration and release, acquisition of memory control, etc.) that, given the level of detail considered in these models, are not relevant to the modeling of bus contention and memory interference. We thus assume these transitions to fire at a very high speed that we set equal to α. If more detailed models are necessary, it is easy to explicitly account for these phenomena by carefully setting the corresponding transition speeds.

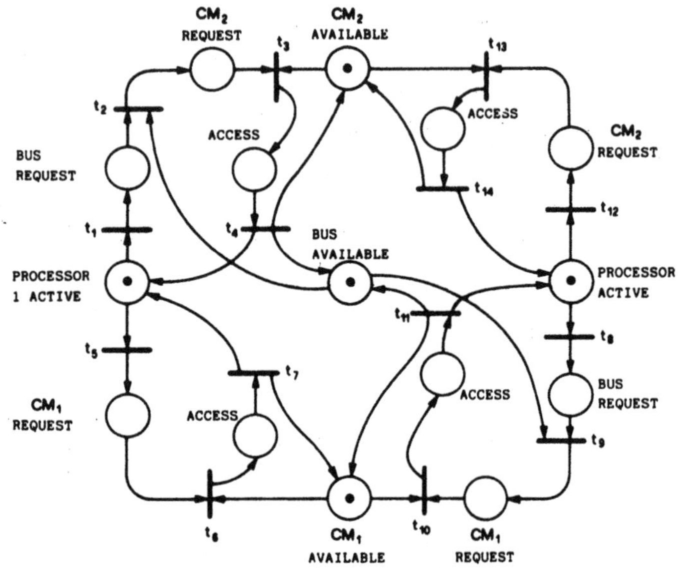

Fig. 3. *SPN* of a two processor system in which the *GB* is occupied also when the requested *CM* is busy.

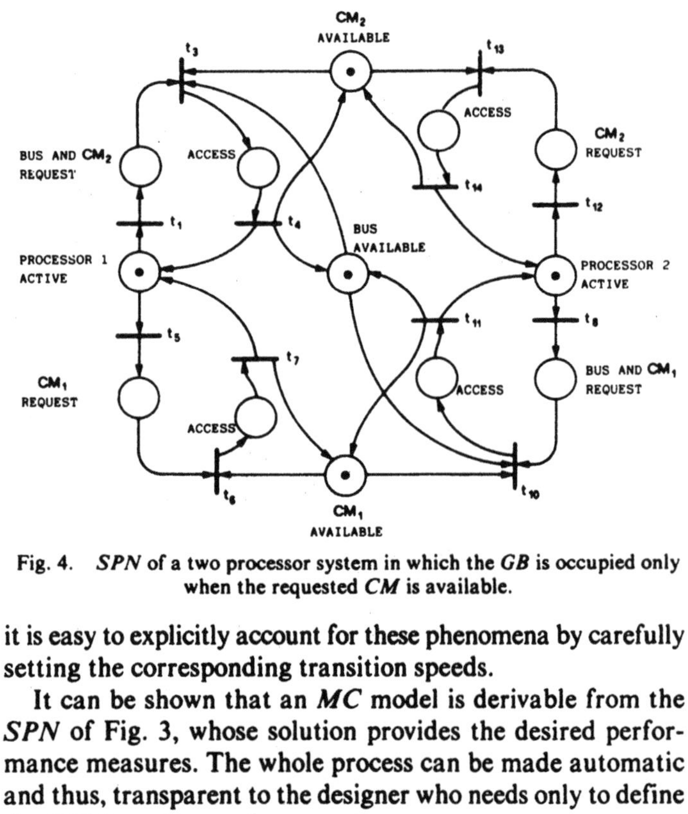

Fig. 4. *SPN* of a two processor system in which the *GB* is occupied only when the requested *CM* is available.

It can be shown that an *MC* model is derivable from the *SPN* of Fig. 3, whose solution provides the desired performance measures. The whole process can be made automatic and thus, transparent to the designer who needs only to define the *SPN* topology and parameters.

Fig. 3 is an *SPN* model of a system in which a processor requesting to access a busy external common memory module can nevertheless occupy the global bus. This may lead to a performance loss when more than two processors are present in the system. If, instead, the bus arbiter prevents the processors from seizing the bus unless the destination memory is free, the *SPN* becomes a little simpler: two places and two transitions are removed in the case of a two processor system. The resulting *SPN* is shown in Fig. 4 in which the firing rates of the remaining transitions are left unchanged with respect to the previous case.

Three things should become clear from these two examples. First of all, *SPN*'s provide a way of obtaining a simple and

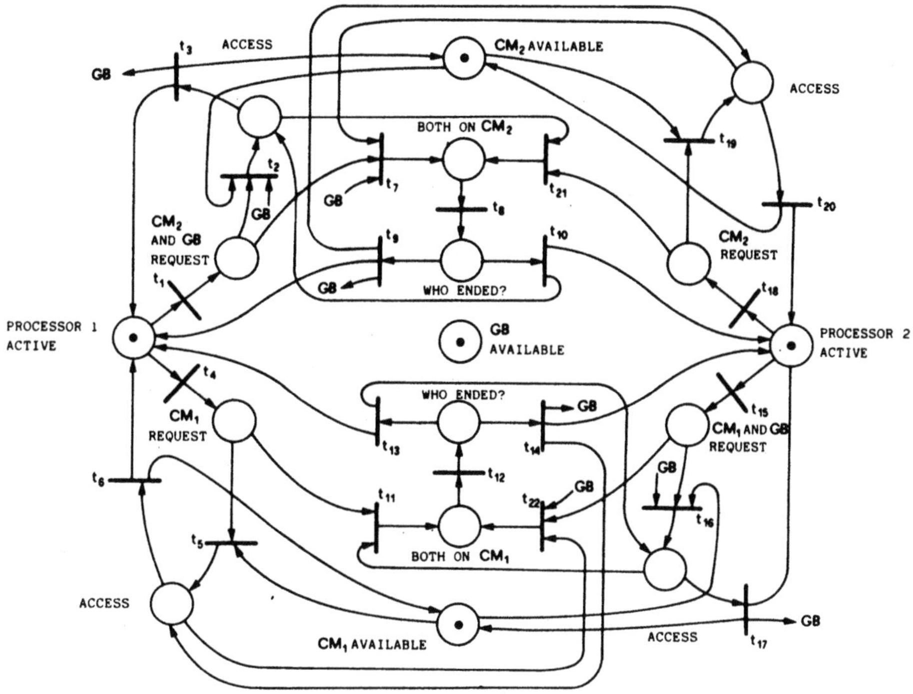

Fig. 5. *SPN* of a two processor system with interleaving of memory accesses.

precise description of the system operation and workload. Secondly, an automated Markovian analysis of the system is possible without having to go through the process of finding the correct state definition and of evaluating the state transition rates. Finally, *SPN*'s are extremely versatile: a change in the assumptions is often immediately represented with a little modification of the net.

To further emphasize these concepts, let us consider a more detailed view of the system operations. Assume the common memory accesses to be actually subdivided into a set of elementary memory operations so that some degree of interleaving is possible: processors trying to access the same memory module will be served in parallel at individual rates smaller than μ, but larger than $\mu/2$. The *SPN* that describes this behavior is easily drawn in the case of a two processor system and is shown in Fig. 5. Since the lengths of the two accesses are independent, identically distributed random variables, the probability of either access ending first is 0.5. We thus have two conflicting transitions, t_9 and t_{10} in one case and t_{13} and t_{14} in the other case, that select which processor must continue accessing the memory while the other returns to its active state. The rates of these transitions are equal so that they fire with equal probability. Transition rates are in this case assigned as follows:

$$g_1 = g_4 = g_{15} = g_{18} = \lambda/2$$
$$g_3 = g_6 = g_{17} = g_{20} = \mu$$
$$g_8 = g_{12} = \mu'. \qquad (4)$$

All other transition rates are set to the already mentioned very high speed α to make negligible the times needed for those operations to occur in our models. The rate μ' represents the speed at which two simultaneous access requests to the same common memory module are served. This rate is contained in the range $(\mu, 2\mu)$ since no interleaving keeps the speed equal to the rate of service of a single request and full interleaving can make the rate twice as large.

A range of operational conditions can be easily inspected exploiting the versatility of the *SPN* model. For instance, if we eliminate transitions t_{10} and t_{13} and set $\mu' = \mu$, the *SPN* reduces to the case in which preemption of the access performed by a processor on its local memory is allowed (i.e., requests coming from external processors through the global bus are given priority). If, instead, in the *SPN* of Fig. 5, we set $\mu' = 2\mu$, the case of dual port memories that can support simultaneous accesses is represented.

We have already said that *SPN*'s are powerful tools for the precise representation of distributed systems characterized by parallelism, contention, and queueing. As any other modeling tool, however, they also have weak points, such as the practical difficulty of representing systems of increasing size and the rapid growth of the number of states of their isomorphic *MC*'s.

As an example, consider the extension of the *SPN* of Fig. 3 to a three processor case which yields the graph of Fig. 6. The *SPN* becomes rather complex despite the introduction of the simplifying assumption of managing the global bus queue with a random selection policy. From a conceptual point of view, the *SPN* representation of the three processor system is no more difficult than that of the two processor case. In fact, a modular description of the *SPN* can be given. The replication of modules with identical structure must, however, be provided with a precise description of the interconnection among them. The increased complexity of the graphical representation of the three processor system is followed by an explosion of the number of states of the associated *MC*. From 26 states in the two processor case we go to 395 states in the three processor case. The *MC* is still solvable; thus the analysis of the system

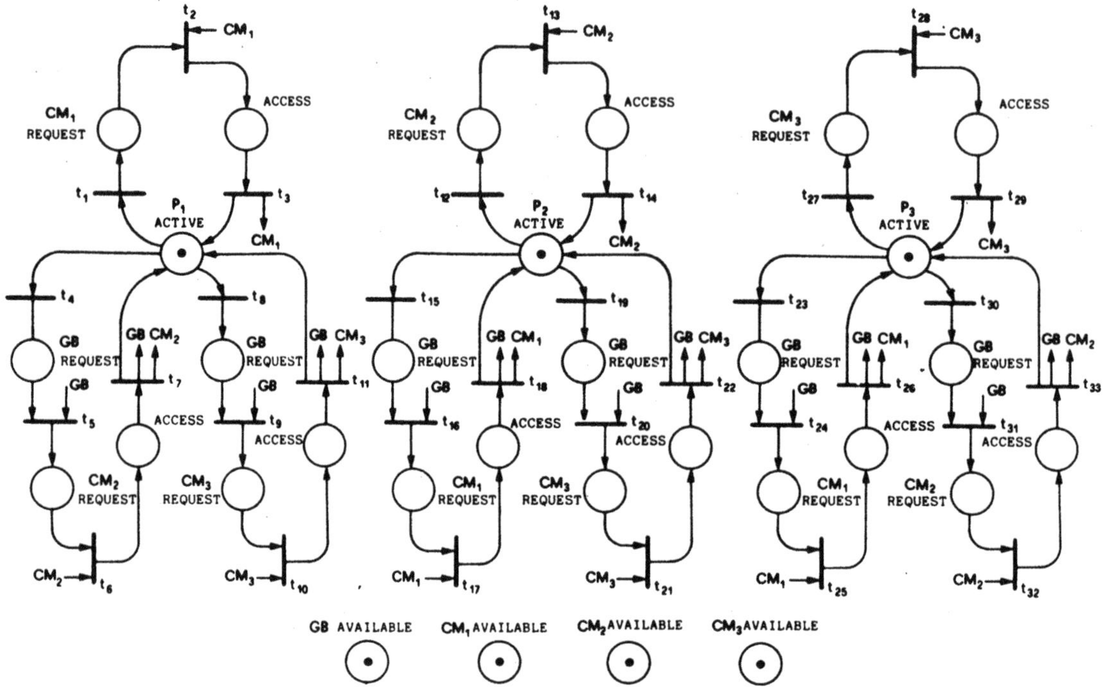

Fig. 6. *SPN* of a three processor system as in Fig. 3.

is still feasible, but this growth indicates that even slightly larger systems become intractable.

The processing power P of a two processor system is presented in Table I. Different values of the load factor are considered as listed in the first column. The second column contains the processing power values obtained from the *SPN*'s of Figs. 3, 4, and 5. The *SPN*'s of Figs. 3 and 4 lead to different processing power values only for systems comprising more than two processors; the *SPN* of Fig. 5 reduces to that of Fig. 3 when no interleaving is considered. The third column contains the processing power values provided by the *SPN* of Fig. 5 when full interleaving is assumed by setting $\mu' = 2\mu$. The last column contains the processing power values obtained with the assumption that external processors may preempt local accesses on common memories.

These results show how changes in the assumptions have a limited impact on processing power values of a two processor system, particularly when the system load is low. More significant differences are expected for larger systems.

TABLE I
PROCESSING POWER OF A TWO PROCESSOR SYSTEM OBTAINED FROM (a) THE *SPN*'S OF FIGS. 3-5, (b) THE *SPN* OF FIG. 5 WITH $\mu' = 2\mu$, AND (c) CONSIDERING PREEMPTION

ϱ	a	b	c
0.01	1.980	1.980	1.980
0.05	1.901	1.904	1.901
0.1	1.807	1.814	1.807
0.2	1.633	1.655	1.633
0.4	1.346	1.400	1.350
0.6	1.131	1.208	1.139
0.8	0.968	1.059	0.979
1.0	0.842	0.941	0.857

V. MARKOVIAN MODELS

The limitations of *SPN* models can be overcome in some cases by a direct study of their underlying Markov processes aimed to obtain a reduction of the state space dimension. Crucial to the success of this reduction step are the symmetry assumptions introduced in the system description. Whereas *SPN*'s allow an automatic generation of the state definition of the underlying Markov process, in this case, the analyst has the responsibility of correctly and carefully choosing the definition of the state of the Markov chain (*MC*). Since the correct choice of the state definition of a reduced *MC* is difficult in general, a convenient strategy is to first define the state of an *MC* that describes the system operations at the same level of detail used in the *SPN* analysis, and then to reduce the size of the state space by applying state aggregation techniques. Any correct choice of the state definition leads to an *MC* isomorphic to the original *SPN*. A proper choice makes the reduction step easy by explicitly considering the system symmetries.

In the case of the architecture of TOMP, a convenient system state definition is provided by the $2N$-tuple

$$(m_1, s_1; m_2, s_2; \cdots; m_N, s_N) \tag{5}$$

where m_i is the index of the memory module referenced by processor i and s_i is the state of processor i. s_i can take the values

- 4 active
- 3 accessing the local common memory module
- 2 accessing an external common memory module
- 1 blocked
- 0 queued for the local common memory
- $-k$ queued for the global bus: kth in queue

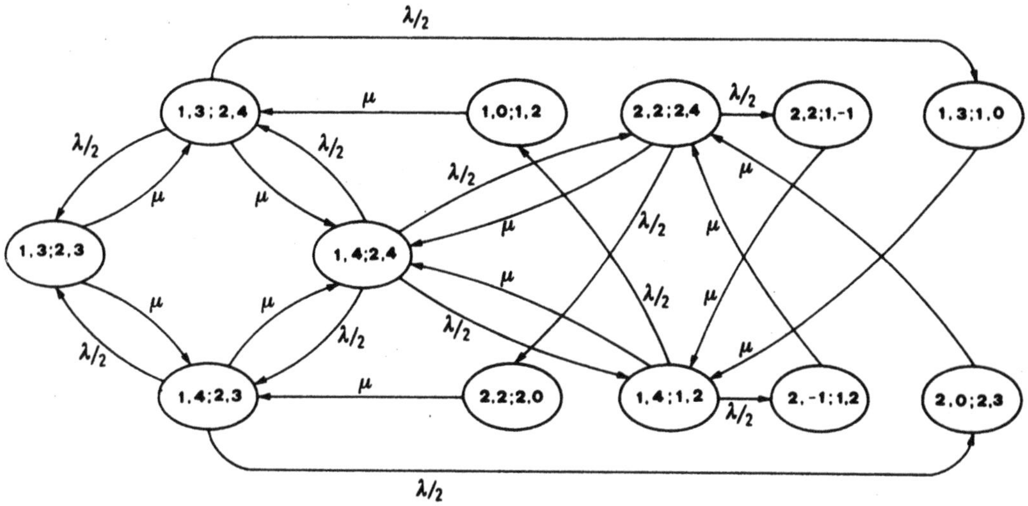

Fig. 7. State transition rate diagram of the *MC* of a two processor system as in Fig. 3.

In the two processor case we obtain the state transition rate diagram shown in Fig. 7. Notice that this state transition rate diagram is a pictorial representation of the stochastic process underlying the *SPN* of Fig. 3. The symmetries of the system can be used to obtain the state definition of the reduced *MC*

$$(m_{1\text{st}}, s_{1\text{st}}; \cdots; m_{i\text{th}}, s_{i\text{th}}; \cdots; m_{N\text{th}}, s_{N\text{th}}). \qquad (6)$$

The structure of this reduced state is similar to that of the original one. The only difference is that processors are ordered according to their activity state (i.e., active processors, queued processors, $\cdots$ are grouped together) without distinguishing among processor indexes, but distinguishing among memory reference indexes. The position of each pair does not necessarily correspond to the index of the associated processor. The memory reference of the ith pair reflects the position occupied in the ordered list by the processor associated with the memory being referenced.

Using this state description, a substantial reduction of the size of the state space is achieved and an algorithm can be devised to automatically generate the transition matrix of the reduced *MC*.

Applying this reduction technique to the two processor chain of Fig. 7, we obtain the state transition rate diagram of Fig. 8, which can be easily solved, giving as a result for the processing power

$$P = \frac{8(\rho + 1)}{7\rho^2 + 8\rho + 4}. \qquad (7)$$

The evaluation of (7) for different values of the load factor produces the numerical results already given in column two of Table I.

Unfortunately, the size of the state space of the reduced chain keeps growing combinatorially with the number of processors considered in the model, making the exact computation of the performance indexes feasible only for small systems. A detailed description of the use of Markov chain methods for the analysis of some multiprocessor architectures (including the one selected for TOMP) can be found in [2].

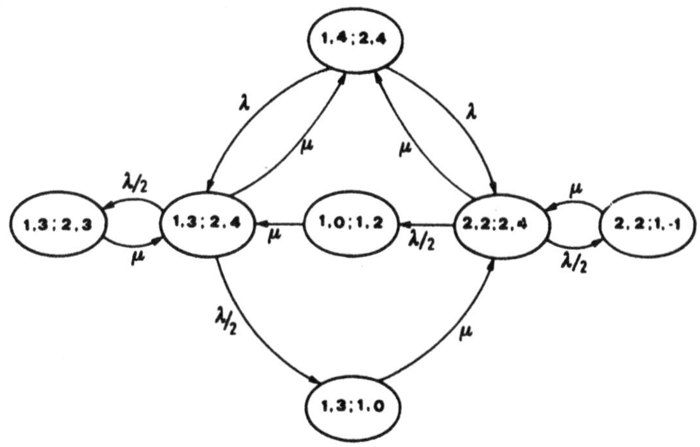

Fig. 8. State transition rate diagram of the reduced *MC* of a two processor system as in Fig. 3.

VI. Queueing Network Models

An alternative approach to the analysis of multiprocessor systems is an explicit representation of the contention for shared resources with a queueing network (*QN*). Fig. 9 depicts a *QN* model of TOMP in which queueing may occur at the global bus and at the common memory modules. Processors are represented as delay elements. Common memory access requests can be viewed as customers that require service from the common memory modules. Upon completion of their service, access requests return to their corresponding processor stations where they are delayed before repeating the memory access cycle. This delay represents processor activity between subsequent access requests (CPU burst).

One class of *QN* models for which computing the exact solution is simple is that of the so-called product form *QN*'s considered by the BCMP theorem [3], [8]. Simultaneous possession of resources (for which individual queues exist) and priority queueing policies normally make *QN* models of multiprocessor systems not product form. Nice computational properties of approximate solutions of non product form *QN* models can, however, be exploited when some additional restrictions are imposed on the behavior of the system repre-

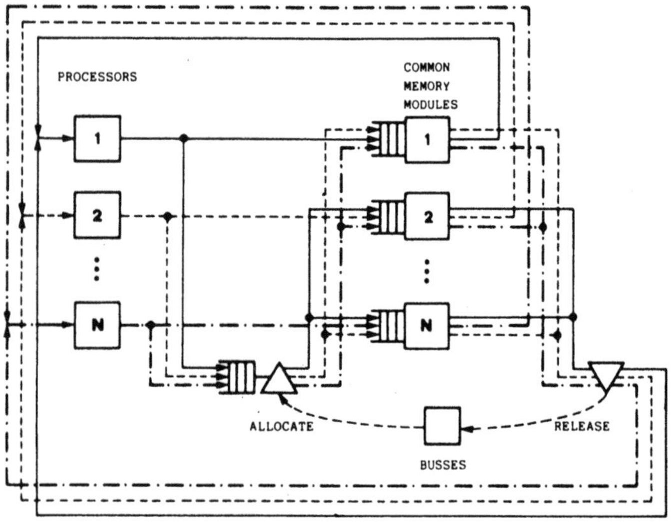

Fig. 9. *QN* representation of a generalization of the TOMP architecture with a multiple bus interconnection network.

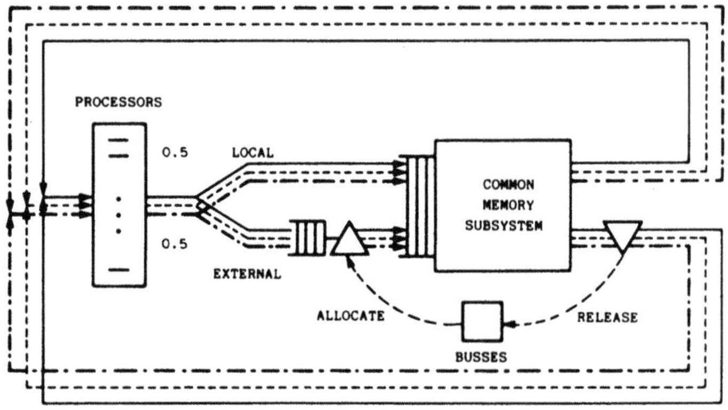

Fig. 10. Flow equivalent representation of the memory subsystem.

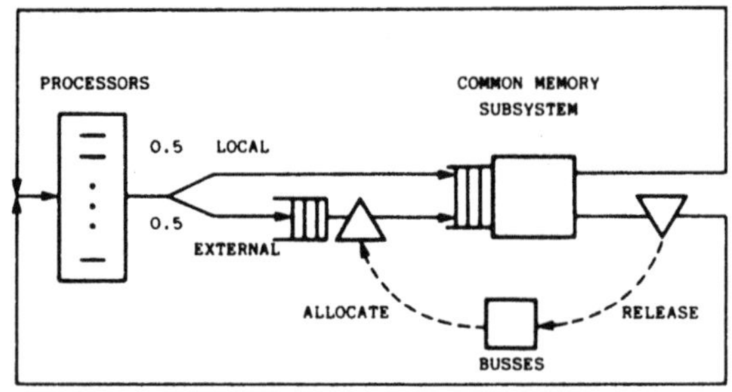

Fig. 11. Aggregate representation of the *QN* of Fig. 9.

sented in Fig. 9. Let us assume that processors trying to reach an external common memory module, having found the global bus free, seize it and, if necessary, wait in queue for the destination memory module to become available without releasing the global bus. Under these operating conditions, the *QN* of Fig. 9 becomes a model with a passive resource (the global bus) [13], [23]. Approximate solutions of these models can be obtained by using decomposition and equivalence techniques [6], [7], [11], [12] that are standard in the *QN* field.

Let us identify the common memory modules as a single common memory subsystem loaded by the processors with memory access requests. At any point in time, up to N access requests can either be queued or receive service from the memory subsystem, but only one of them can be an external request (only one bus is available). An aggregated model such as that of Fig. 10 can be obtained replacing the memory subsystem with an equivalent station whose service characteristics are computed using a set of controlled experiments [13], [16].

Similarly to what we have done with *MC* models, a further simplification can be obtained when the identity of the access requests (issuing processor identifier) is removed and a set of requests belonging to two different classes (the class of local requests, and the class of external requests) is assumed to load the common memory subsystem. This abstract view of the multiprocessor system can be used to represent more general cases in which the architecture considered in this paper is extended to embody an interconnection network comprising an arbitrary, but finite, number B of buses. The resulting model is that of Fig. 11.

The success of this aggregation technique relies on the possibility of replacing the common memory subsystem with a memory flow equivalent station so that the behavior of the processors is left unchanged by such a substitution. The functional characteristics of the equivalent service station are obtained by computing the response time of the memory subsystem to access requests of the two classes, assuming the memory subsystem itself to be kept under a fixed load. This technique is known to be exact when the original model is of the product form type [6], [7], [11], [37] while it provides approximate results in the other cases [12], [34]. The controlled experiments for the computation of the parameters of the equivalent memory station are performed on a model that can be obtained from the original *QN* (Fig. 9) by shortcircuiting the processor and bus servers, and by assuming that fixed mixes of memory access requests are continuously asking for service from the memory modules. Fig. 12 depicts the multiclass network used to perform the controlled experiments in the general case of a N processor system. Each class in this model identifies a closed path throughout the network used by a fixed number of customers. A class is said to be alive if at least one customer of that class is present in the model; it is said to be dead otherwise. In the case of the model of Fig. 12, alive classes have a population of only one customer. The first N classes represent local common memory requests. A fictitious station (with zero mean service time) is added to the model to accumulate the global throughput of local requests provided by the memory subsystem. Local requests do not interfere among each other since they visit different memory modules. The second set of N classes is introduced to represent the external common memory requests. Each one of these classes visits $N - 1$ memory modules. The global behavior of the external access requests is collected adding another fictitious station with zero mean service time (see Fig. 12).

A request mix is characterized by having n classes ($n = 1, 2, \cdots, N$) simultaneously alive. The symmetry of the system allows us to identify a request mix with any distribution of n requests over the $2N$ different classes with the constraints that classes i and $N + i$ ($i = 1, 2, \cdots, N$) cannot be simultaneously alive (a processor issues either a local request or an external

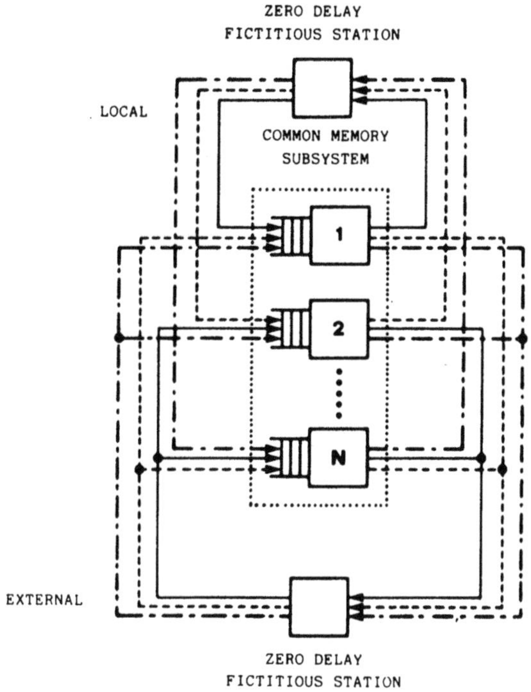

Fig. 12. Multibus model for the computation of the parameters of the equivalent station.

request), and that the number of external classes simultaneously alive cannot exceed the number of available busses *B*. Let *nl* and *ne* represent the number of local and external classes that are alive in a given request mix. A request mix is identified by the pair (*nl*, *ne*). Two request mixes are considered different when the corresponding pairs are different.

Let *Xl*(*nl*, *ne*) represent the throughput of the first fictitious station when the memory subsystem is loaded with the (*nl*, *ne*) request mix; similarly, let *Xe*(*nl*, *ne*) represent the throughput of the second fictitious station under the same subsystem load. These two quantities represent the rates of local and external requests satisfied by the memory subsystem under given loads. Their reciprocals can be interpreted as mean response times. The behavior of the memory subsystem (the service function of the equivalent memory station) is represented by the set of mean response times obtained by loading the memory subsystem with all the possible request mixes.

The computation of the service function of the memory equivalent station is completed assuming that the memory subsystem responds with a rate of service *X*(*nl*, *B*) every time it is actually loaded with a request mix (*nl*, *ne*) such that $ne > B$. When the bus interconnection network is made up of *N* buses and thus, behaves as a crossbar switch, the original model is a product form network and the aggregation process is exact. When the number of buses (*B*) is smaller than the number of processors (*N*), the aggregation process leads to an approximate *QN* model of the multiprocessor system that in general does not satisfy the conditions for a product form solution [6], [7], but that can nevertheless be solved with an efficient technique proposed by Herzog [19]. The accuracy of the approximation degenerates with the decreasing of the number of buses and has a worst case represented by the single global bus interconnection structure.

The results of this approximate analysis of the multiple bus model shown in Fig. 11 have been successfully validated with a detailed simulation of the original system model. Tables II and III present the validation results in which simulation interval estimates are obtained using the regenerative method [22], [25] with 95 percent confidence interval and 5 percent accuracy. The approximation of the analytical results is, in the case we have considered, extremely good so that they are covered by the confidence intervals provided by the simulation. In the analysis of a three processor system and single global bus, the *SPN* model of Fig. 6 provides exact results that can be used to check the behavior of the approximation method in worst case conditions. The very good agreement found between the results obtained with the two techniques suggests the possibility of using this fast aggregation method in the analysis of larger size systems.

VII. Measurements with Exponential Load

Measurements were performed on the three processor TOMP prototype. Each processor runs a cyclic process corresponding to the sequential execution of a CPU burst and a common memory access. The CPU burst consists of a sequence of operations on the private memory. Let *Tp* represent the time required for the execution of each elementary operation, and *Np* the number of operations in a sequence. A common memory access is a sequence of elementary read/write operations on a common memory area that can be either local or external. Each elementary operation requires a time *Ta′* when directed to the local common memory module and a time *Ta″* when directed to an external common memory module. The number of elementary operations needed to perform an external access sequence is *Na*. Following the assumptions introduced in Section II, the probabilities of accessing local or external common memory modules have been set to the following values, respectively,

$$P\{\text{accessing local common memory}\} = 0.5$$

$$P\{\text{accessing each external common memory}\} = 0.25. \quad (8)$$

As we said in the introduction, the aim of the measurements was to validate the stochastic models used in the performance analysis of the system, with respect to the study of contention for physical resources rather than to the modeling of applications or system control software. For this reason, the workload applied to the real system closely approximates the model assumed in Section II. The quantities *Np* and *Na* approximate exponentially distributed random variables with average values $E[Np]$ and $E[Na]$, respectively.

The experimental values of processing power were obtained with direct measurements of three signals on each processor module. These signals (named GREQ, GSERV and LREQ) are active whenever the following conditions hold.

GREQ—the processor has requested the global bus, but access has not been granted yet.

GSERV—the processor is using the global bus to access an external common memory module.

LREQ—the processor is either waiting to access its common memory module or accessing it.

The measurement instrumentation (Fig. 13) is composed of a 5 MHz pulse generator, a simple gating logic circuit, and a set of pulse counters.

TABLE II
PROCESSING POWER OF A THREE PROCESSOR SYSTEM IN THE CASE OF 1, 2, AND 3 BUSES. COMPARISON OF THE APPROXIMATE ANALYTICAL RESULTS OBTAINED WITH A QUEUEING NETWORK AGAINST THE INTERVAL ESTIMATES OBTAINED WITH SIMULATION. IN THE CASE OF 1 BUS, THE EXACT SOLUTION OBTAINED WITH THE SPN OF FIG. 6 IS ALSO PRESENTED

ρ	1 BUS				2 BUSSES			3 BUSSES		
	SPN	QN	simulation low	simulation up	QN	simulation low	simulation up	QN	simulation low	simulation up
0.05	2.850	2.850	2.70	2.99	2.853	2.71	2.99	2.853	2.70	2.99
0.1	2.704	2.701	2.56	2.83	2.713	2.58	2.85	2.713	2.57	2.84
0.2	2.427	2.419	2.29	2.53	2.455	2.34	2.58	2.456	2.38	2.58
0.3	2.189	2.167	2.05	2.26	2.228	2.13	2.35	2.230	2.12	2.34
0.4	1.963	1.948	1.85	2.04	2.030	1.94	2.14	2.033	1.93	2.13
0.5	1.776	1.759	1.73	1.91	1.859	1.78	1.96	1.862	1.78	1.96
0.6	1.616	1.598	1.57	1.73	1.709	1.61	1.77	1.714	1.63	1.80
0.8	1.358	1.340	1.28	1.41	1.466	1.38	1.52	1.473	1.39	1.53
1.0	1.163	1.147	1.11	1.22	1.278	1.21	1.33	1.286	1.21	1.33

TABLE III
PROCESSING POWER OF A FOUR PROCESSOR SYSTEM IN THE CASE OF 1, 2, AND 3 BUSES. COMPARISON OF THE APPROXIMATE ANALYTICAL RESULTS OBTAINED WITH A QUEUEING NETWORK AGAINST THE INTERVAL ESTIMATES OBTAINED WITH SIMULATION

ρ	1 BUS			2 BUSSES			3 BUSSES			4 BUSSES		
	QN	simulation low	simulation up	QN	simulation low	simulation up	QN	simulation low	simulation up	QN	simulation low	simulation up
0.05	3.797	3.61	3.99	3.803	3.62	3.99	3.803	3.62	3.99	3.803	3.62	3.99
0.1	3.592	3.42	3.78	3.615	3.44	3.80	3.615	3.43	3.79	3.615	3.44	3.80
0.2	3.199	3.03	3.34	3.266	3.10	3.41	3.269	3.13	3.46	3.269	3.13	3.46
0.3	2.846	2.71	2.99	2.957	2.80	3.09	2.963	2.82	3.11	2.963	2.79	3.08
0.4	2.542	2.39	2.64	2.686	2.45	2.70	2.698	2.58	2.84	2.698	2.58	2.84
0.5	2.283	2.14	2.36	2.451	2.34	2.59	2.467	2.40	2.66	2.467	2.38	2.61
0.6	2.065	1.97	2.17	2.247	2.10	2.31	2.267	2.16	2.38	2.267	2.15	2.37
0.8	1.723	1.62	1.79	1.915	1.82	2.01	1.941	1.82	2.01	1.943	1.90	2.10
1.0	1.472	1.36	1.50	1.660	1.60	1.77	1.691	1.64	1.81	1.692	1.64	1.81

Defining fm to be the pulse frequency, and Nx to be the number of pulses measured by the counter associated to signal x over a fixed measure time Tm, we obtain the fraction of time during which signal x is active, $F(x)$, as

$$F(x) = \frac{Nx}{fm\ Tm}. \tag{9}$$

The fraction of time during which processor i is not active, $F_i(\text{NACT})$, can be evaluated as

$$F_i(\text{NACT}) = F_i(\text{GSERV}) + F_i(\text{GREQ}) + F_i(\text{LREQ}) \tag{10}$$

and the processing power is obtained as

$$P = 3 - \sum_{i=1}^{3} F_i(\text{NACT}). \tag{11}$$

For each measurement, the value of the load factor ρ may be estimated as

$$\rho = \frac{Na\ Ta}{Np\ Tp} \tag{12}$$

where Ta is the common memory access time.

Since in the TOMP prototype the access time to a common memory module has different values for the local and external processors, we assume (as a first-order approximation) Ta to be the mean of the two values Ta' and Ta''; thus

$$Ta = \frac{Ta' + Ta''}{2}. \tag{13}$$

The measured values of processing power, obtained as in (11) versus the load factor as given by (12) are plotted in Fig. 14(a).

Several approximations introduced in the description of the system workload and some architectural features that were

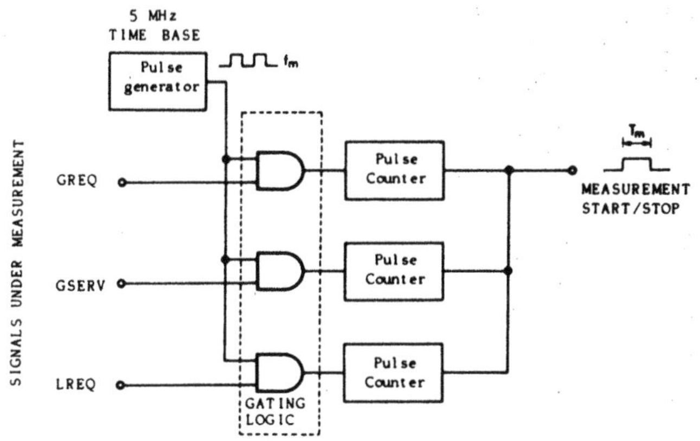

Fig. 13. Block diagram of the measurement setup.

not taken into account in the models make the previously defined parameter ρ not exactly representative of the real load of the multiprocessor system. The impact of these approximations on the estimate of the parameter ρ can be substantial and a more careful derivation of its value is needed. In the following paragraphs we discuss some of these factors to derive a new formula for the evaluation of the load factor.

A. Nonexponential Distributions

At the beginning of each CPU burst, each processor computes three uniformly distributed random numbers by means of a shift register based on an irreducible polynomial of order 32 [31]. The first random number is 2 bits wide and it is used to determine which common memory area is to be accessed during the next access period. The other two random numbers are used as pointers into logarithmic conversion tables to obtain the two random numbers *Na* and *Np*. Therefore, the exponential distributions of the CPU burst and of the access period assumed in Section II are in fact approximated by truncated geometric distributions. *Na* can vary between 1 and 2^{16}, and *Np* can vary between a minimum number *Nc* and a maximum $Nc + 2^{16}$. *Nc* is the number of internal cycles needed to evaluate the three random numbers.

B. Internal Operations

Individual common memory accesses, although part of a single sequence, are separated by a short gap of duration *Ti* corresponding to processor operations (register transfers); this fact allows a partial interleaving of the operations of different processors on the global bus and increases the mean CPU burst duration by a factor proportional to the mean access time. We can then correct the load factor ρ as follows:

$$\rho' = \frac{Na\ Ta}{(Np\ Tp + Na\ Ti)}. \tag{14}$$

C. Memory Refresh

The private memory of the prototype processor was implemented using dynamic memories refreshed by the processor itself. The refresh operations are carried on in parallel with the execution of the workload process and their effect is to increase the CPU burst duration by a factor *Tr/Tir*, where *Tr* is the time required to execute a refresh operation and *Tir* is the time interval between two refreshes. Therefore, the load factor ρ can be further corrected as

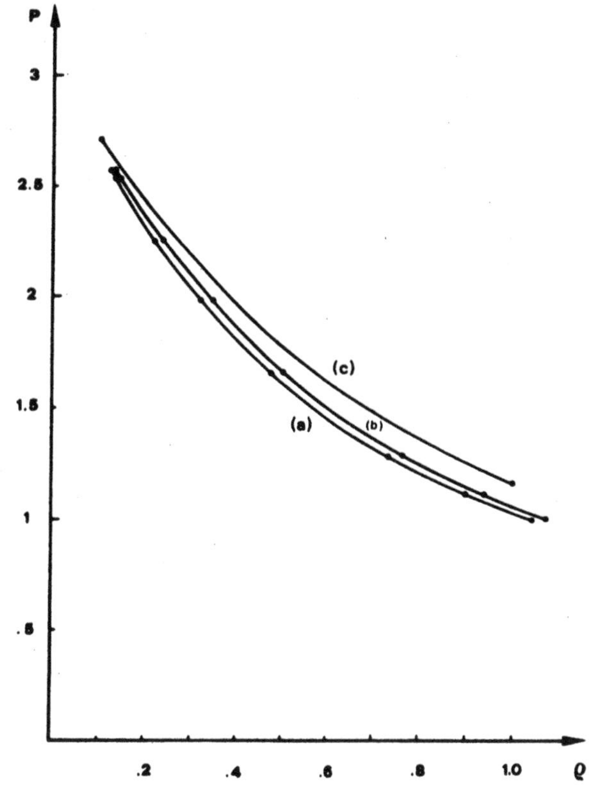

Fig. 14. Processing power of a three processor system. Comparison of the analytical results obtained with the *SPN* of Fig. 6 [curve (c)] against the measurement results [curves (a) and (b)].

$$\rho'' = \frac{Na\ Ta}{(Np\ Tp\ (1 + Tr/Tir) + Na\ Ti)}. \tag{15}$$

D. Global Bus Arbitration

The arbitration is carried on by a distributed synchronous logic that assigns the bus to one processor at the time following a fixed priority policy. The arbitration process lasts a certain amount of time during which all the requesting processors are held waiting. This time can vary between two limits *Tarmn* and *Tarmx*. Thus, in order to consider the global bus arbitration on the load factor ρ, we can add to each external common memory access time *Ta″* the average bus arbitration time *Tar*, estimated as

$$Tar = \frac{Tarmn + Tarmx}{2}; \tag{16}$$

hence, we obtain that the corrected common memory access time *Ta″* is given by

$$Ta''' = \frac{Ta' + Ta'' + Tar}{2}. \tag{17}$$

and the load factor ρ can be finally corrected obtaining

$$\rho''' = \frac{Na\ Ta'''}{(Np\ Tp\ (1 + Tr/Tir) + Na\ Ti)}. \tag{18}$$

The measured values of processing power versus the corrected load factor ρ''' are shown in Fig. 14(b). Fig. 14(c) presents the results given by the *SPN* of Fig. 6. The comparison between the measured values and the analytical model estimates confirms the validity of the modeling approach we have used. The performance predictions are very accurate in spite of the differences between the actual prototype behavior and the assumptions on system operations used in the development of the model, where an abstract view of the system behavior neglects the actual details of the elementary operations executed by the prototype.

VIII. Conclusions

In this paper we have presented stochastic models for the analysis of contention for shared resources in a multiprocessor prototype currently under development at Politecnico of Torino. Three different modeling techniques have been used (stochastic Petri nets, Markov chains, and queueing networks), all based on Markovian assumptions of the system behavior.

These three techniques can be viewed as a single modeling tool since they are all based on the analysis of similar Markovian stochastic processes. The Markovian analysis can, however, be performed at each stage of the study using the most suitable technique. *SPN*'s proved to be a very versatile tool for the precise definition and the performance analysis of small multiprocessor systems. *MC*'s allow the analysis of larger systems provided that some extra modeling effort is made for the reduction of the state-space dimension. The computational complexity of the exact analysis of *SPN* and *MC* models of moderate size systems suggests approximation techniques as strong candidates in the assessment of the performance of large size multiprocessor systems. The aggregated *QN* model we have discussed in this paper is a first step in this direction. The results obtained in this study are promising, but some more work is required to establish the robustness of the method in a more general environment.

The performance predictions yielded by the analysis have been validated using both simulation and measurement results. Measurements on the experimental prototype are in very good agreement with the performance estimates yielded by the model, in spite of the differences between the actual system operations and the abstract view of the system used in the development of the model.

References

[1] M. Ajmone Marsan and M. Gerla, "Markov models for multiple bus multiprocessor systems," *IEEE Trans. Comput.*, vol. C-31, pp. 239-248, Mar. 1982.

[2] M. Ajmone Marsan, G. Balbo, and G. Conte, "Comparative performance analysis of single bus multiprocessor architectures," *IEEE Trans. Comput.*, vol. C-31, pp. 1179-1191, Dec. 1982.

[3] F. Baskett, K. M. Chandy, R. R. Muntz, and F. G. Palacios, "Open, closed and mixed networks of queues with different classes of customers," *J. Ass. Comput. Mach.*, vol. 22, 1975.

[4] F. Baskett and A. J. Smith, "Interference in multiprocessor computer systems with interleaved memory," *Commun. Ass. Comput. Mach.*, June 1976.

[5] D. P. Bhandarkar, "Analysis of memory interference in multiprocessors," *IEEE Trans. Comput.*, vol. C-24, pp. 897-908, Sept. 1975.

[6] G. Balbo and S. C. Bruell, "Aggregation in multiclass queueing networks," in *Proc. CMG XII Conf.*, New Orleans, LA, Dec. 1981.

[7] ——, "Computational aspects of aggregation in multiple class queueing network," to be published in *Perform. Eval.*

[8] S. C. Bruell and G. Balbo, *Computational Algorithms for Closed Queueing Networks.* Amsterdam, The Netherlands: Elsevier, 1980.

[9] R. Bisiani and H. Mauerberg, "Software development for task-oriented multiprocessor architectures," in *Proc. COMPCON 79*, Sept. 1979.

[10] J. P. Buzen and D. Potier, "Accuracy of the exponential assumption in closed queueing models," in *Proc. 1977 SIGMETRICS/CMG Int. Conf. Comput. Perform., Modeling, Measurement, Management*, Washington, DC, Nov. 1977.

[11] K. M. Chandy, U. Herzog, and L. Woo, "Parametric analysis of queueing network models," *IBM J. Res. Dev.*, vol. 19, Jan. 1975.

[12] ——, "Approximate analysis of general queueing networks," *IBM J. Res. Dev.*, vol. 19, Jan. 1975.

[13] K. M. Chandy and C. H. Sauer, "Approximate methods for analyzing queueing network models of computer systems," *Ass. Comput. Mach. Comput. Surveys*, vol. 10, Sept. 1978.

[14] W. Chiarottino, G. Giandonato, S. Giorcelli, and G. Martinengo, "SEM—Studio di Strutture per un Sistema Elaborativo Modulare a Microprocessori," *CSELT Rapporti Tecnici*, vol. 6, June 1978.

[15] G. Conte, D. DelCorso, F. Gregoretti, and E. Pasero, "TOMP80—A multiprocessor prototype," in *Proc. EUROMICRO 81*, Paris, France, Sept. 1981.

[16] P. J. Denning and J. P. Buzen, "The operational analysis of queueing network models," *Ass. Comput. Mach. Comput. Surveys*, vol. 10, Sept. 1978.

[17] F. Fung and H. Torng, "On the analysis of memory conflicts and bus contentions in a multiple-microprocessor system," *IEEE Trans. Comput.*, vol. C-28, pp. 28-37, Jan. 1979.

[18] G. S. Graham, Guest Editor, "Special Issue: Queueing network models of computer systems," *Ass. Comput. Mach. Comput. Surveys*, vol. 10, Sept. 1978.

[19] U. Herzog, L. Woo, and K. M. Chandy, "Solution of queueing problems by a recursive technique," *IBM J. Res. Dev.*, vol. 19, May 1975.

[20] S. Hoener and W. Roeder, "Efficiency of a multiprocessor system with time-shared busses," in *Proc. EUROMICRO 77*, Amsterdam, The Netherlands, Sept. 1977.

[21] C. H. Hoogendoorn, "A general model for memory interference in multiprocessors," *IEEE Trans. Comput.* vol. C-26, pp. 998-1005, Oct. 1977.

[22] L. D. Iglehart, "The regenerative method for simulation analysis," in *Current Trends in Programming Methodology, Vol. III*, K. M. Chandy and R. T. Yeh, Eds. Englewood Cliffs, NJ: Prentice-Hall, 1978.

[23] T. W. Keller, "Computer system models with passive resources," Ph.D. dissertation, Comput. Sci. Dept., Univ. Texas at Austin, 1976.

[24] J. G. Kemeni and J. L. Snell, *Finite Markov Chains.* Princeton, NJ: Van Nostrand, 1960.

[25] S. S. Lavenberg, "Regenerative simulation of queueing networks," IBM Res. Rep. RC-7087, 1978.

[26] J. A. Merlin and D. J. Farber, "Recoverability of communication protocols—Implications of a theoretical study," *IEEE Trans. Commun. Technol.*, vol. COM-24, pp. 1036-1045, Sept. 1976.

[27] M. K. Molloy, "On the integration of delay and throughput measures in distributed processing models," Ph.D. dissertation, Univ. California, Los Angeles, 1981.

[28] S. Natkin, "Reseaux de Petri stochastiques," these de Docteur-Ingenieur, CNAM-Paris, June 1980.

[29] C. B. Newport and P. Kaul, "Communications processors for TELENET's third generation packet switching network," in *Proc. EASCON 1977.*

[30] J. H. Patel, "Processor-memory interconnections for multiprocessors," in *Proc. 6th Annu. Symp. Comput. Architecture*, Apr. 1979.

[31] W. Peterson and E. Weldon, *Error Correcting Codes.* Cambridge, MA: MIT Press, 1961.

[32] J. L. Peterson, "Petri nets," *Ass. Comput. Mach. Comput Surveys*, vol. 9, Sept. 1977.

[33] C. A. Petri, "Communication with automata," Ph.D. dissertation, Tech. Rep. RADC-TR-65-377, New York, Jan. 1966.

[34] C. H. Sauer, "Approximate solution of queueing networks with simultaneous resource possession," IBM Res. Rep. RC 8679, Jan. 1981.

[35] A. S. Sethi and N. Deo, "Interference in multiprocessor systems with localized memory access probabilities," *IEEE Trans. Comput.*, vol. C-28, pp. 157-163, Feb. 1979.

[36] F. J. W. Symons, "Introduction to numerical Petri nets, a general graphical model of concurrent processing systems," *A.T.R.*, vol. 14, Jan. 1980.

[37] H. Vantilborgh, "Exact aggregation in exponential queueing networks," *J. Ass. Comput. Mach.*, vol. 25, Oct. 1978.

[38] T. J. Williams, "Hardware versus functions—A view of distributed and hierarchical industrial control," AFIPS Presidential Address, presented at the Nat. Comput. Conf., Anaheim, CA, June 1978.

[39] P. J. Willis, "Derivation and comparison of multiprocessor contention measures," *IEE J. Comput. Digital Techniques*, Aug. 1978.

[40] W. M. Zuberek, "Timed Petri nets and preliminary performance evaluation," in *Proc. 7th Annu. Symp. Comput. Architecture*, 1980.

Marco Ajmone Marsan (S'76–M'76–S'78–M'78) was born in Torino, Italy, in 1951. He received the Dr.Ing. degree in electronic engineering from Politecnico di Torino, Torino, Italy, in 1974, and the M.S. degree from the University of California, Los Angeles, in 1978.

From 1975 to 1977 he was at Istituto di Elettronica e Telecomunicazioni, Politecnico di Torino, as Acting Assistant Professor. Since November 1978, he has been in charge of a course on elementary probability and signal theory. During the summers of 1980 and 1981 he was with the Research in Distributed Processing Group, Computer Science Department, University of California, Los Angeles. His current interests are in the area of performance evaluation of data communication and computer systems, communication networks, and queueing theory.

Dr. Ajmone Marsan is a member of the Associazione Elettrotecnica Italiana and the IEEE Computer Society.

Gianni Conte (M'82) was born in Torino, Italy, in 1946. He received the Dr.Ing. degree in electronic engineering from the Politecnico of Torino, Torino, Italy, in 1970.

Since 1972 he has been acting as a Researcher at the Department of Electronics, Politecnico of Torino, where he is presently Associate Professor of Electronics. His current research activity includes multiprocessor system design with an emphasis on architecture and performance evaluation. He is also interested on CAD tools for complex digital system design.

Dr. Conte is a member of the Associazione Elettrotecnica Italiana, the Associazione Italiana per il Calcolo Automatico, and the IEEE Computer Society.

Gianfranco Balbo was born in Piossasco, Italy, in 1946. He received the Doctor degree in physics from the University of Torino, Torino, Italy, in 1970, and the M.S. and Ph.D. degrees from Purdue University, West Lafayette, IN, in 1975 and 1979, respectively.

Since 1978 he has been an Acting Assistant Professor in the Department of Computer Science, University of Torino, where he is in charge of an introductory course on performance evaluation of computer systems. His current interests are in the area of performance evaluation of computer systems, queueing network models, and queueing theory.

Dr. Balbo is a member of the Association for Computing Machinery.

Francesco Gregoretti was born in Torino, Italy, in 1951. He received the Dr.Ing. degree in electronic engineering from Politecnico di Torino, Torino, Italy, in 1975.

From 1975 to 1977 he was at Istituto di Elettronica e Telecomunicazioni, Politecnico di Torino, as Acting Assistant Professor. In 1978 he was at Laboratoire de Calculatrices Digitales, Swiss Federal Institute of Technology, Lausanne, Switzerland. Since November 1978 he has again been at Politecnico di Torino as a Researcher. His current interests are in the area of tightly coupled multiprocessor systems and hardware/software tradeoffs.

Chapter 4

DESIGN METHODOLOGY

The current distributed systems design has been done in a rather *ad hoc* way. Many of the system design approaches are on a trial-and-error basis. Such design approaches are often unsatisfactory because in many cases, the systems either do not meet the specified requirements or are designed too conservatively.

One top-down software requirements engineering methodology called SREM has evolved and matured to a point that has been used on a variety of projects at different locations. The first paper in this chapter by Alford presents an overview of the development of SREM, its basic model of requirements, and how the model is implemented in the requirement statement language and supporting software. SREM has been extended from software requirement engineering to specifying such system-level requirements as concurrency, allocation, interface design, and fault tolerance for distributed systems. The second paper by Sheffer, *et al.*, reports the experience of using SREM to a command, control, communication, and intelligence (C^3I) system. The study showed that SREM is a viable approach for specifying C^3I software requirements and also encounter problems in the area of SREM specification language, analysis tools, and trainings. The last paper by Chu and Leung provides an analytical model to estimate the response time for loosely coupled distributed systems. The model considers such factors as the precedence relationships among software modules, interprocessor communication, interconnection network delay, module scheduling policy, and assignment of module to computers. The model may be applied to study such design issues as module assignment, scheduling policies, and data base management algorithms.

SREM at the Age of Eight; The Distributed Computing Design System

Mack Alford
TRW Huntsville Laboratory

SREM has been extended. Now a requirements-driven model for integrated software engineering environments, SREM has new tools to support its application, the Distributed Computing Design System.

Since its development and initial presentation in 1976, Software Requirements Engineering Methodology, or SREM, technology has evolved in both application and research.[1] The methodology and tools have matured to a point where they are being used on a variety of projects at a number of different locations; the research that led to SREM has been extended to address the problems of specifying system-level requirements and defining a distributed or uniprocessor design that satisfies requirements generated with SREM.

This article overviews developments in these areas and summarizes their results. It also describes the origins of SREM, its basic model of requirements, and how the model is implemented in RSL, the Requirements Statement Language, and supporting software.

An overview of SREM

SREM research was prompted by the observation that the requirements documents produced on a number of projects in the late 1960's did not adequately specify the conditions under which specific actions were to occur. The primary reason for the inadequate specification was determined to be the use of hierarchy-of-functions model for specification of requirements.

As Figure 1a indicates, a hierarchy of functions provides a mechanism for dividing a function into a number of smaller pieces and verifying that the inputs and outputs of the function match those of its decomposition. However, as Figure 1b indicates, the arrival of an input message M1 results in invocation of some sequence of bottom-level functions to process it. The specific sequence of functions selected depends on the values of the message and the current values of program variables; these conditions are usually described in the text of the function's descriptions, not in the model. Because the hierarchy-of-functions model does not explicitly represent the conditions or sequences of processing, requirements generated under it are ambiguous with respect to them. Thus, a great deal of manual effort and interpretation is required to identify the bottom-level functions that should process a specific input message and verify consistency.

The Ballistic Missile Defense Advanced Technology Center, or BMDATC, sponsored SREM research in 1973 in an attempt to formalize and automate techniques for specifying software requirements. The results were a language, RSL,[2] for the statement of software requirements; a set of tools—the Requirements Engineering Validation System, or REVS—to translate the language, perform auto-

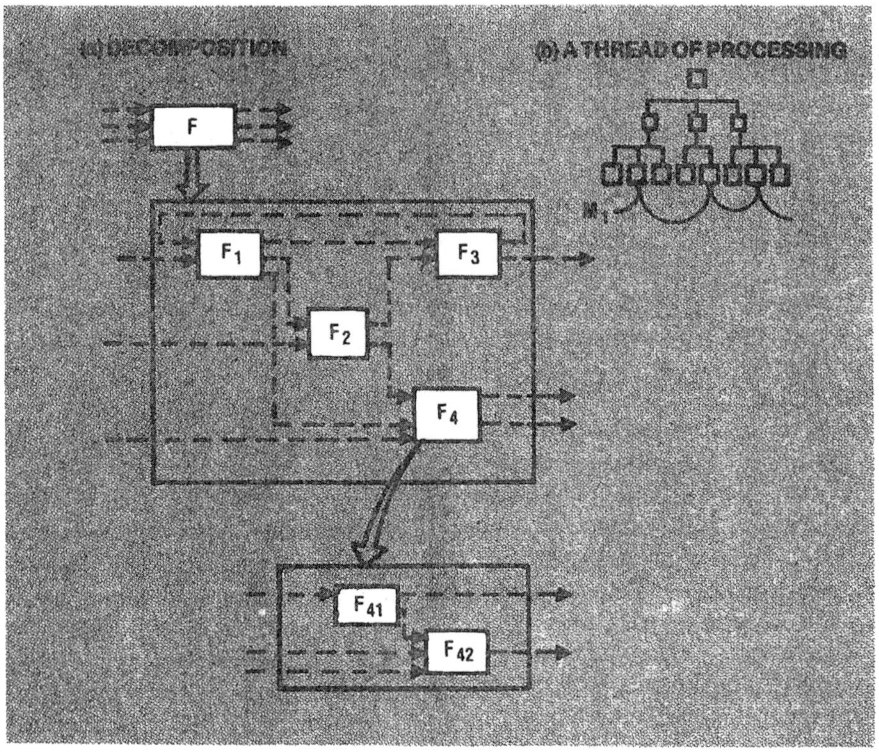

Figure 1. Hierarchy of functions: (a) decomposition, (b) a thread of processing.

mated consistency and completeness analysis, produce documentation, and generate simulators; and the methodology, SREM, which was expressed as a sequence of steps for generating the requirements through use of the language and tools. These results are described below.

The SREM model of functional requirements. The model of software requirements on which SREM is based is that of a highly structured finite state machine. The state-machine model is used to define processing requirements by specifying a set of inputs and outputs, a set of states, and a function that maps inputs plus current state onto outputs plus updated state. The usual limitation of the state-machine model is its inability to describe complex systems. For example, a state transition diagram can be drawn to represent the state of an elevator that stops at three floors, with buttons as inputs; however, the state transition diagram for 13 elevators that stop at 87 floors is too complex to be represented as a single diagram.

SREM overcomes these difficulties by structuring inputs, outputs, state, and processing. The inputs and outputs are structured into messages that cross interfaces to external subsystems. The state is structured into sets of information about objects the data processor knows; as an object's messages are processed, different types of information about the object are kept. Requirements networks, or R-nets, are used to structure the description of the processing. Each R-net specifies the transformation of a single input message plus current state into some number of output messages plus an updated state. Only one R-net is active at a time, consistent with the state-machine model.

Figure 2 presents the nomenclature of the R-net graph. Each R-net is a graph with nodes representing structural nodes and logic nodes. The R-net includes, at most, one input interface that passes a single input message, some number of output interfaces,

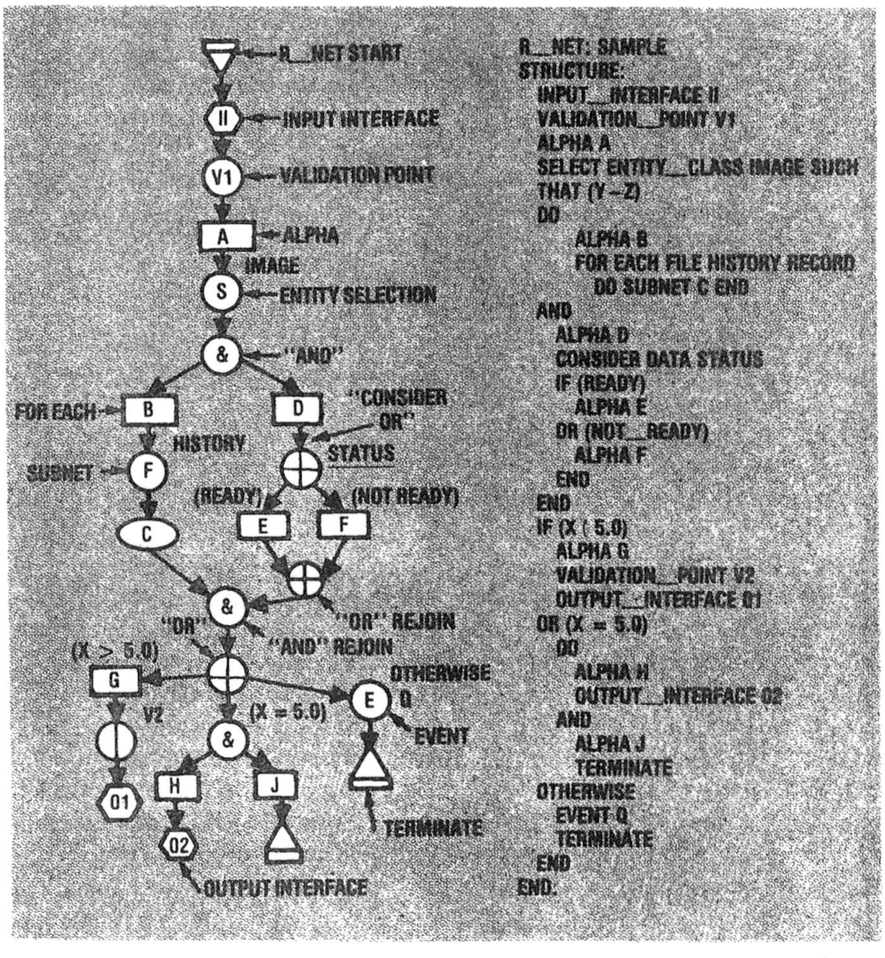

Figure 2. Sample R-net.

some number of ALPHAs specifying transformations, and some number of subnets. The ALPHA, denoted by a rectangle, is used to specify the transformation of an input data set into an output data set, the creation and destruction of state data, and the changing of the kind of state data kept about an object. It can also be used to form a specific output message for an output interface to pass to an external subsystem.

A subnet, represented as an oval, is defined as a processing subgraph with one entrance and one exit point; the subnet is used to show common processing requirements under different conditions and to shorten the length of an R-net.

The graph structure on the R-net uses OR nodes to specify the conditions of processing. Conditions on a path through the graph that leads to an ALPHA imply the conditions under which data are created, accessed, updated, or destroyed. These conditions imply the conditions under which an output message must be produced in response to an input message.

The AND nodes in the graph structure simplify specification of complex processing requirements by representing independent portions of processing. For example, Figure 3 presents an R-net in which processing of an input message can be represented as five independent sets of decisions, each with three choices. The necessary and sufficient condition for this representation is that no data output by any branch of an AND node be input on any other branch. This allows $3 \times 3 \times 3 \times 3 \times 3 = 243$ combinations of output message and state update to be represented in terms of an AND node with five branches, each having three choices, for a total of 15 stimulus-response paths.

The SELECT and FOR_EACH nodes of the R-net are used to select state data to be used in the processing. The SELECT node specifies the conditions for associating an input message with state data about an object called an Entity Class. A FOR_EACH node specifies that each of the elements of a list of data items are to be used for processing. The R-net, thus, provides for explicit specification of the conditions for accessing or updating state data kept about an individual object; thus, it provides the foundation for assuring that no item of data is used before it has been given a value.

The benefits of the structured state-machine model for the statement of processing requirements are several. It lays the foundation for completeness checking (e.g., that the processing has produced all required output messages), consistency checking (e.g., that all data must be produced before it is used), and for specifying the stimulus-response relationships to which response times and accuracy requirements can be attached.

Specification of performance requirements. Accuracy and response-time performance requirements are expressed by means of the concept of a path through the R-nets. A path of processing through an R-net and its associated subnets is specified by attaching named nodes, called *validation points,* onto the R-net graph and then defining the path in terms of a sequence of these validation points (e.g., path V1-V2 in Figure 2). A path can traverse multiple R-nets by using the EVENT node (which enables another R-net) as a connector. The conditions for the path are the sequence of OR_NODE choices that connect its initial point to its terminal point. Response time requirements are expressed in terms of a minimum or maximum response time for a specific path. Accuracy requirements are expressed in terms of data recorded at the validation points.

This approach has the benefit of assuring testability of the requirements and software design; it specifies the measurements that must be taken in order to test the accuracy, and it gives the software designer requirements for the data that should be recorded in order to make the software testable.

The Requirements Statement Language. RSL is based on a set of elements, attributes, relationships, and structures. The elements are its nouns, the relationships its verbs, and the attributes its adjectives. The structures describe the graph of processing requirements. RSL uses 21 different kinds of elements, such as the R-nets, ALPHAs, state data, and messages, to represent the features of the requirements model. Each instance of an element has a unique name. A name can have up to 60 characters; this encourages use of self-descriptive names. For example, an ALPHA might be named

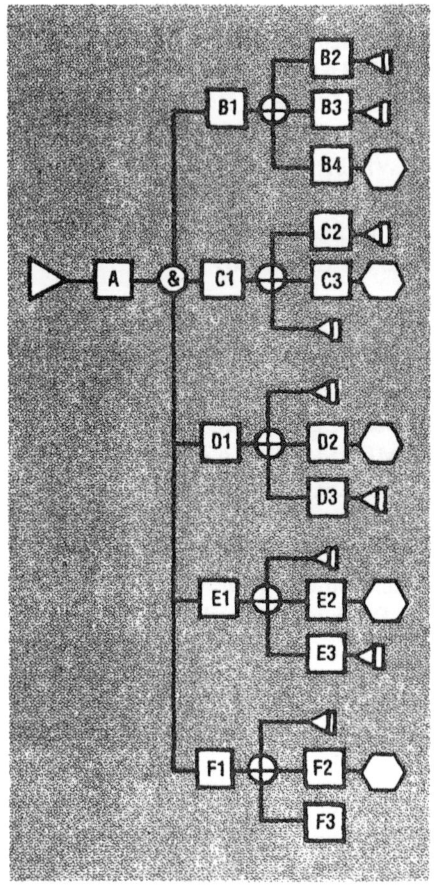

Figure 3. Example of handling complexity.

DETERMINE_IF_MEASUREMENT_IS_WITHIN_RANGE.

The relationships are expressed in terms of a subject, relationship name, and object; a complementary relationship name links object back to subject. RSL uses 23 relationships to express connections between elements. For example, a specification for an ALPHA to transform one data set into another is expressed by

ALPHA DETERMINE_IF_MEASUREMENT_IS_WITHIN_RANGE. INPUTS DATA MEASURED_POSITION, DATA LIMITS. OUTPUTS DATA WITHIN_RANGE.

The data items that comprise a message are defined by

MESSAGE RADAR_RETURN. MADE BY DATA MEASUREMENT_TIME, DATA MEASURED_RANGE, DATA MEASURED_AZIMUTH, DATA MEASURED_ELEVATION.

The requirement for generation of a specific message at the point when an ALPHA is executed is expressed by

ALPHA A.
FORMS MESSAGE WARNING_MESSAGE.

Whenever the user inputs a relationship to the translator, the complementary relationship is automatically added to the data base as well. This provides automatic cross-referencing capability at the requirements level.

The attributes provide various descriptors of the elements. Every element has an attribute DESCRIPTION, which is used to describe the element; a DATA element might have an additional attribute of UNITS, such as the following:

DATA MEASURED_RANGE.
DESCRIPTION: The range between the radar and the object in track.
UNITS: FEET.

As the above examples show, the syntax of the language is simple. An element is identified, then attribute, relationship, and structure sentences are specified in any order.

RSL provides the R-net and subnet structures for representing the sequences of processing of the SREM graph model. As indicated in Figure 2, the text representation is equivalent to the graphic representation.

RSL is not limited to the specification of processing; it can express other concepts, such as traceability, as well. Additional elements are used to identify source documents, requirements in those source documents, and decisions made in deriving the requirements. A traceability relationship is then used to link these originating requirements and decisions to the lower-level requirements expressed in RSL (e.g., ALPHA, MESSAGE, or SUBNETs). The use of these language constructs provides for automated completeness checking (e.g., that every ORIGINATING_REQUIREMENT traces to some lower-level requirement).

In summary, RSL serves two overall purposes: It provides a checklist of characteristics for requirements specification, and it puts the requirements into a machine-readable form that can be translated into a database for automated consistency and completeness analyses.

Supporting tools. A set of tools, called the Requirements Engineering Validation System, or REVS, was developed to support generation and verification of software requirements using SREM. The tools have six kinds of functions:

(1) *extension* of RSL to tailor it to a specific project,
(2) *translation* of the RSL into an automated database,
(3) *analysis* of the database contents against the consistency and completeness criteria,
(4) *extraction* of information from the database,
(5) *generation* of functional or analytical simulators of the required processing from the requirements specification, and
(6) *generation and display* of graphical descriptions of the R-nets and subnets.

Boehm[3] has recently described the tools' ability to automatically verify requirements.

Methodology description. SREM describes a sequence of steps for defining requirements, expressing them in RSL, and using the tools to check consistency and completeness.

Table 1 gives an overview of the seven phases of SREM, the focus of each phase, and some of the criteria that should be satisfied during each phase. Each phase is broken into a number of lower-level steps. Each step is defined in terms of the subset of RSL generated and the subset of the overall consistency/completeness criteria, which the tools verify. This definition by steps provides a structure for generating the requirements information. For example, Table 1 shows

Table 1. SREM phases and criteria.

	PHASE	FOCUS	CRITERIA
(1)	DEFINE KERNEL	Identify all I/O MESSAGES, R-nets, and ALPHAS.	All input messages processed. All output messages generated.
(2)	ESTABLISH BASELINE	Clean up database. Generate plots of R-nets.	All naming consistent.
(3)	DEFINE DATA	Define data input to and output by each ALPHA.	No data used before given a value.
(4)	ESTABLISH TRACEABILITY	Generate consistent traceability requirements.	All top requirements satisfied.
(5)	SIMULATE FUNCTIONALITY	Simulate DP subsystem functions performed.	Validation that all are processed correctly.
(6)	IDENTIFY PERFORMANCE REQUIREMENTS	Define traceable, testable performance requirements for DP subsystem.	Each path constrained by response time and accuracy.
(7)	DEMONSTRATE FEASIBILITY	Rapid prototype of all critical algorithms.	Accuracy requirements satisfied by prototype algorithms.

that that the R-nets are established before the input-output is finalized and that the traceability from top-level requirements to functional requirements is established before the performance requirements are addressed.

The resulting methodology thus guides the requirements developer through the sequence of steps in which the requirements information should be derived and represented in RSL. As early as possible, the tools should be used to check subsets of the consistency criteria and to provide early detection of errors and some objective management milestones for generating the requirements.

Evolution of SREM. The SREM methodology and tool capabilities are essentially the same today as delivered in 1977. Although the tools were originally developed as proof-of-principle prototypes for use in a batch environment, some of their limitations have been removed. For example, in 1981 the tools were transported to the Vax 11/780, significantly enhancing their utility and availability. In 1983, the database management software was rewritten into Pascal, resulting in a significant increase in their performance on the Vax. Work to enhance the user interface—to, for example, provide an interactive forms-entry capability and improve error diagnostics—is under way.

A working knowledge of SREM is acquired in a standard, two-week training course. The first week consists of lectures with some hands-on experience; the second week concentrates on working through an example with an instructor. As of 1985, over 40 organizations have participated in this type of training course.

Benefits and limitations of SREM. As experience in the application of SREM has grown, a number of its benefits and limitations have emerged. Many of the benefits are direct consequences of SREM's state-machine foundation, including:

- an objective stopping point for requirements specification, which includes definition of all state data and conditions for transforming input messages plus current state into an a set of output messages plus updated state;
- verification of data flow consistency—no item of data is used before it is given a value;
- specification of performance in testable terms (i.e., accuracies of calculation and response time limits of paths of processing); and
- traceability of system-level requirements to processing (software) requirements.

The key concept of SYSREM is that a system function acts over a finite time interval.

Many of the perceived limitations of SREM are also direct consequences of its state-machine foundations:

- SREM forces a requirements engineer to express requirements at a level of detail that conventional development techniques do not usually reach until test planning identifies the stimulus-response threads to be tested. SREM requires more effort during the requirements phase.
- SREM does not specify processing in terms of a hierarchy, which is more familiar than the stimulus-response networks.
- SREM does not directly specify a distributed design because its model assumes that a message is completely processed before the next message is input—although SREM can be used to define requirements for such a design.

These perceived limitations result from a combination of two factors. The first is that SREM specifies a state machine. The second, and more fundamental, factor is that SREM was developed as a stand-alone requirements methodology. It is connected neither to a specific method for specifying system-level requirements and allocating them to a data processor nor to a specific method for translating these requirements into a design. Thus, the relationship between the state-machine level of requirements and the other levels of requirements/design information was not made specific. Subsequent DCDS research addressed these problems.

The systems requirements engineering methodology

The first major extension of the SREM concepts sought to address the problem of defining system requirements and allocating them to the data processing subsystem. The result was called the Systems Requirements Engineering Methodology, or SYSREM. The research leading to SYSREM, conducted from 1977 to 1981, was sponsored by BMDATC. This research extended the SREM state-machine model to represent decomposition and concurrency; it used the same language approach and tools.

Overview of SYSREM. The formal foundation for SYSREM is the graph model of decomposition.[4] System requirements are specified in terms of time functions, their decompositions, and their allocation to system components.

The key concept of SYSREM is that a system function acts over a finite interval of time; this system action is represented as a time function that accepts items arriving during the time interval and transforms them into items that are output during the time interval. An item that the function inputs or outputs can be decomposed into sequences and allowed concurrencies of lower-level items. A time function is thus specified in terms of its input items, output items, invariants of its transformation, completion criteria (anything that causes the system to stop performing a function and switch to some subsequent mode of operation), and performance. Performance is defined in terms of one or more metrics describing the efficiency or accuracy of transformation of the input to the output items.

A decomposition of a function is defined as a graph of lower-level functions that must preserve

- any input and output sequences specified,
- any invariants of the transformation,
- the number and kinds of completion criteria (reasons for exiting the function), and
- performance traceability (the original performance function must be computable from the performance functions of the lower-level functions).

The graph model of decomposition has several unique characteristics, which are illustrated by application to the following patient monitoring problem[1,3]:

A hospital requires a patient monitoring program. An analog device monitors each patient's pulse, temperature, blood-pressure, and skin resistance. The program reads these factors at intervals specified for each patient and stores them in a database. For each patient, safe ranges for each factor are specified—for example, patient X's valid temperature range is 98 to 99.5°F. If a factor falls outside the patient's safe range or if an analog device fails, the system notifies the nurse's station.

The unique features of the SYSREM solution to this problem include the following:

(1) *Both sequences and concurrency are represented.* As illustrated in Figure 4, the function MONITOR PATIENTS is decomposed into a replication of concurrent activities, each of which monitors a single patient. The function MONITOR A PATIENT is then decomposed into a sequence of functions—first, CONNECT PATIENT, then MEASURE AND MONITOR PATIENT, then DISCONNECT PATIENT. Thus, the graph explicitly shows that any patient must be connected before being monitored, but that one patient can be in the process of being connected while another is being disconnected.

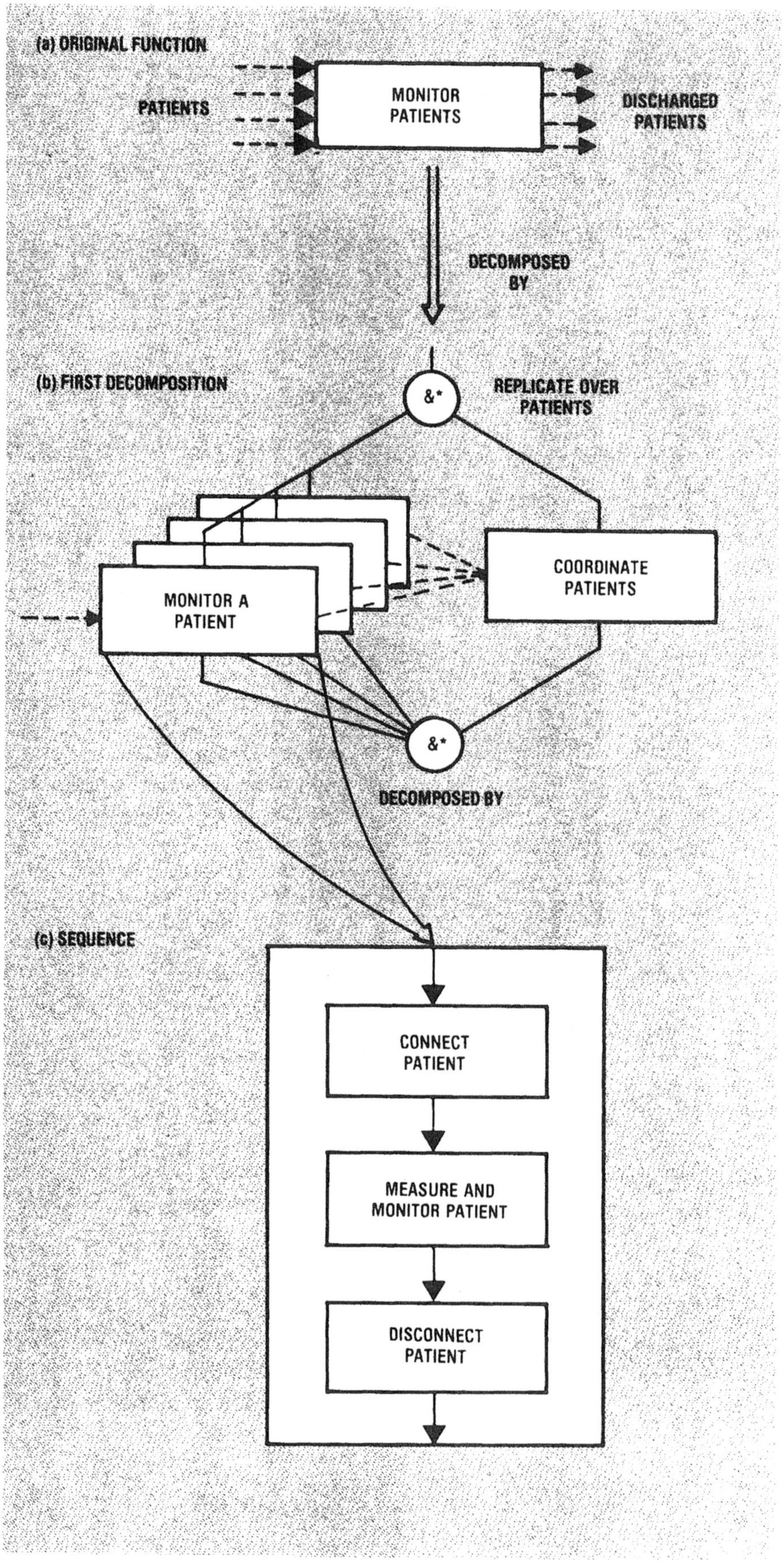

Figure 4. Example SYSREM decompositions: (a) original function, (b) first decomposition, (c) sequence.

(2) *Control functions are derived as an integral part of the decomposition activity.* Whenever a function is decomposed into a set of parallel functions, a control function must be defined to coordinate these functions. This control function accepts status information and issues controls. Figure 4 illustrates this fact: A function MONITOR PATIENTS is decomposed into a replication of functions to monitor each patient and into a control function, COORDINATE PATIENTS, to control conflicts. In this case, conflicts would be due only to resource competition.

(3) *Performance and function are simultaneously decomposed.* Suppose that a performance index of the system is the maximum time it takes to detect and raise an alarm when pulse rate drops for any patient. The overall performance can be decomposed by associating the performance index MAXIMUM TIME TO DETECT AND RAISE AN ALARM FOR THIS PATIENT[3] with each of the lower-level functions MONITOR A PATIENT. The overall maximum response time can be calculated from these individual response times.

(4) *Allocation of function sequences and concurrency to components is another unique feature.* Figure 5a illustrates decomposition of the function MEASURE AND MONITOR PATIENT into concurrent functions of MEASURE PATIENT and MONITOR MEASUREMENTS for each patient. Figure 4 shows that this happens after CONNECT PATIENT and before DISCONNECT PATIENT. These functions are then allocated between the measurement and data processing subsystems. Thus, both concurrency and sequences are required of these components.

(5) *Interface designs are derived.* Figure 5b shows how the allocation of functions to components results in the definition of an interface function that transfers information between subsystems. This interface function is repetitively decomposed and allocated, to yield the layers of interface design necessary to connect the subsystems.

(6) *Exceptions are addressed by defining an additional layer of functions to detect and recover from faults.* Fault detection thus corresponds to taking an exception exit from a function in the standard layer into the layer containing fault-handling functions; fault recovery then corresponds to a transition back to the standard layer.

(7) *The maximum concurrency of the required processing is exposed.* It is exploited later, during the distributed design phase.

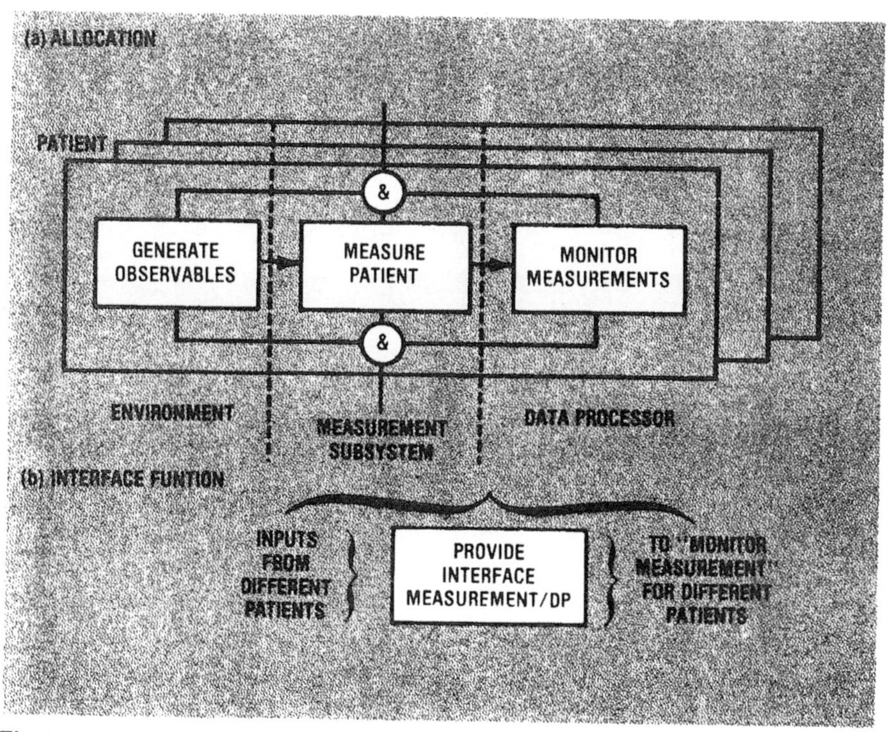

Figure 5. Decomposition of MEASURE AND MONITOR PATIENT; (a) allocation, (b) interface function.

SYSREM/SREM interface. The model used at the system level defines and allocates time functions to a data processing component. These functions are further decomposed to the level at which they accept discrete messages. If the interfaces are serialized (an input must be processed before the next input is addressed), the result is exactly a finite-state machine. These functions can be further decomposed, to the stimulus-response level, by representing them in terms of subnets of RSL, thus yielding the structured state machine of SREM—and providing a smooth transition from system to software requirements. The system specification language was defined to express these concepts.

SSL blends into RSL by relating system-level functions and items to software-level subnets, R-nets, and data. The SSL and RSL languages are thus interlocked and can be viewed as a single language with subsets applying to system and software requirements. Similarly, the methodology steps are interlocked: The end point of SYSREM provides all the information necessary to perform the steps of SREM.

Status. SYSREM is today in a state similar to that of SREM in 1977-78. A SYSREM training course has been developed and used to transfer the technology to several projects.

Distributed computing design system

One of the most significant limitations of SREM was that it left the transition from requirements to design to the ingenuity of the developers. To address this problem, BMDATC in 1981 sponsored research toward a Distributed Computing Design System, or DCDS.

The purpose of this ongoing research is to develop and integrate design languages and tools into the SYSREM/SREM baseline. These languages and tools are to increase reliability and productivity by developing a software engineering environment to record and control the development of requirements, design, code, and tests for a distributed data processing subsystem. Figure 6 presents a conceptual view of the end product: an integrated set of languages, tools, databases, and methods that spans the entire software development cycle.

This research is built on two sets of previous research: the SYSREM/SREM work discussed above, and Mariani and Palmer's[5] approach, also sponsored by BMDATC, to designing distributed processing. A great many published papers have described the results of research on distributed design issues, special problems of communication protocols, distributed database control, distributed failure detection and recovery, etc., but none has demonstrated clear traceability to requirements. The intent of the DCDS is to provide a structure for deriving and considering such problems in a requirements-driven way—and thus eliminate problems of manually translating requirements information into a different representation in order to initiate design. DCDS provides tools to detect and correct errors early and to produce a structure that can be modified and maintained with less effort.

DCDS key concept. The key concept of the DCDS research is the recognition that the SYSREM concepts can be used to define a software design by allocating required processing and state data onto units of code and data structures. The interfaces between these units of code are decomposed and allocated to the level of the functions of the distributed operating system. Fault tolerance is achieved by adding functions to detect and recover from errors, then decomposing and allocating them to units of code assigned to specific processors.

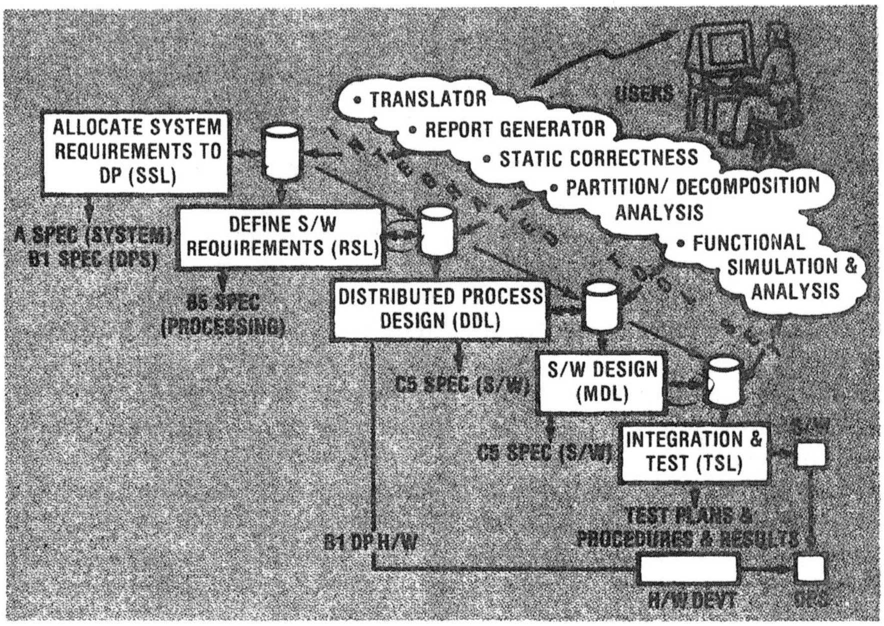

Figure 6. DCDS integrated languages and tools.

A significant result of the research is the recognition that this design model supports separation of the concerns of distributed design from those of algorithm design. Distributed design addresses the problem of selecting the data processor architecture and mapping the required processing onto this architecture to meet the timing and sizing requirements—in other words, it is programming in the large. Module design addresses the problem of constructing the algorithms that accomplish the required transformations and satisfy the overall accuracy requirements; module design is programming in the small. Figure 7 illustrates this approach.

Module design. A module can be viewed as a unit of engineering work in designing and developing an algorithm to accomplish a required transformation. Given no constraints on processor utilization or response time, the first algorithm that satisfies the ac-

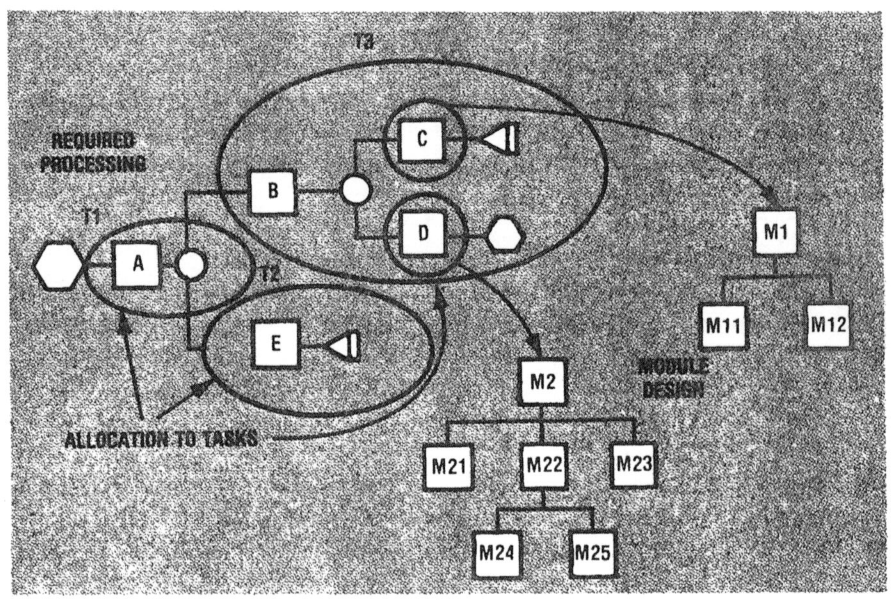

Figure 7. Allocation of required processing to modules and tasks.

curacy requirements is selected for use. Real-time embedded software usually requires more algorithm design effort in order to meet execution time constraints.

A module is designed in two phases, preliminary and detailed design, with a preliminary design review in between. The preliminary design is accomplished by partitioning the required processing, expressed in RSL, into modules. Required data is partitioned into logical units, which are assigned logical types (e.g., an array of real numbers). Algorithms are defined to perform the transformation required of the module; this can result in the definition of lower-level modules and thus a need for further design. In any case, construction preserves the stimulus-response and data-flow properties of the requirements.

The mapping of required processing and data onto modules and data structures is expressed in the Module Design Language; thus, RSL and MDL interlock. For the patient monitoring problem, one might record a design as follows:

MODULE COMPARE_LIMITS.
CONSTITUTES ALPHA: COMPARE_ MEASUREMENT_TO_ LIMITS.
INPUTS VARIABLE V_MEASUREMENT.
OUTPUTS VARIABLE V_RESULT.
VARIABLE V_RESULT.
REPRESENTS DATA MEASUREMENT_STATUS.
RANGE: (ALARM, WARNING, OK).

A module design is expressed in terms of a hierarchy of modules; a program design language, or PDL, can be used to express the logic of each module. Several candidate design approaches can be defined in the Module Design Language. The designer estimates sizing and timing for the algorithms and assesses accuracy characteristics. The designer selects an algorithm approach from these candidates before the preliminary design review, so that it can be assessed against accuracy and loading requirements. Tools are used to verify that the design preserves stimulus-response and data flow properties.

By the time of the preliminary design review, each module is associated with a budget and schedule and assigned to an individual programmer. The preliminary design information is transferred to a unit development folder.[6] For each module, an automated unit development folder tool maintains schedule and status, requirements and design descriptions, a PDL description of the design, test plans, code, and test results.

The distributed design methodology can be viewed as having distributed and task design phases.

In summary, the preliminary design of the modules is performed and recorded in a Module Design Language, and the SREM tools are used to check the consistency/completeness criteria. The detailed design, code, and unit testing employs an automated version of the unit development folder to record all intermediate results. This information base becomes invaluable during integration testing, maintenance, and production of the required design documentation.

Distributed design. The distributed design methodology can be viewed as having two major phases: the distributed process design phase, which defines a configuration of processors, allocates required processing and data to the processors, and verifies satisfaction of required response times; and the task design phase, which transforms this logical design into the design of the units of code in a programming language.

The purpose of the distributed process design is to make the design decisions necessary for transforming the requirements on the data processing subsystem, or DPS, into sets of requirements for hardware/software "processes" and their interprocess communication network. In order to address internode design, the decomposition of processes should proceed to the level that permits packaging the requirements for each single processor. The distributed process design defines the system-wide communication protocols, process schedulers, and design standards that affect the multiple nodes of the DPS. The distributed process design must also address DPS-level requirements for reliability, fault tolerance, reconfiguration, growth, and other ". . .ilities."

As Figure 8 indicates, there are four potential levels of a processor distribution: geographical distribution, local network distribution, computer system distribution, and hardware/software distribution. Each level must address a unique set of problems and trade-offs. The constraints, design variables, and objective functions that drive the design activity vary from one level of design to the next.

Allocation of processing to nodes must balance delay time of intranode communication against the nonfunctional requirements for automomy. Allocation of data to geographic nodes must balance the communication delays of remote access of a single copy of data against replication of the data to achieve tolerance to a single-point failure and against the added complexity of maintaining replicated database consistency. A feasible allocation must satisfy several kinds of constraints: response times must be met, execution time and memory size limitations must not be exceeded at any processing node, and communication resources must not be overloaded. Thus, distributed process design follows the same order described in SYSREM: allocation, interface design, resource estimation, and definition of fault-detection and recovery functions.

The Distributed Design Language is used to define the software processes, their allocation to processor nodes, and their relationships to the software requirements-level R-nets, subnets, and data. The DCDS tools are used to verify the completeness of the allocation. The allocation of processing to tasks—that is, scheduled units of

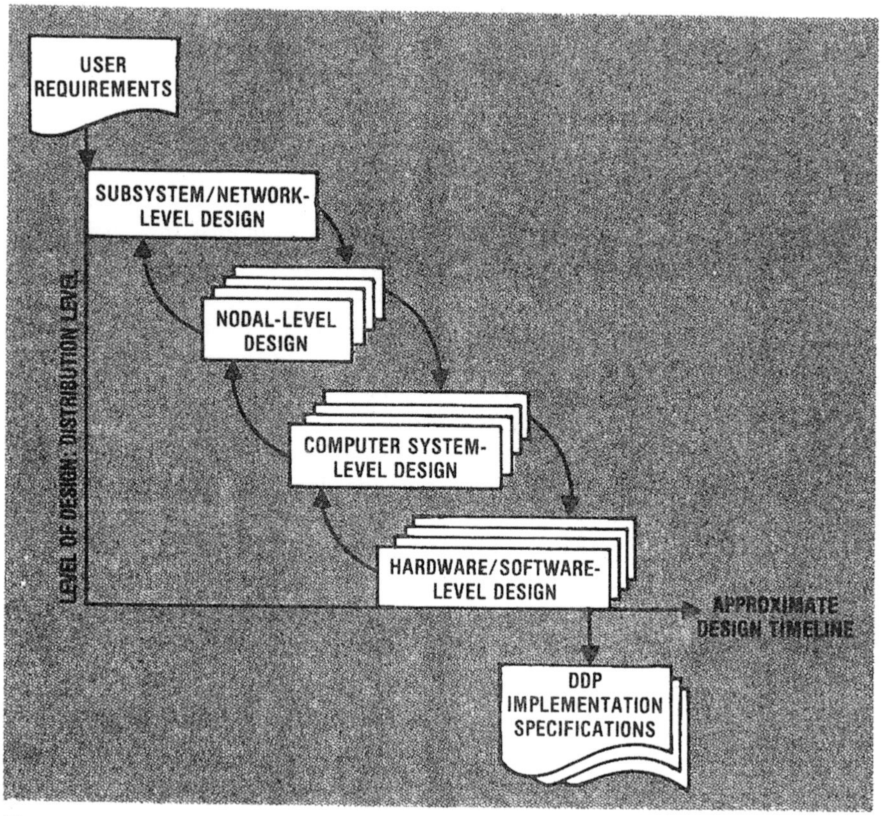

Figure 8. Levels of distributed design.

code—is expressed in a similar fashion. The task read/write relationships to the logical data structures of buffers, messages, and files are recorded. Tools are used to verify that the distributed design preserves the data flow and stimulus-response properties of the requirements. Simulation verifies satisfaction of response times as well as processor and communication constraints.

The process design is complete when the tasks, their scheduling rules, and data structures have been identified and are shown to meet all response times and constraints.

Task design. Task design translates the process design into a design to be coded in a programming language. The logical design phase defines the overall design of the task in terms of a PDL definition of the sequences of reads, writes, and invocations of modules. The physical design then maps this logical design onto data structures and algorithms coded in the selected programming language.

This approach provides for the natural identification of data objects, proposed by Booch[7] and others, for an object-oriented design. The RSL processing requirements define the conditions under which state data is created, selected, accessed, updated, and destroyed. The database is designed by the selection of a data structure and procedures for performing the required data manipulations. The programming language's runtime library or a reusable set of data management utilities can provide these procedures. The data objects can be derived by noting that the allocation of processing between tasks gives rise to the requirement for an interface function between them; this interface function can be decomposed and allocated between a requirement to provide a data object (allocated to the data management system) and requirements for the tasks to use specific read/write mechanisms.

During the physical design phase, the logical data structures are assigned to data structures and declarations, and the logical tasks are coded in the selected programming language. As with the module design, the automated unit development folder tool manages development of the task. A distributed process construction tool uses the DDL definition of design to extract units of code from the AUDF and combine them with operating system code in order to generate the total source code for each node of the distributed processor.

In summary, the Distributed Design Methodology uses a Distributed Design Language to provide traceability from requirements to design and to assure that the stimulus-response and data flow properties of the design are preserved. In addition, the design adds features for detection and recovery from exceptions, thus providing the fault-tolerance features of the design.

Status. An earlier version of the Distributed Design Methodology was successfuly used for the design of a 10-node distributed processing system with software coded in Pascal. TRW in Huntsville is demonstrating the latest version of the methodology and tools with both Pascal and Ada as the target programming languages. Training courses are being developed to initiate transfer of the technology and tools. A Test Specification Language and methodology are also being developed to link the requirements, design, and tests and to verify test coverage completeness.

After eight years of additional research and application, the following conclusion can be made:

(1) SREM demonstrates that it is practical to express processing requirements in terms of a structured finite-state machine. If the effort of test planning and correction of errors discovered during testing are taken into account, SREM appears to require less effort than traditional approaches.

(2) The SREM state-machine model has been extended to address system requirements and designs by representing time sequencing, concurrency, allocation, interface design, fault tolerance, and performance. This ex-

tended model provides a fresh view of the system/software design process.

(3) The sequence of languages—SSL/RSL/MDL/DDL/TSL—is an example of a unified approach to representing intermediate products of software development.

(4) A prototype set of tools sufficient to demonstrate the viability of the approach supports the methodology and languages. Additional productizing of the tools would bring additional benefits to users.

(5) A baseline, requirements-driven methodology that spans the entire life cycle has been developed. It is currently under evaluation to assess its ability to meet its goals of increased reliability and productivity.

During the past eight years, research has been aimed at making SREM evolve into a complete software engineering environment. Considerable growth potential remains, in terms of turning the tools into marketable products, upgrading the technology transfer mechanisms and materials, and extending the DCDS framework to, for example, exploit the state-machine foundations by interfacing with program-proof techniques. □

Acknowledgments

This article presents results of projects sponsored by the Ballistic Missile Defense Advanced Technology Center under contracts DSAS60-78-C-0158 and DASG60-81-C-0059 and by the US Air Force, Rome Air Development Center, under contracts F30602-78-C-0026 and F30602-84-C-0123.

References

1. M. Alford, "A Requirements Engineering Methodology for Real Time Processing Requirements," *IEEE Trans. Software Engineering,* Vol. SE-3, No. 1, Jan. 1977, pp. 60-69.
2. T. E. Bell, D. C. Bixler, and M. E. Dyer, "An Extendable Approach to Computer Aided Software Requirements Engineering," *IEEE Trans., Software Engineering,* Vol. SE-3, No. 1, Jan. 1977, pp. 49-60.
3. B. Boehm, "Verifying and Validating Software Requirements and Design Specifications," *IEEE Software,* Vol. 1, No. 1, Jan. 1984, pp. 75-88.
4. M. Alford. "Requirements for Distributed Data Processing Design," *Proc. First Int'l Conf. Distributed Computing Systems,* Pub. No. CH1445, IEEE Computer Society, Los Alamitos, Calif., Oct. 1979, pp. 1-14.
5. M. P. Mariani et al., *Tutorial: Distributed System Design,* presented at First Int'l Conf. Distributed Computing Systems, Oct. 1979.
6. B. Boehm, *Software Engineering Economics,* Prentice-Hall, Englewood Cliffs, N.J., 1981, pp. 607-612.
7. G. Booch, *Softwre Engineering with Ada,* The Benjamin/Cummings Publishing Company, Inc., 1983, pp. 220-228.

Mack W. Alford is the chief scientist at TRW's Huntsville Engineering and Software Development Facility. He is also the principle investigator of the Distributed Computing Design System project sponsored by BMDATC. His principal research interest is the integration of various system and software design methods into a single structure spanning the entire software development life cycle.

Alford joined TRW in 1961 and started research into software requirements techniques in 1968. He was the manager of the Requirements Engineering Interface Department on the Site Defense Project in 1972-73. He was responsible for methodology development on the SREM project, developed the SREM training classes. and applied SREM to several projects. He was the project manager of the DCDS project and its predecessors from 1978 until 1983.

Alford attended UCLA and received a BA degree in mathematics in 1962, an MA in 1966, and performed postgraduate work as a TRW fellow during 1970-1973.

Questions concerning this article can be addressed to the author at TRW, 213 Wynn Drive, Huntsville, AL 35805.

A Case Study of SREM

Paul A. Scheffer and Albert H. Stone, III
Martin Marietta Denver Aerospace

William E. Rzepka
Rome Air Development Center

This methodology can improve the integrity of a large software system description, but it is labor-intensive and hard to learn.

In 1979 the Rome Air Development Center, Griffiss Air Force Base, New York, initiated a program to investigate whether the Software Requirements Engineering Methodology could specify and analyze software requirements for the embedded computers that are a part of US Air Force Command, Control, Communications, and Intelligence (called C^3I) systems.[1] SREM had been developed in 1977 by TRW, Inc., under contract to the US Army Ballistic Missile Defense Advanced Technology Center. It had been specifically designed to describe and analyze real-time, stimulus-response requirements of single-computer, missile-defense systems.[2] By 1979, the question had arisen whether SREM could be applied to the man-machine interfaces, large databases, and multi-computer, distributed networks that characterize large, C^3I systems.

A C^3I system is a heterogeneous collection of people, procedures, and equipment organized to perform a mission. The specific purpose of the C^3I system is to provide the decision maker with the kind of information he or she needs to effectively manage the mission resources. Equipment typically includes aircraft, sensors, communications circuits, computers, software, shelters, etc. Primary missions include

- *Command and management.* The World Wide Military Command and Control System and North American Air Defense Command Cheyenne Mountain Complex are examples of systems that assimilate information from many sources and process it into a form high-level decision makers can use.
- *Communications.* The Strategic Air Command's Automated Total Information Network is an example of a packet-switching network that connects many military installations.
- *Surveillance and control.* The Joint Surveillance System performs peacetime surveillance of United States and Canadian air space; the Ground-Based Electro-Optical Deep Space Surveillance system is a multi-computer network for telescope-signal processing of space objects.
- *Intelligence.* The Tactical Information Processing and Interpretation system is an intelligence gathering system that involves the collection, processing, and interpretation of large information databases.

To answer the question about SREM's potential for describing C^3I systems, the Rome Air Development

Center effort used SREM to specify the software requirements for a small C^3I subsystem. This work reached two conclusions.

First, SREM in its current state could adequately specify software requirements for command and control systems. This was demonstrated for critical C^3I elements such as the man-machine interface, database, and communications. But, in addition, the evaluation uncovered some aspects of SREM that were not completely responsive to command and control system needs; and the evaluation did not seriously address the performance of the SREM system software, the effectiveness of the SREM training materials, and the utility of the user interface to the SREM tools.

These results led to the second conclusion: further evaluation of SREM on large C^3I systems was needed. This effort would be a technically thorough evaluation of the capabilities of SREM for specifying and analyzing command and control software requirements, and would recommend improvements based on the evaluation. The comprehensive investigation was contracted to Martin Marietta Denver Aerospace in the fall of 1980 and was completed in the spring of 1983.[3] This article describes that work.

Background

In recent years SREM has been the focus of several studies that have either characterized its functionality with respect to some problem domain or attempted to assess the effectiveness of its procedures, specification language, and tools relative to other techniques. Stainer performed a feature comparison of SREM and PSL/PSA[4] that described strong and weak points of each technique.[5] Salwin compared SREM and PSL/PSA in the context of a Navy system for analyzing weapon system readiness data.[6] Slegel examined SREM's ability to validate requirements for maintenance and diagnostic software in a real-time command-and-control system.[7] A McDonnell Douglas group evaluated SREM in the real-time, ballistic-missile-defense context.[8] Its report described SREM's capabilities for displaying requirements and detecting consistency errors and tool costs. Alford has reported the status of SREM's requirements development procedures, requirements specification language, support software, transfer to user organizations, and planned extensions and improvements.[9] Celko compared the specification properties and error-detection capabilities of SREM, PSL/PSA, and IORL[10] as a result of applying these techniques to an Army management information system; he concluded that using any automated tool is superior to manual validation of requirements.[11]

Scope

SREM is a formal, integrated approach to requirements engineering activities. It begins when the system requirements analysis has identified system functions and functional interfaces between subsystems and system operating rules, and the top-level system requirements have been allocated to the computing resource. It is designed to induce certain qualities often lacking in the specification of many large software systems, including internal consistency, explicitness, testability, and traceability.

In addition to the step-by-step requirements engineering techniques, SREM includes a machine-processable, "English-like," Requirements Statement Language and a Requirements Engineering and Validation System to automatically process the requirements statements and to perform a wide range of analyses and simulations on its centralized database. REVS constitutes the automated-tools part of SREM. It uses a relational database (called the Abstract System Semantic Model) to capture requirements processed from RSL.

Functionally, REVS consists of six software components that create the ASSM and examine its contents:

- *RSL* (*RSL translator*). Translates requirements and creates the ASSM;
- *Rslxtnd* (*RSL extend*). Augments/extends the RSL language elements;
- *Radx* (*analysis/data extraction*). Extracts information from the ASSM for analysis and documentation, identifies ASSM subsets for consistency/completeness, and analyzes ASSM content for dataflow;
- *Simgen* (*simulation generation*). Builds a simulation package;
- *Simxqt* (*simulation execute*). Performs the simulation exercises; and
- *Simda* (*simulation data analysis*). Analyzes and documents the simulation.

In the evaluation of SREM that we describe in this article, the primary mechanism consisted of applying it to two typical Air Force systems through the existing specifications that defined these systems. With this exercise, three evaluation aspects could be examined:

- The ability of SREM to describe the software requirements of C^3I systems;
- Where SREM can best be applied in the Air Force software life cycle; and
- The quality of SREM training.

We focus on the first and second evaluation aspects, and discuss each using a common format: assessment goals, evaluation methods, derived results, and recommendations. We address training from the perspective of important evaluation issues.

Applying SREM to C^3I systems

Goals. To determine SREM's applicability to C^3I systems, two areas were examined: specification scope and requirements analysis capabilities.

The first addressed SREM's ability to describe all characteristics of C^3I systems. The characteristics of C^3I

systems that distinguish them from other systems and the ones that the evaluation project tried to express in RSL are

- Real-time and near real-time processing;
- The ability to present data to an analyst and react to his decisions;
- The ability to deal with real-world objects that simultaneously are users of C^3I data, providers of C^3I data, and objects about which the C^3I system maintains data;
- The ability to manipulate static data, such as cartographic or hypsographic information, as well as such dynamic data as tank position or sensor status;
- Distributed processing; and
- Communications processing.

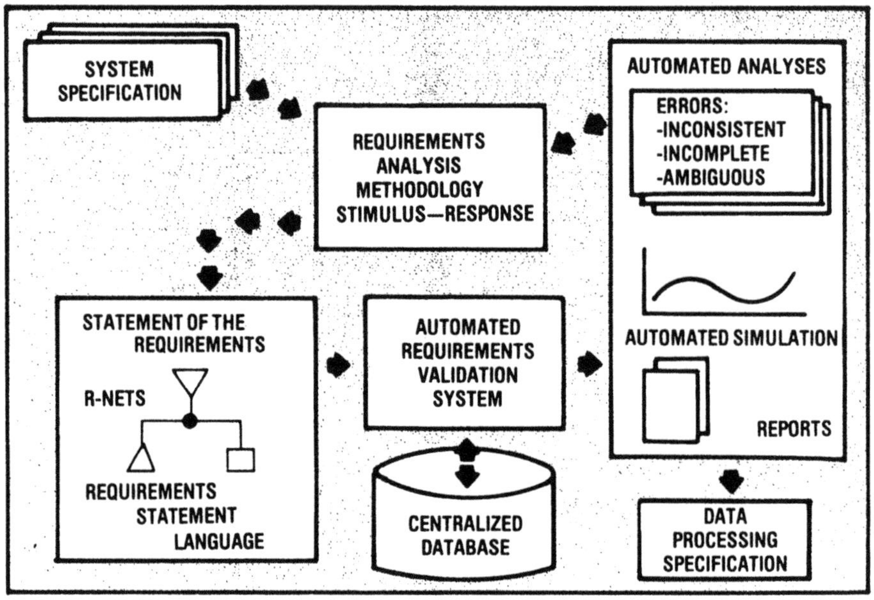

Figure 1. Software Requirements Engineering Methodology.

The second area of concern was SREM's capacity to automatically detect such specification errors as requirement ambiguities, requirement inconsistencies, and specification incompleteness.

Methods. SREM was applied to two systems: the Communications Switch Interface Development system and the Advanced Sensor Exploitation system. CSID is an interactive system for compatibility analysis of communications switching system interface data that is currently operational at the Rome Air Development Center. It is described in a design specification.[12] ASE is a distributed C^3I system responsible for gathering, correlating, and disseminating sensor information. The ASE is described in a software requirements specification.[13] The SREM technique was used to interpret requirements, produce an ASSM, and analyze each system's specification. Functional simulations were only applied to selected ASE subsystems.

The initial input to SREM is a system specification that is translated into RSL and interpreted to determine the interfaces with the outside world, the messages across these interfaces, and the required processing relationships and flows (Figure 1). Next, the details of the functional requirements, including all of the input/output data relationships, their attributes, maximum and minimum values, allowed ranges for non-numeric data, and the processing steps, are completed. RSL is used to input these requirements, described as Requirement Networks, or R_nets, into the REVS, which in turn builds the centralized database called the Abstract System Semantic Model. The automated static analyzer, Radx, is executed to check for errors in element attributes or relationships between elements. When all information has been input and all errors corrected, the result is a formal functional requirements specification.

Before the requirements specification can be considered complete, a system simulation is needed to verify that the envisioned system's interfaces and processing relationships behave as required. Simple functional models are created in Pascal for each of the processing steps that have been identified. These models are embedded directly in the RSL and used as input to a simulation generation function to create a behavioral model of the functional requirements.

When the processing relationships have been verified, performance requirements must still be specified for the functional requirements so that system performance constraints can be tested. Each performance requirement will constrain a processing path within the system. This method of establishing performance requirements allows the traceability of requirements and highlights the system structure for review.

If it is also necessary to verify that the requirements specification is analytically feasible, one more simulation step, called the analytical feasibility demonstration, is performed. This simulation uses actual algorithms of the intended system instead of simple functional models to establish that the identified software requirements can be tested.

All REVS components were used in evaluating SREM. The RSL translator function was used to construct an ASSM for both applications, ASE and CSID. The Radx function served three purposes: first, the Radx analysis capabilities were employed to verify the consistency of the ASSM by examining the attributes associated with the ASSM elements, tracing detected errors to one of two places, either the RSL description or the originating requirements documentation; second,

Table 1. RSL production data.

SPEC	DOCUMENT SIZE (PAGES)	MAN-HOURS[1]	TIME (MONTHS)	ASSM SIZE LINES RLS	NUMBER ELEMENTS[2]	PERCENT DATA[3]	PERCENT PROC[4]	PERCENT OTHER[5]
CSID	196	7498	10	10353	1109	53	40	7
ASE	515	11277	20	35550	3016	46[6]	8.8[6]	44.9[6]
Total	711	18775	30	45903	4125	-	-	-

NOTES:
1 Engineering hours to translate and analyse specification.
2 RSL elements such as data, R_net.
3 Messages, Data, Entity_Classes, etc.
4 R_nets, Subnets, Alphas, etc.
5 Sources, Originating_Requirements, etc.
6 Averaged over six subsystems (last three columns only).

the same analysis capabilities determined the completeness of the formal specification by examining the relationships between elements; and third, the Radx capabilities for user-defined analysis were used to produce a document approximating a MIL-STD-490 type B-5 functional requirements specification. The language extension function, Rslxtnd, of REVS enhanced data requirements descriptions. The Simgen function was used in conjunction with the Simxqt and Simda functions to exercise the dataflow logic. Models of the R_net processing steps were added to allow the Simgen function to construct a simulation program executed by Simxqt with the results analyzed by Simda.

Results. Table 1 shows, for each system studied, the size of the specification used, the time spent creating the ASSM databases, and the size of the ASSMs produced. The following statistics can be derived from the table:

- Approximately 19 lines of correct RSL were produced per eight-hour workday;
- Approximately 1.8 correct RSL element definitions were produced per eight-hour workday;
- While error-occurrence data were not kept for CSID, about 100 specification errors were found when applying the SREM (not necessarily REVS) to ASE, resulting in about 120 man-hours expended per error discovered; and
- A significant disparity occurs in the composition of the databases (Figure 2); in particular, the amounts of information required to describe control flow (40 percent versus 9 percent) and overhead activities, such as configuration management, traceability, and commentary (7 percent versus 45 percent), varied significantly between specifications examined.

The learning curve for the RSL must be considered as well. While RSL was produced at approximately 11 lines per day initially, experienced analysts were able to achieve about 25 lines per day. A similar difference was experienced in the production rate of RSL element definitions (1.2 versus 2.1 elements per day).

Analyst effort needed to achieve these productivity rates averaged 26.4 man-hours per page of specification. Since the project consisted of only the CSID and ASE data points, this average is not considered a reliable predictor of validation effort.

A detailed analysis of specification flaw exposure was done for the ASE system. Table 2 shows error classes and how they were found. Clearly evident here is that the strength of SREM is its methodology as opposed to its automated validation tools. The structure of the methodology guides the analyst to an understanding of the requirements through an iterative learning process that exposes requirement flaws.

In examining the ASE error data and its associated analyst ($372,000) and computer ($20,400) costs, we can conclude that the cost to detect each error was approximately $4785. This result appears to have been influenced by several factors. First, many of the textual descriptions in the ASE system specification were generated from DeMarco dataflow diagrams, resulting in a high-quality specification with relatively few errors. Second, the analysts reported that not all of the errors detected (about 10 percent) were documented. Third, in arriving at the cost/error figure, it was assumed that all of the man-hours (and hence costs) associated with the ASE evaluation were devoted to error detection. However, a significant portion was expended on other activities, such as configuration management, traceability, and textual descriptions. A final perspective from which to view this data is the total cost of developing the ASE system. Approximately $7.5 million has been invested in the design and implementation of the ASE. Hence, the cost of using SREM to specify and analyze the ASE system has been about five percent of the total system development cost.

Caution must be used in comparing the raw error-correction costs from the SREM study to other cost studies published in the literature. The instability of dollar-values over time, and hence labor cost, is a significant variable, as is the influence of two techniques (that is, manual and SREM) since one may pre-expose errors to the other. Moreover, it is not possible to determine how many errors each technique misses. The conclusion that can be reached from these data is that the application of a disciplined methodology like SREM is a cost-effective means of analyzing software requirements.

All of the attributes that characterize C^3I systems were contained in one or both of the specifications. The real-time and near real-time phenomena present throughout the ASE specification proved very difficult to express because many timing requirements spanned several R_nets. RSL is limited to describing such requirements only along control flow paths within an R_net. Decision-making characteristics proved difficult to express when applied to man-machine interfacing in prompt-driven systems. Throughout translation of the CSID specification, the project team found it necessary to add state flags and their related conditional data to describe and correctly associate the CSID user's reply to the prompt that evoked the reply. The additions severely reduced the clarity of the requirements in the ASSM.

C^3I real-world objects were easily transformed into RSL with the element types ENTITY_CLASS and ENTITY_TYPE. The data requirement characteristics were described easily by attributes associated with the element types DATA and FILE. RSL is capable of describing only distributed processing and parallel processing requirements in which the sequence is not important. This generality in processing structure precludes detailed description of distributed and parallel processing situations where time sequences are important, and so SREM is most appropriately used for software requirements analysis or high-level design activities. Communications characteristics are easily described with appropriate RSL attributes of specific element types (for example, value range); detailed information (for example, baud rate) can be associated with the characteristics by appropriate extensions to RSL using the language extension function (Rslxtnd).

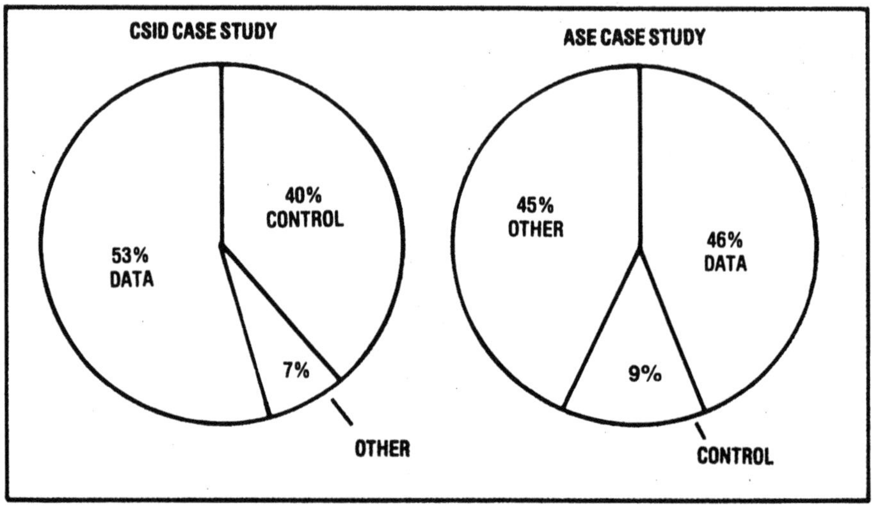

Figure 2. Comparison of requirements databases.

Recommendations. The sample application of SREM to these test systems clearly demonstrated the benefit of disciplined techniques in requirements analysis. A formalized scheme uncovers many problems and questions that help improve the integrity of the system description. But this is true of any disciplined approach to requirements analysis: benefits outweigh costs because flaws are detected early and are not permitted to permeate the system.

The major recommendations that relate specifically to C^3I applicability concern parallel processing and distributed processing capabilities. For appropriate detail, the RSL must be modified to explicitly describe parallel and distributed processing. The RSL modifications would in turn require the modification of Radx to extract and analyze the new information, as well as the modification of Simgen so parallel and distributed processing can be portrayed within the simulations.

Role of SREM in the software life cycle

Goals. The goal here was to determine in which phase or phases of the software life cycle SREM is most appropriate. This goal was approached from three directions:

- Assessment of the methodological technique prescribed for using SREM;
- Evaluation of the ability of the REVS software tools to support SREM; and
- Determination of the best placement of SREM within the software life cycle used by the Air Force.

The term "software life cycle" is used to identify the processes that occur in the development of software systems from initial conception to final realization in an operational environment. The following phases and associated processes are considered.

- *Conceptual.* The need for a system to solve a particular set of problems is identified, with feasibility assessments, tradeoff studies, and analyses being performed. Requirements for computer resources are allocated. The description of the system takes the

Table 2. ASE error data summary.

CLASS	NUMBER	% OF TOTAL	HOW EXPOSED
Inconsistency/misuse	30	36	80% by analyst; 20% by REVS
Ambiguity/lack of detail	17	21	100% by analyst
Incompleteness/non-use	35	43	100% by analyst
	82	100	

form of an initial system specification.

- *Requirements definition.* Requirements are defined for system functions, interfaces, performance, and such non-functional issues as safety, human factors, and reliability. A data dictionary is produced.
- *Design.* The specification for the system envisioned in the requirements phase is transformed into an overall design of how the system is to accomplish its goals. The transformation involves the allocation of system functions to hardware and/or software, a description of the objects the system is to operate on, and a description of the algorithms to be used in operating on those objects.
- *Coding-and-checkout.* The design is translated into a computer language. It is then executed to evaluate its performance.
- *Test-and-integration.* The resulting program is tested to ensure that the software performs as intended, and the system, as implemented, fulfills all system requirements.
- *Operational.* The system is in operation and must be maintained. The maintenance process is invoked to correct problems not previously encountered or to change the system as the needs of its users change.

Methods. As its name suggests, SREM is intended specifically for requirements analysis. Requirements analysis involves functional specification and data description that occur in both the requirements-definition and design phases of the life cycle. The first part of the methodology evaluation addressed whether SREM was an effective technique for defining unambiguous and testable requirements. The second part was a comparative one, to determine whether the requirements produced were of sufficient quality that derived designs would be of higher quality than those produced without the benefit of SREM. Hence, SREM was evaluated by

- Examining the consistency and completeness of the requirements produced;
- Examining the REVS tools products for information content, tool maturity, and utility; and
- Comparing designs produced from both the original specifications (CSID and ASE) and from the translations of those specifications into RSL.

To place SREM correctly in the requirements-definition and design phases of the software life cycle and to identify how well it supported requirements analysis, the completed requirements databases (ASSMs) were using as the basis for validating the original specifications. Databases were built for the CSID system and three ASE subsystems (ASE, C^3I, and NELS). Simultaneously, designs were produced in a conventional fashion by top-down decomposition expressed through Nassi-Schneiderman charts by using only the software specification documents. Figure 3 shows this comparison scheme. The resulting designs were compared on common bases of design walkthroughs, McCabe's complexity measures and Myer's reliability measures,[3] and by subjectively determining if the design characteristics of hierarchical construction and levels of abstraction and information hiding were adequately supported by SREM.

Results. The SREM proved to be of great value for the task of requirements analysis. This structured approach aided the requirements analyst in identifying inconsistencies and ambiguities in the specification as the methodology progressed through all of its steps. However, SREM utility appears to lie within a fairly narrow range of the life cycle. It was developed to specify software requirements after the system requirements analysis phase has been completed, but before any detailed processing algorithms have been formed. The consensus of the analysts using SREM was that its strengths are defining, correcting, or analyzing software-specific requirements of the system.

The RSL Translator cannot adequately recover from a syntax error and continue its error-detection process as if the previous error did not occur. As a result, the phenomena of RSL syntax errors being produced by a previous error was prevalent throughout the entire specification-translation process and caused the project team to become very sensitive to the quality of the RSL syntax being entered into the ASSM.

The Simgen function of REVS was applied to two of the ASE subsystems. The Simgen function itself will automatically run an ASSM data analysis (Radx) every time a simulator generation is attempted. Valuable time and resources may be unnecessarily expended if no significant changes are made to the simulator definition. Moreover, Simgen does not maintain any kind of "error status" flag on the results of the Radx analysis, so that the simulator generation will be run to completion even though the preceding Radx step was in error.

The evaluation of the designs produced from both RSL specifications and the original specification documents (Figure 3) showed no clear advantage for either technique. Both sets of designs were approximately equal in complexity and modularity according to the measures used. However, a controlled experiment was not intended, and the same design team was used for both versions, which certainly influenced the result.

Recommendations. For designs produced directly from specifications or RSL, controlled experiments must be performed to collect sufficient data and to draw conclusions. We recommend that such experiments be conducted.

While the SREM technique itself proved to be valuable in identifying specification problems, REVS left much to be desired. The RSL translator was inefficient and performed error recovery inconsistently; both of these problems should be corrected before REVS is released for general use. Radx has similar problems. Dataflow analysis should be decoupled for Simgen and placed under user control. When a simulation's dataflow has been analyzed once, and as long as it is not modified, the simulation should be executable without another dataflow analysis.

In general, REVS needs to be made more efficient in terms of the computer resources used and convenience. Several basic structural changes would improve the REVS package. The changes to consider are

- Partition the predefined Radx analyses into smaller executable pieces so the Vax version is comparable in modularity to the CDC version.
- Further investigate Vax multitasking to accomplish more parallel activities (expand on simple foreground-background concept).
- The DBMS technique should not use its own paging scheme, which encourages thrashing in a virtual memory system.
- REVS initialization requires inordinate time, indicating extensive processing at each startup. Table-driven or other predefined structures could reduce resource consumption.
- The command language facilities would be improved with a hierarchical Help structure, more detailed prompting levels (indicating which subsystems are available, providing requests for needed input, signaling when a function is complete), and elaborating numeric error codes with meaningful messages.
- Decoupling RSL processing from database creation (syntax-only check) to reduce the time and costs associated with RSL translation.

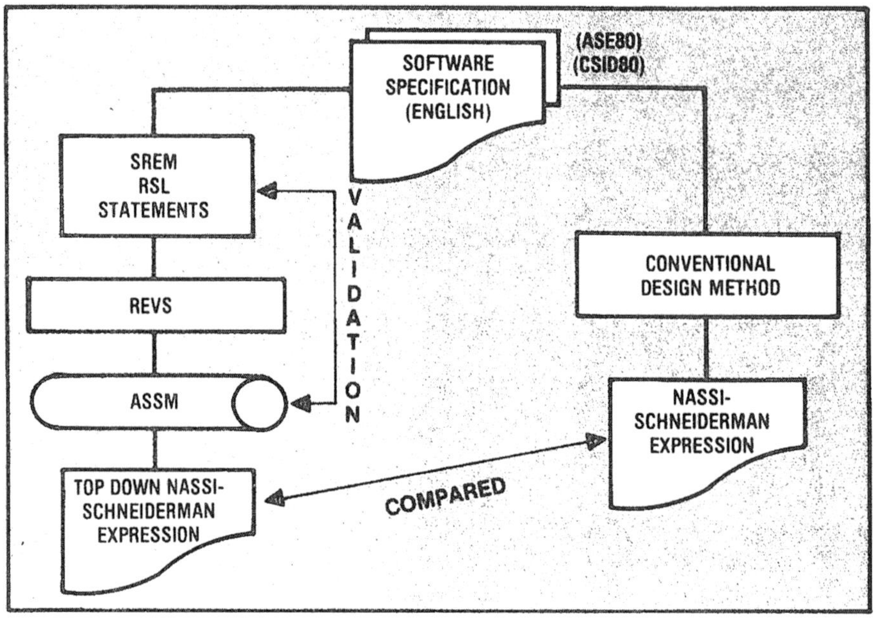

Figure 3. System comparison scheme.

Training evaluation issues

Training is an important element in the successful integration of any methodology into the infrastructure of a software development organization. The organization must determine its availability and quality prior to committing to its routine use. To help in making this determination, it should consider at least three aspects of training. First, the planning and logical structure of the course must be examined with respect to

- *Audience considerations.* What is the target audience and does the course address its needs? Can the course material be reasonably covered in the time allowed?
- *Course overview.* Are the objectives of both the methodology and the training clearly stated?
- *Planned activities.* Do the class exercises support the material covered in the lecture? Is sufficient hands-on experience included?
- *Progress evaluation.* Are criteria given so student progress may be evaluated? Are the criteria related to observable student behavior?
- *Course summary.* Is provision made for summarizing or reviewing difficult concepts?

Second, course execution must be considered, including

- *Teaching methods.* Is the quality and amount of instructor-student interaction adequate? Are discussions encouraged? Are examples used to clarify difficult concepts?
- *Environment.* Are the conditions under which the course is taught comfortable and conductive to learning?

Third, course materials must be evaluated for utility in both learning and using the methodology.

Data gathered during the ASE case study provides some interesting insights into the nature of the requirements engineering process using the SREM model:

- The work of requirements analysts is predominantly the definition, description, and configuration management of data. Process (control flow) descriptions amount to only nine percent of the specifications produced.
- Analyst productivity was 19 lines of formal specification language per day. This is about the same as some higher order programming languages, but is only about half of the productivity rate of Fortran. The rate is probably attributable to the large amount (45 per-

cent) of descriptive information contained in the specifications.

- The cost of learning formal requirements engineering techniques is significant. Analyst productivity during the learning period (first specification) was only one-half of its rate while generating a second specification.
- Requirements engineering, like software development, is highly labor intensive. Computer analysis costs accounted for only five percent of budget.

The evaluation showed that SREM is a viable approach for specifying C^3I software requirements. As with any new and complex technology, however, problems have been encountered. The evaluation team has recommended changes to the SREM specification language, analysis tools, and training.

Since the time of this evaluation, TRW has made several improvements to the internal organization and implementation of REVS, such as a complete reorganization and recoding of the database management system, reportedly improving performance by a factor of 70. Also, RADC has initiated an enhancement effort to improve the "user friendliness" of REVS. R_nets graphics, electronic-forms entry of RSL and REVS commands, user Help facilities, improved error detection, recovery and diagnostics, and requirements documentation generation tools will be available in the fall of 1985. A users group is being organized to distribute and maintain the enhanced REVS software. □

Acknowledgments

The authors wish to thank the following people for their diligent efforts and assistance during the SREM evaluation: Roger Weber of RADC; Chris Beall, Bev Castor, Jim Fullerton, Dave Hartschuh, and Susan Madison of Martin Marietta Denver Aerospace.

References

1. W. E. Rzepka, "Using SREM to Specify Command and Control Software Requirements," technical report RADC-TR-82-319, Rome Air Development Center, Griffiss AFB, NY, Dec. 1982.
2. M. W. Alford, "A Requirements Engineering Methodology for Real-Time Processing Requirements," *IEEE Trans. Software Engineering,* Vol. SE-3, No. 1, Jan. 1977, pp. 366-374.
3. A. H. Stone et al. *"SREM Evaluation, Final Report,"* RADC technical report, contract F30602-80-0272, Apr. 1983, 2 vols.
4. D. Teichroew and E. A. Hershey, "PSL/PSA: A Computer-Aided Technique for Structured Documentation and Analysis of Information Processing Systems," *IEEE Trans. Software Engineering,* Vol. SE-3, No. 1, Jan. 1977.
5. H. M. Stainer, "An Evaluation of PSL/PSA and RSL/REVS—Two Computer-Assisted Software Requirements/Specification/Description Tools," technical report FS-76-205, Fleet Systems Dept., Johns Hopkins University, Applied Physics Laboratory, Laurel, Md., Oct. 1976.
6. A. E. Salwin, "A Test Case Comparison of URL/URA and RSL/ REVS," technical report FS-77-161, Fleet Systems Dept., Johns Hopkins University, Applied Laboratory, Laurel, Md., July 1977.
7. R. C. Slegel, "Applying SREM to the Verification and Validation of an Existing Software Requirements Specification," *Proc. Compsac78.*
8. "SREM Evaluation Results Summary," technical report, McDonnell Douglas, Huntington Beach, Calif., Oct. 1978.
9. M. W. Alford, "Software Requirements Engineering Methodology (SREM) at the Age of Four," *Proc. Compsac80,* Oct. 1980, pp. 366-374.
10. "IORL Language Reference Manual Version 2," technical manual, Teledyne Brown Engineering, Dec. 1982.
11. J. Celko, J. S. Davis, and J. Mitchell, "A Demonstration of Three Requirements Language Systems," *Sigplan Notices,* Vol. 18, No. 1, Jan. 1983.
12. *CSID Interpreter Software Requirements Document,* Harris Corporation, 1980.
13. K. Lubbes et al., *The Advanced Sensor Exploitation (ASE) Analysis/ Design Report,* Pattern Analysis and Recognition Corporation, 1980.

Paul A. Scheffer is manager of software engineering research at Martin Marietta Denver Aerospace, where he has been leading the design and development of an integrated software engineering environment. In addition to research and development in software techniques and tools, he has led other application software development projects, been involved in the Ada effort, and served as program manager for various government agencies. Prior to joining Martin Marietta, he worked for Planning Research Corporation, MITRE, and the federal government.

Scheffer is an IEEE member and received a BS degree in mathematics and an MS in computer science from Purdue in 1964 and 1971, respectively.

Albert H. Stone III is now with the Computer Languages Section of the Software R&D Laboratory at Hewlett Packard's Fort Collins System Division. His primary interest is in the understanding and application of advanced software engineering techniques to the software development process. Prior to joining H-P, he worked at several aerospace companies, where his interests included the development of metrics for measuring and predicting facets of the software development process, as well as tools for modifying that process. He has taught courses at Metropolitan State University and has participated in the IEEE Software Reliability Standards Working Group. He received an IEEE Computer Society outstanding paper award at the Seventh International Conference on Software Engineering. Stone received his Bachelor's degree in Mathematics from San Jose State University in 1976, and is pursuing a Master's degree in Computer Science at Colorado State University.

William E. Rzepka is a guest editor of this issue of *Computer.* His photograph and biography appear on page 12.

Questions about this article can be directed to Paul A. Scheffer, Martin Marietta Denver Aerospace, Mailstop S8030, PO Box 179, Denver CO 80201.

TASK RESPONSE TIME MODEL & ITS APPLICATIONS FOR REAL-TIME DISTRIBUTED PROCESSING SYSTEMS*

Wesley W. Chu and Kin K. Leung

Computer Science Department
University of California, Los Angeles
California 90024

Abstract

Response time is an important system performance measure for real-time distributed processing systems. This paper introduces an analytic model to estimate the task response time for loosely coupled distributed systems. The model considers such factors as the precedence relationships among software modules, interprocessor communication, interconnection network delay, module scheduling policy, and assignment of modules to computers. Simulation experiments are used to validate the assumptions of the analytic model. Applications of the model to the study of such design issues for distributed systems as module assignment, precedence relationships, module scheduling policies, and database management algorithms are discussed.

1. INTRODUCTION

With the advent of low-cost VLSI and communication technologies, distributed processing (DP) has become an economically and technologically attractive computer architecture. The DP system considered in this paper consists of multiple computers, each with its own memory and peripherals, connected by an interconnection network.

In a DP system, an application task is often partitioned into several sub-tasks (i.e., software modules) which are assigned to a set of computers for processing. An example of a task consisting of fifteen modules assigned to a system with three computers is shown in Figure 1. The logical structure and precedence relationships among the software modules may be represented by a task control-flow graph. The task is repeatedly invoked to meet the processing requirements (e.g., processing return signals from a radar). After a module completes its execution, it sends messages to enable (invoke) its succeeding module(s) as indicated in the task control-flow graph. In addition, when a module finishes its execution, it may also send messages to update the shared data files on other computers. Such message exchanges among modules are referred to as intermodule communication (IMC)[1]. The overhead for communications among modules that reside on the same computer is usually small and can be assumed to be negligible. If messages are sent between modules that reside on different computers, the messages are called interprocessor communication (IPC). IPC re-

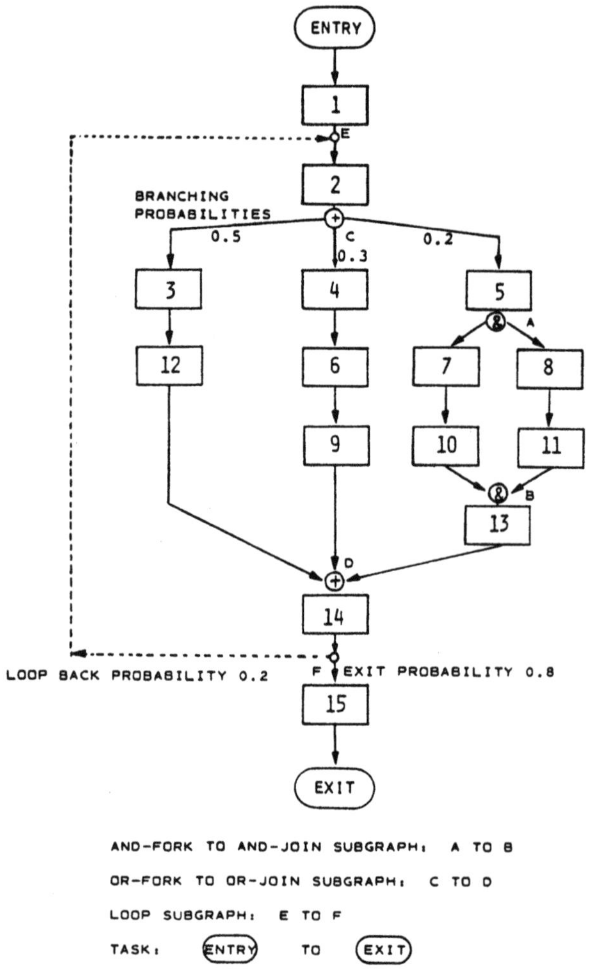

Figure 1a. A Sample Task Control-Flow Graph

*This work was supported by the Ballistic Missile Defense Advanced Technological Center under Contract DASG60-83-C-0019 and the U.C. MICRO Grant P-5607-N-84.

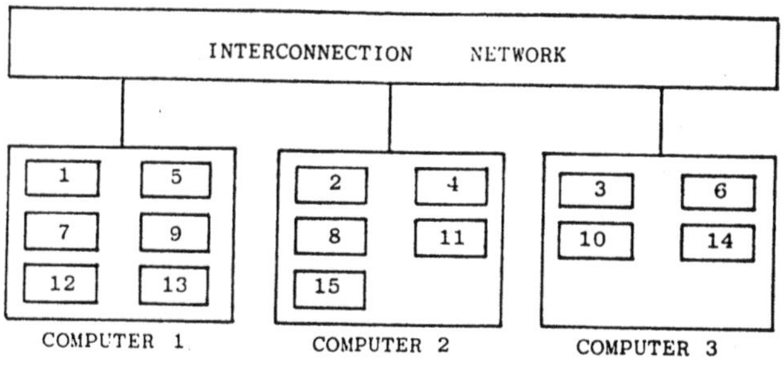

Figure 1b. Assignment of Modules to Computers

quires such extra processing as communication protocol and management of the distributed data files, and incurs interconnection network delay. Therefore IPC has significant impact on the system performance and response time.

If data are shared among modules residing on different computers, to provide fast local accessing and to enhance file availability, some of the shared data files are replicated on several computers. However, maintaining the data consistency of the replicated copies requires the use of a concurrency control mechanism (e.g., locking, timestamp, exclusive-writer protocol). Therefore, planning a DP system is complicated by many such complex and interdependent design issues as module and file assignment[2], module scheduling policy, database management algorithm, etc. Presently, there is no systematic methodology for designing DP systems. Existing system designs use ad hoc methods which result in a trial-and-error approach. Further, since DP systems often are required to perform time critical functions, response time is an important performance measure. Simulation techniques are used to estimate the response time, but such approaches are time-consuming and expensive. This motivates us to develop an analytic model for estimating the response time for DP systems. The model can be used as a unified approach for studying various DP design issues and exploring the tradeoffs among different design choices.

We shall first present our task response time model based on module response times and the weighted task control-flow graph. Next, we present a set of simulation experiments to validate the assumptions used in the model for various types of logical structures and precedence relationships among modules. Finally, we discuss the use of the model to study the interrelationships among task response time, module assignment, precedence relationships, scheduling policy for module executions, and database management algorithms.

2. A TASK RESPONSE TIME MODEL

Queueing networks [3-5] are commonly used to model DP systems. In such models, computers are represented as servers, modules as customers, and task invocations correspond to external arrivals. Customers are routed for service in accordance with the task control-flow graph and the module assignment. In DP systems, a module may enable more than one modules. This is referred to as a FORK in the graph. Alternatively, a module may have several immediate predecessor modules which must complete their executions before the succeeding module can be executed. This is referred to as a JOIN. When a control-flow graph consists of FORKs and JOINs, the routing scheme in the queueing network model is inadequate to represent the logical relationships among modules. Thus the system cannot be represented by a tractable queueing network model. Therefore, we present a new model to estimate the task response time.

Task response time, or *port-to-port* (PTP) time, is the time from the request of a task invocation to the completion of its execution. Since a task may be repeatedly invoked and the modules are enabled according to the sequence as indicated in the control-flow graph, task response time consists of module waiting times, module execution times and precedence waiting times. *Module waiting time* is the time from a module invocation arrival until it starts its execution on a computer. This waiting time is the time spent waiting for module executions and input IPC processings. *Module execution time* is the sum of a module's execution time and its output IPC time. Let the sum of a module's waiting time and execution time be denoted as *module response time*. The *precedence waiting time* is the intermodule synchronization delay due to the precedence relationships among modules. Our task response time model consists of two sub-models: *module response time model* and *weighted control-flow graph model*. The first sub-model computes the module response times, while the latter considers the precedence waiting times.

2.1 Module Response Time Model

For a given module assignment, each computer will execute a fixed set of modules. The response time of a module is the time from its invocation to the completion of its execution. Thus module response time includes waiting (queueing) time and module execution time. If a module needs to send messages to other computers, the output IPC time is included as a part of the module execution time. Further, these IPC's are transmitted over the interconnection network, and eventually arrive at their destinations. These input IPC's on the destination computers can be viewed as a special module which also contends for processing. Based on the module assignment and IMC's among modules, IPC processing times can be obtained. Let the module execution times be characterized by probability distribution functions (PDF's). Then each computer can be modeled as a queueing system with several modules (customers of different types) with specified service distributions. Based on the logical structures among modules and task invocation rate, the invocation rate of each module on the computer can be determined. In queueing terminology, module invocations are customer arrivals. If several modules on the same computer are invoked simultaneously, this results in a bulk module invocation.

In our model, we assume that 1) the module invocation arrival (single or bulk) processes are independent of each other, and 2) module invocation interarrival times are Poisson distributed. To illustrate the concept, let us determine the modules' response times on a computer that uses *first-come-first-serve* (FCFS) scheduling policy* for module executions.

Consider a computer that has n distinct module invocations (single or bulk invocations), and the arrival rate for the ith module invocation be λ_i and the Laplace Transform (L.T.) of the service requirement be $U_i^*(s)$ for $i=1,2,\ldots n$. For a bulk invocation that invokes a set M of distinct modules (referred to as *module bulk),* the corresponding service requirement is $U_i^*(s)= \prod_{m \epsilon M} X_m^*(s)$, where $X_m^*(s)$ is the L.T. of the service time of module m.

Based on the assumptions 1 and 2, this queueing system is an extension of the regular FCFS M/G/1 queue with total arrival rate $\lambda = \sum_{i=1}^{n} \lambda_i$, and the L.T. of service time for each invocation arrival is $U^*(s) = \sum_{i=1}^{n} \frac{\lambda_i}{\lambda} U_i^*(s)$. For the M/G/1 queue, the first two moments of the module bulk waiting time from the bulk invocation arrival until its first module starts to execute are

$$\overline{w} = \frac{\sum_{i=1}^{n} \lambda_i \overline{u_i^2}}{2(1-\rho)} \tag{1}$$

and

$$\overline{w^2} = 2(\overline{w})^2 + \frac{\sum_{i=1}^{n} \lambda_i \overline{u_i^3}}{3(1-\rho)} \tag{2}$$

where:
$\overline{u_i^n} = n^{th}$ moment of service time for i^{th} module invocation,
ρ = server utilization $= \sum_{i=1}^{n} \lambda_i \overline{u_i^1}$,
$\overline{w}$ = average module bulk waiting time.
From Eqs.(1) and (2), we obtained the variance of module bulk waiting time as

$$\sigma_w^2 = \overline{w^2} - (\overline{w})^2 = 2(\overline{w})^2 + \frac{\sum_{i=1}^{n} \lambda_i \overline{u_i^3}}{3(1-\rho)} - \left\{ \frac{\sum_{i=1}^{n} \lambda_i \overline{u_i^2}}{2(1-\rho)} \right\}^2 \tag{3}$$

In a bulk invocation, a set of modules are invoked at the same time. Based on the resource requirements, the operating system schedules the execution sequence for these modules. Let the sequence be $j_1, j_2, \ldots j_k, \ldots j_m$. The response time (a random variable) for module j_k is

$$t(j_k) = w + \sum_{i=1}^{k} x(j_i) \tag{4}$$

where:
w = module bulk waiting time,
$x(j_i)$ = execution time for module j_i.
The average response time $T(j_k)$ for module j_k can be obtained by taking the expected values of Eq.(4). We have

$$T(j_k) = \overline{w} + \sum_{i=1}^{k} \overline{x}(j_i) \tag{5}$$

Since w, $x(j_i)$ and $x(j_k)$ are independent random variables, the variance $\sigma_t^2(j_k)$ of the response time for module j_k is the sum of variances of each component in Eq.(4). Hence

$$\sigma_t^2(j_k) = \sigma_w^2 + \sum_{i=1}^{k} \sigma_x^2(j_i) \tag{6}$$

where $\sigma_x^2(j_k)$ is the variance of execution time for module j_k and σ_w^2 is given in Eq.(3). For the case of a single module invocation, there will be only a single module in the execution sequence.

2.2 Weighted Control-Flow Graph Model

To take into consideration the precedence waiting times due to the intermodule relationships as indicated in the task control-flow graph, we map the mean and variance of the module response times (computed by the module response time model) onto the control-flow graph as arc weights (Figure 2). The response time for module i is assigned as the weights for all arcs emerging from module i in the control-flow graph. After the execution of module i, if it enables module j which is residing on a different computer, the module enablement message is transmitted via the interconnection network. Since the network delay is independent of module response times, the mean and variance of network delay** can be added to the weight of the arc from module i to j. Then the task response time can be estimated from this weighted control-flow graph model.

*The model can be applied to other module scheduling policies with the use of appropriate queueing delay equations.

**Network delays among any pair of computers may be different depending upon the characteristics of the interconnection network.

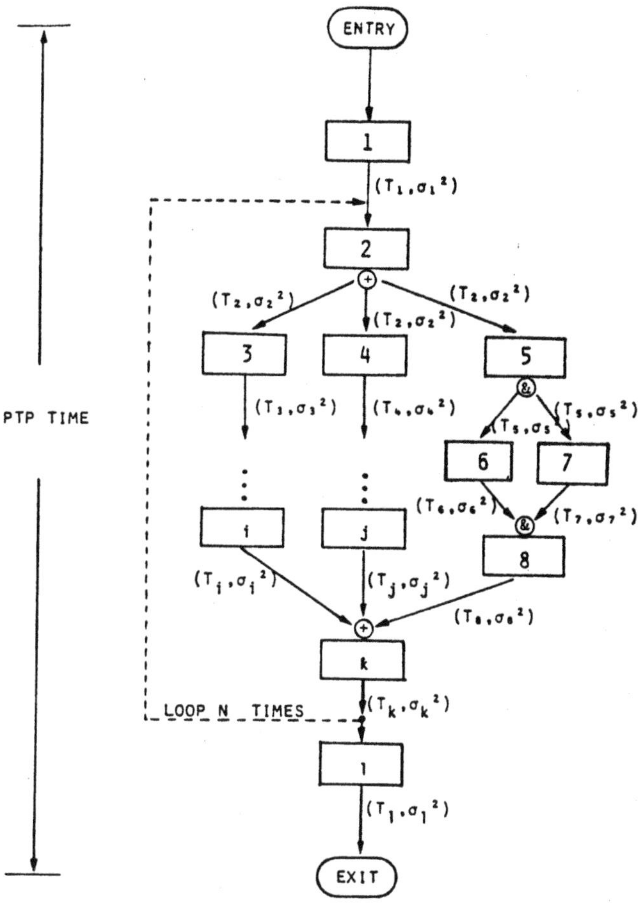

T_i - MEAN MODULE i RESPONSE TIME

σ_i^2 - VARIANCE OF MODULE i RESPONSE TIME

Figure 2. Weighted Control-Flow Graph for Response Time Estimations

According to the logical structures and precedence relationships among software modules, there are four common types of control-flow subgraphs: sequential thread, And-Fork to And-Join, Or-Fork to Or-Join, and loop (Figures 3 to 6). A task control-flow graph may contain a combination of these basic logical relationships among modules. Each of these graphs can be reduced to a single node graph. Such successive graph reductions yield the estimation of the task response time.

2.2.1 Sequential Thread Subgraph

Sequential thread subgraph (Figure 3) is a sequence of modules connected in series in which each module (except the last) has a single successor. Modules execute in the sequence indicated by the thread. Assuming that module response times represented by arc weights are random variables, then the total response time of the thread is the sum of all arc weights of each module.

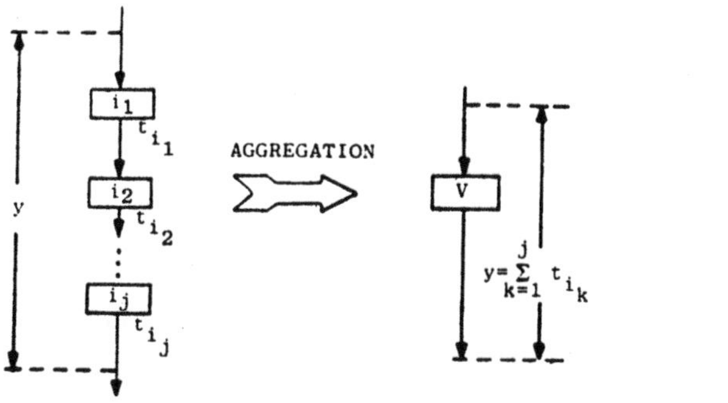

t_{i_j} : RESPONSE TIME OF MODULE i_j (RANDOM VARIABLE)

y : RESPONSE TIME FOR THE SEQUENTIAL THREAD (RANDOM VARIABLE)

Figure 3. Sequential Thread

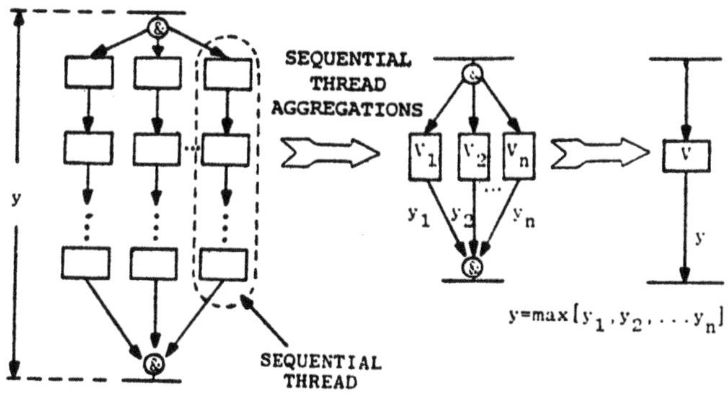

Figure 4. And-Fork To And-Join Subgraph

2.2.2 And-Fork to And-Join Subgraph

This subgraph begins from a module which simultaneously enables several succeeding modules *(an and-fork)* and ends at a module which is enabled only when all of its preceding modules have completed their executions *(an and-join)* as shown in Figure 4. This subgraph may correspond to the case in which the modules assigned to different computers require concurrent processing. Since sequential threads can be reduced to a single node as mentioned above, the and-fork to and-join subgraph can be aggregated into several nodes V_i with response time y_i for $i=1,2,\ldots,n$ (Figure 4). Because of the and-join function, the response time of the subgraph is the maximum of y_i's.

Computing the response time for this subgraph requires the knowledge of the PDF's for y_i's, which is rather complicated. In this study, we shall emphasize mainly the *average* task response time, which usually can be determined by the first two moments of module response times. Therefore, these moments are derived from the module response time model. According to the coefficients of variation of y_i's, they can be approximated by either Erlangian or hyper-exponential distribution functions[6]. Assuming that y_i's are independent, the joint PDF for y_i's can be computed. Thus the mean and variance of the response time for the subgraph can be obtained.

2.2.3 Or-Fork to Or-Join Subgraph

This type of the subgraph consists of an or-fork and an or-join as depicted in Figure 5. At the or-fork, the module enables one of its succeeding modules. This type of subgraph facilitates the system to process one out of several threads based on certain selection criteria. The branching probability to execute each thread can be measured or estimated from the IMC data. The response time for the subgraph is the weighted response times of all these threads.

2.2.4 Loop Subgraph

Loops are often contained in a task control-flow graph for repeatedly processing a set of modules for a task invocation. A loop may contain any of the aforementioned subgraphs. After aggregating these subgraphs, a loop may be represented by a single cyclic node graph as shown in Figure 6. The arc weight is the response time of executing a single loop. The response time of the loop subgraph can be computed from the average number of times that the loop is executed multiplied by the time required to execute a single loop.

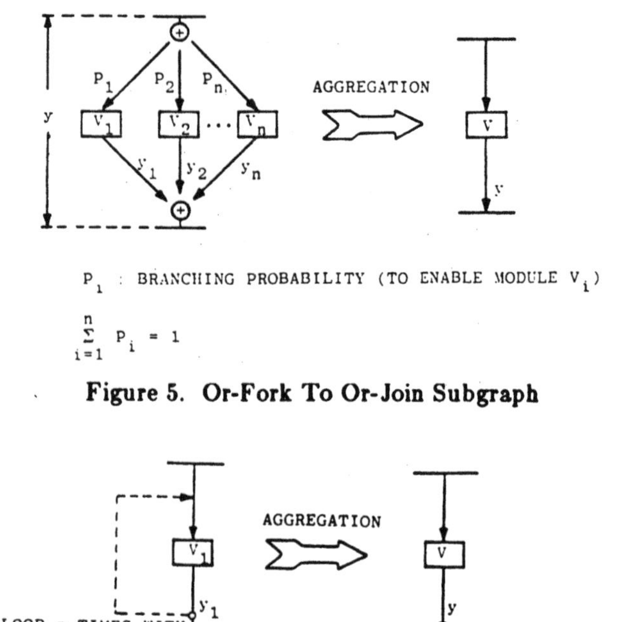

Figure 5. Or-Fork To Or-Join Subgraph

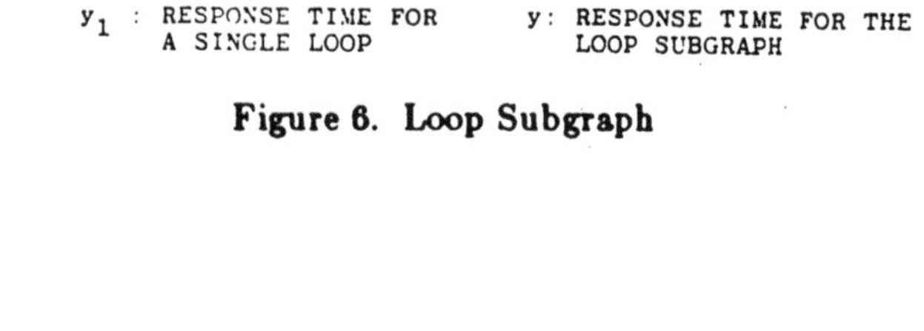

Figure 6. Loop Subgraph

2.3 Module Response Times With Dependent Module Invocations

In Section 2.1, module invocations are assumed to be independent and their interarrival times are Poisson distributed (assumptions 1 and 2). Thus, the logical dependency and the precedence relationships among modules are neglected when computing the module response times. The independence assumption is based on the following observations. Each computer is allocated with several modules which are enabled by modules residing on other computers. Since the operation of each computer is independent of each other, the module invocation arrival processes at each computer are random and thus can be approximated by independent Poisson processes. However, if a module is invoked by another module residing on the same computer (e.g., assigning a sequential thread to the computer), then the module invocations are dependent and non-Poisson arrivals. The error introduced in computing the mean module response times in such cases may be unacceptable. Therefore we introduce the following generalized model to compute the mean module response times for dependent module invocations.

2.3.1 Partitioning the Control-Flow Subgraphs

Based on a module assignment, we partition the control-flow graph into a set of subgraphs such that the modules of each subgraph are allocated to the same computer. Each control-flow subgraph on a computer is invoked by other computers via the interconnection network. Examples of such subgraphs are shown in Figure 7. Due to the relationships among modules as indicated in the subgraphs, the invocations of these modules are dependent upon each other. In addition, the dependency among the modules at the *forks* and *joins* increases the computation complexity for module response times. For tractability while considering the precedence relationships among modules, we further partition the subgraphs into several smaller ones at the forks or joins. As a result, the partitioned subgraphs become sequential threads (Figure 8). Figure 8a is a special case where two sequential threads are invoked simultaneously via bulk module invocations as they succeed an and-fork in the original control-flow subgraph. Further, if a sequential thread has an or-fork (Figure 8f) and the control branches to a module residing on another computer, then the execution terminates at the or-fork.

2.3.2 Mean Module Response Times for Partitioned Subgraphs

Since computing the mean module response time is simpler than computing its variance, we are able to relax assumptions 1 and 2. Let us refer to the first module of each sequential thread in a subgraph as the *entry module*, and other modules as *non-entry modules*. We assume: 1a) the invocations for the entry module(s)

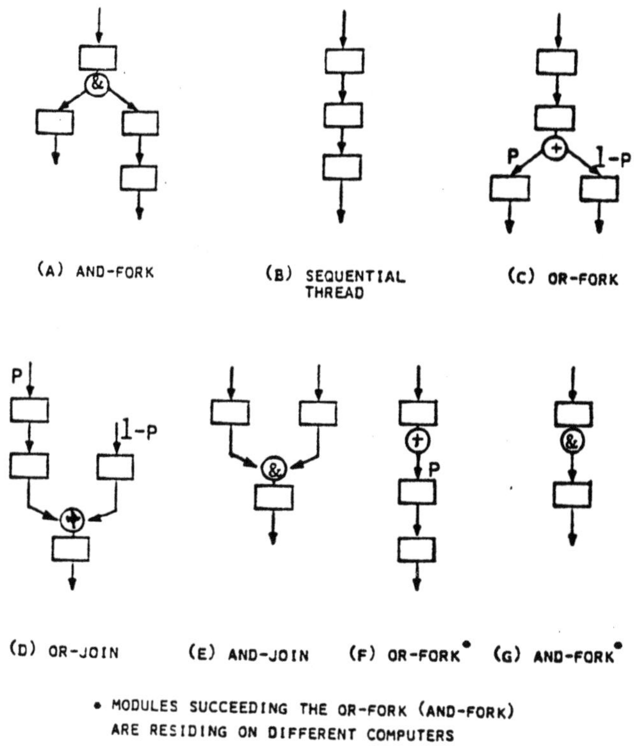

Figure 7. Examples of Control-Flow Subgraphs that Allocated on a Computer

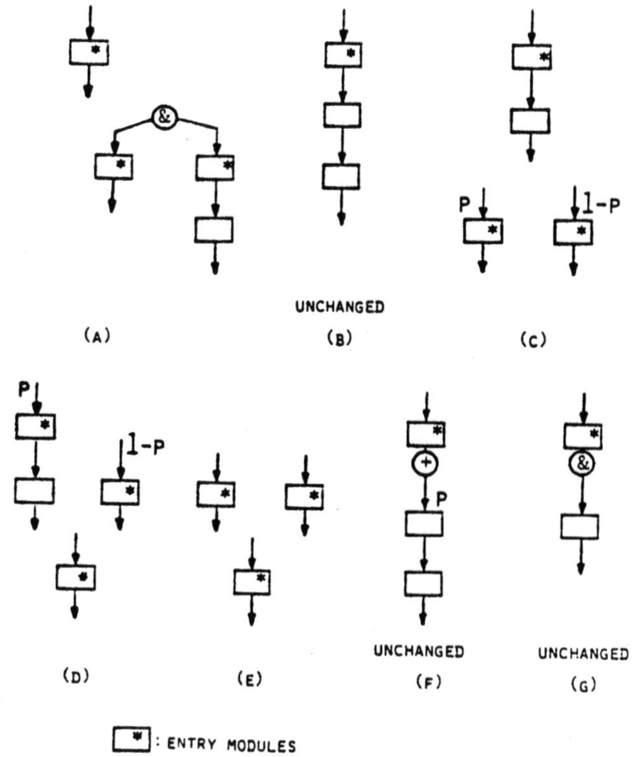

Figure 8. Partitioned Control-Flow Subgraphs of Figure 7

of each subgraph are independent of each other, 2a) the interarrival times of these invocations are exponentially distributed (i.e., Poisson arrival processes). In this case, only the invocations for the entry modules are independent and Poisson arrivals, and the invocations for non-entry modules may be dependent and non-Poisson arrivals. Thus the mean module response times* computed under these relaxed assumptions include such module precedence relationships as sequential threads, bulk module invocations at and-forks, and branching at or-forks.

Let us consider the response times for entry modules. Due to Poisson arrivals, the average waiting time for a given entry module is the processing time required to execute all the module invocations existing (waiting or being executed) on the computer upon the arrival of the entry module invocation. When several entry modules are invoked simultaneously, these modules are executed in a predefined sequence. Except the first module in the sequence, the mean module waiting time for a given entry module is the sum of the module bulk waiting time and the execution times of those modules processed prior to the module (Same as Eq.(4)).

*For mathematical tractability, the variances of module response times are computed under the independent Poisson assumptions.

Let us now consider the waiting times for non-entry modules. After an entry module finishes its execution, it enables its succeeding module as indicated in the subgraph. Since the invocation arrivals for the non-entry modules no longer form a Poisson arrival process, we need to keep track of the 'history' of the module executions since the arrival of that entry module invocation. During the waiting time of the entry module, new module invocations may arrive from other computers, and some of modules waiting in front of the entry module may invoke their succeeding modules. These module executions will become the waiting time for the non-entry module, which can be divided into three components, and computed as shown in the Appendix. The module response times can be obtained by summing the respective waiting and execution times.

Our study reveals that for most subgraphs, the module response times based on independent and Poisson module invocation assumptions are very close to those of the dependent module invocations. The dependent module invocation approach provides more accurate module response times only when the modules assigned on a computer form a long sequential thread. This reveals that assumptions 1 and 2 are reasonable, and provide good approximations for most cases.

3. MODEL VALIDATION

To validate the proposed task response time model, simulation experiments were performed via two simulation packages: a queueing network based simulation package PAWS [7], and a simulator of the Distributed Processing Architecture Design (DPAD) System [8] for real time space defense applications. In the PAWS simulation, computers are modeled as servers, and module invocations are represented as customers which request services from the servers. The service times correspond to the module execution times. After receiving service, a customer is transferred to another server queue according to the task control-flow graph and the module assignment. A customer goes through the interconnection network if it is transferred from one server to another. The network is represented by a server which always delays each customer according to the network delay distribution function before passing the customer to its destination server. As a result, the module invocations are dependent upon each other, and their arrivals are non-Poisson distributed. Further, the queueing discipline on a computer is also used for the corresponding server queue. For an AND-FORK operation, the module invocation is split into several modules and routed to their appropriate servers. For an AND-JOIN operation, the module following the join waits until all precedent modules complete their executions. The precedence and logical relationships among modules are preserved in the simulation. Therefore, PAWS provides a flexibility for testing different types of task control-flow graphs. However, it uses idealized external inputs (e.g., Poisson task invocation arrivals) and does not include the detailed operating system overhead.

We have performed the simulation to obtain the mean PTP times for selected types of task control-flow graphs. To reach the steady state of the queueing systems, the task is invoked ten thousand times for each simulation run. Further, each simulation experiment is repeated five times with different initial random numbers to reduce the statistical fluctuation. In this paper, let us consider the sample task control-flow graph in Figure 1a with its parameters given in Table 1. It consists of sequential threads, an And-Fork to And-Join, an Or-Fork to Or-Join, and a loop. These modules are assigned to three identical computers for processing, and the system has a constant network delay of 0.2 second for message exchanges among computers. Figures 9 to 12 present the mean response times for these subgraphs and the whole task for the module assignments (Table 2). We aggregate the response times of sequential threads, the and-fork to and-join, the or-fork to or-join, and the loop, and finally obtain the PTP time for the entire graph. Besides this control-flow graph, we have also studied the performance of the analytical model for various types of control-flow structures. The fact that mean response times from the analytical model compare closely with that of simulations reveals that the assumptions used in the analytical model (independent and Poisson module invocation arrivals) are good approximations for response time estimations.

The PAWS simulation is very time-consuming. Depending on task invocation rates and control-flow graphs, each simulation point requires five to eight hours of VAX-11/780 processing time. While for the analytical model, the response time computation for a given module assignment under various loading environments requires less that one minute of CPU time. This represents a reduction of three orders of magnitude in computation time!

MODULES	MEAN EXECUTION TIME (in sec)	EXECUTION TIME DISTRIBUTION
1, 2, 3, 4, 5	1	EXPONENTIAL
6, 7, 8, 9, 10	2	EXPONENTIAL
11, 12, 13, 14, 15	3	EXPONENTIAL

Table 1. Module Execution Times for the Sample Control-Flow Graph (Figure 1a)

COMPUTERS / LOADING / ASSIGNMENTS	CPU 1		CPU 2		CPU 3	
	MODULES ASSIGNED	PROCESSING LOAD (SEC) PER TASK INVOCATION	MODULES ASSIGNED	PROCESSING LOAD (SEC) PER TASK INVOCATION	MODULES ASSIGNED	PROCESSING LOAD (SEC) PER TASK INVOCATION
A	1, 5, 7, 9, 12, 13	5.125	2, 4, 8, 11, 15	5.875	3, 6, 10, 14	5.625
B	1, 3, 5, 7, 13	3.125	2, 6, 8, 9, 11, 12, 15	8.875	4, 10, 14	4.625

Table 2. Module Assignments & Computer Processing Load for the Sample Control-Flow Graph

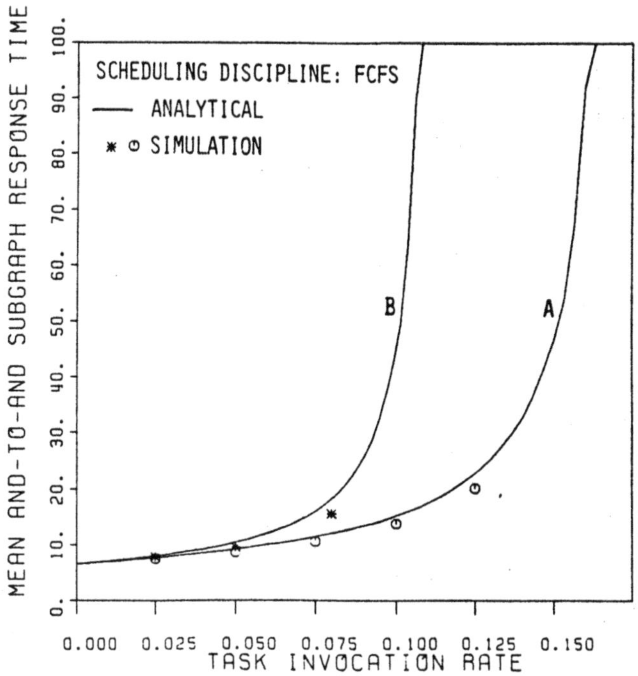

Figure 9. Mean Response Time for the And-Fork to And-Join Subgraph of the Sample Control-Flow Graph (Figure 1a)

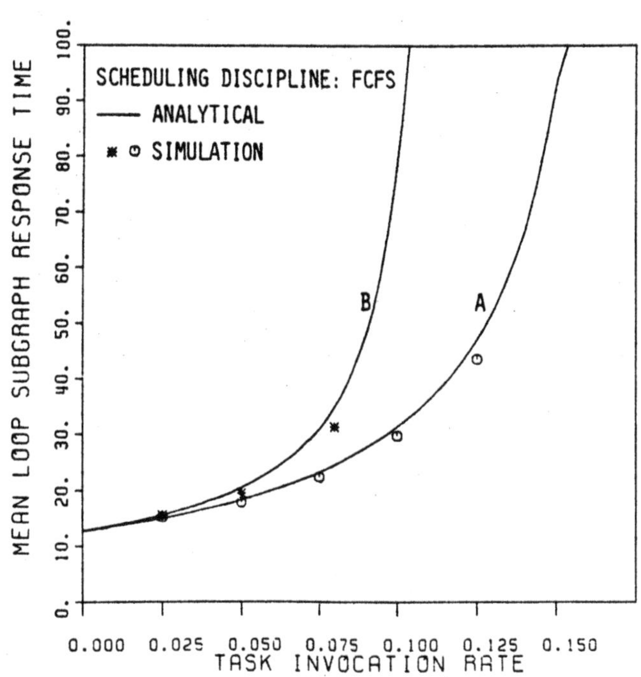

Figure 11. Mean Response Time for the Loop Subgraph of the Sample Control-Flow Graph

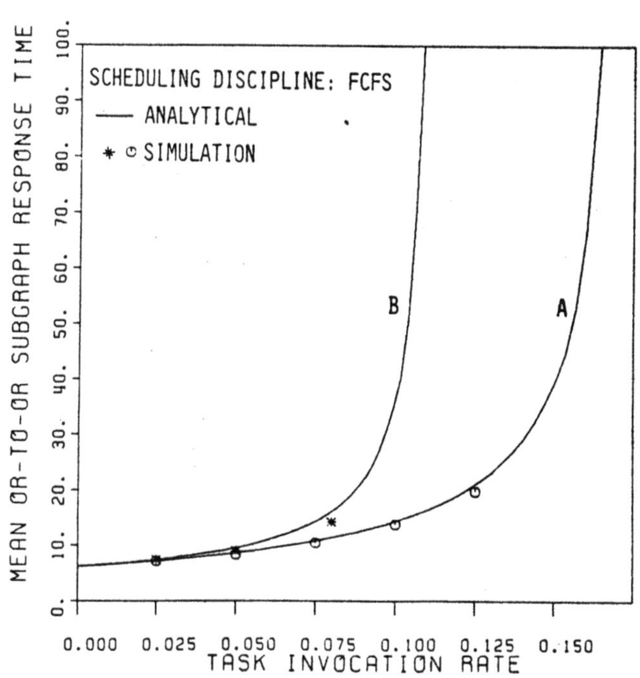

Figure 10. Mean Response Time for the Or-Fork to Or-Join Subgraph of the Sample Control-Flow Graph

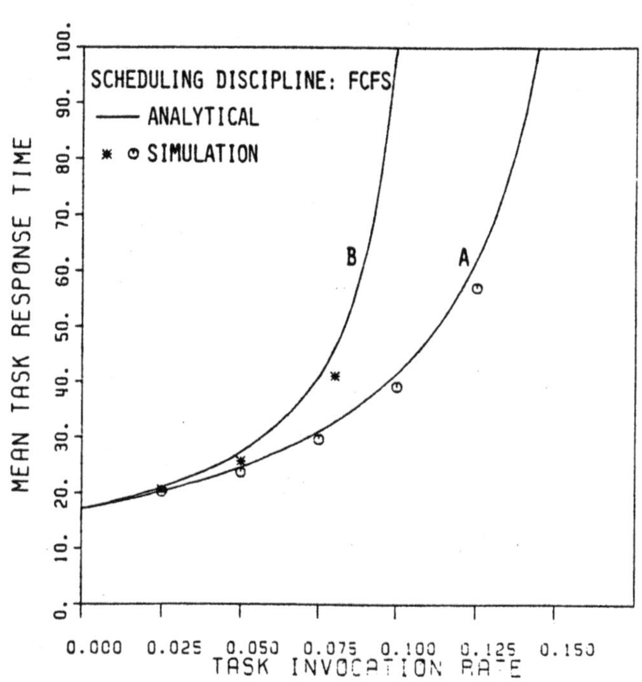

Figure 12. Mean Task Response Time for the Sample Control-Flow Graph

We now describe the model validation via the DPAD simulator+. The DPAD system is a real time DP system which processes radar return signals for space defense applications. The DPAD simulator provides detailed operating system operations for module scheduling and IPC message exchanges among computers. Further, non-Poisson task invocation arrivals are used. Its task control-flow graph is shown in Figure 13. The module assignment and module priorities are shown in Table 3. The processing thread for precision track function is indicated by shaded modules in Figure 13. For input data to the analytical model, we collected the IMC data, module execution times (Table 4) and invocation rates in every 100-msec time interval from the DPAD simulator. Since the DPAD System uses a priority module scheduling policy rather than FCFS, queueing formulas were derived to compute the module response times for this scheduling discipline. The PTP time was generated for each of these time intervals. To obtain the 90% confidence intervals for the task response time, the simulation was repeated five times. From Figure 14, we note that the PTP time predictions are close to the simulation measurements. This indicates that the model also provides a good response time estimation for non-Poisson task invocation arrivals with priority module scheduling policy and IPC overhead.

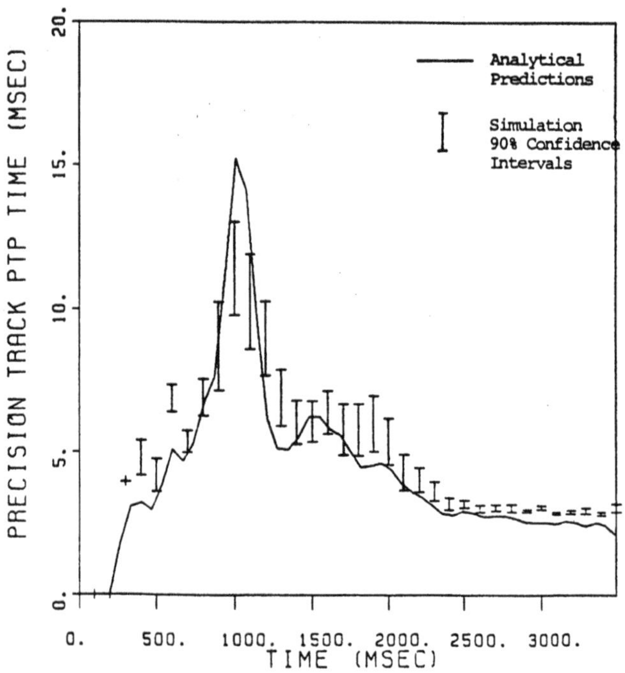

Figure 14. Comparing Analytical Predictions with the DPAD Simulation

+The DPAD simulator was originally developed at TRW and subsequently enhanced at UCLA to include facilities for measuring IMC data, module execution time and invocation statistics.

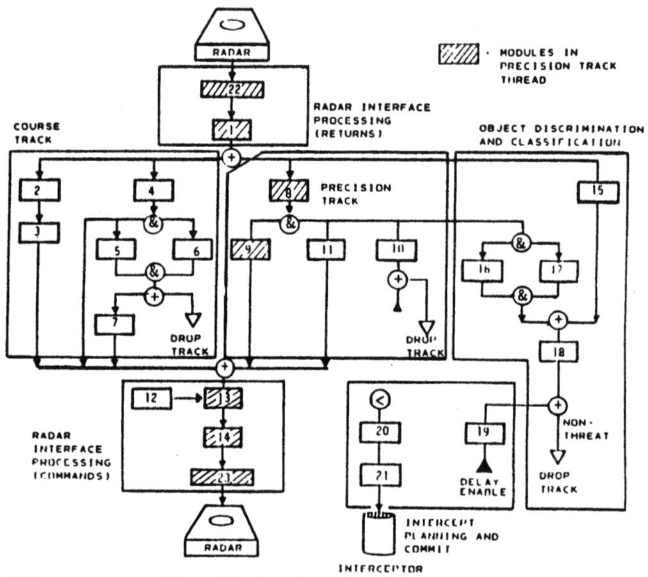

Figure 13. The Task Control-Flow Graph for the DPAD System

COMPUTERS	MODULE ASSIGNMENT
CPU 1	$M_1(1)$, $M_2(1)$, $M_4(1)$, $M_6(1)$, $M_8(1)$, $M_{10}(1)$, $M_{16}(1)$, $M_{22}(4)$
CPU 2	$M_3(1)$, $M_5(1)$, $M_9(1)$, $M_{17}(1)$, $M_{18}(1)$, $M_{19}(5)$, $M_{20}(6)$, $M_{21}(6)$
CPU 3	$M_7(1)$, $M_{11}(1)$, $M_{12}(1)$, $M_{13}(3)$, $M_{14}(2)$, $M_{15}(1)$, $M_{23}(4)$

$M_x(i)$: Module x with priority i. $M_x(i)$ has higher priority than $M_y(j)$ if $i > j$.

Table 3. A Module Assignment for the DPAD System

MODULES	MEAN EXECUTION TIME (ms)	COEF. OF VARIATION
1	0.157043	0.000163
2	0.313522	0.023414
3	0.397477	0.000066
4	0.422061	0.885611
5	0.379197	0.000042
6	0.321836	0.252115
7	0.325322	0.178972
8	1.128163	0.007556
9	0.659989	0.000000
10	0.535785	0.000236
11	0.000000	0.000000
12	0.000000	0.000000
13	0.334381	0.002888
14	0.131086	0.003647
15	0.000000	0.000000
16	0.717703	0.000090
17	1.017310	0.000000
18	0.656880	0.002384
19	3.339637	0.000003
20	6.695341	0.000012
21	0.730000	0.000000
22	0.080373	0.017631
23	0.162269	0.005263

Table 4. Module Execution Times (Including Output IPC) for the DPAD System Averaged over 35 100-msec Time Intervals

4. MODEL APPLICATIONS

The proposed model can be used to study the effect on response time of such design issues as module assignment and precedence relationships, module scheduling disciplines and database management algorithms. With the response time as a performance measure, the model can be used to study the tradeoffs among various design choices and to provide us insight into planning and evaluating distributed systems.

4.1 Module Assignment and Precedence Relationships

The assignment of modules to computers is an important problem in DP system design. Module assignment affects the response time, throughput, and system reliability. The factors that affect the module assignments are: a) computer processing capacities and their utilization factors, b) IMC among modules, and c) logical and precedence relationships among modules. Several approaches to the assignment problem in distributed systems have been proposed [9-12]. However, each of these approaches has its shortcomings such as neglecting queueing effect and precedence relationships. Therefore, the 'optimal' module assignments generated by them do not provide low response times on the actual systems. Our proposed model takes both computer load and precedence relationships into consideration. For a given module assignment, a module scheduling policy and a data management algorithm, the task response time can be estimated from the proposed model. The proposed model can be used to investigate the performance in terms of task response time of module assignment strategies with various module precedence relationships at different operating environments. This study provides insight into the interrelationship among precedence relationships, module assignment and task response time.

4.2 Module Scheduling Disciplines

For a given module assignment, the scheduling policy for module execution affects the response time. For example, to reduce operating system overhead, invocations for the same module may be delayed until a predefined number of module invocations have arrived and are executed in a batch manner. To avoid excessive waiting, a time-out mechanism may be used in conjunction with this scheduling policy. The proposed model can be employed to study the relationships among time-out constant, batch size, operating system overhead and the PTP time for this scheduling algorithm. Further, it can investigate the optimal assignment of module priorities for head-of-line priority scheduling policy and the relationships among scheduling policy, module assignment and the PTP time.

4.3 Database Management Strategies

Distributed systems require protocols to ensure internal and mutual data consistency for simultaneous access of replicated data files. These protocols require extra IPC, processing, and increase module response delays. Commonly used techniques for consistency controls are locking, timestamp, and exclusive-writer protocol [13,14]. In the proposed model, the effect of IPC can be included as a special module execution. If the module execution has to be delayed for handling the data consistency problem, the module execution time is correspondingly prolonged. Thus the model can be used to study the overhead in terms of PTP time of several commonly used database concurrency control algorithms such as locking, timestamping, and the exclusive-writer protocol. The results of these investigations should provide insight into the performance as well as overhead of concurrency control algorithms for distributed systems at various operating environments.

5. CONCLUSIONS

A new task response time model is presented for estimating the PTP time for distributed processing systems. The model maps the module response times into the task control-flow graph as arc weights and estimates the PTP time from the weighted task control-flow graph model. Since this approach considers the queueing effects, the interconnection network delays, and the logical relationships among modules, the model provides accurate PTP time prediction. Simulation experiments reveal that the proposed model provides fairly accurate PTP time. The model can be used to study module assignment problem and the effect of precedence relationships among modules on the PTP time. In addition, it can be used to study other design issues such as module scheduling policy, database management algorithm, etc. Thus this model serves as a valuable tool for the systematic planning and designing of distributed processing systems.

Acknowledgement

The authors wish to thank Min-Tsung Lan of UCLA and Joseph Hellerstein of IBM Thomas J. Watson Research Center (formerly of UCLA) for their effort in collecting various statistics for our DPAD model validation.

REFERENCES

[1] W.W. Chu, M.T. Lan and J. Hellerstein, "Estimation of Intermodule Communication (IMC) and Its Applications in Distributed Processing Systems," *IEEE Trans. on Computers*, Vol.C-33, No.8, Aug. 1984, pp.691-699.

[2] W.W. Chu, L. Holloway, M.T. Lan and Kemal Efe, "Task Allocation in Distributed Processing," *IEEE Computer,* Nov. 1980, pp. 57-69.

[3] F. Basket, K.M. Candy, R. Muntz, and F. G. Palacios, "Open, Closed, and Mixed Networks of Queues with Different Classes of Customers," *Journal of the ACM,* Vol. 22, No. 2, April 1975, pp. 248-260.

[4] P. Heidelberger, and K.S. Trivedi, "Queueing Network Models for Parallel Processing with Asynchronous Tasks," *IEEE Trans. on Computers,* Nov. 1982, pp. 1099-1109.

[5] E.D. Lazowska, J. Zahorjan, G.S. Graham & K.C. Sevcik, *Quantitative System Performance: Computer System Analysis Using Queueing Network Models,* Prentice-Hall, New Jersey (1984).

[6] C.H. Sauer and K.M. Chandy, *Computer Systems Performance Modeling,* Prentice-Hall, New Jersey (1981).

[7] R. Berry, K.M. Chandy, J. Misra, and D. Neuse, *PAWS 2.0 Performance Analyst's Workbench System: User Manual,* Information Research Associates, Austin, Texas, Dec. 1982.

[8] M.L. Green, E.Y.S. Lee, S. Majumdar, and D.C. Shannon, "Phase III of Distributed Processing Architecture Design (DPAD) Program -- The DDP Underlay Simulation Experiment: Tactical Applications and d-RTOS Models," *Special Report* 35010-79-A005, TRW Defense and Space Systems Group, May 15, 1980.

[9] H.S. Stone, "Multiprocessor Scheduling with the Aid of Network Flow Algorithms," *IEEE Trans. on Software Eng.,* Vol.SE-3, No.1, Jan. 1977, pp.85-93.

[10] G.S. Rao, H.S. Stone and T.C. Hu, "Assignment of Tasks in a Distributed Processor System with Limited Memory," *IEEE Trans. on Computers,* Vol.C-28, No.4, April 1979, pp.291-299.

[11] P.Y.R. Ma, E.Y.S. Lee and M. Tsuchiya, "A Task Allocation Model for Distributed Computing System," *IEEE Trans. on Computers,* Vol.C-31, No.1, Jan. 1982, pp.41-47.

[12] T.C.K. Chou and J.A. Abraham, "Load Balancing in Distributed Systems," *IEEE Trans. on Software Eng.,* Vol.SE-8, No.8, July 1982, pp.401-412.

[13] P.A. Bernstein and N. Goodman, "Concurrency Control in Distributed Database Systems," *Computing Surveys* 13, 2, June 1981, pp. 185-221.

[14] W.W. Chu and J. Hellerstein, "The Exclusive-Writer Approach to Updating Replicated Files in Distributed Processing Systems," to appear in *IEEE Trans. on Computer,* 1985.

[15] J.D.C. Little, "A Proof of the Queueing Formula $L = \lambda W$," *Operations Research,* 9, pp.383-387(1961).

Appendix

Computation of Mean Module Response Times with Dependent Invocations

Consider a computer allocated with modules of v distinct control-flow subgraphs. Each subgraph consists of one or more sequential threads which may be invoked simultaneously (See Figure 8a). Assume that the ith subgraph consists of b_i sequential threads, and the jth sequential thread comprises $d_i(j)$ modules for $j=1,2,...b_i$. For a subgraph consists of a single sequential thread, then $b_i = 1$. Let $M_i(j;k)$ be the kth module (starting from the entry module) of the jth sequential thread for the ith subgraph. In addition, let $P_i(j;k,t)$ be the probability of invoking $M_i(j;t)$ given that $M_i(j;k)$ is executed for $i=1,2,...v$, $j=1,2,...b_i$ and $1 \leq k \leq t \leq d_i(j)$. Thus if a subgraph does not contain any or-fork, $P_i(j;k,t) = 1$ for all k and t. For a subgraph containing a branch of an or-fork, the modules in this branch are not invoked if the control branches to the modules that do not reside on the same computer. Thus we have,

$$P_i(j;k,k) = 1 \qquad (A.1)$$

and $$P_i(j;k,k+a) = \prod_{t=k}^{k+a-1} P_i(j;t,t+1) \qquad (A.2)$$

for $1 \leq k \leq k+a \leq d_i(j)$.

Mean Waiting Time for Entry Modules

Let $W_i(j;k)$ be the mean waiting time for module $M_i(j;k)$. According to the assumptions 1a and 2a, the mean waiting time for $M_i(1;1)$ (i.e., an entry module) for all $i=1,2,...v$ under the first-come-first-serve discipline is the average time to complete the current module execution and all the modules in the job queue on the computer when the invocation for $M_i(1;1)$ arrives. Thus we have

$$W_i(1;1) = W_o + \sum_{r=1}^{v} \sum_{s=1}^{b_r} \sum_{t=1}^{d_r(s)} \bar{n}_r(s;t)\, \bar{x}_r(s;t) \qquad (A.3)$$

where:

$\bar{n}_r(s;t) =$ average number of invocations for $M_r(s;t)$ waiting in the job queue,

$\bar{x}_r(s;t) =$ average execution time for $M_r(s;t)$,

$W_o =$ mean residual module execution time

$$= \sum_{r=1}^{r} \sum_{s=1}^{b_r} \sum_{t=1}^{d_r(s)} \frac{1}{2} \lambda_r(s;t)\, \overline{x^2}_r(s;t),$$

$\overline{x^2}_r(s;t) =$ second moment of execution time for $M_r(s;t)$,

$\lambda_r(s;t) =$ invocation rate for $M_r(s;t)$.

Based on Little's result[16] (i.e., $\bar{n}_r(s;t) = \lambda_r(s;t)\, W_r(s;t)$) and substituting the computer utilization of $M_r(s;t)$, $\rho_r(s;t) = \lambda_r(s;t)\, \bar{z}_r(s;t)$, into Eq.(A.3), we have

$$W_i(1;1) = W_o + \sum_{r=1}^{v} \sum_{s=1}^{b_r} \sum_{t=1}^{d_r(s)} \rho_r(s;t)\, W_r(s;t) \qquad (A.4)$$

For simplicity in notation, we can order the thread index j such that the execution sequence for the bulk module invocations is to execute module $M_i(j;1)$ before module $M_i(s;1)$ for $j<s$. Thus the mean waiting time $W_i(j;1)$ is

$$W_i(j;1) = W_i(1;1) + \sum_{s=1}^{j-1} \bar{z}_i(s;1) \qquad (A.5)$$

for $i=1,2,\ldots v$, and $b_i \geq j \geq 2$.

Mean Waiting Time for Non-Entry Modules

Let us consider the waiting time for the non-entry modules $M_i(j;k)$ (i.e., with $k\geq 2$). After completing its execution, a module invokes its succeeding module, if any, and places the invocation at the end of the job queue. Since these invocation arrivals are dependent and non-Poisson distributed, we need to keep track of the invocations generated from the modules residing on the local computer as well as the newly arrived module invocation from other computers. The waiting time for the non-entry modules can be divided into three components. The first component, $W1_i(j;k)$, is due to the executions of the succeeding modules invoked by the module invocations which are being executed or waiting in the job queue upon the arrival of the invocation for $M_i(j;1)$. The second component, $W2_i(j;k)$, is due to the waiting for the module executions invoked by the bulk module invocations (i.e., $M_i(s;1)$, $s = 1, \cdots b_i$ and $s \neq j$). The last component, $W3_i(j;k)$, is the waiting time due to the module invocations from other computers that arrive after the invocation for the entry module and their succeeding modules. Thus,

$$W1_i(j;k) = \sum_{r=1}^{v} \sum_{s=1}^{b_r} \sum_{t=1}^{d_r(s)-k+1} \bar{n}_r(s;t)\, P_r(s;t,t+k-1)\, \bar{z}_r(s;t+k-1)$$

$$+ \sum_{r=1}^{v} \sum_{s=1}^{b_r} \sum_{t=1}^{d_r(s)-k+1} \rho_r(s;t)\, P_r(s;t,t+k-1)\, \bar{z}_r(s;t+k-1) \qquad (A.6)$$

The first term of Eq.(A.6) is the total time for executing the succeeding modules invoked by $M_r(s;t)$ waiting in the job queue upon the arrival of the invocation for $M_i(j;1)$. Similarly, the second term is the execution times of the modules succeeding the module $M_r(s;t)$ which has probability $\rho_r(s;t)$ of being executed when the invocation for $M_i(j;1)$ arrives.

According to the definition of invocation probability $P_r(s;t,t+k-1)$,

$$\lambda_r(s;t+k-1) = \lambda_r(s;t)\, P_r(s;t,t+k-1) \qquad (A.7)$$

Applying Little's result and substituting Eq.(A.7) and $\rho_r(s;t) = \lambda_r(s;t)\, \bar{z}_r(s;t)$ into Eq.(A.6), after some algebraic manipulation, it yields

$$W1_i(j;k) = \sum_{r=1}^{v} \sum_{s=1}^{b_r} \sum_{t=1}^{d_r(s)-k+1} \rho_r(s;t+k-1)[W_r(s;t) + \bar{z}_r(s;t)] \qquad (A.8)$$

The second component of $W_i(j;k)$ is

$$W2_i(j;k) = \sum_{s=1}^{j-1} P_i(s;1,k)\, \bar{z}_i(s;k) + \sum_{s=j+1}^{b_i} P_i(s;1,k-1)\, \bar{z}_i(s;k-1) \qquad (A.9)$$

The first term in Eq.(A.9) is the execution times for the modules succeeding the entry module(s) ($M_i(s;1)$ for $s<j$) that are executed before $M_i(j;1)$ in the bulk module invocation. The second term is the execution times of those modules succeeding the entry module(s) ($M_i(s;1)$ for $s>j$) executed after $M_i(j;1)$.

The third component of $W_i(j;k)$ is used to keep track of the new module invocations that arrive after the invocation for the entry module $M_i(j;1)$ an . their succeeding modules subsequently generated from the newly arrived invocations. Thus, we have

$$W3_i(j;k) = [W_i(j;k-1) + \bar{z}_i(j;k-1)] \sum_{r=1}^{v} \sum_{s=1}^{b_r} \lambda_r(s;1)\, \bar{z}_r(s;1)$$

$$+ [W_i(j;k-2) + \bar{z}_i(j;k-2)] \sum_{r=1}^{v} \sum_{\substack{s=1 \\ d_r(s)\geq 2}}^{b_r} \lambda_r(s;1)\, P_r(s;1,2)\, \bar{z}_r(s;2)$$

$$+ \\ \vdots$$

$$+ [W_i(j;1) + \bar{z}_i(j;1)] \sum_{r=1}^{v} \sum_{\substack{s=1 \\ d_r(s)\geq k-1}}^{b_i} \lambda_r(s;1)\, P_r(s;1,k-1)\, \bar{z}_r(s;k-1) \qquad (A.10)$$

Due to the first-come-first-serve scheduling, those module invocations from other computers arriving during the response time (waiting plus execution) of $M_i(j;k-1)$ contribute a part of the waiting time for $M_i(j;k)$. Thus the first term of Eq.(A.10) is the total time for executing those module invocations arriving during the response time of $M_i(j;k-1)$. Likewise, the remaining terms of Eq.(A.10) are the times for executing those module invocations from the same computer where $P_r(s;1,t)$ represents the probability that $M_r(s;1)$ invokes $M_r(s;t)$. After substituting $\lambda_r(s;t) = \lambda_r(s;1)\, P_r(s;1,t)$ and $\rho_r(s;t) = \lambda_r(s;t)\, \bar{z}_r(s;t)$ into Eq.(A.10), and simplifying, we have

$$W3_i(j;k) = \sum_{t=1}^{k-1} \left\{ [W_i(j;t) + \bar{z}_i(j;t)] \sum_{r=1}^{v} \sum_{\substack{s=1 \\ d_r(s)\geq k-t}}^{b_r} \rho_r(s;k-t) \right\} \qquad (A.11)$$

Therefore, the mean module waiting time for $M_i(j;k)$ is

$$W_i(j;k) = W1_i(j;k) + W2_i(j;k) + W3_i(j;k) \qquad (A.12)$$

for $i=1,2,\ldots v$, $j=1,2,\ldots b_i$, and $d_i(j) \geq k \geq 2$.

The mean module waiting time for each module is expressed in Eq.(A.4), (A.5) or (A.12). They can be determined by solving this set of linear equations. The mean response time for each module is the sum of its mean waiting time and mean execution time.

Chapter 5

FAULT TOLERANT DESIGN OF DISTRIBUTED SYSTEMS

Fault tolerance is an important requirement in modern computer systems. Distributed systems, because of their available multiple processor and memory modules, have the natural capabilities to provide fault tolerance. There are many ways we can implement fault tolerance, for example, hardware replication and voting, software checkpoints, software voting, *et cetera* [IEEE 78]. For a recent survey on this subject, see [RENN 84].

In this chapter, we shall place more emphasis on fault tolerance for distributed systems. The first paper by Siewiorek provides an overview of fault tolerance technique. The second paper by Serlin provides an extensive survey of available commercial fault tolerant computer systems, their hardware features, and fault tolerance principles. The third paper by Wallace and Barnes describes the software fault tolerant design for the Unix RTR operating system. The testing results show that the system achieves high levels of availability. The last paper by Kim explores the concept of distributed execution of recovery block as an approach for unified treatment of hardware and software faults. Experimental results indicate the feasibility of incorporating such a distributed execution scheme into real time computer systems.

Should the system be highly reliable or highly available? This is one of a multitude of questions the architect must answer in developing a fault-tolerant system.

Architecture of Fault-Tolerant Computers*

Daniel P. Siewiorek, Carnegie-Mellon University

System reliability has been a major concern since the beginning of the age of electronic digital computers. The earliest computers were constructed of components such as relays and vacuum tubes that would fail to operate correctly as often as once every hundred, thousand, or million cycles. This error rate was far too high to ensure correct completion of even modest calculations requiring tens of millions of operating cycles. The Bell relay computer (c. 1944) performed a computation twice and compared results; it also employed error-detecting codes. The first commercial computer, the Univac I (c. 1951), utilized extensive parity checking and two arithmetic logic units in a match-and-compare mode. Today, interest in reliability pervades the computer industry, from large mainframe manufacturers to semiconductor fabricators who produce not only reliability-specific chips (such as those used for error-correcting codes) but also entire systems (such as the Intel 432).[2]

Computer designers have to be students of reliability, as do computer system users. Our dependence on computing systems has grown to the extent that it is becoming difficult or impossible to return to less sophisticated mechanisms. When an airline-seat-selection computer fails, for example, the airline can no longer revert to assigning seats from a manual checklist: since the addition of round-trip check-in service, the computer must be consulted to determine which seats have been assigned to passengers who have not yet checked in. The last resort is a free-for-all rush for seats. The computer system user must be able to understand the advantages and limitations of the state-of-the-art in reliability design, determine the impact of those advantages and limitations upon the applications or computation at hand, and specify the requirements for the system's reliability so that the application or computation can be successfully completed.

Fault-tolerant computing is the correct execution of a specified algorithm in the presence of defects. The effect of defects can be overcome by the use of redundancy. This redundancy can be either temporal (repeated executions) or physical (replicated hardware or software).

As in all systems design, system specifications constrain the design space—and thus the design techniques—that can be used. At the highest level of specification, fault-tolerant systems are categorized as either highly available or highly reliable.

The availability of a system as a function of time, $A(t)$, is the probability that the system is operational at the instant of time, t. If the limit of this function exists as time goes to infinity, it expresses the expected fraction of time that the system is available to perform useful computations. Activities such as preventive maintenance and repair reduce the time that the system is available to the user. Availability is typically used as a basis for evaluating systems in which service can be delayed or denied for short periods without serious consequences.

The reliability of a system as a function of time, $R(t)$, is the conditional probability that the system has survived the interval $[0,t]$, given that it was operational at time $t = 0$. Reliability is used to describe systems in which it is not feasible to repair the system "on line" (as in satellite computers) or in which the computer is serving a critical function and cannot be lost even for the duration of a repair (as in flight computers on aircraft) or in which the repair is prohibitively expensive. In general, it is more difficult to build a highly reliable computing system than a highly available one because of the more stringent requirements imposed by the reliability definition. An even more stringent definition sometimes used in aerospace applications is the maximum number of failures anywhere in the system that the system can tolerate and still function correctly.

Taxonomy

There are two approaches to increased reliability: fault avoidance (fault intolerance) and fault tolerance.[3] Fault avoidance results from conservative design practices, such as the use of high-reliability components, component

*This article is based on portions of Chapter 3, "Reliability and Availability Techniques," by S. Elkind, and Introduction to Part II, "The Practice of Reliable System Design."[1]

burn-in, and careful signal-path routing. The goal of fault avoidance is to reduce the possibility of a failure. Even with the most careful fault avoidance, however, failures will eventually occur and result in system failure (hence the name fault intolerance). In fault-tolerant designs, *redundancy* is used to provide the information needed to negate the effects of failures. The redundancy is manifested in one of two ways: extra time or extra components. One form of "time redundancy" involves extra executions of the same calculation, perhaps by different methods. Comparisons or other operations on the multiple results (identical when no errors are present) provide the basis for subsequent action. Time redundancy is usually provid by software. Component redundancy is the use of ext gates, memory cells, bus lines, functional modules, a the like to supply the extra information needed to gua against the effect of failures.

A redundant system may go through as many as stages in response to the occurrence of a failure. The stages—fault confinement, fault detection, fault maskir retry, diagnosis, reconfiguration, recovery, restart, repa and reintegration—are explained in the box belo Designing a redundant system involves the selection of coordinated failure response that combines some or all

The stages in response to failure

Fault confinement. When faults occur, it is desirable to limit the scope of their effects. Fault confinement is achieved by limiting the spread of fault effects to one area of the system, thereby preventing contamination of other areas. Fault confinement can be achieved through liberal use of fault-detection circuits, through consistency checks before performing a function ("mutual suspicion"), and through multiple requests/confirmations before performing a function. These techniques may be applied in both hardware and software.

Fault detection. Most failures eventually result in logical faults. Many techniques are available to detect faults, such as parity, consistency checking, and protocol violation. Unfortunately, these techniques are not perfect, and an arbitrary period of time may pass before detection occurs. This time is called "fault latency." Fault-detection techniques are of two major classes: off-line detection and on-line detection. With off-line detection, the device is not able to perform useful work while under test. Diagnostic programs, for example, run in a stand-alone fashion even if executed on idle devices or multiplexed with the operations software. Thus, off-line detection assures integrity before and possibly at intervals during operation, but not during the entire time of operation. On-line detection, on the other hand, provides a real-time detection capability, for it is performed concurrently with useful work. On-line techniques include parity detection and duplication.

Fault masking. Fault-masking techniques hide the effects of failures. In a sense, the redundant information outweighs the incorrect information. In its pure form, masking provides no detection. However, many fault-masking techniques can be extended to provide on-line detection as well. Otherwise, off-line detection techniques are needed to discover failures. Majority voting is an example of fault masking.

Retry. In many cases, a second attempt at an operation may be successful. This is particularly true of a transient fault that causes no physical damage.

Diagnosis. If the fault-detection technique does not provide information about the failure location and/or properties, a diagnostic step may be required.

Reconfiguration. If a fault is detected and a permanent failure located, the system may be able to reconfigure its components to replace the failed component or to isolate it from the rest of the system. The component may be replaced by backup spares. Alternatively, it may simply be switched off and the system capability degraded: this process is called "graceful degradation."

Recovery. After detection and (if necessary) reconfiguration, the effects of errors must be eliminated. Normally, the system operation is backed up to some point in its processing that preceded the fault detection, and operation recommences from this point. This form of recovery, often called "rollback," usually entails strategies using backup files, checkpointing, and journaling. In recovery, error latency becomes an important issue because the rollback must go far enough to avoid the effects of undetected errors that occurred before the detected one.

Restart. Recovery may not be possible if too much information is damaged by an error, or if the system is not designed for recovery. A "hot" restart—that is, a resumption of all operations from the point of fault detection—is possible only if no damage has occurred. A "warm" restart implies that only some of the processes can be resumed without loss. A "cold" restart corresponds to a complete reload of the system, with no processes surviving.

Repair. When a component is diagnosed as "failed," it is replaced. As with detection, repair (replacing defective components) can be either on-line or off-line. In off-line repair, either the failed component is not necessary for system operation and can be removed without bringing down the system, or the entire system must be brought down to perform the diagnosis and repair. In on-line repair, the component may be replaced immediately by a backup spare in a procedure equivalent to reconfiguration, or operation may continue without the component as is the case with masking redundancy or graceful degradation. In either case of on-line repair, the failed component may be physically replaced or repaired without interrupting system operation.

Reintegration. After the physical replacement of a component, the repaired module must be reintegrated into the system. For on-line repair, reintegration must be accomplished without interrupting system operation.

these stages. The ordering of the stages just mentioned corresponds roughly to the normal chronology although the actual timing may be different in some instances.

Figure 1 depicts one scenario that illustrates some of the preceding concepts. The time line illustrates the stages in fault handling for a nonfault-tolerant system; fault-tolerant systems automate one or more of these stages. Upon detection, a fault-tolerant system is brought down, diagnosed, and manually reconfigured to allow a restart. Before operation recommences, the software process must be rolled back to a point before the errors occurred and then restarted. Finally, after the failed module is repaired and put back on line, the system is halted temporarily to allow the module to be reintegrated into the system. Figure 1 also illustrates some reliability measurement concepts: the mean time to failure, or MTTF; mean time to detection, or MTTD—sometimes called error latency; mean time to repair, or MTTR; and availability.

Taking these system-failure response stages into account, the spectrum of fault-tolerance techniques can be divided into three major classes: *fault detection, masking redundancy,* and *dynamic redundancy.* Figure 2 proposes a taxonomy of system-failure response strategies.

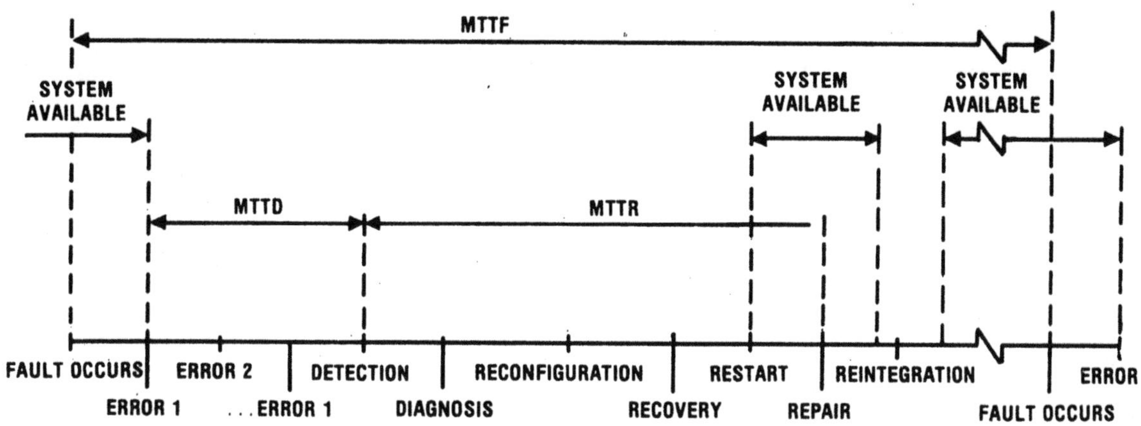

Figure 1. A scenario for on-line detection and off-line repair. The measures—mean time to failure, MTTF, mean time to detect, MTTD, and mean time to repair, MTTR—are the average times to failure, to detection, and to repair, respectively.

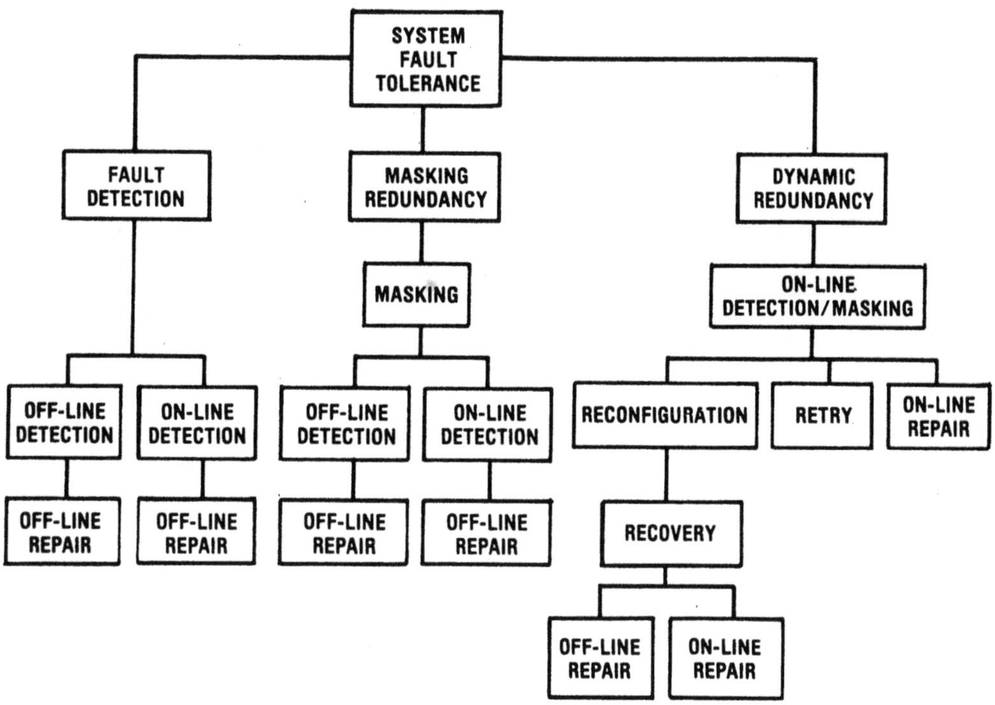

Figure 2. The taxonomy of system fault-tolerance strategies.

Fault detection provides no tolerance to faults, but gives warning when they occur. It is used in many small systems (such as microcomputers and minicomputers), some of which may incorporate simple on-line detection mechanisms. This branch does not represent fault tolerance in the strictest sense: even though faults are detected, they cannot be tolerated (except for retry upon transient faults).

Masking redundancy, also called *static redundancy,* tolerates failures but gives no warning of them. It is used in such systems as computers with error-correcting code memories, or with majority-voted redundancy in a fixed configuration (in the latter, an odd number of redundant copies perfom identical computations, a subsequent vote determines the correct output with the majority prevailing, and circuit elements remain constant).

The rightmost branch of the figure covers those systems whose configuration can be dynamically changed in response to a fault, or in which masking redundancy, supplemented by on-line fault detection, allows on-line repair. Examples are multiprocessor systems, which can degrade gracefully in response to processing element failures, and triplicated systems, which include disagreement detection in the voter and are designed for on-line repair.

The range in cost of fault-tolerant techniques is almost a continuum in terms of percentage of redundancy. Figure 3 depicts three regions of hardware redundancy, each corresponding to one of the three major areas of the fault-tolerance technique spectrum. Even though most techniques in each area fit within these regions, individual techniques may fall well outside of them. The divisions drawn are not exact, however. Some basic techniques have properties pertaining to more than one region and some, while they should be considered basic techniques in their own right, require concurrent use of other techniques (for example, failure detection is needed to invoke replacement of a broken module with a spare).

Table 1 summarizes the major techniques now in use. In many cases, the technique listed is only a representative of a class of similar techniques. The table is partitioned according to the taxonomy in Figure 2. In the following portion of this article, we will briefly discuss the techniques from a historical perspective. More details can be found in other articles in this issue, as well as in the book on which this article is based.[1]

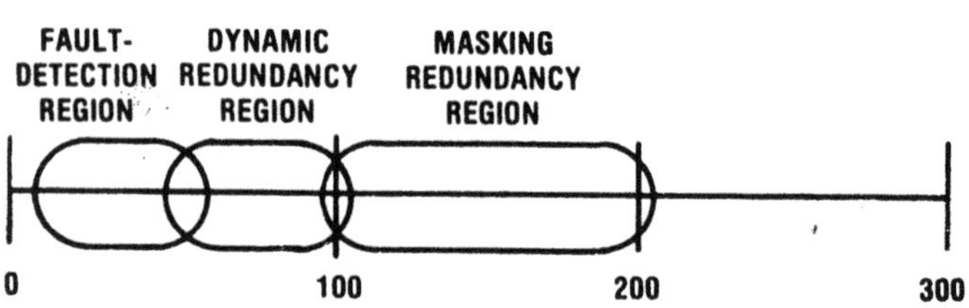

Figure 3. Cost range of fault-tolerance techniques for three areas of hardware redundancy (in terms of the redundancy required).

Fault-avoidance techniques

One method of increasing computer reliability is to lessen the possibility of failures (fault avoidance). If fault avoidance alone cannot economically meet system design goals, fault-detection and/or fault-tolerance techniques must be used. Some fault-avoidance techniques are intended to decrease the possibility of transient faults. Careful signal routing, shielding, cabinet grounding, and input-line static filters are examples of techniques that effectively increase the signal-to-noise ratio. Other techniques are useful against both "hard" and transient faults. A design rule that limits the fan-out of gates to a small number, for example, decreases power dissipation (hence reducing thermal effects) and thus the probability of hard failures. Fan-out limitation also increases the effective noise margin at the inputs of subsequent gates and thus decreases the possibility of a transient fault. Another concern is the avoidance of human errors through such measures as labeling and documentation. In addition, the possibility of assembly errors should be minimized. For example, many manufacturers produce printed circuit boards and connectors that are shaped in such a way that they cannot be plugged in backward or into the wrong slots. System reliability can be improved by changing environmental factors (such as temperature and vibration), improving component quality (for example, by incoming inspection and burn-in), and by increasing the level of circuit integration (thereby reducing solder joints, power dissipation, and physical area).

Table 1. Classification of reliability techniques.

REGION	TECHNIQUE
Fault avoidance	Environment modification
	Quality changes
	Component integration level
Fault detection	Duplication
	Error detection codes
	Parity
	Check sums
	Arithmetic codes
	Cyclic codes
	Self-checking and fail-safe logic
	Watchdog timers and time-outs
	Consistency and capability checks
Masking redundancy	Voting
	Error correcting codes
	Hamming SEC/DED
	Other codes
	Masking logic
	Interwoven logic
	Coded-state machines
Dynamic redundancy	Reconfigurable duplication
	Reconfigurable voting
	Backup sparing
	Graceful degradation
	Reconfiguration
	Recovery

Fault detection at IBM

Table 2 presents the evolution of IBM's maintenance strategy. Detection techniques are listed for a representative machine from each major era. The techniques can be loosely grouped into three major categories: internal hardware error-detection circuits, diagnostics (including software and microcode), and display (such as lights, error logs, and tracing). The IBM strategy has evolved from "failure recreate" to "failure capture." Prior to the S/370, IBM customer engineers attempted to recreate the failure by rerunning diagnostics, sometimes in conjunction with varying voltage and clock frequency, until the failure recurred. The system was placed in a tight programmed loop to produce a continuous failure condition for analysis. In failure capture, hardware circuits detect errors, and information about the current status of the machine state is logged for subsequent analysis.

The features found in the IBM 4300 series are described in the box at the right. The hardware error-detection, error-correction, and monitoring circuits are used in the

Table 2. Evolution of IBM maintenance strategy.

MACHINE	ERA	TECHNIQUES
650	Late 1950's	Six internal checkers Stand-alone diagnostics on punched cards Light and switch panel
1401	Early 1960's	20 internal checkers Stand-alone diagnostics Light and switch panel
S/360-50	Mid-1960's	75 internal checkers OLTEP—On-Line Test Executive Program Microdiagnostics Log fault data to main memory EREP—Error Recording and Edit Program for outputting logged data Maintenance panel
370/168 Mod 3	Early 1970's	Error-detection circuits OLTEP Microdiagnostics for fault isolation Service processor, including trace unit—trace up to 199 fixed and eight movable logic points over 32 machine cycles for intermittent or environmental faults
303X	Mid-1970's	Error-detection circuits OLTS—on-line functional tests Console and processor microdiagnostics EREP Scope loops Support processor, including trace and remote (telephone) access to log data and trace information
4341	Late 1970's	Error-detection circuits 25,000 shadow latches Support processor—error logging and environmental monitoring

Reliability, availability, and serviceability for IBM 4300's

Error-detection/correction circuits

- Single-bit error correction/double-bit error detection in main memory
- Data-path parity
- Store-and-fetch memory access protection
- Instruction retry (model 4341 only). On an error, processor performs a retry and, if successful, loads the machine check interrupt. Options include hard-stop on error, no retry (but logout), disable error report, and stop after logout. During instruction execution, data in certain machine facilities is saved. Prior to instruction re-execution, this data is restored.
- Disk error correction
- I/O retry at both processor and disk controller levels
- Peripheral unit "power off" signal (model 4341 only)
- Disk self-test
- Voltage margin under program control
- Relocatable control storage
- Level-sensitive scan design
- Microdiagnostic locate, field-replaceable unit 80 percent of time
- Halt or trace on address or data match comparisons can be made on any reference, I/O reference, data store, or instruction fetch

Support processor

- Separately powered
- Separate system diskette for microcode loading, system error logging, and storage of microdiagnostics
- Sensors for monitoring power variances, temperature fluctuations, and electrostatic discharge (model 4341 only)
- For both retriable and unretriable errors, the support processor performs an internal logout. Each logout has an identifier that specifies the number of logouts to date.
- Support-processor-generated eight-digit reference code guide to failing unit. Reference code logged on diskette and display console.
- Display console and data link functions for remote support facility

Remote support facility

- Remote monitoring (especially of error registers) and control
- Remote initiation of diagnostics
- Remote examination of error log on system diskette
- Distribute microcode updates

following maintenance scenario. The support processor displays a diagnostic code. A customer engineer is called to the site and examines the error information on the system diskette, executes diagnostics from the system diskette, and uses the support processor to monitor results. For additional information, the customer engineer can telephone a central database (called Retain) for the latest service aids and failure data from other sites. (A specialist from a Field Technical Support Center can use the telephone link to remote monitor and/or control diagnostics on the model 4341.)

The reliability, availability, and serviceability, or RAS, features of the IBM System/360-System/370 are described by Droulette.[4] The goal is high availability with minimized impact of failures. Four stages of corrective action are identified, each with successively larger impact on users: *transparent recovery, one user affected, multiple users affected,* and *down.* The successively increasing severity stage-recovery structure is common in systems with high-availability goals and in real-time data processing environments in which temporary loss of data is tolerable. RAS features in the IBM 3081 are discussed by Bossen and Tendolkar.[5,6]

Fault detection at Univac

The availability, reliability, and maintainability, or ARM, features in the Univac 1100/60 are described by Boone.[7] ARM at Univac emphasizes on-line error detection. Error-detection hardware in the Univac 1100/60 includes:

(1) *Memory.* Double-error-detecting code on memory data and parity on address and control information;

(2) *Cache.* Parity on data, address, and control information;

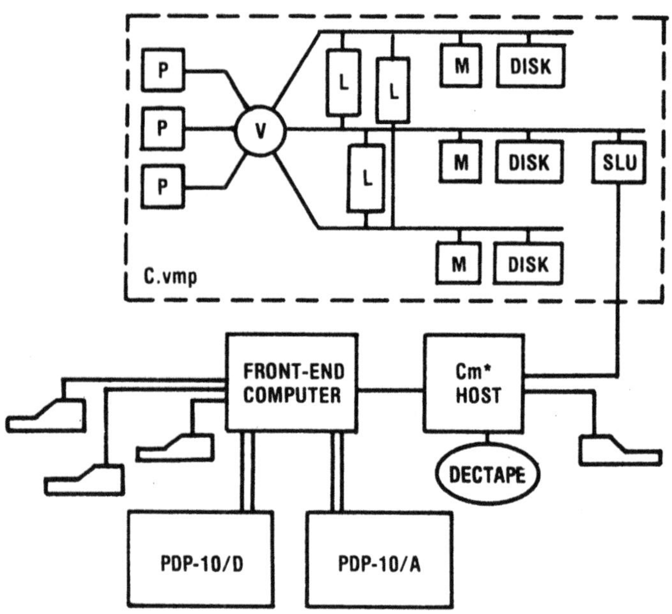

Figure 4. The C.vmp system configuration and connection to Carnegie-Mellon University facilities in which P = processor, L = link, V = voter, M = memory, and SLU = Serial Line Unit.

(3) *I/O unit.* Parity on data and control;

(4) *CPU.* Parity on data paths, parity on control store, and duplication and comparison of control logic.

As indicated, parity on multibit logic and duplication of random logic are primary error-detection techniques employed in the 1100/60. Error recovery in the Univac 1100/60 consists of:

(1) *Memory.* Single-error-correction code on data and retry on address or control information parity error;

(2) *Cache.* Retry on address or control information parity error and disable portions of cache on data parity errors;

(3) *I/O Unit.* Retry on data or control parity errors;

(4) *CPU.* Retry on control store parity error, invert sense of control store, and macroinstruction retry.

Based on the assumption that most errors are transients, recovery consists primarily of retry. Instead of attempting a number of retries immediately after an error is detected, the 1100/60 pauses so that the source of a transient (such as power supply instability) dies out. The pause can be from 5ms to 5s in 1ms increments. The pause value is set to cope with site-dependent conditions. Hard failures are tolerated in main memory through error correcting code, in cache through performance degradation, and in the control store by inverting the bits in the microinstruction (if required for a bit to match a stuck-at-zero or a stuck-at-one value).

An integral part of the 1100/60 ARM philosophy is the system support processor. The SSP combines many features of the IBM 4341 support processor and the Vax-11/780 console processor (see Siewiorek and Swarz, Chapter 8).[3] With the advent of low-cost microprocessors, it became cost-effective to concentrate in a support processor the functionality traditionally provided by front console switches and maintenance panels. Once the basic functionality was provided for system control, expansion to ARM functionality followed naturally. A support processor typically consists of 50K to 100K ips, a small amount of nonvolatile ROM (such as 4K words), RAM (up to 256K words), secondary storage (floppy disk), remote access port, and interfaces to buses and control signals internal to the CPU. Some of the functionality associated with support processors[8] includes:

- System console
- System boot
- System quick test of boot path
- Error logger
- Diagnostic tools (such as microdiagnostics, scan/set/compare internal state, fault injection, and remote diagnosis)
- Error recovery techniques (such as writable control-store reload, transplant state to another processor, and reconfiguration)

Masking redundancy in multiple-computer systems

Fault-detection techniques supply warnings of faulty results. They may also provide diagnostic capabilities, with a determination of some finite number of possible failure locations (such as a device or set of devices causing the fault). However, the use of fault-detection techniques alone does not provide actual tolerance of faults. Fault masking, on the other hand, employs redundancy which provides fault tolerance by either isolating or correcting fault effects before they reach module outputs. Fault masking is a "static" form of redundancy:[9,10] the logical interconnection of the circuit elements remains fixed, and no intervention occurs from elements outside the module. Thus, when the masking redundancy is exhausted by faults in the module, any further faults will cause errors at the output.

Notification of fault occurrence is implicit in fault detection. In its pure form, fault-masking does not provide fault detection: the effects of faults are automatically neutralized without notification of their occurrence. Pure fault-masking thus gives no warning of a deteriorating hardware state until enough faults have accumulated to cause an error. As a result, most fault-masking techniques are extended to provide fault detection as well. The additional redundancy needed for this purpose is usually minor. In the case of a few fault-masking techniques, however, fault detection is either impossible or too costly.

As an example of fault-masking redundancy, consider the three processor-memory pairs, each pair connected by means of a bus as depicted in Figure 4. C.vmp (for computer, voted multiprocessor)[11] is in fact composed of three separate machines capable of operating in independent mode, executing three separate programs. Under the control of an external event or under the control of one of the processors, C.vmp can synchronize its redundant hardware and start executing the critical section of code. Figure 4 is an example of three redundant copies using "bus level" majority voting. A more precise definition of C.vmp would therefore be: a multiprocessor system capable of fault-tolerant operation.

Like fault detection, fault masking can be used in combination with other techniques in a dynamic redundancy scheme. For example, fault masking may be used until its redundancy is exhausted, after which spares may be switched in to renew the redundancy.

Dynamic redundancy in multiple-computer systems

Another approach to increased reliability utilizes redundancy in a dynamic way. Dynamic redundancy techniques involve the reconfiguration of system components in response to failures. The reconfiguration prevents failures from contributing their effects to the system operation. In many instances, reconfiguration amounts to disconnecting the damaged units from the system. If fault masking is used as part of the dynamic redundancy scheme, the removal of failed components may be postponed until enough failures have accumulated to threaten an impending nonmaskable failure.

Reconfiguration is triggered either by internal detection of faults in the damaged subunit or by detection of errors in its output.* Thus, fault-detection techniques (with or without masking) form the basis of dynamic redundancy. A system's chance of successful reconfiguration is greatly dependent on its fault-detection ability. Three issues are involved in the employment of fault detection in a reconfigurable system. The first is the confinement of fault effects before irrecoverable damage occurs; the second is fault detection; and the third is correct diagnosis of the failure location, so that the faulty unit—and only the faulty unit—is marked for remedial action (removal and/or replacement). Thus, the two fault-detection criteria of coverage and diagnosability are important factors in the choice of a detection technique. Detection coverage in particular is commonly used in deriving the reliability formula of a dynamically redundant system. In modeling dynamically redundant systems, coverage is often generalized to mean the probability of a successful reconfiguration; successful fault detection then becomes only one of the factors in determining coverage, along with the probabilities of successful error confinement and resource switching.

Until about 1975, the most common way of increasing availability was to have a complete backup computer system, as depicted in Figure 5(a). If the main computer failed, work would be transferred to the backup computer in a matter of 15 to 30 minutes. The failed system could be repaired while useful processing continued on the backup system. The Sage Air Defense System employed standby redundancy. Subsequently, switches were added to allow peripherals to be attached to either computer, as shown in Figure 5(b). Besides reducing the operator tasks necessary to transfer programs and data, switching reduced the costs of redundancy because it was necessary to replicate only critical components.

The next step was to provide peripherals with "dual ports" as shown in Figure 5(c). The peripherals were online to each computer and the transfer to the backup computer could occur at electronic speeds. An example of dual-ported peripherals can be found in the IBM S/360-S/370 family.[12] An interprocessor communication bus was added, as shown in Figure 5(d), and loosely coupled cooperation between the computers became possible. An operating system optimizes the use of both computers. In the event of a fault, the failed unit is configured out of the system, which is then restarted.

A primary example of "loosely coupled" multicomputer systems is the Tandem 16, the first commercially available, modularly expandable system designed specifically for high availability. Tandem is composed of up to 16 computers interconnected by two message-oriented Dynabuses. All I/O device controllers are dual ported for access by an alternate path in case of processor or I/O failure. Upon this hardware structure the software builds a process-oriented system with all communications handled as messages. This abstraction allows the blurring of the physical boundaries between processors and peripherals. Any I/O device or resource in the system can be accessed by a process, no matter where the resource and process reside.

*Reconfiguration can be performed either automatically by the system itself, (on-line repair) or manually by operations or maintenance personnel (off-line repair). In the first case, the system experiences a temporary pause before operation continues; in the second, the halt is longer and may require complete reinitialization. Hence, on-line repair improves both reliability and availability, whereas off-line repair usually only increases the availability. The emphasis in this section is upon on-line repair.

Data integrity is maintained through the mechanism of I/O *process-pairs*: one I/O process is designated as "primary," the other as "backup." All file modification messages are delivered to the primary I/O process. The primary sends a message with checkpoint information to the backup so that it can take over if the primary's processor or its access path to the I/O device fails. Files can also be duplicated on physically distinct devices controlled by primary and backup members of an I/O process-pair on physically distinct processors. All file modification messages are delivered to both I/O processes. Thus, in the event of physical failure or isolation of the primary, the backup file is up-to-date and available.

User applications can also use the process-pair mechanism. Consider a nonstop application program, *A*, as shown in Figure 6. Program *A* starts a backup process, *A'*, in another processor. There are also duplicate file images, one designated "primary" and the other "backup." Program *A* periodically (at user-specified points) sends checkpoint information to *A'*. *A'* is the same program as *A*, but knows that it is a backup program. *A'* reads checkpoint messages to update its data area, file status, and program counter. *A'* loads and executes if the system reports that *A*'s processor is down (that is, if error messages sent from *A*'s operating system image or *A*'s processor fail to respond to a periodic "I'm alive" message). All file activity by *A* is performed on both the primary and backup file copies. When *A'* starts to execute from the last checkpoint, it may attempt to repeat I/O operations successfully completed by *A*. The system file handler will recognize this and send *A'* a successfully completed I/O message. Program *A* periodically asks the operating system if a backup process exists. If a backup process no longer exists, *A* can

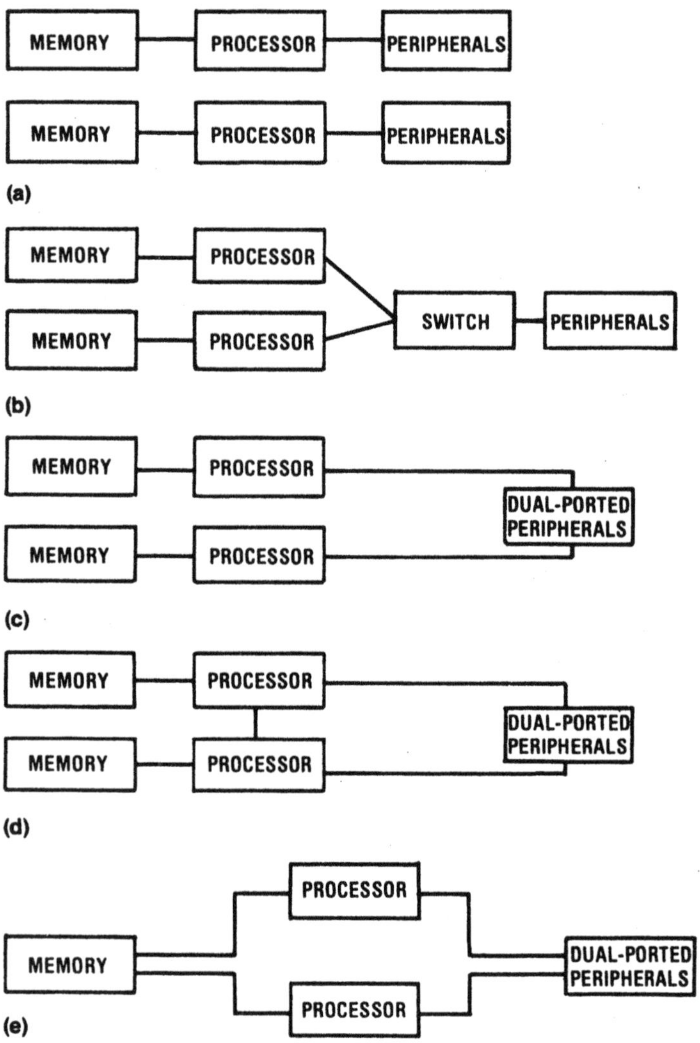

Figure 5. The evolution of systems using dynamic redundancy includes back-up computer systems (a), backup computer systems with switches (b), dual-ported peripherals (c), dual-processor with interprocessor communication (d), and tightly coupled multiprocessors (e).

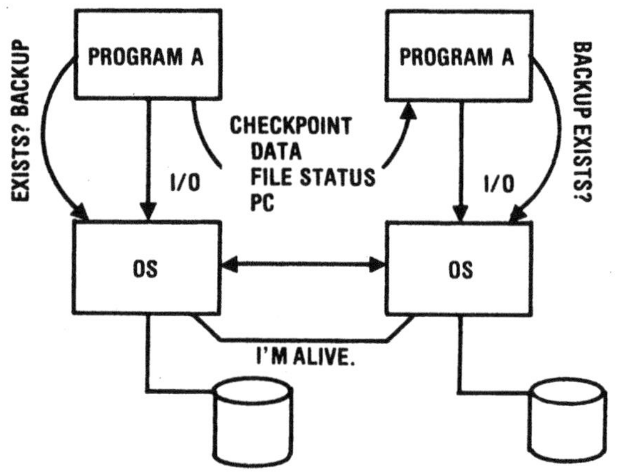

Figure 6. Shadow processing in Tandem consists of a nonstop application program *A* and a backup process, *A'*, in another processor.

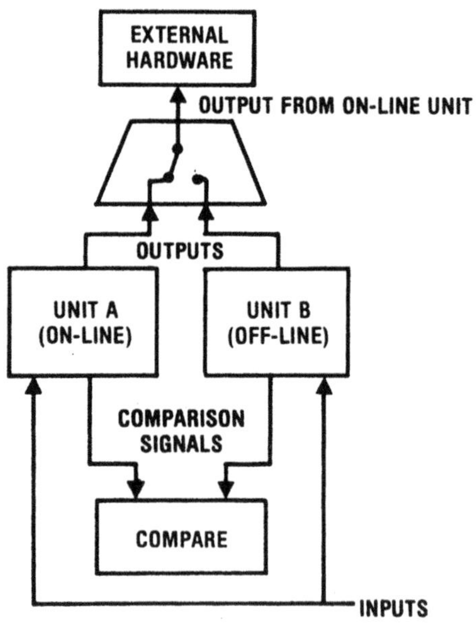

Figure 7. Reconfigurable duplication is characterized by a detected mismatch during comparison of characteristic signals that triggers reconfiguration.

request the creation and initialization of a copy of both the process and file structure. More information on the operating system and the programming of nonstop applications is given by Bartlett.[13] Checkpointing reduces the effective power of a pair of Tandem processors by 15 to 30 percent. Tandem applications include order entry, hospital records, bank transactions, and library transactions.

Another approach to loosely coupled dynamic redundancy employs hardware comparators as shown in Figure 7. In the figure, only one of the duplicated units (the active unit) is connected to the system outputs. The other (standby) unit is functioning in parallel with the active unit, but is not connected to the outputs. In practice, the duplicate modules are often resident on the same bus (or buses), and the switching function is performed by the bus interface unit in each module. When a fault is detected by a mismatch, there are several means of determining the faulty copy and switching it out. Four methods are discussed here. The first is to run a diagnostic program. In the Bell ESS-2,[14] for example, the active processor runs a self-diagnostic program. If the diagnostic fails, control is passed to the standby processor. The faulty processor is taken off line to run maintenance programs that facilitate its rapid repair. Another means of identifying the faulty copy is to include self-checking capabilities on each module. The joint occurrence of an internally detected fault and a mismatch provides immediate detemination of the faulty copy.[14,15] A third approach to determining the faulty processor is to use a watchdog timer. In the Bell ESS-2, for example, the active processor must reset a time periodically. If it fails to do so, the timer automatically invokes a change of control to the standby processor. The fourth method of configuration selection is to use an outside arbiter to control the configuration. In the Comtrac railroad traffic control computer,[16] a mismatch forces both processors to run identical test programs. The test program exercises the entire processor in the course of calculating a single constant. If a failure is present, there is a high probability that the calculation will result in a wrong answer. The results from the two processors are compared with a stored constant by a special controller. Based on the results of the test, the controller performs the proper configuration action.

Stratus and the Intel 432 employ two copies of duplicate logic (that is, a factor of four redundancy). When a mismatch occurs, the pair without mismatch becomes the primary and takes over.

The final step in the evolution of dynamic redundancy is the addition of shared memory [see Figure 5(e)] to produce a tightly coupled multiprocessor. The processors share a common pool of memory and peripherals. Any similar unit can back up a failed component. A single operating system allocates workload to various devices on a first-come, first-serve basis. Examples of shared memory multiprocessors include Pluribus,[17] C.mmp,[11] Intel 432,[1] and Synapse.[18]

Ultimate system goals affect design philosophy and design tradeoffs, and the costs of fault tolerance must be weighed against the cost of errors (including the cost of downtime as well as the expense of correcting incorrect computations). Some system goal considerations that affect design philosophy include: Is the system to be highly reliable or highly availible? Do all outputs have to be correct, or only data committed to long-term storage? How familiar must the user be with the architecture and software redundancy? Is the system constructed so that attributes of the application can be used to simplify fault-tolerant techniques? Is the system constrained to use existing components? Even if the design is new, what is the cost and/or performance penalty to the user who does not require fault tolerance? Is the design stand-alone, or are there other processors that can be called upon to assist in times of failure? These, as well as a multitude of other questions, must be answered by the architect of a fault-tolerant architecture. ✱

References

1. D. P. Siewiorek and R. S. Swarz, *The Theory and Practice of Reliable System Design,* Digital Press, Bedford, Mass., 1982.
2. *IAPX 432 Interconnect Architecture Reference Manual,* Intel Corp., Order No. 17248-001, 1982.
3. A. Avižienis, "Architecture of Fault-Tolerant Computing Systems," *Proc. Fifth Int'l Symp. Fault-Tolerant Computing,* IEEE-CS Press, Los Alamitos, Calif., 1975, pp. 3-16.
4. D. L. Droulette "Recovery Through Programming System/360- System/370," *Proc. AFIPS SJCC,* Vol. 38, AFIPS Press, Montvale, N. J., 1971, pp. 467-476.
5. D. C. Bossen and M. Y. Hsiao, "Model for Transient and Permanent Error-Detection and Fault Isolation," *IBM J. Research and Development,* Vol. 26, No. 1, Jan. 1982, pp. 67-77.
6. N. N. Tendolkar and R. L. Swan, "Automated Diagnostic Methodology for the IBM 3081 Processor Complex," *IBM J. Research and Development,* Vol. 26, No. 1, Jan. 1982, pp. 78-88.
7. L. A. Boone, H. L. Liebergot, and R. M. Sedmak, "Availability, Reliability, and Maintainability Aspects of the Sperry Univac 1100/60," *Proc. 10th Int'l Fault-Tolerant Computing Symp.,* IEEE-CS Press, Los Alamitos, Calif., 1980, pp. 3-8.
8. D. J. Kunshier and D. R. Mueller, "Support Processor-Based System Fault Recovery," *Proc. 10th Int'l Symp. Fault-Tolerant Computing,* IEEE-CS Press, Los Alamitos, Calif., 1980, pp. 197-301.
9. R. A. Short, "The Attainment of Reliable Digital Systems Through the Use of Redundancy: A Survey," *IEEE Computer Group News 2,* Mar. 1968, pp. 2-17.
10. A. Avižienis, "Fault-Tolerant Computing—Progress, Problems, and Prospects," *Proc. IFIP Congress 77,* North Holland Press, New York, 1977, pp. 405-420.

11. D. P. Siewiorek, et al., "A Case Study of C.mmp, Cm*, and C.vmp: Part 1—Experiences with Fault Tolerance in Multiprocessor Systems," *Proc. IEEE,* Vol. 66, No. 10, Oct. 1978, pp. 1178-1199.

12. D. P. Siewiorek, C. G. Bell, and A. Newell, *Computer Structures: Principles and Examples,* McGraw-Hill Book Co., New York, 1982, Chapter 52.

13. J. F. Bartlett, "A 'NonStop' Operating System," *Proc. Hawaii Int'l Conf. System Sciences,* Honolulu, Hawaii, 1978, pp. 103-119.

14. W. N. Toy, "Fault-Tolerant Design of Local ESS Processors," *Proc. IEEE,* Vol. 66, No. 10, Oct. 1978, pp. 1126-1145.

15. M. Morganti, G. Coppadoro, and S. Ceru, "UDET 7116—Common Control for PCM Telephone Exchange: Diagnostic Software Design and Availability Evaluation," *Proc. Eighth Int'l Fault-Tolerant Computing Symp.,* IEEE-CS Press, Los Alamitos, Calif., 1978, pp. 16-23.

16. H. Ihara, K. Fukouka, Y. Kubo, and S. Yokota, "Fault-Tolerant Computer System with Three Symmetric Computers," *Proc. IEEE,* Vol. 66, No. 10, Oct. 1978, pp. 1160-1177.

17. D. Katsuki et al., "Pluribus—An Operational Fault-Tolerant Multiprocessor," *Proc. IEEE,* Vol. 66. No. 10, Oct. 1978, pp. 1146-1159.

18. *Synapse Transaction Processing System Overview,* Synapse Computer Corporation, Milpitas, Calif., 1983.

Daniel P. Siewiorek is a professor of computer science at Carnegie-Mellon University. During his tenure there he helped to initiate and guide the Cm* project, which has culminated in an operational 50-processor multi-microprocessor system. Siewiorek also directed the construction of C.vmp, a triply redundant fault-tolerant computer, and formulated a hardware design automation project.

His current research interests include computer architecture, reliability modeling, fault-tolerant computing, modular design, and design automation. He has served as associate editor of the Computer System Department of the *Communications of the Association for Computing Machinery* and as chairman of the IEEE Technical Committee on Fault-Tolerant Computing. Siewiorek is a member of the IEEE, ACM, Tau Beta Pi, Eta Kappa Nu, and Sigma Xi.

Siewiorek received his BS degree in electrical engineering (summa cum laude) from the University of Michigan, Ann Arbor, in 1968, and the MS and PhD degrees in electrical engineering (minor in computer science) from Stanford University, Stanford, California, in 1969 and 1972, respectively.

Questions about the article can be addressed to the author at Carnegie-Mellon University, Dept. of Computer Science, Pittsburgh, PA 15213.

A wide choice of multiprocessor systems featuring hardware fault tolerance is now available from a growing number of commercial suppliers; fault-tolerant software design remains a problem.

Fault-Tolerant Systems in Commercial Applications

Omri Serlin, ITOM International Company

Although fault-tolerant techniques were employed in some of the earliest digital computers, the advent of solid-state devices—first the transistor, and later integrated circuits—greatly improved the overall reliability of computer systems. One notable exception to this trend, however, is the popular dynamic MOS RAM: memory systems based on such ICs are actually less reliable than the magnetic cores they replaced. In fact, the reliability of solid-state memory systems has been made to equal that of the older, magnetic-core systems only through the use of error correcting codes; however, parity and ECC schemes are applicable only to subsystems that do not perform any data transformations, but perform only pure data transport (such as computer buses and I/O channels) or offer pure storage (such as main memory and disks).

As a result of the improvement in basic component reliability on the one hand and the development of error-correcting codes on the other, the initial interest that computer scientists had in developing fault-tolerant techniques soon faded. During the 1960's and early 1970's, interest in such techniques remained limited to a number of specific applications areas, including computer-controlled telephone switching systems, military and commercial real-time monitoring and control systems, commercial time-sharing systems, and airline reservations systems.

Early dual-processor systems

Computer-controlled, electronic switching systems began to appear in central offices of the public telephone network in the US and in France around 1965. Because of the nature of the services they render, the computers incorporated in such switching complexes must provide very high availability. A typical requirement is that there be no more than two hours of system outage (downtime) in 40 years.

To achieve the goal of high availability, various techniques have been devised by AT&T Bell Laboratories for use in its family of ESS computers, of which the latest is the 3B20D processor used in the No. 5 ESS and recently released as a commercial product (see Figure 1). Details differ in each ESS implementation, but the general scheme is to duplicate all critical components (such as the control unit and memory system). The running system utilizes one set of subsystems, while a duplicate set is either in a "hot backup" mode or is executing synchronously with the on-line set. The system detects errors either by matching the results produced by both sets (as in the No. 1A ESS) or by constructing each set from self-checking modules, which are themselves duplicates that match one another's results (as in the No. 3A ESS and 3B20D).

In real-time monitoring and control applications, a computer system is integrated into its environment through various sensors that permit it to monitor the state of physical devices and processes. If the computer is also entrusted with the task of controlling some devices or processes with a variety of actuators, it becomes a "closed-loop" system. Applications include industrial process control, both continuous and discrete; power plant monitoring, both conventional (fossil fuel) and nuclear; aerospace telemetry and on-board control systems; air traffic control systems; and military command and control systems.

To address the high-availability issues inherent in these applications, dual-processor configurations similar to the one shown in Figure 2 were (and in many cases, still are) employed. The particular system depicted in the figure closely resembles the SEL 88 system, manufactured between 1970 and 1974 by Systems Engineering Laboratories.

In the SEL 88 system, four-port memory modules allowed access from two pairs of CPUs and direct memory access I/O processors. Modules connected in this way created a shared memory region, which mapped into the high end of each processor's address space. This shared memory was typically used to hold "global common" areas (the main programming language was Fortran), which allowed programs running in the two separate processors to share data. In addition, the operating system copy in each processor, which occupied the low end of the address space, could use the shared, high-address locations to communicate with each other at high speeds.

To coordinate the use of shared memory, the system supported a *test bit and set* instruction, which was used to manage semaphores. This instruction read the word containing the addressed bit, set the bit to "one" and the condition code to reflect the status of the bit prior to setting, then rewrote the word into the shared memory—all in one uninterruptible sequence. In this way, a program running in one processor could both test a flag and, upon finding it clear, set the flag to indicate that it was about to modify a certain region of memory; the other CPU was then expected to refrain from modifying (or even reading) the same region.

A special "peripheral switch" permitted I/O controllers to be accessed by either one (but not both) of the I/O processors. Each controller attached to the switch (up to 14 could be accommodated) was actually controlled by a single-pole, double-throw switch, with the peripheral controller at the center position and the I/O processors at the two "throws." This was simplified, since the I/O processor normally communicated with the controllers over coaxial cables in bit-serial fashion, but parallel interfaces could also be similarly switched. Both manual and computer-controlled switching were supported. Typically, the "process I/O" interfaces (such as analog-digital converters and discrete I/O lines) and one or more disk controllers were attached to the peripheral switch.

In addition to the usual parity checking and various error traps, each CPU in this system was equipped with a "watchdog timer" designed to detect "stalls." This timer (actually a downtime counter) could be loaded with an initial count by the CPU; it then counted down at a fixed, clock-controlled rate. The operating system or the applications programs running in each CPU were expected to reload periodically the initial value into their timers. An interrupt signal was sent *to the other CPU* if the program failed to do so before the watchdog timer counted down to zero.

Assuming that no branch of either the system or user programs took longer to execute than the countdown time, such a situation could only come about either because of a complete CPU failure or because of a program bug or hardware error leading to an "infinite loop." In any event, the receipt of the watchdog timer interrupt at a given processor signaled that the other CPU was probably "stalled."

Dual- or multiple-processor systems, similar to the one just described, whether with or without the shared-memory feature, were available from a number of suppliers, including DEC, Data General, and Perkin Elmer's Interdata Division. The five-computer complex that supported the NASA Manned Space Flight Center was of this type, as were the IBM 9020 systems installed in the en-route air

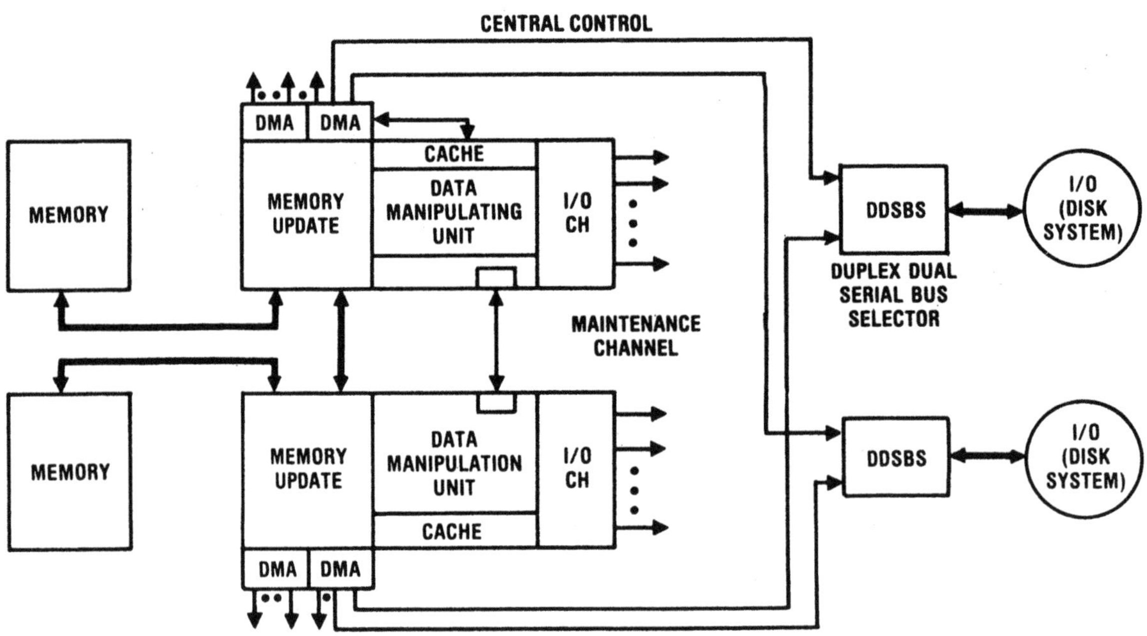

Figure 1. General block diagram of the 3B20D system.

traffic control centers. Variants of this arrangement are still available from several manufacturers, including Hewlett-Packard and, in the UK, Computer Technology, Ltd.

However, these systems provide only the illusion of fault tolerance. For example, they incorporate a number of "critical points," the failure of any of which can bring the entire system down. Examples of such critical points include the shared memory, the peripheral switch, and the shared controllers and devices attached to the switch. Such deficiencies are part of the reason that computer-based "closed-loop" control systems are not permitted in certain critical applications in the US (for example, nuclear power plant control).

Equally serious is the fact that failed components can neither be removed nor be returned to service without powering down one or both processor systems. Furthermore, few of these systems can accept additional processors to accommodate growing workloads.

The most notable limitation of such systems is that they include practically no software support. It is generally left to the end user to supply even the most basic mechanisms for interprocessor communications and control of shared memory and shared peripherals; recovery procedures are entirely within the user's own responsibility.

The main reason for these and other deficiencies is that the elements employed in these multiprocessor systems were never designed for fault-tolerant operation. Indeed, even SEL's four-port memories and bit-serial peripheral controllers were—and still are—highly unusual. By and large, these systems were (and are) "force-fitted" into the fault-tolerant application by incorporating only superficial hardware and software modifications into products that were originally meant to function in a stand-alone, single-processor environment.

Variations of this architecture have been employed in commercial time-sharing systems and in airline reservations systems. Both environments are particularly sensitive to downtime, not only because of the actual monetary losses resulting from such disruptions, but also because of the large number of users affected, both internal employees and outside customers.

On-line transaction processing

Airline reservations systems, initially based on Univac and IBM computers, were quite unlike other real-time systems in several important respects—not least of which was that the hardware manufacturers actually undertook to develop the specialized operating systems, terminal communications protocols, and applications interfaces. This task proved so onerous for Univac, especially at United Airlines, that the company could never recover its original momentum. Only a handful of airlines now use Univac's USAS reservation system.

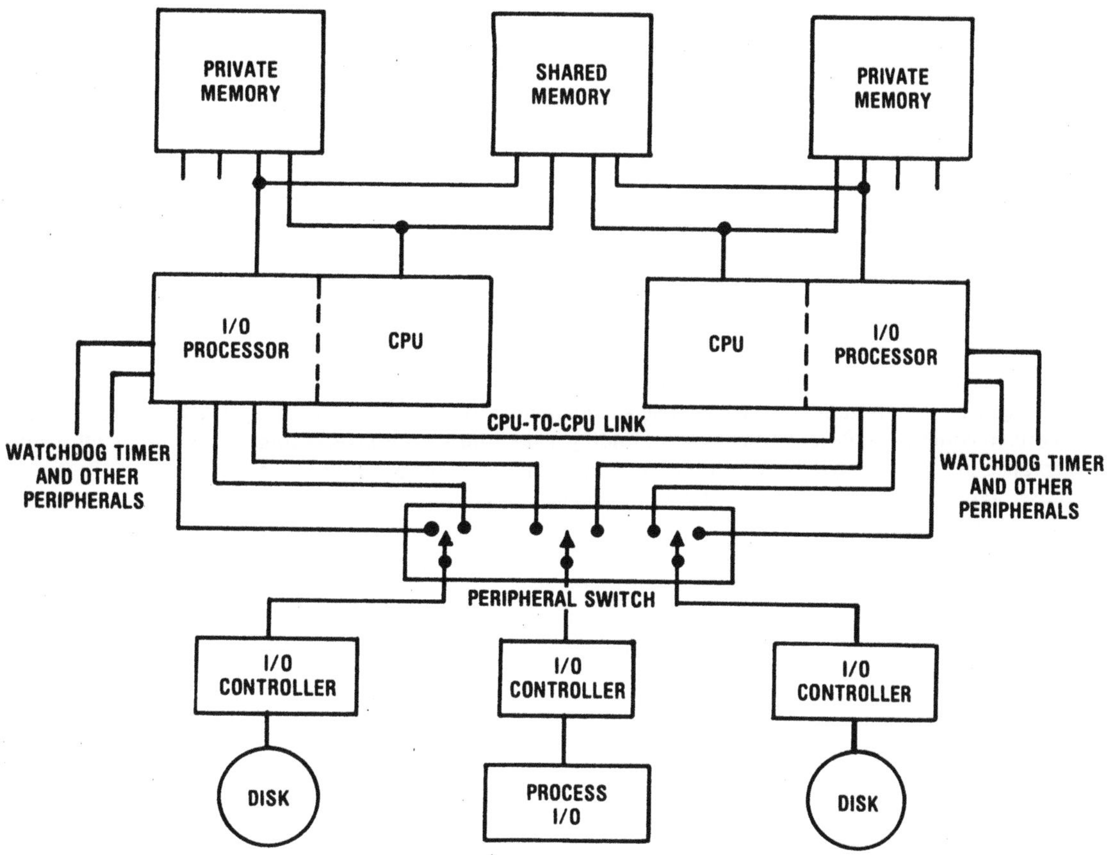

Figure 2. SEL 88-type dual processor (ca.1970).

IBM hardware and the IBM PARS and IPARS software systems became de facto airline industry standards in the US and abroad. The underlying software, the Airline Control Program, is now fully interfaced to SNA, IBM's "grand design" in computer networking. Under SNA's multisystems networking facility, user terminals can access application programs throughout a network of mainframes, even when the application is physically located in a processor to which the terminal has no direct connection. ACP has been so successful that it is now offered by IBM as a more or less standard product for such applications as on-line banking and credit verification.

Unlike real-time monitoring and control systems, which make little use of disk-resident data because disk accesses are too lengthy relative to the required response time, airline reservations systems are created expressly for the manipulation of disk-resident databases. The issues of shared access from a large number of terminals, database consistency and integrity, and system recovery are therefore of prime importance. ACP, for example, includes facilities for periodic dumping of critical data items, called "keypoints" and "globals," to different disk modules. The concepts of checkpointing, audit trails, record locking and disk mirroring or shadowing, also supported by ACP, originated largely from the requirements of on-line transaction processing, or OLTP, of which airline reservations systems were early examples.

The explosive growth in on-line applications is responsible to a large extent for the recent increased interest in FT systems. On-line systems are being installed at ever-increasing rates to handle support of automatic teller machines, automatic gasoline pumps, and other electronic fund-transfer applications; reservations systems for airlines, hotels, and auto-rental agencies; lottery and wagering systems; and videotex or information utilities, to name a few. Even such classical "back office" functions as billing and inventory control are handled increasingly by on-line systems.

The obvious attractions of on-line systems are that they allow a business to increase employee productivity, exercise tighter controls through more up-to-date reporting, and offer new or improved services to customers. These benefits, however, are accompanied by a serious risk: on-line systems at the heart of a business make the business more fragile by sharply increasing the tangible and intangible costs of computer failure. FT systems are finding wide acceptance in OLTP service because they can isolate the end user and the database from the effects of some internal hardware faults.

No FT system can guarantee 100 percent immunity against all faults; such systems can, however, achieve a high level of probability that internal faults will be detected and recovered from before they affect the end users and the database. How well an FT system does this is measured by its *depth,* which is the number of faults of a particular kind that can be handled; and by its *coverage,* which is the range of fault types that the system has been designed to anticipate. FT coverage and depth vary greatly from system to system. Even within a given system, different components may exhibit different depths: ECC-equipped memory systems, for instance, can withstand several successive faults; processors and I/O controllers typically have zero depth in conventional systems and a depth of one or more in FT systems.

The Tandem approach

In 1975, Tandem took a new and more systematic approach to fault tolerance. The Tandem multiprocessor architecture eliminated single points of failure by, among other things, eliminating "master/slave" relations among processors and providing dual paths to all subsystems. Moreover, for the first time in a commercial system, it provided for on-line repair, i.e., the ability to remove defective components (for example, printed circuit boards) and return repaired ones to service without impacting running applications programs. The key architectural features of the Tandem system that underlie these capabilities are processor replication, dual-access I/O controllers, a redundant power system, and a message-based operating system.

A Tandem Nonstop system (Figure 3) includes from two to 16 processors, each with its own memory and I/O channel. These minicomputer-type processors communicate over a high-speed, duplexed, 16-bit parallel bus system called Dynabus. All I/O controllers are dual ported; each is accessible from two I/O channels, typically of two different processors. Disk drives are, in addition, dual-ported; each is attachable to two controllers. Disk data therefore remains accessible even when both a processor and a disk controller have failed.

Should a disk drive fail, the database can still be recovered if the optional disk mirroring has been in effect up to the point of failure. With disk mirroring, the system automatically maintains two identical copies of designated files on two independent drives. A special utility is provided to restore a newly repaired drive to mirror conditions gradually while permitting the surviving drive to satisfy the ongoing workload.

Each processor is individually powered and thus can be shut down for repair independently of other system components. Controllers draw their power from the supplies of both processors to which they are connected; the capacity of each supply is such that the controllers can continue to function even when one processor is shut down.

Each processor in the system contains its own copy of the Guardian operating system, which maintains for each local tables reflecting the status of all available system resources. Stalls (infinite loops) and processor crashes are detected by the absence of "I'm alive" messages, which each processor is required to periodically broadcast over the Dynabus to all other processors.

Checkpointing. Checkpointing is the key recovery mechanism in the Tandem system. For each running process, there is an identical, but semi-inactive, backup process in another processor. The function of the backup is to replace the "primary" process should there be an unrecoverable fault in the primary's processor. The primary process sends its backup periodic "checkpoint messages," which define the state of the process at critical points in the computation. The operating system in each processor "wakes up" the relevant backup process upon discovering that its corresponding primary has failed. The backup can then resume the task from the state defined in the last checkpoint.

Checkpointing is conceptually simple, but its efficient application requires a high degree of programming skill and understanding of system details. Checkpointing is still employed internally by Tandem-supplied system components. One such component is the transaction monitoring facility, or TMF, which maintains database consistency by undoing the effects of aborted or incomplete transactions and supports database recovery. Another checkpointing-based Tandem product, Pathway, is responsible for handling communications with the user terminals. User applications can now be implemented through higher level abstractions called *requesters* and *servers,* which are interjected between the TMF-enhanced DBMS and Pathway. These requesters and servers can be coded as conventional high-level language programs; their loss entails no more than a manual restart of an interrupted transaction.

Message system. Isolation of user processes from configuration details is accomplished by forcing all interprocess communications to be carried out via the *message system.* For example, a user process needing some disk data formulates a "message" addressed to the logical disk controller process. By consulting its resource tables, the local operating system copy determines the actual location of the destination process. The user process therefore does not need to know which two processors are currently connected to the disk in question or which of the two processes is currently the primary.

The isolation of user tasks from configuration details is essential for on-line repair. Furthermore, such isolation facilitates "graceful growth," or the ability to increase the transaction-processing capacity of the system by merely plugging in additional processors. Although this capability is not entirely "seamless," it is, nevertheless, one of the key advantages Tandem has over conventional systems, in which growth involves painful "upgrades." In addition, a

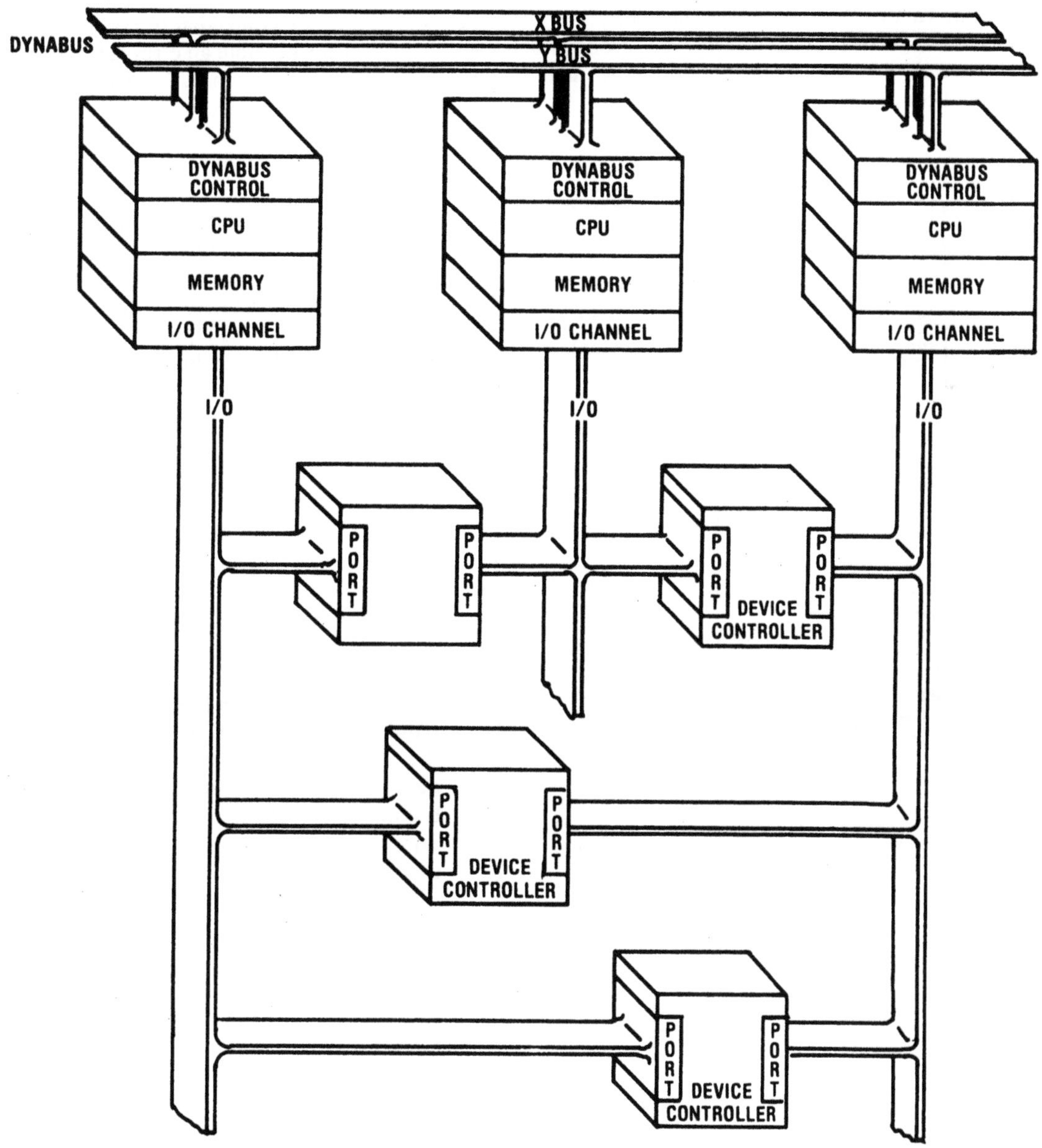

Figure 3. Tandem Nonstop architecture.

network of geographically remote Tandem systems can be created. A relatively minor enhancement to the basic message-based Tandem software is needed to support this important capability.

The Tandem system has undergone a number of notable improvements. Along with enhanced performance, the Nonstop II, introduced in 1981, added "extended addressing" to allow data access beyond the 64K-word limitation of the original product. The Nonstop TXP,[1] introduced in November 1983, achieved a substantially higher performance level through an additional 64K-byte cache and other refinements; the model is expected to receive an enhancement later this year to allow execution of programs larger than 64K-word.

By combining minicomputer technology with architectural innovation, Tandem brought to market an attractive FT system with a substantial price-performance edge over mainframe-based, redundant backup systems. As a result, it enjoyed five years of vigorous growth in revenues and earnings. Despite some recent moderation in its rate of growth, Tandem continues to be the undisputed leader in the FT/OLTP field. It has an especially strong presence in the areas of banking, financial institutions, manufacturing, and communication applications.

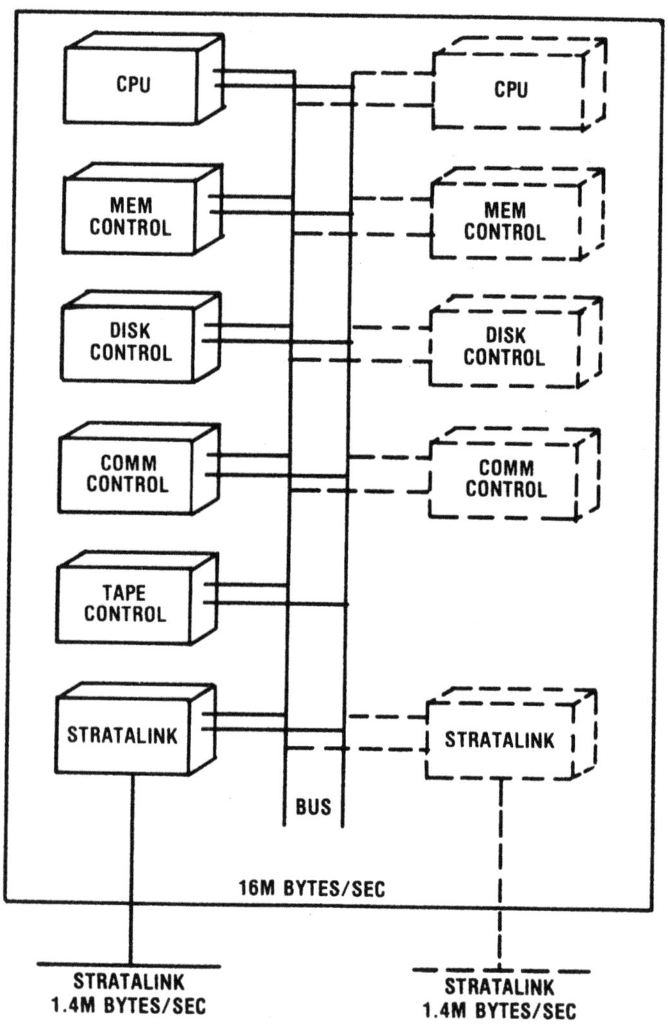

Figure 4. Stratus "pair and spare" architecture.

Over the last several years, a number of new FT/OLTP suppliers have emerged. They are using powerful, low-cost, 16/32 MPUs to create innovative FT designs that were not economically feasible only a few years ago. Most are targeting the OLTP applications that are being addressed by Tandem.[2-5]

Pair and spare

One particularly interesting strategy, dubbed *self-checking,* is employed by Stratus Computer of Natick, Massachusetts, and, to some extent, by the Intel 432 MPU family (see Johnson article, pp. 40-48) and the AT&T 3B20D processor. Stratus, a 1980 start-up which went public in August 1983, developed an architecture (Figure 4), informally known as "pair and spare," in which major functions are replicated four times. First, each subsystem (a printed circuit board) has an identical counterpart, its "spare." Both are self-checking: each consists of a "pair" of identical functions that receive identical inputs; output comparators generate an error signal whenever the paired outputs are mismatched. Normally, a subsystem and its spare are tightly synchronized; should one subsystem detect an internal mismatch, it merely "pulls out" and its spare continues to carry the load, all without missing a beat.

To assure that faulty subsystems are detected rapidly, Stratus equips its systems with automatic dialers that report faults to a support center. When a repaired subsystem is returned to service, an interrupt informs both CPUs (or the spare CPU, if the repaired system is the other CPU). The CPU then brings the repaired system to full synchronism with its running counterpart; for example, a repaired memory subsystem will copy the contents of the functioning memory.

Self-checking is employed throughout the Stratus system;[6] the pair-and-spare strategy is restricted to the CPU and memory proper only. Disk controllers have duplicate read and write circuitry; the controller will not write to the disk, or the duplex system bus, unless both sections agree. Communications controllers are similarly self-checking: each handles half the load, but either can take over all ports.

The Stratus scheme is attractive for several reasons. It requires no recovery from a fault: the work goes on using the "spare" subsystem. Since no recovery is required, neither are such artifices as checkpointing and "I'm alive" broadcasts. To the user (and most system functions), the Stratus computer appears to be a conventional machine that requires no special FT programming considerations.

Stratus is able to implement a degree of redundancy that would have been out of the question with minicomputer technology, and yet offer a surprisingly low price ($180,000 for a typical, basic system) because of its liberal use of off-the-shelf microprocessors. A basic Stratus system may contain as many as 18 Motorola 68000 and Zilog Z80A microprocessors. Because of the product's convincing FT architecture and low system cost, Stratus has had considerable market success, growing from about $5 million in revenues in 1982, its first year of shipments, to $20 million in 1983. A significant number of independent software vendors have adopted vertical market applications, especially in banking and finance, to the Stratus system.

Members of the Intel 432 microprocessor family feature functional redundancy checking, which facilitates the construction of pair-and-spare and/or self-checking systems. The comparators needed to implement self-checking are built into each chip and can be activated with an external signal. Thus, a self-checking module can be created by connecting all corresponding input and output pins of a pair of identical chips. As noted earlier, the AT&T 3B20D processor also employs self-checking and mirror-image memories, although it differs in implementation details from the Stratus approach and cannot be expanded beyond the basic, two-CPU configuration.[7]

Tightly coupled systems

A disadvantage of the pair-and-spare strategy is that when growth becomes necessary, the basic unit must be "cloned" in its entirety. Stratus can accommodate up to 32 processing modules, interconnected over a duplexed, ring-type local area network. However, the PMs are, in effect, stand-alone computers that are not normally able to share resources with other PMs.

Synapse Computer, a well-funded, 1980 start-up in Milpitas, California, has developed an architecture (Figure 5) that avoids this limitation. In this scheme, multiple 68000-based processors are "tightly coupled" through a duplexed, high-speed, 32-bit parallel bus to a common, shared-memory system, which holds the only copy of the operating system. The processors, some of which are specialized for I/O while others concentrate on running the transaction-processing applications, act as a pool from which resources are drawn as required to service the load. The processors are self-dispatching: when idle, they look up work queues in main memory and assign themselves to the next task that needs doing. A somewhat similar architecture is employed in the System 9000 from GEAC Computers International (Markham, Ontario, Canada); variations have been used in the BTI 8000 and the Elxsi systems as well.

Synapse calls its architecture N + 1: by configuring just one more processor than the *N* required to service some workload, essentially the same FT depth can be achieved as in a 2*N* scheme, in which each processor or process is backed by a duplicate counterpart.

Applications and I/O processors schedule work for each other by making entries in various dispatching queues in main memory. I/O processors have substantial local buffers, while each application processor is equipped with a 16K-byte, high-speed cache that minimizes memory bus utilization.

The caches are managed under a "non-write-through" policy,[2] which leaves updated data in the cache as long as possible. This technique improves the hit rate but creates a problem when shared data structures or I/O buffers are involved. Synapse evolved an elegant "ownership" scheme to allow the multiple processors to hold shared data in their caches. It handles read-only accesses, such as instructions, simply by giving each requester a copy of the requested item; shared memory continues to "own" such items.

When a processor issues a write request against a shared data item, ownership of the item, along with the item itself, is transferred from main memory to the requesting processor. Should another processor need access to that item, the owner will either furnish a copy (for read-only access) or generate a "busy" response. All caches monitor bus traffic for requests for the data items they hold. IOPs have special privileges that allow them to write data to shared memory without previously reading it; all caches note such writes and invalidate any corresponding entries.

A high degree of graceful growth is possible with this approach. Additional processors can be added to handle independent growth either in applications (transaction) load or in I/O load.

Processor failures are handled through a semitransparent checkpointing system. Users need not code explicit checkpoint calls; they must instead build their applications from small "program units" by following a set of design rules. The system then undertakes to insert checkpoints automatically between such program units; this activity can be suppressed. A relational database

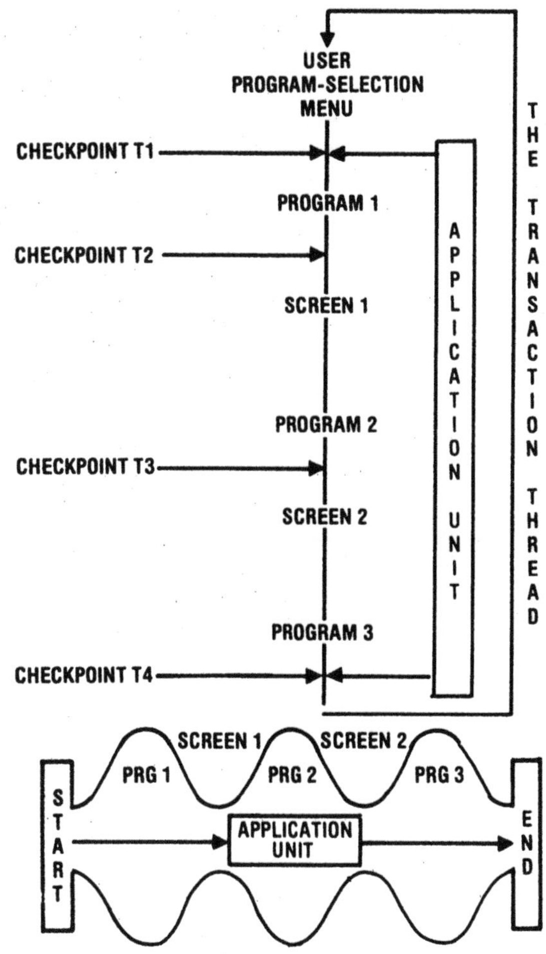

Figure 5. Synapse checkpoint model.

system, integrated with (rather than grafted onto) the operating system facilitates a "Commit" strategy which assures transaction atomicity (that is, the transaction either completes successfully or its effects are removed). A "write-ahead log" technique is used.

The shared-memory system is a single point of failure. A memory failure is the most severe problem that can occur, since it can wipe out work queues, the disk buffers, or parts of the operating system. The memory controller detecting the fault deals with this problem by interrupting all running processors. The mass-storage controller in the highest-priority I/O slot then reloads the operating system, taking care to bypass the failed memory module. Should it fail to do so within a given time period, the next-highest priority I/O controller will try. After a successful reboot, the database recovery process examines the mirrored log file and proceeds to implement all pending committed transactions while undoing the effects of uncommitted (incomplete) transactions. End users should suffer no more than the loss of the screen data they were manipulating at the time of the crash. This recovery process may take up to a few minutes.

Other approaches

Auragen Systems of Fort Lee, New Jersey, also a 1980 start-up, has developed an architecture that is conceptually similar to Tandem's but includes several interesting hardware and software improvements. The system[8] is composed of multiple "clusters" connected to a duplexed, 32-bit, parallel-bus system. Each cluster contains at least three 68010-based processors: two of them execute user tasks and global system processes, while the third manages the system's bus interface and executes most operating system kernel functions. The operating system is based on Unix System III but is modified both internally (to support FT, a message system, and a multiprocessor environment) and externally (to present a more friendly user interface).

For fault recovery, Auragen employs "synchronization" (Figure 6), an interesting variation of the checkpointing idea. After a primary process and its backup have been brought to identical states (synchronized), the backup receives and saves all messages sent to its primary; it also keeps track of the number of messages issued by its primary since the last synchronization. Should the primary fail, the backup would reprocess the saved input messages, suppressing output messages already issued by the primary while it was still functioning.

Synchronization occurs under system control and requires no insertion of checkpoints in the applications code. Moreover, synchronization can occur at a lower frequency than conventional checkpointing and involves less data. The penalty is that more processing steps are involved during recovery, since the backup goes through the motions of some of the actions already completed by the primary. The suggested justification is that the reduction in overhead during normal operation is well worth the longer recovery from rare (one hopes) faults.

Tolerant Systems (San Jose, California), founded in 1982, also employs a synchronization scheme but within the context of a distributed architecture. The basic system building blocks, each based on a pair of National Semiconductor Corporation's NS16000 microprocessors, are interconnected over a duplexed Ethernet local area network.[9]

Computer Consoles, Inc., (Rochester, New York), is developing a multiple processor architecture based on its successful Directory Assistance System. The CCI FT system, dubbed Power 5/55, provides full point-to-point connections among as many as eight 68000-based processors and eight disk controllers. These connections enable the system to implement an interesting generalization of the disk-mirroring scheme: multiple copies of the database are automatically maintained by the system to reduce greatly the response time for inquiry-only transactions, which generally constitute 70 to 90 percent of the transaction load. A local area network connects all pro-

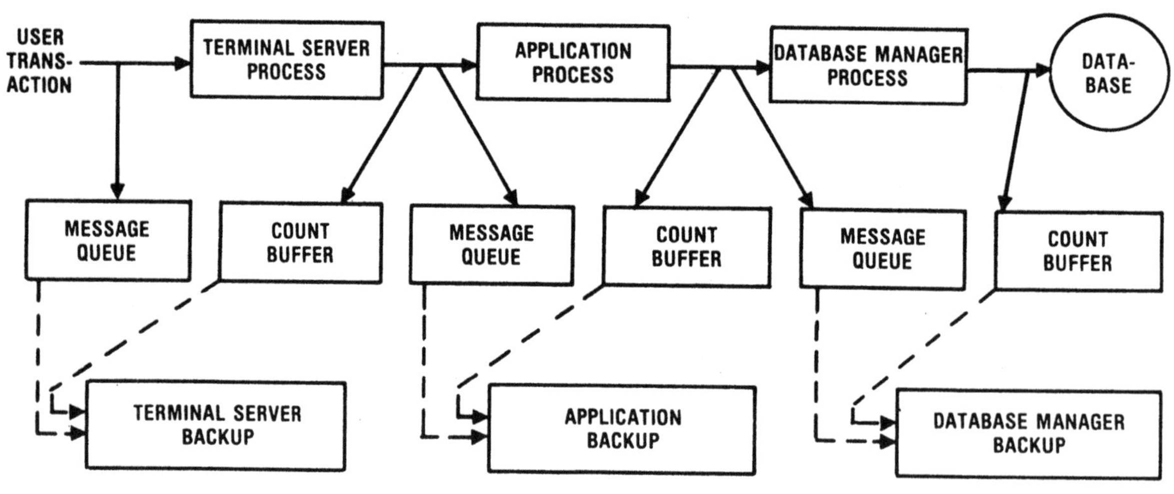

Figure 6. Auragen synchronization scheme (simplified).

cessors to all front-end communications and terminal controllers.

Sequoia Systems (Marlboro, Massachusetts), founded in 1981, is preparing to introduce an FT/OLTP system that combines self-checking processors within a tightly coupled, shared-memory architecture.[10] Encore Computer is also believed to be developing a transaction-processing system along similar lines. Interestingly, Stratus has recently introduced new, "extended architecture" models in which four or six self-checking processors share the duplexed memory system within a Processing Module.

A few firms are addressing FT systems to the special needs of the process control and industrial automation environments. August Systems (Tigard, Oregon) has a system that employs TMR in its front end (analog/ digital interfaces) while the triple-processor main engine runs an interesting variation of TMR called SIFT (software-implemented fault tolerance). The three 8086-based processors perform identical computations and periodically "vote" on the results by reading each other's memory (the links are strictly read-only to prevent one processor from corrupting another's memory). The repetitive nature of the computation involved in process applications makes this approach viable. Voting occurs just prior to launching the next iteration of the algorithm.[11]

Autech (Pompano Beach, Florida) has a system in which duplexed basic units, designed and packaged for harsh-environment service, can be interconnected over a duplexed local area network to a supervisory computer. Hewlett-Packard offers a conventional, hot backup, dual-processor system—dubbed Systemsafe 1000—for supervisory control applications.

The comparison table on pp. 28-29 summarizes the salient features and intended applications of several FT systems now being offered commercially by US manufacturers.

Some open issues

Moves by the established suppliers. Most of the established mainframe and minicomputer manufacturers are known to be considering FT systems. The problem they face is that offering convincing FT architectures may well cause them to lose a great part of their large investments in existing software. This loss clearly would be unacceptable to both vendors and users. Consequently, the established manufacturers can be expected to introduce a variety of solutions involving slightly modified existing products. Examples of this approach are the Vax Cluster from DEC, the NCR V8500/V8600 cluster, the IBM Series/1 ring, and the Perkin Elmer Series 3200 Resilient System, to name a few.

The absence of the established manufacturers from the FT/OLTP scene is both a boon and an obstacle for the existing FT suppliers. Lack of competition from the established vendors helps the newcomers sell their solutions. However, the proprietary nature of the new architectures is limiting their appeal to new applications only: the effort involved in converting existing applications may be too large. This has been a problem for Tandem and is likely to continue to be the principal factor limiting the acceptance of the new FT systems.

Long-range prospects. As more functions are compressed onto fewer and fewer chips, the reliability of a system providing constant functionality and performance can be expected to improve. The suggestion has been made that this will eventually lead to a loss of interest in FT techniques.

A much more likely scenario is that very simple machines, equivalent to today's desktop microcomputers, will indeed become so reliable as to obviate the necessity of equipping them with special FT features. Even today it can be argued plausibly that the correct FT strategy for desktop systems is to stock spare machines and simply replace a malfunctioning unit.

However, the spread of such desktop computing resources is likely to create demand for "file servers" at several levels of the corporate hierarchy. Such file servers, or "group computers," will be used mainly as custodians of shared data (database managers) and as electronic mail hubs, rather than as shared computing (time-sharing) resources.

These computers are likely to continue to be fairly complex. Furthermore, as more workers begin to depend on file servers for the performance of their daily duties, the demand for FT features in such systems will intensify.

Reliable power. As fewer electronic parts are required to implement computing systems, the role of factors other than electronics in system availability will become more pronounced. Several firms (Arete, No Halt, Parallel Computers) are beginning to offer built-in battery-backup systems to counteract the effects of power failures, already a major source of system downtime. Due to the reduced power requirements of today's smaller disks and progress in small-battery technology, such systems can often maintain the complete computer configuration for up to several hours.

Transaction throughput. Almost without exception, today's FT architectures are based on multiplicities of relatively low-powered processors. While these architectures are justified by the nature of transaction processing, which is characterized by relatively limited CPU requirements and fairly heavy I/O loads, they are inherently less efficient than ones in which a relatively small number of very powerful processors can take advantage of economies of scale. It is likely that both approaches will eventually find market acceptance. Meanwhile, FT suppliers are answering the need for higher throughput by adding performance-enhancing features within the context of their basic architectures. The Tandem TXP and the Stratus XA models are examples of such moves.

Software fault tolerance. As the hardware becomes more reliable, software faults—already recognized as being more of a problem than hardware faults in many situations—will become even more visible. High hopes raised by a variety of panaceas ("structured programming," "correctness proofs," "reusable software," "recovery blocks," etc.) have proven premature.

COMMERCIAL FAULT-TOLERANT SYSTEMS

COMPANY/SYSTEM	ADDRESS & PHONE	TARGET MARKETS	CPU TECHNOLOGY	OPERATING SYSTEM NAME & TYPE
August Systems, Inc./ Can't Fail 300	18277 SW Boones Ferry Rd. Tigard, OR 97223 (503) 684-5330	Industrial automation and process monitoring/ control.	Three Intel Corp. 8086-based processors run identical code when in FT mode.	RTTS (real-time task scheduler), one copy per CPU.
Auragen Systems Corp./ System 4000	2 Executive Dr. Ft. Lee, NJ 07024 (201) 461-3400	On-line transaction processing (OLTP); medium to large applications.	Up to 32 clusters of three Motorola 68010 each; clusters interconnect over a high-speed, duplex 32-bit bus.	AT&T Bell Laboratories' Unix with internal modifications: one copy per cluster.
Autech Corp./ DAC-6000	Data Systems Division 1301 W. Copens Rd., Pompano Beach, FL 33064 (305) 979-2700	Industrial automation and process monitoring/ control.	Dual 68000-based Displaymaster and Decmaster. Zilog, Inc., Z80A-based process I/O modules.	Aide process control development system plus read-only memory routines in Decmaster's controller and process I/O modules.
Computer Consoles, Inc./ Power 55/5	97 Humboldt St. Rochester, NY 14609 (716) 482-5000	OLTP, medium to large applications.	Up to eight 68000-based CPUs with 68000-based disk and terminal controllers.	Perpos (perpetual processing OS), Unix-based, one copy per CPU plus special control in inter-computer controllers. (ICC).
Hewlett-Packard Co./ Systemsafe/1000	Data Systems Division 11000 Wolfe Rd. Cupertino, CA 95014 (408) 257-7000	Industrial automation and process monitoring/ control.	Two HP1000 Models 60 or 65 working in "hot backup" mode (16-bit, microprogrammed).	RTE-6/VM, real-time, multitasking, virtual memory, one copy per CPU.
Parallel Computers, Inc./ Parallel 300	3004 Mission St. Santa Cruz, CA 95060 (408) 429-1338	OLTP, very small to small applications.	Two 68010's on a multi-bus.	Berkeley Unix; kernel in both CPUs; one does I/O.
Sequoia Systems/ No Name Yet	3 Metropolitan Corp. Center Marlboro, MA 01752 (617) 480-0800	OLTP, medium to large applications.	Up to 64 CPUs and 96 IOPs, all 68010-based and self-checking.	UNIX-based with new kernel, one copy in shared memory.
Stratus Computer, Inc./ FT200, XA400, XA600	17 Strathmore Rd. Natick, MA 01760 (617) 653-1466	OLTP, small to large applications.	Self-checking CPUs based on Motorola 68000s. Each Processing Module can have duplexed CPU, memory and controllers. Maximum 32 Processing Modules on a ring-type local area network.	VOS (Virtual OS), one copy per CPU (FT200) or four CPUs (XA400) or six CPUs (XA600).
Synapse Computer Corp./ Synapse N+1	801 Buckeye Ct. Milpitas, CA 95035 (408) 946-3191	OLTP, medium to large applications.	Up to 28 68000-based CPUs and IOPs (I/O processors) working with a shared memory via a duplexed, high-speed 32-bit parallel bus.	Synthesis, one copy in shared memory.
Tandem Computers, Inc./ NonStop I, II, TXP	19333 Vallco Pkwy. Cupertino, CA 95014 (408) 725-6000	OLTP, medium to large applications.	Up to 16 CPUs on a duplexed, high-speed, 16-bit parallel bus. CPU is 16-bit microprogrammed.	Guardian, one copy per CPU.
Tolerant Transaction Systems/Eternity	81 E. Daggett Dr. San Jose, CA 95134 (408) 946-5567	OLTP, small to medium applications. Also real time.	Two National Semiconductor Corp. 16000's in each system building block.	Transaction executive, transaction operator interface elements may be replicated in same or multiple system building blocks.

MEMORY SYSTEM	PERFORMANCE/CPU (MIPS and TPS)	FT STRATEGY	CPU FAULT DETECTION*	RECOVERY SCHEME
32K bytes per CPU on-board; up to 1M byte per CPU on Multibus.	Approximately 0.4 MIPS—up to 256 A/D points. TPS not relevant.	CPUs: SIFT; analog front end: TMR	At start of each iteration, three CPUs check state data and vote out odd processor.	Repaired processor reads programs from read-only link or from disk; synchronized at next voting point.
Up to 8M bytes per cluster (1M byte/board).	0.85 MIPS/cluster (company figure). Nominally 27 MIPS/system at full expansion. 1.5 TPS/CPU (estimate).	Queue and count	Self-detect via idle diagnostics and absence of "I'm alive" messages.	Backup process reprocesses input messages since last sync, discarding outputs already effected.
64K bytes to 256K bytes per CPU, with parity; battery backup on board; CMOS static.	Decmaster supports up to 256 process points. TPS: not relevant.	Hot backup	Timeouts, cross diagnostics.	Auto switchover to backup Decmaster on stall (timeout).
512K bytes to 4M bytes per CPU, error checking and correction, battery backup. Each of two ICCs has 512K bytes.	Nominally 5.6 MIPs (0.7 per 68000). Two TPS/CPU (ITOM estimate) due to multicopy database.	Checkpointing	ICC timeout transactions; bad ICCs detected by CPU voting scheme.	Next available CPU completes stalled transaction.
256K bytes to 2M bytes per CPU; 1 parity bit/16 bits of data.	1 MIPS (200K floating-point operation/sec mod 65); TPS not relevant.	Hot backup	Watchdog timer times out.	Peripheral switch flips over, hot backup CPU informed via interrupt.
Maximum 4M bytes/processor.	0.7 MIPS.	Hot backup	Hardware and software synchronization between CPUs.	Manual replace and restart.
2M bytes to 64M bytes with ECC (seven bits per 32-bit word).	Sequoia claims up to 40 MIPS at full expansion.	Automatic reassignment	Self-checking subsystem electrically disconnects.	Next available CPU picks up stalled transaction.
FT200: 8M bytes logical XA400: (16M bytes physical) XA600: 16M bytes logical (32M bytes physical).	0.7, 2.0, 3.0 MIPS; 2, 4, 6 TPS; for FT200, XA400, and XA600, respectively.	Pair and spare	Self-checking subsystem pulls out and generates red-light interrupt to operating system.	Re-education procedures synchronize repaired module with one that's running.
16M bytes/system (1M byte boards), error checking and correction.	0.7 MIPS/CPU; system MIPS depend on how many CPUs configured. 2 TPS/CPU (ITOM estimate) if supported by enough I/O processors.	Checkpointing	Timeout mechanisms.	Next available processor picks up stalled transaction that's been checkpointed into shared memory.
8M bytes/CPU (2M bytes/board), error checking and correction.	0.7, 0.8, 2 MIPS; 1, 1.5, 5 to 6 TPS for Nonstop I, II, and TXP, respectively.	Checkpointing	Absence of "I'm alive" message; each CPU must broadcast over Dynabus each second.	Backup process in another CPU picks up transaction from last good checkpoint sent by primary.
1M byte to 4M bytes per system building block.	1.5 MIPS/system building block (Tolerant estimate).	Checkpointing	Timeouts and "I'm alive" message.	Backup system building block takes over.

*Beyond conventional parity and error traps.

An intriguing idea is that software creation might be brought up to a fault-free level comparable to that of hardware design if software designers had available the equivalent of computer chips—small, well-tested, widely used off-the-shelf packages. With the increasing popularity of rehostable-kernel operating systems, such as Unix, universally applicable packages could become a reality within the foreseeable future. Still, the design of reliable software is very much an intractable problem today. Whoever solves it will gain a well-deserved place of honor in the history of computing. ✱

References

1. R. Horst and S. Metz, "New System Manages Hundreds of Transactions/Second," *Electronics,* Apr. 19, 1984, pp. 147-151.
2. O. Serlin, "New Microprocessor-Based Computer Architectures," *AFIPS Conf. Proc.*, Vol. 54, 1984 NCC, AFIPS Press, Reston, Va.
3. O. Serlin, "Fault Tolerance," *Computerworld Buying Guide,* Aug. 1983.
4. O. Serlin, *Fault-Tolerant Transaction Systems,* Datamation (OEM edition), Jan. 1983.
5. O. Serlin, *Fault-Tolerant Systems,* ITOM International Co., Aug. 1982.
6. R. Freiburghouse, "Making Processing Fail-Safe," *Mini-Micro Systems,* May 1982.
7. W. N. Toy and L. E. Gallaher, "Overview and Architecture of the 3B20D Processor," *Bell System Technical J.,* Jan. 1983, part 2.
8. A. Borg, J. Baumbach, and S. Glazer, "A Message System Supporting Fault Tolerance," *Proc. Ninth ACM Symp. Operating Systems Principles,* Oct. 1983.
9. "Computer System Isolates Faults," *Computer Design,* Nov. 1983.
10. "Sequoia Unveils Self-Checking, Shared-Memory FT System," *FT Systems Newsletter,* ITOM International Co., May 1984, pp. 2-7.
11. J. H. Wensley, "Industrial Control System" *Electronics,* Jan. 27, 1983, pp. 98-102.

Omri Serlin heads ITOM International Company, a research and consulting firm in Los Altos, California, which he established in January 1980. For 18 years prior to establishing ITOM, he worked in various technical, management and product planning capacities in the computer industry. He is the author of a popular market research study on fault-tolerant systems and writes a monthly newsletter on the subject. Among his other interests are supermicros and local area networks. He is a member of the IEEE 802 Committee.

Serlin received a BS degree in electrical engineering from Bridgeport University in 1961 and an MS degree in the same field from Rutgers University in 1964.

His address is ITOM International Company, PO Box 1415, Los Altos, CA 94022.

Although most efforts to provide fault tolerance have concentrated on hardware solutions, to achieve ultrahigh availability, designers must also develop software solutions.

Designing for Ultrahigh Availability: The Unix RTR Operating System

John J. Wallace and Walter W. Barnes, AT&T Bell Laboratories

Early designers of highly available computers concentrated on recovery from hardware failures to keep downtime to a minimum. But as hardware became more reliable, and systems (particularly software) became more complex, the percentage of downtime caused by hardware decreased. Achieving ultrahigh availability—on the order of a few minutes of downtime per year—requires far more than just reliable hardware. This can be seen from Table 1, which gives causes of downtime for both electronic switching[1-3] and transaction processing.[4]

Although the numbers differ, in both cases the hardware accounts for less than half the downtime. The other causes include the following:

- Software might cause a crash or other type of unavailability. (For example, an unintentionally locked semaphore might cause a service to be unavailable.)
- Recovery software might respond to a hardware fault incorrectly and fail to construct a viable collection of hardware components even though one is possible.
- Incorrect operator procedures might cause downtime. Examples of this abound, including powering down the wrong unit, failing to back up a critical database, or following incorrect procedures in a manual.
- Installation of new hardware or software might require downtime.

Consequently, designers of ultrahigh availability computers must consider many causes of downtime, not just hardware.

Tackling downtime

Developing a computer that operates with practically no downtime, planned or unplanned, requires a thorough understanding and treatment of all the areas of reliability, maintainability, and availability. The terms reliability, maintainability, and availability have specific meanings here. *Reliability* refers to the failure rate of hardware and software components, that is, how often a component fails to perform its intended operation. *Maintainability* refers to techniques to repair and upgrade hardware and software. *Availability* refers to the probability that a system is operational at any given time. Note that although availability is a function of reliability, a highly available system can be created by replicating unreliable hardware components. Furthermore, a highly reliable system may not be highly available if there are no procedures for on-line maintenance.

Some areas that affect reliability, maintainability, and availability are examined in the following paragraphs.

Hardware. Besides techniques to improve hardware availability, which are discussed elsewhere,[3,5] designers of ultra-available computers must also consider two other issues:

- Environmental hardening. The hardware should tolerate high temperatures and extremes of humidity from air conditioner outages. Depending on locale, the hardware may need to withstand high altitudes, dusty air, or violent shocks from earthquakes. Backup electrical power is usually required.

Table 1. Causes of downtime.

CAUSE OF DOWNTIME	ELECTRONIC SWITCHING (%)	TRANSACTION PROCESSING (%)
Hardware failure, environment	20	45
Software failure, incorrect recovery	50	30
Incorrect procedures	30	20
Other, such as updates	Included in preceding values	5

- Maintenance. Traditional fault-tolerant architectures have duplicated units, and their availability decreases with the square of repair time.[5] Consequently, a short repair time is critical for these architectures. For this reason, remote maintenance, error containment, automatic and accurate diagnostics, and adequate supplies of spares need to be carefully considered.

Intelligent fault recovery. The fault-recovery system is responsible for maintaining a usable collection of hardware and software components in the face of failures. Therefore, *to minimize errors*, the recovery should be limited to the area immediately affected by the failure; *to minimize system disruption*, the recovery effort should be the minimum necessary to attempt correcting the failure; and, finally, *if this recovery does not correct the failure*, a more drastic recovery should be tried.

High software reliability. As hardware availability improves, software failures will cause most of the downtime and will ultimately limit the system's availability. Consequently, software reliability must also improve. Aside from techniques to ensure high-quality software, additional techniques can be used for software systems that operate continuously for months or years. First, processes should have individual fault recovery and rollback mechanisms to recover from hardware or "transient" software failures. Second, system integrity software should monitor correct operation of the entire hardware and software system. Third, audits should validate data consistency and reclaim lost resources. Finally, overload controls should ensure the availability of resources and prevent catastrophic failures.

Update procedures. It should be possible to install new hardware and software without taking the system down. Therefore, (1) procedures are needed to change hardware (such as the amount of memory or the types of peripherals) and software (to incorporate new features or correct bugs) with no disruption of service; (2) for ultra-available computers, it should be possible to install completely new releases of hardware, firmware, and software or replace an entire hardware unit, such as a processor, with minimum disruption; (3) it should be possible to back out any updates that are found to contain errors; and, finally, (4) an update should be automatically backed out if it is suspected of causing a failure that disrupts operation.

Operator interface. When each minute of downtime may cost thousands of dollars of lost revenue, the operator's interface to the computer must help effect a quick repair. The operator interface should provide immediate feedback on the status of the system and help the operator make quick, accurate decisions. Furthermore, it should prevent dangerous mistakes by the operator. Finally, it should provide positive control over all parts of the system independent of hardware or software integrity.

Assuring ultrahigh availability. All of the preceding techniques will fail to produce an ultra-available system unless high availability is treated as one of the system's primary features. Therefore, availability should be accurately modeled throughout the product life cycle; the system should be thoroughly debugged and tested to ensure high quality, correct operation, and the required availability; site experience should be carefully tracked to ensure that problems are fixed quickly and availability objectives are met; and, finally, all problems should be resolved in a controlled manner.

Methods of improving software quality and reducing maintenance costs are used in computer systems that do not have ultrahigh availability as a primary goal. These methods include inspections, quality controls, and automated project-control tools. Since improved quality gives improved availability, high quality is also necessary for highly available computers.

The AT&T 3B20 Duplex computer and Unix RTR operating system

The AT&T 3B20 Duplex computer (3B20D) and Unix RTR operating system* provide a fault-tolerant base for applications needing ultrahigh availability.† Together they make up the latest in a series of ultra-available computers designed by AT&T Bell Laboratories and manufactured by AT&T Technologies. Introduced in September 1981, they now serve over 200 systems in 12 applications.

Every essential unit, that is, every unit needed for a usable system, is duplicated in the hardware architecture, shown in Figure 1. Duplication ensures a viable configuration in the face of any single hardware failure and some multiple failures, giving a theoretical mean time between disabling hardware failures of over 400 years (depending on specific configuration).

The duplicated CPUs are self-checking, each with private, error-correcting memory. Self-checking ensures the discovery of failures before data is corrupted. The processors run active/standby, in which a failure in the active processor causes a switch to the standby processor without any degradation in processing power. The contents of both processors' memories are kept identical through the use of a memory-update link.

I/O processors and disk controllers are duplicated and dual-ported to both processors. Peripherals attached to the I/O processor can be duplicated, dual-ported, or single-ported, thus allowing the peripheral's availability to match its importance. In a typical configuration, critical data links are duplicated, the system console and printer are dual-ported, and normal terminals are single-ported. Disk drives can be mirrored, with each of the mirrored twins connected to a different disk controller. Consequently, a processor, a disk controller or a disk, and an I/O processor can fail without degrading the system's capabilities or incurring downtime.

The hardware is environmentally hardened to ensure continuous operation in the face of high temperature and humidity (such as can be caused by air conditioner failures), earthquakes, and other environmental catastrophes. Further, an uninterruptible power system with battery backup is available to provide continuous power.

*The Unix RTR operating system was formerly named the Duplex Multi-Environment Real Time (DMERT) operating system.

†An issue of *The Bell System Technical Journal* is devoted to describing the first release of this system.[6]

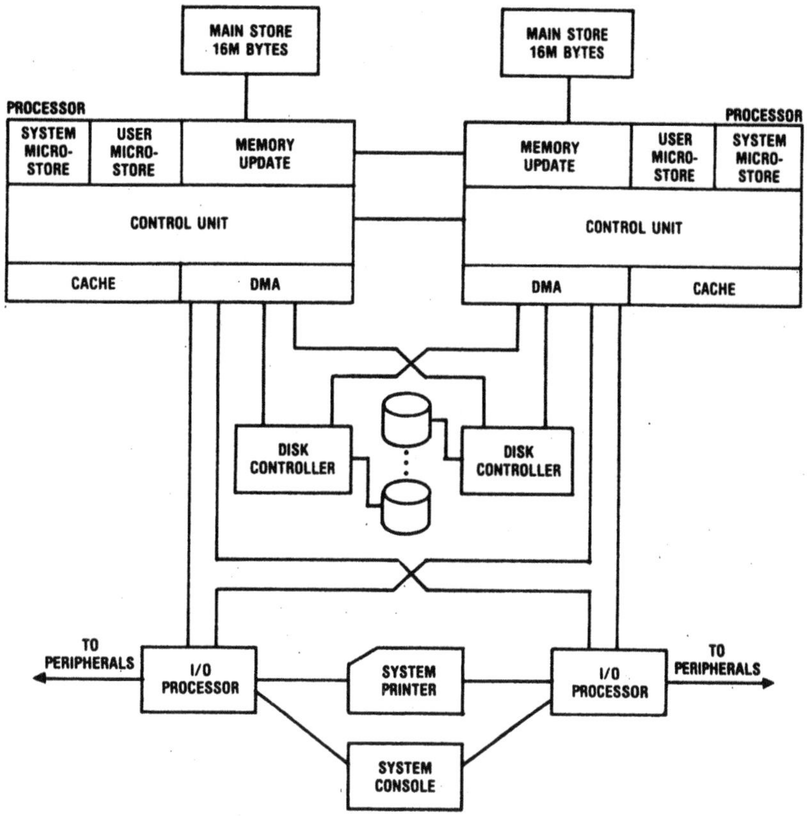

Figure 1. The architecture of the AT&T 3B20 Duplex system.

The design of the 3B20D hardware and Unix RTR operating system not only provides typical Unix operating system services but also provides a fault-tolerant safety net, as shown in Figure 2. This approach uses a combination of fault prevention and fault tolerance. Fault prevention attempts to eliminate faults through techniques such as verification and testing; these are discussed below in the section on "Assuring ultrahigh availability." Since there are many causes of faults and all faults cannot be eliminated, fault-tolerant techniques attempt to recover from faults that do occur.

Intelligent fault recovery

The Unix RTR system's fault-recovery strategy is to maintain a collection of hardware units that provides full capabilities in spite of failures. Fault recovery combines the following techniques to provide a system that, while complete in itself, allows applications to tailor the system to the users' needs.[7]

Centralized decision making. The fault-recovery system provides central configuration management through the following software: a configuration administrator and a database. When a failure occurs, the administration software accesses information in the database (kept in main memory) to quickly determine an alternate configuration of hardware units. Since there is one central database, the administration software can access the status of all hardware in the system to make an intelligent recovery.

Configuration database. The on-line configuration database provides a high-level description of hardware units, including their status, replication, whether they are essential to operation, how they are connected, and their error counts and thresholds. Short-term error counts and thresholds help detect failures, while long-term counts and thresholds help detect erratic, transient behavior.

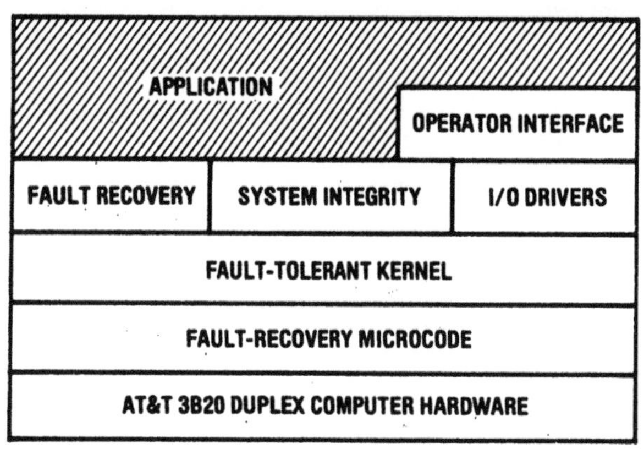

Figure 2. The fault-tolerant safety net.

Distributed recovery. Although the administration software makes central decisions regarding the hardware configuration, individual drivers are responsible for carrying out those decisions. This approach is taken for all types of units and permits customer hardware to be included in the database and administered even though the Unix RTR system does not know the device's characteristics.

Progressive recovery. The system matches the type of recovery to the severity of the fault. In traditional operating systems, the recovery action is often more disruptive than the fault it is intended to correct. Instead of taking a "sledgehammer" approach to recovery, the Unix RTR system takes minimal action to recover from faults, thereby disrupting processing as little as possible. For both hardware and software component failures, a localized recovery is first attempted to minimize the effect on unrelated parts of the system. Localized recovery is possible since the 3B20D's extensive fault-detection mechanisms find failures early. If the effect of the failure is not local, but rather has affected many processes or hardware units, then a system-wide rollback is attempted. Most work in progress is continued or restarted automatically. If this type of recovery is not successful, then automatic recovery escalates to various severities of bootstraps. By monitoring recovery and using escalating levels of initialization, the system ensures the correction of the failure, but at the lowest possible recovery level so as not to reduce availability unnecessarily.

Progressive recovery reduces the disruption caused by failures. Table 2 lists remedial actions and the typical resultant downtime (as seen by critical processing) caused by different levels of recovery. To provide applications with continuity across a bootstrap, the system preserves specific segments of their data in main memory. This data area is cleared only during the most severe recovery, which must be requested manually by the operator.

Downtime does not increase much as recovery escalates to more drastic actions beyond a bootstrap. However, disruption to an application's users (seen as aborted transactions, etc.) does increase as recovery becomes more drastic. Notice that "progressive recovery" is not always synonymous with "fastest recovery," since attempts to recover at lower levels may fail. But if most faults can be handled at the lower levels, disruption to the application is minimized.

Table 2. Progressive levels of recovery.

LEVEL OF RECOVERY	ACTION	APPROXIMATE DOWNTIME (SECONDS)
Local	Local recovery	None
1	Unix RTR operating system and I/O driver software rollback	0.15
2	Quick bootstrap	11
3	Complete bootstrap: reloading the configuration database	11
4	Manual only: Perform 3 (above), but also clear all memory	11

Automatic and manual reconfiguration. For the failure of a component, such as a disk-head crash, the system automatically reconfigures to bypass the malfunctioning unit. The operator may also reconfigure the system manually. In most cases, recovery is local and no downtime results from the reconfiguration.

As mentioned previously, for duplicated hardware architectures such as the 3B20D, availability is inversely proportional to the square of repair time. To reduce repair time, the system automatically schedules diagnostics on faulty units, thus eliminating a manual (and time-consuming) step towards repair. Obviously, accurate diagnostics are needed.

Reliable software

To reduce downtime due to software failures, high-availability systems should possess facilities to recover from software faults and minimize their disruptive effects. For this reason, we present the following techniques for increasing software reliability and isolating software faults for quick recovery.

Process fault recovery. Some categories of software faults are detected by the operating system (such as illegal system calls) or by the hardware (for example, illegal memory references). However, any high-availability operating system must report these faults to any process (program) that could encounter the faults; the process, in turn, conducts a recovery. The Unix RTR operating system—upon detecting any of several, similar faults—transfers control to the fault-handling routine of a process. This routine may then perform appropriate corrective action.

For noncritical programs, the corrective action often consists of terminating the process and restarting it. To continue work in progress, important information may be saved for the subsequent invocation of the program. However, system software often includes critical processes that cannot be terminated. These programs are often "servers," such as device drivers, file managers, and transaction monitors. They are occasionally subject to "transient" software faults, which result from unusual requests or sequences of requests. Often these bugs are difficult to find during testing and survive to be shipped to customers. Our experience has shown that often a simple rollback and retry will effect recovery from these transient faults.

System integrity. A large computer system includes many software subsystems. To provide high availability, the integrity of all software must be assured. Similarly, applications software subsystems must be monitored to ensure continuous operation.

The Unix RTR operating system provides these capabilities. During recovery, system integrity software makes sure that all major software systems start up properly. Recovery is automatically escalated if any systems fail to operate correctly. During operation, critical parts of the system—such as the operator interface, file system, maintenance control, software update, and system integrity software itself—are monitored by the system integrity software. If any of these parts fail, they are automatically restarted.

The system integrity software also provides applications facilities to monitor the integrity of their own software modules. Thus, the application can specify integrity constraints and have them enforced in the same manner as is done for Unix RTR system software.

Audits. If software is expected to operate for a year or more without reinitialization, facilities must be provided to detect and correct occasional corruption of internal data structures and reclaim "lost" system resources. Data structures should contain redundant information to aid this effort.[8]

There are many sources of data corruption. Sometimes multiple errors will interact to produce corruption. For example, suppose a process fails to return some system resource due to a bug. If another bug in the operating system's termination logic fails to reclaim the resource, the resource may become inaccessible for further use.

The Unix RTR operating system provides audits, which run periodically. These audits check various internal data structures for consistency and lost elements. Errors are reported and, where possible, corrected. Some examples of these audits follow:

- The program-administration audit checks the data structures that compose the process table. This audit can detect and correct such anomalies as processes indefinitely blocked during initialization or termination.
- The configuration-database audit checks the internal structure of the database to detect and correct structural errors, such as broken links.
- The file-manager audit checks many internal data structures for consistency.
- The message-buffer audit identifies lost message buffers and returns them to the system's message-buffer pool.

Overload. An overloaded system may be incapable of performing some tasks and is therefore partially unavailable. Worse yet, overload may result in a software crash. A high-availability computer system must detect overload and take appropriate corrective action.

The Unix RTR operating system monitors resources to detect overload conditions. Some of these resources correspond to physical entities—such as main memory, disk space, and processor time. Other elements monitored include operating system resources—such as free buffers and unused entries in various system tables.

Corrective actions are taken in response to detected overload. Depending on the type of overload, these actions may include removing a noncritical process that is consuming a great deal of a particular resource. For example, when overload is detected, automatically scheduled audits or diagnostics might be suspended. The strategy in case of extreme overload may be to reinitialize.

In all cases, the application is warned that an overload condition exists. It may be possible for the application to respond to the overload. For example, in a process control system, the scan rate of noncritical inputs might be decreased. In a transaction-processing system, some terminals or transactions might be made temporarily unavailable or be artificially throttled.

Update

Most computer systems must suspend processing to install new software or hardware. This downtime is unacceptable for a system that must be continuously available. The system must be able to accept new software (including an entirely new operating system) and new hardware (including a new processor) with little or no downtime.

Software update. The Unix RTR operating system provides a means of updating software with no downtime.[9] Software replacement of whole functions or just a few bytes is possible for critical processes. For less critical programs that may be stopped and restarted, file replacement updates the executable image on-disk. Some of these steps may be combined and installed as an atomic update so no inconsistent states are introduced.

Irrespective of the means used to update a running process, the programmer is presented with a high-level language interface. The programmer need only supply the new high-level language source files associated with the update. The software development system compiles the new source, compares the new object code with the old object code, determines what kinds of replacements to use, and generates the replacement files to be sent to the customer.

The operator interface supports the application of updates and, at a later time, the permanent inclusion of updates. At any time before the updates are made permanent, they may be backed out by the operator. Furthermore, if software recovery is required during a user-specified acceptance interval, the update will be automatically backed out. If a bootstrap occurs, all temporary updates will be backed out.

Update tracking is provided by the system. An update database of site history is maintained that includes lists of such information as updates that have been received but not applied, applied but not made permanent, or applied but backed out.

System update. A special case of software update is the installation of an entirely new operating system and new application. The Unix RTR system supports installing all new system and application software with a single bootstrap. To minimize the bootstrap's impact, specified application data can be preserved. During system update, one of the pair of duplicated system disks is taken off line. This disk is rewritten with the new software. The system is then booted from this disk. The new software may be used during an acceptance interval, during which time the system may be rolled back to the old software with a bootstrap. Ultimately, the new software will be marked "permanent" and copied to the other system disk.

Hardware update. To provide high system availability, it must be possible to change the system's hardware without incurring downtime. The Unix RTR operating system provides this capability. Since essential hardware units are duplicated, they may be taken out of service, powered down, modified, tested, and integrated back into the system with no system downtime. The flexible configuration database supports these activities. Using this facility, peripherals, peripheral controllers, I/O processors, memory, CPUs, and such may be installed or repaired with no downtime. While hardware is being updated the ability to survive some hardware failures is reduced.

Processor replacement. The ultimate hardware update is one in which the entire processor is replaced—often with a newer, more powerful one. Such updates should incur minimum downtime. The 3B20D processors have replaced older, less cost-effective processors; such processor replacement capabilities must be designed in close cooperation with the applications and are often application-specific. Close to 70 such processor replacements have been completed using the 3B20D/Unix RTR system. With few exceptions, each processor replacement caused less than a minute of downtime.

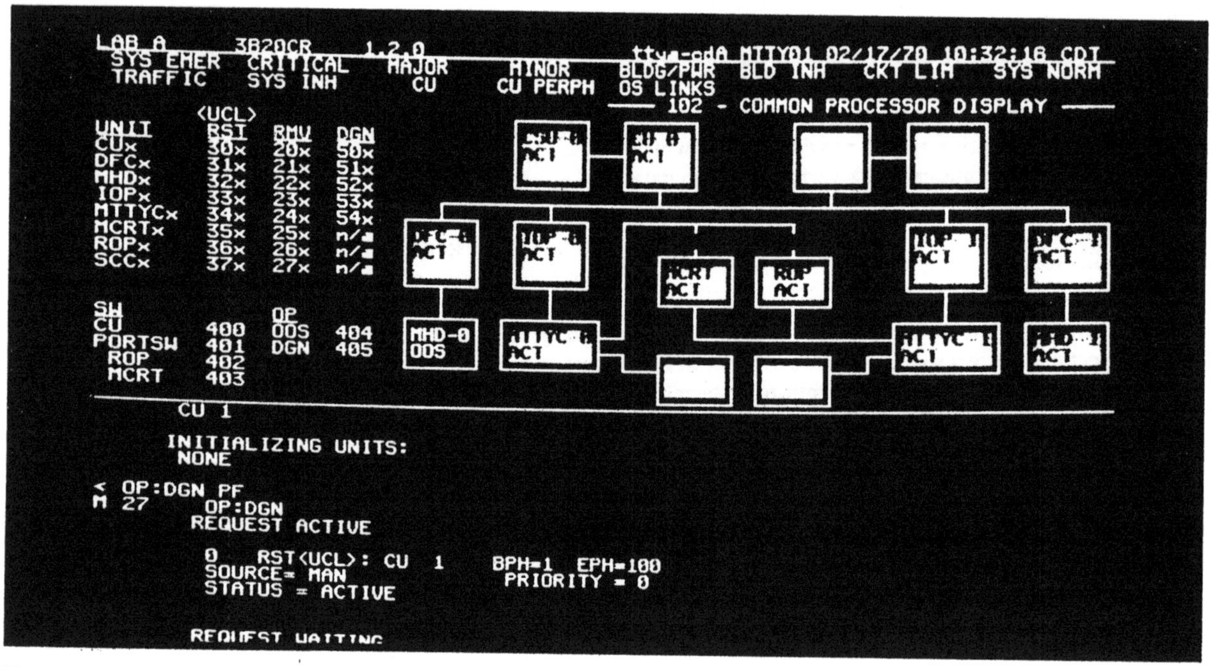

Figure 3. Multiwindow operator screen.

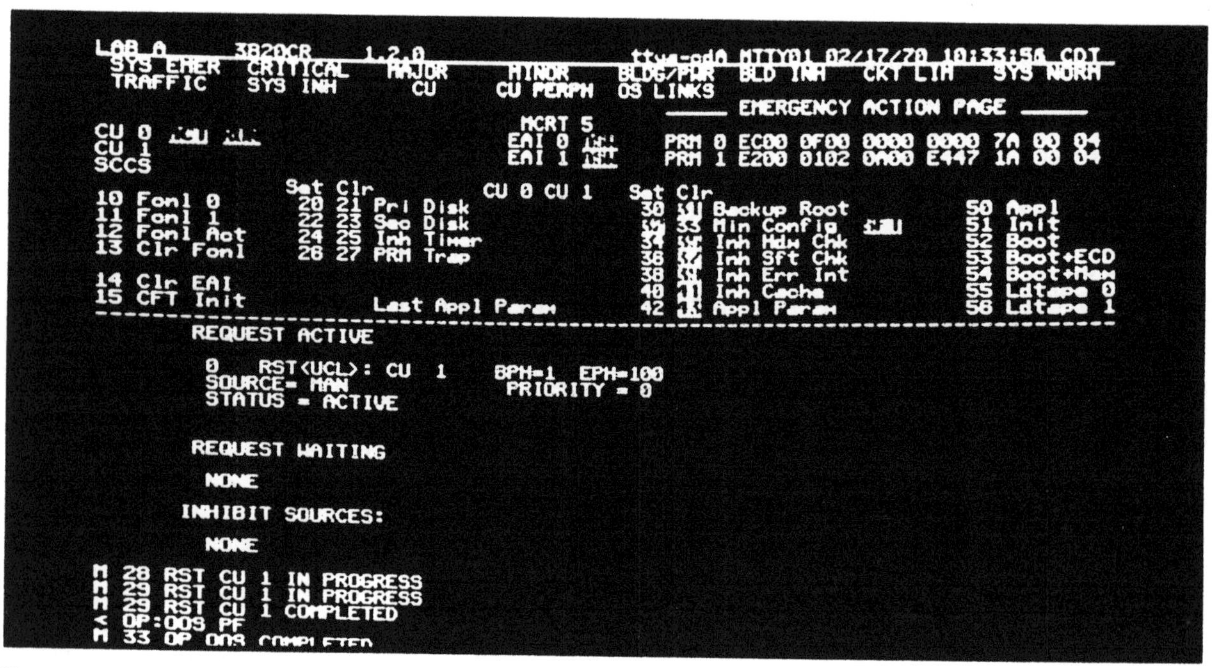

Figure 4. Menu of critical commands.

On-site debugging. While the vast majority of debugging is complete before a product is shipped to customers, some amount of on-site debugging is inevitable. Sometimes a problem is dependent on the particular set of updates in use at a site and cannot be recreated in the development laboratory. Other problems occur only with a particular load and must be studied while the system is in operation. High-availability systems have particular needs for on-site debugging tools. These tools must be completely noninterfering—that is, they should not degrade system availability. The tools should also be as productive as possible in order to help locate problems quickly.

The 3B20D/Unix RTR system can be debugged on-site using the Field Test Set. This is a self-contained, portable debugger that may be carried to a site, installed, used, and removed with no impact on system availability. The use of this debugger cannot affect system function, performance, or availability, since it traces the execution of instructions and data references in the CPU with no interference by passively monitoring the system bus.

Operator interface

Erroneous operator input or the lack of timely operator input may result in downtime. The operator interface of a high-availability system must minimize downtime due to these causes. Such an operator interface must be both easy to use and powerful (to promote correctness and timeliness), but must also protect the system from erroneous input.

Status information. The operator must be able to determine the status of the system quickly and easily. The Unix RTR operating system provides a brief indication of system status—it is always shown at the top of the operator's CRT console. In addition, a status page displays a block diagram of the system's configuration by using color graphics (for example, units in service are shown in green, out-of-service units are red, and standby units are blue).

An example of a multiwindow operator screen is shown in Figure 3. The first window contains one line at the top of the screen showing site name, software release identification, terminal name, date, and time. The second window contains lines two and three and displays an abbreviated status report. ("CU PERPH" is shown in red to indicate that a peripheral is out of service.) The third window includes lines four through 21 and shows a color, block diagram of the system, including a menu of commands available to the operator. For example, to diagnose moving-head disk 0, shown out of service in the block diagram, the operator would type 520. The fourth window contains lines 22 through 48 (not shown). This area scrolls and is used for textual input and output.

Ease of use. An operator interface must be easy to use to limit operator errors. The system's operator interface uses menus and provides positive feedback to acknowledge user input. In addition, a form interface (like those used for data entry in some transaction-processing systems) is provided to query and update the configuration of the system.

Operator guidance. Where possible, the operator should choose from a limited number of selections, which are optimized for the task at hand. Menus have traditionally been used for this purpose. Additional operator guidance should be used where possible. For example, the system's operator interface uses color to highlight menu selections particularly appropriate for the task at hand.

In Figure 3, the out-of-service moving-head disk is shown in red, and the menu selection that instructs the system to diagnose and restore the disk is also shown in red to provide operator guidance.

Minimized dangerous errors. The operator interface of a high-availability computer must protect the system from erroneous commands that might degrade availability. The Unix RTR system's operator interface protects the invocation of some critical commands (such as "boot" and "inhibit hardware checks") by placing them on a special menu, away from other, more common commands. In addition, the commands most likely to impact system availability, such as "boot," are further protected. The operator is asked "Are you sure?" when any of these commands are invoked and has 45 seconds in which to respond "yes." If the operator responds "no" or makes no response, the operation is not performed.

The menu of critical commands is shown in Figure 4. Notice that this page begins with a brief indication of system status. Beneath this are additional status information and the menu selections that implement positive control of the 3B20D hardware.

Positive control. In the event of a system failure where automatic recovery is unsuccessful, the operator must respond quickly to reconfigure the system and reboot. Such control of the 3B20D/Unix RTR system is provided by independent, duplicated microprocessors. When the system is operating normally, these microprocessors serve as peripheral controllers for the operator's console. In the event of a total system failure, they allow the operator to interactively specify a desired configuration for the 3B20D processor and initiate a bootstrap without resorting to front panel switches or the like (see Figure 4).

Assuring ultrahigh availability

To assure that availability goals are met, it is important not only to design for availability, but also to accurately model, test, track, and control it.

Modeling. When designing an ultrahigh availability computer, availability must be modeled and predicted early in the system requirements analysis. Downtime objectives should be established and allocated to the different hardware and software components. (Table 1 could be used to help determine these allocations.)

Hardware availability can be modeled using traditional approaches based on failure rates of components, repair times, and replication strategies.[5] Estimating software reliability is harder, since it is not as well understood. However, since software reliability depends partially on software quality, Unix RTR software developers use methods, not models, to ensure high-quality software. These methods include requirement and design reviews, code inspections, and extensive testing; they are similar to methods discussed elsewhere.[10,11]

Testing. The product must be rigorously tested before its release to determine whether it meets its predicted availability. Adequate testing is particularly important when a manufacturer expects a rapid product buildup, since unexpected downtime will harm customer relations and burden support personnel.

As the product matures and becomes more reliable, testing must become more rigorous because problems will be harder to find. Aside from traditional test methods, such as acceptance and first customer (beta-site) testing, other methods are used for the Unix RTR operating system. These additional methods include the following:

- Physical fault-insertion, in which faults are placed in the hardware circuitry, typically by way of the backplane. Through tests that simulate most hardware failures, we make sure that fault-recovery mechanisms and diagnostics operate correctly and that there is no single point of failure that could cripple the entire system.
- Software fault-insertion, in which faults are placed in software components to test local recovery and make sure that the software recovers correctly.

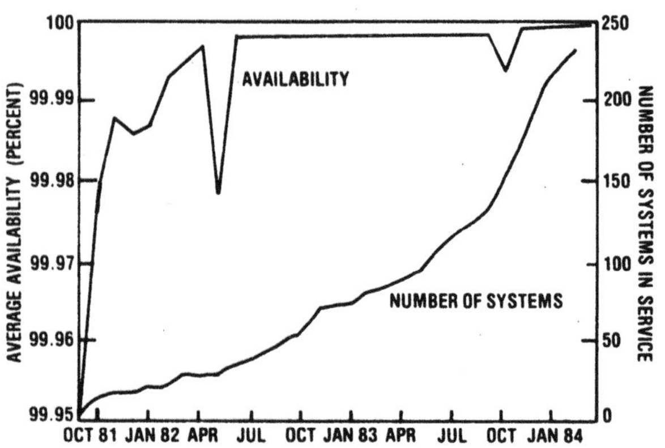

Figure 5. The observed availability and the number of 3B20D/Unix RTR systems in service.

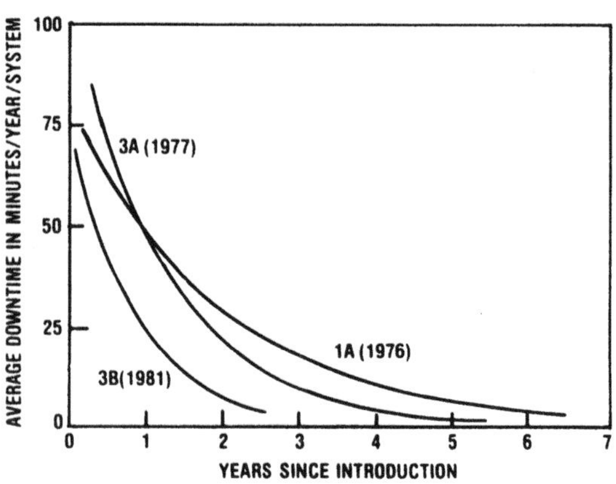

Figure 6. Downtime versus time since introduction for three high-availability computers.

- Stress testing, performed at full load, in which it is determined whether all hardware and software components operate correctly when pushed to their limits. Furthermore, stress testing can be used to estimate how well the system is meeting its availability objectives.[12]
- Software debugging-and-testing systems that allow the programmer to debug and test in high-level languages; they improve software quality and, hence, availability.
- Regression tests which check that, as new features are introduced, old features are not broken and availability is not sacrificed.

Typically, a system will experience a maturing period, during which its availability will start relatively low but, after time, will approach its objectives. Figure 5 shows this to be the case for the 3B20D/Unix RTR system. It experienced about 250 minutes average downtime per year when it was first introduced in September 1981. Within one year, over 50 systems were in operation and experienced less than 10 minutes average downtime per year. (These downtime figures, from a telephone switching environment, are based on monthly average availability data and include downtime due to hardware, software, and procedural errors attributed to the 3B20D/Unix RTR system.)

We expect to continue improving system availability. However, each new major release introduces a somewhat immature system and brings with it the possibility of regressing to lower levels of availability. So, as a product matures, testing becomes even more important to avoid these lapses in high availability.

Tracking. Throughout testing, installation at customer sites, and operation, systems should be tracked to monitor how well they are meeting their availability objectives.[13] It is important to track each problem's symptoms, stimuli, and effects in addition to its frequency and type. The Unix RTR system keeps this information in activity logs, which can be queried remotely on each system. Through accurate tracking, problems can be identified early and a solution effected before the impacts on availability are drastic. The information tracked includes downtime, hardware failures, transient hardware errors, software errors, recoveries caused by software, software audit failures, software overloads, and operator input.

The importance of tracking is emphasized by the spike for May 1982 shown in Figure 5. This lapse in availability was caused by a hardware problem that forced a recovery that was too drastic for the fault. By tracking and responding to this problem quickly, we were able to both improve the recovery (to minimize downtime) and remove the source of the fault: a noisy power supply.

Control. All problems discovered through testing and site experience must be solved quickly: these problems have causes that must be determined and corrected. However, without proper controls and procedures, problems may be ignored, especially when programmers are isolated from customer sites or test facilities.

To make sure that problems are solved, we use automated tools and assign responsibility for each problem to specific programmers and their management. Through these tools, we can also query and track the status and priority of a problem, print reports, and estimate staff usage. Since all development work is linked to a specific problem or a new feature request, we also have added project control.

Although the techniques discussed in this article will improve a system's availability, the development costs of such a system may be higher than for a conventional system. There are many reasons for this. First, more effort is required to design, implement, and test systems by using some of these techniques. For example, including software recovery, audits, and overload controls may double the lines of code for some software components. Second, some features, such as on-line update, require development of hardware and software not otherwise needed. Third, testing is more rigorous. The system must be of high quality to ensure high availability, and this requires extensive, thorough testing. Furthermore, once a system has achieved a high level of availability, there are fewer failures and the average time between failures is increased. Therefore, finding failures through testing and site experience and improving availability becomes more costly. Finally, large gains in availability can be made in early refinement of the system. Yet, improvements become difficult after a point since they involve complex changes to algorithms and design rather than simple bug fixes. (Notice the asymptotic nature of the availability curve in Figure 5.)

Figure 6 shows downtime data for three AT&T computer systems, including the 3B20D. Each has achieved high levels of availability. However, by refining and improving the techniques discussed in this article, each computer approached its availability objectives more quickly than its predecessor. (Downtime data in Figure 6 includes both planned and unplanned downtime from the computer hardware and operating system software. For comparison, the downtime data has been fit to an exponential decay function.) *

Acknowledgments

The authors gratefully acknowledge the contributions of Al Burger, Rich Buttenhoff, Betty Cox, Tony Guercio, Keith Johnson, Jesse Kartus, Tim Surratt, Joseph Tam, Charles Wrobel, and the reviewers. The design, implementation, and support of the 3B20 Duplex computer and its Unix RTR operating system required the cooperative efforts of hundreds of people within Bell Laboratories and AT&T Technologies; the authors wish to acknowledge the contributions of all whose work is summarized here.

References

1. P. W. Bowman et al., "Maintenance Software," *Bell System Technical J.*, Vol. 56, No. 2, Feb. 1977, pp. 255-287.
2. W. N. Toy, "Fault-Tolerant Design of Local ESS Processors," *Proc. IEEE*, Vol. 66, No. 10, Oct. 1978, pp. 1126-45.
3. T. Anderson and P. A. Lee, *Fault-Tolerance Principles and Practice*, Prentice-Hall International, Inc., London, 1981, p. 97.
4. S. E. Jones, "Synapse's Approach to High Application Availability," *Digest of Papers, Compcon Spring 83*, pp. 12.17.
5. G. D. Kraft and W. N. Toy, *Microprogrammed Control and Reliable Design of Small Computers*, Prentice-Hall, Inc., Englewood Cliffs, N.J., 1981, p. 163-196.
6. J. O. Becker, guest editor, "The 3B20D Processor and DMERT Operating System," *Bell System Technical J.*, Vol. 62, No. 1, Part 2, Jan. 1983.
7. D. J. Fitch, A. M. Guercio, K. W. Johnson, and G. T. Surratt, "DMERT: A Fault-Tolerant Environment for Diverse Applications," *Proc. 14th Int'l Conf. Fault-Tolerant Computing*, June 1984.
8. J. R. Connet, E. J. Pasternak, and B. D. Wagner, "Software Defenses in Real-Time Control Systems," *Digest of Papers, Second Int'l Symp. Fault-Tolerant Computing*, pp. 94-99.
9. R. L. Engram, P. A. Shannon, and S. S. Weber, "Transparent Software and Hardware Changes in a Telecommunications System," *Proc. Fifth Int'l Conf. Software Eng. for Telecommunication Switching Systems*, July 1983, pp. 157-162.
10. R. L. Glass, *Software Reliability Guidebook*, Prentice-Hall, Inc., Englewood Cliffs, N.J., 1979.
11. M. E. Fagan, "Design and Code Inspections to Reduce Errors in Program Development," *IBM Systems J.*, Vol. 15, No. 3, 1976, pp. 61-66.
12. D. S. Trushin and D. J. Fitch, "Attaining Objectives in a High-Availability System," *Third Annual Int'l Phoenix Conf. Computers and Communications*, Mar. 1984, pp. 221-225.
13. N. O. Whittington, L. C. Brown, and N. X. Delessio, "3B20D Computer System Field Experience—The First 250 Systems," *Proc. Eleventh Int'l Switching Symp.*, May 1984.

John J. Wallace is a member of the technical staff at AT&T Bell Laboratories in Naperville, Illinois. He has worked in the Operating Systems Laboratory on the Unix RTR kernel since 1980 and is currently designing the kernel for a distributed multiprocessor system.

Wallace received a BS in computer science from Worcester Polytechnic Institute in 1978 and an MS in electrical engineering (computer engineering) from Carnegie-Mellon University in 1979. He is a member of the IEEE Computer Society and ACM.

Walter W. Barnes is a member of the technical staff at AT&T Bell Laboratories in Naperville, Illinois. His research interests include fault-tolerant distributed systems and computer security. He is currently designing the operating system for a fault-tolerant, distributed computer.

Barnes received a BGS in computer science from Kansas University in 1978 and an MS in computer science from Northwestern University in 1983. He is a member of IEEE and ACM.

Questions about this article can be directed to either author at AT&T Bell Laboratories, Naperville-Wheaton Rd., Naperville, IL 60566.

DISTRIBUTED EXECUTION OF RECOVERY BLOCKS: AN APPROACH TO UNIFORM TREATMENT OF HARDWARE AND SOFTWARE FAULTS

K. H. Kim
Department of Computer Science & Engineering
University of South Florida
Tampa, Florida 33620

Abstract

This paper explores the concept of distributed execution of recovery blocks as an approach for unified treatment of hardware and software faults. A useful characteristic of the approach is the relatively small time cost it requires and thus the approach is suitable for incorporation into real-time computer systems. Three different schemes for distributed execution of recovery blocks are discussed. One of them called Scheme C here looks particularly promising. The possibility of combining Scheme C with a load-sharing multiprocessing scheme is also discussed. Finally, experimental results that strongly indicate the feasibility of incorporating the distributed execution schemes into a broad range of real-time computer systems are presented.

1. Introduction

As computers are increasingly used in critical real-time applications such as space navigation, air-traffic control, patient monitoring, power plant control, etc., users' demands for fault tolerance capabilities of such computers are also steadily increasing. Such computer systems should be capable of tolerating failures of not only their hardware components but also their software components.

In many of the fault tolerance schemes explored in the past, efficient recovery of the system from the detected fault depended upon the success in locating the extent of the fault with high precision [K1]. However, distinguishing hardware faults from software faults in a real-time computer system has often been a problem troubling the system designers. For example, symptoms of transient hardware faults and those of software faults are often very similar. If their effects are detected when the result of a computing task is rejected by an acceptance test or run-time assertion check, then the system may run a hardware diagnosis but it won't reveal any fault in the system hardware. The only way to tell whether the rejection of the task result was due to a transient hardware fault or a software fault is to retry the task with the same software. If the result is rejected again, then it is reasonable to conclude that the software is faulty. Or if the result is accepted this time, then a reasonable conclusion is that a transient hardware fault occurred during the previous execution of the task.

Therefore, distinguishing hardware faults from software faults is costly even if it is logically feasible. Also, introducing different treatments for all possible different faults can quickly add up to an intolerable system complexity. Naturally, computer system disigners have long sought for techniques for unified treatment of both hardware and software faults.

The purpose of this paper is to show that distributed execution of recovery blocks, a combination of both distributed processing and recovery block concepts, is a promising approach for unified treatment of both hardware and software faults. Recovery block consists of one or more routines, called try blocks here, designed to compute the same or similar results, and an acceptance test which is an expression of the criterion used for accepting the results of try blocks [H2,R1]. A try (i.e., execution of a try block) is thus always followed by an acceptance test. In the next section, three different schemes for distributed execution of recovery blocks will be presented in the increasing order of their potential in system reliability enhancement. A discussion on the possibility of combining the distributed execution schemes with a load balancing scheme will then follow in Section 3. In order to test the execution efficiency of the schemes, two experimental implementations and measurements have been done, one in the Reliable Distributed Microcomputing Laboratory (RDML) of the University of South Florida and the other in the BMD Advanced Research Center, Huntsville [W1]. Section 4 is a brief summary of the experiment results.

2. Schemes for Distributed Execution of Recovery Blocks

+ This work was supported partly by U.S. Army BMD Advanced Technology Center under Contract No. DASG60-83-C-0042.

Throughout this paper, only two try blocks, i.e., the primary and the alternate, are used to illustrate distributed execution of a recovery block for the sake of simplicity. Also, a watch-dog timer used to ensure timely completion of tries is an integral part of the recovery block discussed in this paper [H1]. Therefore, the acceptance test can be viewed as a combination of both "logic acceptance test" and "time acceptance test". Furthermore, the recovery block discussed in this paper does not contain global variables.

2.1 Scheme A

Figure 1 depicts Scheme A for distributed execution of a recovery block. The primary node contains only the primary try block whereas the alternate try block and the logic and time acceptance tests run on the backup node. Therefore, the backup node is solely responsible for acceptance testing and recovery. Both nodes receive the same data set simultaneously from the predecessor computing station. The backup node turns its watch-dog timer on as soon as it receives a data set. Both nodes process the data set using the try blocks contained in them. When the primary node has completed processing of the data set, the result is sent to the backup node for checkout by use of the logic acceptance test. If the result does not arrive at the backup node in time, then the watch-dog timer in the backup node generates a "fault" signal. If the result arrives in time and passes the logic acceptance test, then the result is forwarded to the successor computing station. On the other hand, if the result from the primary node fails in the logic acceptance test or the watch-dog timer generates a "fault" signal, i.e., the result fails in the time acceptance test, then the result from the alternate try block is checked out by use of the logic acceptance test. On passing the test, the result from the alternate try block is forwarded to the successor computing station.

Therefore, both the primary and alternate try blocks are executed concurrently. The failure of the primary node in producing an acceptable result can be caused by hardware faults, residual design errors in the primary try block or both. The exact cause needs not be identified for recovery purpose.

However, the scheme suffers from a major drawback. That is, if the backup node is lost, the entire computing station crashes because the decision-making mechanism, i.e., the acceptance test, is in the backup node. If the backup node hardware is functioning but the alternate try block behaves in an undesirable manner, the computing station can continue to function as long as the primary node produces acceptable results.

2.2 Scheme B

Figure 2 depicts Scheme B which is a result of an attempt to remove the major weakness of Scheme A. The logic acceptance test is now duplicated in both the primary and backup nodes. Therefore, the result of each try block is checked out in the node in which the try block is running. If the primary node fails in its logic acceptance test, then it sends a notice to the backup node. The latter responds by forwarding its result generated from execution of the alternate try block to the successor computing station, provided that the result has passed both the logic and time acceptance tests.

In this scheme, the computing station does not crash even if the backup node is lost. Whether the primary node fails due to hardware faults or the imperfect primary try block, the backup node takes the same recovery action.

One drawback of this scheme is that the primary node is abandoned when it fails to produce an acceptable result due to a residual design error in the primary try block. Therefore, a poor utilization of hardware resources can result and cause an unnecessary shortening of the life-time of the computing station.

2.3 Scheme C

Scheme C, depicted in Figure 3, is a way to remove the drawback of Scheme B. This scheme is different from Scheme B in two major ways. First, the complete acceptance test consisting of logic and time tests is now duplicated in both the primary and backup nodes. Secondly, the two try blocks are duplicated in both nodes. However, the roles of the two try blocks are not the same in the two nodes. The primary node uses try block A as the primary try block initially, whereas the backup node uses try block B as the initial primary. Therefore, until a fault is detected, both nodes receive the same input data, process them by use of two different try blocks, and check the results by use of the acceptance test. Both nodes perform all these tasks concurrently. The time acceptance test in the backup node is used to ensure timely behavior of both nodes.

Once the primary node fails in producing an acceptable result, the roles of the primary and backup nodes are reversed as well as the roles of the primary and backup try blocks within the failed node. Therefore, the new primary node continues to use try block B as the primary try block while the new backup node picks try block B as the primary try block. If the former primary node is dead due to permanent irreparable hardware faults, converting it into the new backup node is meaningless. However, if the former primary node failed merely was due to an error in the former primary try block (A), then converting it into the new backup node with try block B as the new primary try block is worthwhile; when the new primary node is lost, the backup node is available for a take-over and continued service.

As soon as the new backup node picks try block B as the primary try block, it makes a retry in processing the data set with B as an effort to keep the database in the node up to date. If the next data set arrives before the new backup node succeeds in the retry, then it must be queued in the input buffer; this means that the new backup node starts lagging behind the new primary node. In order for this scheme to work, the data arrival rate should be such that the new backup node may catch up with the primary node even if the former lags temporarily behind the latter. In fact, if try block B contains a residual design error, both nodes can fail to process a certain data set. In that case, both nodes will retry with try block A and if successful, both nodes will use A as their new primary try blocks. The roles of the nodes may remain as before.

On the other hand, if the backup node fails first, then the primary node needs not be disturbed. The backup node will just try to pick try block A as its new primary try block. Again, if the backup node was completely lost, this arrangement is useless. However, if the failure was due to an error in try block B, then picking try block A as the new primary can result in the backup node being available for continued service when the primary node fails later.

It is also conceivable to design a failed node to stay with the same try block used before for the sake of keeping diversity in the try blocks used by the two nodes. The roles of the nodes are still reversed. For example, if the primary node in Figure 3 fails first, then it becomes the new backup node and makes a retry with the previously used try block A. If successful, the new backup node stays with try block A as its primary. Therefore, the two nodes continue to run two different try blocks. An advantage is that if a data set causes one of the try blocks to fail but not both of them, then one acceptable result can be sent to the successor computing station with little delay. However, if the failure of the former primary node was caused by a residual design error in try block A, the retry by the node with A after it assumes the role of the new backup node will fail. Therefore, the node will have to switch to try block B after two consecutive failures; it will lag much behind the new primary node. Several other strategies for using try blocks are conceivable. Hopefully future experiments will provide insight into the merits and weaknesses of various conceivable strategies.

This scheme does not have the drawbacks of Scheme A and Scheme B. Both hardware and software faults are treated in a unified manner in this scheme. Yet the scheme does not require any additional software design. It is just an efficient way of utilizing both hardware and software resources to maximally prolong the life-time of a computing station. The recovery time is minimal since maximum concurrency is exploited.

3. Scheme C with load balancing

In the case where a computing station uses multiple nodes for the purpose of multiprocessing, i.e., for the purpose of obtaining a throughput higher than what is obtainable with a single node, it is not cost-effective to divide the nodes into an equal number of primary nodes and backup nodes. A reasonable approach is to connect the nodes loosely through queues containing data sets and allow each node to dynamically pick the next task among the primary try block, the alternate try block, and the acceptance test. Figure 4 depicts such an approach. This is essentially the approach used in [W1]. In this scheme, each node may pick up its next job from any of the four queues. If it picks a data set from the "input data" queue, it executes the primary try block (A) and deposits the result (together with the original input data) into the "try results" queue. If its next job has come from the "try results" queue, then it first locates a record in the "arrival time record" queue that corresponds to the data set just picked up from the "try results" queue. The record should contain both the arrival time and the maximum expected processing time of the data set. This information is used by the node in determining if a timing fault has occurred or not. If it concludes that a timing fault has occurred, the result data set is rejected and the corresponding original input data set is moved to the "retry data" queue. Otherwise, the node executes the logic acceptance test. If the result is acceptable, an irrevocable update of the database with the result is carried out and then the result is moved into the "validated results" queue for pickup by the successor computing station. If not acceptable, the data set is moved to the "retry data" queue. If a node picks its next job from the "arrival time record" queue, then it checks if the record is too old. If so, then the node moves the corresponding data set in the "input data" queue into the "retry data" queue. If a node picks its next job from the "retry data" queue, then it executes the alternate try block (B) and deposits the result into the "try results" queue.

One drawback of this scheme is that a "crazy" node can disrupt a significant portion of the network, thereby causing a significant performance degradation. For example, it may get stuck to a queue or repeatedly pick up new data sets and produce unacceptable results. Or it may continue to pick up data sets from the "try results" queue and reject them even if they are good. However, it may be possible to implement the scheme in such a way that the probability of a "crazy" node causing a significant disturbance becomes very small. This is a subject worth further study. It seems also a worthwhile research topic to explore some other possible ways of combining Scheme C and load balancing schemes.

4. Experimental Validation

In this section, two experiments carried out in order to test the time overhead of the distributed execution schemes, are briefly described. One experiment was carried out at the author's location and the other at the U.S. Army BMD Advanced Research Center, Huntsville, Alabama [W1].

The performance of a distributed execution scheme is a function of several factors. For example, the type of communication medium used to connect computer nodes is a major factor in determining the performance. The higher the communication bandwidth is, the better the performance becomes. The networks used in both experiments are tightly coupled ones.

4.1 Experiment conducted at USF RDML with Scheme C

The network configurations used are depicted in Figure 5. Node 3 in the figure was used as a backup to node 2 (Analyzer-1). A node used here is a Z8000-based single-board microcomputer. The connection medium used between nodes is a two-port buffer memory consisting of two independent memory banks of 16K bytes each. Nodes can exchange data through a two-port buffer memory nearly at the rate of local (on-board) memory access.

The nature of the application program written in Extended Concurrent Pascal [K2] is as follows. Node 6 (Data generator) simulates a real-time device which generates stimulus data to the rest of the network and accepts the response (command). The remaining four data processing nodes contain an input (i.e., stimulus data) classification process, various analysis processes, which constitute the intelligence of the solution algorithm, and a control command scheduler process that delivers the network's response to the real-time device. The stimulus data from Node 6 is first handled by the input classification process which distributes inputs to the rest of the network. The command scheduler process basically honors requests from various analysis processes for scheduling commands to the real-time device.

Since the purpose of this experiment was to measure the time overhead, only hardware faults were injected and only one try block was used in both Node 2 and Node 3. Measurement was made of the time taken for data sets to reach Node 5 (Command scheduler) from Node 1 (Input classifier). Figure 6-a shows the data travel time measured when no faults were injected. The solid curve in the figure corresponds to the case of the network without Scheme C, i.e., without use of Node 3 whereas the dotted curve is for the case of the network with Scheme C incorporated by use of Node 3 as the backup node. The delay shown in the figure is less than 100mS. Figure 6-b shows the data travel time measure when Node 2 was turned off, i.e., disabled, during the measurements. It shows that the time-out and recovery actions contributed to about 250mS delay in the data travel time when the fault was injected.

It is clear that there are many real-time applications where the distributed execution schemes can be used with tolerable amounts of time overhead.

4.2 Experiment conducted at BMD ARC

The details on this experiment are referred to [W1]. Only the measurement results are briefly mentioned here. The distributed execution scheme that was experimented is essentially Scheme C with load balancing depicted in Figure 4. A simulated time scale rather than an absolute clock time was used. The time taken for data sets to travel from the "input data" queue to the "validated results" queue was measured. It was reported that incorporation of the distributed execution scheme contributed on the average 1mS increase in the travel time. When a fault was injected into one node, the time-out (30mS) and recovery actions caused the travel time of the affected data set to jump to 32mS while the average travel time in a fault-free mode is about 5mS. However, this jump was mainly because the watch-dog timer had been set with the waiting period of 30mS. The absolute values of the numbers reported are not so much significant as the fact that this experiment also indicated the feasibility of using a distributed execution scheme in many real-time applications which impose very stringent response time requirements.

5. Conclusion

Several schemes for distributed execution of recovery blocks were explored in this paper. They are the results of a search for techniques for unified treatment of hardware and software faults in real-time computer systems. The experimental results, although limited, are encouraging in that they match with our expectation on the small time costs of the distributed execution schemes. The cases of nested recovery blocks should pose no serious problems since enclosing recovery blocks and nested recovery blocks can be assigned to different nodes. Some of the basic questions related to the effective use of recovery blocks for software fault tolerance still remain unsatisfactorily answered and not helped by the distributed execution schemes. Until those questions are settled, the recovery block approach to software fault tolerance remains an immature technology.

ACKNOWLEDGEMENT: The author wishes to thank Howard Welch and Bill McDonald for inspiring suggestions during the work summarized in this paper. He would also like to thank S. Heu, P. Rehm, S. Yang, and J. Yoon for their assistance during this work.

References

[H1] Hecht, H., "Fault-Tolerant Software for Real-Time Applications", Computing Surveys, Dec. 1976, pp.391-407.

[H2] Horing, J.J., Lauer, H.C., Melliar-Smith, P.M., and Randell, B., "A Program Structure for Error Detection and Recovery", Lecture Notes in Comp. Sci., vol. 16, Springer-Verlag, 1974, pp.171-187

[K1] Kim, K.H., Hecht, H., Huang, J., and Naghibzadeh, M., "Strategies for Structured and Fault-Tolerant Design of Recovery Programs", Proc. IEEE Computer Society's Int'l Computer Software and Applications Conf. (COMPSAC), Nov. 1978, pp.651-656.

[K2] Kim, K.H., "Evolution of a Virtual Machine Supporting Fault-Tolerant Distributed Processes at a Research Laboratory", Proc. IEEE Computer Society's Int'l Conf. on Data Engineering, Los Angeles, April 1984.

[R1] Randell, B., "System Structure for Software Fault Tolerance", IEEE Trans. on Software Engr., June 1975, pp.220-232.

[W1] Welch, H., "Distributed Recovery Block Performance in a Real-Time Control Loop", Proc. 1983 Real-Time Systems Symposium, Dec. 1983.

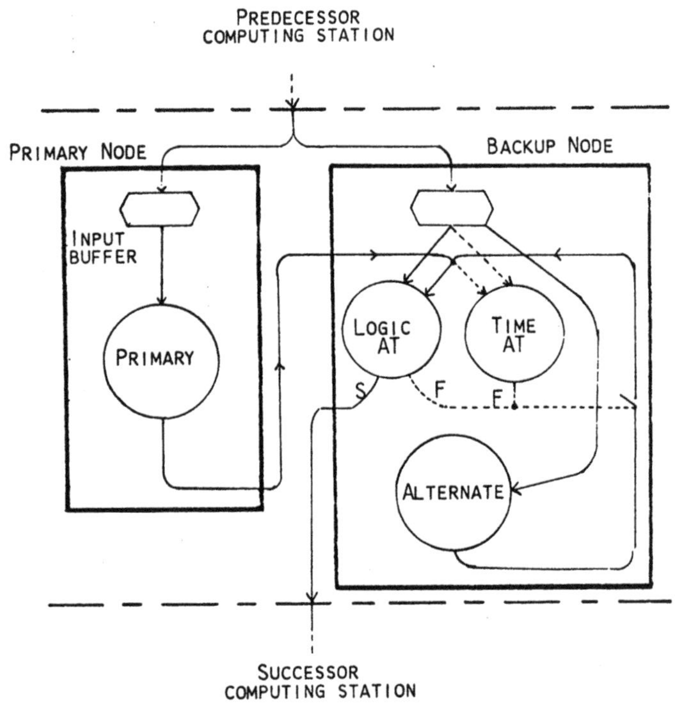

FIGURE 1. SCHEME A

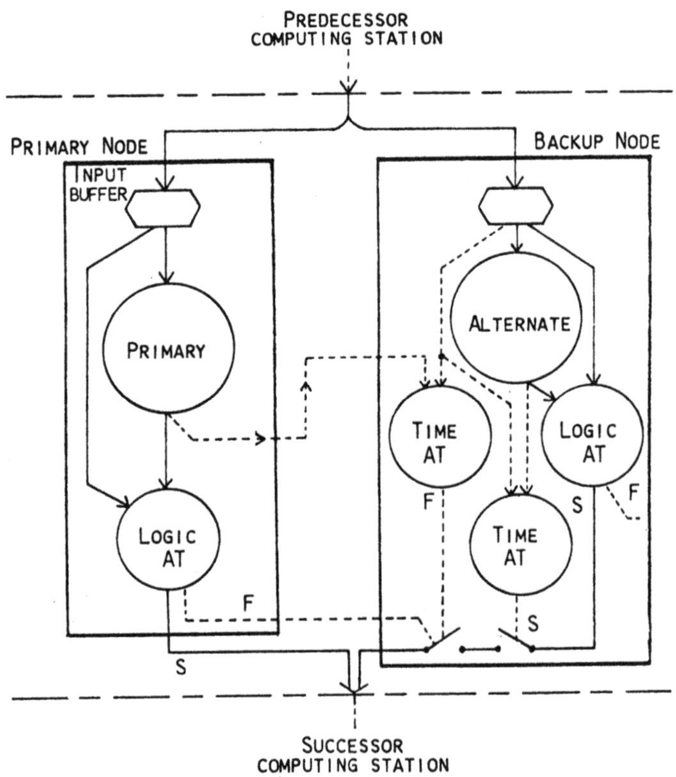

FIGURE 2. SCHEME B

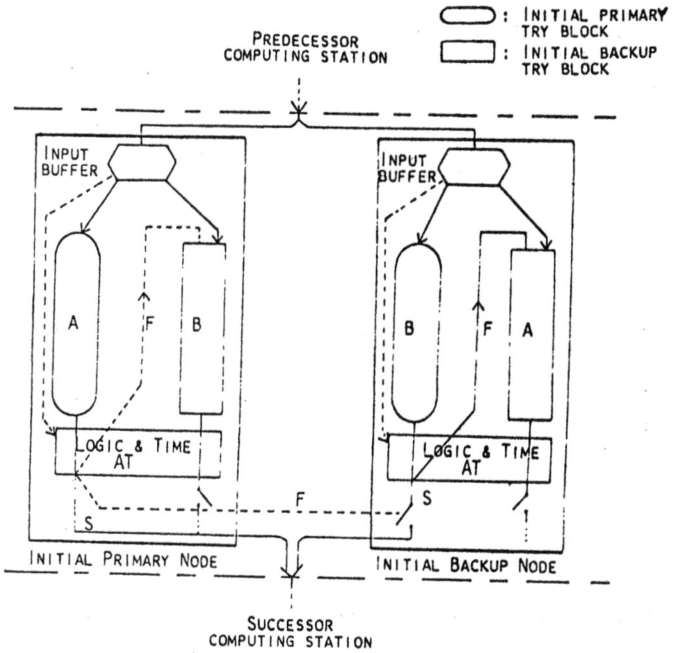

Figure 3. Scheme C

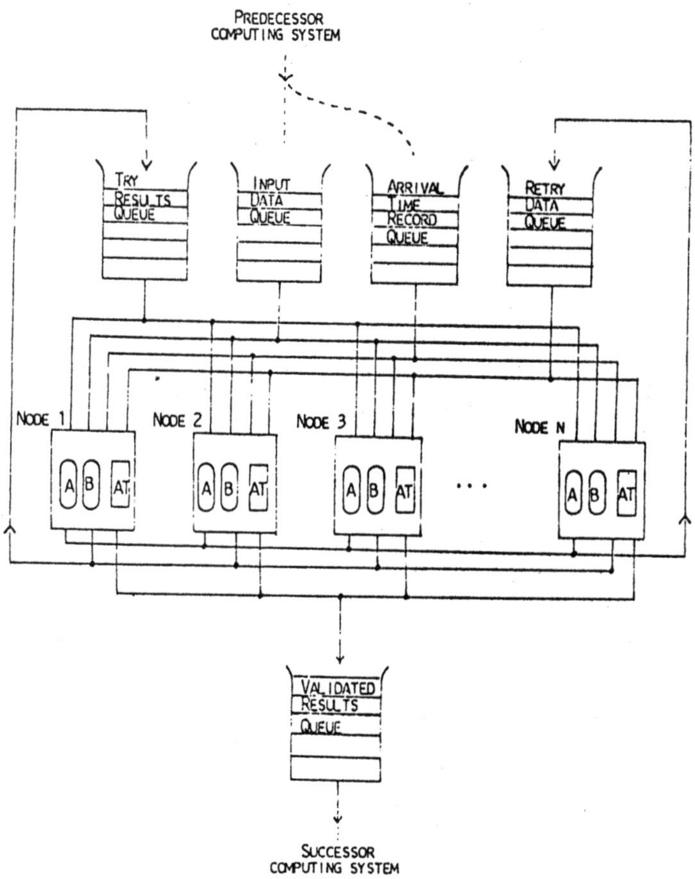

Figure 4. Scheme C with load balancing

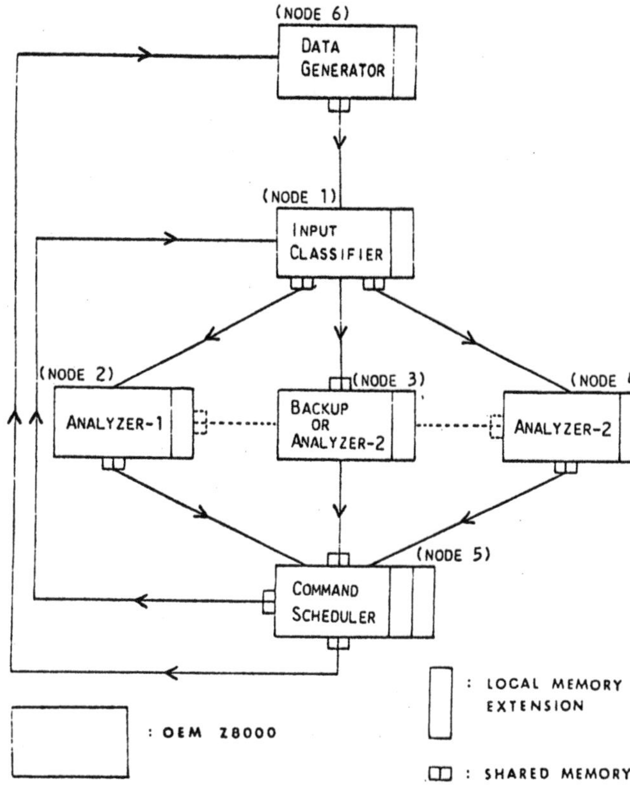

Figure 5. Network configuration used at USF RDML for experimentation with Scheme C

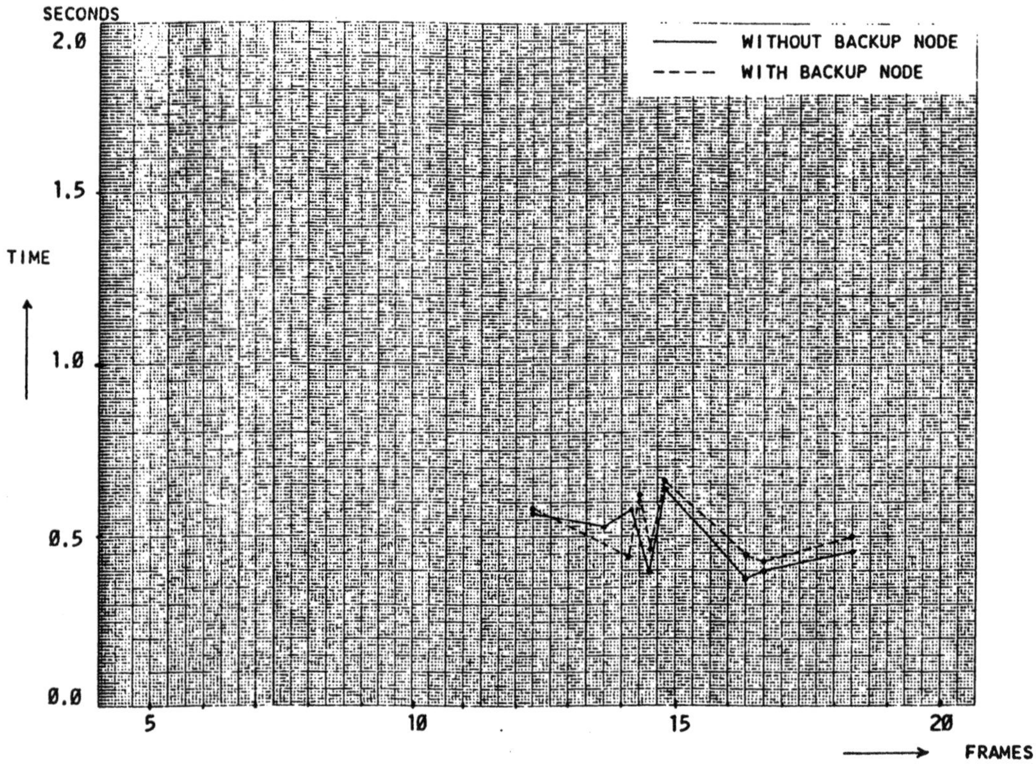

FIGURE 6-A. DATA TRAVEL TIME MEASURED WITH THE SETUP IN FIGURE 5.

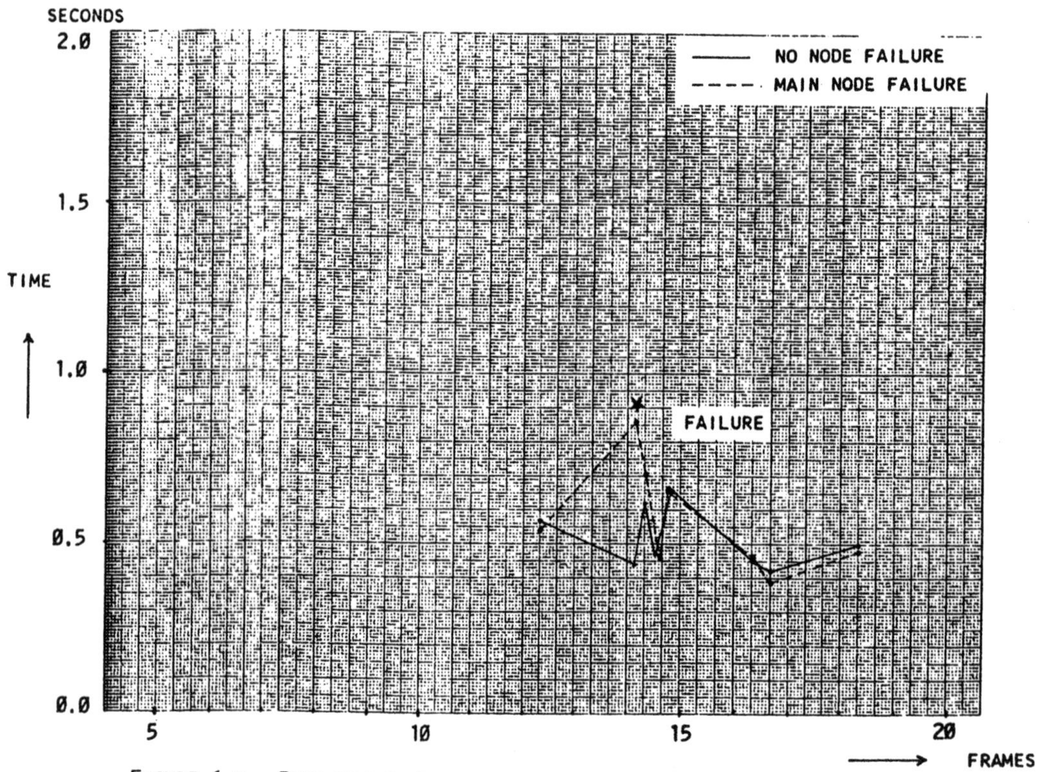

FIGURE 6-B. DATA TRAVEL TIME MEASURED WITH THE SETUP IN FIGURE 5.

Chapter 6

CACHE MEMORY FOR DISTRIBUTED SYSTEMS

Cache memory can be used to reduce the amount of traffic between processors and memories in a distributed system, thus improving the system performance. One of the key problems is the cache coherence, that is, the value of a given data item that resides on several caches is consistent after its modification.

In this chapter, we shall present several techniques for handling the cache coherence problem. The first paper by Archibald and Baer proposes a "global directory" approach for cache coherence in tightly coupled multiple processor systems. They also provide the limit (number of processors and level of sharing) within which this approach is viable. The second paper by Goodman proposes a new write strategy: write once, to guarantee consistent data among multiple processors and better performance than write-back or write-through in many instances. Such a write strategy may be used in the loosely coupled system.

For an approximate analytical model for estimating the performance of multiprocessors with private cache memories with a single main memory, the interested reader should refer to [PATE 82]. The parameters used in the model are the size and type of interconnection network, the cache miss-ratio, the cache block transfer time, and read-write policies. For more information on cache consistency, the interested reader should refer to [TANG 76, CENS 78, YEN 82, SMIT 82, GOOD 86].

An Economical Solution to the Cache Coherence Problem

James Archibald and Jean-Loup Baer[1]

Department of Computer Science, FR-35
University of Washington
Seattle. Wa, 98195

Abstract

In this paper we review and qualitatively evaluate schemes to maintain cache coherence in tightly-coupled multiprocessor systems. This leads us to propose a more economical (hardware-wise), expandable and modular variation of the "global directory" approach. Protocols for this solution are described. Performance evaluation studies indicate the limits (number of processors, level of sharing) within which this approach is viable.

1. Introduction

The cache coherence problem arises in multiprocessors configured with private caches. In such systems each processor has associated with it a cache or fast memory to store the contents of the most recently accessed locations in main memory. If several caches can contain a copy of the same memory location, and there are no means to prevent processors from simultaneously modifying their respective copies, inconsistencies can arise, i.e., the "data base" can become incoherent. Mechanisms are required to either:

1. have main memory always contain the most up-to-date information and operate the caches in *de facto* read-only mode;
2. allow multiple copies but restrict them to be for private data and read-only code and data (this requires either cache flush and possibly writebacks at context switch or forcing suspended processes to resume on their original processor);
3. allow sharable write data (this requires invalidating and eventually purging copies in individual caches).

Independently of the chosen method, we will say that a multiprocessor system is *cache coherent* if a read access to any block always returns the most recently written value of that block.

This paper focuses on one particular solution, which we call the two-bit solution, to the cache coherence problem that allows sharable data. A description of the proposed solution and its associated protocols is included in Section 3, following a brief review in Section 2 of solutions previously implemented or described in the literature. Performance evaluations of the two-bit design relative to other approaches and possible extensions to improve performance will be the subject of Section 4.

[1]This work was supported in part by NSF Grant MCS 80-25616 and MCS 83-04534

2. A Spectrum of Solutions to the Cache Coherence Problem

2.1. Spectrum of Solutions

In this section we briefly review existing or proposed schemes for solving the cache coherence problem in a tightly-coupled multiprocessor. We start with the static, software enforced solution which allows sharing of read-only and private data and is dependent on software (compiler) assist. The second scheme examined is the most rigid approach, often called the "classical" solution, where it is insured that main memory is always up-to-date. The third scheme, the dynamic solution which has several variations, uses a map or directory and requires hardware assists. The last group of methods are intended for shared bus systems.

2.2. Static, or Software Enforced, Solutions

The presence of two local caches for each processor, one for code and one for data, has been advocated for a long time. In the case of uniprocessors with a small cache it was found that the added logical complexity was not worthwhile [1]. But the magnitude of the cache coherence problem can be significantly reduced by this separation in a multiprocessor environment. Assuming that code is read-only (an assumption that is not valid for all systems; see, e.g., IBM System/370) only data references and data caches need be considered for consistency purposes. This two-cache approach has been implemented in uniprocessors such as the Data General MV/8000 and in the S-1 multiprocessor.

Data coherence can be further simplified if only private data is allowed to be cached. This can be implemented by appending a tag to each main memory block, at compile or link time, indicating whether it is code, private or public (sharable) data. On a cache miss to a public block, no loading in the cache takes place, and hence the public data is always up-to-date in main memory. If the granularity at the block level seems to be too fine, the tags can be set at the page level with a potential loss of space efficiency due to internal fragmentation. This approach is particularly attractive for the proponents of object-oriented systems.

This solution is appealing for new systems that do not require software compatibility with previous architectures. It will yield good performance if the amount of public data is limited, e.g., to semaphores and system tables. However, if the processors are used cooperatively on a common application sharing a large data base, then degradations due to memory access, and hence interference, are likely to be felt.

It is important to note that this software solution is not sufficient by itself if we allow process migration. I/O handling in the case of a write-back policy (that is, stores initially modify the cache and are transmitted to memory only when the modified block is to be replaced) raises also some difficulties. Perhaps it is for this reason that the software solution should be limited to "read-only" caches with the advantages of simpler cache designs and the disadvantages of less speed-up and dependency on the software.

2.3. Classical Solution

This approach resolves coherence problems by informing all caches of all writes--that is, each cache broadcasts to all other caches the address of the block being modified. The receiving caches examine their directories for the block in question, invalidating it if it is present. The scheme is typically used in conjunction with write-through (i.e, stores modify both the cache and main memory) but could be adapted for write-back. This approach is the one used in the dual processors IBM 370/168 and 3033 (cf. [6, 7]). It is also common in uniprocessors, such as the VAX 11/780, for insuring data coherence between memory accesses by the central processor and those generated by I/O traffic.

The main advantage of this solution is that it does not require changes in the uniprocessor architectures and hence no changes need to be made to the existing software of the uniprocessors. The addition of a cache invalidation line is necessary but the listening and invalidating logic of the caches may already be present for I/O concurrency purposes. Although this scheme appears to be easily expandable, performance degradation is unavoidable as the number of processors increases and this factor is in effect the most damaging drawback to the method. The traffic generated on the cache invalidation line, traffic that is certainly accentuated by the constraint of a write-through policy, becomes rapidly prohibitive. The number of cache cycles spent in processing invalidation requests can be minimized by a "BIAS memory" which filters out repeated invalidation requests for the same block (cf. reference [BAEN 79] in [7]).

2.4. Dynamic Directory Schemes

The methods described in this section all maintain some type of table, map, or directory that serves to reduce the traffic and overhead produced by the coherence enforcement mechanism. These directories can be viewed as filters, since they filter out much or all of the unnecessary overhead incurred in a scheme like the classical one described above. (For example, only those caches with copies of a block being written into need to receive invalidation signals.) Although the schemes can be implemented for both write-through and write-back, we assume a write-back policy for the discussion that follows. The approaches differ in how the directories are maintained, where they are located, and how the information is stored in the directory. All the schemes mentioned here provide sufficient information about each memory block to determine its global state as exactly one of the following:

1. not present in any cache or "Absent";
2. present in one or more caches (and which ones) in a read only mode or "Present+";
3. present in one cache (and which one) and modified or "PresentM".

Additionally, each cache keeps its usual local information, that is, a valid bit and a modified bit for each block.

When the processor references a memory location there are two instances where the cache's local information is sufficient to allow execution to proceed, namely a cache hit on read and a cache hit on an already modified block on write. However, independently of the scheme being used, the global state of a block must be determined at the following times with the corresponding actions being taken:

1. Replacement of a block. If the block to be replaced is valid and unmodified, its global state might change from Present+ to Absent (if it was the only copy being cached) or remain in state Present+ but with one less owner. If the block is valid and modified, it will be written back and its state changed from PresentM to Absent.
2. Read Miss. If the global state is Absent change state to Present+. If the global state is Present+ indicate the new ownership. If the global state is PresentM, the owning cache must be directed to write-back the missed block to main memory before it can be loaded in the requesting cache, with a corresponding change in the global and local states.
3. Write Miss. If the global state is Absent, load the block from main memory and change its global state to PresentM. But if the global state is Present+ all owning caches must be directed to invalidate their copy of that block, and if the state is PresentM, the owning cache must first write-back the missed block and then invalidate its copy, before the block can be loaded and its state set to PresentM.
4. Write Hit on Previously Unmodified Block. The only possible global state is Present+. All other owning caches (if any) must each invalidate their copy before execution can proceed. The state of the block is set to PresentM.

2.4.1. Cache Directory Duplication

This approach [8] uses a central memory controller which contains a duplicate of each cache's directory. This would require a controller with a large amount of processing power since all copies of the directories must be searched (presumably in parallel for an efficient implementation) to determine the global state. To our knowledge there exists no published design for such a controller. Its implementation could be rather simple if the number of caches were limited (e.g., 8), if all caches were organized in a similar fashion, and if they used low set associativity (even better would be a direct mapping organization which could be viable if data and instruction caches were separated), but these conditions are too restrictive for the type of machines we would like to consider. Note also that the design of the controller would depend on the number of processors in the system and hence limit and possibly prohibit expanding the system by adding processors. Finally, since all cache directory changes, in addition to all global state queries and updates, have to be sent to a central controller, the overall performance of this method could be severely limited by a controller bottleneck.

2.4.2. Full Distributed Map

The second approach first published in [2], and since preferred by most authors and reportedly to be implemented on the S-1 [9], consists of appending to each main memory block a vector of bits with one bit/cache, say e_k for cache C_k, indicating the presence or absence of the block in C_k and an extra bit, say m, indicating whether the block has been modified or not. Thus, Absent is such that all e_k are 0, Present+ implies that m is 0 and one or more e_k are 1's, and PresentM requires that m and one and only one e_k be 1. Since the information can be localized at the memory controller and retrieved directly, it will be easier to design a faster controller than in the previous solution but it will be quite costly in memory. For example, if the block size is 16 bytes and there are 16 processors in the system, a tag of 17 bits is required for each block of 256 bits (assuming 8 bit bytes), requiring a total of almost 15% extra memory. Although it is not space efficient, this method is very time efficient. If the memory is organized such that a block resides completely in a single memory module, with possible internal interleaving, the map can be distributed over the memory modules, since each controller need only concern itself with that portion of the map for the blocks in its module. This eliminates the potential bottleneck of a centralized controller. Like the cache directory duplication method outlined above, this approach has the disadvantage of limiting expansibility, since the length of the vector of bits determines the maximum system size. Any expansion must be envisioned at the design stage of the memory controllers.

2.4.3. Full Map With Added Local State

An extension [10] of the previous method involves the addition of a local state to blocks in the cache. This new state informs the cache that it has the only copy of an unmodified block, thus allowing writes on unmodified (unshared) blocks to proceed without first consulting the global table. This improves performance but it also introduces additional synchronization problems (not fully resolved in [10]) having to do with correct information being present in the global map. The global map actually contains the same information as in the previous approach but, due to the added local states, the underlying protocols are changed significantly.

2.5. Bus Schemes

These schemes are based on the assumption that the interconnection network in the multiprocessor is a shared bus. In this case, each cache can monitor other caches requests by listening to the bus. This allows clever and efficient solutions to the coherence problem by distributing the information contained in the global maps (as in the previous section) over the local caches [4, 5].

For example the "write-once" scheme [4] can be seen as a decentralization of the cache directory duplication method with the addition of an added local state, while at the same time taking advantage of the broadcast feature of the classical solution. More specifically, the states Absent (either by omission or through an invalid bit), Present+ and PresentM are encoded locally. Furthermore, PresentM is divided into "Reserved" (i.e., written once with a copy in main memory) and "Dirty" (i.e., with the only valid copy in the cache). On cache misses, each other cache in the system is aware of the address of the desired block, and takes action as necessary if it owns a copy of that block. For instance, on a read miss all caches listen to the request but at most one will respond, i.e., the one, if any, that has the desired block and has modified it (with respect to main memory: state PresentM "Dirty"). Similar protocols relying on all caches listening to the request on the bus are necessary in the cases of write miss and first write to an umodified block.

In a system without a shared bus interconnection network, it is much more difficult for each cache to be aware of all other cache requests and therefore the bus oriented schemes do not easily generalize. A distributed global map at the main memory level appears to be the most promising method for general interconnection networks.

3. The Two-bit Directory Scheme

3.1. General Presentation

We introduce now a more economical and expandable solution to the global directory approach. This approach combines features of the classical broadcast approach with features of the full distributed map approach. We associate with each memory block only four global states, namely:

1. not present in any cache or "Absent" ;
2. present in one cache in read-only mode or "Present1";
3. present in 0 or more caches in read-only mode or "Present*";[2]
4. present in one cache and modified or "PresentM".

Since there are exactly four possible states for a block, we can encode the information in two bits. The main difference between this scheme and the full map approach is that the identities of owning caches are not known. Thus, when it is necessary for a signal to be sent to a cache that did not initiate the transaction, it must be broadcast to all caches as in the classical method. Note however, that these signals are only necessary in the case of actual sharing or task migration and not on every cache miss as in the bus schemes. Therefore, any difference between the full map scheme and the partial two-bit map approach depends on the extent of sharing of writeable data.

The map is, however, significantly smaller and each tag is of fixed size, allowing for easy expansion in the number of processor-cache pairs. Our rationale is that in the situations where read sharing and write sharing are rare the degradation of performance due to this lack of knowledge will not be significant. In essence, we follow the philosophy that has made virtual memory systems successful, that is, most of the time the lack of knowledge will be transparent; when exceptions occur (actual read/write sharing of blocks) the overhead will be higher in clearing them but overall we have a system performing almost as well and more flexibly with a much smaller hardware investment.

A common problem in previous papers outlining alternative solutions to the cache coherence problem is a failure to be specific about the nature and location of the directory and the exact actions of the coherence mechanism. Attempts to outline the underlying protocols have been incomplete and unsatisfactory, blending actions local to each processor-cache (P_i-C_i in Figure 3.1), actions local to the memory controller-memory storage complex (K_j-M_j), and data transfers and control messages on the interconnection network linking the processors with main memory. In addition, synchronization problems have not been completely resolved. Since these problems must necessarily be solved before a successful implementation of the method can be realized, we present here the protocol specifications necessary to implement the two-bit scheme. This is part of an effort at the University of Washington to fabricate a controller chip incorporating this scheme in the larger context of a system as the one shown in Figure 3.1. As in the full distributed map, each controller is

[2] This apparent anomaly will be explained soon

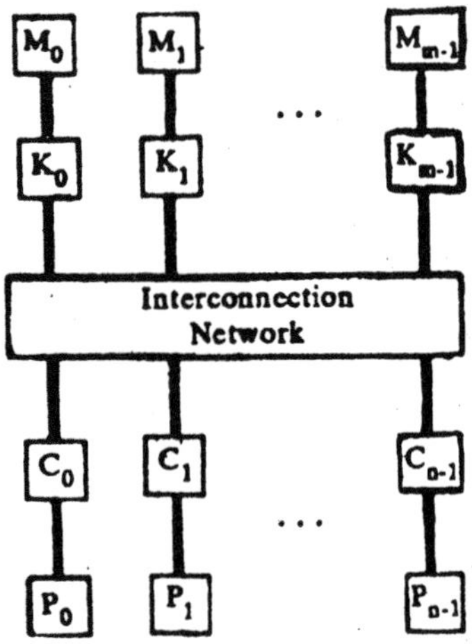

Figure 3-1: Multiprocessor with private caches

responsible only for the blocks pertaining to its module. It incorporates the bit-map (2 bits/block) as well as the necessary logic.

3.2. Protocol Specifications

The commands generated at each locus of control are shown in Table 3.1. The ensuing protocols for the 4 instances delineated previously, namely: replacement algorithm under a write-back policy, read miss, write miss and write hit on previously unmodified block are then specified. We note where the incomplete information of the two-bit map imposes additional overhead.

The following notation will be used throughout.

- *k* will be the index of the processor and associated cache generating a load or store request. Other processor-caches will be denoted by *i*, and, if need be, by $i_1, i_2, \ldots, i_m$.
- *a* is the address of the block being addressed. *d* is the displacement within that block of the i-unit (word, byte) being referenced.
- *a* is at position b_k in cache C_k if a hit occurs; otherwise b_k is the position in C_k of the block chosen to be replaced. A copy of *a* present in some cache C_i will be in position b_i.
- *olda* is the address of the block being replaced.
- control commands are written in capital letters and data transfers in italics.

3.2.1. Replacement of a Block

The protocol is initiated after a LOAD(*a*,*d*) or STORE(*a*,*d*) from the processor is acknowledged with a VALIDHIT(*a*, *false*, b_k) from the cache. Three cases are to be considered depending on the status of the valid and modified bits associated with b_k, namely:

1. Valid bit is off. There is no need to perform any replacement nor to change the global state map.
2. Valid bit is on and modified bit is off. The block does not have to be written back but its global state might change. An EJECT(*k*,*olda*,"*read*") will be sent to the appropriate memory controller. If the state of *olda* is Present1 it will be changed to Absent by SETSTATE(*olda*,"*Absent*"), otherwise it will remain at Present*.
3. Valid bit and modified bit are on. An EJECT(*k*,*olda*,"*write*") will be sent followed by a data transfer *put*(b_k,*olda*). After the data is received the controller will perform SETSTATE(*olda*,"*Absent*").

(Note: EJECT(*k*,*olda*,"*read*") could be ignored - in case 2 - and the protocols to follow still be correct. This stems from the fact that state Present1 is subsumed in Present*; however keeping Present1, and allowing the transition from Present1 to Absent, will reduce the number of broadcasts.)

P_k - C_k	P_k - K_j
LOAD(*a*,*d*)	REQUEST(*k*,*a*,*rw*)
STORE(*a*,*d*)	MREQUEST(*k*,*a*)
VALIDHIT(*a*,*horm*,b_k)	EJECT(*k*,*olda*,*wb*)
ld(*a*,b_k)	*put*(b_k,*olda*)
st(*a*,b_k)	
setmod(b_k)	

K_j - P_i	K_j - M_j
BROADINV(*a*,*i*)	SETSTATE(*a*,*st*)
BROADQUERY(*a*,*rw*)	*get*(*k*,*a*)
MGRANTED(*k*,*yorn*)	
put(b_i,*a*)	

Table 3-1: Control commands and data transfers

3.2.2. Read Miss

On a read miss, after replacement of a block b_k as specified above, a REQUEST(*k*,*a*,"*read*") will be sent to the memory controller. Depending on the state of *a*, we have:

1. *a* is in state Absent (resp. Present1, Present*). A data transfer *get*(*k*,*a*) will be generated followed by SETSTATE(*a*,"*Present1*") (resp. SETSTATE(*a*,"*Present**"), SETSTATE(*a*,"*Present**")).
2. *a* is in state PresentM. Its contents have to be retrieved from the cache *i* that has modified it and transferred to cache *k*. At the same time we write-back in main memory and change the global state and the local state in cache *i*. However, the two-bit scheme does not identify *i*. Therefore a BROADQUERY(*a*,"*read*") is broadcast to all caches. All caches check for a copy of *a* and only cache *i* will respond by a *put*(b_i,*a*) and will also reset the modified bit associated with b_i. When the data is received by the controller, it is written back in main memory and transmitted to cache *k* via *get*(*k*,*a*), the latter being followed by SETSTATE(*a*,"*Present1*").

Here the overhead with respect to the full map scheme is in the BROADQUERY directed to all caches instead of a PURGE(*a*,*i*,"*read*") directed only to cache *i*.

3.2.3. Write Miss

On a write miss, after replacement b_k, a REQUEST(k,a,"*write*") will be sent to the memory controller. We have three cases:

1. a is in state Absent. A data transfer *get*(k,a) will be generated followed by SETSTATE(a,"*PresentM*").
2. a is in state Present1 or Present*. All copies of a, if any, must be invalidated. Since the controller does not know the identities of the caches holding copies of a, it broadcasts this invalidation to all caches via BROADINV(a,k) (the parameter k is not necessary here but will become mandatory in the next protocol). Upon reception of this command, all caches, except cache k, will check if they have a copy of a and if so will invalidate it. After the broadcast the controller proceeds with *get*(k,a) followed by SETSTATE(a,"*PresentM*").
3. a is in state PresentM. We proceed as in the Read miss case 3, with a BROADQUERY(a,"*write*") instead of a BROADQUERY(a,"*read*"), the resetting of the local valid bit instead of the modify bit and a SETSTATE(a,"*PresentM*").

In the write miss protocols the added overhead of the two-bit scheme appears in both cases 2 and 3.

3.2.4. Write Hit on Previously Unmodified Block

A block loaded on a read miss cannot be modified by a processor without checking whether its cache owns the only copy of it. Thus on a write hit to a block whose modified bit is off, an MREQUEST(k,a) is sent to the appropriate controller. Then either:

1. a is in state Present1. The controller will acknowledge with an MGRANTED(k,true) (this justifies keeping the encoding of Present1).
2. a is in state Present*. Then the controller will send a BROADINV(a,k). All caches except cache k will invalidate their copy of a. After sending the broadcast, the controller will grant the request. Now we see why we need the parameter k. If it were not there cache k would invalidate the block it wants to modify!

Here the added overhead is in the broadcast of case 2.

3.2.5. Synchronization Issues

Until now we have not addressed the synchronization issues. Although a detailed analysis is not included in this paper, the following example gives an idea of the range of problems to be solved. These problems are not inherent to the two-bit solution; they were not considered in [2] and only alluded to in [10].

Example. Cache i and cache j hold copies of a. "At the same time" processor i wants to execute STORE(a,d_i) and processor j wants to execute STORE(a,d_j). Processor i sends an MREQUEST(i,a) to the controller while processor j sends MREQUEST(j,a). The controller must enforce the completion of one MREQUEST before considering the second. Two possible implementations are:

- Allow the controller to treat only one command at a time. This restriction seems too stringent and could lead to important performance degradation.
- Oblige the controller to treat commands related to a given block only one at a time. This requires a slightly more complex design.

In either case a possible scenario from the controller's viewpoint could be:

> Receives MREQUEST(i,a)
> Receives MREQUEST(j,a)
> Enqueues MREQUEST(j,a)
> a being in state Present*, sends BROADINV(i,a)
> Sends MGRANTED(i,true)
> Deletes MREQUEST(j,a) from the queue.

Upon receipt of BROADINV(i,a), cache j should invalidate its copy of a and in effect treat BROADINV as an MGRANTED(j,*false*). Processor j next action will therefore be a REQUEST(j,a,"*write*").

We now briefly mention the requirements for the design of a controller and the modifications that have to be made to local caches in order to support the various protocols. The controller must consist of:

- A bit map of the blocks stored in the module under control. This bit map consists of a 2 bit/block encoding of the 4 states.
- A control unit (finite state automaton) to implement the protocols specified above with the restriction that only one request at a time will be serviced.
- A queue for temporary storing of requests arriving while the current one is being serviced and logic to insert and delete (anywhere) elements in the queue.
- Local buffers and associated control to interact with the memory module on the one hand and the interconnection network on the other.

An addition that one would like to make to this basic design is to allow for multiprogramming capabilities in the controller so that it can process requests for various blocks simultaneously. The controller state (at command switch time) would consist of the state of the protocol (including flags), the identity of the local processor-cache pair initiating the command, and the memory address of the block being processed. This multiprogramming capability implies that a new process (request) must check all active ones for potential conflict on the block being accessed. Additional buffers and queuing control will be necessary at the memory and interconnection network interfaces.

Logic to capture invalidation requests at the local cache level can be designed in the same way as the one used in conventional uniprocessor systems for the classical solution. The main modification that has to be made is the ability to purge, i.e., write-back a block, when this action is not dictated by the processor to which the cache is attached.

4. Performance Evaluation

4.1. Assumptions

We wish to compare the performance of the two-bit scheme with the performance of the full distributed (n+1 bit) map approach described above. Specifically, we derive an expression for the added overhead of the partial map approach relative to the full map method in implementations where all other factors remain the same. The major difference between the two schemes is that the two-bit scheme loses the identity of owning caches necessitating a broadcast in those cases when a command must be sent to a cache. Extra commands necessitated by the two-bit scheme can be viewed as a check for the absence of a block in a cache since the number of "forced" write-backs and invalidations are independent of the mapping method. We assume that all other differences are negligible, that is, time to write-back or load a block are the same, as are cache hit ratios and other system characteristics. Some differences more likely to be apparent are the time required to access the global map, and the time required for a memory controller to send commands to caches. It could be argued that the smaller size of the two-bit map will allow it to be accessed more quickly than the larger map but we assume that access times are independent of the method. Since the n+1 bit scheme requires the sending of PURGE and INVALIDATE commands to all owning caches, effectively any subset of the total number of caches, this approach requires time to select the recipients and sequential message handling. In contrast, the two-bit approach does not have these requirements but its broadcasts do increase the probability of conflicts in the interconnection network. However, for the following analysis we assume that the differences are negligible.

4.2. Derivation of Extra Overhead

Consider a model (similar to that developed in [3]) in which the stream of memory references is the merging of a stream of references to private or read-only shared blocks (or simply 'private') with a stream of references to writeable shared blocks (or simply 'shared'). Let q be the probability that the next reference is to a shared block, w the probability that a reference to a shared block is a write, h the hit ratio of shared blocks in the cache, and n the number of caches in the system. Also let $P(PM)$ be the probability that a shared block has global state PresentM, $P(P1)$ the probability that a shared block has global state Present1, and $P(P^*)$ the probability that a shared block has global state Present*. Note that there is no additional overhead of the two-bit scheme resulting from accesses to private blocks; effects due to process migration are not included but could be accounted for by adjusting the level of sharing. Broadcasts are only required in the following three cases:

1. *Read miss.* A broadcast is required only if the global state of the block is PresentM. Since only one cache owns the block and the requesting cache is in an idle state (and hence never loses a cycle) the broadcast has an overhead of n-2 unnecessary commands. The average number of extra commands per memory request resulting from a read miss is therefore:

$$T_{RM} = (n - 2)q(1 - w)(1 - h)P(PM).$$

2. *Write miss.* A broadcast is required if the block has any global state other than Absent. The overhead for PresentM and Present1 is n-2 commands while the overhead for Present* can be n-1. The average number of extra commands per memory request resulting from a write miss is therefore:

$$T_{WM} = (n - 2)qw(1 - h)(P(PM) + P(P1)) + (n - 1)qw(1 - h)P(P^*).$$

3. *Write hit.* A broadcast is required only if the global state of the block is Present*. Since in the worst case the block is present in no caches the broadcast could have an overhead of n-1 extra commands. Also, since the block is present in at least one cache a conditional global state probability must be used. The average number of extra commands per memory request resulting from a write hit is therefore:

$$T_{WH} = (n - 1)qwhP(P^*)/(P(P1)+P(PM)+P(P^*)).$$

Combining the above, the total number of extra cache commands in the system resulting from a single memory request is:

$$T_{SUM} = T_{RM} + T_{WH} + T_{WM}.$$

Since each cache in the system causes this much overhead, the total seen by a single cache (resulting from all other caches but itself) is $(n\text{-}1)T_{SUM}$.

4.3. Parameter Values and Results

Since the added overhead of the two-bit scheme is very dependent on the degree of sharing, it would be expected to give good performance for a low level of sharing, while a high level of sharing should result in more significant degradation.

To evaluate the performance of the two-bit scheme, consider the following cases reflecting three different degrees of sharing:

1. Low sharing. q is 0.01 and h is 0.95. Additionally, we assume the following values: $P(P1)$ is 0.06, $P(P^*)$ is 0.01, and $P(PM)$ is 0.03.
2. Moderate sharing. q is 0.05 and h is 0.90 (slightly lower due to more sharing). In addition: $P(P1)$ is 0.25, $P(P^*)$ is 0.05, and $P(PM)$ is 0.10.
3. High sharing. q is 0.10 and h is 0.80 (much lower due to high level of sharing). Additionally, $P(P1)$ is 0.35, $P(P^*)$ is 0.10, and $P(PM)$ is 0.35.

Table 4.1 shows the value $(n\text{-}1)T_{SUM}$ for the three cases over the values indicated.

n:	4	8	16	32	64
case 1:					
w = 0.1	0.000	0.005	0.025	0.109	0.449
w = 0.2	0.002	0.010	0.047	0.203	0.840
w = 0.3	0.003	0.015	0.070	0.298	1.231
w = 0.4	0.004	0.020	0.092	0.392	1.622
case 2:					
w = 0.1	0.009	0.055	0.263	1.146	4.773
w = 0.2	0.015	0.089	0.422	1.827	7.593
w = 0.3	0.021	0.123	0.580	2.508	10.413
w = 0.4	0.027	0.157	0.739	3.188	13.233
case 3:					
w = 0.1	0.057	0.382	1.887	8.314	34.839
w = 0.2	0.072	0.470	2.304	10.118	42.336
w = 0.3	0.087	0.559	2.721	11.923	49.833
w = 0.4	0.102	0.647	3.138	13.727	57.330

Table 4-1: Added overhead of two-bit scheme in commands per memory reference.

In addition to the above analysis we applied the model developed in [3] to the two-bit solution. In this model an expression is derived for the total traffic received at the cache per memory reference, called T_R. The model assumes a full map is used and therefore a minimal number of commands are sent. An approximation of the added overhead of the two-bit method can be obtained by multiplying T_R by the number of other processors in the system, since each cache will see all broadcasts (except those it caused). Table 4.2 shows the results obtained by evaluating the expression $(n\text{-}1)T_R$ of the model for the values indicated. As above, the unit of measure is the number of commands received in each cache per memory reference. For the results shown in the table, the cache size is

n:	4	8	16	32	64
q = 0.01:					
w = 0.1	0.007	0.028	0.091	0.253	0.599
w = 0.2	0.013	0.046	0.131	0.315	0.684
w = 0.3	0.017	0.057	0.152	0.344	0.730
w = 0.4	0.020	0.065	0.163	0.360	0.756
q = 0.05:					
w = 0.1	0.047	0.175	0.517	1.312	3.005
w = 0.2	0.079	0.259	0.682	1.583	3.425
w = 0.3	0.100	0.308	0.769	1.724	3.655
w = 0.4	0.114	0.338	0.819	1.804	3.786
q = 0.10:					
w = 0.1	0.095	0.351	1.036	2.628	6.018
w = 0.2	0.158	0.518	1.365	3.170	6.859
w = 0.3	0.200	0.616	1.540	3.453	7.319
w = 0.4	0.228	0.676	1.641	3.613	7.582

Table 4-2: Added overhead derived from model in [3].

128 blocks, the number of shared blocks is 16, and the probability that a shared block reference is to a particular shared block is 1/16.

Although the actual numbers differ, the two different methods of analysis agree well on the limitations of this approach. The level to which the degradation remains acceptable depends on several factors, including the percentage of total cycles that the cache is actually busy servicing memory requests, and the desired application of the multiprocessor. For values of $(n\text{-}1)T_{SUM}$ near 1.0, each cache receives on average one command (requiring one lost cycle to service) for each memory request it services. Since in most caches a substantial number of cache cycles (to 50%) are spent in an idle state (not servicing memory requests) much of the overhead of stolen cycles can be hidden from the processor. The lost cycle only affects performance if a memory request from the processor is delayed. Based on this assumption, it can then be observed from the tables that the two-bit approach can give acceptable performance with up to 64 processors, assuming a low level of sharing such as in the case of execution of independent processes. For a more moderate level of sharing, performance is acceptable up to 16 processors. If the sharing is very high and particularly write intensive, the unmodified two-bit solution is appropriate only for configurations with 8 or less processors.

Of more concern is the effect of the broadcasts on traffic in the interconnection network. This estimate of performance gives an idea of the magnitude of the increased traffic due to broadcasts but gives no corresponding measure as to how the overall performance of the system is affected. Short of simulation, there are few alternatives to determine the effects of this traffic. This will be investigated in future studies, but we assume here that for values of $(n\text{-}1)T_{SUM}$ less than 1.0 this traffic is not prohibitive. There are, however, modifications in the design of the two-bit scheme that can significantly reduce this bus traffic as well as reducing the lost or stolen cycles in the local cache. These are explained in the next section.

4.4. Enhancements

The two degradations resulting from the additional commands that must be sent in the two bit approach are the wasted cycles at the local cache and the additional traffic in the interconnection network. Each of the following modifications is directed at reducing the effects of one of these two sources of degradation.

The first approach involves using a parallel cache controller design similar to that proposed in [4]. Duplicate copies of the cache directory are kept, allowing cache directory searches to be completed without slowing the cache. Only when the broadcast block is present in the cache would the cache lose a cycle as it must then respond to the command. Therefore the performance of the cache is affected only when blocks are actually shared--from the viewpoint of the cache this is equivalent to the distributed full map scheme. However, this alternative does nothing to reduce the potentially prohibitive bus traffic; the commands are still broadcast, they are only dealt with more efficiently at the receiving cache. Therefore, performance improvements resulting from this design would be limited.

A second and more promising approach involves adding to each memory controller a translation buffer or cache memory in which to store the identities of caches which own copies of blocks from that module. In those cases where a broadcast is needed in the unmodified two-bit scheme, the controller would first determine if the identity of the owner (or owners) is present in the translation buffer. If so, selective message handling can be performed just as with the n+1 bit approach; if not, a broadcast must be used as in the unmodified two-bit scheme. Although this could add to the time required to send commands, much of the unnecessary bus traffic and commands are eliminated. For example, if a 90% hit ratio on this translation buffer could be maintained, 90% of the added overhead resulting from the broadcasts is eliminated. In general the performance can achieve any desired approximation of the full bit map approach by ensuring that the hit ratio in the translation buffer is sufficiently high.

5. Conclusion

In this paper we have reviewed several schemes to enforce cache coherence in a tightly coupled multiprocessor system. We have proposed an economical, expandable and modular global directory approach. Hardware assists in the form of controllers associated with memory modules are the additional components of the system. Protocols between these controllers and the processor-cache pairs have been defined. The hardware overhead is small and independent of the number of processor-cache pairs at the expense of some degradation of performance when there is heavy sharing.

The protocols and associated hardware design need to be refined (and proven correct). To obtain a more precise performance analysis better estimates of parameters relative to the behavior of concurrent programs must be obtained. Because of the importance of expandable tightly-coupled multiprocessor systems we plan to address these problems in the near future.

Acknowledgment

We thank Professor C.Girault for numerous discussions that helped us better understand the intricacies of data coherence and protocol design.

USING CACHE MEMORY TO REDUCE PROCESSOR-MEMORY TRAFFIC

James R. Goodman

Department of Computer Sciences
University of Wisconsin-Madison
Madison, WI 53706

ABSTRACT—The importance of reducing processor-memory bandwidth is recognized in two distinct situations: single board computer systems and microprocessors of the future. Cache memory is investigated as a way to reduce the memory-processor traffic. We show that traditional caches which depend heavily on spatial locality (look-ahead) for their performance are inappropriate in these environments because they generate large bursts of bus traffic. A cache exploiting primarily temporal locality (look-behind) is then proposed and demonstrated to be effective in an environment where process switches are infrequent. We argue that such an environment is possible if the traffic to backing store is small enough that many processors can share a common memory and if the cache data consistency problem is solved. We demonstrate that such a cache can indeed reduce traffic to memory greatly, and introduce an elegant solution to the cache coherency problem.

1. Introduction

Because there are straightforward ways to construct powerful, cost-effective systems using random access memories and single-chip microprocessors, semiconductor technology has, until now, had the greatest impact through these components. High-performance processors, however, are still beyond the capability of a single-chip implementation and are not easily partitioned in a way which can effectively exploit the technology and economics of VLSI. An interesting phenomenon has occurred in the previous decade as a result of this disparity. Memory costs have dropped radically and consistently for computer systems of all sizes. While the component cost of a CPU (single-chip implementations excluded) has declined significantly over the same period, the reduction has been less dramatic. A result is that the amount of memory thought to be appropriate for a given speed processor has grown dramatically in recent years. Today small minicomputers have memory as large as that of the most expensive machines of a decade ago.

The impact of VLSI has been very different in microprocessor applications. Here memory is still regarded as an expensive component in the system, and those familiar primarily with a minicomputer or mainframe environment are often scornful of the trouble to which microprocessor users go to conserve memory. The reason, of course, is that even the small memory in a microprocessor is a much larger portion of the total system cost than the much larger memory on a typical main frame system. This results from the fact that memory and processors are implemented in the same technology.

1.1. A Super CPU

With the advances to VLSI occurring now and continuing over the next few years, it will become possible to fabricate circuits that are one to two orders of magnitude more complex than currently available microprocessors. It will soon be possible to fabricate an extremely high-performance CPU on a single chip. If the entire chip is devoted to the CPU, however, it is not a good idea. Extrapolating historical trends to predict future component densities, we might expect that within a few years we should be able to purchase a single-chip processor containing at least ten times as many transistors as occur in, say, the MC68000. For the empirical rule known as Grosch's law [Grosch53], $P = k\ C^g$, where P is some measure of performance, C is the cost, and k and g are constants, Knight[Knight66] concluded that g is at least 2, and Solomon[Solomon66] has suggested that $g \approx 1.47$. For the IBM System/370 family, Siewiorek determined that $g \approx 1.6$ [Siewiorek82]. While Grosch's law breaks down in the comparison of processors using different technology or architectures, it is realistic for predicting improvements within a single technology. Siewiorek in fact suggests that it holds "by definition."

Assuming $g = 1.5$ and using processor-memory bandwidth as our measure of performance, Grosch's law predicts that a processor containing 10 times as many transistors as a current microprocessor would require 30 times the memory bandwidth.[1] The Motorola MC68000, running at 10 MHz, accesses data from memory at a maximum rate of 5 million bytes per second, using more than half its pins to achieve this rate. Although packaging technology is rapidly increasing the pins available to a chip, it is unlikely that the increase will be 30-fold (the 68000 has 64 pins). We would suggest a factor of two is realistic. Although some techniques are clearly possible to increase the transfer rate into and out of the 68000, supplying such a processor with data as fast as needed is a severe constraint. One of the designers of the 68000, has stated that all modern microprocessors — the 68000

[1]This is a conservative estimate, in fact, because it ignores predictable decreases in gate delays.

included – are already bus-limited [Tredennick82].

1.2. On-chip Memory

One alternative for increased performance without proportionately increasing processor-memory bandwidth is to introduce memory on the same chip with the CPU. With the ability to fabricate chips containing one to two million transistors, it should be possible – using only a portion of the chip – to build a processor significantly more powerful than any currently available single-chip CPU. While devoting the entire chip to the CPU could result in a still more powerful processor, introducing on-chip memory offers a reduction in memory access time due to the inherently smaller delays as compared to inter-chip data transfers. If most accesses were on-chip, it might actually perform as fast as the more powerful processor.

Ideally, the chip should contain as much memory as the processor "needs" for main storage. Conventional wisdom today says that a processor of the speed of current microprocessors needs at least 1/4 megabytes of memory [Lindsay81]. This is certainly more than is feasible on-chip, though a high performance processor could probably use substantially more than that. Clearly all the primary memory for the processor cannot be placed on the same chip with a powerful CPU. What is needed is the top element of a memory hierarchy.

1.3. Cache Memory

The use of cache memory, however, has often aggravated the bandwidth problem rather than reduce it. Smith [Smith82] says that optimizing the design has four general aspects:

(1) maximizing the hit ratio,

(2) minimizing the access time to data in the cache,

(3) minimizing the delay due to a miss, and

(4) minimizing the overheads of updating main memory, maintaining multicache consistency, etc.

The result is often a larger burst bandwidth requirement from main storage to the cache than would be necessary without a cache. For example, the cache on the IBM System/370 model 168, is capable of receiving data from main memory at a rate of 100 megabytes per second [IBM76]. It supplies data to the CPU at less than 1/3 that rate. The reason is that to exploit the spatial locality in memory references, the data transferred from backing store into the cache is fetched in large blocks, resulting in requirements of very high bandwidth bursts of data. We have measured the average bandwidth on an IBM System/370 model 155, and concluded that the *average* backing-store-to-cache traffic is less than the cache-to-CPU traffic.

The design of cache memory for mini-computers demanded greater concern for bus bandwidth. The designers of the PDP-11 models 60 and 70 clearly recognized that small block sizes were necessary to keep main memory traffic to a minimum [Bell78].

Lowering the bandwidth from backing store to the cache can be accomplished in one of two ways:

(1) small blocks of data are brought from backing store to the cache, or

(2) long delays occur while a block is being brought in, independent of (and in addition to) the access time of the backing store.

While it is possible to bring in the word requested initially (read through), thus reducing the wait on a given reference, the low bandwidth memory interface will remain busy long after the initial transfer is completed, resulting in long delays if a second backing storage operation is required.

We therefore have explored the effectiveness of a cache which exploits primarily or exclusively temporal locality, i.e., the blocks fetched from backing store are only the size needed by the CPU (or possibly slightly larger). In considering ways to evaluate this strategy, we identified a commercial environment that contained many of the same constraints and seemed amenable to the same kinds of solutions. This environment is the marketplace of the single-board computer running on a standard bus such as Multibus[2] or Versabus.[3] We have chosen to study this environment in an attempt to gain insight into the original, general scheme.

2. The Single Board Computer Application

A single board computer typically contains a microprocessor and a substantial amount of memory, though small enough that it must be used carefully. If needed, access to additional random access memory is through the bus, which is designed for generality and simplicity, not for high performance. Multibus, in particular, was defined in the early 70's to offer an inexpensive means of communication among a variety of subsystems. Although originally introduced by Intel Corporation, it has found wide acceptance, having been proposed – in a slightly modified form – as the IEEE P796 bus standard [IEEE80]. Currently, several hundred vendors offer Multibus-compatible cards.

While the market has rapidly developed for products using this bus, its applications are limited by the severe constraint imposed by the bandwidth of Multibus. Clearly the bus bandwidth could be increased by increasing the number of pins, and by modifying the protocol. Its broad popularity and the availability of components to implement its protocol mean, however, that it is likely to survive many years in its present form. Thus a large market exists for a computer-on-a-card which, much as if it were all on a single chip. has severe limitations on its communications with the rest of the system.

We decided to determine if a cache memory system could be implemented effectively in the Multibus environment. To that end we have designed a cache to be used with a current-generation microprocessor. In addition, we have done extensive simulation of cache performance, driven by memory trace data. We have identified a new component which is particularly suited for VLSI implementation and have demonstrated its feasibility by designing it [Ravishankar83]. This component, which implements the tag memory for a dynamic RAM cache intended for a microprocessor, is similar in many respects to the recently announced TMS 2150 [TI82].

Multibus systems have generally dealt with the problem of limited bus bandwidth by removing most of the processor-memory accesses from the bus. Each processor card has its own local memory, which may be addressable to others through the Multibus. While this approach has much in common with ours, we believe that the allocation of memory – local or remote – should be handled by the system, freeing the programmer of this task. In typical Multibus applications, considerable effort is expended guaranteeing that the program running is primarily resident on-board. This approach is viable for a static partitioning of tasks. Results to date have been much less satisfactory, however, for the more general situation where a number of processors are dynamically allocated. (For efficiency reasons it also precludes the use of shared code segments).

---

[2] Multibus is a trademark of Intel Corporation.

[3] Versabus is a trademark of Motorola.

In many environments, a simple dynamic hardware allocation scheme can efficiently determine what memory locations are being accessed frequently and should therefore be kept in local memory – better than the programmer who often has little insight into the dynamic characteristics of his program. There are environments where the programmer is intimately familiar with the behavior of his program and can generate code to take advantage of it. In this environment the time spent running a program is often much more substantial than the time developing the program. This explains, for example, why an invisible cache is not appropriate on the CRAY-1. We believe that freeing the programmer from concern about memory allocation is essential where programmer productivity is critical.

2.1. A Single-Board Computer with Cache

To evaluate our approach, we proposed a single-board computer containing, (possibly along with other things) a CPU and no local memory except a cache, with backing store provided through Multibus. Thus we picked an important problem in its own right: Can we build a cache that works with a Multibus system supporting multiple processors? In particular, how many processors can we support running in parallel on Multibus? We believe that a system which could reasonably support five to 10 processors would be a significant advance. This can't be compared directly against current systems because a single processor overloads the Multibus. Thus local memories must be heavily exploited if performance is important.

Earlier analyses [Kaplan73, Bell74, Rao78, Patel82] have used the cache hit ratio or something closely related to measure performance. The important criterion here is to maximize use of the bus, not the hit ratio, or even necessarily to optimize processor performance. We optimize system performance by optimizing bus utilization, achieving higher performance by minimizing individual processors' bus requirements, and thereby supporting more processors reasonably well. We allow individual processors to sit idle periodically rather than tie up the bus fetching data which they might not use. This implies that the cache stale data problem must be solved effectively. We present a new solution in section 3.

2.2. Switching Contexts

Where bus bandwidth is limited, a task switch is a major disturbance, since the cache must effectively be reloaded at this time. The processor is momentarily reduced to accesses at the rate at which the bus can supply them. While this problem seems unavoidable, it need not be serious if task switching is minimized. We are providing an environment which allows many processors to work out of a single monolithic memory in parallel. If more parallel tasks are required, more processors can be used. We point out that the current Multibus alternative is to move the program into local memory, an operation which also swamps the bus. The task switch merely makes this operation implicit, and avoids bringing across the bus data which are never actually used. Writing the old data out is also no worse than the alternative, since we only write that which has been changed and which has not been already purged.

There may be certain cases – an interrupt handling program, for example – where a particular program does not flush the cache, but uses only a small portion of it. Provisions could be made to allow such a program to be locked in the cache. Alternatively, a separate cache might be provided for such a program Our studies indicate that a relatively small cache can be effective for a single program, so it may be possible to keep separate caches around for individual processes if the number is small. We would suggest taking this one step further and providing an additional processor for each cache. An interesting question then arises as to the cost of dynamically assigning processes to processors. Our proposal allows this assignment, though clearly at some performance penalty.

3. Cache Coherency

It is well-known that multiple caches present serious problems because of the redundancy of storage of a single logical memory location [Tang76, Censier78, Rao78]. The most common method among commercial products for dealing with this, the stale data problem, is to create a special, high-speed bus on which addresses are sent whenever a write operation is performed by any processor. This solution has weaknesses [Censier78] which have generally limited commercial implementations to two processors. In the single-chip processor or single-board computer environments, it has the added weakness that it requires a number of extra I/O pins.

An alternative approach, implemented in C.mmp [Hoogendoorn77] and proposed by Norton [Norton82], is to require the operating system to recognize when inconsistencies might occur and take steps to prevent them under those circumstances. This solution is unappealing because the cache is normally regarded as an architecture-independent feature, invisible to the software.

A third approach, variations of which have been proposed by Censier and Feautrier [Censier78], Tang [Tang76], Widdoes [Widdoes79], and Yen and Fu [Yen82], is to use some form of tagged main memory, keeping track of individual blocks in this way to prevent inconsistency. Individual blocks are temporarily designated as *private* for a particular processor so that it may modify it repeatedly without reference to main memory. The tag must be set whenever such a critical section is entered and reset whenever the critical section is left, i.e., the modified word is written back to main storage. This approach requires substantial hardware, and appears infeasible for a large number of caches, since an operation in a central place is required at the entry or exit of any critical section.

Our approach has much in common with the third approach, but allows the critical section information to be distributed among the caches, where it already resides. In addition, we use the normal read and write operations, with no tag bits in main memory, to accomplish the synchronization. A related scheme [Amdahl82] which uses a special bus to convey the notice of entry or exit from a critical section, has been implemented in a commercial product, but has not been published to our knowledge. We call our scheme *write-once*.

3.1. Write-Through or Write-Back?

While the choice between write-through (also known as store-through) and write-back (also known as store-back or copy-back) has no bearing on the read hit ratio, it has a major impact on bus traffic, particularly as the hit ratio approaches 100%. In the limit, when the hit ratio is 100%, write-back results in no bus traffic at all, while write-through requires at least one bus cycle for each write operation. Norton [Norton82] concluded that using write-back instead of write-through for a hypothetical processor typically would reduce the bus traffic by more than 50% and if the processes ran to completion bus traffic would be decreased by a factor of 8. For typical read-to-write and hit ratios and when task switching is infrequent, our simulations have given strong evidence that write-back generates substantially less bus traffic than write-through.

But write-back has more severe coherency problems than write-through, since even main memory does not always contain the current version of a particular memory location.

3.2. A New Write Strategy: Write-Once

We propose a new write strategy which solves the stale data problem and produces minimal bus traffic. The replacement technique requires the following structure. Associated with each block in the cache are two bits defining one of four states for the associated data:

Invalid There is no data in the block.

Valid There is data in the block which has been read from backing store and has not been modified.

Reserved The data in the block has been locally modified exactly once since it was brought into the cache and the change has been transmitted to backing store.

Dirty The data in the block has been locally modified more than once since it was brought into the cache and the latest change has not been transmitted to backing store.

Write-once requires rapid access to the address tags and state bit pairs concurrently with accesses to the address tags by the CPU. This can most easily be achieved by creating two (identical) copies of the tag memory. Censier [Censier78] claims that duplication is "the usual way out" for resolving collisions between cache invalidation requests and normal cache references. This is not a large cost, since a single chip design of this part of the cache – using present technology – is quite feasible. Further, we have discovered a way to reduce substantially the number of tags required. In addition, the same chip type could be used for both instances. This is a natural way to partition the cache in VLSI because it results in a maximal logic-to-pin ratio. We have designed and submitted for fabrication such a chip [Ravishankar83].

The two copies always contain exactly the same address data, because they are always written simultaneously. While one unit is used in the conventional way to support accesses by the CPU, a second monitors all accesses to memory via the Multibus. For each such operation, it checks for the address in the local cache. If a match is found on a write operation, it notifies the cache controller, and the appropriate block in the cache is marked *invalid*. If a match is found on a read operation, nothing is done unless the block has been modified, i.e., its state is *reserved* or *dirty*. If it is just *reserved*, the state is changed to *valid*. If it is *dirty*, the local systems inhibits the backing store from supplying the data. It then supplies the data itself.[4] On the same bus access or immediately following it, the data must be written to backing store. In addition, for either *reserved* or *dirty* data, the state is changed to *valid*.

This scheme achieves coherency in the following way. Initially write-through is employed. However, an additional goal is achieved upon writing. All other caches are purged of the block being written, so the cache writing through the bus now is guaranteed the only copy except for backing store. It is so identified by being marked *reserved*. If it is purged at this point, no write is necessary to backing store, so this is essentially write-through. If another write occurs, the block is marked *dirty*. Now write-back is employed and, on purging, the data must be rewritten to backing store.

[4]There is a mechanism in Multibus which allows this capability. Unfortunately, it is rarely used, not well-defined, and requires that local caches respond very rapidly. Versabus has a much cleaner mechanism by which this end can be accomplished.

Write-once has the desirable feature that units accessing backing store need not have a cache, and need not know whether others do or not. A cache is responsible for maintaining consistency exactly for those cases where it might create a violation, i.e., whenever it writes to a location. Thus it is possible to mix in an arbitrary way systems which employ a cache and those which do not; the latter would probably be I/O devices. Considerable care must be exercised, however, when a write operation over the bus modifies less than an entire block.

4. Simulation

We designed a cache memory system to work on Multibus. To validate our design before building it we did extensive simulation using memory trace data. To date we have performed extensive simulations for six traces, all running under UNIX:[5]

EDC	The UNIX editor *ed* running a script.
ROFFAS	The old UNIX text processor program *roff*.
TRACE	The program, written in assembly language, which generated the above traces for the PDP-11.
NROFF	The program *nroff* interpreting the Berkeley macro package *-me*.
CACHE	The trace-driven cache simulator program.
COMPACT	A program using an on-line algorithm which compresses files using an adaptive Huffman code.

The first three traces are for a PDP-11, while the latter three are for a VAX. While the PDP-11 does not run on Multibus, its instruction set is similar to many microprocessors which do, and the programs used for tracing were of the kind we envision for such a system. The PDP-11 is similar in many ways to the MC68000, and has in common with the 8086 a limited addressing capability.

While the VAX also does not run on Multibus, it is an example of a modern instruction set and, therefore is a reasonable example of the kind of processor likely to appear in a single-chip CPU in the future. It also has a larger address space which, as shown in section 4.3, is significant. We are actually using virtual addresses, but all of the programs we ran are small enough to fit into main memory. Since we are tracing only a single process, we conclude that there is no significant difference between virtual and real addresses.

In addition to cache parameters, miss ratios vary greatly depending on the program running. For the each of the above traces, a wide and unpredictable variation occurred as we varied a single parameter. Thus plotting parameters for the individual traces was often not enlightening. Averaging over the three traces in each category gave much more revealing results, providing data that suggested a continuous function for many of the variables studied. Thus all our results are actually the average of three programs, each running alone.

4.1. Effect of Write Strategy on Bus Traffic

Although write-through normally generates less bus traffic than write-back, the latter can be worse if the hit ratio is low and the block size is large. Under write-back, when a dirty block is purged, the entire block must be written out. With write-through, only that portion which was modified must be written. We found that write-back is decisively superior to write-through except (1) when cache blocks are very large, or (2) when the cache size is very small.

[5]UNIX and NROFF are trademarks of Bell Laboratories.

Write-once results in bus traffic roughly equal to the better of the two. We have found cache parameters for which it actually performs better on the average than either write-through or write-back for a number of programs. This was a surprising result, since write-once was developed to assure coherency, not to minimize bus traffic. The replacement scheme outperforms both write-through and write-back whenever the total number of sets is about 16. For example, for a 4-way set associative, 2048-byte cache with a block size of 32 bytes, the average bus traffic for three PDP-11 programs for which we have traces was 30.768% for write-through, 17.55% for write-back, and 17.38% for write-once.

4.2. Cold Start vs. Warm Start

An important consideration in determining cache hit ratio and bus traffic is the cold start period known as the *lifetime function* [Easton78], during which time many misses occur because the cache is empty. This is defined as the period until as many cache misses have occurred as the total number of blocks in the cache. This initial burst of misses is amortized over all accesses, so the longer the trace analyzed, the lower the miss ratio obtained. In addition to the initiation of a program and occasional switches of environments, a cold start generally occurs whenever there is a task switch. Thus an important assumption in traditional cache evaluation is the frequency of task switching. We have argued that task switching must be very infrequent in our system. Thus we can more nearly approach in practice the warm start hit ratios, and thus it is appropriate to use very long traces of a single program, and assume a warm start. We did that initially, using the full length of the PDP-11 traces available to us (1,256,570 memory accesses). We noted, however, that for even much shorter traces than we were running, there was little difference between warm start and cold start statistics. Since cold start statistics are easier to generate, we normally used them. Unless stated otherwise, our results are from cold start, but at least 10 times the lifetime function in total length.

4.3. Cache Size

In general, we were surprised at the effectiveness of a small cache. For the PDP-11 traces with a cache of 2K bytes or larger, we discovered that essentially no misses occurred after the cold start period. These are not trivial programs, but were run on a machine which has only 64K bytes for both instructions and data. The programs are very frugal in their use of memory, and the entire working set apparently can fit in the cache.

The VAX traces do not exhibit the same locality observed with the PDP-11, and a 64K-byte cache was not large enough to contain the entire working set of the program. This may be a result of the larger address space available, the more complex instruction set, or more complex programs. In all cases the programs were spread out over a much larger memory space than for the PDP-11 traces. For this comparison we used a small block size of 4 bytes. This may have had a greater impact on the VAX than on PDP-11 traces.

We found that reducing the size of the cache (below 4K bytes for the PDP-11) increased the miss ratio and the bus traffic – in general the two correlate well with respect to this parameter. Fig. 1 shows the average miss ratio and bus traffic as a function of total cache size for the PDP-11 traces. For this and all results given, the miss ratio includes writes. The bus traffic is given as a percent of the number of accesses that would be required if no cache were present. Fig. 2 shows the same data for the VAX traces.

4.4. Block Size

Our cache design incorporates extremely small blocks, depending heavily on temporal locality. Easton and Fagin [Easton78] claim that page size and miss ratios are independent for warm start, but highly dependent for cold start. If true, this can be explained by the observation that hits in the cache on cold start depend heavily on spatial locality, while temporal locality provides many hits when it is warm. Spatial locality, however, is strongly correlated to block size, being directly proportional in the extreme case of strictly sequential memory accesses. Our simulations partially confirm Easton's observation. In particular, we found that, as block size is increased, miss ratios generally decline up to a point, then increase for either warm or cold starts. However, for small block sizes, the warm start miss ratio is marginally lower than for the cold start case, while for large block sizes, the two numbers are nearly identical. See figs. 3-7. This is encouraging since we have argued for restricted task switches: our environment is more that of a warm start than is the traditional environment. In many simulations we were able to get very high hit ratios once the cold start period ended. For small blocks transferred, however, this period (the lifetime function) is longer. Our simulations show very clearly that reducing the block size down to a single transfer across the bus dramatically decreases the hit ratio, particularly for cold starts, but also decreases bus traffic significantly. In general, we observed that increasing the transfer block size from one bus cycle to two typically decreases the miss ratio by 30 to 50%, while increasing the bus traffic by 10 to 20%. This relation holds for the first two doublings. These results, e.g., fig. 3, are relatively more pessimistic for small block sizes than those reported by Strecker in [Bell78].

We have made the assumption that access time is related linearly to block size. In many cases this is not true. It is essentially true for the Multibus, since only two bytes can be fetched at a time, and arbitration is overlapped with bus operations. For a single-chip implementation, it would almost certainly be worthwhile to provide the capability for efficient multiple transfers over a set of wires into the processor. This has not been incorporated in our analysis, but will undoubtedly suggest a somewhat larger transfer block size.

4.4.1. Lowering the Overhead of Small Blocks

Small blocks are costly in that they greatly increase the overhead of the cache: an address tag and the two state bits are normally stored in the cache for each block transferred. We reduced this overhead by splitting the notion of block into two parts:

(1) The *transfer block* is the amount of data transferred from backing store into the cache on a read miss.

(2) The *address block* is the quantum of storage for which a tag is maintained in the cache. It is always a power of two larger than a transfer block. An effective cache can be implemented by keeping the transfer block small but making the address block larger.

For most commercial products containing a cache, the address block size is the same as the transfer block size, though we know of one example [IBM74] where the address block contained two transfer blocks. The IBM System/360 Model 85 [Liptay68] in fact is a special case of this, *viz.*, a direct-mapped cache, where the Model 85 "sector," consisting of 1K bytes, corresponds to our address block. Each sector contains 16 transfer blocks, which were called simply "blocks."

4.4.2. The Effect of Large Address Blocks

The use of address blocks larger than transfer blocks means that only data from one address block in backing store can occupy any of the blocks making up an address block in the cache. There are cases where the appropriate transfer block is empty, but other transfer blocks in the same address block must be purged so that the new address block can be allocated. We examined this for various sizes of address blocks and found that the miss ratio increased very slowly up to a point. For the situation shown in fig. 7, the miss ratio had only risen by about 30% when the address block contained 64 bytes for the PDP-11 traces. That point was reached for the VAX traces when it contained 32-byte address blocks.

We predicted that the bus traffic would correlate well with miss ratio with respect to this parameter. To our surprise, the bus traffic actually *declined* initially as we increased the address block size. The decline was small, but consistent for the PDP-11 trace tapes, eventually climbing over the base line when the address block was 16 or 32 transfer blocks. The phenomenon was smaller, but discernible for the VAX traces as well, though in all cases the bus traffic started increasing sooner. This situation is shown in fig. 8.

We initially suspected that our simulation might be faulty. That was not the case, and eventually we were able to explain it and verify it. The write-once algorithm requires a bus operation whenever a block is modified initially (set to *reserved.)* However, reservations could be made on the basis of either transfer blocks or address blocks. We had put the choice into the simulator, but had not experimented with it, reserving at the address block level. This in fact reduces the number of bus writes necessary for reservation because of spatial locality of writes: an address block already *reserved* need only be marked *dirty* when any transfer block within it is modified. This would seem to increase greatly the traffic whenever the block is purged from the cache, but in fact the effect is small: only those transfer blocks which have actually been modified need be written back.

We demonstrated that this was indeed responsible for the behavior noted by changing the reservations to the transfer block level. The simulation results then exhibited the originally predicted behavior, correlating closely with the miss ratio.

We conclude that minimum bus traffic is generated with minimum transfer block sizes. The miss ratio may be substantially improved by using slightly larger transfer blocks, in which case bus traffic does not increase greatly. Using larger address blocks reduces the cost of the tag memory considerably. It initially has only a minor effect on miss ratio, which is more than offset by the savings in writes due to the more efficient reservation of modified blocks

4.5. Other Design Aspects Studied

4.5.1. Write Allocation

Write allocation, also known as *fetch on write*, means that a block is allocated in the cache on a write miss as well as on a read miss. While it seems natural for write-back, it typically is not used with write-through. It is essential for write-once to assure coherency. Our early simulations showed that it was highly desirable for write-back and write-once, and superior even for write-through with small blocks. This was true using both the measures of miss ratio and bus traffic. In all results presented, write allocation was employed.

4.5.2. Associativity

We ran a number of simulations varying the associativity all the way from direct mapped to fully associative. While this is clearly an important parameter, we have little new to report, i.e., fully associative cache is the best, but 2-way set associative is not much worse, and 4-way set associative is somewhere in between. (But see [Smith83]). We had hoped to find that a high degree of associativity would improve performance, because such an organization is much more feasible in the VLSI domain, but results were negative. For results reported here we have assumed a 4-way, set associative cache.

4.5.3. Replacement Algorithm

Replacement strategy has been the subject of another study using the same simulator and traces [Smith83]. In order to limit its significance, which seems to be orthogonal to the issues raised here, we have assumed true LRU replacement among the elements of each set in all cases.

4.5.4. Bus Width

The width of the data paths between units is an important parameter in that it is closely related to bandwidth. We have the capability to specify the bus width both from backing store to cache and from cache to CPU. For the purposes of this study, we have assumed in all cases that the VAX memory supplies 4 bytes to the cache in one bus cycle, while the PDP-11 memory supplies 2 bytes. An 8-byte transfer therefore is counted as two cycles for the VAX and 4 for the PDP-11.

We assumed that the cache supplied one word – 16 bits for the PDP-11 and 32 bits for the VAX – to the CPU on each request. However, the intelligence of the processor determines how often the same word must be fetched. The trace tapes contain all memory references. We filtered these with the assumption that on instruction fetches the same word would not be fetched without an intervening instruction fetch. No filtering was done on data fetches.

5. Summary

Our simulations indicate that a single board computer with a 4K-byte cache can perform reasonably well with less than 10% of the accesses required to its primary memory without a cache. The PDP-11 traces suggest a number as low as 3%. While the VAX numbers are higher, additional declines will be experienced by increasing the size of the cache beyond 4K bytes.

An important result is the use of the write-once algorithm to guarantee consistent data among multiple processors. We have shown that this algorithm can be implemented in a way that degrades performance only trivially (ignoring actual collisions, which are rare), and performs better than either pure write-back or write-through in many instances.

The use of small transfer block sizes can be coupled with large address blocks to build an inexpensive cache which performs effectively in the absence of frequent process switches. The low bus utilization and the solution to the stale data problem make possible an environment for which this condition is met. Even though the miss ratio increases, bus traffic initially declines as the address block is enlarged, holding the transfer block constant. Therefore larger address blocks should be used for reserving memory for modification even if small blocks are used for transfer of data.

The approach advocated here is appropriate only for a system containing a single logical memory. This is significant because it depends on the serialization of memory accesses to assure consistency. It has applications beyond those studied here, however. For example, the access path to memory could be via a ring network, or any other technique in which every request passes every processor. This extension seems particularly applicable at the for maintaining consistency for a file system or a common virtual memory being supplied to multiple processors through a common bus such as Ethernet.

Clearly there are many environments for which this model is inappropriate — response to individual tasks may be unpredictable, for example. However, we believe that such a configuration has many potential applications and can be exploited economically if the appropriate VLSI components are designed. We have investigated the design of such components and believe that they are both feasible and well-suited for VLSI [Ravishankar83].

Our analysis indicates that the cache approach is reasonable for a system where bandwidth between the CPU and most of its memory is severely limited. We have demonstrated through simulation of real programs that a cache memory can be used to significantly reduce the amount of communication a processor requires. While we were interested in this for a single-chip microcomputer of the future, we have also demonstrated that such an approach is feasible for one or more currently popular commercial markets.

6. Acknowledgements

This material is based upon work supported by the National Science Foundation under Grant MCS-8202952.

We thank Dr. A. J. Smith for providing the PDP-11 trace tapes upon which much of our early work depended. We also wish to thank T.-H. Yang for developing the VAX trace facility. P. Vitale and T. Doyle contributed much through discussions and by commenting on an early draft of the manuscript.

7. References

[Amdahl 82] C. Amdahl, *private communication*, March 82.

[Bell 74] J. Bell, D. Casasent, and C. G. Bell, "An investigation of alternative cache organizations," *IEEE Trans. on Computers*, Vol. C-23, No. 4, April 1974, pp. 346-351.

[Bell 78] C. Bell, J. Judge, J. McNamara, *Computer engineering: a DEC view of hardware system design*, Digital Press, Bedford, Mass., 1978.

[Censier 78] L. M. Censier and P. Feautrier, "A new solution to coherence problems in multicache systems," *IEEE Trans. on Computers*, Vol. C-27, No. 12, December 1978, pp. 1112-1118.

[Easton 78] M. C. Easton and R. Fagin, "Cold-start vs. warm-start miss ratios," *CACM*, Vol. 21, No. 10, October 1978, pp. 866-872.

[Grosch 53] H. A. Grosch, "High Speed Arithmetic: the Digital Computer as a Research Tool," *Journal of the Optical Society of America*, Vol. 43, No. 4, (April 1953).

[Hoogendoorn 77] C. H. Hoogendoorn, "Reduction of memory interference in multiprocessor systems," *Proc. 4th Annual Symp. Comput. Arch.*, 1977, pp. 179-183.

[IBM 74] "System/370 model 155 theory of operation/diagrams manual (volume 5): buffer control unit," IBM System Products Division, Poughkeepsie, N.Y., 1974.

[IBM 76] "System/370 model 168 theory of operation/diagrams manual (volume 1)," Document No. SY22-6931-3, IBM System Products Division, Poughkeepsie, N.Y., 1976.

[IEEE 80] "Proposed microcomputer system bus standard (P796 bus)," *IEEE Computer Society Subcommittee Microcomputer System Bus Group*, October 1980.

[Kaplan 73] K. R. Kaplan and R. O. Winder, "Cache-based computer systems," *Computer*, March 1973, pp. 30-36.

[Knight 66] J. R. Knight, "Changes in computer performance," *Datamation*, Vol. 12, No. 9, September 1966, pp. 40-54.

[Lindsay 81] "Cache Memory for Microprocessors," *Computer Architecture News, ACM - SIGARCH*, Vol. 9, No. 5, (August 1981), pp. 6-13.

[Liptay 68] "J. S. Liptay, "Structural aspects of the System/360 Model 85, Part II: the cache," *IBM Syst. J.*, Vol. 7, No. 1, 1968, pp. 15-21.

[Norton 82] R. L. Norton and J. L. Abraham, "Using write back cache to improve performance of multiuser multiprocessors," *1982 Int. Conf. on Par. Proc.*, IEEE cat. no. 82CH1794-7, 1982, pp. 326-331.

[Patel 82] "Analysis of multiprocessor with private cache memories," J. H. Patel, *IEEE Trans. on Computers*, Vol. C-31, No. 4, April 1982, pp. 296-304.

[Rao 78] G. S. Rao, "Performance Analysis of Cache Memories," *Journal of the ACM*, Vol. 25, July 1978, pp. 378-395.

[Ravishankar 83] C. V. Ravishankar and J. Goodman, "Cache implementation for multiple microprocessors," *Digest of Papers, Spring COMPCON 83*, IEEE Computer Society Press, March 1983.

[Siewiorek 82] D. P. Siewiorek, C. G. Bell, and A. Newell, *Computer Structures: Principles and Examples*, McGraw-Hill, New York, N.Y., 1982.

[Smith 82] A. J. Smith, "Cache memories," *Computing Surveys*, Vol. 14, No. 3, September 1982, pp. 473-530.

[Smith 83] J. E. Smith and J. R. Goodman, "A study of instruction cache organizations and replacement policies," *Tenth Annual Symposium on Computer Architecture*, June 1983.

[Solomon 66] M. B. Solomon, Jr., "Economies of Scale and the IBM System/360," *CACM*, Vol. 9, No. 6, June 1966, pp. 435-440.

[Tang 76] C. K. Tang, "Cache system design in the tightly coupled multiprocessor system," *AFIPS Proc., NCC*, Vol. 45, pp. 749-753, 1976.

[TI 82] *Texas Instruments MOS Memory Data Book*, Texas Instruments, Inc., Memory Division, Houston, Texas, pp. 106-111, 1982.

[Tredennick 82] N. Tredennick, "The IBM micro/370 project," public lecture for *Distinguished Lecturer Series*, Computer Sciences Department, University of Wisconsin-Madison, March 31, 1982.

[Widdoes 79] L. C. Widdoes, "S-1 Multiprocessor architecture (MULT-2)," *1979 Annual Report – the S-1 Project, Volume 1: Architecture*, Lawrence Livermore Laboratories, Tech. Report UCID 18619, 1979.

[Yen 82] W. C. Yen and K. S. Fu, "Coherence problem in a multicache system," *1982 Int. Conf. on Par. Proc.*, IEEE cat. no. 82CH1794-7, 1982, pp. 332-339.

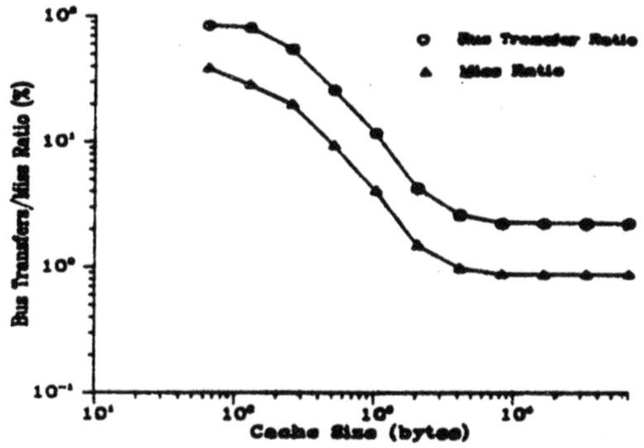

Fig. 1. Bus Transfer and Miss Ratios vs. Cache Size; blocks are 4 bytes; PDP-11 traces. The bus transfer ratio is the number of transfers between cache and main store relative to those necessary if there were no cache.

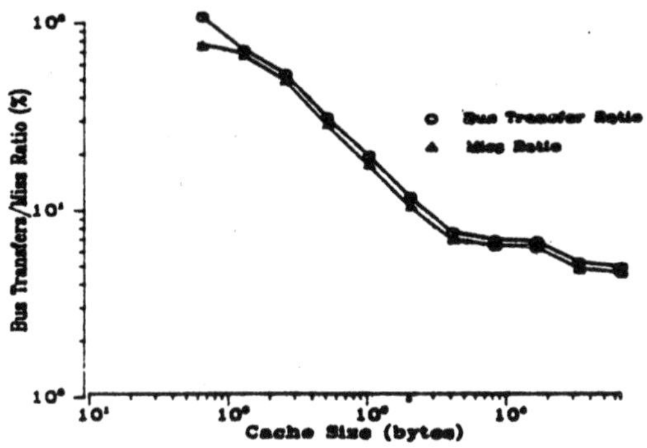

Fig. 2. Bus Transfer and Miss Ratios vs. Cache Size; 4-byte blocks; VAX-11 traces.

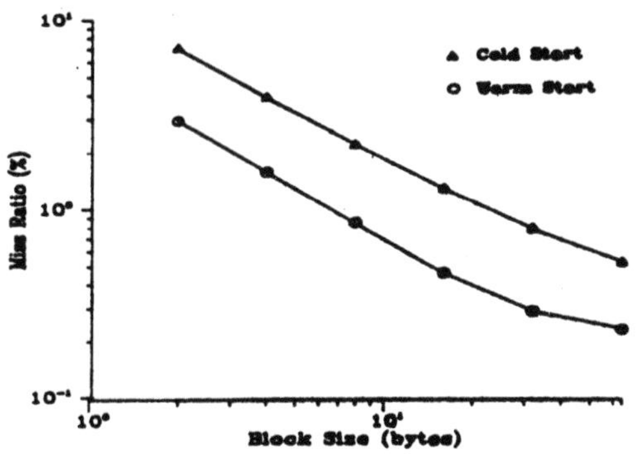

Fig. 3. Miss Ratio vs. Block Size for warm and cold starts; PDP-11 traces.

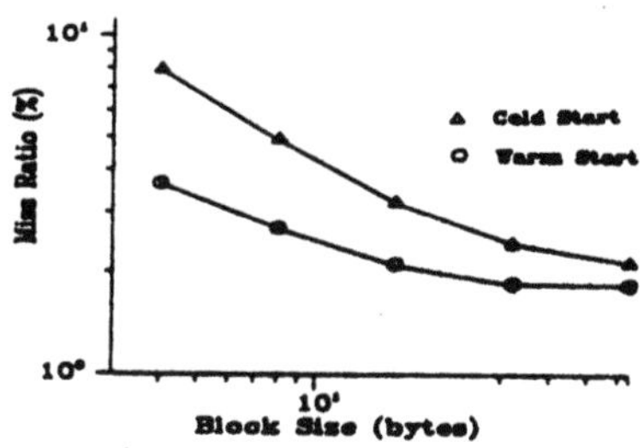

Fig. 4. Miss Ratio vs. Block Size for warm and cold starts; VAX-11 traces.

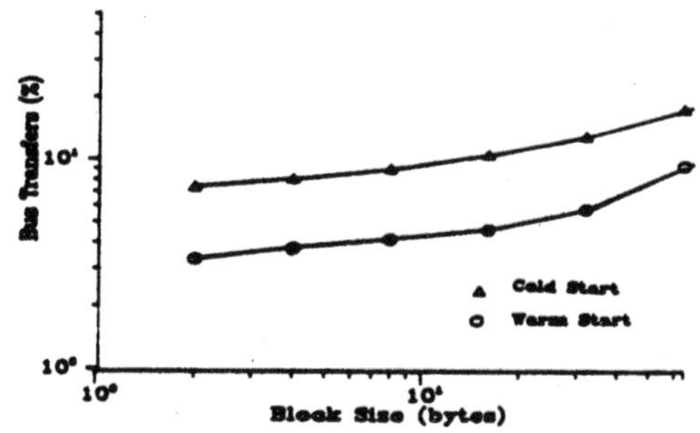

Fig. 5. Bus Transfer Ratio vs. Block Size for warm and cold starts; PDP-11 traces.

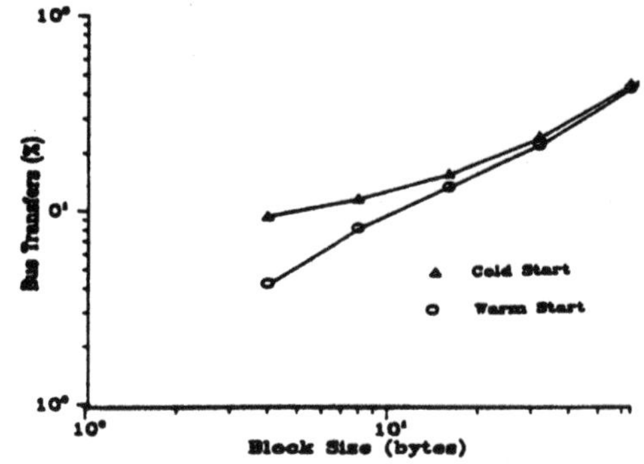

Fig. 6. Bus Transfer Ratio vs. Block Size for warm and cold starts; VAX-11 traces.

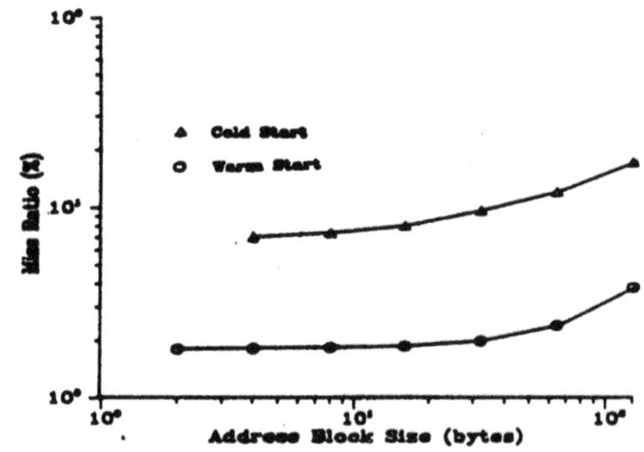

Fig. 7. Miss ratio vs. Address Block Size for PDP-11 and VAX-11 traces.
The triangles indicate the VAX-11 trace (not cold start); the circles indicate the PDP-11 trace (not warm start).

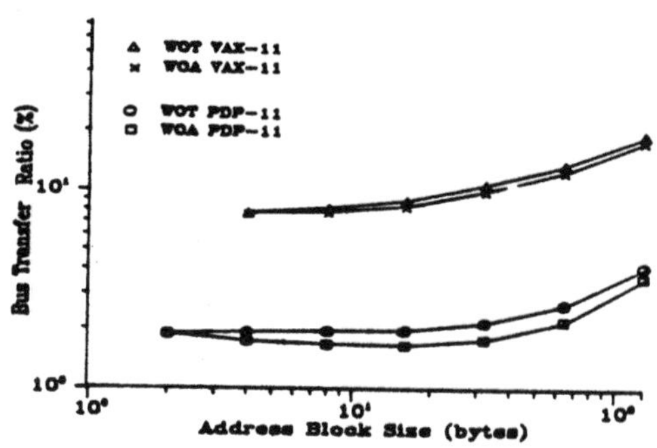

Fig. 8. Bus Transfer Ratio vs. Address Block Size for warm and cold starts; WOA: address blocks are reserved. WOT: transfer blocks are reserved.

Chapter 7

CASE STUDIES

There are many distributed systems that have been constructed as prototypes, test beds, and commercial products. In this chapter, we shall provide three commercial products: Pluribus, Tandem System, and Stratus; and a distributed test bed system for real time applications developed by System Development Corporation, Huntsville.

The first three papers are related with the Tandem Systems. The paper by Horst and Chou presents the Tandem hardware architecture and its performance. The paper by Bartlett describes the key parameters of the kernel of the Tandem System which provides fault tolerant transaction processing in a distributed environment. The paper by Borr discusses the transaction monitoring facility, distributed data base management systems for the Tandem System which provide fault tolerant transaction processing in a distributed environment. The paper by Freiburghouser presents the Stratus architecture, operating system software, and transaction processing. The last paper by McDonald and Smith describes distributed test beds for performance experiments to support the development, analysis, evolution, and validation of research in distributed computing for real time applications. The flexible reconfigurable test bed enables realistic investigation of a variety of candidate hardware and software solutions for the specific application.

There are many interesting distributed systems that have been built, such as Pluribus, C.mmp, Cm*, C.vmp, SIFT, and FTMP, all of which appeared in an excellent special issue of *IEEE Proceedings on Fault Tolerant Systems* [IEEE 78].

The Hardware Architecture and Linear Expansion of Tandem NonStop Systems

Robert Horst and Timothy Chou

Tandem Computers Incorporated - 19333 Vallco Parkway - Cupertino, CA USA

ABSTRACT

The Tandem NonStop TXP is a commercially available multiple processor system that delivers mainframe class performance for transaction processing applications. Several sixteen-processor systems may be configured in a ring structure using fiber optics. This structure allows from two to over two hundred processors to be applied to a single online application. Benchmark results are presented to demonstrate the linear growth of system performance as processors are added.

TANDEM HARDWARE ARCHITECTURE EVOLUTION: 1976-1981

The market for high volume transaction processing has increased rapidly. In the 60s, only large airlines required large on-line transaction processing (OLTP) systems. These requirements were filled by centralized mainframe computers running specialized, highly tuned applications. They suffered from limited expandability, a costly applications environment, and the requirement to program in assembly language[5].

Today, many other industries are taking advantage of OLTP systems. Some of these applications include on-line banking, credit authorization, debit cards, teletext, telephone billing, electronic mail, medical information systems and paperless factories. These markets have similar systems requirements: the system must continue to operate despite hardware failures, it must be expandable, and it must be capable of high transaction throughput.

In 1976 Tandem introduced a new system architecture specifically designed to address the problems of OLTP. Designated the NonStop I, this system consisted of from two to sixteen loosely coupled processors which communicated with each other over dual high speed busses[2,10]. The Tandem hardware architecture is illustrated in Figure 1. This loosely coupled architecture has proven to be effective for transaction processing by supporting incremental expansion, high availability, and high performance[8]. The loose coupling does not limit performance since transaction processing, unlike most scientific processing, is easily partitioned into multiple relatively independent processes.

Briefly, each CPU runs at one to two mips, memory is from 1 to 16 megabytes, each IO channel runs at 5 megabytes/second, and each interprocessor bus (Dynabus) runs at a peak rate of 13 megabytes per second.

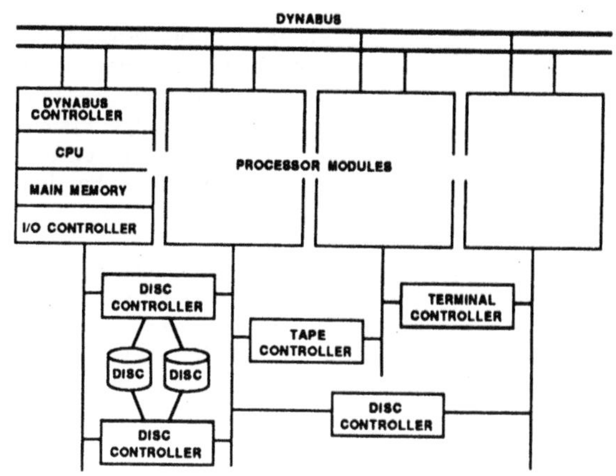

Figure 1: A diagram of Tandem's NonStop System architecture.

In 1981, the NonStop II was introduced to remove addressing limitations of the 16-bit NonStop I. Many new software features have been added to the basic offering. The system was expanded into a network of up to 255 systems, a relational data base management system as well as transaction management software[1,3,4] were also added. These products allowed users to develop distributed fault tolerant OLTP applications without worrying about the underlying system implementation.

TANDEM HARDWARE ARCHITECTURE EVOLUTION: 1981-1985

The Tandem system as it stood in 1981 solved all of the requirements for OLTP, but the performance required for some large applications was beyond the reach of a 16-processor system. The network provided a way to apply more than one system to a single application without reprogramming; however, the relatively slow speed of data communications lines and software overheads of long-haul communication protocols proved to be a bottleneck in high volume applications. It was apparent that there was a need for systems able to support high volume transaction processing. The need was addressed on two fronts. A project was started to expand the number of processors which could be applied to a single application, and another project was started to develop a higher performance processor.

FIBER OPTIC EXTENSION (FOX)

The most obvious way to increase the number of processors in a Tandem system is to extend the high-speed interprocessor busses to handle more processors. While this is not difficult from a hardware design standpoint, there are drawbacks. All processors would be required to be in close physical proximity in order to keep from degrading the bus performance. This would cause a physical space problem in some computer rooms—the associated discs and communications gear require considerable space. In addition, allowing a single system to expand to more processors does not help existing customers who already have several systems requiring higher bandwidth communications.

An alternative approach to adding processors in the same system is to use a high speed connection between systems. This effectively adds another level of interconnection hierarchy between the 26 Mbytes/sec inter-CPU links, and the 56 Kbit/sec network links. Figure 2 illustrates the Tandem solution which uses fiber-optics to link up to fourteen systems.

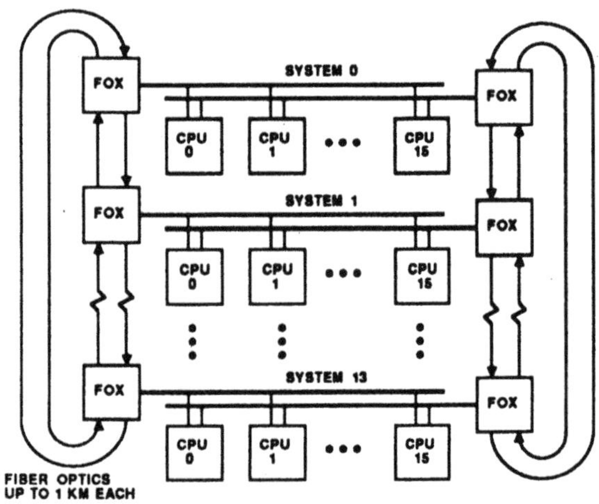

Figure 2: The connectivity of the FOX fiber optic ring. It connects up to 14 systems and up to 224 processors.

Each node can accept or send up to 4 Mbytes/sec. With this additional bandwidth, a cluster of up to 224 CPUs can be configured to handle a single on-line transaction processing application.

The topology of the FOX connection is a store-and-forward ring structure. Four fibers are connected between a system and each of its two neighbors. Each interprocessor bus is extended by a pair of fibers, which allows messages to be sent in either direction around the ring. The four paths provided between any pair of systems assures that communication is not lost if a system is disabled (due to a power-fail perhaps) or if an entire four fiber bundle is severed. The ring topology also has advantages over a star in that there is no central switch which could be a single point of failure. In addition, cable routing is easier with a ring than with a star.

In a ring structure, bandwidth increases as additional nodes are added. The total bandwidth available in a FOX network depends on the amount of passthrough traffic. In a 14 node FOX ring if each node sends to all other nodes with equal probability the network has a usable bandwidth of 10 Mbytes/sec. With no passthrough traffic the bandwidth increases to 24 Mbytes/sec. Theoretically an application generating 3K bytes of traffic per transaction, at 1,000 transactions per second, would require a FOX ring bandwidth of only 3 Mbytes/second. This would put total utilization of the FOX network at less than 30% of the total available bandwidth.

Fiber optic links were chosen both to solve technical and practical problems in configuring large clusters. Since fiber optics are not susceptible to electromagnetic interference, they provide a reliable connection even in noisy environments. They also provide high bandwidth communications over fairly large distances (1 km). This eases the congestion in the computer room and allows many computers in the same or nearby buildings to be linked. Fiber optic cables are also flexible and of small diameter, thus easing installation. Figure 3 provides additional details on FOX.

- Ring-configured fiber optic inter-system link
- Links up to 14 systems of 16 processors
- Up to 1km between any two adjacent nodes
- Data rate: 4 mbyte/sec per node, max 28 mbyte/sec per ring
- Light source: Light emitting diodes
- Receiver: PIN (Positive Intrinsic Negative) photodiodes
- Cable: Glass fiber optics, attenuation 6dB/km max

Figure 3. Fox fact sheet.

TXP PROCESSOR DESIGN RATIONALE

Once a system architecture can apply a large number of processors to a single application, there is still a question of what the characteristics of the processor should be. The possibilities span a large range of performance levels. At the low end of the performance range are microprocessor based designs. These may be based on one chip microprocessors such as the Motorola 68000 family, the Intel 8086 family or the National 32000. In the midrange are designs based on medium-scale integration or gate arrays. Such designs are typified by mini/supermini computers such as the Digital VAX series, Hewlett-Packard 3000 and the IBM 4300 series. At the high end are designs based on the most aggressive IC, packaging, and cooling technologies. Examples of this type of design are mainframes such as the IBM 3090, Amdahl 580, and high end machines from Sperry, Burroughs, CDC and Cray.

Many factors need to be analyzed in order to decide whether the micro, mini, or mainframe approach should be preferred for the processors in a high volume transaction processing system. These factors include cost-performance, granularity of fault tolerance, granularity of adding performance, and ease of managing the system.

In a system which is modularly expandable, cost-performance is the driving force in the development of a new processor. Improving cost-performance by lowering costs is difficult. Even using a microprocessor, which may be nearly free, may not significantly reduce costs over a minicomputer-style design due to the many fixed costs which make up a system. The cost of main memory, packaging, power and cabling are not reduced in proportion to CPU cost reductions.

It is easier to improve cost-performance by increasing the performance of the processor. This might seem to favor a mainframe as the best choice for a multiprocessor system. Unfortunately, the complexity of a mainframe design requires a large development cost and long development time. In addition, in trying to improve uniprocessor performance some nonlinearities are encountered. For instance, the jump from air to liquid cooling constitutes a large cost increment.

Other factors influence the choice of processors. If the processor is too small, the number of processors required to perform a large application can become so large as to be unmanageable. In addition, if the system is not carefully designed, performance improvements can cease to be linear beyond some number of processors.

On the other hand, if the processor is so powerful that the application can be handled by a single processor, fault tolerance can suffer. Today the only fault tolerant configurations of mainframes require an expensive duplicated hot standby. Even if these machines could be incorporated into the Tandem architecture in which the second machine can do useful work, the failure of one of the mainframes would remove half the computing power from the system. In extremely critical applications, it may not be tolerable to degrade performance while a hardware failure is being repaired. If the application requires only one processor to handle the peak load, a second processor is needed in case of failure, for a 100% overhead. In contrast, if four less powerful processors are used to handle the same workload, only one extra processor is needed in case of failure for a 25% overhead.

THE NONSTOP TXP PROCESSOR

Based on the above rationale, Tandem introduced the NonStop TXP processor in 1983. Its primary design objectives were to improve both cost-performance and absolute performance over the NonStop II[7]. The initial pricing of the NonStop TXP offered a 50% improvement in price-performance over the NonStop II at about 2.5 times its performance.

In the NonStop TXP design, the emphasis on cost-performance extended all the way to the component level. One of the first decisions to be made was the selection of static RAMs to be used in the cache memory and control store. The most advanced RAMs at that time were organized as 4Kx4 and 16Kx1 bits with access times of 45ns. These were four times the density of and 10 ns faster than the RAMs used in the NonStop II.

To implement logic functions, advanced MSI Schottky technology and programmable array logic were chosen. An extensive analysis of LSI alternatives available in 1981 showed that a gate array machine would have been about the same performance level, higher cost, and would have required a much longer development cycle.

Once a technology was chosen, the next challenge was to develop an architecture which could utilize the improved components to improve performance and cost-performance. One such area was the cache memory design. Although extensive academic research in cache memories was available during the NonStop TXP design[11], most of the studies did not anticipate the impact of large RAMs on cache organizations. Using 16K static RAMs, a 64K byte cache requires only 32 components (not including parity or the tag comparison RAMs or logic). This makes it much more economical to design a large "dumb" cache (direct mapped) than a smaller "smart" cache (set associative). After performing some real time emulation of different cache organizations, the final cache design for the NonStop TXP was chosen. It is a 64K byte direct mapped virtual cache with hashing of some of the address bits. Hit ratios for the cache have been measured between 96% and 99% while performing transaction processing workloads.

Other tradeoffs were also made in the interest of cost performance. In order for the NonStop TXP to be plug-compatable with the NonStop II processor, the CPU was required to fit on four circuit boards. Had it overflowed those boards, a large jump in cost would have occurred. For this reason, the NonStop TXP relies on microcode to perform some of the functions done in hardware on many machines. For instance, after every cache access, the microcode must perform a conditional branch to test for a cache miss. If a miss occurred, the microcode fetches the block from memory and refills the cache block. Performance could have been improved a few percent by providing additional control and data path hardware to perform the cache refill directly. However, since this hardware would have required an additional logic board, it would have adversely affected cost-performance.

Many of the tradeoffs made in the NonStop TXP design were based on detailed measurements of the NonStop II performance. A complex performance analyzer, named XPLOR, was designed and built solely for that purpose. XPLOR was used to perform the cache emulation experiments. In addition, it provided data on instruction frequencies, percent time spent in each instruction, and the memory reference activity of each instruction. This allowed hardware to be saved in the support of less frequent instructions and applied to accelerating the more frequent instructions. XPLOR also provided data which enabled the microcode to be optimized for the more frequent paths through complex instructions.

The final result is a processor which has a 83.3 ns microcycle time and can execute simple instructions in only two cycles. In typical applications, the NonStop TXP executes about 2 million instructions per second. This new processor has not uncovered any bottlenecks in the I/O or message system; hence, the improvements in CPU performance have been directly translated into transaction processing performance. Figure 4 summarizes the TXP features.

- DYNABUS : 26Mbytes/sec
- 2 MIPs per processor
- 83.3 nsec microcycle time
- Three stage microinstruction pipelining
- Three stage macroinstruction pipelining
- Dual data paths and dual arithmetic-logic units
- Two level control store - 8K x 40 bits and 4K x 84 bits
- Extensive parity and selfchecking
- 64 Kbyte cache memory - 96% to 99% hit ratio
- 64-bit access of main memory
- 2-8 Mbytes physical memory (64K DRAMs)
- 1 Gbytes virtual memory addressing
- Basic instruction set of 220 instructions
- Optional decimal and floating point instruction sets
- 3 - 12 hour battery backup of main memory
- Plug-compatible with NonStop II processor
- 5 Mbyte/sec burst-multiplexed channel per processor
- Up to 32 I/O controllers per processor
- Up to 256 I/O devices per processor
- Data communications:
  - Byte synchronous - 80kbps
  - Bit synchronous - 56kbps
  - Asynchronous - 50bps to 19.2kbps

Figure 4. TXP Fact sheet.

PERFORMANCE BENCHMARKS

Recently several customer benchmarks have been run which demonstrate the capability of the Tandem architecture to support high volume, high performance on-line transaction processing. Two of these benchmarks are described below.

BANKING BENCHMARK

In the summer of 1984 a major European bank benchmarked a Tandem system to support a bank card and electronic funds transfer application. The data base for the application consisted of the following files:

Card	:	1.2 million records of credit cards
Account	:	2.4 million records of account balances
Log	:	History of updates to Accounts
Customer	:	4 million records about customers

The application was described by five major types of transactions. The two most frequent transactions were the DEBIT and LOOKUP transactions.

DEBIT Transaction Profile:
X.25 Message in;
Read random Card;
Read random Account;
X.25 Message out;
X.25 Message in;
Read random with lock same Account;
Rewrite Account;
Sequential write to log of Account update;
X.25 Message out.

LOOKUP Transaction Profile:
X.25 Message in;
Read random Card;
Read random Account;
X.25 Message out;
X.25 Message in;
Read random Customer;
X.25 Message out;

In this benchmark, 50% of the transactions were DEBIT, 40% were LOOKUP, and 10% were other transactions.

The benchmark was done on a 4, 8, 12, and 16 processor single system as well as 1, 2, 3 and 4 4-CPU systems FOXed together. The results are shown in Figure 5. Note that the transaction rate grows linearly in the case where the processors are interconnected via the Dynabus. This is also true when processors are interconnected via FOX. In addition, FOX introduces almost no throughput degradation.

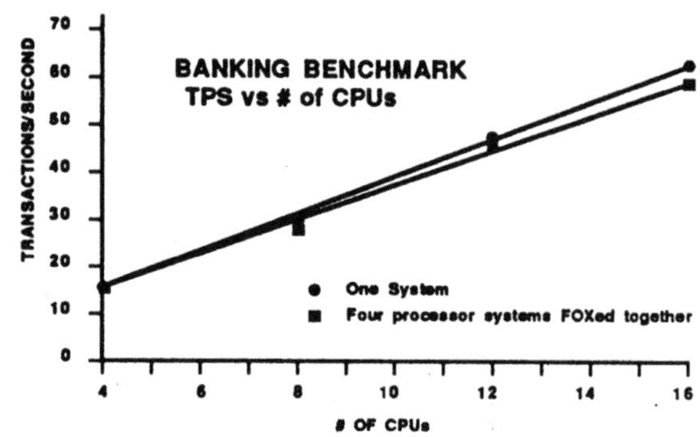

Figure 5. A benchmark to demonstrate Dynabus and Fox linearity. Transaction throughput vs the number of cpus on the DynaBus, and vs the number of CPUs on a FOX ring.

RETAILING BENCHMARK

In the fall of 1984 a major American retailer benchmarked a retail credit authorization application. The requirements were for three individual sites, each site providing 100+ authorization transactions per second for its area. Each site will be connected through a large SNA network and can communicate directly with the other two when necessary for processing out-of-area authorizations. The data base for the application consisted of the following files:

Authorization	:	20 million records
Bankcard Negative	:	10 million records
Out-of-Area Index	:	10 million records
Transaction Journal	:	Large entry sequenced file

The application was composed largely of one transaction, MAIN, which was nearly 75% of all transactions.

MAIN Transaction Profile:
SNA Message in;
Five in-memory table lookups;
Random Read with Lock of Authorization file;
Write Authorization file;
Write Transaction Journal SNA Message out;

As with the banking benchmark, the retail benchmark showed linear growth in transaction throughput as processors and discs are added. By doubling the number of cpus and discs, the benchmark got twice the throughput for the same response time—less than 1.7 seconds for 90% of the transactions. This is illustrated in Figure 6.

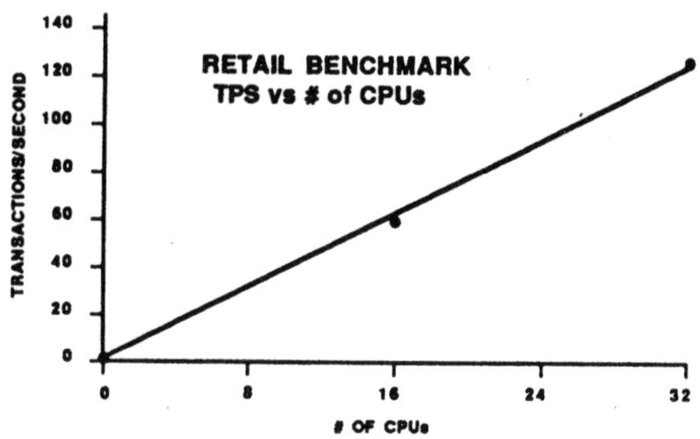

Figure 6. Linearity of transaction throughput for a retailing benchmark.

SUMMARY

Both of these benchmarks demonstrate the capability for this system architecture to provide high volume transaction processing. The actual transaction throughputs are shown in Figure 6. Response times in both benchmarks averaged 1 second. Figures 5 and 6 graphically illustrate both the linearity and processing power in the region between 2 and 32 processors.

These graphs do not contain a wealth of data points because each benchmark is expensive in both time and equipment. However, they do represent real measurements as opposed to theoretical modeling results.

There is a great temptation to extrapolate these curves to 224 processors (the total number in a FOX ring). Assuming linear growth the transaction rate that hypothetically could be supported is somewhere over 800 transaction per second. In reality this may or may not be achievable; however, we hope at some point in time to be able to ascertain this experimentally. Once again, it should be noted that building a 224 processor system and benchmarking it is extremely costly in both time and equipment.

CONCLUSIONS

For a number of years there has been academic interest and hypotheses[9] that a number of small processors could be tied together in some way to provide the computing power of a larger machine. While this may not be true in general, this paper illustrates that it is possible in on-line transaction processing.

Ordinary OLTP systems bottleneck at 50 transactions per second while high performance OLTP systems achieve 200 transactions per second. Beyond these rates, users have been forced to build their applications using ad hoc techniques rather than general purpose systems. Even using these ad hoc techniques, the highest transaction throughput claimed by any mainframe manufacturer is somewhere near 800 transactions per second[6]. Our experimental results to date indicate that the Tandem architecture, a general purpose multiprocessor, is capable of supporting high volume transaction processing.

ACKNOWLEDGEMENTS

The authors would like to thank Jim Gray, Harald Sammer, Eric Chow, Joan Zimmerman, and Hoke Johnson for providing many helpful remarks and suggestions. The reported benchmarks were done by Harald Sammer's Frankfurt High Performance Research Center and by Tom Houy's Large Systems Support group at Tandem.

—A version of this paper appears in: Proceedings of 12th International Symposium on Computer Architecture, June 1985.

REFERENCES

[1]Arceneaux, G. et al., "A Closer Look at Pathway," Tandem Computers, SEDS-003, June 1982.

[2]Bartlett, J., "A NonStop Kernel," Proceedings of the Eighth Symposium on Operating System Principles, pp. 22-29, December 1981.

[3]Borr, A., "Transaction Monitoring in ENCOMPASS," Proceedings of the Seventh International Conference on Very Large Databases, September 1981. Also Tandem Computers TR 81.2.

[4]Borr, A., "Robustness to Crash in a Distributed Database: A Non Shared-Memory Multi-processor Approach," Proceedings of the Tenth International Conference on Very Large Databases, September 1984.

[5]Gifford, D., Spector, A., "The TWA Reservation System," Communications of the ACM, vol. 27, no. 7, pp. 650-665, July 1984.

[6]Gray, J. et al., "One Thousand Transactions Per Second", in the Proceedings of the IEEE COMPCON-85, San Francisco. Also Tandem Computers TR 85.1.

[7]Horst, R. and Metz, S.,"New System Manages Hundreds of Transactions/Second," Electronics, pp. 147-151, April 19, 1984. Also Tandem Computers TR 84.1.

[8]Kim, W., "Highly Available Systems for Database Applications," Computing Surveys, vol. 16, no. 1, pp. 71-98, March 1984.

[9]Satyanarayanan, M., "Multiprocessing: An Annotated Bibliography," Computer, pp. 101-116, May 1980.

[10]Siewiorek, D., Bell, C.G., Newell, A., Computer Structures: Principles and Examples. McGraw Hill Book Company, 1982.

[11]Smith, A. J., "Cache Memories," Computing Surveys, vol. 14, no. 3, pp. 473-530, Sept. 1984.

A NonStop* Kernel

Joel F. Bartlett
Tandem Computers Inc.
Cupertino, Ca.

Abstract

The Tandem NonStop System is a fault-tolerant [1], expandable, and distributed computer system designed expressly for online transaction processing. This paper describes the key primitives of the kernel of the operating system. The first section describes the basic hardware building blocks and introduces their software analogs: processes and messages. Using these primitives, a mechanism that allows fault-tolerant resource access, the process-pair, is described. The paper concludes with some observations on this type of system structure and on actual use of the system.

Introduction

Fault-tolerant computing systems have been built over the last two decades in a number of places to satisfy a variety of goals. These results and differing approachs have been summarized in [1,3,11]. In the past, many of these systems have been designed for specific tasks, such as telephone switching, where the costs of failure are significant. In addition, the designers of most of the systems did not intend to provide general purpose hardware and software modules which the end user would customize to form a reliable system.

An increasing number of online applications in commercial data processing has created a demand for fault-tolerant general purpose computing. These applications are also characterized by their high rate of growth, which requires that the computing system be significantly expanded over its lifetime. The Tandem system is intended to fit these requirements.

* NonStop and Tandem are Trademarks of Tandem Computers Inc.

1. Hardware Organization

A network consists of up to 255 nodes. Each node is composed of multiple processor and I/O controller modules interconnected by redundant buses [2,3] as shown in PMS [3] notation in Figure 1. A node consists of two to sixteen processors, where each processor (Pcentral) has its own power supply, memory, backup battery, and I/O channel (Sio). All processors are interconnected by redundant interprocessor buses (Sipb). Each I/O controller (Kdisc, Ksync, etc.) is connected to two I/O channels and is powered from two different power supplies using a diode ORing scheme. Finally, dual-ported I/O devices such as discs (Tdisc) may be connected to a second I/O controller. The contents of a disc may be "mirrored" on a second volume, but this function is supported primarily by software rather than by hardware. I/O devices other than discs are normally single ported and are connected to one I/O controller.

The processors are 16 bits wide with up to 2mb of memory per processor. The internal clock speed of the processor is 100ns, resulting in a register-to-register add in .6 microseconds and a load of a word from memory in 1.1 microseconds.

The two interprocessor buses (Sipb) provide each processor with two point-to-point paths to each other processor and to itself. Data transfers to and from the buses are buffered in high speed 16-word packet buffers in each processor, allowing data transfers at a rate of 13.5 megabytes/sec. This is more than three times faster than the processor's memory, which assures that interprocessor messages are not delayed by the bus bandwidth.

1.1 Hardware fault model

The system design goal is to provide continuous operation in the presence of a single fault. This requires that all single faults be detectable, diagnosable, and repairable online. In addition, the software must allow reintegration of the repaired module into the system.

Error recovery analysis needs some assumptions to be made about the types of faults that the system can tolerate. First, a fault in either a processor, its memory, or its power supply must be contained in and therefore at most disable that processor. Second, a fault in either an interprocessor bus or an I/O channel will at most disable that bus. Third, a fault in an I/O controller will at most disable that I/O controller. With these assumptions, it can be seen that a single fault will at most make I/O devices attached only to one controller unavailable.

Physical events affecting the system's hardware can be divided into three classes [1]. The first class, permanent hardware failures, will be detected either on the initial instance of the failure or shortly thereafter by background tests. These give rise to two kinds of problems: error in recovery algorithms and contamination of data bases that takes place before failure detection.

Intermittent component failures share the previously mentioned problem areas. In addition, unless there is immediate detection, there is a far higher probability of data base corruption as the background tests are much less likely to see the problem.

A final source of problems, and perhaps the most serious in actual operation, is that caused by external interference with the system. This class includes such items as air conditioning failures, but is primarily composed of operational errors by either the computer operator or service personnel. Sometimes these occur during normal operations, but often their actions are in response to another fault at which point a single misstep may cause the entire system to fail.

2. Software Structure

The operating system [4] provides many of the user services usually associated with medium-size systems: multiprogramming, access to a gigabyte of virtual memory per processor, a file system, and extensive communications facilities. However, it offers these services in a fault-tolerant manner on a modular, expandable computer system. To do this, its structure has been designed as an analogue of the hardware structure. As the hardware consists of multiple processors and I/O controllers, the operating system functions are distributed over multiple processes; and as the hardware modules are interconnected via redundant buses, the operating system processes communicate via fault-tolerant messages.

At the time this structure was proposed and development started, December 1974, there were few precedents for it. Our main inspiration was found in the work of Dijkstra [5] and Brinch Hansen [6], whose ideas and examples provided the key kernel primitives and structure for the system design.

2.1 Processes

Each processor supports up to 256 concurrent processes. Each process has a private data space, but may share code with other processes in the same processor. A major portion of the cost of a process switch is chargeable to memory mapping which is required to designate the new process' code and data spaces. This

```
.-------------------.--------------------.-----------Sipb
|                   |                    |
|-.-----------------|-.------------------|-.---------Sipb
| |                 | |                  | |
 Pcentral            Pcentral             Pcentral
 |                   |                    |
 Sio                Sio                  Sio
 |---Kdisc-----------|----Ksync------------|
 |   |               |    |
 |   |----Tdisc----| |    |---Tmodem (to another node)
 |   |             | |    |
 |   |----Tdisc----| |    |---Tmodem (to another node)
 |                   |
 |-------------Kdisc---|
 |                   |
 |--------Ktape--------|
 |        |          |
 |        Ttape      |
 |                   |
 |--------Kasync-------|
          |
      Tterminal's
```

Figure 1: PMS Diagram of a Node.

results in a cost of approximately .5 milliseconds to switch processes.

All processors contain both a monitor process and a memory manager process. The Monitor's functions include process management within its processor (e.g., process creation and deletion), information return, message system control, and fault recovery. When a process is created, it is given a unique "processid" composed of two parts. The first is its location (node number, processor number, and process number) and the second is either a unique timestamp or a symbolic name.

Process synchronization primitives include counting semaphores and process-local event flags. Semaphores are used within the kernel to control such things as access to shared I/O controllers. Event flags are used to signal a process that events such as device interrupt, message arrival, and message completion have occurred. These primitives were chosen using the author's experience at the time rather than following an exhaustive survey of available methods. They have been more than adequate for the resource control involved in I/O operations and in the implementation of the message system. More complex resource control is handled by requesters sending messages to the process which "owns" the resource.

2.2 Messages

Almost all information flow, even within a single processor, is carried in messages rather than through shared storage. Each process has a message queue where all messages sent to it by other processes are placed. Messages are queued in either a FIFO manner or according to the sender's priority, at the receiver process's option. The message system is designed to provide a process-to-process communication mechanism which is independent of the location of the processes and transparent to interprocessor bus transmission errors.

A message consists of a request for a service and a reply by the server. For example, if a process wishes to create another process, it calls the procedure NEWPROCESS which in turn sends a message to the Monitor process in the processor where the process is to be created. The sender will then wait for the message reply. When the Monitor retrieves the request from its message queue, it creates the process, and then replies to the message (which awakes the sender) with either the new processid or an error indication.

This model is similar to that discussed by Cheriton in [7] and has the desirable property that it is an analogue of an operating system procedure that is called by the application program to perform a specific service and return a result. Inherent in it is a positive acknowledgement for each logical request, which is the first key to providing fault tolerance in this system.

In addition, the application program is not allowed direct access to the message system. This is done by providing a conventional user/privileged mode in the processor. User programs may only enter the operating system (and privileged mode) at certain defined entry points, e.g. NEWPROCESS in the previous example. This restriction provides obvious protection and information hiding benefits and allows the operating system to control error recovery on message failures, a second key to the system's fault tolerance.

2.2.1 Message primitives

Before the error recovery strategies can be shown, the kernel's message primitives must be introduced. A message exchange using these primitives takes the following form:

A process "R", the requestor, sends a message to process "S", the server, by calling the procedure LINK. The caller supplies a processid, six message parameter words, and an optional resident buffer which may contain additional data related to the message or may be used to return a result. If the message can be sent, then the address of the sender's Link Control Block (LCB) is returned to R, a matching LCB (which contains the six message parameter words, R's processid, S's processid, and the address of R's LCB) is queued on S's message queue, and S is awakened on the event LREQ (request pending).

When S is ready to process a request, it calls the procedure LISTEN, which dequeues the first LCB from its message queue. The returned LCB contains the six message parameters and the size of the data buffer that the caller supplied to LINK. If there is any data that must be retrieved from R before the operation is performed, S calls the procedure READLINK with the addresses of its data buffer and LCB. READLINK copies the data from R's buffer to S's buffer.

S then performs the appropriate operation and returns the results to R by calling the procedure WRITELINK with the appropriate LCB and, optionally, a buffer whose contents are to be returned. Prior to this call, S may alter the message parameter words in its LCB to return status to R. WRITELINK causes S's buffer and message parameter words to be copied into R's buffer and LCB. A "done" flag is set in R's LCB, and then R is awakened on the event LDONE (request complete).

At this point, S is finished with the message and may go on to other things. R can examine the results of the request and then return its LCB and buffer (if any) to the system by calling BREAKLINK.

2.2.2 Message properties

The previous example illustrates several key aspects of the message system. First, all messages are sent by value. By having no shared data structures, the message system looks the same irrespective of the relative locations of the processes R and S.

Since information transfer between R and S only occurs via message system primitives, which in turn only work when the supplied LCB's match (processid's for R and S and R's LCB address are identical in both LCB's), the message is always abortable by either R or S. The requestor, R, can terminate the message by calling BREAKLINK. If the message has not been completed, a cancel flag will be set in S's LCB and S will be awakened on the event LCAN (request cancellation). The server, S, may also terminate the message by setting the cancel flag in its LCB and calling WRITELINK without specifying a buffer. This will result in the requestor being awakened on LDONE with both the completion and the cancel flag set in its LCB.

Completion of a message with the cancel flag set provides a uniform mechanism for signaling failures. It allows outstanding messages to be cleaned up on a process or processor failure by setting the cancel flag, mimicking cancellation by the failed end of the message.

Certain system status messages that need no reply, such as processor failure or reload, are sent by system processes to application processes. It is important that the system process not be blocked if the application process does not pick up the message. Hence the sender calls BREAKLINK immediately after calling LINK, terminating its end of the message. This technique can only be used when the information can fit in the six message parameter words.

A server process is free to pick up multiple requests through LISTEN, queue them internally, and not READLINK or WRITELINK the request until it is ready to process the request or reply to it. For example, a process controlling a disc may need to block certain requests that need to access a locked record until the record is unlocked.

Conversely, a process may have multiple LINK's outstanding at any time. This allows an application process to keep a read request posted for each terminal that it manages, processing the input data as requests complete.

2.2.3 Message system resource control

In a message-based system, allocation of control blocks and buffers is a potential source of resource contention and deadlock. No formal limits on process interaction via messages have been defined. This approach allows flexible application design, but at some risk. The resource allocation strategies that have been devised are not "correct" in a formal sense, but they do minimize this risk.

First, LCB allocation is controlled by providing both "reserved" and "pool" LCB's. A process may reserve some number of LCB's to queue incoming messages and some number of LCB's to send messages. If a process has all of its reserved (possibly none) LCB's in use, then pool LCB's will be allocated if they are available. If an LCB cannot be obtained within 10 seconds, then the call to LINK will fail. System server processes reserve one or more LCB's for incoming messages and a sufficient number (dependent solely on the servers' needs during request processing) for outgoing messages to assure that they can complete any request made of them.

Message buffer allocation is managed by several techniques. First, data buffers for incoming messages are not allocated until the server process is ready to request the data via READLINK. Second, allocation is made from different storage pools on the basis of the type of request. For example, buffers for reads from terminals are separated from buffers for disc requests since these two buffer types are usually held for significantly different periods of time. In addition, certain types of system server processes have permanently allocated buffers so that they may always service requests.

2.2.4 Interprocessor bus protocol

While messages between two processes in the same processor can be sent using standard mutual exclusion primitives and moves, messages between processes in different processors must flow over the interprocessor buses.

In order to make messages useful as an abstraction, it is important that the message primitives recover from bus errors and fail only if the other process does not exist, the other processor is down, or there are no free LCB's. In addition, localized error detection and correction is required for fault isolation and repair. These arguments for local robustness should not be interpreted as arguments against end-to-end checking as encouraged by Saltzer in [7]. On the contrary, the author believes that they are both necessary in fault-tolerant systems.

From an implementation and confidence viewpoint, it is desirable that the error recovery scheme be as simple as possible yet still detect misrouted, inserted, or lost packets. In addition, the two physical buses must support an arbitrary number of logical connections between processes so that transmissions can be multiplexed.

With these requirements in mind, a bus protocol, similar in spirit to HDLC [8], was designed which uses sequenced packets and positive acknowledgements. When the sender processor sends data, it is divided into 16-word packets consisting of the sender and receiver processor numbers, a sequence number, 13 information words, and a checksum. Following transmission, the request waits on the wait acknowledge (WACK) list. If the request is still on the WACK list after one second, it is resent on the other bus. This cycle repeats until either the transmission is acknowledged or the receiving processor is declared down. Repeated failures to acknowledge transmission over a bus to another processor cause that path to be marked as down. The sender processor may send up to three logical transfers ahead of the last acknowledged logical transfer. Additional transfers will be queued until the previous transfers are acknowledged.

Each processor maintains a Bus Receive Table (BRT) entry for incoming data from each processor, which includes a buffer address, a transfer count, and the next expected sequence number. When a packet arrives on either bus, it is checked for correct routing, moved into memory as its checksum is computed, and the checksum and the sequence number verified. A good packet causes the BRT entry to be updated. When the transfer count becomes zero or a packet error occurs, an interrupt is posted. On detecting a bus receive error, the processor need only note the type of error and flush the packet; error recovery is the responsibility of the sending processor.

An area of concern in this error recovery mechanism is the time lost to timeouts or packet flushing. This time is minimal, as the bus error rate is very low: errors are only observed when a hardware fault has occurred. For example, a month's error log for the system that this paper was prepared on contained no bus error messages. Given this error rate, the correctness of the error recovery scheme is far more important than its efficiency.

An example of the low-level protocol is the action taken when a server, S, WRITELINKs data to its requestor, R. First, the request is queued on the Send Data List (SDL), and a sequence number assigned to it. Then S is suspended, the request is added to the WACK list, and a here's data back (PHDB) control packet and the data block packet(s) are sent to R's processor.

R's processor sees a bus receive interrupt for the PHDB packet, sets the BRT buffer address to R's buffer, sees a data completion interrupt after the data block packet(s) have been received, and then queues an acknowledgement for S's processor. The acknowledgement is either sent as an unsequenced control packet or piggy-backed on some control packet that is part of another request. When the packet holding the acknowledgement arrives, S's processor completes the request and activates S.

Every second, each processor sends an unsequenced acknowledgement packet over each bus to every processor. This packet has two purposes: to recover from lost acknowledgements and to tell the other processors that this processor is up. Every two seconds, each processor checks whether it has received an unsequenced packet from each other processor. If not, it considers that processor to be down, and cancels all messages from it as described earlier.

2.2.5 Message system performance

Sample program segments and performance data are shown below. Neither process does any processing on the message, and message buffers are preallocated. The requestor process executes:

```
while  true  do
   begin
   LINK( ... );
   wait for message completion;
   BREAKLINK( ... );
   end;
```

and the server process executes:

```
while  true  do
   begin
   wait for a message;
   LISTEN;
   READLINK( ... )
   WRITELINK( ... )
   end;
```

with the results:

READLINK (bytes)	WRITELINK (bytes)	Elapsed time/msg (ms) intracpu	intercpu
0	0	2.1	2.6
0	200	2.3	2.9
200	0	2.4	4.2
2000	2000	4.6	7.0

The asymmetry between the second and the third example occurs because a WRITELINK must always be performed to complete the message, but a READLINK is only performed when data must be moved from R to S.

3. Process-pairs

Processes and messages provide a method for hiding processor boundaries and inter-processor bus errors. Associating a process with a resource provides a method of addressing and accessing it. The next step is to build a protocol that provides fault-tolerant access to the resource, protecting against information loss due to a processor failure.

A pair of processes and a symbolic name are associated with each I/O device or application server process. Requests are sent to the "primary" process of the "process-pair", which handles the request and controls the resource. When the primary receives a request for an operation such as a file open or close, the primary process "checkpoints" the request to the "backup" process via the message system. These checkpoints ensure that the backup process has all information that it will need to assume control of the device in the event of an I/O channel error or a fault of the primary process' processor. When the primary fails, the backup process "takes over" and becomes the primary.

The message system directs messages to process-pairs as follows. Each processor maintains a name table, associating a symbolic name with two processids in the node. When a message is sent to a named process, the first processid of the pair is used. If that process does not exist or is not currently the primary process, then the message fails; the processids in the table are exchanged, and the message is resent to the other half of the process-pair.

3.1 Error recovery using process-pairs

Unfortunately, not all requests for service are arbitrarily retryable. For example, writing a record into a key-sequenced file causes a duplicate key error to be returned if the record already exists. Hence, it is important that a server process-pair do the actual processing of a non-retryable request exactly once (see [7] for a discussion of this problem of "atomicity"). Requests are assigned sequence numbers and the server is required to track non-retryable requests by saving their sequence numbers and status, so that it may simply return the status on a duplicated request.

For example, let R and R' be primary and backup requestor processes and S and S' be primary and backup server processes. A sequence number is kept for each opener of a file by both the requestor and the server. When the file is opened, the initial state has all sequence numbers equal to zero. When R wishes to write a record into a disc file controlled by S, R sends S a message:

(1)   R' seq=0   R seq=0 -> S seq=0   S' seq=0

S picks up the message and performs the following check to see if this is a redundant operation:

```
(2) if   requestor seq < my seq
    then  return  saved status
```

The amount of previous status that must be saved here is dependent upon the processes involved. Here, S is the standard disc process so R would have had to specify the number of previous results to save at the time the file was opened.

If the check for a saved result fails, then the operation is performed. S reads the disc block, checks if the record already exists, and then checkpoints the request and the new block to its backup, S'.

(3)   R' seq=0   R seq=0   S seq=0 -> S' seq=0

The block is written to disc(s), the completion status is saved and checkpointed to S', and both S and S' increment their sequence number.

(4)   R' seq=0   R seq=0   S seq=1 -> S' seq=1

The result is then returned to R, who also increments his sequence number.

(5)   R' seq=0   R seq=1 <- S seq=1   S' seq=1

Finally, R checkpoints the result to R', who increments his sequence number, returning the system to a state indicating that there are no requests in progress.

(6)   R' seq=1 <- R seq=1   S seq=1   S' seq=1

Failure recovery during a request takes the following forms:

First, R' or S' may fail during the request without affecting the operation, as it can be carried out even if the checkpoints fail.

Second, if R fails following step (1), then S performs the operation, but is unable to return the result. When R' becomes R, it repeats the request starting at (1); but since its sequence number is still zero, the test in (2) returns the result that would have been returned had R not failed, and the operation is not repeated.

Finally, if S fails during the operation, S' becomes S and either does nothing or completes the operation using the checkpointed information, saving the completion status and incrementing its sequence number. When R resends the request (1) to the new S, it either does the operation or returns the saved result.

It should be emphasized that this checkpoint and error recovery process is independent of the location of the processes, the number of processors in the system, and the other message traffic in the system. By confining the recovery actions to the processes directly involved, the mechanism is both simple and arbitrarily expandable.

3.2 Process-pair maintainence

Process-pairs for I/O processes are created at system configuration time. A memory image for each processor is created with all necessary data structures. At initial load time, a processor is loaded from the disc. Each configured process will test to see if its other half exists, and observing that it does not, it will become the primary. An initial command interpreter will be created by the Monitor process which can then be used to issue RELOAD commands to load the rest of the processors.

When a processor is reloaded at an initial load or following repair, the configured processes will start execution. Each will observe that the other half of its process-pair is up, and therefore it is the backup. While this is going on, the process which reloaded the processor will be notifying all interested processes in the system that the processor is now up. The primary of each process-pair will then checkpoint its current state to the backup.

Application process-pairs are created in a more general manner. An initial primary process will be created in a processor. The process will in turn select some other processor and create its backup there. If the primary fails, then the backup will take over and it may select another processor to create a new backup, or, as is usually done, it will wait for the original processor to be repaired and reloaded before creating a backup. The primary of any process-pair may switch roles with its backup. This is generally done to balance the load on a system following the repair and reintegration of a processor.

4. Observations

The system does tolerate faults, they are repaired online and reintegrated into running systems. More specific reliability and availability statements are best left for our users to make.

System performance is likewise difficult to comment upon. In the example of section 3.1, the process R might be able to originate ten of these requests per second. However, it must be emphasized that there is no such thing as a "standard transaction" and specific applications must be examined for accurate measurements. The reader is directed to [9] for the description and results of an extensive benchmark involving this and other systems.

A system structured around process-pairs communicating via messages has already faced some of the major problems involved in distributed computing systems: decentralized control, partial system failure, and reintegration of repaired components. Two logical extensions to the system have been done to allow distributed systems to be connected into a network: the inclusion of a node specifier in processids, and the extension of message destinations to include processes in other nodes with communication provided by more conventional data communications equipment.

The advantages and disadvantages of multiple-processor computer systems have been explored in some detail in [11] and need not be restated here. However, there is no question that there is some cost associated with the use of a message system rather than shared memories in either a uni- or a multiprocessor configuration. The additional system resources consumed by a message system are processor time and memory, which are becoming the cheapest part of the system. This "penalty" has to be offset against the system's fault tolerance, the ease of system expansion, and the possibilities for system evolution (as shown by the addition of a network capability) that such a structure provides.

It is reasonable to ask whether users can write application process-pairs. Many do, and if the design has been done carefully, they will recover correctly from single faults. A detailed discussion of the various techniques for checkpointing is presented in [10]. However, the use of higher-level tools for terminal management functions and transaction backout [12] allows users to write server processes in COBOL which do not have backup processes, do not issue checkpoints, nor concern themselves with failure recovery. Thus, the application's fault tolerance need not rely heavily on the user's ability to design and implement correct error recovery.

Unfortunately, the hard problem is not the handling of the fault tolerance, but the design of a reasonable online system. Many user's initial reaction to this design problem is to try to create a monolithic application program to do all functions. Such a user often is from a batch data processing shop which is attempting to develop its first online application. This approach may get early results, but the program will be very hard to maintain and it will not scale up as it cannot be split across multiple processors for higher throughput. Another reaction (which sometimes follows the first) is to divide the application into countless processes which all must be used to process the simplest terminal inquiry. This is often combined with a very ornate key-sequenced data base. The result of this can be an application which handles two transactions per minute.

Application design and system sizing are still art rather than science. We have developed tools and guidelines for application design, for simulation and modelling to aid in system sizing [13], and for measurement of the resultant system

[14]. These are extensively used in developing quotes for systems and tend to eliminate disappointment upon system delivery.

Transaction systems have needs that differ somewhat from those of general-purpose computing systems. The primary function of a processor in a transaction system is to move data between discs and terminals, with a surprisingly small amount of processing done along the way. The high demands for message and I/O buffers may force the purchase of additional processors to gain buffer address space, rather than to increase processor power.

Therefore, extensions to the system architecture to improve memory access can be more useful than reimplementation of the hardware for greater speed. The former direction has been taken by our NonStop II system, which is a compatible extension of our 16-bit architecture to provide a 32-bit logical address space. This additional addressing capability eliminates many processor limitations that could be traced to small address spaces.

The decision to build a complex system based entirely upon processes interacting via messages has been the proper one for us. It has allowed us to construct reliable transaction systems differing in cost by an order of magnitude which can be constructed with the same modules and run the same software. It has also provided a flexible base on which to do significant software extensions without major redesign of existing system software.

5. Acknowledgements

This kernel has evolved over a period of time and it reflects the contributions of many people. In particular, I would to like to acknowledge the efforts of Dennis McEvoy, David Hinders, Jerry Held, Mike Green, Harald Sammar and Wendy Bartlett. I would also like to thank Wendy Bartlett, Jim Gray and the referees for their criticism which improved the presentation of this material.

6. References

[1] Avizennis, A., Architecture of Fault-Tolerant Computing Systems, FTC-5, IEEE and F.N.I.E., Paris, (June 1975), pp 3-16.

[2] Katzman, J. A., A Fault-Tolerant Computing System, Eleventh Hawaii International Conference on System Sciences, (January 1978), pp 85-102.

[3] Siewiorek, D. P, Bell, C. G., and Newell, A., Computer Structures: Readings and Examples, McGraw-Hill, Inc., (1982).

[4] Bartlett, J. F., A NonStop Operating System, Eleventh Hawaii International Conference on System Sciences, (January 1978), pp 103-117.

[5] Dijkstra, E. W., The Structure of the "THE" Multiprogramming System, Comm. ACM 11, (May 1968), pp 341-346.

[6] Brinch Hansen, P., The Nucleus of a Multi-programming System, Comm. ACM 13, (April 1970), pp 238-241, 250.

[7] Liskov, B., Report on the Workshop on Fundamental Issues in Distributed Computing, Operating Systems Review, (July 1981), pp 9-38.

[8] CCITT, recommendation X.25, Level 2, Geneva,(1976).

[9] Gleser, Malcolm A., Bayard, J., and Lang, D. D., Benchmarking for the Best, Datamation, (May 1981).

[10] Tom, G. F., Checkpointing Techniques for Fault-Tolerant Process-Pairs, BS Thesis at MIT, (June 1981).

[11] Enslow, P. H. Jr., Multiprocessor Organization - A Survey, Computing Surveys, Vol 9, Number 1, (March 1977), pp 103-129.

[12] Borr, A. J., Transaction Monitoring in ENCOMPASS: Reliable Distributed Transaction Processing, 7th International Conference on Very Large Data Bases, (September 1981).

[13] Blake, Russ, Tailor: A Simple Model That Works, Proc. of Conf. on Simulation, Measurement, and Modelling of Computer Systems, ACM SIGMETRICS, Boulder, (August 1979).

[14] Blake, Russ, XRAY: Instrumentation for Multiple Computers, Proc. Int'l. Symp. on Computer Performance, Modelling, Measurement, and Evaluation, ACM SIGMETRICS and IFIP WG7.3, Toronto, (May 1980).

TRANSACTION MONITORING IN ENCOMPASS [TM]: RELIABLE DISTRIBUTED TRANSACTION PROCESSING

Andrea J. Borr

Tandem Computers Incorporated
19333 Vallco Parkway
Cupertino, California 95014

ABSTRACT: A transaction is an atomic update which takes a data base from a consistent state to another consistent state. The Transaction Monitoring Facility (TMF), is a component of the ENCOMPASS distributed data management system, which runs on the Tandem [TM] computer system. TMF provides continuous, fault-tolerant transaction processing in a decentralized, distributed environment. Recovery from failures is transparent to user programs and does not require system halt or restart. Recovery from a failure which directly affects active transactions, such as the failure of a participating processor or the loss of communications between participating network nodes, is accomplished by means of the backout and restart of affected transactions. The implementation utilizes distributed audit trails of data base activity and a decentralized transaction concurrency control mechanism.

CONTENTS

INTRODUCTION

The Tandem NonStop [TM] System architecture --hardware and software--is designed to provide failure-tolerance, expandability, and distributed data processing in an on-line transaction processing environment. The architectural overview which follows shows how such features as continuous availability, tolerance of single-module failures, fail-safe structural integrity of files, and I/O device fault tolerance derive from the design. The extension of the operating system to support a network of Tandem nodes is discussed. The network extension is reliable, highly available, and provides geographic independence. These features provide the foundation upon which to build a reliable distributed data management system; however, reliable distributed transaction processing requires that another layer of failure protection be provided for the data base. Logical data base consistency must be guaranteed despite processor failure, application process failure, network partition, transaction deadlock, or application-requested transaction abort. The means used by ENCOMPASS to provide these features are examined.

ARCHITECTURAL OVERVIEW

Hardware Architecture

The Tandem system is based on multiple, independent processors. Figure 1 illustrates the architecture of a typical three-processor system. The hardware structure consists of from 2 to 16 processor modules, each with its own power supply, up to two megabytes of memory, and I/O channel, interconnected by dual high-speed (13.5 megabytes/sec) interprocessor buses. Each I/O controller is redundantly powered and connected to two I/O channels. Disc drives may be connected to two I/O controllers, and discs themselves may be duplicated, or "mirrored", to provide data base access despite disc failures. At least two paths connect any two components in the system. Thus, hardware redundancy is arranged so that the failure of a single module does not disable any other module or

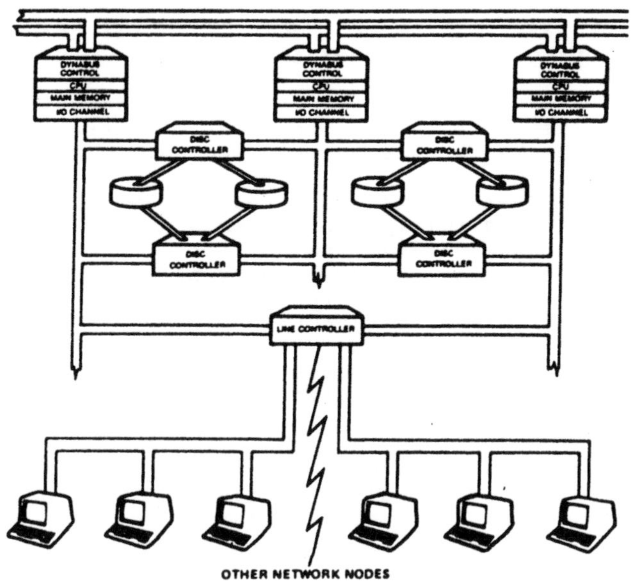

FIGURE 1. THE TANDEM NONSTOP HARDWARE ARCHITECTURE

disable any inter-module communication. Normally, all components are active in processing the workload. However, when a component fails, the remaining system components automatically take over the workload of the failed component [4].

The Tandem Operating System

System resources are managed by a message-based operating system which decentralizes information and control. The operating system resides in each component processor. The relationship among the processors of a system is characterized by symmetry and the absence of any master-slave hierarchy.

The operating system provides the software abstractions, processes and messages, necessary for decentralized control of the distributed components. All communications between processes is via messages. The Message System makes the physical distribution of hardware components transparent to processes. User processes access the Message System through the File System. The Message System and the File System effectively transform the multiple-computer structure into a unified multiprocessor at the user level.

System-wide access to I/O devices is provided by the mechanism of the I/O "process-pair". An I/O process-pair consists of two cooperating processes which run in the two processors physically connected to a particular I/O device. One of these processes, designated the "primary", controls the I/O device, handling all requests to perform I/O on the device. The other process, designated the "backup", functions as a stand-by in case of failure of the primary path to the device. The primary process sends the backup process "checkpoints", via the Message System, which ensure that the backup process has all the information that it would need in the event of failure to assume control of the device and carry through to completion any operation initiated by the primary. During normal operation, the backup is passive, acting only to receive the primary's checkpoints. In the event of an I/O channel error or a failure of the primary's processor, the backup process takes control of the device and becomes the primary.

The process-pair is a general mechanism utilized within the operating system to make system resources and services available to all processes in a fault-tolerant manner. An example of the use of the process-pair mechanism for a system process other than an I/O process is the "operator" process-pair, which is responsible for formatting and printing error messages on the system console. The primary and backup of the operator process run in two processors of the system. In the event of a failure of the primary's processor, the backup is able to continue offering this service. The continuous service provided by the process-pair is the essence of the feature termed NonStop.

The concept of the process-pair extends to application processes as well as to system processes. User-callable operating system routines are provided for creating a backup process and sending checkpoints to it. As shown by Bartlett [2], a process-pair application can provide continuous fault-tolerant processing despite module failure.

The design of the Tandem operating system is described in more detail in [1] and [2].

The Tandem Network

The message-based structure of the Tandem operating system allows it to exert decentralized control over a local network of processors. Since it already addresses some of the problems of controlling a distributed computing system, the operating system has a natural extension to support a data communications network of Tandem nodes, each node containing up to 16 processors. (Henceforth, the terms "system" and "node" will be used interchangeably, and the term "network" will be used to refer to a collection of Tandem nodes connected by data communications links).

The extension of the operating system to the network operating system involves the generalization of message destinations to include processes in other nodes. This extension of the Message System beyond the boundaries of a single system allows a process anywhere in the network to send or receive a message from any other process in the network.

Features of the Tandem network include the following:

(1) fault-tolerant nodes for high availability and data integrity;

(2) user-level transparency of access to geographically distributed system resources;

(3) decentralized control, characterized by the absence of a network master;

(4) dynamic best-path message routing, including automatic re-routing in the event of a communications line failure;

(5) automatic packet forwarding via an end-to-end protocol which assures that data transmissions are reliably received.

The design of the Tandem network system is described in more detail in [5].

DATA MANAGEMENT SYSTEM OVERVIEW

ENCOMPASS

The ENCOMPASS Distributed Data Management System performs the functions required for the development and operational control of on-line application systems. The basic functions provided by ENCOMPASS components include: (1) data base management; (2) terminal management; (3) transaction flow and application control; and, (4) transaction management.

Data Base Management

The data base management component of ENCOMPASS provides a data definition language, a data dictionary, a relational data base manager, and a high-level non-procedural relational query/report language.

Among the features provided by the ENCOMPASS data base manager are the following:

(1) three types of structured file organizations: key-sequenced, relative, and entry-sequenced;

(2) multi-key access to records with automatic maintenance of the indices during file update;

(3) data and index compression;

(4) partitioning of files--by key value range--across multiple disc volumes (possibly on multiple nodes);

(5) security controls by function, user class, network node, application program, and specified terminal;

(6) a cache buffering scheme designed to keep the most recently referenced blocks of data in main memory.

The ENCOMPASS data base manager distributes data across multiple processors and discs, providing multiple points of control. Implemented as an I/O process-pair per disc volume, designated the DISCPROCESS, it protects the structural integrity of individual files through active checkpointing of process state and data, and recovery in the case of processor, I/O channel, or disc drive failure. The DISCPROCESS controls all access to a logical disc volume, which in the case of a mirrored device pair includes two physical disc drives and all primary and backup access paths (I/O channels and I/O controllers).

The DISCPROCESS protects the integrity of the files resident on its volume by maintaining control information and data in two processors--the processors in which the primary and backup DISCPROCESSes reside. If a failure occurs which prevents the primary DISCPROCESS from completing an operation it has started, the backup DISCPROCESS automatically takes over and completes the operation.

Two granularities of locking are provided for concurrency control: file and record. Record level locking operates on the primary key of an individual logical data record. (There is no locking at the block or index level.) Locks on existing records are obtained at read time by explicit application program request. All locks are exclusive mode.

Each DISCPROCESS maintains the locking control information for those records and files resident on its volume only. Thus, concurrency control for ENCOMPASS is decentralized and is effectively distributed among the DISCPROCESSes; no central lock manager exists. Deadlock detection is by timeout, the interval being specified as part of the lock request.

Terminal Management

The terminal management component of ENCOMPASS, known as the Terminal Control Process (TCP), provides screen formatting, data validation, screen sequencing, and data mapping. A TCP controls up to 32 terminals and supports a variety of terminal types and communication lines. The application interface to each terminal is defined by the user in a high-level language known as Screen COBOL (a COBOL-like language with extensions for screen handling). The user's Screen COBOL program is interpreted by the TCP to perform screen sequencing, data mapping, and field validation for a single terminal. A TCP supervises the interleaved execution of Screen COBOL programs, each associated with one of the terminals under control of the TCP. Multiple TCP's can be run to provide better distribution of available resources or to support large numbers of terminals.

TCP's are configured as process-pairs. As a result of the fault tolerance thus provided, the terminal user has continuous access to the executing Screen COBOL program despite module failure, including processor failure.

Transaction Flow and Application Control

ENCOMPASS applications have user-defined transactions that originate at terminals and access data bases. In addition to providing a Screen COBOL program defining the screen formats and controls for a terminal, the ENCOMPASS user provides a set of application program modules, known as application "server" programs, which access and update data base files. Screen COBOL programs and application server programs communicate by exchanging request and reply messages. Communication between a Screen COBOL program and a server is initiated by the Sceen COBOL "SEND" verb. Under control of the SEND verb, the TCP, using the File System, passes a transaction request message to a server. The server performs the application function against the data base. The structure of an application server program is simple and single-threaded: (1) read the transaction request message; (2) perform the data base function requested; (3) reply. A server must be "context free" in the sense that it retains no memory from the servicing of one request to the next. Application servers are written to be independent of terminal and communications considerations. Servers may be written in available commercial languages such as COBOL.

ENCOMPASS application control provides monitoring of applications which are spread across a single system or network. It provides for the dynamic creation and deletion of application server processes to ensure good response time and utilization of resources as the workload on the system changes. Figure 2 shows a typical ENCOMPASS configuration.

Transaction Management

The transaction management component of ENCOMPASS is known as the Transaction Monitoring Facility (TMF). TMF implements the concept of a transaction as defined in the following.

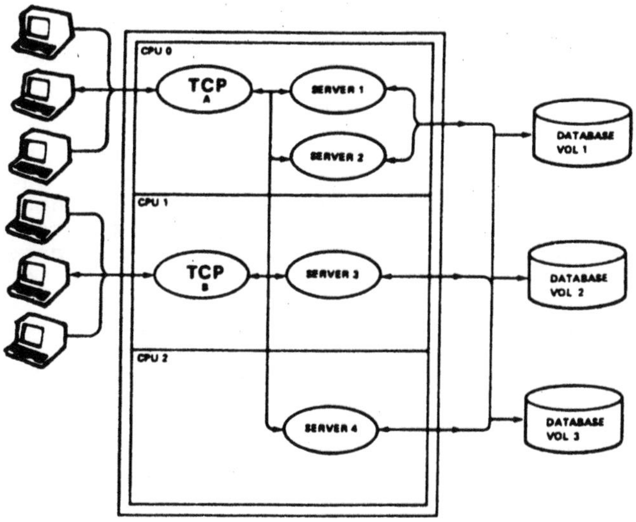

FIGURE 2. A TYPICAL ENCOMPASS CONFIGURATION

A transaction is a (possibly multi-step) logical update which takes the data base from a consistent state to another consistent state. A consistent data base is one which satisfies an application-dependent set of assertions concerning the relationships between files, records, fields, and secondary indices, the truth of which is required for the data base to effectively model the application's world of reference.

In order for data base consistency to be maintained, a transaction must have the property of atomicity: either all of its effects persist or none of its effects persist. This in turn requires that a transaction which aborts for any reason, by user request or due to a failure, be backed out so that none of its effects persist. On the other hand, a transaction which completes reaches a point at which it abdicates the right to back out. At this point, the transaction is said to commit: all of its effects will persist regardless of subsequent failures.

Prior to the existence of TMF in ENCOMPASS, data base consistency had to be preserved by application fault-tolerance. The application had to be coded as a process-pair, which by careful design of checkpoint logic could recover correctly from single-module failures. (The run-time systems of COBOL and FORTRAN automated process-pair coordination and error-recovery to some extent.) Since process-pairs always carried forward to completion processing interrupted by failure, transactions always committed. The reversal of a transaction had to be coded by the user, as there was no automated transaction backout. Furthermore, there was no protection for the data base in the event of multiple-module failure. If a disc's primary and backup processors failed simultaneously, data on the disc could be left in an unrecoverable or inconsistent state.

The introduction of transaction backout by TMF makes it unnecessary to code the application as a process-pair. Without TMF, the application process must maintain correct state in a backup process in case the primary fails. With TMF, the state of progress of an incomplete transaction is immaterial, since failure will cause the transaction to be automatically backed out, restoring data base consistency. TMF further provides voluntary transaction backout, making it unnecessary for the user to code transaction reversal. Data base protection in the event of multiple-module failure is provided by the ROLLFORWARD facility described in a later section.

The ENCOMPASS user's interface to TMF is through use of the Screen COBOL verbs BEGIN-TRANSACTION, END-TRANSACTION, ABORT-TRANSACION, and RESTART-TRANSACTION.

BEGIN-TRANSACTION is used to mark the beginning of a sequence of operations which should be treated as a single transaction. For the Screen COBOL program, BEGIN-TRANSACTION marks the beginning of a series of one or more SEND's of transaction request messages to application server processes. The network location of the application server process and, in fact, of the data base itself, is transparent to the Screen COBOL program. The server, the data base, or part of the database (in any combination) may reside on remote network nodes. For example, a server may transparently access data base files residing on any network node. A transaction may do work at multiple nodes and involve multiple server requests.

Execution of BEGIN-TRANSACTION causes a unique transaction identifier, or "transid", to be generated. The transid consists of a sequence number, qualified by the number of the processor in which BEGIN-TRANSACTION was called, qualified by the number of the network node which originated the transaction, designated the "home" node for the transaction. The Screen COBOL special register TRANSACTION-ID is set to contain the new transid, and the terminal is said to enter "transaction mode".

BEGIN-TRANSACTION marks a restart point in case of failure while the terminal is in transaction mode. If the transaction fails for any reason except an explicit ABORT-TRANSACTION by the Screen COBOL program (and the number of restarts has not exceeded a configurable "transaction restart limit"), the terminal's execution is restarted at BEGIN-TRANSACTION after TMF backs out any data base updates that have been performed for the current transid. A new transid is obtained for the new attempt at executing the logical transaction.

The types of failures which would result in the automatic abort, backout, and restart of a transaction by the system include: (1) failure of the primary TCP's processor (i.e. primary process of the process-pair); (2) failure of an application server's processor while that server was working on the transaction; (3) complete loss of communication with a network node which participated in the transaction. On the other hand, recovery from the failure of a component such as a primary DISCPROCESS' processor, an individual network communication line, a power supply, I/O controller, or disc drive is handled automatically by the operating system transparently to transaction processing.

The effect of a processor or other single module failure, which would necessitate crash restart and data base recovery on a conventional system, is limited to the on-line backout of those transactions in process on the failed module. Transactions uninvolved in the failure continue processing. Because the TCP checkpoints data extracted by the Screen COBOL program from input screen(s) to its backup, in many cases the restart of a logical transaction may not require re-entering the input screen(s).

All SEND's executed by a Screen COBOL program whose terminal is in transaction mode have the terminal's current transid automatically appended to the interprocess message by the File System. When the application server reads the transaction request message, the terminal's current transid becomes the "current process transid" for the application process. When the application process then executes a statement requiring disc I/O and/or record or file locking, the File System automatically appends the application process' current transid to the request message which is sent to the DISCPROCESS.

When all the SEND's required for the transaction's execution are complete, the Screen COBOL program indicates that the transaction should be committed by executing the END-TRANSACTION verb. At the completion of the execution of this verb, the transaction's data base updates become permanent and will not under any circumstances be backed out. The Screen COBOL program's END-TRANSACTION request can, however, be rejected because the transaction has been aborted by the system due to one of the causes of automatic abort, e.g. network partition. If so, the Screen COBOL program may be restarted at the BEGIN-TRANSACTION point.

If the Screen COBOL program, or any of the servers to which it has done a SEND, detects a need to abort and back out a transaction--without automatic restart by the TCP--the Screen COBOL program executes the ABORT-TRANSACTION verb.

Finally, RESTART-TRANSACTION is used to indicate that the current attempt to execute the transaction has failed due to a transient problem and so should be backed out and restarted. For example, a server may request a data base record lock with a timeout interval specified; then, in case the timeout occurs, it would recover from a possible deadlock by replying to the SEND with an error result indicating that the Screen COBOL program should call RESTART-TRANSACTION.

TMF DESIGN OVERVIEW

Concurrency Control

Gray defines a transaction that sees a consistent data base state as one that (a) does not overwrite dirty data of other transactions; (b) does not commit any writes until the end of transaction; (c) does not read dirty data from other transactions; and (d) prior to its completion, does not permit any data it reads to be dirtied by other transactions. If all transactions observe these protocols, then transaction backout produces a consistent state [3].

TMF enforces clauses (a), (b), and (c) as follows. It verifies that all records updated or deleted by a transaction have been previously locked by that transaction. (A lock on an existing record is acquired at record read time by explicit application request.) TMF automatically generates locks on all new records inserted by a transaction and on the primary key values of all records deleted by a transaction. Clause (d) insures that the reads performed by a transaction are repeatable [3]. The observance of clause (d) is recommended to writers of TMF transactions, but for system performance reasons is not enforced, as enforcement would require the generation of a lock for each record read by a transaction.

Audit Trails

TMF maintains distributed audit trails of logical data base record updates on mirrored disc volumes. An audit trail is a numbered sequence of disc files whose volume of residence is configurable and whose creation and purging is managed by TMF. The locations of audit trails for disc volumes containing data base files designated by the user as "audited" are independently configurable. Each DISCPROCESS which manages a disc volume configured as "audited" (i.e. capable of containing audited data base files) automatically provides "before-images" and "after-images" of data base updates by application processes to an AUDITPROCESS (of which several, each a process-pair, are configurable), which writes to an audit trail. All audited discs on a given controller share an AUDITPROCESS and an audit trail. Multiple controllers may be configured to use the same or different AUDITPROCESSes and audit trails. Auditing of data base updates is totally transparent to application programs. For transactions that span data bases on multiple nodes of a network, all audit images for records residing on a particular node are contained in audit trails at that node. This enables transaction backout at a node to occur without the need for communication with other nodes. Transaction backout is performed by the BACKOUTPROCESS (a process-pair), using the transaction's before-images recorded in the audit trails.

The implementation of the DISCPROCESS as a process-pair, residing in two processors, eliminates the necessity for the protocol, termed "Write Ahead Log" by Gray [3], which requires before-images to be write-forced to the audit trail prior to performing any update of the data base on disc. The Write Ahead Log protocol enables restart after system crash using conventional recovery techniques. In the NonStop approach to handling failure, checkpoint is the functional equivalent of Write Ahead Log. By checkpointing the audit records generated by an update request to its backup prior to performing the update, the primary DISCPROCESS assures the feasibility of transaction backout even in the event of the failure of the primary's processor. As in Write Ahead Log, however, all audit records generated by a transaction are write-forced to disc as part of the two-phase transaction commit protocol.

In addition to the data base audit trails, TMF maintains, at each node, a "Monitor Audit Trail" which contains a history of transaction completion statuses: commits and aborts. A transaction commits at the time its commit record is written to the Monitor Audit Trail.

Transaction State Change

A transaction goes through several state changes during the commit or abort protocol. All transaction state changes are broadcast, via the interprocessor bus, to all processors within a single node. This is done regardless of which processors actually participated in the transaction. In contrast, in the network case only those nodes which participated in the transaction are notified of transaction state change.

The decision to broadcast transaction state change information to all processors within a single system was taken because of the speed and reliability of the interprocessor bus as a communication medium.

A summary of the possible states of a transaction follows:

(1) Active. A transaction has this state after BEGIN-TRANSACTION has been called but before commit or abort has been requested. BEGIN-TRANSACTION broadcasts the transid in "active" state to all processors in the system. The possible states which can follow are "ending" or "aborting".

(2) Ending. A transaction has this state after END-TRANSACTION has been called but before the transaction commit record has been written to the Monitor Audit Trail. During "ending" state, all the transaction's audit records are written to the audit trails. This constitutes "phase one" of transaction commit. The possible states which can follow are "ended" or "aborting".

(3) Ended. A transaction has this state after the transaction commit record has been written to the Monitor Audit Trail. Once the transaction has entered the "ended" state, the Screen COBOL END-TRANSACTION verb completes, and participating DISCPROCESSes are notified to release the committed transaction's locks. This constitutes "phase two" of transaction commit. Once the "ended" state has completed, the transid leaves the system.

(4) Aborting. A transaction has this state after the decision to back out the transaction has been taken, but before any of its locks are released. While the transaction is in "aborting" state, all of its audit records are written to the audit trails and the transaction's data base updates are backed out by the BACKOUTPROCESS. "Aborting" and "ending" are parallel states. The only possible following state is "aborted".

(5) Aborted. A transaction has this state after the transaction has been backed out. Once the transaction has entered "aborted" state, participating DISCPROCESSes are notified to release the backed out transaction's locks. "Aborted" and "ended" are parallel states. Once the "aborted" state has completed, the transid leaves the system.

The state transitions of a transaction are illustrated in Figure 3.

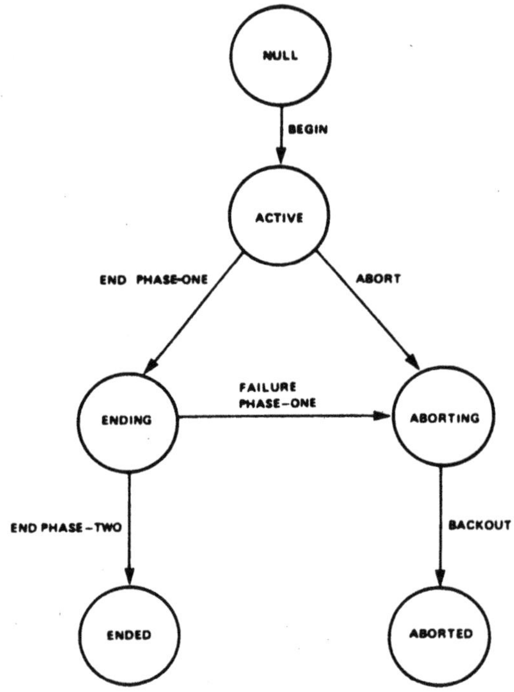

FIGURE 3. STATE TRANSITIONS OF A TRANSACTION

For transactions which stay within a node, TMF uses an abbreviated two-phase commit protocol. Its purpose is to ensure that all audit records generated by a transaction are written to disc prior to unlocking the transaction's locks, thus making the transaction's output visible to concurrent transactions. This guarantees that a transaction, once committed, can always be recovered using ROLLFORWARD, a TMF utility which can be used to apply after-images from the audit trails to a previously archived copy of the data base. ROLLFORWARD is discussed in a later section.

Distributed Transaction Processing

Transactions can originate on any node of the network and can be transmitted by any path to any number of other network nodes through SEND's from a TCP to remote servers or I/O requests from servers to remote discs. TMF ensures data base consistency both within a single node and across nodes by treating all data base updates performed by a transaction as a group, identified network-wide by the transid. All of the updates in the group are made permanent by the execution of the Screen COBOL END-TRANSACTION verb. If a failure occurs, the transaction's updates are backed out on all participating nodes.

The strategy, used in the single-node case (up to 16 processors), of broadcasting transaction state change information to all processors, regardless of their participation in the transaction, is clearly too expensive to use in the network case. Furthermore, the information is likely to be useless to most of the network. Therefore, only nodes participating in the transaction receive state change information.

Coordination of distributed transactions is one of the functions of the "Transaction Monitor Process" (TMP), a process-pair which is configured for each network node that participates in the distributed data base. Whenever a transid is transmitted by the File System to a remote node (as a result of a SEND to a remote server or an I/O request to a remote audited data base file), the TMP on the sending node determines whether the destination node has received a previous transmission of the requesting transid from the sending node. If not, the TMP on the sending node notifies the TMP on the destination node to broadcast the transid in "active" state to all processors on its node. This "remote transaction begin" occurs prior to any transmission of the transid by the File System to a server or DISCPROCESS on the destination node.

Distributed Commit Protocol

In a distributed data base environment, where a single transaction may result in the update of files on multiple nodes, loss of communication between nodes may cause data base inconsistency. TMF uses a more elaborate two-phase commit protocol for distributed transactions than that used for single-node transactions, due to the unreliability of the communication medium and the loose coupling of the nodes. The distributed commit protocol allows any participating node to unilaterally abort a transaction. The purpose of phase one is twofold. First, it serves to ensure that all audit records generated by a transaction are written to the audit trails on all participating nodes prior to allowing the unlocking of any of the transaction's locks. Secondly, it guarantees that the decision to commit or abort a transaction is uniform across all nodes, even in the event of loss of communications between participating nodes or the catastrophic failure of a node.

In the distributed case, transaction state change is accomplished by TMP-to-TMP messages sent over the network. Each participating node sends transaction state change messages to the TMP on all nodes for which it was the direct source of transid transmission. On receipt of a transaction state change message, the TMP broadcasts the state change to all processors within its node.

Certain network TMP message types are termed "critical response". For critical response messages, the destination TMP must be accessible at the time the message is initiated, and it must reply with an affirmative response in order for the transaction state change to proceed. Examples of critical response messages to remote TMP's are the network message requesting remote transaction begin and that requesting phase one of commit (i.e. transaction state change to "ending").

Other network TMP message types are termed "safe-delivery". For safe-delivery messages, the destination TMP need not be accessible at the time the message is initiated, and the reply serves only to acknowledge receipt of the message rather than to signify concurrence. The sending of safe-delivery messages--whenever transmission becomes possible--is guaranteed, but their delivery is not time-critical to the transaction's state change. Examples of safe-delivery messages to remote TMP's are the network message requesting transaction state change to "ended" (phase two of commit) and that requesting transaction state change to "aborting" (requesting transaction backout). Following transaction backout, state change to "aborted" on each participating node is accomplished under local control, without need for further network communication.

The critical response message requesting phase one of commit is initially transmitted over the network by the TMP on the transaction's home node in response to the Screen COBOL program's END-TRANSACTION call. For phase one to complete successfully, each node to which the home node directly transmitted the transid must be accessible and must reply affirmatively after having written the transaction's audit records to disc on its node and after having assured, transitively, that all nodes to which the transid was further transmitted have done likewise. The existence of a node participating in the transaction which is either inaccessible at phase-one time, or which responds negatively to the phase-one request because it has previously decided to abort the transaction (e.g. due to a prior loss of communications) will cause the commit attempt to fail. The TMP on the transaction's home node will transmit transaction backout messages in this case. The successful completion of phase one, on the other hand, will cause the home node TMP to transmit phase-two messages, causing the release of the transaction's locks throughout the network and the completion of the END-TRANSACTION call.

For example, suppose a TCP on node 1 SENDs to a server on node 2, which in turn updates a record via a DISCPROCESS on node 3. The TMP on node 1 remembers that it transmitted the transaction to node 2, but does not know that node 2 transmitted it to node 3. The TMP on node 2 remembers that it transmitted the transaction to node 3. When END-TRANSACTION is called on node 1, "ending" state is broadcast to all processors on node 1. The TMP on node 1 receives this broadcast and sends a network message to the TMP on node 2. The latter broadcasts to all processors on node 2 and in addition sends a network message to the TMP to node 3, which broadcasts to all processors on its node. This causes the transaction to go into "ending" state on all processors of all participating nodes. This is the first phase of the commit protocol. The second phase is similar.

Once phase one has completed successfully, the inability to communicate with all participating nodes during phase two (lock release) does not impede the completion of the Sceen COBOL programs's END-TRANSACTION call on the home node. It merely means that records locked by the committed transaction on inaccessible remote nodes will remain locked until such time as communication is restored.

Until a non-home node has replied affirmatively to the phase-one message, it can unilaterally abort the transaction, and then force network consensus to abort by replying negatively to the phase-one message when it is received. Once a non-home node has replied affirmatively to the phase-one message, however, it must hold the transaction's locks until notification of the transaction's final disposition (i.e. to state "ended" or to state "aborting") is received (possibly indirectly) from the transaction's home node. If communication is lost at this point, the transaction's locks on the inaccessible node will be held until communication is restored. The manual override for this situation requires the following steps: (1) use of a TMF utility on the home node to determine the transaction's disposition; (2) a telephone conversation (for example) between operators on the home node and on the inaccessible non-home node; and, finally, (3) use of the TMF utility on the non-home node to force like disposition of the transaction.

ROLLFORWARD

Conventional transaction management systems must be optimized for quick restart in the event of total node failure. NonStop systems allow optimization of normal processing at the expense of restart time. For example, audit records need not be written to disc prior to updating the data base. On the other hand, however rare the occurrence of total node failure (e.g. simultaeous failures of two processors hosting a process-pair), TMF must have a provision for recovering the data base.

TMF's approach to recovery from total node failure is based on occasional archived copies of audited data base files, plus an archive of all audit trails written since the data base files were archived. These copies can be created during normal transaction processing. TMF reconstructs any files open at the time of a total node failure by using the after-images from the audit trail to reapply the updates of committed transactions. ROLLFORWARD negotiates with other nodes of the network about transactions which were in "ending" state at the time of the node failure.

A DISTRIBUTED DATA BASE APPLICATION

Tandem's Manufacturing Division uses ENCOMPASS to implement a reliable distributed data base to coordinate its four manufacturing facilities in Cupertino (California), Santa Clara (California), Reston (Virginia), and Neufahrn (West Germany). Manufacturing is one application of Tandem's 50-node corporate network. (The network grows at a rate of about two nodes per month; the manufacturing application adds approximately two nodes yearly.) The network for the manufacturing system is shown in Figure 4.

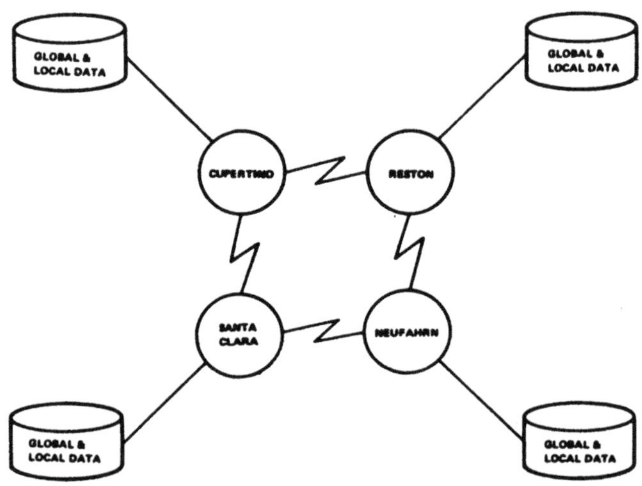

FIGURE 4. MANUFACTURING NETWORK

Each node has a copy of the "global" files: Item Master File, Bill of Materials File, and the Purchase Order Header File. In addition, each node has a set of "local" files: Stock File, Work-in-Progress File, Transaction History File, and the Purchase Order Detail File.

The global files are replicated at all nodes for reasons of performance and availability. Most transactions access and update only local files. Transactions which reference global files access only a few records and occur infrequently. Transactions which update global files can originate at any node.

The designers of the system were faced with two conflicting goals: (1) the maintenance of consistency among the global file copies; and (2) node autonomy: the ability for a node to carry on its processing, including the update of global data, despite network partition or the unavailability of other nodes.

If consistency were the only goal, straightforward application of TMF to the problem would have been the solution. All global files would be TMF-audited. All reads of a record in a global file would be directed to the local copy. Updates of global files would be applied to all copies, within the scope of a single TMF transaction. Unfortunately, this simple approach fails to address the goal of node autonomy, since no node can run a global update transaction at a time when any other node is unavailable.

The actual design compromises the goal of replica consistency somewhat for the sake of node autonomy. As in the above design, all files are TMF-audited and reads are always directed to the local record copy. For the purpose of update, however, each global file record is assigned a master node, the name of which is stored in each record instance. The update of a global record can occur only if its master node is available. An update request is sent to a server on the record's master node. The server executes a TMF transaction which updates the master copy of the record and queues "deferred" update requests for the non-master copies of the record in a "suspense file" at the record's master node. A dedicated process, called the "suspense monitor", scans the suspense file looking for work to do. When it finds a deferred update record for a node which is currently accessible, the suspense monitor executes a TMF transaction which sends the update to a server at the non-master node and deletes the suspense file entry.

It is important that the deferred updates for non-master copies of records at a node occur in suspense file order. If a node becomes disconnected from the network, deferred updates for it accumulate in the suspense files of other nodes, and the disconnected node's suspense file accumulates updates for other nodes. When the network is re-connected and all accumulated updates are applied, global file copies converge to a consistent state.

CONCLUSIONS

The design of TMF is seen to rely heavily on the concept of NonStop, Tandem's unique approach to fault tolerance which provides continuous operation despite single module failures. Unlike conventional data base recovery techniques, which are oriented to repairing the data base after a system halt and restart, TMF maintains data base consistency through failures via the on-line backout of those individual transactions affected by the failure.

Since a Tandem node is in itself a local network of up to 16 processors, the techniques used to implement such features as transaction concurrency control and transaction commit coordination within a single node are of necessity oriented to the distributed environment. Consequently, their extension to a network is a relatively straightforward extrapolation of the single-node implementation. The differences between the handling of the single-node case and the network case are largely accounted for by the significant disparity in the speed and reliability of the communication media.

ACKNOWLEDGEMENTS

I would like to acknowledge the contributions of Glenn Peterson, Keith Hospers, Bill Earl, Gary Kelly, Keith Stobie, Jerry Held, Dennis McEvoy, and Glenn Linderman in the design, implementation, and testing of TMF. The design of Tandem's manufacturing data base is due to Jim Gray and Vince Sian. Thanks are furthermore due to Jim Gray for editorial suggestions whose implementation improved the presentation of this material.

REFERENCES

1. Bartlett, J. F., "A 'NonStop' Operating System", Eleventh Hawaii International Conference on System Sciences, 1978.

2. Bartlett, J. F., "A NonStop Kernel", Proceedings of Eighth Symposium on Operating Systems Principles, ACM, 1981 (also Tandem TR 81.4).

3. Gray, J. N., "Notes on Data Base Operating Systems", IBM Research Report: RJ 2188, February 1978.

4. Katzman, J. A., "A Fault-Tolerant Computing System", Eleventh Hawaii International Conference on System Sciences, 1978.

5. Katzman, J. A., and Taylor, R. H., "GUARDIAN/EXPAND, a NonStop Network" (submitted for publication).

6. Smith, L., "Designer's Overview of Transaction Processing", (submitted for publication).

Making processing fail-safe

ROBERT FREIBURGHOUSE, Stratus Computer, Inc.

Any number of modules, each configurable to be fully redundant, achieves 'continuous processing' for the Stratus/32

Buyers who must have a computer system that continues to function despite failures have not had much of a selection, but their choice has been broadened by the introduction of the Stratus/32 system from Stratus Computer, Inc., Natick, Mass. With 4M bytes of memory, dual 143M-byte disks, a 600-lpm printer and magnetic tape, a typical Stratus/32 sells for $172,000, including COBOL and VOS software licenses. Based on COBOL benchmarks, the system's performance equals or surpasses that of several popular superminis.

The Stratus/32 multiprocessor, fault-tolerant system for commercial applications supports on-line transaction processing, batch processing, word processing and interactive program development. It uses a combination of hardware and software that provides continuous processing of user programs during computer failure without checkpoint/restart programming at the user or system level. Central to the system's fail-safe operation are processing modules, each of which has redundant logic and communication paths, logic and CPU boards and main and disk memory. Twin components operate in parallel with each other; when one fails, its partner carries on.

Architectural overview

The Stratus/32 processing modules are connected via

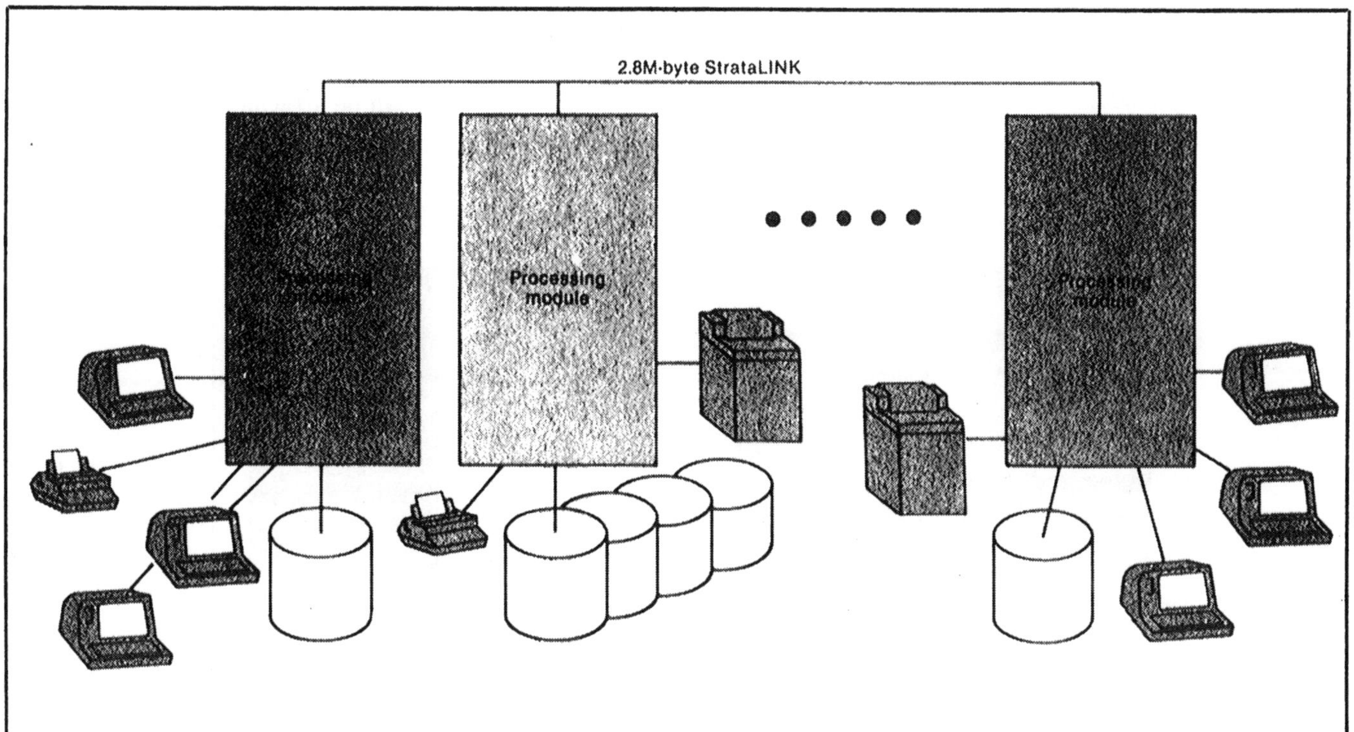

Fig. 1. A Stratus/32 system consists of as many as 32 processing modules *connected by a high-speed coaxial link. The modules can be located anywhere within an office building or can be adjacent to each other.*

Each processing module can be configured as fully redundant, partially redundant or non-redundant.

the StrataLINK high-speed coaxial link. Each processing module consists of memory, two Motorola Corp. 68000 CPUs, at least one disk and various peripheral controllers and devices (Fig. 1). Both 68000 CPUs are visible to the operating system, and each executes its own instruction stream using a shared memory.

Each processing module can be configured as fully redundant, partially redundant or non-redundant. The degree of a module's redundancy determines the module's resistance to hardware failure. A fully redundant module can withstand failure of essentially any component in the module without performance or data loss and without user program interruption. Multiple modules are used only to achieve greater system capacity; they never serve as backup for other modules.

Stratus's distributed virtual operating system (VOS) runs in each of the processing modules. All modules are equal and can operate independently, but through the use of transparent local networking software, VOS makes the entire set of processing modules appear as a single computer system to programs, programmers and application users.

Although each peripheral device is attached to a processing module, VOS makes all devices available to programs running in any module. Similarly, a program running in a module creates processes to run in the same module or in others. An interactive terminal user can create processes to execute commands or to run programs in any module. The users need not be aware of the module they are using. Likewise, batch jobs can run anywhere in the system.

All VOS service requests have a uniform interface that is independent of the processing module on which the work will be performed. For example, a request to open a file has the same form and arguments regardless of where the file resides. VOS examines the file name, looks in a device table to determine the module that owns the device and performs the requested operation or makes a network request over the StrataLINK to the VOS running the owning module. The requesting program does not see the network request. Consequently, user programs are unaware of the location of files or devices and see the multiple-module network as a single virtual-computer system (Fig. 2).

Examining the hardware

A processing module includes one or more cabinets that contain a complete computer with a logic-board chassis, dual power supplies, peripheral devices and and terminal port. A single cabinet holds a fully redundant module consisting of two 143M-byte disk drives, a magnetic tape, 16M bytes of memory, redundant CPU boards and a set of redundant peripheral controllers (Fig. 3).

A high-speed bus with a 125-nsec. cycle time is central to processing-module organization The bus—virtually two buses operating in parallel—has two sets of data and control-logic paths. The data path on each bus is 32 bits wide, and data can be put on the bus every bus cycle. This results in a potential bus rate of 32M bytes per sec., although processor/memory boards now run at 16M bytes per sec. By comparison a VAX/11-780 bus runs at 13M bytes per sec.

Each logic board that can be attached to the bus can

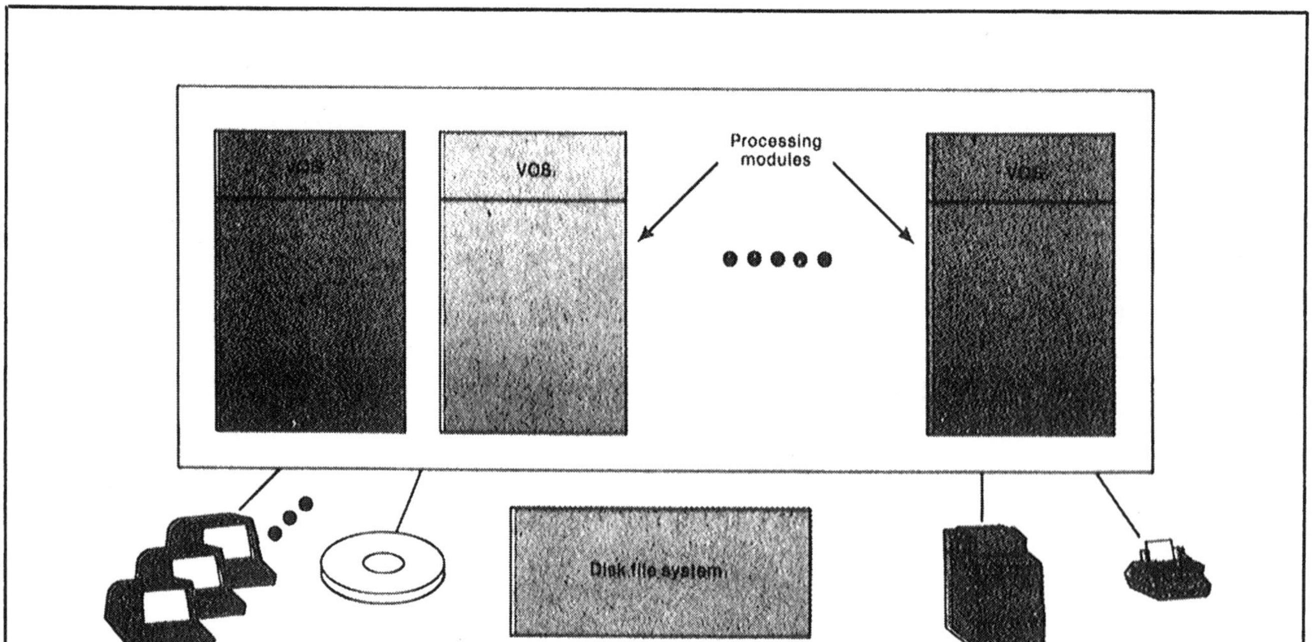

Fig. 2. The Stratus/32 virtual operating system (VOS) *makes all processing modules appear as part of a single virtual system in which all devices, files and system resources are accessible as if it were a single computer.*

The bus—virtually two buses operating in parallel—has two sets of data and control-logic paths.

detect its own failure and shut itself down. It can also run with a redundant board that continues to operate in the event of its partner's failure. Neither logic board is primary, and neither is aware of the other. The pair of boards appears collectively to other system components as a fail-safe entity.

The self-checking technique used by each type of board differs slightly, but generally involves the use of two sets of logic on a board. Each set performs every operation in parallel with the other. When data are to be sent to the bus or to a device, the results produced by the two sets of logic are compared. If identical, the result is sent onto the bus or to the device. Dissimilar results indicate a board failure, and no data are sent. In this case, a red LED on the board is lit, and an interrupt signal is sent on the bus. Until the board is tested and logically reconnected by maintenance software, it remains off-line. The board's redundant partner continues to operate, and no other component of the system is aware of the failure (Fig. 4).

The CPU board contains two complete sets of logic and is self-checking. Four Motorola 68000 processors provide each board with two processors visible to the operating system (Fig. 5). A redundant partner CPU board ensures continuous processing in the event of a failure of a CPU board. At a component price of approximately $100 for each 68000, this is a cost-effective solution to continuous processing that was not practical until the availability of VLSI technology.

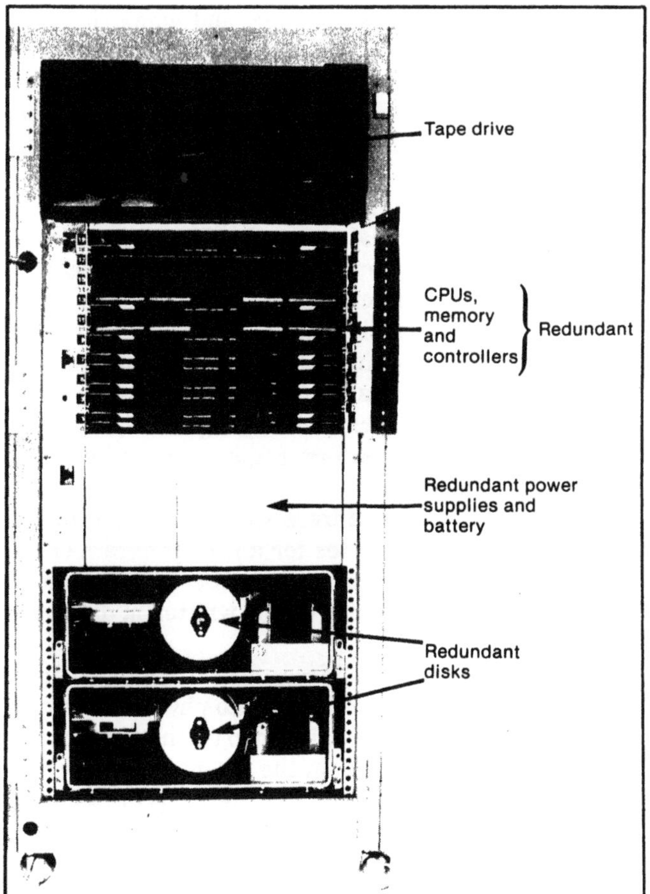

Fig. 3. A Stratus/32 processing module *can contain 16M bytes of memory, a full set of redundant controllers, two 143M-byte disks, a tape drive and two software-visible CPUs. (Additional disks and tapes are held in adjacent cabinets.)*

Redundancy is achieved by using a pair of logic boards for each logical entity in the system. Each board is attached to both halves of the bus, and both boards operate in parallel, performing identical operations. The output of both boards is placed on the bus at the same instant and is guaranteed to be identical.

Memory is duplicated in a redundant system so that N megabytes of program-visible memory is implemented using 2NM bytes of physical memory with N megabytes attached to each of two memory controllers. When data are written to a given memory location, both memory controllers respond and write the data into their memory. When data are read from memory, both controllers respond and read from their memory.

The controllers and the memory are synchronized and appear to the rest of the system as a single logical entity. Memory subsystems are not paired with CPUs, bus halves or other system components. Memory is implemented from 64K RAMs and is packaged on 1M- or 2M-byte boards. It has a 375-nsec. read-cycle time and is four-way interleaved. A typical processing module has 4M or 8M bytes of memory. In packaged configurations, Stratus sells memory for $5000 per megabyte. A 2M-byte array board lists for $20,000.

The memory system can be dynamically reconfigured to be redundant or non-redundant. This allows a module to use all available memory when full redundancy is not needed. Reconfiguration can occur on-line without affecting running programs.

Disks cannot run completely synchronized with each other; they require help from the operating system to provide continuous processing. Each disk can be configured to have a duplicate. The mirror disk is attached to a separate controller to protect from controller failure. When a program writes a record to a redundant disk, the operating system writes records to the disk and to its mirror. When a program reads from the disk, the operating system reads from the disk that is not busy or whose heads are best positioned to read the record. If a read error occurs, the record is read from the other disk.

An error-correction code stored with each disk record detects media failures during a read. A read error from a redundant disk results in reading the same record from its partner. Non-redundant disks are vulnerable to total disk failure, but are protected from media failures by VOS, which verifies each write. A record that cannot be verified is rewritten to another disk block, and the bad block is removed from the available disk space.

StrataLINKs, like disks, cannot run synchronized.

The CPU board contains two complete sets of logic and is self-checking.

However, the operating system has sufficient software error detection to run dual StrataLINKs as separate parallel links until one fails. Failure of a link is detected, and data are retransmitted over the other link without affecting users of the link. A link failure could cause some performance loss because a dual link has a 2.8M-byte-per-sec. transmission rate, while a single link has a 1.4M-byte-per-sec. rate. But because most links do not operate even close to their maximum rates, it is unlikely that an application would notice the performance difference.

A failure scenario

When a logic board or an attached peripheral device fails, it puts itself off-line, lights a red light on the board and transmits an interrupt to the operating system. Maintenance software in the system then tests the failed board to determine if the failure was transient or hard. In either case, the failure is noted in a hardware-failure log file, and selected terminals are notified of the failure. If the board passes the maintenance-software check, it is resynchronized with its redundant partner and put back on-line, and its red light is turned off. If the board fails the software check, it remains off-line, and a red light on the system control panel is lit.

A failed board can be replaced in a running system by a nontechnical person without special tools and without affecting any user's program. VOS dynamically reconfigures itself when a board is added or removed from the system.

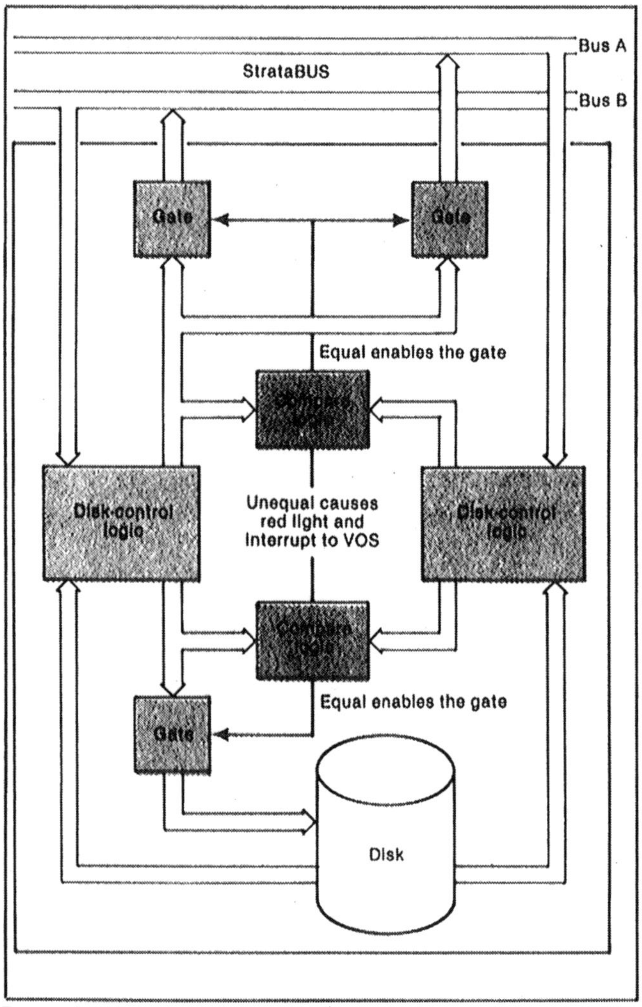

Fig. 4. Self-checking disk controller. *Two sets of logic operate in parallel with each other. If their results differ, a warning light goes on, and no data are sent until the situation is corrected.*

Operating-system software

Each processing module contains two software-visible 68000 processors and a software-visible Z80 μp on each peripheral controller. The VOS off-loads detailed I/O processing to the Z80s and uses one of the 68000s to respond to interrupts and to execute the word processor. The other 68000 executes user code and non-interrupt-driven system code. For example, a user program that calls VOS to perform disk I/O has the user 68000 enter VOS and set up the disk-I/O command chain. The user 68000 is then rescheduled to execute another user's program. The disk-I/O operations are executed by the Z80 on the disk controller, and when the disk operation completes, the "executive" 68000 responds to the interrupt and posts a notification to the scheduler that this I/O event is complete. Depending on the setting of the scheduler's parameters, the user 68000 can be rescheduled to execute the user's program then or at the next scheduling interval.

A "process" is a virtual CPU and a 16M-byte address space in which a sequence of user programs can be executed. A process is created when a user logs onto the system, and is terminated when a user logs off. A process can create additional processes that operate independently of the creating process. VOS uses system processes to monitor terminals for log-in requests, to run the spooler and to perform requests made by other processing modules.

Each process has an address space consisting of 4M bytes for VOS and 12M bytes for a user program (Fig. 6). A program consists of any number of separately compiled subroutines, which can be written in different source languages.

The 16M-byte virtual address space is divided into 4096-byte pages that are mapped into physical memory pages by an address-translation map on the CPU board. The translation occurs within the 125-nsec. clock cycle and does not slow the CPU. The user's program and most of the programs in VOS see only the virtual address space and are unaware of the translation.

The hardware address-translation map informs the scheduling and paging algorithms of which physical pages were recently used and which virtual pages of each process were recently used by that process. Thus, it is possible to determine quickly the real working set

When data are written to a given memory location, both memory controllers respond and write the data into their memory.

of each process and which physical page of memory to replace when a new page is required.

Sharing and protection.

Each page of a process's address space has an associated access code that allows execution, read/write or read-only. The processor has supervisor and user execution states, and, for each state, it has potentially separate access codes for each page of the address space. These access codes are stored in the address-translation map used to translate virtual to physical addresses, and are enforced for every memory reference in both user and supervisor states.

All users share the physical pages of VOS and appear in the address space of each process. Likewise, user programs are shared if executed by more than one process. Sharing user programs and system commands and utilities requires no action on the part of a user and occurs with no visible effect to the user. All code produced by Stratus compilers is pure and reentrant.

A user's program is protected from destruction because each page of program instructions is given an execute-only access code. A user's data are protected from other users because they exist only in the address space of the user. The data are also protected from execution to aid debugging of users' programs.

Inter-process communication facilities of VOS allow a multi-process application to be developed on a single-module configuration and run later without modification on a distributed configuration consisting of multiple processing modules, or even on multiple Stratus systems connected by StrataNET. Consequently, the mechanisms used to start, stop or synchronize processes do not use shared memory; they use the file system as a high-level shared memory.

Every file in the file system has an associated lock and an associated event. In addition, each record in a file has an associated lock. Locks synchronize file access between two or more processes and can be set or reset to indicate reading or updating of the file or records.

Simple notification and waiting for events between processes are performed using event counts. An event count is a large integer that is incremented each time that it is notified by a process.

Most inter-process communication is related to files and consists of notifying processes that data are available to be processed or of waiting for data to arrive for processing. The use of events and locks associated with files is consequently natural and efficient.

User-visible software

The Stratus/32 was introduced with a host of native-mode software, including:

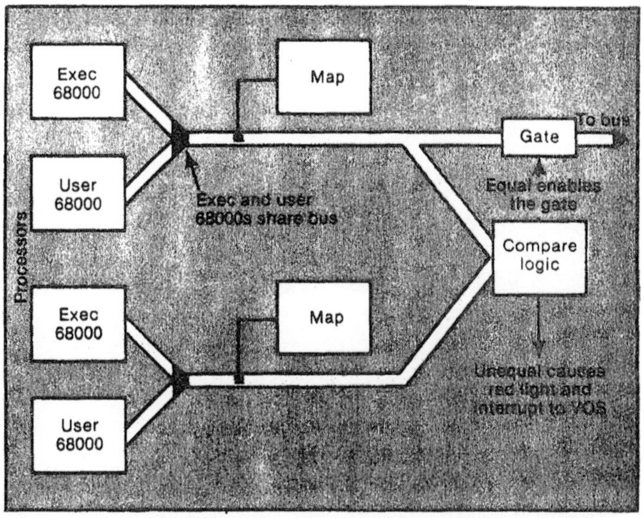

Fig. 5. A single Stratus/32 CPU board contains four Motorola 68000 processors *that provide two software-visible processors. The board is fully self-checking and contains redundant virtual/physical address-translation maps.*

- **CRT menu-oriented commands.** The VOS command interpreter accepts all commands in two forms: a conventional line-oriented form suitable for use on hard-copy terminals or from within command language programs called command macros, and a CRT menu form that displays all command options and their default values. The CRT menu form is invoked by typing the name of the command followed by a function key. A command reference manual is unnecessary.
- **Five industry-standard languages.** These include COBOL 74, FORTRAN 78, PL/I-G, Pascal and BASIC. All languages are supported by optimizing compilers that share an optimizer and a code generator that produces highly optimized relocatable binary code. Subroutines written in all languages can be combined into a program, and all languages can call all VOS service subroutines. All compiled code is pure and reentrant.
- **Program debugging.** Program development in any high-level language can be done entirely within that language without the programmer's knowing the instruction set, data formats or register arrangement of the 68000 processor. For all languages, the debugger can set breakpoints on statements, display variables, make assignments to variables, execute calls and functions, execute gotos, step through the program and execute conditional breakpoints. The debugger can be entered to start execution of a program, when a program fails or to examine a snapshot of a program that has failed.
- **Data security.** Each file has an access-control list consisting of pairs of user IDs and associated access rights (execute, read or read/write). Access rights can be specified by a user or groups of users and are enforced by the VOS I/O system. Access-control lists provide file security without embedding passwords into programs. The lists operate on the basis of people or groups who access the file; consequently, they are easy to administer and use. Security is provided regardless

All languages are supported by optimizing compilers that share an optimizer and a code generator that produces highly optimized relocatable binary code.

of what programs or system commands are used to access files.

• **Networking.** StrataNET permits two or more Stratus systems to run as if they were one system. Just as users of individual processing modules of a system have access to their entire system, users of a networked system have access to the entire network without any network-oriented requests or commands. Normal file operations and inter-process communication operate transparently to the user's program.

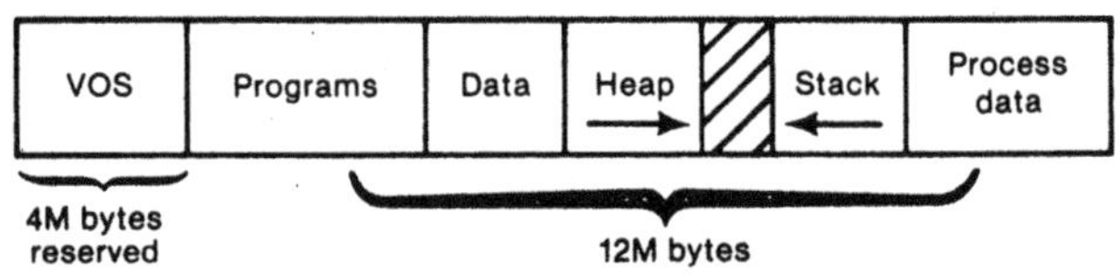

Fig. 6. Stratus/32 virtual address space provides as much as 12M bytes of program and data space per user program. *The stack is the interrupt directory; the heap is handy for temporary data that must be stored randomly. Both expand and contract as needed. User programs and system code are shared without user involvement, and no segment limits are imposed on programs or data.*

• **Transaction processing.** VOS supports the development of transaction-oriented applications by providing CRT forms-design utility and forms I/O statements in all high-level programming languages, multi-terminal transaction control in all high-level programming languages, individual record and file locking, multi-key indexed file access, queued file access and file-system operations to ensure the integrity of transactions.

Data representing a transaction can be processed directly by a user-written transaction-control program, or data can be written into a queued file to be processed by other programs, called transaction servers, which operate asynchronously with respect to the transaction-control program. Transaction servers can run in any processing module, not just modules running the transaction-control program. Likewise, transaction-control programs can run in several modules. The number and distribution of transaction servers can be dynamically altered in response to changes in the transaction rate. ■

Robert Freiburghouse is co-founder and vice president of software engineering, at Stratus Computer, Inc., Natick, Mass.

A reconfigurable multi-microcomputer system with 64 nodes and 64 shared memories is being developed incrementally. Numerous experiments have already been run on the existing nucleus network.

A Flexible Distributed Testbed for Real-Time Applications

William C. McDonald
System Development Corporation

R. Wayne Smith, TRW, Inc.

The complexity and sophistication of the real-time data processing problems encountered in computer-based weapon systems severely tax all aspects of advanced data processing technology. Typically, these systems impose requirements in reliability, availability, cost, performance, and growth that stress today's data processing technology.[1] Furthermore, data processing solutions are required for a wide range of system concepts and operational environments.[2] Although proven conventional techniques such as pipelining and cache memory have significantly improved computer performance and advances in circuit technology have increased processor capacity, current and projected needs still represent significant challenges.

In real-time systems such as those for ballistic missile defense, the data processing problem is dominated by the necessity of meeting port-to-port response times while achieving total system throughput requirements. Response times may be as low as a few milliseconds with throughput requirements ranging up to tens of millions of instructions per second. Frequently, the data processing system must also remain dormant for months, activate on minutes' notice, and operate unattended with ultra-reliability for periods ranging from a few hours to several days.

Distributed computing promises to satisfy the requirements of these systems by utilizing moderately priced, contemporary hardware in networks. To achieve this promise, research and development is being pursued in all aspects of real-time distributed computing technology.[3,4] Many techniques have been proposed for achieving reliability through redundancy, detecting and recovering from errors, distributing and managing shared data, communicating reliably between processes, allocating and scheduling resources in the presence of failures and overloads, and achieving high throughput through architectural innovation. These techniques must be proven experimentally before they can be used in a real-time system. Individually and collectively they impose overheads that create problems in satisfying real-time requirements. As a result, solutions to the problems of real-time distributed computing must be proven in a realistic environment for the specific real-time application.

Two approaches can be considered for the development, evaluation, and demonstration of candidate solutions to the problems of real-time distributed computing. The first uses dedicated hardware and software resources for each application. This approach provides high-fidelity results, but the diversity of applications and candidate architectural, hardware, and software solutions makes it prohibitively expensive and time-consuming. The second approach uses a highly flexible testbed that enables rapid, realistic investigation of a variety of candidate solutions for the specific application. This approach, although initially more expensive, is now cost-effective because of the availability of (1) low-cost, 16-bit microcomputers that can be used to develop flexible multi-microcomputer systems and (2) well-supported minicomputers that act as centralized coordination facilities for software development, interactive access, and experiment control and monitoring.

This article describes a flexible distributed testbed that is being developed to support the development, analysis, test, evaluation, and validation of research in distributed computing for real-time applications. The testbed not only provides the resources for experimentally obtaining quantitative results, but also serves as a focal point for the research, integrating related research activities and providing a mechanism for technology transfer to associated research efforts.

Distributed testbed overview

The distributed testbed's hardware and software resources support quantitative investigations into distributed computing techniques for a variety of real-time applications. Hardware resources include a nucleus network of VAX 11/780 computers, a CDC 6400/7600 complex, and three multi-microcomputer systems. Software resources include an architecture description language, ADL, that provides the user interface to the testbed, several operating system components to support the control and use of testbed resources, system software to support application program development, and network services to support distributed operation of the nucleus.

The nucleus network of eight Digital Equipment Corporation VAX 11/780 computers[5] supports both local and remote interactive access to the distributed testbed. It also provides resources for application software development, supports ADL and its software, hosts the multi-microcomputer systems, and provides high-performance computing elements and a variety of interconnect mechanisms to support distributed computing experiments. The nucleus is also interfaced with a CDC 6400/7600 complex that supports large-scale simulation and analysis.

The multi-microcomputer systems are composed of Zilog Z8001 MCB single-board microcomputers (CPU with local memory), shared memory buffers, and high-speed switching networks acting under the coordination of a central control facility (i.e., a VAX 11/780). Together, these facilities provide the structural and functional flexibility for effective modeling and evaluation of a wide variety of conceptual distributed architectures.

Three interconnected multi-microcomputer systems—a crossbar, ring, and banyan, each hosted by a VAX 11/780—are under development and evaluation in the distributed testbed. The long-range goal is to develop a large reconfigurable multi-microcomputer testbed for investigating distributed architectures for a class of real-time data processing problems encountered in ballistic missile defense.[6] Following a period of evaluation, either the ring or the banyan system will be expanded to form a large reconfigurable multi-microcomputer system, LRMS, composed of 64 processing elements and 64 shared memories.

ADL is a high-order language that enables user-description of arbitrary architectures. The architecture description is used by the architecture description system, ADS, to construct an experiment that is executed, monitored, and evaluated on the testbed. ADL/ADS is hosted by the VAX 11/780.

The operating system support for experimentation on the distributed testbed is supplied by three major components—the master operating system, MOS; the application operating system, AOS; and the kernel operating system, KOS. MOS provides global testbed control, performing activities that require a global view of the system. It supports interactive access to the multi-microcomputer testbeds through the VAX, permits simultaneous experimentation on the testbed, and provides services to ADL/ADS for developing, configuring, loading, and executing experiments. AOS provides execution-time resource control, performing activities that require knowledge of an experimenter's specific needs. It is application-specific and controls the experimenter's virtual architecture and applications processes. AOS is generated from the ADL description by ADS. KOS provides low-level direct hardware control, performing activities requiring knowledge of the processor's local state. KOS, which resides in each microcomputer and includes low-level debug aids, coordinates all local activities and provides services to AOS and MOS.

The distributed testbed nucleus uses the VAX/VMS operating system software. VMS services are extended over the nucleus network to provide generalized communication among processes and system services to support distributed operation of the nucleus.

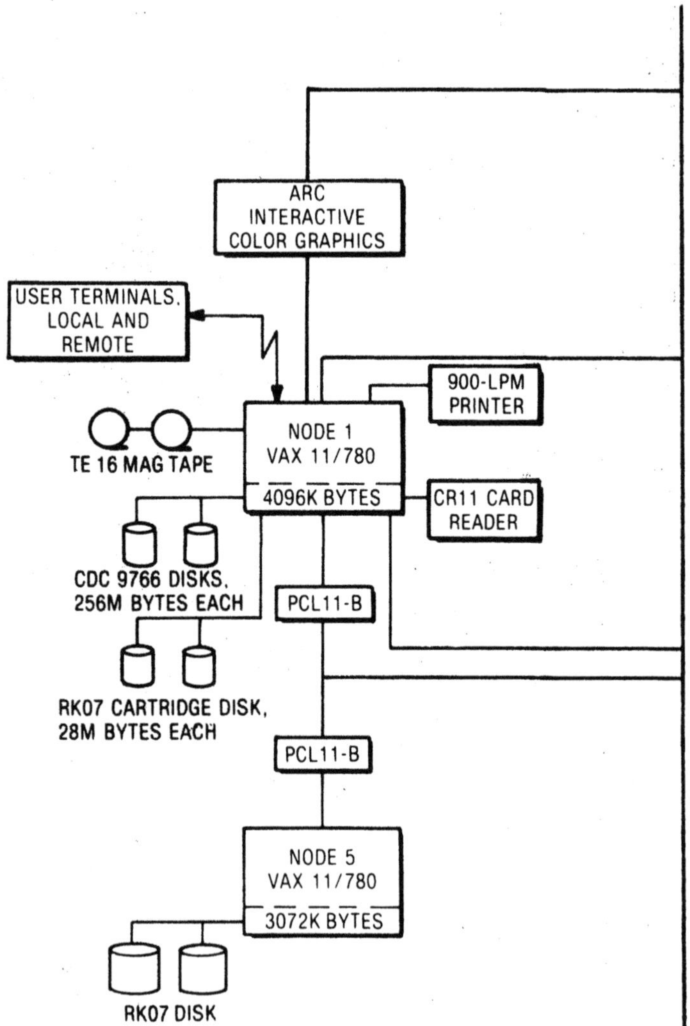

Figure 1. Distributed testbed nucleus.

Hardware resources

Nucleus network. The nucleus network (Figure 1) is composed of eight VAX 11/780 computers interconnected by a parallel bus. Two machines (nodes 1 and 8) are equipped to support software development and to host a distributed computing design system. The remaining six machines are used to host the multi-microcomputer systems, to host hardware-in-the-loop experiments, and to support experiments in distributed computing.

The primary network in the nucleus is the DEC PCL11-B, a parallel time-division-multiplexed bus. Bandwidth can be dynamically allocated under software control so that some processors can receive a higher fraction of the total available bandwidth. High-speed synchronous DMC-11 links are used to form a sequentially connected four-node subnetwork. This network provides program transferability during system software development. Links can be easily moved as required to support specific experiments. Four of the VAX 11/780 computers are interconnected to the CDC 6400 and CDC 7600 with a carrier-sense multiple-access network, Network Systems Corporation's HYPERchannel. Two DEC MA780 multiport shared memories are used to interconnect six of the VAX 11/780 computers. Each shared memory has four ports and includes selective cache invalidation and 2M bytes of memory. This system is used to support shared memory experiments in the nucleus network and to provide high-bandwidth, low-latency communication paths between processors.

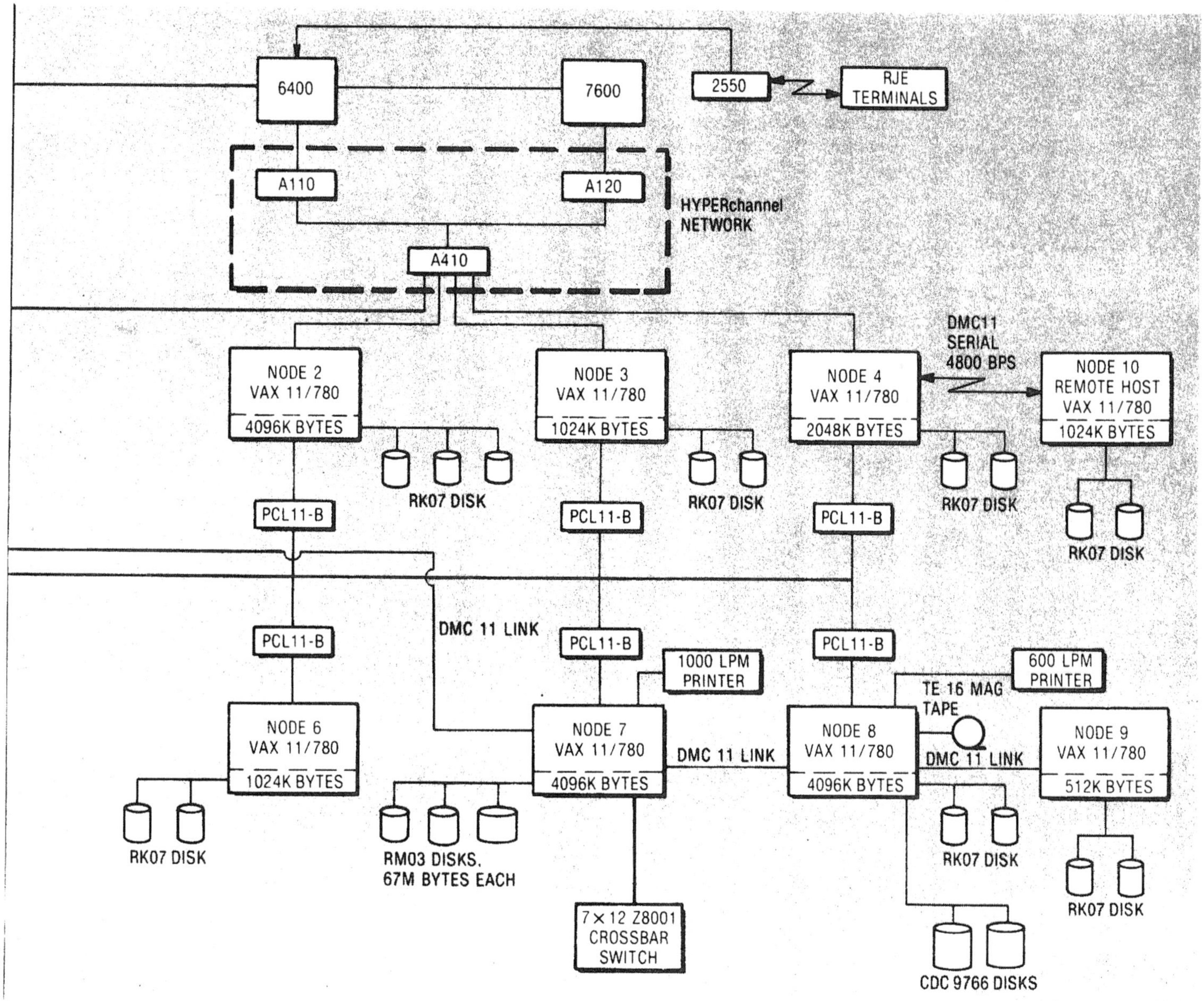

Two additional VAX 11/780 machines are attached to the testbed nucleus. One is a remote host connected to the nucleus network through a 4800-baud serial DEC DMC-11 link. The other is located on-site and primarily supports microprogramming research and development, using the VAX 11/780 writable control store.

Crossbar multi-microcomputer system. The CMS is composed of six Z8001 MCB processing elements interconnected with 12 shared memory buffers by a crossbar switch as illustrated in Figure 2. The fully parallel crossbar switch transfers the normal Z8001 memory access signals (address, data, control) directly to the shared memory. Each shared memory buffer is assigned to a separate 64K-byte memory space segment in the Z8001 address space, and shared memory access is by normal Z8001 memory read/write operations. Memory-mapped access to special functions, such as a real-time clock, interprocessor interrupt facilities, and synchronization flag registers, is provided in the same manner. One VAX 11/780 has access to the shared memories via its I/O transactions.

The crossbar system is designed using low-power Schottky TTL logic components. The entire system is driven from a single 6-MHz clock to simplify design and test. Each processing element has 32K bytes of local RAM plus ROM located in segment zero and can access any location in shared memory at any time. Each shared memory buffer includes an arbitration unit that implements a first-come, first-served policy for resolution of conflicting memory requests, and a fixed priority scheme resolves simultaneous requests. Byte, word, and long-word access modes are supported, and instructions are executable from shared or local memory.

The real-time clock is 32 bits wide and is incremented at a 250-kHz rate. The clock has two segment addresses for its two 16-bit halves, but it has no interrupt capability and cannot be set.

Each microcomputer and the VAX 11/780 have associated interrupt registers. A processor is interrupted by writing data to its interrupt register. The interrupted processor can then read the data; subsequent writes to that register will be blocked until completion of the read. Any processor can interrupt itself or read the contents of any interrupt register.

Flag registers provide synchronization mechanisms. The first access to a flag register by a processor (read or write) locks the register. A subsequent access by a different processor is blocked, and the processor attempting access is placed in the WAIT state. The second access by the original processor unlocks the register, and the blocked access is allowed to proceed. Processors have equal priority for flag register access.

The VAX 11/780 has access to the switch through a general-purpose Unibus interface that supports five types of transfers: shared memory access, interrupt request, read 32-bit real-time clock, flag register operations, and microprocessor reset. A serial RS-232 link between VAX and the microcomputers supports diagnostics, debugging, and data collection.

Ring multi-microcomputer system. The RMS is composed of 16 Z8001 MCB processing elements interconnected with 16 shared memory buffers by a high-speed

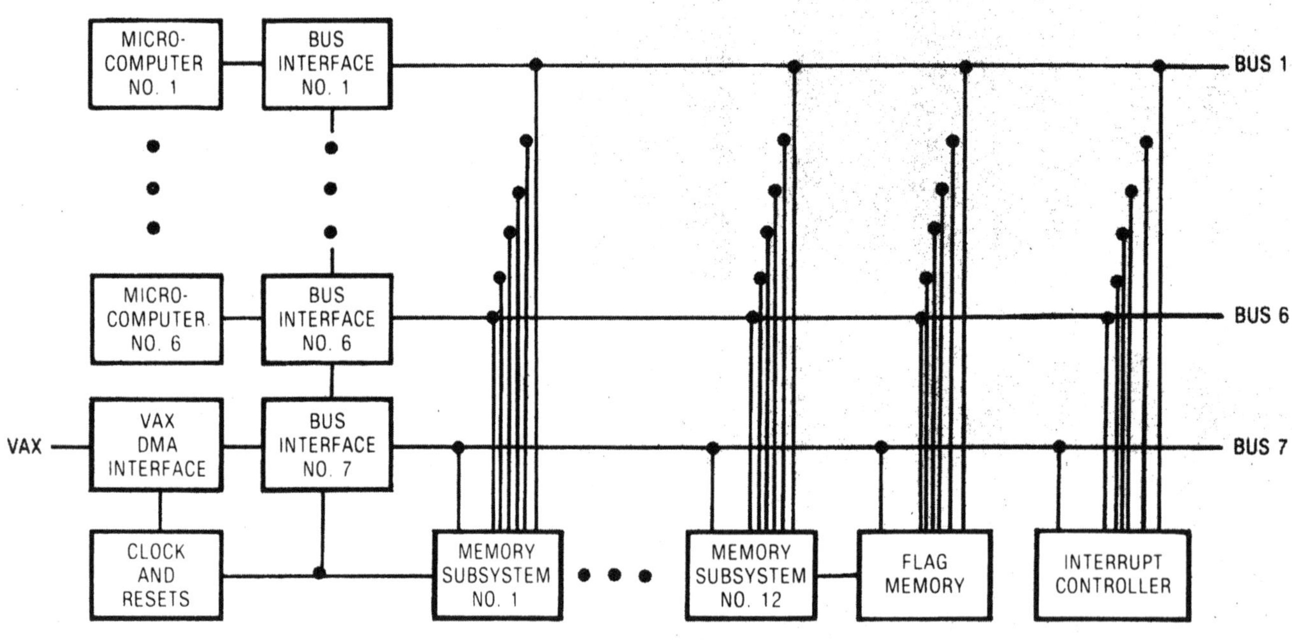

Figure 2. Crossbar multi-microcomputer system.

Pierce[7] ring as illustrated in Figure 3. The ring moves fully parallel single-word packets from the ith ring node to the ith + 1 ring node each clock cycle. All transfers are via transparent reads and writes to the shared memory over the network. A microprocessor may interrupt any other processor over the network. All write and interrupt requests are acknowledged to provide flow control in the network.

Ten packet types are provided: read request, read response data, write request, write acknowledgment, dump local shared memory, dump acknowledgment, test and set request, test and set response data, interrupt request, and interrupt acknowledgment. The total packet width is 60 bits. Six bits are used for routing tags (destination node address). Data are 16 bits. Eighteen bits are used for shared memory addressing at the node. Five bits are used for packet type. Source address is 6 bits. Single error correction and double error detection are performed over the full width of the packet.

The ring interface provides the logical and electrical interface between the Z8001 MCB, the ring node, and the shared memory co-located with each microcomputer. The interface performs packet assembly and disassembly; error coding, checking, and correcting; and acknowledgment packet generation. The interface also provides a short path to the local shared memory, supports shared memory management with the Zilog Z8010 memory mapping unit, and handles interrupts. An input register removes packets from the ring node, and an interrupt queue prevents system deadlock. If the input register is full, subsequent packets will be rerouted around the ring. This protocol utilizes the ring to buffer packets and avoids the need for high-speed queues in the interface. The interface also includes programmable interval timers, a real-time clock, and several counters and registers for instrumenting the system.

Central network control resides within a dedicated VAX 11/780. A control node interfaces the ring to the VAX 11/780 Unibus adapter through a general-purpose interface device. This gives the VAX access to the shared memories and allows any processor to interrupt, or be interrupted by, the VAX. The control node also monitors ring activity and can delete packets that satisfy specific conditions. A serial control network between the VAX and the microprocessors supports experiment control, debugging, data collection, and system maintenance, and special control signals are provided to reset individual processors and real-time clocks from the VAX.

The ring node is designed using 100K ECL with a goal of 75-100 MHz for the ring clock in the LRMS. The interface is designed using advanced Schottky with an interface clock rate of 25-33 MHz. The entire system is synchronous.

Banyan multi-microcomputer system. The BMS is composed of 15 Z8001 MCB processing elements interconnected with 15 shared memory buffers by a fully parallel, unidirectional, packet-switched banyan network with a switching node fanout and spread of four,[8,9] as illustrated in Figure 4. The VAX 11/780 is provided access via I/O transactions.

An interface unit connects the processing elements and shared memory buffers to both inputs and outputs of the banyan network. Packets are transferred through the

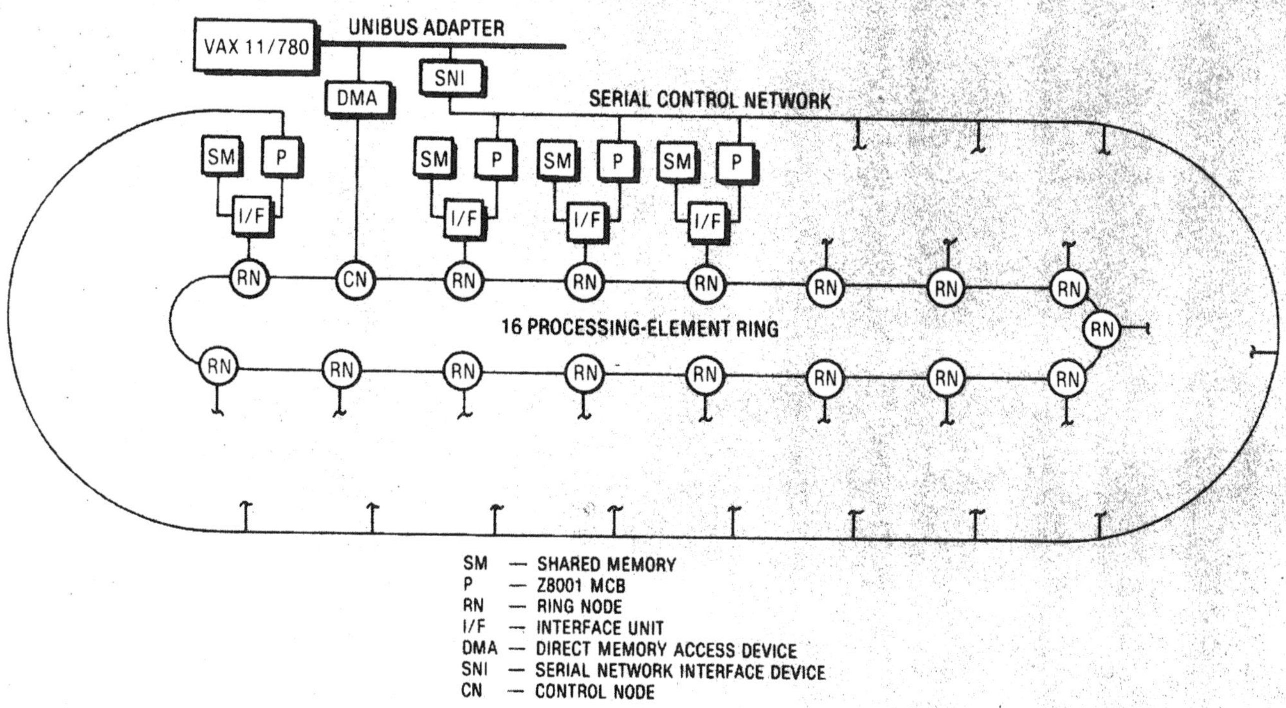

Figure 3. Ring multi-microcomputer system.

switch, one stage per switch clock cycle, unless blocked.

The banyan switching node is a 4 × 4 crossbar.[10] Conflicts between packets at a switching node are resolved by first-in-first-out transmission with rotating priorities to resolve ties. Three protocols are being investigated for movement of packets through the network. The first protocol requires that a packet wait until the next stage is empty; it then moves on the next clock cycle. The second protocol requires that a packet move when the blocking packet moves; movement occurs on the same switch clock cycle. The third protocol uses high-speed FIFO queues at each input to each switch node, and packets move on each switch cycle.

The second protocol requires propagation of a busy signal back through the network to all preceding stages. For a large system, propagation delays through the system limit network speed; known as pipelining the switch, this gives rise to the busy-ripple-back problem. The first protocol avoids this problem, but some performance is lost under heavy loads. Queues at the switching nodes restore this performance but introduce complexity at the node.

Packet width, types, and fields are the same as in the ring multi-microcomputer system. The interface unit is also very similar to the one in the RMS. The principal difference is that FIFO queues are included to remove packets from the network as rapidly as possible to reduce blocking in the network.

Central network control resides in a dedicated VAX 11/780. One switch node input and output is interfaced with the VAX 11/780 Unibus adapter through a general-purpose interface device. A serial control network is provided for experiment control, debugging, diagnostics, and data collection. Special control signals are provided to reset individual processors and real-time clocks and to clear the switch from the VAX.

Banyan switch node designs with a switch clock rate of 10-20 MHz have been investigated in 10K ECL and advanced Schottky. The entire BMS is driven from a single system clock.

Architecture description language

Overview. The architecture description language and its support software, the architecture description system, serve as the user interface to the testbed. ADL/ADS provides the user with the capability to describe arbitrary

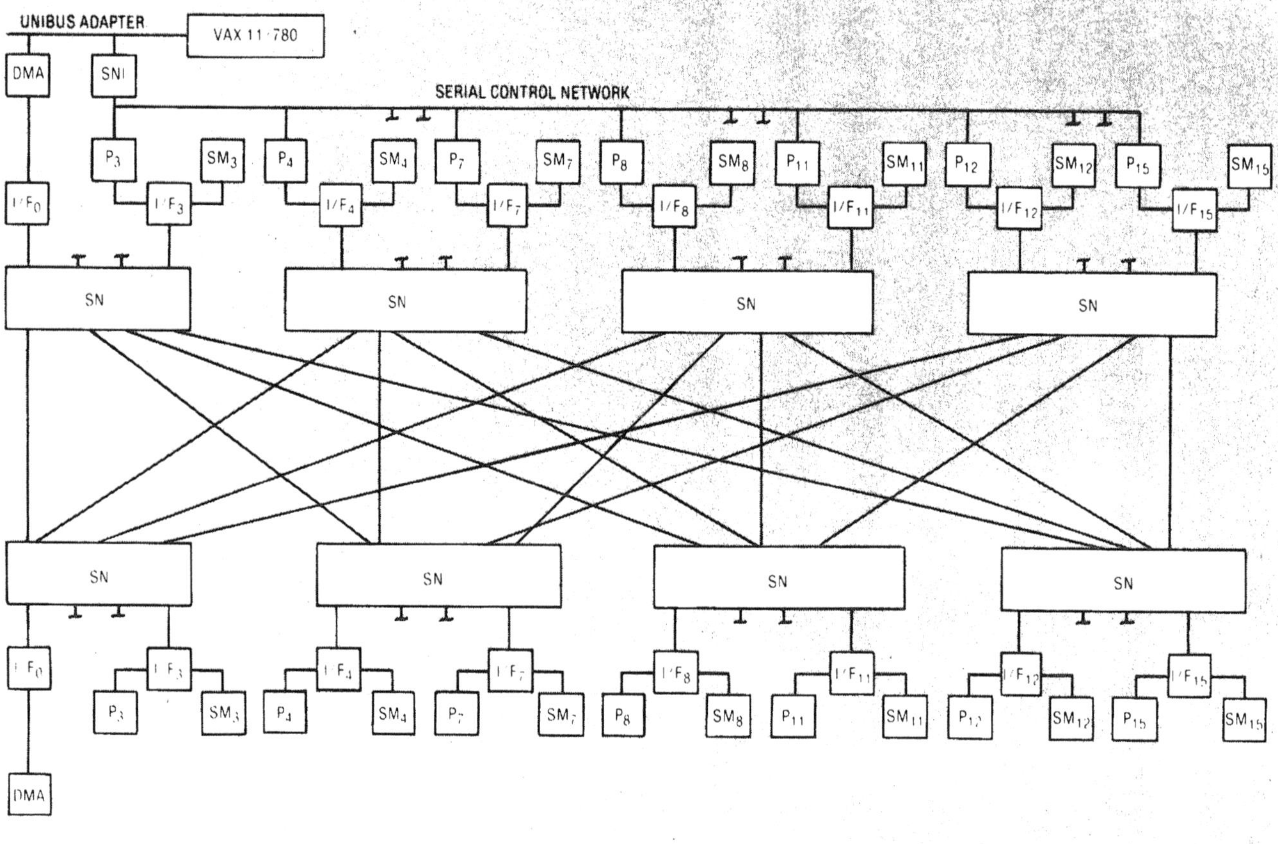

Figure 4. Banyan multi-microcomputer system.

distributed computing architectures. The architecture description is used to construct an experiment that is executed, monitored, and evaluated on the testbed with the aid of ADS.

A major purpose of ADL/ADS is to support the development of experiments evaluating potential solutions to critical research and design issues of distributed computing architectures. These include issues associated with the computing system structure, the partitioning and allocation of application software and data, and the distribution of control software and data. The rationale for a capability such as ADL is that it will (1) simplify use of the testbed, thus allowing the user to concentrate on his design problem without detailed involvement with the testbed; (2) provide a standard experimental approach for evaluating alternative designs, thus increasing confidence in design decisions; and (3) reduce error rate and implementation time.

An overview of the ADL system is given in Figure 5. The user initially describes an architecture, which is maintained in a database. Static analysis tools aid in testing the completeness and consistency of the description (e.g., whether all tasks are allocated). When the user is satisfied with the description, the architecture is constructed by binding, compiling, and loading the experiment onto the portion of the testbed selected by the user. In the construction phase, an application operating system is generated that is tailored to the user's specific needs. Once the experiment is loaded, it can be executed under the user's monitor and control. With the final ADL capability, post-execution analysis, results of the experiment can be replayed and summarized.

ADL is an ambitious effort that involves several issues including (1) the development of language concepts that are appropriate for distributed computing architecture specification; (2) the ability to automate the generation of an AOS; (3) the identification of information to be monitored in an experiment and an efficient method for performing the monitoring; (4) the development of a system with these diverse capabilities that is "user friendly" and is easy to learn and remember.

Fundamental concepts and models. A greal deal of effort has been devoted to defining language concepts that serve the development of software in distributed computing systems, especially methods for communicating among multiprocesses.[11-15] Although suggested implementations range from job control languages to ex-

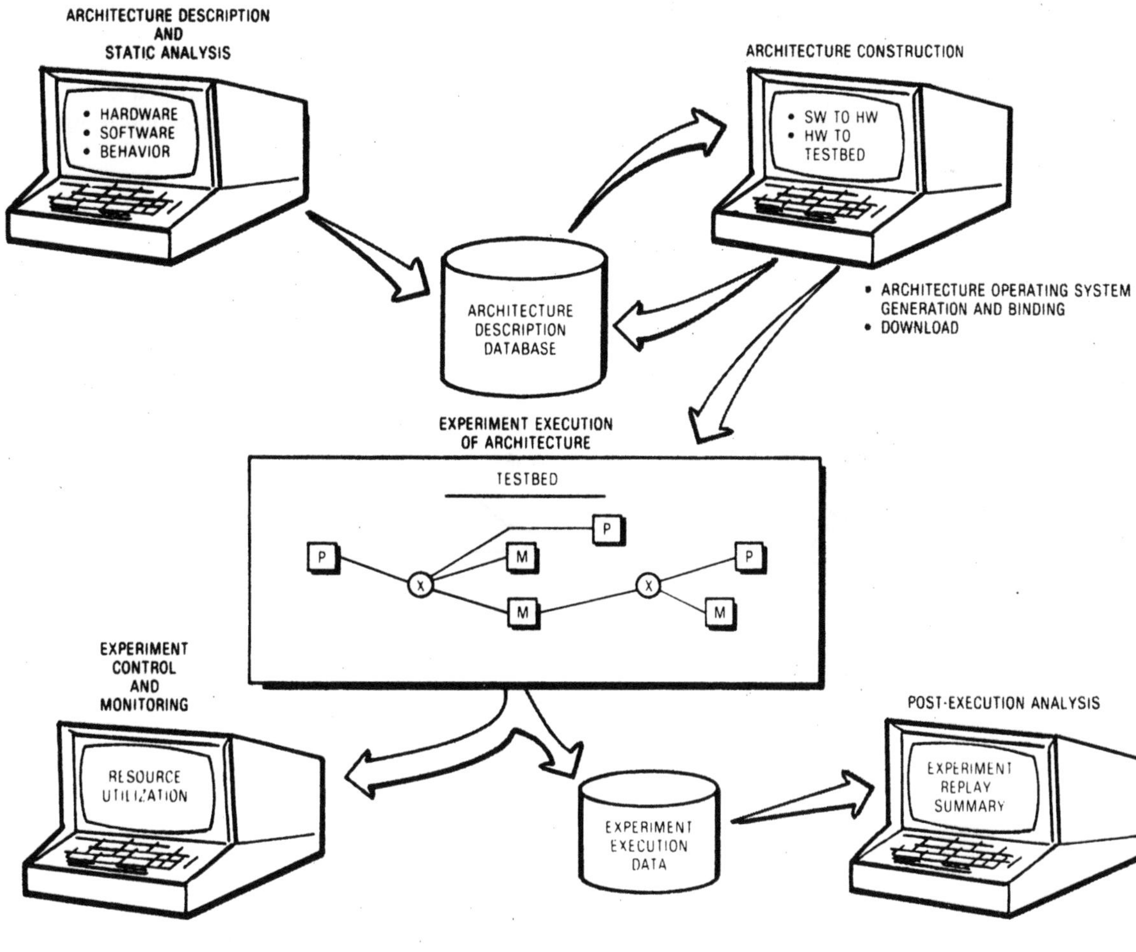

Figure 5. Functional capabilities of the architecture description language.

tensions of current programming languages, most of the concepts rely on modularity, a principle that supports the development of a robust system.

The development of ADL has followed the same general thrust—that is, defining concepts based on certain modularity principles and creating an object-oriented language that specifically addresses the objects of distributed computing architectures. The concepts in ADL are based on two fundamental models of a distributed architecture. The first model, the architecture description model (Figure 6), provides the environment for the description of a user's virtual architecture. It consists of an object space and a behavior space. The object space consists of hardware objects interconnected by a variety of devices and application software objects connected to provide communication among the objects. Finally, certain software objects are allocated to particular hardware objects.

In the behavior space, the architecture model is described in terms of high-level control policies. These control policies interact with the hardware and software objects in terms of (1) requests from the application software and (2) behavior variables produced by the hardware/software objects (e.g., a change in the state of a processor). The application software objects can also issue service requests for execution by the control policies, which can be activated as a function of time.

The second fundamental model (Figure 7), the architecture execution model, presents the concepts of experiment execution and user control and monitoring of the experiment. In the model, the distributed computing system performs as described by the architecture description model. The software objects interact on the hardware objects as specified by actions from the control policies resulting from behavior variables and service requests.

Object space definition. ADL currently supports architecture description at the processor-memory-switch[16] level of hardware detail and the task-message-file level of software detail. The characteristics of objects include their type, name, attributes, and relationships with other objects.

The hardware objects that can be used to describe a distributed computing architecture are

- Processor—logical processing element containing a CPU and a local memory for user-task execution and residence.
- Memory—data storage using random-access memory for transfer of messages among tasks via buffers associated with messages.
- Switch—interconnection mechanism used in conjunction with links and buses.
- Bus—bidirectional transfer media used for interconnection.
- Link—unidirectional transfer media between two hardware components.

The software objects that can be used to describe a distributed computing architecture are

- Task—identifies a closed and self-contained act of user code for performing some computation using messages as input and output.

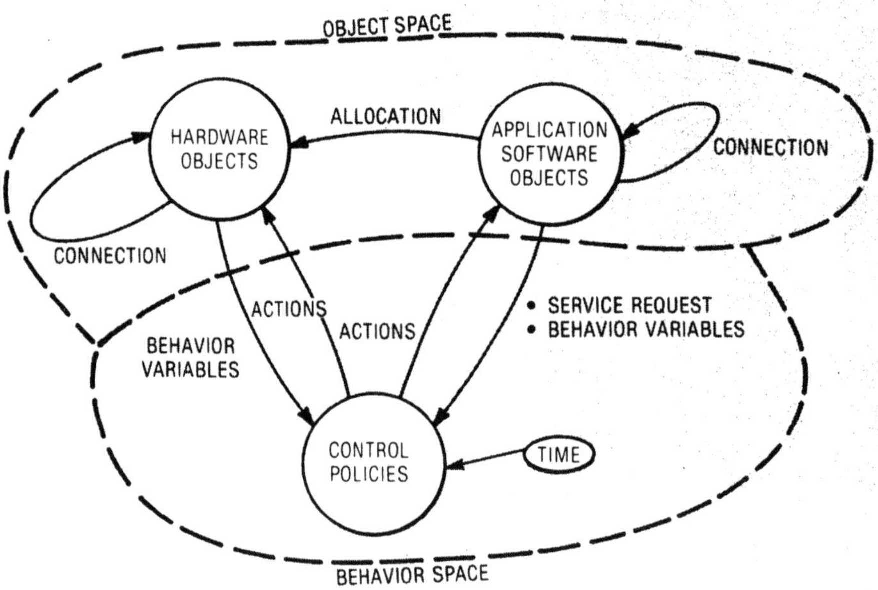

Figure 6. Architecture description model.

- Message—data-set instance originating from a sending task.
- Buffer—location for placing a message sent from a task. The receiving task, or tasks, owns the buffer.
- File—repetitive data set containing multiple instances of the same type of data structure.

These objects have associated attributes, such as size, execution rate, and priority, that are used to specify important object characteristics. Three classes of relationships specify interactions among objects. Software-to-software relationships describe the way that software objects interact via either data or control. Hardware-to-hardware relationships describe the manner in which the hardware objects are interconnected and thus define data transmission paths (e.g., which processor and memories are attached to which buses). Software-to-hardware relationships describe the allocation of the software objects onto the hardware objects (e.g., the initial allocation of tasks to processors).

The implementation of ADL is supported by both textual and graphics descriptions. Figure 8 is an example of a graphics description of a partial hardware structure.

Behavior space definition. The behavior of the architecture is expressed in terms of control policies. Alternative approaches[17] for specifying the control policies include state diagrams, programming languages, and graph models such as Petri nets. The selected technique is a graph model called a C-net for control network.

The graph model contains nodes that specify the entry and exit from a control policy, conditional branch, or processing node. Associated with the entry node is a Boolean expression specifying the object code condition necessary for C-net activation. The terms in the condition are limited to tests concerning attribute values, relationship instances, and time. The conditional expression associated with a branch node has the same form as the one associated with the entry node.

Processing nodes can remember part or all of the state of the distributed computing system in terms of attributes and relationships or can perform actions that change the state of the system. The actions are limited to effecting the concepts in the object space by changing attribute values and relationships. For example, since STATE is an attribute of a TASK, STATE (TI) : = READY is a legal action indicating that task TI is ready for execution.

At first glance, limiting the control space to dealing with object space attributes and relationships may appear overly restrictive. However, this approach provides a feasible method for generating a functional operating system consistent with the level of detail given in the object space for hardware and software elements. If the ADL is extended to include detail about the object space (in terms of new objects, attributes, or relationships),

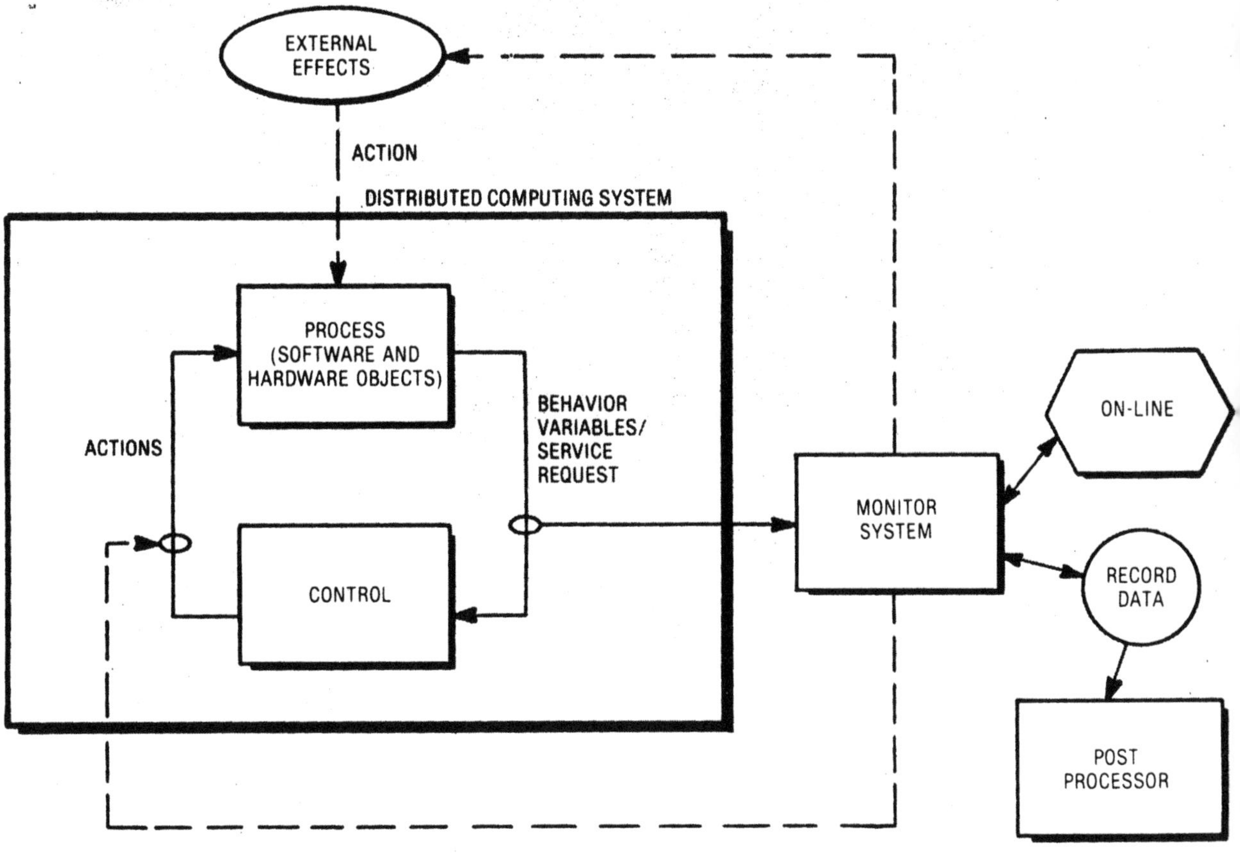

Figure 7. Architecture execution model.

then corresponding extensions can be made to specify the policies that control the new information.

Architecture construction. Following the definition of the architecture in ADL, the user defines its mapping onto the testbed hardware. He then invokes the AOS generation tool which automatically generates an application operating system tailored to the user's architecture. Finally, the necessary interaction with the testbed support software (e.g., compilers, downloaders) is handled automatically by ADS to bind the user-provided application tasks with the ADS-generated AOS.

The ultimate goal is to completely generate an application operating system from the control policies specified by C-nets. However, the initial version of AOS implemented for the crossbar multi-microprocessor system is designed with fixed functionality capabilities that are parameterized from the user's architecture description model. This fixed functionality provides task control, message, and lock control services to the application programs. The task control services are parameterized with task allocation information that allows implementation of almost unrestricted and arbitrary user scheduling policies for the experiment. The message services are parameterized according to buffering and routing information described in the architecture description model and provide send/receive/test capabilities for use by the application programs. Finally, the lock control services allow tasks on the same processor or on separate processors to implement appropriate synchronization techniques.

The AOS makes use of a runtime database constructed by the AOS generation function of the ADS program on the VAX. The runtime database is downloaded into the CMS shared memory during experiment construction and provides the basis for the AOS parameterization performed during AOS initialization. The runtime database is then used by AOS during experiment execution to coordinate the actions of each AOS component on each microprocessor. The database provides a consistent view of the overall system and prevents incompatible actions such as multiple allocation of resources.

Execution and monitoring. During the execution of an experiment, the user can dynamically control and monitor the experiment in an on-line mode. For example, the user can freeze—and later resume—any or all processors or tasks via AOS control to examine snapshots of the experiment environment or to inject artificial external effects to study issues such as fault tolerance. The user can also display combinations of the available monitored data for each of the hardware and software objects. The data that can be monitored include the status of objects (e.g., whether a processor is up or down), the value of objects and their relationships (e.g., the number of times a task has to be executed), and the utilization of objects (e.g., the amount of time that a processor has been busy).

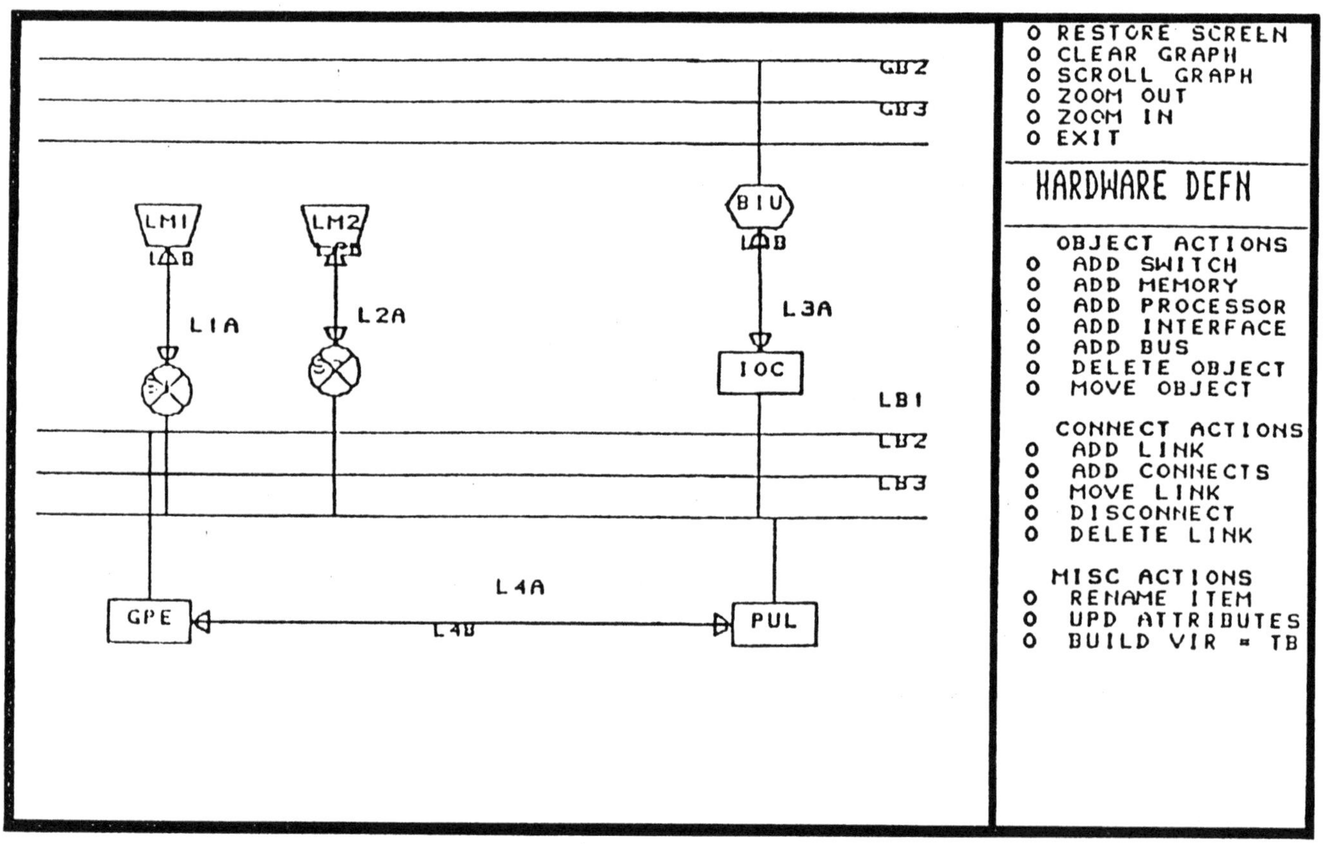

Figure 8. Graphics description of virtual hardware structure.

The final capability is post-execution analysis. All of the monitored data, stored in the experiment execution data file, are available to the post-execution function for a replay of the experiment or for a variety of experiment analyses. Even if the user chooses to display only part of the available data, all of the monitored data are stored in the file. Thus, the user can turn off the on-line monitoring function and use the post-execution function to analyze the stored data.

Testbed system software

Overview. The distributed testbed nucleus uses VAX/VMS operating system software, application programming tools, compilers, assemblers, and program development and test tools. VMS services have been extended over the network to provide generalized system services for distributed operation of the testbed nucleus.

A powerful higher-order language, PDL,[18] is provided for development of microcomputer and VAX software. Derived from Pascal, PDL contains features that make it well suited for both real-time applications and system programming. Among these are a type transfer capability for direct access to special address areas (e.g., local and global memory, real-time clock, interrupt registers, lock registers), special procedure calls for interfacing to a developing operating system, and utilities for tasking and synchronization. A summary of the PDL language is given in Figure 9.

Additional software development tools include a design builder that tracks the parts of a process, beginning with the requirements and evolving into the implementation activity, and a configuration manager that automatically provides separate compilation down to the procedure level of program elements affected by a modification or specified by a programmer.

In addition to the AOS generated by ADL, the distributed testbed supplies a master operating system and a kernal operating system to support experimentation on the multi-microcomputer systems. Figure 10 illustrates the relationship of these OS components to each other, to ADL, and to the application program for the initial implementation on the crossbar multi-microprocessor system.

Nucleus network services. The VAX/VMS operating system supports virtual devices called mailboxes for communication between processes residing in the same processor, and this concept has been extended for communication between processes anywhere in the network. Three network software components—a communications supervisor, a communications monitor, and an I/O interface—support remote mailbox communications. The communications monitor initiates and terminates communications for processes and passes the information to the communications supervisor, which verifies the availability of the required network resources, establishes and abolishes logical networks on existing hardware, and checks the legality of communication requests. The I/O interface, the major execution-time component in interprocess communication, receives data written to a remote mailbox and relays data received from a testbed device to the appropriate destination mailbox.

Two types of services are provided by the testbed network communications software: operations and support services and network system services. Operations and support services permit user entry of network and interprocessor support commands and initiation of virtual terminal operations. Network commands are provided to connect a local terminal to a remote node, to copy files from a local node to a remote node, to queue a local file for printing at a remote node, to delete old versions of specified files on remote nodes, to delete files on a remote node, and to enter a command procedure in the job queue of a remote node. Network system services are provided to sign on/off the network, to create mailboxes and assign channels, to delete mailboxes, to assign/deassign mailboxes, to submit remote command procedures, to copy files to a remote node, to assign a unique name on the network, and to translate logical names. These services are called using the standard VAX-11 procedure calling con-

Declarations

Constant identifiers: explicit constant or constant expression.

Type identifiers: Pascal-like with extensions.
RESTRICT attribute on a type allows use only in certain procedures.
PACKED applies to subranges and enumerations.

Variable identifiers: Pascal-like.

Procedures-function and routine identifiers:
Pascal-like. More flexible arguments, e.g., variable-length arrays.
Routines are not nested.

Common identifiers: for Fortran interface.

Control statements

Assignment
IF-THEN-ELSEIF-ENDIF
CASE-ENDCASE
Loop-Statements-Iteration-Statements-ENDLOOP
WITH-ENDWITH . . . Abbreviations enable use of multiple records of same type in the same width.
LABL:BEGIN-END . . . Labels can be mnemonic.
ESCAPE
ASSERT
GO TO

Features

Local routines
Tasking and synchronization built in
Block-structured, nested scope
Recursive
Type transfer can be used in code
Makes full use of byte, word, and long-word addressing
Powerful diagnostics
- Compile and runtime range checks using interval arithmetic
- Probes in code for testing
- Complete dumps
- Runtime tracebacks

Figure 9. PDL language summary.

vention. All network system services may be used as either external subroutines or external functions.

Master operating system. MOS coordinates system-wide activities, providing the support ADS needs to build and execute its systems. The initial MOS implementation for the crossbar multi-microcomputer system includes capabilities to download tasks and data; to allocate and deallocate memory resources; to send messages to tasks; to start, stop, or resume executing tasks on a given processor; to determine the status of processor and memory resources; to reset processes; to restart main tasks; to clear a processor of all tasks; to copy shared memory blocks; and to handle disk I/O requests.

A downloader loads programs or data into the multi-microcomputer system global shared memory as special messages and notifies the kernel operating system. The message format indicates the address to which the code or data should be moved. In the case of program code, the KOS enters it as a task to be executed.

A message handler provides services to support communication between processes. The processes involved may be a KOS in each of several microcomputers, AOS and its subprocesses in several microcomputers, or a process in the VAX. Processes can send messages to themselves. But user processes in the microcomputers send messages by calling for a KOS service, and messages between the microcomputers and the VAX use the MOS service. The message format includes destination process identifier, source process identifier, length of message, and message data.

Interrupts from the multi-microcomputer system are handled by VAX asynchronous system trap routines through direct passing of data or an interrupt control block.

File storage for the multi-microcomputer systems is on disks attached to the VAX. Processes on the microcomputers must be able to read and write to these files. MOS includes a file manager to create, open, access, and close files using calls to the VAX/VMS operating system. Operations on these files may come as a result of requests from KOS, ADS, or other VAX resident processes. Requests are passed as a message to the file manager. The message specifies the file identifier, operation code, and other parameters appropriate for operations such as record lengths and output buffer addresses. The operation code specifies whether the data are character, text, or numeric.

Kernel operating system. KOS, which is resident in each microcomputer, manages the resources, scheduling, and communications that support the execution of tasks including AOS. Facilities are provided to load tasks; to support I/O to terminal or disk; to allocate memory; to transmit messages; to schedule tasks; to create, suspend, ready, dispatch, and terminate tasks; to synchronize tasks; to provide clock services; and to support time-slicing.

KOS performs task management through the use of task control blocks built when a task is requested. A task

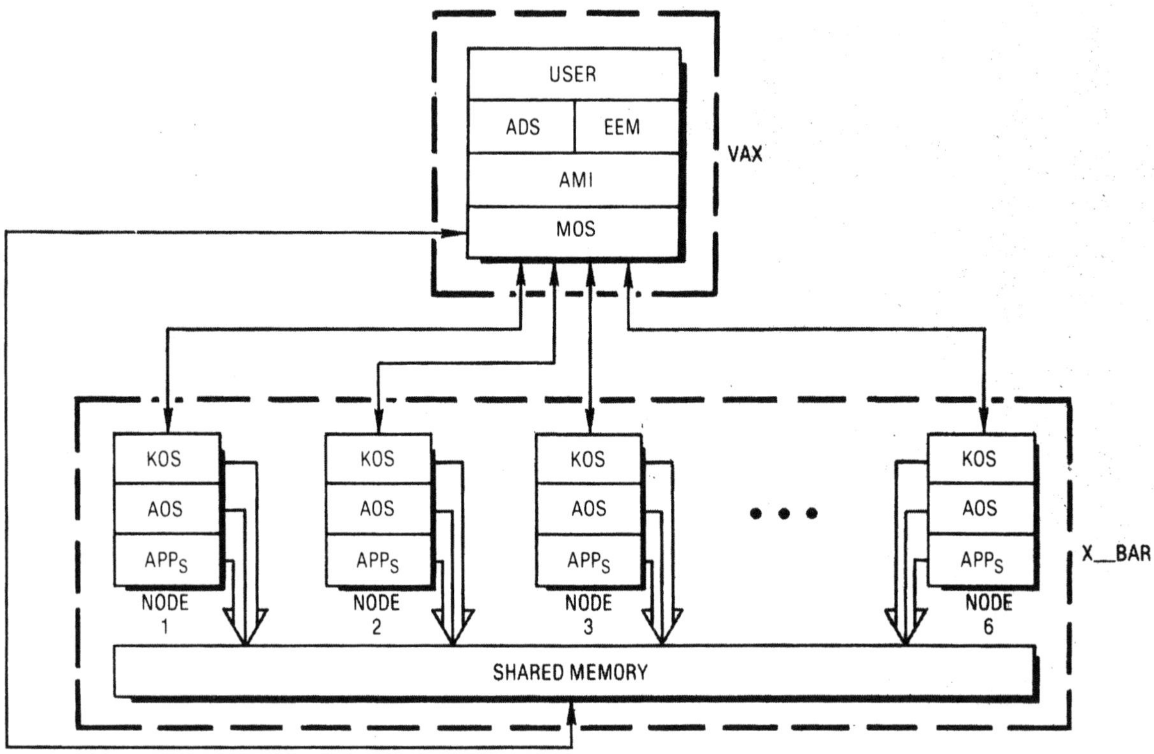

Figure 10. Crossbar multi-microcomputer system software configuration.

may be created from a program and downloaded from the VAX using the master operating system, or it may be created as a subtask by the application operating system. KOS is designed to support AOS, which directly serves the user application program. To achieve this, AOS maintains its own task control system and uses KOS task control facilities only for dispatching the application program.

KOS transmits messages between tasks using data in the message header. Since delivery is not guaranteed, the sender may test the status to see if the message reached its destination. The sending task is not delayed after message initiation. When a message arrives, KOS takes action to notify AOS of message arrival. These actions enable AOS to control the sending of messages and to take appropriate action when a message is received. KOS provides specific services to send a message, to test the status of a sent message, to request a queued message, and to accept a message.

KOS manages local and shared memory. It allocates local memory, which is reserved for system use, to provide stack space for tasks and space for the task code. Shared memory is allocated on a dynamic basis according to user request and system needs using a first-fit strategy. Since no garbage collection, or manipulation of allocated blocks, is performed, it is the responsibility of AOS or the user task to avoid fragmentation of the available memory through proper allocation and deallocation requests. The KOS memory management capabilities are normally utilized indirectly through PDL language constructs.

Synchronization of parallel tasks that access common data requires locks or flags that can be tested and set or reset in an indivisible operation. By using hardware guard registers and flags in global memory, KOS can allocate a lock, deallocate a lock, test and set a lock, and test and reset a lock.

A processor can interrupt any other processor by means of an interrupt register associated with each processor. Writing into the interrupt register generates a nonvectored interrupt, and an interrupt handler then uses the data in the register to determine the required action.

KOS provides services for reading the real-time clock and for setting the interval timer. Time-slicing is effected by a hardware interval timer and a software counter decremented at each interrupt by the interval interrupt handler. When the software counter reaches zero, the current task is suspended and the next task on the READY queue is put into execution. The time-slice length is given as a parameter in the CREATE process and thus entered in the task control block. This time is put into the software interval counter when the task is moved from the READY queue into execution.

Status, experience, and future plans

The VAX 11/780 distributed testbed nucleus, established in 1979, has been used extensively to develop software and to implement distributed computing experiments for real-time applications. For example, it has hosted and supplied realistic data for a number of hardware-in-the-loop experiments designed to test and evaluate special-purpose hardware, including a radar digital beam-forming processor,[19] logic-enhanced memories for multistatic radar deghosting,[20] and an optical signal processor for moving target indication.[21] The system has also been used for experiments in distributed simulation[22] and distributed software development and test[23,24]; detailed evaluations of a distributed real-time operating system,[25] a real-time resource manager,[26] a distributed database manager,[27] and a task allocation scheme[28] for a search, detection, and tracking radar system; investigation of a real-time system, environment, and threat simulation[29] to provide realistic loading for a tactical processor; and extensive experiments and tests to support studies in the distribution of algorithms for processing optical sensor data.[30,31]

Although these experiments demonstrated the flexibility of the nucleus network, particularly the network software, experiment construction was error-prone and time-consuming. As a consequence, ADL/ADS was conceived and implemented for the crossbar multi-microcomputer system, and the need for greater flexibility in distributed hardware architectures led to the development of multi-microcomputer systems.

Since communication delays in the nucleus network were excessive for many real-time applications, the system has recently been augmented with multiport memories to support shared memory experiments in the nucleus and to provide faster process-to-process communication than is possible over the PCL11-B bus. Studies are currently underway to obtain a high-speed, low-latency interconnect to replace the PCL11-B parallel bus.

The nucleus network software has been implemented to support the PCL11-B. Because it is an extension of the VAX/VMS capabilities, users can easily migrate large, centralized processes into distributed processes on the testbed. The network software was initially implemented in macro-assembly language. It has recently been reimplemented in Bliss to improve reliability and error tolerance, to increase network efficiency, to make the system more maintainable, and to incorporate additional features. In the future it will be extended to other networks.

An engineering model of the crossbar multi-microcomputer system has been built and used to support development of the ADL/ADS system, MOS, AOS, KOS, and a real-time radar control experiment. The final CMS system is currently being implemented. Comprehensive experiments in decentralized operating systems, decentralized control, task scheduling, distributed data management, interprocess communications, real-time status monitoring, real-time error recovery, fault detection and system reconfiguration, and nuclear circumvention are planned for the CMS and other multi-microcomputer systems.

Extensive simulation and analysis of ring and banyan network topologies has been performed to predict the performance of a 64-node system. A fully parallel Pierce ring and a packet-switched banyan with fanout and spread of four have been selected. Breadboard prototypes of the ring node and the banyan switch node have been built and demonstrated. Plans are to build a 16-node prototype RMS and a 16-node prototype BMS. Following a period of evaluation, one of the prototype systems will be expanded to a 64-node reconfigurable multi-microcomputer system. Currently a hierarchy of eight interconnected rings of eight processing nodes each appears best suited for the LRMS.

When the concept of the ADL/ADS was conceived by testbed researchers, the eventual goal was to provide access to all resources within the distributed testbed. To achieve that goal, the research and development of ADL/ADS has been, and will continue to be, pursued in incremental steps. The first step involved the definition of a complete language. The current version of ADL/ADS provides a subset of that language and a software system for user interface with the CMS component of the testbed. That language and software have been evaluated and modified accordingly, and the CMS language and software have served as a model for further research into additional language concepts and capabilities that are being incorporated in a system to provide access to the VAX network. The original complete language is being investigated, refined, and expanded by expressing sample VAX-related problems in the language. ■

Acknowledgments

A project with the scope of the real-time distributed testbed cannot be accomplished without the efforts of many people. The authors wish to acknowledge the technical staffs of TRW, System Development Corporation, and General Research Corporation in Huntsville for their contributions. In particular, we would like to recognize the contributions of Glenn Cox, Wayne Crouch, John Ellis, Newman Vosbury, and Tom Williams.

References

1. C. G. Davis and R.L. Couch, "Ballistic Missile Defense: A Supercomputer Challenge," *Computer*, Vol. 13, No. 11, Nov. 1980, pp. 37-46.
2. William A. Davis, Jr., "Ballistic Missile Defense Will Work," *National Defense*, Vol. LXVI, No. 373, Dec. 1981, pp. 16-22.
3. C. R. Vick and J. M. Williams, "The Requirements for a New Generation of Real-Time Data Processing Technology," *Proc. Hawaii Int'l Conf. System Sciences*, Jan. 1977, pp. 1-16.
4. C. R. Vick, J. E. Scalf, and W. C. McDonald, "Distributed Data Processing for Real-Time Application," *Proc. Sixth Texas Conf. Computing Systems*, " Nov. 1977, pp. 1B-1 through 1B-12.
5. P. Hsia et al., "A Configurable Testbed for Distributed Processing," *Journal of Digital Systems*, Vol. 5, No. 3, Fall 1981, pp. 251-264.
6. W. C. McDonald and T. G. Williams, "Evaluation of Multi-Microprocessor Interconnection Networks for a Class of Sensor Data Processing Problems," *Real-Time Signal Processing III, Proc. SPIE*, Vol. 241, July 1980, pp. 238-248.

7. J. R. Pierce, C. H. Coker, and W. J. Kropfl, "Network for Block Switching of Data," *IEEE Convention Record,* New York, Mar. 1971, pp. 34-38.

8. G. R. Goke and G. J. Lipovski, "Banyan Networks for Partitioning Multiprocessor Systems," *First Annual Symp. Computer Architecture,* Dec. 1973, pp. 21-28.

9. H. J. Siegel and R. L. McMillen, "The Cube Network as a Distributed Processing Testbed Switch," *Proc. Second Int'l Conf. Distributed Computing Systems,* Apr. 1981, pp. 377-387.

10. A. C. Hung and M. Malek, "A 4×4 Crossbar Design for the Multistage Interconnection Networks," *Proc. Real-Time Systems Symp.,* Dec. 1981, pp. 3-12.

11. V. Lessor, D. Serrain, and J. Bonar, "PCL: A Process-Oriented Job Control Language," *Proc. First Int'l Conf. Distributed Computing Systems,* Oct. 1979, pp. 315-329.

12. B. H. Liskov, "On Linguistic Support for Distributed Programs," *IEEE Trans. Software Eng.,* Vol. SE-8, May 1982, pp. 203-210.

13. B. H. Liskov, "Primitives for Distributed Computing," *Proc. Seventh Symp. Operating System Principles,* Dec. 1979, pp. 33-42.

14. Chung-Ming Li and Ming T. Liu, "Communicating Distributed Processes: A Language for Distributed Programming in Distributed Data Base Systems," *Proc. First Int'l Conf. Distributed Computing Systems,* Oct. 1979, pp. 47-60.

15. T. W. Mao and R. T. Yeh, "Communication Port: A Language Concept for Concurrent Programming," *IEEE Trans Software Eng.,* Vol. SE-6, Mar. 1980, pp. 194-204.

16. C. G. Bell and A. Newell, "The PMS and ISP Descriptive Systems for Computer Structures," *AFIPS Conf. Proc.,* Vol. 36, 1970 SJCC, pp. 351-374.

17. C. Sunshine, "Formal Techniques for Protocol Specification and Verification," *Computer,* Vol. 12, No. 9, Sept. 1979, pp. 20-27.

18. N. A. Vosbury, "The Process Design System (PDS)," *Proc. Compsac 79,* Nov. 1979, pp. 374-379.

19. E. E. Swartzlander, Jr., and J. M. McKay, "Digital Beam Forming Processor," *Real-Time Signal Processing III, Proc. SPIE,* Vol. 241, July 1980, pp. 232-237.

20. P. T. Alexander et al., "Special Purpose Logic-Enhanced Memories," *Proc. Compsac 77,* Nov. 1977, pp. 780-784.

21. W. Von der Ohe et al., "Optical Signal Processor for Moving Target Indication," *Effective Utilization of Optics in Radar Systems, Proc. SPIE,* Vol. 128, Sept. 1977, pp. 210-213.

22. W. C. McDonald et al., "Distributed Simulation Host: A Distributed Testbed," *Proc. Compsac 80,* Oct. 1980, pp. 562-568.

23. R. H. Hoffman et al., "Simulation Software Development for the BMDATC DDP Underlay Experiment," *Proc. Compsac 80,* Oct. 1980, pp. 569-577.

24. R. H. Hoffman and R. W. Smith, "Applied Techniques for Testing Distributed Data Processing Software," *Proc. Distributed Data Acquisition, Computing, and Control Symp.,* Dec. 1980, pp. 202-212.

25. M. L. Green et al., "A Distributed Real Time Operating System," *Proc. Distributed Data Acquisition, Computing, and Control Symp.,* Dec. 1980, pp. 175-184.

26. S. Majumdar and M. L. Green, "A Distributed Real Time Resource Manager," *Proc. Distributed Data Acquisition, Computing, and Control Symp.,* Dec. 1980, pp. 185-193.

27. E. Y. S. Lee et al., "A Distributed Data Base Manager," *Proc. Distributed Data Acquisition, Computing, and Control Symp.,* Dec. 1980, pp. 194-201.

28. P. Ma et al., "On the Design of a Task Allocation Scheme for Time-Critical Application," *Proc. Real-Time Systems Symp.,* Dec. 1981, pp. 121-126.

29. H. S. Ostrowsky and D. F. Palmer, "SETS: The Distributed Driver," *Proc. Compsac 80,* Oct. 1980, pp. 584-590.

30. D. M. Wilcox, "Super Resolution Algorithms in Distributed Real-Time Signal Processing Systems," *Real-Time Signal Processing III, Proc. SPIE,* Vol. 241, July 1980, pp. 220-223.

31. D. M. Wilcox and R. J. Nichols, "Optical Sensor Signal Processing Requirements for Ballistic Missile Defense," *Real-Time Signal Processing III, Proc. SPIE,* Vol. 241, July 1980, pp. 2-10.

William C. McDonald is principal engineer of requirements analysis and support software for the System Development Corporation Advanced Research Center in Huntsville, Alabama. His research interests include distributed architectures for real-time applications, distributed real-time operating systems, and distributed testbeds. From 1963 to 1973, he was with The Boeing Company where he was involved in the design, development, and analysis of computer and electronic systems for several missile systems and the space program. In 1973, he joined System Development Corporation where he has been engaged in BMD data processing requirements analysis and distributed processing research.

He received his BS in electrical engineering from Mississippi State University in 1963 and his MS in engineering from Southeastern Institute of Technology in 1978. He is a member of the IEEE Computer Society and the IEEE Aerospace and Electronic Systems Society.

R. Wayne Smith, manager of the Systems Software Department for the TRW Software Development and Systems Engineering Laboratory in Huntsville, Alabama, has worked for TRW since 1969. For most of his career he has been involved in the research, development, and application of tools and techniques for software development. This has included work on the Requirements Engineering and Validation System for the Ballistic Missile Defense Agency and the Automated Verification System for NASA/JSC. His research interests include software productivity, higher order languages, software tools and techniques, and distributed computing systems.

A member of the IEEE, Smith received his BS degree in computer science and statistics from the University of Southern Mississippi in 1969.

REFERENCES FOR ADDITIONAL READING

[ADIB 78a] Adiba, M., and D. Portal, "A Cooperation System for Heterogeneous Database Management Systems," *Information Systems*, Vol. 3, No. 3, pp. 209–215, 1978.

[ADIB 78b] Adiba, M., et al., "Issues in Distributed Data Base Management Systems: A Technical Overview," *Proc. 1978 VLDB*, pp. 89–100, Sept. 1978.

[AJMO 83] Ajmone Marsan, M., et al., "Modeling Bus Contention and Memory Interference in a Multiprocessor System," *IEEE Transactions on Computers*, Vol. C-32, No. 1, pp. 60–72, Jan. 1983.

[ALLE 82] Allen, F.W., M.E.S. Loomis, and M.V. Mannino, "The Integrated Dictionary/Directory System," *Computing Surveys*, Vol. 14, No. 2, pp. 245–286, June 1982.

[ALSB 76] Alsberg, P.A., and J.D. Day, "A Principle for Resilient Sharing of Distributed Resources," *Proc. 2nd International Conference on Software Engineering*, pp. 562–570, 1976.

[APER 84] Apers, P., and G. Wiederhold, "Transaction Classification to Survive a Network Partition," Stanford University Technical Report, STAN-CS-85-1053, Aug. 1984.

[APER 80] Apers, P.M.G., "Data Allocation and Distributed Query Processing," *Proc. ACM Pacific Conference*, San Francisco, 1980.

[AVIZ 78] Avizienis, A., "Fault-Tolerance: The Survival Attribute of Digital Systems," *Proc. IEEE*, Vol. 66, No. 10, pp. 1109–1125, Oct. 1978.

[BADA 80] Badal, C.Z., "The Analysis of the Effect of Concurrency Control on Distributed Database System Performance," *Proc. 6th International Conf. on VLDB*, pp. 376–383, Oct. 1980.

[BARN 81] Barnes, G.H., and S.F. Lundstrom, "Design and Validation of a Connection Network for Many-Processor Multiprocessor Systems," *Computer*, Vol. 14, No. 12, pp. 31–41, Dec. 1981.

[BASK 77] Baskett, F., J.H. Howard, and J.T. Mantague, "Task Communication in DEMOS," *Proc. 6th ACM Symposium on Operating System Principles*, published as *Operating Systems Review*, Vol. 11, No. 5, pp. 23–31, Nov. 1977.

[BERN 84] Bernstein, P., and N. Goodman, "Algorithm for Concurrency Control and Recovery in Replicated Distributed Databases," *ACM Transactions on Database Systems*, Vol. 9, No. 4, Dec. 1984.

[BERN 81a] Bernstein, R., and D. Chiu, "Using Semijoins to Solve Relational Queries," *Journal of the ACM*, Vol. 28, No. 1, pp. 25–40, 1981.

[BERN 81b] Bernstein, P., N. Goodman, E. Wong, C. Reeve, and J. Rothnie, "Query Processing in a System for Distributed Databases (SSD-1)," *ACM Transactions on Database Systems*, Vol. 6, No. 4, pp. 602–625, 1981.

[BIRR 83] Birrell, A.D., and B.J. Nelson, "Implementing Remote Procedure Calls," *Proc. 9th Symposium on Operating Systems Principles*, Vol. 17, No. 5, 3 pp., 1983.

[BIRR 82] Birrell, A.D., R. Levin, R. Needham, and M. Schroeder, "Grapevine: An Exercise in Distributed Computing," *Communications of the ACM*, Vol. 25, No. 4, pp. 260–274, April 1982.

[BOKH 79] Bokhari, S.H., "Dual Processor Scheduling With Dynamis Reassignment," *IEEE Transactions on Software Engineering*, Vol. SE-5, No. 4, pp. 341–349, July 1979.

[BRYA 81] Bryant, R.M., and R.A. Finkel, "A Stable Distributed Scheduling Algorithm," *Proc. 2nd International Conference on Distributed Computing Systems*, April 1981.

[CARD 83] Cardenas, A., *Data Base Management Systems*, Chapter 10, Second Edition, Allyn and Bacon, Inc., Boston, MA, 1983.

[CASE 72] Casey, R.G., "Allocation of Copies of Files in an Information Network," *AFIPS Spring Joint Computer Conference*, Vol. 40, AFIPS Press, pp. 617–625, 1981.

[CENS 78] Censier, L.M., and R. Feautrier, "A New Solution to Coherent Problems in Multicache Systems," *IEEE Transactions on Computers*, Vol. C-27, No. 12, pp. 1112–1118, Dec. 1978.

[CERI 86] Ceri, S., G. Gottlob, and G. Pelagatti, "Taxomony and Formal Properties of Distributed Joins," to appear in *Information Systems*, Vol. 11, Nov. 1, 1986.

[CERI 84] Ceri, S., and G. Pelagatti, *Distributed Databases, Principles and Systems*, McGraw-Hill, New York, 1984.

[CERI 83a] Ceri, S., and S.B. Navathe, "A Methodology for the Distribution Design of Databases," *IEEE*, pp. 426–431, 1983.

[CERI 83b] Ceri, S., S. Navathe, and G. Wiederhold, "Distribution Design of Logical Database Schemas," *IEEE Transactions on Software Engineering*, Vol. SE-9, No. 4, pp. 487–504, July 1983.

[CHAN 82] Chang, J., "A Heuristic Approach to Distributed Query Processing," *Proc. 8th International Conference on VLDB*, Mexico City, VLDB Endowment, Saratoga, CA, pp. 54–61, 1982.

[CHEN 84] Chen, P.P., "An Algebra for a Directional Binary Entity-Relationship Model," *Proc. International Conference on Data Engineering*, pp. 37–40, April 1984.

[CHEN 80] Chen, P.P.S., and J. Akoka, "Optimal Design of Distributed Information Systems," *IEEE Transactions on Computers*, Vol. C-29, No. 12, pp. 1068–1080, Dec. 1980.

[CHEN 76] Chen, P.P., "The Entity-Relationship Model: Towards a Unified View of Data," *ACM Transactions on Database Systems*, Vol. 1, No. 1, pp. 9–36, March 1976.

[CHIU 80] Chiu, D.M., and Y.C. Ho, "A Methodology for Interpreting Tree Queries into Optimal Semijoin Expressions," *ACM Transaction on Database Systems*, Vol. 5, No. 4, pp. 169–178, Dec. 1980.

[CHOU 82] Chou, T.C.K., and J.A. Abraham, "Load Balancing in Distributed Systems," *IEEE Transactions on Software Engineering*, Vol. SE-8, No. 4, pp. 401–412, July 1982.

[CHU 86] Chu, W.W., and L. Lan, "Task Allocation and Precedence Relations for Distributed Real-Time Systems," submitted to *IEEE Transactions on Computers*, for publication, 1985.

[CHU 84b] Chu, W.W., "Distributed Data Base Systems," *Handbook of Software Engineering*, Chapter 13, Vick and Rahmoorthy, eds., 1984.

[CHU 79] Chu, W.W., and V. To,"A Hierarchical Conceptual Data Model for Data Translation in a Heterogeneous Database System," *Proc. International Conference on Entity-Relational Approach to Systems Analysis and Design*, Los Angeles, pp. 647–648, Dec. 10–12, 1979.

[CHU 78] Chu, W.W., D. Lee, and B. Iffla, "A Distributed Processing System for Naval Data Communication Networks," *AFIPS Proc.*, Vol. 47, pp. 783–793, 1978.

[CHU 74] Chu, W.W., and G. Ohlmacher,"Avoiding Deadlocking in Distributed Databases," *Proc. ACM National Symposium*, Vol. 1, pp. 156–160, March 1974.

[CODD 70] Codd, E.F., "A Relation Model of Data for Large Shared Data Banks," *CACM*, Vol. 13, pp. 377–387, 1970.

[COFF 81] Coffman, E.G., Jr., et al., "Optimization of the Number of Copies in a Distributed Database," *IEEE Transactions on Software Engineering*, Vol. SE-7, No. 1, pp. 78–84, Jan. 1981.

[DAVI 84] Davidson, S., "Optimism and Consistency in Partitioned Distributed Database Systems," *ACM Transactions on Database Systems*, Vol. 9, No. 4, Dec. 1984.

[DESJ 83] DesJardins, R., "International Standards for Open Systems Interconnection," *SIGCOMM 83 Tutorial*, University of Texas, Austin, March 1983.

[DIAS 81] Dias, D.M., and J.R. Jump, "Packet Switching Interconnection Networks for Modular Systems," *Computer*, Vol. 14, No. 12, pp. 43–53, Dec. 1981.

[DOWD 82] Dowdy, L.W., and D.V. Foster, "Comparative Models of the File Assignment Problem," *Computing Surveys*, Vol. 14, No. 2, pp. 287–313, June 1982.

[EFE 82] Efe, K., "Heuristic Models of Task Assignment Scheduling in Distributed Systems," *Computer*, Vol. 15, No. 6, pp. 50–56, Dec. 1984.

[ELLI 77] Ellis, C.A., "A Robust Algorithm for Updating Duplicate Databases," *Proc. 2nd Berkeley Workshop on Distributed Data Management and Computer Networks*, 1977.

[ELMA 85] Elmasri, R., J. Weeldryer, and A. Hevner, "The Category Concept: An Extension to the Entity-Relationship Model," *Data Knowledge and Engineering*, Vol. 1, No. 1, pp. 75–116, June 1985.

[EPST 78] Epstein, R., M. Stonebraker, and E. Wong, "Distributed Query Processing in Relational Database Systems," *SIGMOD Proc.*, pp. 169–180, May 1978.

[ESWA 74] Eswaran, K.P., "Placement of Records in a File and File Allocation in a Computer Network," *Information Processing 74*, IFIPS, North Holland Publishing Co., 1974.

[ESWA 76] Eswaran, K.P., et al., "The Notions of Consistency and Predicate Locks in a Database System," *Communications of the ACM*, Vol. 19, No. 11, pp. 624–633, Nov. 1976.

[FERR 82] Ferrier, A., and C. Stangret, "Heterogeneity in a Distributed Database Management System SIRIUS-DELTA," *Proc. 8th International Conf. on VLDB*, Mexico City, Sept. 8–10, pp. 45–53, 1982.

[GARC 82] Garcia-Molina, H., and G. Wiederhold, "Read-Only Transactions in a Distributed Database," *ACM Transactions on Database Systems*, Vol. 7, No. 2, pp. 209–234, June 1982.

[GARC 78] Garcia-Molina, H., "Performance Comparisons of Two Update Algorithms for Distributed Databases," *Proc. 3rd Berkeley Workshop on Distributed Databases and Computer Networks*, Aug. 1978.

[GARD 80] Gardarin, G., and W.W. Chu, "A Distributed Control Algorithm for Reliably and Consistently Updating Replicated Databases," *IEEE Transactions on Computers*, pp. 1060–1068, Dec. 1980.

[GARY 78] Gary, J.N., "Notes on Database Operating Systems," *Operating Systems: An Advanced Course, Lecture Notes in Computer Science 60*, Goos and Hartmanis, eds., Springer-Verlag, pp. 393–481, 1978.

[GAVE 76] Gaver, D.P., S.S. Lavenberg, and T.G. Price, "Exploratory Analysis of a Data Base Management System," *IBM Journal of Research and Development*, Vol. 20, No. 5, Sept. 1976.

[GELE 78] Gelenbe, E., and K. Sevick, "An Analysis of Update Synchronization for Multiple Copy Databases," *Proc. 3rd Berkeley Workshop on Distributed Data Management and Computer Networks*, pp. 69–90, Aug. 28–31, 1978.

[GOOD 86] Goodman, J.R., "Cache Memory Optimization to Reduce Processor/Memory Traffic," submitted for publication to *ACM Transaction on Computer Systems*, Jan. 31, 1985.

[GRAY 81] Gray, J., "The Transaction Concept: Virtues and Limitations," *Proc. 1981 VLDB*, pp. 144–154, Sept. 1981.

[GYLY 76] Gylys, V.B., and J.A. Edwards, "Optimal Partitioning of Workload for Distributed Systems," *Proc. COMPCON Fall 76*, pp. 353–357, Sept. 1976.

[HAAS 82] Haas, L.M., et al., "R*: A Research Project on Distributed Relational DBMS," IBM Research Report RJ 3653, San Jose, CA, Oct. 21, 1982.

[HABE 69] Haberman, A.N., "Prevention of System Deadlocks," *Communications of the ACM*, Vol. 12, No. 7, pp. 373–377, 385, July 1969.

[HAMM 80] Hammer, M., and D. Shipman, "Reliability Mechanisms for SDD-1: A System for Distributed Databases," *ACM Transactions on Database Systems*, Vol. 5, No. 4, pp. 431–466. Dec. 1980.

[HAMM 78] Hammer, M., and D. Shipman, "An Overview of Reliability Mechanism for a Distributed Database," *Proc. COMPCON 78*, pp. 63–65, March 1978.

[HELL 80] Hellerstein, J., and W.W. Chu, "Some Potential Deadlocks in Layered Communications Architectures," *AFIPS Proc.*, Vol. 50, pp. 137–140, 1980.

[HEVN 85] Hevner, A.R., O. Wu, and S.B. Yao, "Query Optimization on Local Area Networks," *ACM Transactions on Office Information Systems*, Vol. 3, No. 1, pp. 35–62, Jan. 1985.

[HEVN 79] Hevner, A.R., and S.B. Yao, "Query Processing in Distributed Database Systems," *IEEE Transactions on Software Engineering*, Vol. SE-5, No. 3, pp. 177–187, May 1979.

[HOLT 72] Holt, R.C., "Some Deadlock Properties of Computer Systems," *Computing Surveys*, Vol. 4, No. 3, pp. 179–196, Sept. 1972.

[HOPK 78] Hopkins, A.L., Jr., T.B. Smith, III, and J.H. Lala, "FTMP — A Highly Reliable Fault-Tolerant Multiprocessor for Aircraft," *Proc. IEEE*, Vol. 66, No. 10, pp. 1221–1239, Oct. 1978.

[IEEE 78] "Special Issue on Fault-Tolerant Digital Systems," *Proc. IEEE*, Vol. 66, No. 10, Oct. 1978.

[IRAN 82] Irani, K.B., and K.W. Chen, "Minimization of Interprocessor Communication for Parallel Computation," *IEEE Transactions on Computers*, Vol. C-31, No. 11, pp. 1067–1075, Nov. 1982.

[JENN 77] Jenny, C.J., "Process Partitioning in Distributed Systems," *Proc. NTC 1977*, pp. 31:1-1–31:1-10, 1977.

[JONE 79] Jones, A.K., et al., "A Multiprocessor Operating System for the Support of Talk Forces," *Proc. 7th Symposium on Operating System Principles*, pp. 159–165, Nov. 1980.

[JONE 79] Jones, L.B., and D.V. Foster, "Toward a Multiple Copy File Assignment Model for Files in a Computer System," *Proc. 17th Annual Southeast Regional ACM Conference*, Orlando, FL, April 1979.

[KATS 78] Katsuki, D., et al., "Pluribus — An Operational Fault-Tolerant Multiprocessor," *Proc. IEEE*, Vol. 66, No. 10, pp. 1146–1159, Oct. 1978.

[KATZ 79] Katzman, J.A., "A Fault-Tolerant Computing System," *Proc. 11th Hawaii International Conference on System Science*, 1978.

[KERS 82] Kerschberg, L., P.D. Ting, and S.B. Yao, "Query Optimization in Star Computer Networks," *ACM Transactions on Database Systems*, Vol. 7, No. 4, pp. 678–711, 1982.

[KING 84] King, R., and S. Melville, "Ski: A Semantics Knowledgeable Interface," *Proc. 1984 VLDB*, pp. 30–33, Aug. 1984.

[KING 73] King, P.F., and A.J. Collmeyer, "Database Sharing — An Efficient Mechanism for Supporting Concurrent Processes," *Proc. 1973 National Computer Conference and Exposition*, Vol. 42, pp. 271–275, June 1973.

[KRIS 84] Krishnamurthy, R., and S.P. Morgan, "Query Processing on Personal Computers — A Pragmatic Approach," *Proc. 1984 VLDB*, pp. 26–29, Aug. 1984.

[KRUE 84] Krueger, P., and R. Finkel, "An Adaptive Load Balancing Algorithm for a Multicomputer," Technical Report #539, Computer Sciences Dept., University of Wisconsin, Madison, April 1984.

[KRUS 83] Kruskal, C.P., and M. Snir, "The Performance of Multistage Interconnection Networks for Multiprocessors," *IEEE Transactions on Computers*, Vol. C-32, No. 12, pp. 1091–1098, Dec. 1983.

[LAMP 82] Lampson, B., and H. Sturgis, "Crash Recovery in a Distributed Data Storage System," Technical Report, Xerox Palo Alto Research Center, Palo Alto, CA, 1979.

[LAMP 81a] Lampson, B., "Atomic Transactions," *Distributed Systems — Architecture and Implementation, Lecture Notes in Computer Science 105*, Springer-Verlag, pp. 246–264, 1981.

[LAMP 81b] Lampson, B., "Ethernet, Pub and Violet," *Distributed Systems — Architecture and Implementation, Lecture Notes in Computer Science 105*, Springer-Verlag, pp. 446–484, 1981.

[LIN 83] Lin, K.W., J. Nolte, P.A. Bernstein, and N. Goodman, "Distributed Database System Designer Handbook," Technical Report, *Computer Corporation of America*, Jan. 1983.

[LYNG 84a] Lyngbaek, P., and D. McLeod, "A Personal Data Manager," *Proc. 1984 VLDB*, pp. 14–25, Aug. 1984.

[LYNG 84b] Lyngbaek, P., and D. McLeod, "An Approach to Object Sharing in Distributed Database Systems," *Proc. 1984 VLDB*, pp. 364–375, Aug. 1984.

[MA 82] Ma, P.Y.R., E.T.S. Lee, and M. Tsuchiya, "A Task Allocation Model for Distributed Computig Systems," *IEEE Transactions on Computers*, Vol. C-31, No. 1, pp. 41–47, Jan. 1982.

[MAHM 76] Mahmoud, S., and J.S. Riordan, "Optimal Allocation of Resources in Distributed Information Networks," *ACM Transactions on Database Systems*, Vol. 1, No. 1, pp. 66–78, March 1976.

[MENA 78] Menasce, D.A., and R.R. Muntz, "Locking and Deadlock Detection in Distributed Databases," *Proc. 3rd Berkeley Workshop on Distributed Data Management and Computer Networks*, pp. 215–234, Aug. 28–31, 1978.

[METC 76] Metcalfe, R.M., and D.R. Boggs, "D.R. Ethernet: Distributed Packet Switching for Local Computer Networks," *Communications of the ACM*, Vol. 19, No. 7, pp. 395–404, July 1976.

[MINO 82] Minoura, T., and G. Wiederhold, "Resilient Extended True-Copy Token Scheme for a Distributed Database System," *IEEE Transactions Software Engineering*, Vol. SE-8, No. 3, pp. 173–189, May 1982.

[MORG 77] Morgan, H.L., and K.D. Levin, "Optimal Program and Data Location in Computer Networks," *Communications of the ACM*, Vol. 20, No. 5, pp. 315–322, May 1977.

[NAVA 84] Navathe, S., S. Ceri, G. Wiederhold, and J. Dou, "Vertical Partitioning Algorithms for Database Design," *ACM Transactions on Database Systems*, Vol. 9, No. 4, Dec. 1984.

[PADM 83] Padmanbhan, K., and D. Lawrie, "A Class of Redundant Path Multistage Interconnection Networks," *IEEE Transactions on Computers*, Vol. C-32, No. 12, pp. 1099–1107, Dec. 1983.

[PASS 77] Passafiume, J.J., and S. Wecker, "Distributed File Access in DECNET," *Proc. 2nd Berkeley Workshop on Distributed Databases and Networking*, Lawrence Berkeley Laboratory, Berkeley, CA 1977.

[PATE 82] Patel, J., "Analysis of Multiprocessors with Private Cache Memories," *IEEE Transactions on Computers*, Vol. C-31, No. 4, pp. 296–304, April 1982.

[POPE 81] Popek, G., et al., "Locus: A Network Transparent, High Reliability Distributed System," *Proc. 8th Symposium on Operating Systems Principles*, Pacific Grove, Ca, Dec. 1981.

[RAO 79] Rao, G.S., H.S. Stone, and T.C. Hu, "Assignment of Tasks in a Distributed Processing System with Limited Memory," *IEEE Transactions on Computers*, Vol. C-28, No. 4, pp. 291–299, April 1979.

[RAVI 83] Ravishankar, C.V., and J.R. Goodman, "Cache Implementation for Multiple Microprocessors," *IEEE*, pp. 346–350, 1983.

[RENN 84] Rennels, D.A., "Fault-Tolerant Computing — Concepts and Examples," *IEEE Transactions on Computers*, Vol. C-33, No. 12, pp. 1116–1129, Dec. 1984.

[RIES 81] Ries, D.R., and G.C. Smith, "Nested Transaction in Distributed Systems," *Proc. Symposium on Reliability in Distributed Software and Database Systems*, pp. 117–123, July 1981.

[RIES 82] Ries, D.R., ed., *An Architectural Framework for Database Standardization*, Computer Corporation of America,July 1982.

[RODR 76] Rodriguez-Rosell, J., "Empirical Data Reference Behavior in Data Base Systems," *Computer*, Vol. 9, No. 11, Nov. 1976.

[ROTH 80] Rothnie, J.B., Jr., et al., "Introduction to a System for Distributed Databases (SDD-1)," *ACM Transaction on Database Systems*, Vol. 5, No. 1, pp. 1–17, March 1980.

[SARR 84] Sarrazin, D.B., and M. Malek, "Fault-Tolerant Semiconductor Memories," *Computer*, Vol. 17, No. 8, pp. 49–56, Aug. 1984.

[SELI 80] Selinger, P.G., and M. Adiba, "Access Path Selection in Distributed Database Systems," IBM Research Report RJ 2883, San Jose, CA, Aug. 1980.

[SIEG 81a] Siegel, H.J., and R.J. McMillen, "The Multistage Cube: A Versatile Interconnection Network," *Computer*, Vol. 14, No. 12, pp. 65–76, Dec. 1981.

[SIEG 81b] Siegel, H.J., and R.J. McMillen, "Using the Augmented Data Manipulator in PASM," *Computer*, Vol. 14, No. 2, pp. 25–33, Feb. 1981.

[SIEW 84] Siewiorek, D.P., "Architecture of Fault-Tolerant Computers," *Computer*, Vol. 17, No. 8, pp. 9–18, Aug. 1984.

[SIEW 78] Siewiorek, D.P., et al., "A Case Study of C.mmp, Cm*, and C.vmp: Part I — Experiences with Fault Tolerance in Multiprocessor Systems," *Proc. IEEE*, Vol. 6, No. 10, pp. 1178–1199, Oct. 1978.

[SIEW 78] Siewiorek, D.P., V. Kini, R. Joobbani, and H. Bellis, "A Case Study of C.mmp, Cm*, and C.vmp: Part II — Predicting and Calibrating Reliability of Multiprocessor Systems," *Proc. IEEE*, Vol. 66, No. 10, pp. 1200–1220, Oct. 1978.

[SKEE 82] Skeen, D., "A Quorum-based Commit Protocol," *Proc. 6th Berkeley Workshop on Distributed Data Management and Computer Networks*, pp. 69–80, May 1982.

[SKEE 81] Skeen, D., "Nonblocking Commit Protocol," *SIGMOD International Conference on Management of Data*, Ann Arbor, MI, pp. 133–142, 1981.

[SMIT 82] Smith, A.J., "Cache Memories," *Computing Surveys*, Vol. 14, No. 3, pp. 473–530, Sept. 1982.

[SPEC 85] Spector, A.Z., D. Daniels, D. Duchamp, J. Eppinger, R. Pausch, "Distributed Transactions for Reliable Systems," Technical Report CMU-CS-85-117, Carnegie-Mellon University, Sept. 1985.

[STAN 84] Stankovic, J.A., "A Perspective on Distributed Computer Systems," *IEEE Transactions on Computers*, Vol. C-33, No. 12, pp. 1102–1115, Dec. 1984.

[STON 84] Stonebraker, M., and L. Rowe, "Database Portals — A New Application Program Interface," *Proc. 1984 VLDB*, pp. 3–13, Aug. 1984.

[STON 82] Stonebraker, M., et al., "Performance Analysis of Distributed Data Base Systems," *IEEE Database Engineering*, Vol. 5, No. 4, pp. 58–65, 1982.

[STON 77] Stonebraker, M., and E. Nenhold, "A Distributed Data Base Version of INGRES," *Proc. 2nd Berkeley Workshop on Distributed Data Management and Computer Networks*, Lawrence Berkeley Laboratories, Berkeley, CA, pp. 19–36, May 1977.

[SVOB 81] Svobodova, L., "A Reliable Object-Oriented Data Repository For a Distributed Computer," *Proc. 8th Symposium on Operating Systems Principles*, Dec. 1981.

[SWAN 77] Swan, R.J., S.H. Fuller, and D.P. Siewiorek, "Cm* A Modular Multi-Microprocessor," *Proc. National Computer Conference*, pp. 636–644, June 1977.

[TANE 81] Tanenbaum, A.S., and S.J. Mullender, "An Overview of the Amoeba Distributed Operating System," *Operating Systems Review*, Vol. 15, No. 3, pp. 51–64, July 1981.

[TANG 76] Tang, C.K., "Cache System Design in the Tightly Coupled Multiprocessor System," *Proc. National Computer Conference*, pp. 749–753, 1976.

[THOM 78] Thomas, R.H., "A Solution to the Concurrency Control Problem for Multiple Copy Databases," *Proc. COMPCON 78*, pp. 56–62, March 1978.

[THOM 73] Thomas, R.H., "A Resource Sharing Executive for the ARPANET," *ARIPS Proc.*, Vol. 42, NCC, pp. 155–163, 1973.

[TRAI 82] Traiger, I.L., J. Gray, C.A. Galtier, and B.G. Lindsay, "Transactions and Consistency in Distributed Database Systems," *ACM Transactions on Database Systems*, Vol. 7, No. 3, pp. 323–342, Sept. 1982.

[VANT 84] van Tilborg, A.M., and L.D. Wittie, "Wave Scheduling — Decentralized Scheduling of Task Forces in Multicomputers," *IEEE Transactions on Computers*, Vol. C-33, No. 9, pp. 835–844, Sept. 1984.

[WAH 80] Wah, B.W., "An Efficient Heuristic for File Placement on Distributed Databases," *IEEE COMPSAC*, pp. 462–468, 1980.

[WAH 84] Wah, B.W., and Y. Lien, "The File-Assignment and Query-Processing Problems in Local Multiaccess Networks," *Proc. International Conference on Data Engineering*, Los Angeles, pp. 228–235, April 1984.

[WENS 78] Wensley, J.H., et al., "SIFT: The Design and Analysis of a Fault-Tolerant Computer for Aircraft Control," *Proc. IEEE*, Vol. 66, No. 10, pp. 1240–1254, Oct. 1978.

[WONG 83] Wong, E., "Dynamic Rematerialization: Processing Distributed Queries Using Redundant Data," *IEEE Transactions on Software Engineering*, Vol. SE-9, No. 3, pp. 228–232, 1983.

[WONG 76] Wong, E., and K. Youssefi, "Decomposition — A Strategy for Query Processing," *ACM Transactions on Database Systems*, Vol. 1, No. 3, pp. 223–241, 1976.

[YEN 82] Yen, W.C., and K.S. Fu, "Coherence Problem in Multicache System," *1982 International Conference on Parallel Processing*, pp. 332–339, 1982.

www.ingramcontent.com/pod-product-compliance
Ingram Content Group UK Ltd.
Pitfield, Milton Keynes, MK11 3LW, UK
UKHW051458290926
15471UKWH00008B/1270

9 780890 062128